Foundations of Business Thought

Foundations of Business Thought

First Edition

With contributions by

Calvin M. Boardman
Professor of Finance
Bill Daniels Chair in Business Ethics
David Eccles School of Business
University of Utah

Alan N. Sandomir
Associate Professor (Lecturer) of Marketing
David Eccles School of Business
University of Utah

Harris Sondak
Professor of Management
David Eccles Faculty Scholar
David Eccles School of Business
University of Utah

PEARSON

Boston   Columbus   Indianapolis   New York   San Francisco   Upper Saddle River
Amsterdam   Cape Town   Dubai   London   Madrid   Milan   Munich   Paris   Montreal   Toronto
Delhi   Mexico City   São Paulo   Sydney   Hong Kong   Seoul   Singapore   Taipei   Tokyo

Editor In Chief: Stephanie Wall
Acquisitions Editor: James Heine
Director of Editorial Services: Ashley Santora
Editorial Project Manager: Karin Williams
Editorial Assistant: Ashlee Bradbury
Permissions Manager: Melissa Pellerano
Director of Marketing: Patrice Lumumba Jones
Senior Marketing Manager: Nikki Ayana Jones
Assistant Marketing Manager: Ian Gold
Production Project Manager: Clara Bartunek
Creative Art Director: Jayne Conte
Cover Designer: Suzanne Behnke
Full-Service Project Management: Niraj Bhatt, Aptara®, Inc.
Printer/Binder: Edwards Brothers Malloy
Cover Printer: Lehigh / Phoenix Hagerstown
Text Font: 10.5/13.5 Palatino

Credits and acknowledgments borrowed from other sources and reproduced, with permission, in this textbook appear on the appropriate page within text or on page 533.

Library of Congress Cataloging-in-Publication Data
Boardman, Calvin M.
   Foundations of business thought / Calvin M. Boardman, Alan N. Sandomir, Harris Sondak.
      p. cm.
   Includes index.
   ISBN-13: 978-0-13-285607-2
   ISBN-10: 0-13-285607-7
 1. Business. I. Sandomir, Alan N.   II. Sondak, Harris.   III. Title.
   HF1008.B63 2013
   658--dc23

2012016039

10 9 8 7 6 5 4 3 2 1

PEARSON

ISBN 10:   0-13-285607-7
ISBN 13: 978-0-13-285607-2

Contents

Foundations of Business Thought

FOREWORD

Think of *Foundations of Business Thought* as a journey through the ages of written business history—a flight through the "wormhole" of philosophy, literature, economics, and politics. This voyage is mapped out for us *not* by commentators on the subject of business; rather, our "navigators" are the original authors. These original authors invite us to experience the primary works themselves. They guide us through an arc of interdisciplinary subjects and illuminate more than 2,000 years of thinking about the subject of commerce and its meaning in our lives. This is not a brief journey; of course, it is not a brief subject either. After all, we find ourselves, here in the twenty-first century, surrounded by commerce.

If there is, as the famous social scientist Herbert Simon has suggested, a human world of "bounded rationality" where everything that we think and understand has a limit and beyond which we can neither conceive nor even conceive of conceiving, then commerce has a place of near-dominance in that world of "bounded rationality." Little of what we know does not find a point of convergence with commerce, either in the financing and tracking; the manufacturing; or the distributing, promoting, and selling of it. Many would say that even our ideas about God and faith are subsumed and even regulated by commerce. The subject could just be too large to manage. The best we can do

is to introduce some of its foundations and to remind ourselves that we are searching for answers but not necessarily for truth. The search is truth enough for us right now.

Henry David Thoreau, one of our navigators, tells us why this "historic arc" is crucial to our search. "No wonder," he exclaims, "that Alexander carried the *Iliad* with him on his expeditions in a precious casket. A written word is the choicest of relics. It is something at once more intimate with us and more universal than any other work of art. It is the work of art nearest to life itself." The intimacy forged by experiencing the original text engages our passions. These passions are the fundamental fuels of our personal search for meaning. And our search for meaning is the most essential expedition of our lives.

On our voyage, we come to understand that the nature of business is in part just a reflection of our own personal natures. When it is grand, it is because we, too, are grand. And when it is grim, it is because we, too, are grim. We see in the proximate relationships between enterprise and wealth, and politics and religion, the story of business played out by a cast of characters we recognize. Those characters represent us, after all, even when we observe them acting small, mean, and contemptible or acting noble, virtuous, and reasonable. We recognize ourselves and are moved closer to a comprehension of what it means to be us, living at this time, preparing for our encounter with what we call "the business world"—a world that, for all its careful exploration by those who have come before us, still requires that each of us set out on our own personal exploration. Finally, and in every generation, we are left to make sense of it all for ourselves.

We live and work beneath many layers of history—a record of ideas and activities that we have created in seeking ways to satisfy our needs and wants. We illuminate this canopy with the lights of marketing, accounting, finance, management, and production—we see before us a bright new world of business. We are more curious than before and we ask bigger and bolder questions. No longer interested singularly in the physical—the techniques that inform this business matter—we flow into more speculative channels. We want to know and understand more. What forces direct business? Why do these forces exist? How do we affect them? How do they affect us? Is this the perfect arrangement of means by which we shall improve and advance? Are there conflicts within it that we cannot avoid? How did it all happen? What is the purpose of it all?

The historic arc impels us into territory where the past, present, and future coexist. Our search begins at a place where time runs in cross-currents through Confucion China, Periclean Greece, Thomistic Rome, and Jeffersonian America. Our search begins in a recognition that all business thinking that has preceded us now serves as the foundation of our own business thoughts. How we comprehend and then amend these foundations puts a stamp on generations to follow. ♦

I

INTRODUCTION

A WRITTEN WORD IS THE CHOICEST OF RELICS

Foundations of Business Thought is an eclectic guide through the historic and socio-philosophic maze of our distant and recent business past. Threading its way through, and past, some musty and anachronistic corridors and around some modern and abstract corners, the path it cuts is designed to illuminate alternative entrances and exits. It is a seeker's blueprint to the intellectual architecture of the business world, rather than a static, or passive, consumer's nuts-and-bolts template that, like many standard introduction texts to business, exists to introduce you as efficiently as possible into the mechanical processes of commerce.

The readings prepare you to think about what it means, in the most personal terms, to be part of the commercial world. Most contributors to business texts avoid this kind of exposition, averting the philosophical in deference to the practical. Rather than ask you to study why debt transmogrifies into credit or what it means to act categorically, as if money were an end rather than a means to an end, they ask you to study isolated strains such as the mathematics of finance and the strategies and tactics of contemporary consumer marketing where the primary purposes of capitalization and generating revenue sit like lonely thoughts on a sea of rudimentary ideas.

There is something very partial about the usual approach because it reduces the world to a pursuit of money and a set of life goals built around getting and spending. This is a reduction because it narrows the study of business to a single, how-to program and cuts equally serious inquiries into commerce away from the connective tissues of philosophy, psychology, sociology, history, biology, chemistry, and even physics. Worse, it makes the search for self an absurdly narrow affair. Any short-course, programmatic presentation of business disciplines compresses all possible joys from business into the "neutron star" of profit and its own "Four Weighty P's" of power, position, privilege, and place. Once captured by this academic/social singularity, the moral and intellectual velocity required to escape its gravity is too great for most of us. This is how the business world often imprisons rather than liberates.

Francis Bacon, the early seventeenth-century essayist and philosopher whose own desire for power in excess "caused the angels to fall," has presented the picture in lucid fashion:

> It may be truly affirmed, that no kind of men love business for itself but those who are learned; for other persons love it for profit, as an hireling, that loves the work for the wages; or for honour, as because it beareth them up in the eyes of men, and refresheth their reputation, which otherwise would wear; or because it put-teth them in mind of their fortune, and giveth them occasion to pleasure and displeasure; or because it excerciseth some faculty wherein they take pride, and so entertaineth them in good humour and pleasing conceits toward themselves; or because it advanceth any other their ends. So that as it is said of untrue valours, that some

men's valours are in the eyes of them that look on; so such men's industries are in the eyes of others, or at least in regard of their own designments: only learned men love business as an action according to nature, as agreeable to health of mind as exercise is to health of body, taking pleasure in the action itself, and not in the purchase: so that of all men they are the most indefatigable, if it be towards any business which can hold or detain their mind.

Francis Bacon,
Advancement of Learning

Bacon, whose own mischievous business behavior landed him as a prisoner in the Tower of London with a fine of 40,000 pounds, concluded during his final years that the world of business was a great deception. Bacon observed that men in business were an unstudious, limited, and blinkered lot whose faith in their own certainties was unassailable. These certainties, which he describes in the passage above, caused business practitioners to be certain that competitive engagement in the commercial world, galvanized by self-interest and catalyzed by the promise of self-advancement, would purchase the ephemeral and the eternal, a mortal home on some vast estate and an immortal, celestial home in an infinite firmament. Do the following notions strike you as "certainties"?

1. Business brings profit, and love of profit is a powerful seduction;

2. Business (especially business success) brings in honor, which is a revitalizing bath of the all-consuming will to power;

3. Business builds assets that provide the otherwise hollow practitioner with current, capital, and intangible occupants for the many vacancies of one's life;

4. Business generates pride, which, when felt for others, is not such a bad thing, but when operating self-referentially is just hubris; and

5. Business advances the practitioner's ends. There is no need for self-improvement because self-advancement eliminates the "need."

These are the certainties that bought a prison sentence for Bacon. Later in his life, he concluded that he had an oversupply of unevaluated certainties. "If a man will begin with certainties," he said, "he shall end in doubts: but if he be content to begin with doubt, he shall end in certainties." Bacon applied the scientific method—even to the studies of philosophy and business and could see that the two respective disciplines needed one another. He added natural science, behaviorism, and even religion. The more fields of study he mustered, the more doubts appeared. The more doubts he mastered, the more certainties, of a new and better evaluated variety, emerged. He arranged them all in a utopic synthesis called *The New Atlantis*. The world of business thought figures prominently in this visionary epic. Henry Thomas, in his *Biographical Encyclopedia of Philosophy*, calls *The New Atlantis* "a Utopia in which he [Bacon] pictured a race of men dedicated to the study of nature and God."

In this ideal state, there is no strife for the simple reason that there is no greed. Nobody tries to surpass his neighbors in the personal acquisition of wealth. All the goods and funds are fairly distributed among all the people for "money is like muck, not good unless it be spread."

The business . . . is of the most unusual sort. "We maintain a trade, not of gold, silver, or jewels, nor of silks, nor for spices, nor for any other [material] commodity . . . but only for God's first creature, which was light; To have light of the growth of all parts of the world." For this purpose, the Utopians maintain a class of businessmen called Merchants of Light—philosophers and scientists who traveled throughout the world for the international exchange of new ideas and fair play.

Imagine a world where business practitioners are not foreigners in the land of philosophy and faith.

Imagine a world where the material manifest of business is to secure essential needs and necessary wants and thus provide time for the most important business of all—study and illumination.

Imagine a world where business is conducted by learned people who are energized by every encounter between commerce and its sister disciplines—philosophy, faith, science, history, and even the arts.

This is the world of the learned business practitioner, according to Bacon. And it is a world that cannot even be conceived without the confluent streams of diverse, multidisciplinary inquiry into the study of business. Those in business are not excused from becoming, as Henry David Thoreau states it, "acquainted with wiser men. . . ."

Thoreau is often thought of as a foreigner in the land of commerce. This is an incorrect belief about the man. He tells us in *Walden*, his magnum opus on the joys of living within nature rather than outside it, that his experience at Walden was, in great part, about determining just how he might use business rather than allowing business to use him. Thoreau seems like the outsider. He wants to live an unadorned life of the land, yet at the same time he wants to live within the confines of his own human nature. There are two natures at play in *Walden*—topographic nature and human nature, and without a certain synchrony, there can be only doubt and frustration. This is a very wise conclusion for a young man. (Thoreau was not yet thirty years old when he conducted his Walden experiment.)

Thoreau says that understanding business is crucial to learning how to avoid being crushed by it—that an education in business allows for maximum utility. The more one understands business, the more productive one becomes (which is a central tenet of commercial thinking). For Thoreau, the goal of efficiency is not to increase profit; rather, it is to reduce the amount of time necessary to the earning of a living. It is this logic that he employs to liberate himself from the burdens of giving himself over to a world of work. To live within one's own nature, he tells us, requires time and study—usually of the most pleasant variety. What we generally find, he tells us, is that most luxuries are hindrances to living well and that business, properly understood, is best employed to serve our basic needs only. Thereafter, we are free when we live on our own terms. For Thoreau, this kind of freedom is the foundation for an ideal life.

An idealized life seems to be a common goal for most people. Thoreau traces this kind of thinking to the classic Athenian thinkers, Plato and Aristotle, though he pleads the case for all great thinkers. How to live the ideal life generates different ideas. Many of these ideas are already available in books. Thoreau is adamant about independent thinking and behavior, but he believes that serious reading is essential. The most intelligent ideas and the most judicious judgments need the support of serious reading (such as the readings to be found in Foundations of Business Thought). We need to know the best that has been thought in order to temper our own impressions and conclusions. If we want to live idealized lives, we need to think of serious reading as the kind of refraction that precedes reflection. "I aspire to be acquainted with wiser men than this, our Concord soil, has produced. . . . As if Plato were my townsman," he says. And, as if to pinch just a bit of salt into the language, he adds, "It is not all books that are as dull as their readers." Henry David Thoreau's *Walden* is part of our serious reading in this Introduction. What you learn, as you begin your study of the following readings, will add brilliant color to the business life you will one day lead. What you remember will give dynamic and protean shape to the business and therefore personal relationships you will one day forge.

Your business life could well be a work of the learned imagination that could free you to seek your own nature in the world of commerce and the community of all living things. If you fail to comprehend these foundations now, your work—your life—may become leaden and uninspired—unexceptional in concept and unappealing in design. All hope for a full and healthy personal development might be lost if you thoughtlessly adopt the shallow certainties of an encapsulated, predigested business mind-set.

W. E. B. DuBois suggests that it is nothing less than civilization you are building—a civilization of men and women, people and culture. And for this, he says, "We must have ideals." DuBois is asking you to see that ideals and meaning are tied to your education. You will think and feel as deeply as your "vocabulary" allows. Your own internal logic should suggest that the status quo requirements of contemporary business—unlimited profit, infinite growth of capital, assets, and markets, and finally, self-interest untethered to the interests of an integrated, fully inclusive ecological community—are inadequate to your potential to see wider, think deeper, and act better. ♦

Of Studies from *The Essays*

Francis Bacon (1561–1626)

Studies serve for pastimes, for ornaments, for abilities; their chief use for pastimes is in privateness and retiring; for ornaments in discourse; and for ability in judgment; for expert men can execute, but learned men are more fit to judge and censure. To spend too much time in them is sloth; to use them too much for ornament is affectation; to make judgment wholly by their rules is the humor of a scholar; they perfect nature, and are themselves perfected by experience; crafty men condemn them, wise men use them, simple men admire them; for they teach not their own use, but that there is a wisdom without them and above them won by observation. Read not to contradict nor to believe, but to weigh and consider. Some books are to be tasted, others to be swallowed, and some few to be chewed and digested: that is, some are to be read only in parts, others to be read but curiously, and some few to be read wholly with diligence and attention. Reading maketh a full man, conference in reading, and writing, an exact man; therefore, though a man write little, he had need of a great memory; if he confer little, he had need of a present wit; and if he read little, he had need of much cunning to seem to know that he do not know. Histories make wise men; poets witty; the mathematics subtile; natural philosophy deep; moral grave: logic and rhetoric able to contend. ♦

Questions

1. What are the alternative uses of studies? What are they good for?

2. What are the risks of overdoing the pursuit of study?

Reading from *Walden*

Henry David Thoreau (1817–1862)

With a little more deliberation in the choice of their pursuits, all men would perhaps become essentially students and observers, for certainly their nature and destiny are interesting to all alike. In accumulating property for ourselves or our posterity, in founding a family or a state, or acquiring fame even, we are mortal; but in dealing with truth we are immortal, and need fear no change nor accident. The oldest Egyptian or Hindoo philosopher raised a corner of the veil from the statue of the divinity; and still the trembling robe remains raised, and I gaze upon as fresh a glory as he did, since it was I in him that was then so bold, and it is he in me that now reviews the vision. No dust has settled on that robe; no time has elapsed since that divinity was revealed. That time which we really improve, or which is improvable, is neither past, present, nor future.

My residence was more favorable, not only to thought, but to serious reading, than a university; and though I was beyond the range of the ordinary circulating library, I had more than ever come within the influence of those books which circulate round the world, whose sentences were first written on bark, and are now merely copied from time to time on to linen paper. Says the poet Mîr Camar Uddîn Mast, "Being seated to run through the region of the spiritual world; I have had this advantage in books. To be intoxicated by a single glass of wine; I have experienced this pleasure when I have drunk the liquor of the esoteric doctrines." I kept Homer's Iliad on my table through the summer, though I looked at his page only now and then. Incessant labor with my hands, at first, for I had my house to finish and my beans to hoe at the same time, made more study impossible. Yet I sustained myself by the prospect of such reading in future. I read one or two shallow books of travel in the intervals of my work, till that employment made me ashamed of myself, and I asked where it was then that I lived.

The student may read Homer of Æschylus in the Greek without danger of dissipation or luxuriousness, for it implies that he in some measure emulate their heroes, and consecrate morning hours to their pages. The heroic books, even if printed in the character of our mother tongue, will always be in a language dead to degenerate times; and we must laboriously seek the meaning of each work and line, conjecturing a larger sense than common use permits out of what wisdom and valor and generosity we have. The modern cheap and fertile press, with all its translations, has done little to bring us nearer to the heroic writers of antiquity. They seem as solitary, and the letter in which they are printed as rare and curious, as ever. It is worth the expense of youthful days and costly hours, if you learn only some words of an ancient language, which are raised out of the trivialness of the street, to be perpetual suggestions and provocations. It is not in vain that the farmer remembers and repeats the few Latin words which he has heard. Men sometimes speak as if the study of the classics would at length make way for more modern and practical studies; but the adventurous student will always study classics, in whatever language they may be written and however ancient they may be. For what are the classics but the noblest recorded thoughts of man? They are the only oracles which are not decayed, and there are such answers to the most modern inquiry in them as Delphi and Dodona never gave. We might as well omit to study Nature because she is old. To read well, that is, to read true books in a true spirit, is a noble exercise, and one that will task the reader more than any exercise which the customs of the day esteem. It requires a training such as the athletes underwent, the steady intention almost of the whole life to this object. Books must be read as deliberately and reservedly as they were written. It is not enough even to be able to speak the language of that nation by which they are written, for there is a memorable interval between the spoken and the written language, the language heard and the language read. The one is commonly transitory, a sound, a tongue, a dialect merely, almost brutish, and we learn it unconsciously, like the brutes, of our mothers. The other is the maturity and experience of that; if that is our mother tongue, this is our father tongue, a reserved and select expression, too significant to be heard by the ear, which we must be born again in order to speak. The crowds of men who merely spoke the Greek and Latin tongues in the middle ages were not entitled by the accident of birth to read the works of genius written in those languages; for these were not written in that Greek or Latin which they knew, but in the select language of literature. They had not learned the nobler dialects of Greece and Rome, but the very materials on which they were waste paper to them, and they prized instead a cheap contemporary literature. But when the several nations of Europe had acquired distinct though rude written languages of their own, sufficient for the purposes of their rising literatures, then first learning revived, and scholars were enabled to discern from that remoteness the treasures of antiquity. What the Roman and Grecian multitude could not hear, after the lapse of ages a few scholars read, and a few scholars only are still reading it.

However much we may admire the orator's occasional bursts of eloquence, the noblest written words are commonly as far behind or above the fleeting spoken language as the firmament with its stars is behind the clouds. There are the stars, and they who can may read them. The astronomers forever comment on and observe them. They are not exhalations like our daily colloquies and vaporous breath. What is called eloquence in the forum is commonly found to be rhetoric in the study. The orator yields to the inspiration of a transient occasion, and speaks to the mob before him, to those who can hear him; but the writer, whose more equable life is his occasion, and who would be distracted by the event and the crowd which inspire the orator, speaks to the intellect and heart of mankind, to all in any age who can understand him.

No wonder that Alexander carried the Iliad with him on his expeditions in a precious casket. A written word is the choicest of relics. It is something at once more intimate with us and more universal than any other work of art. It is

the work of art nearest to life itself. It may be translated into every language, and not only be read but actually breathed from all human lips;—not be represented on canvas or in marble only, but be carved out of the breath of life itself. The symbol of an ancient man's thought becomes a modern man's speech. Two thousand summers have imparted to the monuments of Grecian literature, as to her marbles, only a maturer golden and autumnal tint, for they have carried their own serene and celestial atmosphere into all lands to protect them against the corrosion of time. Books are the treasured wealth of the world and the fit inheritance of generations and nations. Books, the oldest and the best, stand naturally and rightfully on the shelves of every cottage. They have no cause of their own to plead, but while they enlighten and sustain the reader his common sense will not refuse them. Their authors are a natural and irresistible aristocracy in every society, and, more than kings or emperors, exert an influence on mankind. When the illiterate and perhaps scornful trader has earned by enterprise and industry his coveted leisure and independence, and is admitted to the circles of wealth and fashion, he turns inevitably at last to those still higher but yet inaccessible circles of intellect and genius, and is sensible only of the imperfection of his culture and the vanity and insufficiency of all his riches, and further proves his good sense by the pains which he takes to secure for his children that intellectual culture whose want he so keenly feels; and thus it is that he becomes the founder of a family.

Those who have not learned to read the ancient classics in the language in which they were written must have a very imperfect knowledge of the history of the human race; for it is remarkable that no transcript of them has ever been made into any modern tongue, unless our civilization itself may be regarded as such a transcript. Homer has never yet been printed in English, nor Æschylus, nor Virgil even—works as refined, as solidly done, and as beautiful almost as the morning itself; for later writers, say what we will of their genius, have rarely, if ever, equalled the elaborate beauty and finish and the lifelong and heroic literary labors of the ancients. They only talk of forgetting them who never knew them. It will be soon enough to forget them when we have the learning and the genius which will enable us to attend to and appreciate them. That age will be rich indeed when those relics which we call Classics, and the still older and more than classic but even less known Scriptures of the nations, shall have still further accumulated, when the Vaticans shall be filled with Vedas and Zendavestas and Bibles, with Homers and Dantes and Shakspeares, and all the centuries to come shall have successively deposited their trophies in the forum of the world. By such a pile we may hope to scale heaven at last.

The works of the great poets have never yet been read by mankind, for only great poets can read them. They have only been read as the multitude read the stars, at most astrologically, not astronomically. Most men have learned to read to serve a Paltry convenience, as they have learned to cipher in order to keep accounts and not be cheated in trade; but of reading as a noble intellectual exercise they know little or nothing; yet this only is reading, in a high sense, not that which lulls us as a luxury and suffers the nobler faculties to sleep the while, but what we have to stand on tiptoe to read and devote our most alert and wakeful hours to.

I think that having learned our letters we should read the best that is in literature, and not be forever repeating our a b abs, and works of one syllable, in the fourth or fifth classes, sitting on the lowest and foremost form all our lives. Most men are satisfied if they read or hear read, and perchance have been convicted by the wisdom of one good book, the Bible, and for the rest of their lives vegetate and dissipate their faculties in what is called easy reading. There is a work in several volumes in our Circulating Library entitled Little Reading, which I thought referred to a town of that name which I had not been to. There are those who, like cormorants and ostriches, can digest all sorts of this, even after the fullest dinner of meats and vegetables, for they suffer nothing to be wasted. If others are the machines to provide this provender, they are the machines to read it. They read the nine thousandth tale about Zebulon and Sephronia, and how they loved as none had ever loved before, and neither did the course of their true love run smooth,—at any rate, how it did run and stumble, and get up again and go on! how

some poor unfortunate got up onto a steeple, who had better never have gone up as far as the belfry; and then, having needlessly got him up there, the happy novelist rings the bell for all the world to come together and hear, O dear! how he did get down again! For my part, I think that they had better metamorphose all such aspiring heroes of universal noveldom into man weathercocks, as they used to put heroes among the constellations, and let them swing round there till they are rusty, and not come down at all to bother honest men with their pranks. The next time the novelist rings the bell I will not stir though the meeting-house burn down. "The Skip of the Tip-Toe-Hop, a Romance of the Middle Ages, by the celebrated author of 'Tittle-Tol-Tan,' to appear in monthly parts; a great rush; don't all come together." All this they read with saucer eyes, and erect and primitive curiosity, and with unwearied gizzard, whose corrugations even yet need no sharpening, just as some little four-year-old bencher his two-cent gilt-covered edition of Cinderella,—without any improvement, that I can see, in pronunciation, or accent, or emphasis, or any more skill in extracting or inserting the moral. The result is dulness of sight, a stagnation of the vital circulations, and a general deliquium and sloughing off of all the intellectual faculties. This sort of gingerbread is baked daily and more sedulously than pure wheat or rye-and-Indian in almost every oven, and finds a surer market.

The best books are not read even by those who are called good readers. What does our Concord culture amount to? There is in this town, with a very few exceptions, no taste for the best or for very good books even in English literature, whose words all can read and spell. Even the college-bred and so called liberally educated men here and elsewhere have really little or no acquaintance with the English classics; and as for the recorded wisdom of mankind, the ancient classics and Bibles, which are accessible to all who will know of them, there are the feeblest efforts any where made to become acquainted with them. I know a wood-chopper, of middle age, who takes a French paper, not for news as he says, for he is above that, but to "keep himself in practice," he being a Canadian by birth; and when I ask him what he considers the best thing he can do in this world, he says, beside this, to keep up and add to his English. This is about as much as the college bred generally do or aspire to do, and they take an English paper for the purpose. One who has just come from reading perhaps one of the best English books will find how many with whom he can converse about it? Or suppose he comes from reading perhaps one of the best English books will find how many with whom he can converse about it? Or suppose he comes from reading a Greek or Latin classic in the original, whose praises are familiar even to the so called illiterate; he will find nobody at all to speak to, but must keep silence about it. Indeed, there is hardly the professor in our colleges, who, if he has mastered the difficulties of the language, has proportionally mastered the difficulties of the wit and poetry of a Greek poet, and has any sympathy to impart to the alert and heroic reader; and as for the sacred Scriptures, or Bibles of mankind, who in this town can tell me even their titles? Most men do not know that any nation but the Hebrews have had a scripture. A man, any man, will go considerably out of his way to pick up a silver dollar; but here are golden words, which the wisest men of antiquity have uttered, and whose worth the wise of every succeeding age have assured us of;—and yet we learn to read only as far as Easy Reading, the primers and classbooks, and when we leave school, the "Little Reading," and story books, which are for boys and beginners; and our reading, our conversation and thinking, are all on a very low level, worthy only of pygmies and manikins.

I aspire to be acquainted with wiser men than this our Concord soil has produced, whose names are hardly known here. Or shall I hear the name of Plato and never read his book? As if Plato were my townsman and I never saw him,—my next neighbor and I never heard him speak or attended to the wisdom of his words. But how actually is it? His Dialogues, which contain what was immortal in him, lie on the next shelf, and yet I never read them. We are underbred and low-lived and illiterate; and in this respect I confess I do not make any very broad distinction between the illiterateness of my townsman who cannot read at all, and the illiterateness of him who has learned to read only what is for children and feeble intellects. We should be as good as the worthies of antiquity, but partly by first knowing how good they were. We are a race of tit-men, and soar but little higher in our intellectual flights than the columns of the daily paper.

It is not all books that are as dull as their readers. There are probably words addressed to our condition exactly, which, if we could really hear and understand, would be more salutary than the morning or the spring to our lives, and possibly put a new aspect on the face of things for us. How many a man has dated a new era in his life from the reading of a book. The book exists for us perchance which will explain our miracles and reveal new ones. The at present unutterable things we may find somewhere uttered. These same questions that disturb and puzzle and confound us have in their turn occurred to all the wise men; not one has been omitted; and each has answered them, according to his ability, by his words and his life. Moreover, with wisdom we shall learn liberality. The solitary hired man on a farm in the outskirts of Concord, who has had his second birth and peculiar religious experience, and is driven as he believes into silent gravity and exclusiveness by his faith, may think it is not true; but Zoroaster, thousands of years ago, travelled the same road and had the same experience; but he, being wise, knew it to be universal, and treated his neighbors accordingly, and is even said to have invented and established worship among men. Let him humbly commune with Zoroaster then, and, through the liberalizing influence of all the worthies, with Jesus Christ himself, and let "our church" go by the board.

We boast that we belong to the nineteenth century and are making the most rapid strides of any nation. But consider how little this village does for its own culture. I do not wish to flatter my townsmen, nor to be flattered by them, for that will not advance either of us. We need to be provoked,—goaded like oxen, as we are, into a trot. We have a comparatively decent system of common schools, schools for infants only; but excepting the half-starved Lyceum in the winter, and latterly the puny beginning of a library suggested by the state, no school for ourselves. We spend more on almost any article of bodily aliment or ailment than on our mental aliment. It is time that we had uncommon schools, that we did not leave off our education when we begin to be men and women. It is time that villages were universities, and their elder inhabitants the fellows of universities, with leisure—if they are indeed so well off—to pursue liberal studies the rest of their lives. Shall the world be confined to one Paris or one Oxford forever? Cannot students be bearded here and get a liberal education under the skies of Concord? Can we not hire some Abelard to lecture to us? Alas! what with foddering the cattle and tending the store, we are kept from school too long, and our education is sadly neglected. In this country, the village should in some respects take the place of the nobleman of Europe. It should be the patron of the fine arts. It is rich enough. It wants only the magnanimity and refinement. It can spend money enough on such things as farmers and traders value, but it is thought Utopian to propose spending money for things which more intelligent men know to be of far more worth. This town has spent seventeen thousand dollars on a town-house, thank fortune or politics, but probably it will not spend so much on living wit, the true meat to put into that shell, in a hundred years. The one hundred and twenty-five dollars annually subscribed for a Lyceum in the winter is better spent than any other equal sum raised in the town. If we live in the nineteenth century, why should we not enjoy the advantages which the nineteenth century offers? Why should our life be in any respect provincial? If we will read newspapers, why not skip the gossip of Boston and take the best newspaper in the world at once?—not be sucking the pap of "neutral family" papers, or browsing "Olive-Branches" here in New England. Let the reports of all the learned societies come to us, and we will see if they know anything. Why should we leave it to Harper & Brothers and Redding & Co. to select our reading? As the nobleman of cultivated taste surrounds himself with whatever conduces to his culture,—genius—learning—wit—books—paintings—statuary—music—philosophical instruments, and the like; so let the village do,—not stop short at a pedagogue, a parson, a sexton, a parish library, and three selectmen, because our pilgrim forefathers got through a cold winter once on a bleak rock with these. To act collectively is according to the spirit of our institutions; and I am confident that, as our circumstances are more flourishing, our means are greater than the nobleman's. New England can hire all the wise men in the world to come and teach her, and board them round the while, and not be provincial at all. That is the uncommon school we want. Instead of noblemen, let us have noble villages of men. If it is necessary, omit one bridge over the river, go round a little there, and throw one arch at least over the darker gulf of ignorance which surrounds us. ♦

QUESTIONS

1. According to Thoreau, why are books so special?

2. How should books be read?

FROM *THE SOULS OF BLACK FOLK*

W. E. B. DuBois (1868–1963)

The function of the university is not simply to teach bread-winning, or to furnish teachers for the public schools, or to be a centre of polite society; it is, above all, to be the organ of that fine adjustment between real life and the growing knowledge of life, an adjustment which forms the secret of civilization. Such an institution the South of today sorely needs. She has religion, earnest, bigoted:—religion that on both sides the Veil often omits the sixth, seventh, and eighth commandments, but substitutes a dozen supplementary ones. She has, as Atlanta shows, growing thrift and love of toil; but she lacks that broad knowledge of what the world knows and knew of human living and doing, which she may apply to the thousand problems of real life today confronting her. The need of the South is knowledge and culture,—not in dainty limited quantity, as before the war, but in broad busy abundance in the world of work; and until she has this, not all the Apples of Hesperides, be they golden and bejewelled, can save her from the curse of the Boeotian lovers.

The Wings of Atlanta are the coming universities of the South. They alone can bear the maiden past the temptation of golden fruit. They will not guide her flying feet away from the cotton and gold; for—ah, thoughtful Hippomenes!—do not the apples lie in the very Way of Life? But they will guide her over and beyond them, and leave her kneeling in the Sanctuary of Truth and Freedom and broad Humanity, virgin and undefiled. Sadly did the Old South err in human education, despising the education of the masses, and niggardly in the support of colleges. Her ancient university foundations dwindled and withered under the foul breath of slavery; and even since the war they have fought a failing fight for life in the tainted air of social unrest and commercial selfishness, stunted by the death of criticism, and starving for lack of broadly cultured men. And if this is the white South's need and danger, how much heavier the danger and need of the freedmen's sons! How pressing here the need of broad ideals and true culture, the conservation of soul from sordid aims and petty passions! Let us build the Southern university—William and Mary, Trinity, Georgia, Texas, Tulane, Vanderbilt, and the others—fit to live; let us build, too, the Negro universities:—Fisk, whose foundation was ever broad; Howard, at the heart of the Nation; Atlanta at Atlanta, whose ideal of scholarship has been held above the temptation of numbers. Why not here, and perhaps elsewhere, plant deeply and for all time centres of learning and living, colleges that yearly would send into the life of the South a few white men and a few black men of broad culture, catholic tolerance, and trained ability, joining their hands to other hands, and giving to this squabble of the Races a decent and dignified peace?

Patience, Humility, Manners, and Taste, common schools and kindergartens, industrial and technical schools, literature and tolerance, —all these spring from knowledge and culture, the children of the university. So must men and nations build, not otherwise, not upside down.

Teach workers to work,—a wise saying; wise when applied to German boys and American girls; wiser when said of Negro boys, for they have less knowledge of working and none to teach them. Teach thinkers to think,—a needed knowledge in a day of loose and careless logic; and they whose lot is gravest must have the carefulest training to think aright. If these things are so, how foolish to ask what is the best education for one or seven or sixty million souls! shall we teach them trades, or train them in liberal arts? Neither and both: teach the workers to work and the thinkers to think; make carpenters of carpenters, and philosophers of philosophers, and fops of fools. Nor can we pause here. We are training not isolated men but a living group of men, nay, a group within a group. And the final product of our training must be neither a psychologist nor a brickmason, but a man. And to make men, we must have ideals, broad, pure, and inspiring ends of living,—not sordid money-getting, not apples of gold. The worker must

work for the glory of his handiwork, not simply for pay; the thinker must think for truth, not for fame. And all this is gained only by human strife and longing; by ceaseless training and education; by founding Right on righteousness and Truth on the unhampered search for Truth; by founding the common school on the university, and the industrial school on the common school; and weaving thus a system, not a distortion, and
10 bringing a birth, not an abortion.

When night falls on the City of a Hundred Hills, a wind gathers itself from the seas and comes murmuring westward. And at its bidding, the smoke of the drowsy factories sweeps down upon the mighty city and covers it like a pall, while yonder at the University the stars twinkle above Stone Hall. And they say that yon gray mist is the tunic of Atlanta pausing over her golden apples. Fly, my maiden, fly, for yonder comes Hippomenes! ♦
20

QUESTIONS

1. According to DuBois, what kind of education is fundamental and most important?

2. What is the main goal of education?

Selections from *The Business Guide*

J. L. Nichols (1851–1895)

How to Do Business

Business, in every age of the world, has been the chief pioneer in the march of man's civilization. Blessings everywhere follow its advancing footsteps. It travels over no bloodstained fields to secure its noble ends, but everywhere brings man into friendly and harmonious intercourse. It removes local prejudices, breaks down personal antipathies, and binds the whole family of man together by strong ties of association and of mutual and independent interests. It brings men together, and towns and cities are built; it makes man venture upon the seas in ships, and traverse continents on iron pathways, and wherever we go, whether abroad or at home, it is business that controls the great interests of the world, and makes the affairs of men mighty.

SELECTION FROM *THE BUSINESS GUIDE*

SELECTION FROM *THE BUSINESS GUIDE*
J. L. Nichols (1851–1895)

Practical Rules for Success

"Economy is itself a great revenue"—Cicero
"Be not simply good, be good for something"—Thoreau

1. Keep your health good by adopting regular and steady habits.
2. Never be afraid to say no. Every successful man must have the backbone to assert his rights.
3. Remember that steady, earnest effort alone leads to wealth and high position.
4. Be not ashamed to work, for it is one of the conditions of our existence. There is not a criminal who does not owe his crime to some idle hour.
5. Never covet what is not your own.
6. Remember that time is gold.
7. To industry and economy add self-reliance. Do not take too much advice, think for yourself. Independence will add vigor and inspiration to your labors.
8. Don't be selfish. Selfishness is the meanest of vices, and the parent of a dozen more. Selfishness keeps a penny so close to the eye that it can't see a dollar beyond.
9. Never forget a favor, for ingratitude is the basest trait of a man's mean character.
10. Never taste or touch that which befogs the mind or dethrones the reason. A drunken man is always at the mercy of his enemies.

II

MOTIVATION FOR THE DEVELOPMENT OF COMMERCE

INTRODUCTION: ALL THAT IS SOLID MELTS INTO AIR

A company's growth is tied to many commitments. Depending on who we talk to on the inside, we may hear that such growth depends on the generation of new products, or on sound credit policies, or on competent management of the company's resources. Representatives from areas such as research and development, finance, and human resources may differ on which commitment is most important. But they will all agree that all commitments rely on one: the development of new business.

New business opportunities drive technology, profit, and employment. While such opportunities drive the small company to new objectives and goals, they also move civilization itself. Cities, states, and nations are built on the activities born from opportunities for business development. At a more personal level, our day-to-day lives are structured around business and, to a large extent, the value of our lives is measured by not only how we direct business, but how we are directed by business.

It was devotion to the Virgin Mary and the suffering of Christ that built the great cathedrals at Mont St. Michel and Chartres, according to historian Henry Adams. It is devotion to technology and business that built Chicago and New York and Main Street, USA. And behind it all is the push to develop ourselves by developing the businesses that give shape to the still incomplete world.

It is clear from the most rudimentary reading of journals written by early Spanish, Portuguese, Dutch, and English explorers of the New World that economic development was the primary motivation for their expeditions. History has often smoothed over the astringent nature of a motivation so seemingly base as "economic" by layering this purpose with alternative motivations, such as escape from religious persecution and diffusion of God's word to "savages," noble and ignoble. But always secure as a foundation for bold exploration is the desire for development of human power, privilege, and place, a common triad of economic design.

The "Diario" of the first recorded voyage to the New World, by Christopher Columbus, is replete with the passion and wonder of discovery. Columbus writes voluminously and rapturously of the many marvels of this newly claimed world. He nearly bursts with colorful outpourings that describe the topographical and biological wealth of the New Indies. At the same time, he is almost unemotional in his observations of the many diametrically opposed kindnesses and atrocities committed by the Spanish explorers in the process of "winning over" the indigenous colonies of natives. Despite the obvious mistakes upon arrival, due to both misreading of natives and rapacity of human nature, Columbus is alight with pride at having provided his royal Spanish sponsors opportunities to develop the resources. The islands would be mined for gold and ores, the Indians would be mined for labor and future loyalty to crown and Christ, and the Indies would be mined for geopolitical and commercial profit.

Columbus doesn't give voice to whether such singular discoveries will magnify his own efforts at personal development. We might infer from his journal entries that he perceives people (the natives) as human capital, assets from whom some considerable return might be recovered. But we might just as easily deduce that Columbus claims, in addition to this human wealth, all other forms of organic and inorganic wealth of the islands, not only for the power and privilege of Spanish Royalty, but for the place of God's greater glory. As Columbus unifies the material and the spiritual, he articulates opposing views for future "developers." For the unlearned pirates who sail the seas of commerce, he establishes a beachhead of deplorable intent—where there is always a disingenuously higher justification for the unmoderated pursuit of pelf. For the curious voyagers on that same body of water, he carves out a harbor where there exists, at least, a genuinely higher possibility for commerce—so that its material nature might be married to its spiritual purpose.

That spiritual purpose is, in part, clarified by the early fifteenth-century Franciscan Fray Bernardino de Sahagun. Bernardino is often thought of as an early ethnographer whose empathy for the true American natives, so brutally mismanaged by Spanish expeditionary forces, allowed him to record their social and cultural lives with an almost orthodox, scientific objectivity. He observed with an admirable detachment from his own culture but was careful to interview indigenous populations as well. In this, one might say that he had many well-informed collaborators.

Bernardino introduces the idea that trade and commerce were not distant from religious belief and ritual. To engage in trade was to put the Indian in touch with the "god of merchants" and with friends and foes alike. They were accustomed to the practices of wholesaling and selling. Though they understood the need to sell "to the buyers' interests," this did not always protect them from peril. Trade could be dangerous, yet it could also be a celebration of the higher and more spiritual callings in life.

Bernal Diaz Del Castillo writes what is called a true history of the conquest of New Spain. Use of the term *conquest* reminds us that the birth of Mexico begins with the Spanish elimination of a thriving cultural and commercial Aztec empire. Diaz offers a firsthand account of the Aztec prince Montezuma. The description of Montezuma's household and belongings offers insight into the layers of a native marketplace. It is apparent from the detail Diaz brings to his writing, that the culture is already capable of intricate production of a rainbow of goods. He reports a visit to the marketplace by his captain, Cortes, and a group of Spanish soldiers. The exchange of common and, what seemed to Cortes and his men, the uncommon in this colorful New World emporium of goods demonstrates the sophistication of this native culture. The opportunities for the development of mutually profitable trade between Spain and New Spain are obvious, though this is an ironic counterpoint to actual history.

John Locke's thinking about the nature of human beings, his writings on religious toleration, and his two treatises on government are early influences on eighteenth-century philosophers such as David Hume, Jean Jacques Rousseau, and Immanuel Kant. Thomas Jefferson and other American revolutionary statesmen of the late eighteenth century also viewed Locke as essential to their own intellectual and political positions. Locke's idea that we are not born with innate ideas did not run counter to the obvious evidence for our grasping and accumulative natures.

Reason, Locke asserted, is the means by which we find a way to seek and hold the property that Thomas Hobbes suggested we would, otherwise, wolfishly struggle to hold for ourselves to the detriment of our neighbors. How might we enter into business relations if our nature served as a vicious impediment to rational allocation of goods? What justification might exist, should we all agree to some kind of social contract, that could account for the property we own? Beyond this, how might we justify ownership of property that exceeds our actual needs?

Just as there is, said Locke, a theory of mind, of human consciousness that makes of experience the only knowledge we may have, there is a theory of property. It is based on labor. Locke's labor theory of value lays a simple foundation. The ownership of property, regardless of self-interested or even selfish motives, is relative to the labor we exert on the property. Labor itself justifies property. It is, said Locke, a divine idea with a very real natural consequence—a healthy consequence, too. As it is a natural right, everyone, regardless of intention and motive, can claim property. There need not be a grand scheme. A business world that holds property as the grand prize will draw in those with desires to bridge property to macroschemes for social advancement or with microschemes for personal improvement. It may also attract, in the main, those with no higher aim than the act of having itself. For Locke, it is only the labor that matters.

It could be said, without irony and without error, that Chief Joseph's story is one that rips Lockeanism from its posts, casting it into the fire of human ignorance, inconsistency, contrariness, and acquisitiveness. How is it possible, a student of commerce asks, that by the nineteenth century, representatives of an American government, founded upon democratic principles and Locke's labor theory of value, could so summarily execute a program of property theft against Indian nations whose title to "American" property was so obvious? A simple answer might include some aspect of Friedrich Nietzsche's idea of "the will to power," the notion that "might makes right" or that power presupposes its own justification. If property is wealth, and the pioneering Americans are seeking wealth, then business as usual includes the concentration of that wealth—within the boundaries of laws that, as Chief Joseph notes, are hardly understood and rarely practiced with any consistency, save the intent to incorporate wealth. Nietzsche might easily have pointed out that American Manifest Destiny was really just an example of the disguised will to power—

disguised because it hid behind a veil of ardent nationalism and was supported by the belief in a Christian destiny, charted by biblical text that some might see as myth reified into fact and chartered by a god who others might claim can neither be proven nor disproven. Indian nations had their gods and destinies, too, but they did not support such notions as facts. In this case, however, the magnitude of American military power trumped all.

Chief Joseph, despite his unfamiliarity with all of the foundations of Manifest Destiny, is wise enough to know a con game when he sees one. Like modern business practitioners who recognize that their businesses are under assault, he sees that the playing field is uneven. He repeatedly asks for a fair deal. He never overextends his requests and, in so doing, makes many allowances for cooperation and sharing. Despite his attempts to get a fair deal, however, he is depreciated and deceived at every turn.

Today, we understand that legal and regulatory codes are designed, in part, to create a level playing field. We also understand that, were such codes not in place, the nature of men and women, fueled by a "will to power" and driven toward personal development and infininite expansion, might run us down. This is the "hit and run" approach experienced by Chief Joseph and his people.

Goethe's cautionary poem *Faust* is the story of a man who craves development. Already a success in the day-to-day world of affairs, he recognizes that two souls exist within his breast: a soul that expresses itself through the phenomenon of materialism, and a soul, in embryonic state, that wishes to express itself through the less tangible phenomenon of spiritualism. He yearns to give spirit to his physical world—to breathe spiritualism into materialism and in the final mix, to grow as much as any human can without offending the Maker of Souls.

Faust's relationship with dark forces, in the person of Mephistopheles, represents the difficulties that arise when taking action in the physical world. The "deal with the devil" is negotiated at the price of Faust's soul. So, any action he takes to spiritualize his material world comes with diabolical strings attached.

Though Faust chooses to give flight to his spirit through the unleashing of titanic human energies combined to build no less an edifice than civilization itself, he must accept that in the business of marshaling such powers for the good of humanity, such modern thinking produces a darker reality. It is the darkness created when advancing civilization fails to preserve the values, traditions, and environments that preceded it. Complexity erodes simplicity. Material living erodes plain living. Industrialism erodes agrarianism. Progress erodes tradition. And, sometimes, the business of building civilization erodes our own souls.

Thus, business developers, who are at the heart of advancing civilization, sometimes cut a deal with the devil to justify progress itself. As Faust is judged, so contemporary explanations and justifications for business development must be judged.

Henry David Thoreau, as the leading character in his magnum opus *Walden,* stands in colorful contrast to Faust. He makes no deals. Life is to be lived close to the earth, not as a seeker of the forces and capital that give rise to business development, but as a seeker of the secrets and clues that give rise to inner human development. Unlike Faust, he does not believe that such a search for human truth must lead inevitably to the development of industry and infrastructure. Interior dreams do not have to take tangible, marketable shapes. The soul must be developed as an outgrowth of the search for truth, and truth must be discovered as an outgrowth of the search for meaning. Developing business, which often takes a toll on our external and internal landscapes, seems a morally questionable and potentially damning method for freeing the spirit that resides in the breast. Such efforts are progressive but not necessarily liberating. And what is the point of progress if it enslaves us to another person's view of what constitutes human perfection?

Thoreau leaves the comfortable city of Concord, Massachusetts, to transact a different kind of business at Walden Pond; yet it is still a business. He wants to be his own businessman— to engage in work that satisfies his own simple needs and to make all work and business secondary to the quest for consciousness. Perhaps,

he is entrepreneurial in spirit. If this is the case, then he is an entrepreneur who wishes to find whatever successes await him without becoming overly dependent on others who act as suppliers, employees, or customers. As an autonomous man, outside the ordinary business orientations of the world, he sees that most people are enslaved by the work that they do. Worse, he observes that the many meaningless labors of his fellow man are accepted without question. Why would a person enter into the world of commerce without first thinking about purpose? Why would a person commit to an unconscious life of meaningless labor? Is money the only motivator? And if this is so, then how genuine a life could such a person live? Might not such inauthenticity be the source of significant unhappiness in the world?

Thoreau advises us to sell our clothes but to keep our thoughts. In this admonition, he takes a different turn than does Faust. There is really only one business in life, he intones—the business of developing our interior selves while leaving other exterior environments relatively pristine so that they might serve as multiform means to spiritual development.

It might seem odd to conceive of one generation at odds with another—to think of generations engaged in argument. This is a helpful way, however, to understand some of William Wordsworth's poetry, especially, the case of his poem "The World Is Too Much with Us."

Wordsworth is writing as one of the founding fathers of the English Romantic movement. The early Romantics took a strong position against the rationalism of seventeenth- and eighteenth-century thought. Such rationalism supported applied science, which, by the mid-eighteenth century, had begun to undermine religion as the genuine force behind human progress. It became clear that James Watt and his improved steam engine really could do what prayer and supplication could not—it could produce and deliver the goods that might eliminate the scarcity that had haunted human history for thousands of years. The science of early industrialization could easily become the dyanamo of progress and the *raison d'etre* of life. Were this to be the case, what would happen to faith? What would become of religious values were they to be supplanted by the material values that industrialization canonized? This concern often motivates Wordsworth.

Wordsworth is a pastoral poet. He sees nature as consistent with religious values, and he cannot accept the idea of worldliness, which turns people toward cities and factories where nature is transformed into industrial work and transmuted into exchange values. The result of this type of transformation is that people become habituated to the idea of labor designed to generate demand for goods. Then demand for goods compels people to even more labor.

Nature, Wordsworth tells us, is lost in the bargain. The archetypal Romantic poet calls people back to nature.

Columbus builds modern Spanish civilization in the New World as an expression of the eternal human duality, to extend the reach of the Spanish kingdom and to expand the self; he wants to link the glory of God to the infinite possibilities of European destiny. Faust builds markets and communities as an expression of the spiritual quest for self-development. Thoreau builds a deeper architecture of the soul as an expression of that same quest. ◆

From *The Journal of Christopher Columbus*

*Christopher Columbus (1451–1506), Clements Robert Markham,
and Paolo del Pozzo Tonscanelli*

Sunday, 16th of December.

At midnight the Admiral made sail with the land-breeze to get clear of that gulf. Passing along the coast of Española on a bowline, for the wind had veered to the east, he met a canoe in the middle of the gulf, with a single Indian in it. The Admiral was surprised how he could have kept afloat with such a gale blowing. Both the Indian and his canoe were taken on board, and he was given glass beads, bells, and brass trinkets, and taken in the ship, until she was off a village 17 miles from the former anchorage, where the Admiral came to again. The village appeared to have been lately built, for all the houses were new. The Indian then went on shore in his canoe, bringing the news that the Admiral and his companions were good people; although the intelligence had already been conveyed to the village from the place where the natives had their interview with the six Spaniards. Presently more than five hundred natives with their king came to the shore opposite the ships, which were anchored very close to the land. Presently one by one, then many by many, came to the ship without bringing anything with them, except that some had a few grains of very fine gold in their ears and noses, which they readily gave away. The Admiral ordered them all to be well treated; and he says: "for they are the best people in the world, and the gentlest; and above all I entertain the hope in our Lord that your Highnesses will make them all Christians, and that they will be all your subjects, for as yours I hold them." He also saw that they all treated the king with respect, who was on the sea-shore. The Admiral sent him a present, which he received in great state. He was a youth of about 21 years of age, and he had with him an aged tutor, and other councillors who advised and answered him, but he uttered very few words. One of the Indians who had come in the Admiral's ship spoke to him, telling him how the Christians had come from heaven, and how they came in search of gold, and wished to find the island of *Baneque*. He said that it was well, and that there was much gold in the said island. He explained to the alguazil of the Admiral[1] that the way they were going was the right way, and that in two days they would be there; adding, that if they wanted anything from the shore he would give it them with great pleasure. This king, and all the others, go naked as their mothers bore them, as do the women without any covering, and these were the most beautiful men and women that had yet been met with. They are fairly white, and if they were clothed and protected from the sun and air, they would be almost as fair as people in Spain. This land is cool, and the best that words can describe. It is very high, yet the top of the highest mountain could be ploughed with bullocks; and all is diversified with plains and valleys. In all Castille there is no land that can be compared with this for beauty and fertility. All this island, as well as the island of Tortuga, is cultivated like the plain of Cordova. They raise on these lands crops of yams, which are small branches, at the foot of which grow roots[2] like carrots, which serve as bread. They powder and knead them, and make them into bread; then they plant the same branch in another part, which again sends out four or five of the same roots, which are very nutritious, with the taste of chesnuts. Here they have the largest the Admiral had seen in any part of the world, for he says that they have the same plant in Guinea. At this place they were as thick as a man's leg. All the people were stout and lusty, not thin, like the natives that had been seen before, and of a very pleasant manner, without religious belief. The trees were so luxuriant that the leaves left off being green, and were dark coloured with verdure. It was a wonderful thing to see those valleys, and rivers of sweet water, and the cultivated fields, and land fit for cattle, though they have none, for orchards, and for anything in the world that a man could seek for.

In the afternoon the king came on board the ship, where the Admiral received him in due form, and caused him to be told that the ships belonged to the Sovereigns of Castille, who were the greatest Princes in the world. But neither the Indians who were on board, who acted as interpreters, nor the king, believed a word of it. They maintained that the Spaniards came from heaven, and that the Sovereigns of Castille must be in heaven, and not in this world. They placed Spanish food before the king to eat, and he ate a mouthful, and gave the rest to his councillors and tutor, and to the rest who came with him.

"Your Highnesses may believe that these lands are so good and fertile, especially these of the island of Española, that there is no one who would know how to describe them, and no one who could believe if he had not seen them. And your Highnesses may believe that this island, and all the others, are as much yours as Castille. Here there is only wanting a settlement and the order to the people to do what is required. For I, with the force I have under me, which is not large, could march over all these islands without opposition. I have seen only three sailors land, without wishing to do harm, and a multitude of Indians fled before them. They have no arms, and are without warlike instincts; they all go naked, and are so timid that a thousand would not stand before three of our men. So that they are good to be ordered about, to work and sow, and do all that may be necessary, and to build towns, and they should be taught to go about clothed and to adopt our customs."

MONDAY, 17TH OF DECEMBER.

It blew very hard during the night from E.N.E., but there was not much sea, as this part of the coast is enclosed and sheltered by the island of Tortuga. The sailors were sent away to fish with nets. They had much intercourse with the natives, who brought them certain arrows of the *Caribas* or *Canibales*. They are made of reeds, pointed with sharp bits of wood hardened by fire, and are very long. They pointed out two

men who wanted certain pieces of flesh on their bodies, giving to understand that the *Canibales* had eaten them by mouthfuls. The Admiral did not believe it. Some Christians were again sent to the village, and, in exchange for glass beads, obtained some pieces of gold beaten out into fine leaf. They saw one man, whom the Admiral supposed to be Governor of that province, called by them *Cacique,* with a piece of gold leaf as large as a hand, and it appears that he wanted to barter with it. He went into his house, and the other remained in the open space outside. He cut the leaf into small pieces, and each time he came out he brought a piece and exchanged it. When he had no more left, he said by signs that he had sent for more, and that he would bring it another day. The Admiral says that all these things, and the manner of doing them, with their gentleness and the information they gave, showed these people to be more lively and intelligent than any that had hitherto been met with. In the afternoon a canoe arrived from the island of Tortuga with a crew of forty men; and when they arrived on the beach, all the people of the village sat down in sign of peace, and nearly all the crew came on shore. The Cacique rose by himself, and, with words that appeared to be of a menacing character, made them go back to the canoe and shove off. He took up stones from the beach and threw them into the water, all having obediently gone back into the canoe. He also took a stone and put it in the hands of my Alguazil,[3] that he might throw it. He had been sent on shore with the Secretary[4] to see if the canoe had brought anything of value. The Alguazil did not wish to throw the stone. That Cacique showed that he was well disposed to the Admiral. Presently the canoe departed, and afterwards they said to the Admiral that there was more gold in Tortuga than in Española, because it is nearer to Baneque. The Admiral did not think that there were gold mines either in Española or Tortuga, but that the gold was brought from *Baneque* in small quantities, there being nothing to give in return. That land is so rich that there is no necessity to work much to sustain life, nor to clothe themselves, as they go naked. He believed that they were very near the source, and that our Lord would point out where the gold has its origin. He had information that from here to *Baneque*[5] was four days' journey, about 34 leagues, which might be traversed with a fair wind in a single day.

TUESDAY, 18TH OF DECEMBER.

The Admiral remained at the same anchorage, because there was no wind, and also because the Cacique had said that he had sent for gold. The Admiral did not expect much from what might be brought, but he wanted to understand better whence it came. Presently he ordered the ship and caravel to be adorned with arms and dressed with flags, in honour of the feast of Santa Maria de la O—,[6] or commemoration of the Annunciation, which was on that day, and many rounds were fired from the lombards. The king of that island of Española had got up very early and left his house, which is about five leagues away, reaching the village at three in the morning. There were several men from the ship in the village, who had been sent by the Admiral to see if any gold had arrived. They said that the king came with two hundred men; that he was carried in a litter by four men; and that he was a youth, as has already been said. Today, when the Admiral was dining under the poop, the king came on board with all his people.

The Admiral says to the Sovereigns: "Without doubt, his state, and the reverence with which he is treated by all his people, would appear good to your Highnesses, though they all go naked. When he came on board, he found that I was dining at a table under the poop, and, at a quick walk, he came to sit down by me, and did not wish that I should give place by coming to receive him or rising from the table, but that I should go on with my dinner. I thought that he would like to eat of our viands, and ordered them to be brought for him to eat. When he came under the poop, he made signs with his hand that all the rest should remain outside, and so they did, with the greatest possible promptitude and reverence. They all sat on the deck, except the men of mature age, whom I believe to be his councillors and tutor, who came and sat at his feet. Of the viands which I put before him, he took of each as much as would serve to taste it,[7] sending the rest to his people, who all partook of the dishes. The same thing in drinking: he just touched with his lips, giving the rest to his followers. They were all of fine presence and very few words. What they did say, so far as I could make out, was very clear and intelligent. The two at his feet watched his mouth, speaking to him and for him, and with much reverence. After dinner, an attendant brought a girdle, made like those of Castille, but of different material, which he took and gave to me, with pieces of worked gold, very thin. I believe they get very little here, but they say that they are very near the place where it is found, and where there is plenty. I saw that he was pleased with some drapery I had over my bed, so I gave it him, with some very good amber beads I wore on my neck, some coloured shoes, and a bottle of orange-flower water. He was marvellously well content, and both he and his tutor and councillors were very sorry that they could not understand me, nor I them. However, I knew that they said that, if I wanted anything, the whole island was at my disposal. I sent for some beads of mine, with which, as a charm, I had a gold *excelente*,[8] on which your Highnesses were stamped. I showed it to him, and said, as I had done yesterday, that your Highnesses ruled the best part of the world, and that there were no Princes so great. I also showed him the royal standards, and the others with a cross, of which he thought much. He said to his councillors what great lords your Highnesses must be to have sent me from so far, even from heaven to this country, without fear. Many other things passed between them which I did not understand, except that it was easy to see that they held everything to be very wonderful."

When it got late, and the king wanted to go, the Admiral sent him on shore in his boat very honourably, and saluted him with many guns. Having landed, he got into his litter, and departed with his 200 men, his son being carried behind on the shoulders of an Indian, a man highly respected. All the sailors and people from the ships were given to eat, and treated with much honour wherever they liked to stop. One sailor said that he had stopped in the road and seen all the things given by the Admiral. A man carried each one before the king, and these men appeared to be among those who were most respected. His son came a good distance behind the king, with a similar number of attendants, and the same with a brother of the king, except that the brother went on foot, supported under the arms by two honoured attendants. This brother came to the ship after the king, and the Admiral presented him with some of the things used for barter. It was then that the Admiral learnt that a king was called *Cacique* in their language. This day little gold was got by barter, but the Admiral heard from an old man that there were many neighbouring islands, at a distance of a hundred leagues or more, as he understood, in which much gold is found; and there is even one island that was all gold. In the others there was so much that it was said they gather it with sieves, and they fuse it and make bars, and work it in a thousand ways. They explained the work by signs. This old man pointed out to the Admiral the direction and position, and he determined to go there, saying that if the old man had not been a principal councillor of the king he would detain him, and make him go, too; or if he knew the language he would ask him, and he believed, as the old man was friendly with him and the other Christians, that he would go of his own accord. But as these people were now subjects of the King of Castille, and it would not be right to injure them, he decided upon leaving him. The Admiral set up a very large cross in the centre of the square of that village, the Indians giving much help; they made prayers and worshipped it, and, from the feeling they show, the Admiral trusted in our Lord that all the people of those islands would become Christians.

SATURDAY, 22ND OF DECEMBER.

At dawn the Admiral made sail to shape a course in search of the islands which the Indians had told him contained much gold, some of them having more gold than earth. But the weather was not favourable, so he anchored again, and sent away the boat to fish with a net. The Lord of that land,[9] who had a place near there, sent a large canoe full of people, including one of his principal attendants, to invite the Admiral to come with the ships to his land, where he would give him all he wanted. The Chief sent, by this servant, a girdle which, instead of a bag, had attached to it a mask with two large ears made of beaten gold, the tongue, and the nose. These people are very openhearted, and whatever they are asked for they give most willingly; while, when they themselves ask for anything, they do so as if receiving a great favour. So says the Admiral. They brought the canoe alongside the boat, and gave the girdle to a boy; then they came on board with their mission. It took a good part of the day before they could be understood. Not even the Indians who were on board understood them well, because they have some differences of words for the names of things. At last their invitation was understood by signs. The Admiral determined to start tomorrow, although he did not usually sail on a Sunday, owing to a devout feeling, and not on account of any superstition whatever. But in the hope that these people would become Christians through the willingness they show, and that they will be subjects of the Sovereigns of Castille, and because he now holds them to be so, and that they may serve with love, he wished and endeavoured to please them. Before leaving, to-day, the Admiral sent six men to a large village three leagues to the westward, because the Chief had come the day before and said that he had some pieces of gold. When the Christians arrived, the Secretary of the Admiral, who was one of them, took the Chief by the hand. The Admiral had sent him, to prevent the others from imposing upon the Indians. As the Indians are so simple, and the Spaniards so avaricious and grasping, it does not suffice that the Indians should give them all they want in exchange for a bead or a bit of glass, but the Spaniards would take everything without any return at all. The Admiral always prohibits this, although, with the exception of gold, the things given by the Indians are of little value. But the Admiral, seeing the simplicity of the Indians, and that they will give a piece of gold in exchange for six beads, gave the order that nothing should be received from them unless something had been given in exchange. Thus the Chief took the Secretary by the hand and led him to his house, followed by the whole village, which was very large. He made his guests eat, and the Indians brought them many cotton fabrics, and spun-cotton in skeins. In the afternoon the Chief gave them three very fat geese and some small pieces of gold. A great number of people went back with them, carrying all the things they had got by barter, and they also carried the Spaniards themselves across streams and muddy places. The Admiral ordered some things to be given to the Chief, and both he and his people were very well satisfied, truly believing that the Christians had come from heaven, so that they considered themselves fortunate in beholding them. On this day more than 120 canoes came to the ships, all full of people, and all bringing something, especially their bread and fish, and fresh water in earthen jars. They also brought seeds of good kinds, and there was a grain which they put into a porringer of water and drank it. The Indians who were on board said that this was very wholesome.

WEDNESDAY, 26TH OF DECEMBER.

To-day, at sunrise, the king of that land came to the caravel *Niña*, where the Admiral was, and said to him, almost weeping, that he need not be sorry, for that he would give him all he had; that he had placed two large houses at the disposal of the Christians who were on shore, and that he would give more if they were required, and as many canoes as could load from the ship and discharge on shore, with as many people as were wanted. This had all been done yesterday, without so much as a needle being missed. "So honest are they," says the Admiral, "without any covetousness for the goods of others, and so above all was that virtuous king." While the Admiral was talking to him, another canoe arrived from a different place, bringing some pieces of gold, which the people in the canoe wanted to exchange for a hawk's bell; for there was nothing they desired more than these bells. They had scarcely come alongside when they called and held up the gold, saying *Chuq chuq* for the bells, for they are quite mad about them.

After the king had seen this, and when the canoes which came from other places had departed, he called the Admiral and asked him to give orders that one of the bells was to be kept for another day, when he would bring four pieces of gold the size of a man's hand. The Admiral rejoiced to hear this, and afterwards a sailor, who came from the shore, told him that it was wonderful what pieces of gold the men on shore were getting in exchange for next to nothing. For a needle they got a piece of gold worth two *castellanos*, and that this was nothing to what it would be within a month. The king rejoiced much when he saw that the Admiral was pleased. He understood that his friend wanted much gold, and he said, by signs, that he knew where there was, in the vicinity, a very large quantity; so that he must be in good heart, for he should have as much as he wanted. He gave some account of it, especially saying that in *Cipango*, which they call *Cibao*, it is so abundant that it is of no value, and that they will bring it, although there is also much more in the island of *Española*, which they call *Bohio*, and in the province of *Caritaba*. The king dined on board the caravel with the Admiral and afterwards went on shore, where he received the Admiral with much honour. He gave him a collation consisting of three or four kinds of yams, with shellfish and game, and other viands they have, besides the bread they call *cazavi*. He then took the Admiral to see some groves of trees near the houses, and they were accompanied by at least a thousand people, all naked. The Lord had on a shirt and a pair of gloves, given to him by the Admiral, and he was more delighted with the gloves than with anything else. In his manner of eating, both as regards the high-bred air and the peculiar cleanliness he clearly showed his nobility. After he had eaten, he remained some time at table, and they brought him certain herbs, with which he rubbed his hands. The Admiral thought that this was done to make them soft, and they also gave him water for his hands. After the meal he took the Admiral to the beach. The Admiral then sent for a Turkish bow and a quiver of arrows, and took a shot at a man of his company, who had been warned. The chief, who knew nothing about arms, as they neither have them nor use them, thought this a wonderful thing. He, however, began to talk of those of *Caniba*, whom they call *Caribes*. They come to capture the natives, and have bows and arrows without iron, of which there is no memory in any of these lands, nor of steel, nor any other metal except gold and copper. Of copper the Admiral had only seen very little. The Admiral said, by signs, that the Sovereigns of Castille would order the Caribs to be destroyed, and that all should be taken with their heads tied together. He ordered a lombard and a hand-gun to be fired off, and seeing the effect caused by its force and what the shots penetrated, the king was astonished. When his people heard the explosion they all fell on the ground. They brought the Admiral a large mask, which had pieces of gold for the eyes and ears and in other parts, and this they gave, with other trinkets of gold that the same king had put on the head and round the neck of the Admiral, and of other Christians, to whom they also gave many pieces. The Admiral received much pleasure and consolation from these things, which tempered the anxiety and sorrow he felt at the loss of the ship [the Santa Maria ran aground on December 25, 1492, and was lost]. He knew our Lord had caused the ship to stop here, that a settlement might be formed. "From this", he says, "originated so many things that, in truth, the disaster was really a piece of good fortune. For it is certain that, if I had not lost the ship, I should have gone on without anchoring in this place, which is within a great bay, having two or three reefs of rock. I should not have left people in the country during this voyage, nor even, if I had desired to leave them, should I have been able to obtain so much information, nor such supplies and provisions for a fortress. And true it is that many people had asked me to give them leave to remain. Now I have given orders for a tower and a fort, both well built, and a large cellar, not because I believe that such defences will be necessary. I believe that with the force I have with me I could subjugate the whole island, which I believe to be larger than Portugal, and the population double. But they are naked and without arms, and hopelessly timid. Still, it is advisable to build this tower, being so far from your Highnesses. The people

may thus know the skill of the subjects of your Highnesses, and what they can do; and will obey them with love and fear. So they make preparations to build the fortress, with provision of bread and wine for more than a year, with seeds for sowing, the ship's boat, a caulker and carpenter, a gunner and cooper. Many among these men have a great desire to serve your Highnesses and to please me, by finding out where the mine is whence the gold is brought. Thus everything is got in readiness to begin the work. Above all, it was so calm that there was scarcely wind nor wave when the ship ran aground." This is what the Admiral says; and he adds more to show that it was great good luck, and the settled design of God, that the ship should be lost in order that people might be left behind. If it had not been for the treachery of the master and his boat's crew, who were all or mostly his countrymen,[10] in neglecting to lay out the anchor so as to haul the ship off in obedience to the Admiral's orders, she would have been saved. In that case, the same knowledge of the land as has been gained in these days would not have been secured, for the Admiral always proceeded with the object of discovering, and never intended to stop more than a day at any one place, unless he was detained by the wind. Still, the ship was very heavy and unsuited for discovery. It was the people of Palos who obliged him to take such a ship, by not complying "with what they had promised to the King and Queen, namely, to supply suitable vessels for this expedition. This they did not do. Of all that there was on board the ship, not a needle, nor a board, nor a nail was lost, for she remained as whole as when she sailed, except that it was necessary to cut away and level down in order to get out the jars and merchandise, which were landed and carefully guarded." He trusted in God that, when he returned from Spain, according to his intention, he would find a ton of gold collected by barter by those he was to leave behind, and that they would have found the mine, and spices in such quantities that the Sovereigns would, in three years, be able to undertake and fit out an expedition to go and conquer the Holy Sepulchre. "Thus," he says, "I protest to your Highnesses that all the profits of this my enterprise may be spent in the conquest of Jerusalem. Your Highnesses may laugh, and say that it is pleasing to you, and that, without this, you entertain that desire." These are the Admiral's words.

SUNDAY, 13TH OF JANUARY.

The Admiral did not leave the port, because there was no land-breeze with which to go out. He wished to shift to another better port, because this was rather exposed. He also wanted to wait, in that haven, the conjunction of the sun and moon, which would take place on the 17th of this month, and their opposition with Jupiter and conjunction with Mercury, the sun being in opposition to Jupiter, which is the cause of high winds. He sent the boat on shore to a beautiful beach to obtain yams for food. They found some men with bows and arrows, with whom they stopped to speak, buying two bows and many arrows from them. They asked one of them to come on board the caravel and see the Admiral; who says that he was very wanting in reverence, more so than any native he had yet seen. His face was all stained with charcoal, but in all parts there is the custom of painting the body different colours. He wore his hair very long, brought together and fastened behind, and put into a small net of parrots' feathers. He was naked, like all the others. The Admiral supposed that he belonged to the Caribs, who eat men, and that the gulf he had seen yesterday formed this part of the land into an island by itself. The Admiral asked about the Caribs, and he pointed to the east, near at hand, which means that he saw the Admiral yesterday before he entered the bay. The Indian said there was much gold to the east, pointing to the poop of the caravel, which was a good size, meaning that there were pieces as large. He called gold *tuob*, and did not understand *caona*, as they call it in the first part of the island that was visited, nor *nozay*, the name in San Salvador and the other islands. Copper is called *tuob* in Española. He also spoke of the island of *Goanin*, where there was much *tuob*. The Admiral says that he had received notices of these islands from many persons; that in the

other islands the natives were in great fear of the *Caribs,* called by some of them *Caniba,* but in Española *Carib.* He thought they must be an audacious race, for they go to all these islands and eat the people they can capture. He understood a few words, and the Indians who were on board comprehended more, there being a difference in the languages owing to the great distance between the various islands. The Admiral ordered that the Indian should be fed, and given pieces of green and red cloth, and glass beads, which they like very much, and then sent on shore. He was told to bring gold if he had any, and it was believed that he had, from some small things he brought with him. When the boat reached the shore there were fifty-five men behind the trees, naked, and with very long hair, as the women wear it in Castille. Behind the head they wore plumes of feathers of parrots and other birds, and each man carried a bow. The Indian landed, and signed to the others to put down their bows and arrows, and a piece of a staff, which is like … …., very heavy, carried instead of a sword. As soon as they came to the boat the crew landed, and began to buy the bows and arrows and other arms, in accordance with an order of the Admiral. Having sold two bows, they did not want to give more, but began to attack the Spaniards, and to take hold of them. They were running back to pick up their bows and arrows where they had laid them aside, and took cords in their hands to bind the boat's crew. Seeing them rushing down, and being prepared—for the Admiral always warned them to be on their guard—the Spaniards attacked the Indians, and gave one a stab with a knife in the buttocks, wounding another in the breast with an arrow. Seeing that they could gain little, although the Christians were only seven and they numbered over fifty, they fled, so that none were left, throwing bows and arrows away. The Christians would have killed many, if the pilot, who was in command, had not prevented them. The Spaniards presently returned to the caravel with the boat. The Admiral regretted the affair for one reason, and was pleased for another. They would have fear of the Christians, and they were no doubt an ill-conditioned people, probably

Caribs, who eat men. But the Admiral felt alarm lest they should do some harm to the 39 men left in the fortress and town of *Navidad*, in the event of their coming here in their boat. Even if they are not Caribs, they are a neighbouring people, with similar habits, and fearless, unlike the other inhabitants of the island, who are timid, and without arms. The Admiral says all this, and adds that he would have liked to have captured some of them. He says [10] that they lighted many smoke signals, as is the custom in this island of Española. ◆

ENDNOTES

1. Diego de Arana of Cordova, a near relation of Beatrix Henriquez, the mother of the Admiral's son Fernando.

2. *Dioscorea alata.* The stem has a woody tissue, with a large farinaceous tuber attached, which sometimes weighs 30 lbs.

3. Diego de Arana.

4. Rodrigo de Escobedo.

5. Las Casas suggests that this name *Baneque* may possibly mean Jamaica or the mainland.

6. The Feast of the Annunciation. *(Las Casas.)*

7. "Hacer la salva," the quantity taken by the taster before it was eaten by guests.

8. A coin worth two *castellanos*. The *castellano* was worth 490 *maravedis*.

9. This was Guacangari, Lord of Marien, afterwards the tried and steadfast friend of the Admiral.

10. Juan de la Cosa, the master, was a native of Santoña, on the north coast of Spain. There were two other Santoña men on board, and several from the north coast.

QUESTIONS

1. What was (were) Columbus's original goal(s)?

2. What goal(s) emerged once he arrived in the West Indies?

3. What did Columbus consider the local inhabitants to have become by the fact of his arrival?

4. How did Columbus contrast the Indians and the Spaniards?

5. Who were the Caribs and why did Columbus seek them out?

6. What did Columbus urge the king and queen of Spain to do with the profits made from his discovery and conquest?

A HISTORY OF THE ANCIENT WORLD

Fray Bernardino De Sahagun (1499–1590)

It is supposed that Yiacatecutli, god of merchants, was the one who started trading among those people, and that for this reason the guild of the merchants adopted him as their god and honored him in different ways, one being to offer him paper with which they covered his statues wherever they found them. They also venerated the cane (stick) with which they walked, which was a solid cane called utatl (also otate). They have still another kind of cane or walking stick made of a solid light black cane without a knot, and which looks like reed such as is used in Spain.[1] All merchants used that kind of cane on the road. When they reached the place where they were to spend the night, they would gather all their canes and tie them into one bundle, which they then stuck at the head of the sleeping place or camp. They would sprinkle blood in front of this bundle, which blood they obtained by bleeding their own ears, tongue, arms or legs. Then they offered incense by building a fire and burning copal in front of this bundle of sticks, which they considered as the image of the god Yiacatecutli, and by this means they asked him to protect them from all danger. These merchants traveled over the whole land, bartering, trading, buying in some place and selling in another what they had purchased. They also travel through towns, along the seashore, and in the interior. There isn't a place they do not pry into and visit, here buying, there selling; it is neither too hot for them in this place nor too cold in that one. They don't shun a road because it is too rough nor too difficult to search for whatever is there, either pretty or valuable or advantageous to buy and sell again. These traders suffer great hardships and are exceedingly daring; they go anywhere, even if it should be an enemy's domain and they are very sly in their deals with strangers, in learning their languages, as well as in their tactics, attaining through kindness what they want, thus gaining their confidence. They find out where the feathers (plumes) and the precious stones can be had, or the gold; there they purchase them and take them to where they are worth a great deal. They also know where to go to find exquisite and valuable skins of beasts, and where to resell them at high prices. Likewise do they deal in precious cups of many different kinds and material adorned with diverse painted figures, and which are used in all the different districts; some of these cups have covers made of tortoise shell and spoons of the same to stir the cocoa; there are cups with covers painted in different colors and figures, made to resemble a leaf of the "vinarbol"[2] and with various kinds of beautiful sticks with which they stirred their cocoa. If they are forced to enter an enemy's realm, they first learn the language of these people; they adopt their mode of dress so they might not be taken for strangers, but for people of that same country. It often happened that the enemy recognized them, capturing and killing them. If one or two or more were able to escape, they were wont to notify the chief or principal lord of the province, as, for instance, Moteccuzuma or any of his predecessors, bringing him as an offering some of the treasures of those countries, making a present of these things in remuneration of their sufferings, and in order to be honored by their people and considered courageous. They would give him an amber bib, which is a large, transparent, yellow stone which hangs from the lower lip as a sign that he was brave and noble, too; this bib was highly valued.

Whenever these traders or merchants left for such a voyage to foreign lands they took leave of their relatives amid great ceremonies, in accordance with ancient rites. They remained absent many years, and when they returned they brought back great riches (many treasures). In order to display what they had and to give an account of the countries they had visited and the things they had seen, soon upon their return they would invite all the traders (merchants), especially the principal ones, as well as the chieftains of the town, and arranged a great festivity for them. These festivities they called "washing of feet." The guests did great honor to the cane (walking-stick) with which the traveler had gone and come back; considered it the image of Yiacatecutli, god of the merchants, who had favored them to travel the roads and brought them back safely. In order to do due honor to the cane they placed it in one of the temples they had in the different quarters of the town, and which they call calpulli, which means church of the district or parish. In the calpulli to which this particular trader belonged, he put the cane in an honored place, and when the dinner was served to his guests, he first placed food, flowers, and acayietl (small tube containing incense of odoriferous herbs which was burned in front of the stick); and even afterwards, after the invitation was over, each time the trader was about to eat he first placed food and all the other things in front of the stick (cane), which he now kept in his own home, in the private oratory thereof. All these traders, after returning from one of their voyages, as they now were wealthy, would buy male and female slaves, whom they offered to their god on his feast, this generally being Yiacatecutli, who had five brothers and one sister, all being held as deities, and according to the size of their devotion, they would sacrifice slaves to each one of them separately on his personal feast, or to all together, or to the sister alone.

ENDNOTES

1. The well known Malacca cane.
2. Probably a name for the grape-vine.

QUESTIONS

1. Where do Aztec merchants travel, according to Sahagun?

2. How long are they on the road at a time?

3. What kind of specialized knowledge do they have?

From *The True History of the Conquest of New Spain*

Bernal Díaz Del Castillo (1492–1581)

Chapter XCI.

Of the manner and appearance of the Great
Montezuma and what a great Prince he was.

The Great Montezuma was about forty years
old, of good height and well proportioned,
slender, and spare of flesh, not very swarthy,
but of the natural colour and shade of an
Indian. He did not wear his hair long, but so as
just to cover his ears, his scanty black beard
was well shaped and thin. His face was somewhat long, but cheerful, and he had good eyes
and showed in his appearance and manner
both tenderness and, when necessary, gravity.
He was very neat and clean and bathed once
every day in the afternoon.[1] He had many
women as mistresses, daughters of Chieftains,
and he had two great Cacicas as his legitimate
wives, and when he had intercourse with them
it was so secretly that no one knew anything
about it, except some of his servants. He was
free from unnatural offenses. The clothes that
he wore one day, he did not put on again until
four days later. He had over two hundred
chieftains in his guard, in other rooms close to
his own, not that all were meant to converse
with him, but only one or another, and when
they went to speak to him they were obliged to
take off their rich mantles and put on others of
little worth, but they had to be clean, and they
had to enter barefoot with their eyes lowered
to the ground, and not to look up in his face.
And they made him three obeisances, and said:
"Lord, my Lord, my Great Lord," before they
came up to him, and then they made their
report and with a few words he dismissed
them, and on taking leave they did not turn
their backs, but kept their faces toward him
with their eyes to the ground, and they did not
turn their backs until they left the room. I
noticed another thing, that when other great
chiefs came from distant lands about disputes
or business, when they reached the apartments
of the Great Montezuma, they had to come
barefoot and with poor mantles, and they
might not enter directly into the Palace, but
had to loiter about a little on one side of the
Palace door, for to enter hurriedly was considered to be disrespectful.

For each meal, over thirty different dishes
were prepared by his cooks according to their
ways and usage, and they placed small pottery
brasiers beneath the dishes so that they should
not get cold. They prepared more than three
hundred plates of the food that Montezuma
was going to eat, and more than a thousand for
the guard. When he was going to eat, Montezuma would sometimes go out with his chiefs
and stewards, and they would point out to him
which dish was best, and of what birds and
other things it was composed, and as they
advised him, so he would eat, but it was not
often that he would go out to see the food, and
then merely as a pastime.

I have heard it said that they were wont to
cook for him the flesh of young boys, but as he
had such a variety of dishes, made of so many
things, we could not succeed in seeing if they
were of human flesh or of other things, for they
daily cooked fowls, turkeys, pheasants, native
partridges, quail, tame and wild ducks, venison, wild boar, reed birds, pigeons, hares and
rabbits, and many sorts of birds and other
things which are bred in this country, and they
are so numerous that I cannot finish naming
them in a hurry; so we had no insight into it,
but I know for certain that after our Captain
censured the sacrifice of human beings, and the
eating of their flesh, he ordered that such food
should not be prepared for him thenceforth.

Let us cease speaking of this and return to
the way things were served to him at meal
times. It was in this way: if it was cold they
made up a large fire of live coals of a firewood
made from the bark of trees which did not give
off any smoke, and the scent of the bark from

which the fire was made was very fragrant, and so that it should not give off more heat than he required, they placed in front of it a sort of screen adorned with figures of idols worked in gold. He was seated on a low stool, soft and richly worked, and the table, which was also low, was made in the same style as the seats, and on it they placed the table cloths of white cloth and some rather long napkins of the same material. Four very beautiful cleanly women brought water for his hands in a sort of deep basin which they call "xicales,"[2] and they held others like plates below to catch the water, and they brought him towels. And two other women brought him tortilla bread, and as soon as he began to eat they placed before him a sort of wooden screen painted over with gold, so that no one should watch him eating. Then the four women stood aside, and four great chieftains who were old men came and stood beside them, and with these Montezuma now and then conversed, and asked them questions, and as a great favor he would give to each of these elders a dish of what to him tasted best. They say that these elders were his near relations, and were his counselors and judges of law suits, and the dishes and food which Montezuma gave them they ate standing up with much reverence and without looking at his face. He was served on Cholula earthenware either red or black. While he was at his meal the men of his guard who were in the rooms near to that of Montezuma, never dreamed of making any noise or speaking aloud. They brought him fruit of all the different kinds that the land produced, but he ate very little of it. From time to time they brought him, in cup-shaped vessels of pure gold, a certain drink made from cacao which they said he took when he was going to visit his wives, and at the time he took no heed of it, but what I did see was that they brought over fifty great jugs of good cacao frothed up, and he drank of that, and the women served this drink to him with great reverence.

Sometimes at meal-times there were present some very ugly humpbacks, very small of stature and their bodies almost broken in half, who are their jesters, and other Indians, who must have been buffoons, who told him witty sayings, and others who sang and danced, for Montezuma was fond of pleasure and song, and to these he ordered to be given what was left of the food and the jugs of cacao. Then the same four women removed the table cloths, and with much ceremony they brought water for his hands. And Montezuma talked with those four old chieftains about things that interested him, and they took leave of him with the great reverence in which they held him, and he remained to repose.

As soon as the Great Montezuma had dined, all the men of the Guard had their meal and as many more of the other house servants, and it seems to me that they brought out over a thousand dishes of the food of which I have spoken, and then over two thousand jugs of cacao all frothed up, as they make it in Mexico, and a limitless quantity of fruit, so that with his women and female servants and bread makers and cacao makers his expenses must have been very great.

Let us cease talking about the expenses and the food for his household and let us speak of the Stewards and the Treasurers and the stores and pantries and of those who had charge of the houses where the maize was stored. I say that there would be so much to write about, each thing by itself, that I should not know where to begin, but we stood astonished at the excellent arrangements and the great abundance of provisions that he had in all, but I must add what I had forgotten, for it is as well to go back and relate it, and that is, that while Montezuma was at table eating as I have described, there were waiting on him two other graceful women to bring him tortillas, kneaded with eggs and other sustaining ingredients, and these tortillas were very white, and they were brought on plates covered with clean napkins, and they also brought him another kind of bread, like long balls kneaded with other kinds of sustaining food, and "pan pachol" for so they call it in this country, which is a sort of wafer. There were also placed on the table three tubes much painted and gilded, which held *liquidambar* mixed with certain herbs which they call *tabaco,* and when he had finished eating, after they had danced before him and sung and the table was removed, he inhaled the smoke from one of those tubes, but he took very little of it and with that he fell asleep.

Let us cease speaking about the service of his table and go back to our story. I remember that at that time his steward was a great Cacique to whom we gave the name of Tápia, and he kept the accounts of all the revenue that was brought to Montezuma, in his books which were made of paper which they call *Amal*, and he had a great house full of these books. Now we must leave the books and the accounts for it is outside our story, and say how Montezuma had two houses full of every sort of arms, many of them richly adorned with gold and precious stones. There were shields great and small, and a sort of broad-swords, and others like two-handed swords set with stone knives which cut much better than our swords, and lances longer than ours are, with a fathom of blade with many knives set in it, which even when they are driven into a buckler or shield do not come out, in fact they cut like razors so that they can shave their heads with them. There were very good bows and arrows and double-pointed lances and others with one point, as well as their throwing sticks, and many slings and round stones shaped by hand, and some sort of artful shields which are so made that they can be rolled up, so as not to be in the way when they are not fighting, and when they are needed for fighting they let them fall down, and they cover the body from top to toe. There was also much quilted cotton armour, richly ornamented on the outside with many coloured feathers, used as devices and distinguishing marks, and there were casques or helmets made of wood and bone, also highly decorated with feathers on the outside, and there were other arms of other makes which, so as to avoid prolixity, I will not describe, and there were artizans who were skilled in such things and worked at them, and stewards who had charge of the arms.

Let us leave this and proceed to the Aviary, and I am forced to abstain from enumerating every kind of bird that was there and its peculiarity, for there was everything from the Royal Eagle and other smaller eagles, and many other birds of great size, down to tiny birds of many-coloured plumage, also the birds from which they take the rich plumage which they use in their green feather work. The birds which have

these feathers are about the size of the magpies in Spain, they are called in this country *Quezales*, and there are other birds which have feathers of five colours—green, red, white, yellow and blue; I don't remember what they are called; then there were parrots of many different colours, and there are so many of them that I forget their names, not to mention the beautifully marked ducks and other larger ones like them. From all these birds they plucked the feathers when the time was right to do so, and the feathers grew again. All the birds that I have spoken about breed in these houses, and in the setting season certain Indian men and women who look after the birds, place the eggs under them and clean the nests and feed them, so that each kind of bird has its proper food. In this house that I have spoken of there is a great tank of fresh water and in it there are other sorts of birds with long stilted legs, with body, wings and tail all red; I don't know their names, but in the Island of Cuba they are called *Ypiris*, and there are others something like them, and there are also in that tank many other kinds of birds which always live in the water.

Let us leave this and go on to another great house, where they keep many Idols, and they say that they are their fierce gods, and with them many kinds of carnivorous beasts of prey, tigers and two kinds of lions, and animals something like wolves which in this country they call jackals and foxes, and other smaller carnivorous animals, and all these carnivores they feed with flesh, and the greater number of them breed in the house. They give them as food deer and fowls, dogs and other things which they are used to hunt, and I have heard it said that they feed them on the bodies of the Indians who have been sacrificed. It is in this way: you have already heard me say that when they sacrifice a wretched Indian they saw open the chest with stone knives and hasten to tear out the palpitating heart and blood, and offer it to their Idols in whose name the sacrifice is made. Then they cut off the thighs, arms and head and eat the former at feasts and banquets, and the head they hang up on some beams, and the body of the man sacrificed is not eaten but given to these fierce animals. They also have in that cursed house many vipers and poisonous snakes which carry on their tails things that sound like bells. These are the worst vipers of all, and they keep them in jars and great pottery vessels with many feathers, and there they lay their eggs and rear their young, and they give them to eat the bodies of the Indians who have been sacrificed, and the flesh of dogs which they are in the habit of breeding. We even knew for certain that when they drove us out of Mexico and killed over eight hundred of our soldiers that they fed those fierce animals and snakes for many days on their bodies, as I will relate at the proper time and season. And those snakes and wild beasts were dedicated to those savage Idols, so that they might keep them company.

Let me speak now of the infernal noise when the lions and tigers roared and the jackals and the foxes howled and the serpents hissed, it was horrible to listen to and it seemed like a hell. Let us go on and speak of the skilled workmen he [Montezuma] employed in every craft that was practised among them. We will begin with lapidaries and workers in gold and silver and all the hollow work, which even the great goldsmiths in Spain were forced to admire, and of these there were a great number of the best in a town named Atzcapotzalco,[3] a league from Mexico. Then for working precious stones and chalchihuites, which are like emeralds, there were other great artists. Let us go on to the great craftsmen in feather work, and painters and sculptors who were most refined; from what we see of their work to-day we can form a judgment of what they did then, for there are three Indians to-day in the City of Mexico named Marcos de Aquino, Juan de la Cruz and El Crespillo, so skillful in their work as sculptors and painters, that had they lived in the days of the ancient and famous Apelles, or of Michael Angelo Buonarotti, in our times, they would be placed in the same company. Let us go on to the Indian women who did the weaving and the washing, who made such an immense quantity of fine fabrics with wonderful feather work designs; the greater part of it was brought daily from some towns of the province on the north coast near Vera Cruz called Cotaxtla, close by San Juan de Ulua, where we disembarked when we came with Cortés.

In the house of the Great Montezuma himself, all the daughters of chieftains whom he had as mistresses always wore beautiful things, and there were many daughters of Mexican citizens who lived in retirement and wished to appear to be like nuns, who also did weaving but it was wholly of feather work. These nuns had their houses near the great Cue of Huichilobos and out of devotion to it, or to another idol, that of a woman who was said to be their mediatrix in the matter of marriage, their fathers placed them in that religious retirement until they married, and they were [only] taken out thence to be married.

Let us go on and tell about the great number of dancers kept by the Great Montezuma for his amusement, and others who used stilts on their feet, and others who flew when they danced up in the air, and others like Merry-Andrews, and I may say that there was a district full of these people who had no other occupation. Let us go on and speak of the workmen that he had as stone cutters, masons and carpenters, all of whom attended to the work of his houses, I say that he had as many as he wished for. We must not forget the gardens of flowers and sweet-scented trees, and the many kinds that there were of them, and the arrangement of them and the walks, and the ponds and tanks of fresh water where the water entered at one end and flowed out at the other; and the baths which he had there, and the variety of small birds that nested in the branches, and the medicinal and useful herbs that were in the gardens. It was a wonder to see, and to take care of it there were many gardeners. Everything was made in masonry and well cemented, baths and walks and closets, and apartments like summer houses where they danced and sang. There was as much to be seen in these gardens as there was everywhere else, and we could not tire of witnessing his great power. Thus as a consequence of so many crafts being practised among them, a large number of skilled Indians were employed.

As I am almost tired of writing about this subject and my interested readers will be even more so, I will stop talking about it and tell how our Cortés in company with many of our captains and soldiers went to see Tlaltelolco,[4] which is the great market place of Mexico, and how we ascended the great Cue where stand the Idols Tezcatepuca and Huichilobos. This was the first time that our Captain went out to see the City, and I will relate what else happened.

Chapter XCII.

How our Captain went out to see the City of Mexico and Tlaltelolco, which is the great market place, to find the great Cue of Huichilobos, and what else happened.

As we had already been four days in Mexico and neither the Captain nor any of us had left our lodgings except to go to the houses and gardens, Cortés said to us that it would be well to go to the great Plaza and see the great Temple of Huichilobos, and that he wished to consult the Great Montezuma and have his approval. For this purpose he sent Jerónimo de Aguilar and the Doña Marina as messengers, and with them went our Captain's small page named Orteguilla, who already understood something of the language. When Montezuma knew his wishes he sent to say that we were welcome to go; on the other hand, as he was afraid that we might do some dishonour to his Idols, he determined to go with us himself with many of his chieftains. He came out from his Palace in his rich litter, but when half the distance had been traversed and he was near some oratories, he stepped out of the litter, for he thought it a great affront to his idols to go to their house and temple in that manner. Some of the great chieftains supported him with their arms, and the tribal lords went in front of him carrying two staves like sceptres held on high, which was the sign that the Great Montezuma was coming. (When he went in his litter he carried a wand half of gold and half of wood, which was held up like a wand of justice.) So he went on and ascended the great Cue accompanied by many priests, and he began to burn incense and perform other ceremonies to Huichilobos.

Let us leave Montezuma, who had gone ahead as I have said, and return to Cortés and our captains and soldiers, who according to our custom both night and day were armed, and as Montezuma was used to see us so armed when we went to visit him, he did not look upon it as anything new. I say this because our Captain and all those who had horses went to Tlaltelolco on horseback, and nearly all of its soldiers were fully equipped, and many Caciques whom Montezuma had sent for that purpose went in our Company. When we arrived at the great market place, called Tlaltelolco, we were astounded at the number of people and the quantity of merchandise that it contained, and at the good order and control that was maintained, for we had never seen such a thing before. The chieftains who accompanied us acted as guides. Each kind of merchandise was kept by itself and had its fixed place marked out. Let us begin with the dealers in gold, silver, and precious stones, feathers, mantles, and embroidered goods. Then there were other wares consisting of Indian slaves both men and women; and I say that they bring as many of them to that great market for sale as the Portuguese bring negroes from Guinea; and they brought them along tied to long poles, with collars round their necks so that they could not escape, and others they left free. Next there were other traders who sold great pieces of cloth and cotton, and articles of twisted thread, and there were *cacahuateros* who sold cacao. In this way one could see every sort of merchandise that is to be found in the whole of New Spain, placed in arrangement in the same manner as they do in my own country, which is Medina del Campo, where they hold the fairs, where each line of booths has its particular kind of merchandise, and so it is in this great market. There were those who sold cloths of henequen and ropes and the *cotaras*[5] with which they are shod, which are made from the same plant, and sweet cooked roots, and other tubers which they get from this plant, all were kept in one part of the market in the place assigned to them. In another part there were skins of tigers and lions, of otters and jackals, deer and other animals and badgers and mountain cats, some tanned and others untanned, and other classes of merchandise.

Let us go on and speak of those who sold beans and sage and other vegetables and herbs in another part, and to those who sold fowls, cocks with wattles, rabbits, hares, deer, mallards, young dogs and other things of that sort in their part of the market, and let us also mention the fruiterers, and the women who sold cooked food, dough and tripe in their own part of the market; then every sort of pottery made in a thousand different forms from great water jars to little jugs, these also had a place to themselves; then those who sold honey and honey paste and other dainties like nut paste, and those who sold lumber, boards, cradles, beams, blocks and benches, each article by itself, and the vendors of *ocote*[6] firewood, and other things of a similar nature. I must furthermore mention, asking your pardon, that they also sold many canoes full of human excrement, and these were kept in the creeks near the market, and this they use to make salt or for tanning skins, for without it they say that they cannot be well prepared. I know well that some gentlemen laugh at this, but I say that it is so, and I may add that on all the roads it is a usual thing to have places made of reeds or straw or grass, so that they may be screened from the passers by, into these they retire when they wish to purge their bowels so that even that filth should not be lost. But why do I waste so many words in recounting what they sell in that great market, for I shall never finish if I tell it all in detail. Paper, which in this country is called *Amal*, and reeds scented with *liquidambar*, and full of tobacco, and yellow ointments and things of that sort are sold by themselves, and much cochineal is sold under the arcades which are in that great market place, and there are many vendors of herbs and other sorts of trades. There are also buildings where three magistrates sit in judgment, and there are executive officers like *Alguacils* who inspect the merchandise. I am forgetting those who sell salt, and those who make the stone knives, and how they split them off the stone itself; and the fisherwomen and others who sell some small cakes made from a sort of ooze which they get out of the great lake, which curdles, and from this they make a bread having a flavour something like cheese. There are for sale axes of brass and copper and tin, and gourds and gaily painted jars made of wood. I could wish that I had finished telling of all the things which are sold there, but they are so numerous and of such different quality and the great market place with its surrounding arcades was so crowded with people, that one would not have been able to see and inquire about it all in two days.

Then we went to the great Cue, and when we were already approaching its great courts, before leaving the market place itself, there were many more merchants, who, as I was told, brought gold for sale in grains, just as it is taken from the mines. The gold is placed in thin quills of the geese of the country, white quills, so that the gold can be seen through, and according to the length and thickness of the quills they arrange their accounts with one another, how much so many mantles or so many gourds full of cacao were worth, or how many slaves, or whatever other thing they were exchanging.

Now let us leave the great market place, and not look at it again, and arrive at the great courts and walls where the great Cue stands. Before reaching the great Cue there is a great enclosure of courts, it seems to me larger than the plaza of Salamanca, with two walls of masonry surrounding it and the court itself all paved with very smooth great white flagstones. And where there were not these stones it was cemented and burnished and all very clean, so that one could not find any dust or a straw in the whole place.

When we arrived near the great Cue and before we had ascended a single step of it, the Great Montezuma sent down from above, where he was making his sacrifices, six priests and two chieftains to accompany our Captain. On ascending the steps, which are one hundred and fourteen in number, they attempted to take him by the arms so as to help him to ascend, (thinking that he would get tired,) as they were accustomed to assist their lord Montezuma, but Cortés would not allow them to come near him. When we got to the top of the great Cue, on a small plaza which has been made on the top where there was a space like a platform with some large stones placed on it, on which they put the poor Indians for sacrifice, there was a bulky image like a dragon and other evil figures and much blood shed that very day.

When we arrived there Montezuma came out of an oratory where his cursed idols were, at the summit of the great Cue, and two priests came with him, and after paying great reverence to Cortés and to all of us he said: "You must be tired, Señor Malinche, from ascending this our great Cue," and Cortés replied through our interpreters who were with us that he and his companions were never tired by anything. Then Montezuma took him by the hand and told him to look at his great city and all the other cities that were standing in the water, and the many other towns on the land round the lake, and that if he had not seen the great market place well, that from where they were they could see it better.

So we stood looking about us, for that huge and cursed temple stood so high that from it one could see over everything very well, and we saw the three causeways which led into Mexico, that is the causeway of Iztapalapa by which we had entered four days before, and that of Tacuba, along which later on we fled on the night of our great defeat, when Cuitlahuac[7] the new prince drove us out of the city, as I shall tell later on, and that of Tepeaquilla,[8] and we saw the fresh water that comes from Chapultepec which supplies the city, and we saw the bridges on the three causeways which were built at certain distances apart through which the water of the lake flowed in and out from one side to the other, and we beheld on that great lake a great multitude of canoes, some coming with supplies of food and others returning loaded with cargoes of merchandise; and we saw that from every house of that great city and of all the other cities that were built in the water it was impossible to pass from house to house, except by drawbridges which were made of wood or in canoes; and we saw in those cities Cues and oratories like towers and fortresses and all gleaming white, and it was a wonderful thing to behold; then the houses with flat roofs, and on the causeways other small towers and oratories which were like fortresses.

After having examined and considered all that we had seen we turned to look at the great market place and the crowds of people that were in it, some buying and others selling, so that the murmur and hum of their voices and words that they used could be heard more than a league off. Some of the soldiers among us who had been in many parts of the world, in Constantinople, and all over Italy, and in Rome, said that so large a market place and so full of people, and so well regulated and arranged, they had never beheld before. ♦

ENDNOTES

1. Blotted out in the original: "about the hour of (Ave Maria) evening prayer."—G. G.

2. Gourds.

3. Escapuçalco in the text.

4. Tutelulco in the text.

5. Sandals.

6. Pitch-pine for torches.

7. Cuedlabaca in the text.

8. Guadelupe.

QUESTIONS

1. What products were for sale in the marketplace in Tenochtitlan and how was gold used as currency?

2. Why would the Aztecs place a screen in front of Montezuma while he was eating?

3. What kinds of arms did Diaz say that Montezuma used?

4. How skilled were the Aztec artisans?

5. What was the "cue" (a word apparently invented by Diaz and pronounced *cué*)? What went on there?

6. Why would Diaz depict these details?

OF PROPERTY

FROM *THE SECOND TREATISE OF CIVIL GOVERNMENT*

John Locke (1632–1704)

Whether we consider natural reason, which tells us that men being once born have a right to their preservation, and consequently to meat and drink and such other things as nature affords for their subsistence; or Revelation, which gives us an account of those grants God made of the world to Adam, and to Noah and his sons, 'tis very clear that God, as King David says, Psalm cxv. 16, "has given the earth to the children of men," given it to mankind in common. But this being supposed, it seems to some a very great difficulty how any one should ever come to have a property in anything. I will not content myself to answer that if it be difficult to make out property upon a supposition that God gave the world to Adam and his posterity in common, it is impossible that any man but one universal monarch should have any property upon a supposition that God gave the world to Adam and his heirs in succession, exclusive of all the rest of his posterity. But I shall endeavour to show how men might come to have a property in several parts of that which God gave to mankind in common, and that without any express compact of all the commoners.

God, who hath given the world to men in common, hath also given them reason to make use of it to the best advantage of life and convenience. The earth and all that is therein is given to men for the support and comfort of their being. And though all the fruits it naturally produces, and beasts it feeds, belong to mankind in common, as they are produced by the spontaneous hand of nature; and nobody has originally a private dominion exclusive of the rest of mankind in any of them as they are thus in their natural state; yet being given for the use of men, there must of necessity be a means to appropriate them some way or other before they can be of any use or at all beneficial to any particular man. The fruit or venison which nourishes the wild Indian, who knows no enclosure, and is still a tenant in common, must be

his, and so his, *i.e.*, a part of him, that another can no longer have any right to it, before it can do any good for the support of his life.

Though the earth and all inferior creatures be common to all men, yet every man has a property in his own person; this nobody has any right to but himself. The labour of his body and the work of his hands we may say are properly his. Whatsoever, then, he removes out of the state that nature hath provided and left it in, he hath mixed his labour with, and joined to it something that is his own, and thereby makes it his property. It being by him removed from the common state nature placed it in, it hath by this labour something annexed to it that excludes the common right of other men. For this labour being the unquestionable property of the labourer, no man but he can have a right to what that is once joined to, at least where there is enough, and as good left in common for others.

He that is nourished by the acorns he picked up under an oak, or the apples he gathered from the trees in the wood, has certainly appropriated them to himself. Nobody can deny but the nourishment is his. I ask, then, When did they begin to be his—when he digested, or when he ate, or when he boiled, or when he brought them home, or when he picked them up? And 'tis plain if the first gathering made them not his, nothing else could. That labour put a distinction between them and common; that added something to them more than Nature, the common mother of all, had done, and so they became his private right. And will any one say he had no right to those acorns or apples he thus appropriated, because he had not the consent of all mankind to make them his? Was it a robbery thus to assume to himself what belonged to all in common? If such a consent as that was necessary, man had starved, not-withstanding the plenty God had given him. We see in commons which remain so by compact that 'tis the taking any part of what is common and removing it out of the state nature leaves it in, which begins the property; without which the common is of no use. And the taking of this or that part does not depend on the express consent of all the commoners. Thus the grass my horse has bit, the turfs my servant has cut, and the ore I have dug in any place where I have a right to them in common with others, become my property without the assignation or consent of anybody. The labour that was mine removing them out of that common state they were in, hath fixed my property in them.

By making an explicit consent of every commoner necessary to any one's appropriating to himself any part of what is given in common, children or servants could not cut the meat which their father or master had provided for them in common without assigning to every one his peculiar part. Though the water running in the fountain be every one's, yet who can doubt but that in the pitcher is his only who drew it out? His labour hath taken it out of the hands of Nature, where it was common, and belonged equally to all her children, and hath thereby appropriated it to himself.

Thus this law of reason makes the deer that Indian's who hath killed it; 'tis allowed to be his goods who hath bestowed his labour upon it, though before it was the common right of every one. And amongst those who are counted the civilised part of mankind, who have made and multiplied positive laws to determine property, this original law of nature, for the beginning of property in what was before common, still takes place; and by virtue thereof, what fish any one catches in the ocean, that great and still remaining common of mankind, or what ambergris any one takes up here, is, by the labour that removes it out of that common state nature left it in, made his property who takes that pains about it. And even amongst us, the hare that any one is hunting is thought his who pursues her during the chase. For being a beast that is still looked upon as common, and no man's private possession, whoever has employed so much labour about any of that kind as to find and pursue her has thereby removed her from the state of nature wherein she was common, and hath begun a property.

It will perhaps be objected to this, that if gathering the acorns, or other fruits of the earth, &c., makes a right to them, then any one may engross as much as he will. To which I answer, Not so. The same law of nature that does by this means give us property, does also bound that property too. "God has given us all things richly" (1 Tim. vi. 17), is the voice of reason confirmed by inspiration. But how far has He given it us? To enjoy. As much as any one can make use of to any advantage of life before it spoils, so much he may by his labour fix a property in; whatever is beyond this, is more than his share, and belongs to others. Nothing was made by God for man to spoil or destroy. And thus considering the plenty of natural provisions there was a long time in the world, and the few spenders, and to how small a part of that provision the industry of one man could extend itself, and engross it to the prejudice of others—especially keeping within the bounds, set by reason, of what might serve for his use—there could be then little room for quarrels or contentions about property so established.

But the chief matter of property being now not the fruits of the earth, and the beasts that subsist on it, but the earth itself, as that which takes in and carries with it all the rest, I think it is plain that property in that, too, is acquired as the former. As much land as a man tills, plants, improves, cultivates, and can use the product of, so much is his property. He by his labour does as it were enclose it from the common. Nor will it invalidate his right to say, everybody else has an equal title to it; and therefore he cannot appropriate, he cannot enclose, without the consent of all his fellow-commoners, all mankind. God, when He gave the world in common to all mankind, commanded man also to labour, and the penury of his condition required it of him. God and his reason commanded him to subdue the earth, *i.e.,* improve it for the benefit of life, and therein lay out something upon it that was his own, his labour. He that, in obedience to this command of God, subdued, tilled, and sowed any part of it, thereby annexed to it something that was his property, which another had no title to, nor could without injury take from him.

Nor was this appropriation of any parcel of land, by improving it, any prejudice to any other man, since there was still enough and as good left; and more than the yet unprovided could use. So that in effect there was never the less left for others because of his enclosure for himself. For he that leaves as much as another can make use of, does as good as take nothing at all. Nobody could think himself injured by the drinking of another man, though he took a good draught, who had a whole river of the same water left him to quench his thirst; and the case of land and water, where there is enough of both, is perfectly the same.

God gave the world to men in common; but since He gave it them for their benefit, and the greatest conveniences of life they were capable to draw from it, it cannot be supposed He meant it should always remain common and uncultivated. He gave it to the use of the industrious and rational (and labour was to be his title to it), not to the fancy or covetousness of the quarrelsome and contentious. He that had as good left for his improvement as was already taken up, needed not complain, ought not to meddle with what was already improved by another's labour; if he did, it is plain he desired the benefit of another's pains, which he had no right to, and not the ground which God had given him in common with others to labour on, and whereof there was as good left as that already possessed, and more than he knew what to do with, or his industry could reach to.

It is true, in land that is common in England, or any other country where there is plenty of people under Government, who have money and commerce, no one can enclose or appropriate any part without the consent of all his fellow-commoners: because this is left common by compact, *i.e.*, by the law of the land, which is not to be violated. And though it be common in respect of some men, it is not so to all mankind; but is the joint property of this country, or this parish. Besides, the remainder, after such enclosure, would not be as good to the rest of the commoners as the whole was, when they could all make use of the whole; whereas in the beginning and first peopling of the great common of the world it was quite otherwise. The law man was under, was rather for appropriat-

ing. God commanded, and his wants forced him, to labour. That was his property, which could not be taken from him wherever he had fixed it. And hence subduing or cultivating the earth, and having dominion, we see are joined together. The one gave title to the other. So that God, by commanding to subdue, gave authority so far to appropriate. And the condition of human life, which requires labour and materials to work on, necessarily introduces private possessions.

The measure of property nature has well set by the extent of men's labour and the convenience of life. No man's labour could subdue or appropriate all; nor could his enjoyment consume more than a small part; so that it was impossible for any man, this way, to intrench upon the right of another, or acquire to himself a property to the prejudice of his neighbour, who would still have room for as good and as large a possession (after the other had taken out his) as before it was appropriated. Which measure did confine every man's possession to a very moderate proportion, and such as he might appropriate to himself without injury to anybody, in the first ages of the world, when men were more in danger to be lost by wandering from their company in the then vast wilderness of the earth than to be straitened for want of room to plant in. And the same measure may be allowed still without prejudice to anybody, as full as the world seems. For supposing a man or family in the state they were at first peopling of the world by the children of Adam or Noah; let him plant in some inland vacant places of America, we shall find that the possessions he could make himself, upon the measures we have given, would not be very large, nor, even to this day, prejudice the rest of mankind, or give them reason to complain or think themselves injured by this man's encroachment, though the race of men have now spread themselves to all the corners of the world, and do infinitely exceed the small number that was at the beginning. Nay, the extent of ground is of so little value without labour, that I have heard it affirmed that in Spain itself a man may be permitted to plough, sow, and reap, without being disturbed, upon land he has no other title to but only his making use of it. But, on the contrary, the inhabitants think themselves beholden to him who by his industry on neglected and consequently waste land has increased the stock of corn which they wanted. But be this as it will, which I lay no stress on, this I dare boldly affirm—that the same rule of propriety, viz., that every man should have as much as he could make use of, would hold still in the world without straitening anybody, since there is land enough in the world to suffice double the inhabitants, had not the invention of money, and the tacit agreement of men to put a value on it, introduced (by consent) larger possessions and a right to them; which how it has done I shall by-and-bye show more at large.

This is certain, that in the beginning, before the desire of having more than man needed had altered the intrinsic value of things, which depends only on their usefulness to the life of man; or had agreed that a little piece of yellow metal which would keep without wasting or decay should be worth a great piece of flesh or a whole heap of corn, though men had a right to appropriate by their labour, each one to himself, as much of the things of nature as he could use, yet this could not be much, nor to the prejudice of others, where the same plenty was still left to those who would use the same industry.

Before the appropriation of land, he who gathered as much of the wild fruit, killed, caught, or tamed as many of the beasts as he could; he that so employed his pains about any of the spontaneous products of nature as any way to alter them from the state which nature put them in, by placing any of his labour on them, did thereby acquire a propriety in them. But if they perished in his possession without their due use; if the fruits rotted, or the venison putrefied before he could spend it, he offended against the common law of nature, and was liable to be punished; he invaded his neighbour's share, for he had no right further than his use called for any of them and they might serve to afford him conveniences of life.

The same measures governed the possessions of land, too. Whatsoever he tilled and reaped, laid up, and made use of before it spoiled, that was his peculiar right; whatsoever he enclosed and could feed and make use of, the cattle and product was also his. But if either the grass of his enclosure rotted on the ground, or the fruit of his planting perished without gathering and laying up, this part of the earth, notwithstanding his enclosure, was still to be looked on as waste, and might be the possession of any other. Thus, at the beginning, Cain might take as much ground as he could till and make it his own land, and yet leave enough for Abel's sheep to feed on; a few acres would serve for both their possessions. But as families increased, and industry enlarged their stocks, their possessions enlarged with the need of them; but yet it was commonly without any fixed property in the ground they made use of, till they incorporated, settled themselves together, and built cities; and then, by consent, they came in time to set out the bounds of their distinct territories, and agree on limits between them and their neighbours, and, by laws within themselves, settled the properties of those of the same society. For we see that in that part of the world which was first inhabited, and therefore like to be the best peopled, even as low down as Abraham's time they wandered with their flocks and their herds, which were their substance, freely up and down; and this Abraham did in a country where he was a stranger: whence it is plain that at least a great part of the land lay in common; that the inhabitants valued it not, nor claimed property in any more than they made use of. But when there was not room enough in the same place for their herds to feed together, they by consent, as Abraham and Lot did (Gen. xiii. 5), separated and enlarged their pasture where it best liked them. And for the same reason Esau went from his father and his brother, and planted in Mount Seir (Gen. xxxvi. 6).

And thus, without supposing any private dominion and property in Adam over all the world, exclusive of all other men, which can no way be proved, nor any one's property be made out from it; but supposing the world given as it was to the children of men in common, we see how labour could make men distinct titles to several parcels of it for their private uses, wherein there could be no doubt of right, no room for quarrel.

Nor is it so strange, as perhaps before consideration it may appear, that the property of labour should be able to overbalance the community of land. For it is labour indeed that puts the difference of value on everything; and let any one consider what the difference is between an acre of land planted with tobacco or sugar, sown with wheat or barley, and an acre of the same land lying in common without any husbandry upon it, and he will find that the improvement of labour makes the far greater part of the value. I think it will be but a very modest computation to say that of the products of the earth useful to the life of man nine-tenths are the effects of labour; nay, if we will rightly estimate things as they come to our use, and cast up the several expenses about them—what in them is purely owing to nature, and what to labour—we shall find that in most of them ninety-nine hundredths are wholly to be put on the account of labour.

There cannot be a clearer demonstration of anything than several nations of the Americans are of this, who are rich in land and poor in all the comforts of life, whom nature having furnished as liberally as any other people with the materials of plenty—*i.e.*, a fruitful soil, apt to produce in abundance what might serve for food, raiment, and delight—yet, for want of improving it by labour, have not one-hundredth part of the conveniences we enjoy. And a king of a large and fruitful territory there, feeds, lodges, and is clad worse than a day-labourer in England.

To make this a little clearer, let us but trace some of the ordinary provisions of life through their several progresses before they come to our use, and see how much they receive of their value from human industry. Bread, wine, and cloth are things of daily use and great plenty; yet, notwithstanding, acorns, water, and leaves or skins, must be our bread, drink, and clothing, did not labour furnish us with these more useful commodities. For whatever bread is more worth than acorns, wine than water, and cloth or silk than leaves, skins, or moss, that is wholly owing to labour and industry: the one of these being the food and raiment which unassisted nature furnishes us with; the other, provisions which our industry and pains prepare for us; which how much they exceed the other in value when any one hath computed, he will then see how much labour makes the far greatest part of the value of things we enjoy in this world. And the ground which produces the materials is scarce to be reckoned in as any, or at most but a very small, part of it; so little that even amongst us land that is left wholly to nature, that hath no improvement of pasturage, tillage, or planting, is called, as indeed it is, "waste," and we shall find the benefit of it amount to little more than nothing.

An acre of land that bears here twenty bushels of wheat, and another in America which, with the same husbandry, would do the like, are without doubt of the same natural intrinsic value; but yet the benefit mankind receives from the one in a year is worth £5, and from the other possibly not worth a penny, if all the profit an Indian received from it were to be valued and sold here; at least, I may truly say, not one thousandth. 'Tis labour, then, which puts the greatest part of value upon land, without which it would scarcely be worth anything; 'tis to that we owe the greatest part of all its useful products, for all that the straw, bran, bread, of that acre of wheat is more worth than the product of an acre of as good land which lies waste, is all the effect of labour. For 'tis not barely the ploughman's pains, the reaper's and thresher's toil, and the baker's sweat, is to be counted into the bread we eat; the labour of those who broke the oxen, who dug and wrought the iron and stones, who felled and framed the timber employed about the plough, mill, oven, or any other utensils, which are a vast number, requisite to this corn, from its sowing, to its being made bread, must all be charged on the account of labour, and received as an effect of that. Nature and the earth furnished only the almost worthless materials as in themselves. 'Twould be a strange catalogue of things that industry provided, and made use of, about every loaf of bread before it came to our use, if we could trace them—iron, wood, leather, bark, timber, stone, bricks, coals, lime, cloth, dyeing drugs, pitch, tar, masts, ropes, and all the materials made use of in the ship that brought any of the commodities made use of by any of the workmen to any part of the work, all which it would be almost impossible—at least, too long—to reckon up.

From all which it is evident that, though the things of nature are given in common, yet man, by being master of himself and proprietor of his own person and the actions or labour of it, had still in himself the great foundation of property; and that which made up the great part of what he applied to the support or comfort of his being, when invention and arts had improved the conveniences of life, was perfectly his own, and did not belong in common to others.

Thus labour, in the beginning, gave a right of property, wherever any one was pleased to employ it upon what was common, which remained a long while the far greater part, and is yet more than mankind makes use of. Men at first, for the most part, contented themselves with what unassisted nature offered to their necessities; and though afterwards, in some parts of the world (where the increase of people and stock, with the use of money, had made land scarce, and so of some value), the several communities settled the bounds of their distinct territories, and, by laws within themselves, regulated the properties of the private men of their society, and so, by compact and agreement, settled the property which labour and industry began—and the leagues that have been made between several states and kingdoms, either expressly or tacitly disowning all claim and right to the land in the other's possession, have, by common consent, given up their pretences to their natural common right, which originally they had to those countries; and so have, by positive agreement, settled a property amongst themselves in distinct parts of the world—yet there are still great tracts of ground to be found which, the inhabitants thereof not having joined with the rest of mankind in the consent of the use of their common money, lie waste, and are more than the people who dwell on it do or can make use of, and so still lie in common; though this can scarce happen amongst that part of mankind that have consented to the use of money.

The greatest part of things really useful to the life of man, and such as the necessity of subsisting made the first commoners of the world look after, as it doth the Americans now, are generally things of short duration, such as, if they are not consumed by use, will decay and perish of themselves: gold, silver, and diamonds are things that fancy or agreement have put the value on more than real use and the necessary support of life. Now, of those good things which nature hath provided in common, every one hath a right, as hath been said, to as much as he could use, and had a property in all he could effect with his labour—all that his industry could extend to, to alter from the state nature had put it in, was his. He that gathered a hundred bushels of acorns or apples had thereby a property in them; they were his goods as soon as gathered. He was only to look that he used them before they spoiled, else he took more than his share, and robbed others; and, indeed, it was a foolish thing, as well as dishonest, to hoard up more than he could make use of. If he gave away a part to anybody else, so that it perished not uselessly in his possession, these he also made use of; and if he also bartered away plums that would have rotted in a week, for nuts that would last good for his eating a whole year, he did no injury; he wasted not the common stock, destroyed no part of the portion of goods that belonged to others, so long as nothing perished uselessly in his hands. Again, if he would give his nuts for a piece of metal, pleased with its colour, or exchange his sheep for shells, or wool for a sparkling pebble or a diamond, and keep those by him all his life, he invaded not the right of others; he might heap up as much of these durable things as he pleased, the exceeding of the bounds of his just property not lying in the largeness of his possessions, but the perishing of anything uselessly in it.

And thus came in the use of money—some lasting thing, that men might keep without spoiling, and that, by mutual consent, men would take in exchange for the truly useful but perishable supports of life.

And as different degrees of industry were apt to give men possessions in different proportions, so this invention of money gave them the opportunity to continue and enlarge them; for supposing an island, separate from all possible commerce with the rest of the world, wherein there were but a hundred families—but there were sheep, horses, and cows, with other useful animals, wholesome fruits, and land enough for corn for a hundred thousand times as many, but nothing in the island, either because of its commonness or perishableness, fit to supply the place of money—what reason could any one have there to enlarge his possessions beyond the use of his family and a plentiful supply to its consumption, either in what their own industry produced, or they could barter for like perishable useful commodities with others? Where there is not something both lasting and scarce, and so valuable to be hoarded up, there men will not be apt to enlarge their possessions of land, were it never so rich, never so free for them to take; for I ask, what would a man value ten thousand or a hundred thousand acres of excellent land, ready cultivated, and well stocked too with cattle, in the middle of the inland parts of America, where he had no hopes of commerce with other parts of the world, to draw money to him by the sale of the product? It would not be worth the enclosing, and we should see him give up again to the wild common of nature whatever was more than would supply the conveniences of life to be had there for him and his family.

Thus in the beginning all the world was America, and more so than that is now, for no such thing as money was anywhere known. Find out something that hath the use and value of money amongst his neighbours, you shall see the same man will begin presently to enlarge his possessions.

But since gold and silver, being little useful to the life of man in proportion to food, raiment, and carriage, has its value only from the consent of men, whereof labour yet makes, in great part, the measure, it is plain that the consent of men have agreed to a disproportionate and unequal possession of the earth—I mean out of the bounds of society and compact; for in governments the laws regulate it; they having, by consent, found out and agreed in a way how a man may rightfully and without injury possess more than he himself can make use of by receiving gold and silver, which may continue long in a man's possession, without decaying for the overplus, and agreeing those metals should have a value.

And thus, I think, it is very easy to conceive without any difficulty how labour could at first begin a title of property in the common things of nature, and how the spending it upon our uses bounded it; so that there could then be no reason of quarrelling about title, nor any doubt about the largeness of possession it gave. Right and conveniency went together; for as a man had a right to all he could employ his labour upon, so he had no temptation to labour for more than be could make use of. This left no room for controversy about the title, nor for encroachment on the right of others; what portion a man carved to himself was easily seen, and it was useless, as well as dishonest, to carve himself too much, or take more than he needed.

***

OF PATERNAL POWER

IT MAY perhaps be censured as an impertinent criticism in a discourse of this nature to find fault with words and names that have obtained in the world, and yet possibly it may not be amiss to offer new ones when the old are apt to lead men into mistakes, as this of paternal power probably has done, which seems so to place the power of parents over their children wholly in the father, as if the mother had no share in it; whereas, if we consult reason or revelation, we shall find she hath an equal title. Which may give one reason to ask whether this might not be more properly called parental power? For whatever obligation nature and the right of generation lays on children, it must certainly bind them equal to both the concurrent causes of it. And accordingly we see the positive law of God everywhere joins them together without distinction when it commands the obedience of children. "Honour thy father and thy mother" (Exod. xx. 12); "Whosoever curseth his father or his mother" (Lev. xx. 9); "Ye shall fear every man his mother and his father" (Lev. xix. 3); "Children, obey your parents," &c. (Eph. vi. I), is the style of the Old and New Testaments.

Had but this one thing been well considered, without looking any deeper into the matter, it might, perhaps, have kept men from running into those gross mistakes they have made about this power of parents; which, however it might without any great harshness bear the name of absolute dominion and regal authority when, under the title of paternal power, it seemed appropriated to the father, would yet have sounded but oddly, and in the very name shown the absurdity, if this supposed absolute power over children had been called parental, and thereby have discovered that it belonged to the mother too. For it will but very ill serve the turn of those men who contend so much for the absolute power and authority of the fatherhood, as they call it, that the mother should have any share in it. And it would have but ill supported the monarchy they contend for, when by the very name it appeared that that fundamental authority from whence they would derive their government of a single person only, was not placed in one, but two persons jointly. But to let this of names pass.

Though I have said . . . that all men by nature are equal, I cannot be supposed to understand all sorts of equality. Age or virtue may give men a just precedency. Excellency of parts and merit may place others above the common level. Birth may subject some, and alliance or benefits others, to pay an observance to those to whom nature, gratitude, or other respects may have made it due. And yet all this consists with the equality which all men are in, in respect of jurisdiction or dominion, one over another; which was the equality I there spoke of as proper to the business in hand, being that equal right that every man hath to his natural freedom, without being subjected to the will or authority of any other man.

Children, I confess, are not born in this full state of equality, though they are born to it. Their parents have a sort of rule and jurisdiction over them when they come into the world, and for some time after, but 'tis but a temporary one. The bonds of this subjection are like the swaddling clothes they are wrapped up in and supported by in the weakness of their infancy. Age and reason, as they grow up, loosen them, till at length they drop quite off, and leave a man at his own free disposal. ♦

QUESTIONS

1. What does Locke suggest are the sources of rights to private property?

2. What is the first and universal property right?

3. Is the consent of other people necessary for the appropriation of resources from the environment?

4. Are there any boundaries to what an individual may appropriate from the common pool of natural resources?

5. What does Locke think is hardly possible in a money economy?

1879 Speech to Congress

In-mut-too-yah-lat-lat, also known as Chief Joseph (1840–1904)

My friends, I have been asked to show you my heart. I am glad to have a chance to do so. I want the white people to understand my people. Some of you think an Indian is like a wild animal. This is a great mistake. I will tell you all about our people, and then you can judge whether an Indian is a man or not. I believe much trouble and blood would be saved if we opened our hearts more. I will tell you in my way how the Indian sees things. The white man has more words to tell you how they look to him, but it does not require many words to speak the truth. What I have to say will come from my heart, and I will speak with a straight tongue. Ah-cum-kin-i-ma-me-hut (the Great Spirit) is looking at me, and will hear me.

My name is In-mut-too-yah-lat-lat (Thunder traveling over the Mountains). I am chief of the Wal-lam-wat-kin band of Chute-pa-lu, or Nez Perces (nose-pierced Indians). I was born in eastern Oregon, thirty-eight winters ago. My father was chief before me. When a young man, he was called Joseph by Mr. Spaulding, a missionary. He died a few years ago. There was no stain on his hands of the blood of a white man. He left a good name on the earth. He advised me well for my people.

Our fathers gave us many laws, which they had learned from their fathers. These laws were good. They told us to treat all men as they treated us; that we should never be the first to break a bargain; that it was a disgrace to tell a lie; that we should speak only the truth; that it was a shame for one man to take from another his wife, or his property without paying for it. We were taught to believe that the Great Spirit sees and hears everything, and that he never forgets; that hereafter he will give every man a spirit-home according to his deserts: if he has been a good man, he will have a good home; if he has been a bad man, he will have a bad home. This I believe, and all my people believe the same.

We did not know there were other people besides the Indian until about one hundred winters ago, when some men with white faces came to our country. They brought many things with them to trade for furs and skins. They brought tobacco, which was new to us. They brought guns with flint stones on them, which frightened our women and children. Our people could not talk with these white-faced men, but they used signs which all people understand. These men were Frenchmen, and they called our people "Nez Perces," because they wore rings in their noses for ornaments.

Although very few of our people wear them now, we are still called by the same name. These French trappers said a great many things to our fathers, which have been planted in our hearts. Some were good for us, but some were bad. Our people were divided in opinion about these men. Some thought they taught more bad than good. An Indian respects a brave man, but he despises a coward. He loves a straight tongue, but he hates a forked tongue. The French trappers told us some truths and some lies.

The first white men of your people who came to our country were named Lewis and Clarke. They also brought many things that our people had never seen. They talked straight, and our people gave them a great feast, as a proof that their hearts were friendly. These men were very kind. They made presents to our chiefs and our people made presents to them. We had a great many horses, of which we gave them what they needed, and they gave us guns and tobacco in return. All the Nez Perces made friends with Lewis and Clarke, and agreed to let them pass through their country, and never to make war on white men. This promise the Nez Perces have never broken. No white man can accuse them of bad faith, and speak with a straight tongue. It has always been the pride of the Nez Perces that they were the friends of the white men. When my father was a young man there came to our country a white man (Rev. Mr. Spaulding) who talked spirit law. He won the affections of our people because he spoke good things to them. At first he did not say anything about white men wanting to settle on our lands. Nothing was said about that until about twenty winters ago, when a number of white people came into our country and built houses and made farms. At first our people made no complaint. They thought there was room enough for all to live in peace, and they were learning many things from the white men that seemed to be good. But we soon found that the white men were growing rich very fast, and were greedy to possess everything the Indian had. My father was the first to see through the schemes of the white men, and he warned his tribe to be careful about trading with them. He had suspicion of men who seemed so anxious to make money. I was a boy then, but I remember well my father's caution. He had sharper eyes than the rest of our people.

Next there came a white officer (Governor Stevens), who invited all the Nez Perces to a treaty council. After the council was opened he made known his heart. He said there were a great many white people in the country and many more would come; that he wanted the land marked out so that the Indians and white men could be separated. If they were to live in peace it was necessary, he said, that the Indians should have a country set apart for them, and in that country they must stay. My father, who represented his band, refused to have anything to do with the council, because he wished to be a free man. He claimed that no man owned any part of the earth, and a man could not sell what he did not own.

Mr. Spaulding took hold of my father's arm and said, "Come and sign the treaty." My father pushed him away, and said: "Why do you ask me to sign away my country? It is your business to talk to us about spirit matters, not to talk to us about parting with our land." Governor Stevens urged my father to sign his treaty, but he refused. "I will not sign your paper," he said; "you go where you please, so do I; you are not a child, I am no child; I can think for myself. No man can think for me. I have no other home than this. I will not give it up to any man. My people would have no home. Take away your paper. I will not touch it with my hand."

My father left the council. Some of the chiefs of the other bands of the Nez Perces signed the treaty, and then Governor Stevens gave them presents of blankets. My father cautioned his people to take no presents, for "after a while," he said, "they will claim that you have accepted pay for your country." Since that time four bands of the Nez Perces have received annuities from the United States. My father was invited to many councils, and they tried hard to make him sign the treaty, but he was firm as the rock, and would not sign away his home. His refusal caused a difference among the Nez Perces.

Eight years later (1863) was the next treaty council. A chief called Lawyer, because he was a great talker, took the lead in this council, and sold nearly all the Nez Perces country. My father was not there. He said to me: "When you go into council with the white man, always remember your country. Do not give it away. The white man will cheat you out of your home. I have taken no pay from the United States, I have never sold our land." In this treaty Lawyer acted without authority from our band. He had no right to sell the Wallowa (*winding water*) country. That had always belonged to my father's own people, and the other bands had never disputed our right to it. No other Indians ever claimed Wallowa.

In order to have all people understand how much land we owned, my father planted poles around it and said:

"Inside is the home of my people—the white man may take the land outside. Inside this boundary all our people were born. It circles around the graves of our fathers, and we will never give up these graves to any man."

The United States claimed that they had bought all the Nez Perces country outside of Lapwai Reservation, from Lawyer and other chiefs, but we continued to live on this land in peace until eight years ago, when white men began to come inside the bounds my father had set. We warned them against this great wrong, but they would not leave our land, and some bad blood was raised. The white men represented that we were going on the war-path. They reported many things that were false.

The United States Government asked for a treaty council. My father had become blind and feeble. He could no longer speak for his people.

It was then that I took my father's place as chief. In this council I made my first speech to white men. I said to the agent who held the council:

"I did not want to come to this council, but I came hoping that we could save blood. The white man has no right to come here and take our country. We have never accepted any presents from the Government. Neither Lawyer nor any other chief had authority to sell this land. It has always belonged to my people. It came unclouded to them from our fathers, and we will defend this land as long as a drop of Indian blood warms the hearts of our men."

The agent said he had orders, from the Great White Chief at Washington, for us to go upon the Lapwai Reservation, and that if we obeyed he would help us in many ways. "You *must* move to the agency," he said. I answered him: "I will not. I do not need your help: we have plenty, and we are contented and happy if the white man will let us alone. The reservation is too small for so many people with all their stock. You can keep your presents; we can go to your towns and pay for all we need; we have plenty of horses and cattle to sell, and we won't have any help from you; we are free now; we can go where we please. Our fathers were born here. Here they lived, here they died, here are their graves. We will never leave them." The agent went away, and we had peace for a little while.

Soon after this my father sent for me. I saw he was dying. I took his hand in mine. He said: "My son, my body is returning to my mother Earth, and my spirit is going very soon to see the Great Spirit Chief. When I am gone, think of your country. You are the chief of these people. They look to you to guide them. Always remember that your father never sold his country. You must stop your ears whenever you are asked to sign a treaty selling your home. A few years more, and white men will be all around you. They have their eyes on this land. My son, never forget my dying words. This country holds your father's body. Never sell the bones of your father and your mother." I pressed my father's hand and told him I would protect his grave with my life. My father smiled and passed away to the spirit-land. I buried him in that beautiful valley of winding waters. I love that land more than all the rest of the world. A man who would not love his father's grave is worse than a wild animal.

For a short time we lived quietly. But this could not last. White men had found gold in the mountains around the land of winding water. They stole a great many horses from us, and we could not get them back because we were Indians. The white men told lies for each other. They drove off a great many of our cattle. Some white men branded our young cattle so they could claim them. We had no friend who would plead our cause before the law councils. It seemed to me that some of the white men in Wallowa were doing these things on purpose to get up a war. They knew that we were not strong enough to fight them. I labored hard to avoid trouble and bloodshed. We gave up some of our country to the white men, thinking that then we could have peace. We were mistaken. The white man would not let us alone. We could have avenged our wrongs many times, but we did not. Whenever the Government has asked us to help them against other Indians, we have never refused. When the white men were few and we were strong we could have killed them all off, but the Nez Perces wished to live at peace.

If we have not done so, we have not been to blame. I believe that the old treaty has never been correctly reported. If we ever owned the land we own it still, for we never sold it. In the treaty councils the commissioners have claimed that our country had been sold to the Government. Suppose a white man should come to me and say, "Joseph, I like your horses, and I want to buy them." I say to him, "No, my horses suit me, I will not sell them." Then he goes to my neighbor, and says to him: "Joseph has some good horses. I want to buy them, but he refuses to sell." My neighbor answers, "Pay me the money, and I will sell you Joseph's horses." The white man returns to me, and says, "Joseph, I have bought your horses, and you must let me have them." If we sold our lands to the Government, this is the way they were bought.

On account of the treaty made by the other bands of the Nez Perces, the white men claimed my lands. We were troubled greatly by white men crowding over the line. Some of these were good men, and we lived on peaceful terms with them, but they were not all good.

Nearly every year the agent came over from Lapwai and ordered us on to the reservation. We always replied that we were satisfied to live in Wallowa. We were careful to refuse the presents or annuities which he offered.

Through all the years since the white men came to Wallowa we have been threatened and taunted by them and the treaty Nez Perces. They have given us no rest. We have had a few good friends among white men, and they have always advised my people to bear these taunts without fighting. Our young men were quick-tempered, and I have had great trouble in keeping them from doing rash things. I have carried a heavy load on my back ever since I was a boy. I learned then that we were but few, while the white men were many, and that we could not hold our own with them. We were like deer. They were like grizzly bears. We had a small country. Their country was large. We were contented to let things remain as the Great Spirit Chief made them. They were not; and would change the rivers and mountains if they did not suit them.

Year after year we have been threatened, but no war was made upon my people until General Howard came to our country two years ago and told us that he was the white war-chief of all that country. He said: "I have a great many soldiers at my back. I am going to bring them up here, and then I will talk to you again. I will not let white men laugh at me the next time I come. The country belongs to the Government, and I intend to make you go upon the reservation."

I remonstrated with him against bringing more soldiers to the Nez Perces country. He had one house full of troops all the time at Fort Lapwai.

The next spring the agent at Umatilla agency sent an Indian runner to tell me to meet General Howard at Walla Walla. I could not go myself, but I sent my brother and five other head men to meet him, and they had a long talk.

General Howard said: "You have talked straight, and it is all right. You can stay in Wallowa." He insisted that my brother and his company should go with him to Fort Lapwai.

When the party arrived there General Howard sent out runners and called all the Indians in to a grand council. I was in that council. I said to General Howard. "We are ready to listen." He answered that he would not talk then, but would hold a council next day, when he would talk plainly. I said to General Howard: "I am ready to talk to-day. I have been in a great many councils, but I am no wiser. We are all sprung from a woman, although we are unlike in many things. We can not be made over again. You are as you were made, and as you were made you can remain. We are just as we were made by the Great Spirit, and you can not change us; then why should children of one mother and one father quarrel? Why should one try to cheat the other? I do not believe that the Great Spirit Chief gave one kind of men the right to tell another kind of men what they must do."

General Howard replied: "You deny my authority, do you? You want to dictate to me, do you?"

Then one of my chiefs—Too-hool-hool-suit—rose in the council and said to General Howard: "The Great Spirit Chief made the world as it is, and as he wanted it, and he made a part of it for us to live upon. I do not see where you get authority to say that we shall not live where he placed us."

General Howard lost his temper and said: "Shut up! I don't want to hear any more of such talk. The law says you shall go upon the reservation to live, and I want you to do so, but you persist in disobeying the law" (meaning the treaty). "If you do not move. I will take the matter into my own hand, and make you suffer for your disobedience."

Too-hool-hool-suit answered: "Who are you, that you ask us to talk, and then tell me I sha'n't talk? Are you the Great Spirit? Did you make the world? Did you make the sun? Did you make the rivers to run for us to drink? Did you make the grass to grow? Did you make all these things, that you talk to us as though we were boys? If you did, then you have the right to talk as you do."

General Howard replied: "You are an impudent fellow, and I will put you in the guard-house," and then ordered a soldier to arrest him.

Too-hool-hool-suit made no resistance. He asked General Howard: "Is that your order? I don't care. I have expressed my heart to you. I have nothing to take back. I have spoken for my country. You can arrest me, but you can not change me or make me take back what I have said."

The soldiers came forward and seized my friend and took him to the guard-house. My men whispered among themselves whether they should let this thing be done. I counseled them to submit. I knew if we resisted that all the white men present, including General Howard would be killed in a moment, and we would be blamed. If I had said nothing, General Howard would never have given another unjust order against my men. I saw the danger, and, while they dragged Too-hool-hool-suit to prison, I arose and said: *I am going to talk now. I don't care whether you arrest me or not."* I turned to my people and said: "The arrest of Too-hool-hool-suit was wrong, but we will not resent the insult. We were invited to this council to express our hearts, and we have done so." Too-hool-hool-suit was a prisoner for five days before he was released.

The council broke up for that day. On the next morning General Howard came to my lodge, and invited me to go with him and White-Bird and Looking-Glass, to look for land for my people. As we rode along we came to some good land that was already occupied by Indians and white people. General Howard, pointing to this land, said: "If you will come on to the reservation, I will give you these lands and move these people off."

I replied: "No. It would be wrong to disturb these people. I have no right to take their homes. I have never taken what did not belong to me. I will not now."

We rode all day upon the reservation, and found no good land unoccupied. I have been informed by men who do not lie that General Howard sent a letter that night, telling the soldiers at Walla Walla to go to Wallowa Valley, and drive us out upon our return home.

In the council, next day, General Howard informed me, in a haughty spirit, that he would give my people *thirty days* to go back home, collect all their stock, and move on to the reservation, saying. "If you are not here in that time, I shall consider that you want to fight, and will send my soldiers to drive you on."

I said: "War can be avoided, and it ought to be avoided. I want no war. My people have always been the friends of the white man. Why are you in such a hurry? I can not get ready to move in thirty days. Our stock is scattered, and Snake River is very high. Let us wait until fall, then the river will be low. We want time to hunt up our stock and gather supplies for winter."

General Howard replied, "If you let the time run over one day, the soldiers will be there to drive you on to the reservation, and all your cattle and horses outside of the reservation at that time will fall into the hands of the white men."

I knew I had never sold my country, and that I had no land in Lapwai; but I did not want bloodshed. I did not want my people killed. I did not want anybody killed. Some of my people had been murdered by white men, and the white murderers were never punished for it. I told General Howard about this, and again said I wanted no war. I wanted the people who lived upon the lands I was to occupy at Lapwai to have time to gather their harvest.

I said in my heart that, rather than have war, I would give up my country. I would give up my father's grave. I would give up everything rather than have the blood of white men upon the hands of my people.

General Howard refused to allow me more than thirty days to move my people and their stock. I am sure that he began to prepare for war at once.

When I returned to Wallowa I found my people very much excited upon discovering that the soldiers were already in the Wallowa Valley. We held a council, and decided to move immediately, to avoid bloodshed.

Too-hool-hool-suit, who felt outraged by his imprisonment, talked for war, and made many of my young men willing to fight rather than be driven like dogs from the land where they were born. He declared that blood alone would wash out the disgrace General Howard had put upon him. It required a strong heart to stand up against such talk, but I urged my people to be quiet, and not to begin a war.

We gathered all the stock we could find, and made an attempt to move. We left many of our horses and cattle in Wallowa, and we lost several hundred in crossing the river. All of my people succeeded in getting across in safety. Many of the Nez Perces came together in Rocky Canon to hold a grand council. I went with all my people. This council lasted ten days. There was a great deal of war-talk, and a great deal of excitement. There was one young brave present whose father had been killed by a white man five years before. This man's blood was bad against white men, and he left the council calling for revenge.

Again I counseled peace, and I thought the danger was past. We had not complied with General Howard's order because we could not, but we intended to do so as soon as possible. I was leaving the council to kill beef for my family, when news came that the young man whose father had been killed had gone out with several other hot-blooded young braves and killed four white men. He rode up to the council and shouted: "Why do you sit here like women? The war has begun already." I was deeply grieved. All the lodges were moved except my brother's and my own. I saw clearly that the war was upon us when I learned that my young men had been secretly buying ammunition. I heard then that Too-hool-hool-suit, who had been imprisoned by General Howard, had succeeded in organizing a war-party. I knew that their acts would involve all my people. I saw that the war could not then be prevented. The time had passed. I counseled peace from the beginning. I knew that we were too weak to fight the United States. We had many grievances, but I knew that war would bring more. We had good white friends, who advised us against taking the war-path. My friend and brother, Mr. Chapman, who has been with us since the surrender, told us just how the war would end. Mr. Chapman took sides against us, and helped General Howard. I do not blame him for doing so. He tried hard to prevent bloodshed. We hoped the white settlers would not join the soldiers. Before the war commenced we had discussed this matter all over, and many of my people were in favor of warning them that if they took no part against us they should not be molested in the event of war being begun by General Howard. This plan was voted down in the war-council.

There were bad men among my people who had quarreled with white men. They talked of their wrongs until they roused all the bad hearts in the council. Still I could not believe that they would begin the war. I know that my young men did a great wrong, but I ask, Who was first to blame? They had been insulted a thousand times; their fathers and brothers had been killed; their mothers and wives had been disgraced; they had been driven to madness by whisky sold to them by white men; they had been told by General Howard that all their horses and cattle which they had been unable to drive out of Wallowa were to fall into the hands of white men; and, added to all this, they were homeless and desperate.

I would have given my own life if I could have undone the killing of white men by my people. I blame my young men and I blame the white men. I blame General Howard for not giving my people time to get their stock away from Wallowa. I do not acknowledge that he had the right to order me to leave Wallowa at any time. I deny that either my father or myself ever sold that land. It is still our land. It may never again be our home, but my father sleeps there, and I love it as I love my mother. I left there, hoping to avoid bloodshed.

If General Howard had given me plenty of time to gather up my stock, and treated Too-hool-hool-suit as a man should be treated, there *would have been no war*. My friends among white men have blamed me for the war. I am not to blame. When my young men began the killing, my heart was hurt. Although I did not justify them, I remembered all the insults I had endured, and my blood was on fire. Still I would have taken my people to the buffalo country without fighting, if possible.

I could see no other way to avoid a war. We moved over to White Bird Creek, sixteen miles away, and there encamped, intending to collect our stock before leaving; but the soldiers attacked us, and the first battle was fought. We numbered in that battle sixty men, and the soldiers a hundred. The fight lasted but a few minutes, when the soldiers retreated before us for twelve miles. They lost thirty-three killed, and had seven wounded. When an Indian fights, he only shoots to kill; but soldiers shoot at random. None of the soldiers were scalped. We do not believe in scalping, nor in killing wounded men. Soldiers do not kill many Indians unless they are wounded and left upon the battlefield. Then they kill Indians.

Seven days after the first battle, General Howard arrived in the Nez Perces country, bringing seven hundred more soldiers. It was now war in earnest. We crossed over Salmon River, hoping General Howard would follow. We were not disappointed. He did follow us, and we got back between him and his supplies, and cut him off for three days. He sent out two companies to open the way. We attacked them, killing one officer, two guides, and ten men.

We withdrew, hoping the soldiers would follow, but they had got fighting enough for that day. They intrenched themselves, and next day we attacked them again. The battle lasted all day, and was renewed next morning. We killed four and wounded seven or eight.

About this time General Howard found out that we were in his rear. Five days later he attacked us with three hundred and fifty soldiers and settlers. We had two hundred and fifty warriors. The fight lasted twenty-seven hours. We lost four killed and several wounded. General Howard's loss was twenty-nine men killed and sixty wounded.

The following day the soldiers charged upon us, and we retreated with our families and stock a few miles, leaving eighty lodges to fall into General Howard's hands. Finding that we were outnumbered, we retreated to Bitter Root Valley. Here another body of soldiers came upon us and demanded our surrender. We refused. They said, "You can not get by us." We answered, "We are going by you without fighting if you will let us, but we are going by you anyhow." We then made a treaty with these soldiers. We agreed not to molest any one, and they agreed that we might pass through the Bitter Root country in peace. We bought provisions and traded stock with white men there.

We understood that there was to be no more war. We intended to go peaceably to the buffalo country, and leave the question of returning to our country to be settled afterward.

With this understanding we traveled on for four days, and, thinking that the trouble was all over, we stopped and prepared tent-poles to take with us. We started again, and at the end of two days we saw three white men passing our camp. Thinking that peace had been made, we did not molest them. We could have killed or taken them prisoners, but we did not suspect them of being spies, which they were.

That night the soldiers surrounded our camp. About day-break one of my men went out to look after his horses. The soldiers saw him and shot him down like a coyote. I have since learned that these soldiers were not those we had left behind. They had come upon us from another direction. The new white war-chief's name was Gibbon. He charged upon us while some of my people were still asleep. We had a hard fight. Some of my men crept around and attacked the soldiers from the rear. In this battle we lost nearly all our lodges, but we finally drove General Gibbon back.

Finding that he was unable to capture us, he sent to his camp a few miles away for his big guns (cannons), but my men had captured them and all the ammunition. We damaged the big guns all we could, and carried away the powder and lead. In the fight with General Gibbon we lost fifty women and children and thirty fighting men. We remained long enough to bury our dead. The Nez Perces never make war on women and children; we could have killed a great many women and children while the war lasted, but we would feel ashamed to do so cowardly an act.

We never scalp our enemies, but when General Howard came up and joined General Gibbon, their Indian scouts dug up our dead and scalped them. I have been told that General Howard did not order this great shame to be done.

We retreated as rapidly as we could toward the buffalo country. After six days General Howard came close to us, and we went out and attacked him, and captured nearly all his horses and mules (about two hundred and fifty head).

We then marched on to the Yellowstone Basin. On the way we captured one white man and two white women. We released them at the end of three days. They were treated kindly.

The women were not insulted. Can the white soldiers tell me of one time when Indian women were taken prisoners, and held three days and then released without being insulted? Were the Nez Perces women who fell into the hands of General Howard's soldiers treated with as much respect? I deny that a Nez Perce was ever guilty of such a crime.

10   A few days later we captured two more white men. One of them stole a horse and escaped. We gave the other a poor horse and told him he was free.

   Nine days' march brought us to the mouth of Clarke's Fork of the Yellowstone. We did not know what had become of General Howard, but we supposed that he had sent for more horses and mules. He did not come up, but another new war-chief (General Sturgis) attacked us. We held him in check while we

20 moved all our women and children and stock out of danger, leaving a few men to cover our retreat. Several days passed, and we heard nothing of General Howard, or Gibbon, or Sturgis. We had repulsed each in turn, and began to feel secure, when another army, under General Miles, struck us. This was the fourth army, each of which outnumbered our fighting force, that we had encountered within sixty days.

30   We had no knowledge of General Miles's army until a short time before he made a charge upon us, cutting our camp in two and capturing nearly all our horses. About seventy men, myself among them, were cut off. My little daughter, twelve years of age, was with me. I gave her a rope, and told her to catch a horse and join the others who were cut off from the camp. I have not seen her since, but I have learned that she is alive and well.

40   I thought of my wife and children, who were now surrounded by soldiers, and I resolved to go to them or die. With a prayer in my mouth to the Great Spirit Chief who rules above, I dashed unarmed through the line of soldiers. It seemed to me that there were guns on every side, before and behind me. My clothes were cut to pieces and my horse was wounded, but I was not hurt. As I reached the door of my lodge, my wife handed me my rifle,

50 saying: "Here's your gun. Fight!"

The soldiers kept up a continuous fire. Six of my men were killed in one spot near me. Ten or twelve soldiers charged into our camp and got possession of two lodges, killing three Nez Perces and losing three of their men, who fell inside our lines. I called my men to drive them back. We fought at close range, not more than twenty steps apart, and drove the soldiers back upon their main line, leaving their dead in our hands. We secured their arms and ammuni- 60 tion. We lost, the first day and night, eighteen men and three women. General Miles lost twenty-six killed and forty wounded. The following day General Miles sent a messenger into my camp under protection of a white flag. I sent my friend Yellow Bull to meet him.

   Yellow Bull understood the messenger to say that General Miles wished me to consider the situation; that he did not want to kill my people unnecessarily. Yellow Bull understood 70 this to be a demand for me to surrender and save blood. Upon reporting this message to me, Yellow Bull said he wondered whether General Miles was in earnest. I sent him back with my answer, that I had not made up my mind, but would think about it and send word soon. A little later he sent some Cheyenne scouts with another message. I went out to meet them. They said they believed that General Miles was sincere and really wanted peace. 80 I walked on to General Miles's tent. He met me and we shook hands. He said, "Come, let us sit down by the fire and talk this matter over." I remained with him all night; next morning Yellow Bull came over to see if I was alive, and why I did not return.

   General Miles would not let me leave the tent to see my friend alone.

   Yellow Bull said to me: "They have got you in their power, and I am afraid they will never 90 let you go again. I have an officer in our camp, and I will hold him until they let you go free."

   I said: "I do not know what they mean to do with me, but if they kill me you must not kill the officer. It will do no good to avenge my death by killing him."

   Yellow Bull returned to my camp. I did not make any agreement that day with General Miles. The battle was renewed while I was with him. I was very anxious about my people. 100

I knew that we were near Sitting Bull's camp in King George's land, and I thought maybe the Nez Perces who had escaped would return with assistance. No great damage was done to either party during the night.

On the following morning I returned to my camp by agreement, meeting the officer who had been held a prisoner in my camp at the flag of truce. My people were divided about surrendering. We could have escaped from Bear Paw Mountain if we had left our wounded, old women, and children behind. We were unwilling to do this. We had never heard of a wounded Indian recovering while in the hands of white men.

On the evening of the fourth day General Howard came in with a small escort, together with my friend Chapman. We could now talk understandingly. General Miles said to me in plain words, "If you will come out and give up your arms, I will spare your lives and send you to your reservation." I do not know what passed between General Miles and General Howard.

I could not bear to see my wounded men and women suffer any longer; we had lost enough already. General Miles had promised that we might return to our own country with what stock we had left. I thought we could start again. I believed General Miles or *I never would have surrendered.* I have heard that he has been censured for making the promise to return us to Lapwai. He could not have made any other terms with me at that time. I would have held him in check until my friends came to my assistance and then neither of the generals nor their soldiers would have ever left Bear Paw Mountain alive.

On the fifth day I went to General Miles and gave up my gun, and said, "From where the sun now stands I will fight no more." My people needed rest—we wanted peace. I was told we could go with General Miles to Tongue River and stay there until spring, when we would be sent back to our country. Finally it was decided that we were to be taken to Tongue River. We had nothing to say about it. After our arrival at Tongue River, General Miles received orders to take us to Bismarck. The reason given was, that subsistence would be cheaper there.

General Miles was opposed to this order. He said: "You must not blame me. I have endeavored to keep my word, but the chief who is over me has given the order, and I must obey it or resign. That would do you no good. Some other officer would carry out the order."

I believe General Miles would have kept his word if he could have done so. I do not blame him for what we have suffered since the surrender. I do not know who is to blame. We gave up all our horses (over eleven hundred) and all our saddles (over one hundred) and we have not heard from them since. Somebody has got our horses.

General Miles turned my people over to another soldier, and we were taken to Bismarck. Captain Johnson, who now had charge of us, received an order to take us to Fort Leavenworth. At Leavenworth we were placed on a low river bottom, with no water except river-water to drink and cook with. We had always lived in a healthy country, where the mountains were high and the water was cold and clear. Many of my people sickened and died, and we buried them in this strange land. I can not tell how much my heart suffered for my people while at Leavenworth. The Great Spirit Chief who rules above seemed to be looking some other way, and did not see what was being done to my people.

During the hot days (July, 1878) we received notice that we were to be moved farther away from our own country. We were not asked if we were willing to go. We were ordered to get into the railroad-cars. Three of my people died on the way to Baxter Springs. It was worse to die there than to die fighting in the mountains. We were moved from Baxter Springs (Kansas) to the Indian Territory, and set down without our lodges. We had but little medicine, and we were nearly all sick. Seventy of my people have died since we moved there.

We have had a great many visitors who have talked many ways. Some of the chiefs (General Fish and Colonel Stickney) from Washington came to see us, and selected land for us to live upon. We have not moved to that land, for it is not a good place to live.

The Commissioner Chief (E. A. Hayt) came to see us. I told him, as I told every one, that I expected General Miles's word would be carried out. He said it "could not be done; that white men now lived in my country and all the land was taken up: that, if I returned to Wallowa, I could not live in peace; that law-papers were out against my young men who began the war, and that the Government could not protect my people." This talk fell like a heavy stone upon my heart. I saw that I could not gain anything by talking to him. Other law chiefs (Congressional Committee) came to see me and said they would help me to get a healthy country. I did not know who to believe. The white people have too many chiefs. They do not understand each other. They do not all talk alike.

The Commissioner Chief (Mr. Hayt) invited me to go with him and hunt for a better home than we have now. I like the land we found (west of the Osage reservation) better than any place I have seen in that country; but it is not a healthy land. There are no mountains and rivers. The water is warm. It is not a good country for stock. I do not believe my people can live there. I am afraid they will all die. The Indians who occupy that country are dying off. I promised Chief Hayt to go there, and do the best I could until the Government got ready to make good General Miles's word. I was not satisfied, but I could not help myself. Then the inspector Chief (General McNiel) came to my camp and we had a long talk. He said I ought to have a home in the mountain country north, and that he would write a letter to the Great Chief at Washington. Again the hope of seeing the mountains of Idaho and Oregon grew up in my heart.

At last I was granted permission to come to Washington and bring my friend Yellow Bull and our interpreter with me. I am glad we came. I have shaken hands with a great many friends, but there are some things I want to know which no one seems able to explain. I can not understand how the Government sends a man out to fight us, as it did General Miles, and then breaks his word. Such a Government has something wrong about it. I can not understand why so many chiefs are allowed to talk so many different ways, and promise so many different things. I have seen the Great Father Chief (the President), the next Great Chief (Secretary of the Interior), the Commissioner Chief (Hayt), the Law Chief (General Butler), and many other law chiefs (Congressmen), and they all say they are my friends, and that I shall have justice, but while their mouths all talk right I do not understand why nothing is done for my people. I have heard talk and talk, but nothing is done. Good words do not last long unless they amount to something. Words do not pay for my dead people. They do not pay for my country, now overrun by white men. They do not protect my father's grave. They do not pay for all my horses and cattle. Good words will not give me back my children. Good words will not make good the promise of your War Chief General Miles. Good words will not give my people good health and stop them from dying. Good words will not get my people a home where they can live in peace and take care of themselves. I am tired of talk that comes to nothing. It makes my heart sick when I remember all the good words and all the broken promises. There has been too much talking by men who had no right to talk. Too many misrepresentations have been made, too many misunderstandings have come up between the white men about the Indians. If the white man wants to live in peace with the Indian he can live in peace. There need be no trouble. Treat all men alike. Give them all the same law. Give them all an even chance to live and grow. All men were made by the same Great Spirit Chief. They are all brothers. The earth is the mother of all people, and all people should have equal rights upon it. You might as well expect the rivers to run backward as that any man who was born a free man should be contented when penned up and denied liberty to go where he pleases. If you tie a horse to a stake, do you expect he will grow fat? If you pen an Indian up on a small spot of earth, and compel him to stay there, he will not be contented, nor will he grow and prosper. I have asked some of the great white chiefs where they get their authority to say to the Indian that he shall stay in one place, while he sees white men going where they please. They can not tell me.

I only ask of the Government to be treated as all other men are treated. If I can not go to my own home, let me have a home in some country where my people will not die so fast. I would like to go to Bitter Root Valley. There my people would be healthy; where they are now they are dying. Three have died since I left my camp to come to Washington.

When I think of our condition my heart is heavy. I see men of my race treated as outlaws and driven from country to country, or shot down like animals. I know that my race must change. We can not hold our own with the white men as we are. We only ask an even chance to live as other men live. We ask to be recognized as men. We ask that the same law shall work alike on all men. If the Indian breaks the law, punish him by the law. If the white man breaks the law, punish him also.

Let me be a free man—free to travel, free to stop, free to work, free to trade where I choose, free to choose my own teachers, free to follow the religion of my fathers, free to think and talk and act for myself—and I will obey every law, or submit to the penalty.

Whenever the white man treats the Indian as they treat each other, then we will have no more wars. We shall all be alike—brothers of one father and one mother, with one sky above us and one country around us, and one government for all. Then the Great Spirit Chief who rules above will smile upon this land, and send rain to wash out the bloody spots made by brothers' hands from the face of the earth. For this time the Indian race are waiting and praying. I hope that no more groans of wounded men and women will ever go to the ear of the Great Spirit Chief above, and that all people may be one people.

In-mut-too-yah-lat-lat has spoken for his people.

Young Joseph.
Washington City, D.C.

QUESTIONS

1. Why does Joseph emphasize that Indians are not wild animals but human beings?

2. What is Joseph's attitude toward white people?

3. What does he think of the motivation of white people for coming to his country?

4. What is Joseph's notion of property?

5. Why did the Nez Perce end up going to war?

6. What does Joseph want from Congress?

FROM *FAUST PART TWO*

Johann Wolfgang von Goethe (1749–1832)

ACT FOUR

HIGH MOUNTAINS

[*Rugged forbidding peaks. A cloud drifts up, leans against
the cliff, settles on a projecting spur of rock, and divides.*]

FAUST [*stepping out of it*].
Gazing at those deep solitudes beneath my feet,
I tread with circumspection this high mountain-brink,
Dismissing now my cloudy vehicle, which has brought
Me gently through bright daylight over land and sea.
Slowly it has released me, yet does not disperse.
Towards the east it strives, a dense and vaporous mass;
The astonished eye strives after it in wonderment.
It parts as it moves on, in shifting, billowing change:
Yet seeks a shape.—Yes! now my eye is not deceived!—
On softest bedding, sun-gleamed, splendid there she lies,
A woman's form, most godlike, giant-like indeed:
I see it! It is like Juno, Leda, Helena;
With what majestic charm it hovers in my sight!
Alas, already it drifts away: amorphous, broad,
Its icy summits towering in the distant east
Reflect the dazzling greatness of these fleeting days.

But round my breast and brow there hovers soil, so cool,
So pleasing and caressing a bright wisp of cloud.
Now lightly, hesitantly higher it ascends,
And shapes itself.—Does joy delude, or do I see
That first, that long-lost, dearest treasure of my youth?
They rise to view, those riches of my deepest heart,
That leapt so lightly in the early dawn of love;
That first look, quickly sensed and hardly understood:
No precious jewel could have outshone it, had I held
It fast. Oh lovely growth, oh spiritual form!
Still undissolving, it floats skywards on and up,
And draws my best and inmost soul to follow it.

[*A seven-league boot touches the ground. A second follows
immediately.* MEPHISTOPHELES *dismounts. The boots hurry on.*]

MEPHISTOPHELES. Well, that's quick marching, I must say!—
Now, what are your intentions, pray?
Why choose this savage place to pause,
Where rocks upfang their dreadful jaws?
I know them, though from elsewhere, very well:
This place was once, in fact, the floor of hell.

FAUST. Another of your foolish tales, no doubt;
Such stuff you never tire of handing out.

MEPHISTOPHELES [*seriously*].
    When the Lord God—and I could tell you why—
    Hurled me and my lot headlong from the sky
    Into the fiery depths, the central flame
    For ever burning, evermore the same,
    We found ourselves, by this bright conflagration,
    In a most incommodious situation.
    The devils all began to cough, to utter
    Much belching back and front, to sneeze and splutter;
10   Hell filled with sulphurous acid fumes, expelling
    Its brimstone stench, like a great gasbag swelling!
    Until such monstrous force, as soon it must,
    Shattered the dry lands of the earth's thick crust.
    Now, things are upside down: the great abyss
    Of former times has become peaks like this.
    And on this, too, their orthodoxy's based,
    With nethermost by uppermost replaced;
    For when we fled the hot pit's servitude,
    Our lordship of the upper air ensued.
20   An open secret, kept till now with care;
    Lately revealed to the nations everywhere. (*Eph.* 6:12)

FAUST. Mountains keep noble silence; let them be!
    Their whence and why's no puzzlement to me.
    When Nature's reign began, pure and self-grounded,
    Then this terrestrial globe it shaped and rounded.
    Glad of their peaks and chasms, it displayed
    Mountains and mountains, rocks and rocks it made;
    The soft-curved hills it shaped then, gentling down
    Into the valleys; there all's green and grown.
30   Thus Nature takes her pleasure, never troubling
    With all your crazy swirl and boil and bubbling.

MEPHISTOPHELES. Well, so you say; to you it seems just so.
    But I was there, my dear sir, and I know!
    I saw it all: the lower regions seethed,
    They swelled and spilled, great streams of fire they breathed,
    And Moloch's hammer forging rock to rock,
    Scattered the fragments with its mighty knock.
    The land's still stiff with alien lumps of stone:
    How's such momentum possible? The sages
40   Try to explain, but still untouched for ages
    Those boulders lie, the answer's still unknown.
    We rack our brains to death: what more
    Can thinking tell us?—Only the old lore
    Of simple folk has understood, they've read it
    In their tradition's ripe unchanging store:
    Wonders they see, and Satan gets the credit!
    So on faith's crutch my hobbling wanderer goes:
    Devil's Rock, Devil's Bridge are all he knows.

FAUST. An interesting viewpoint, I must say,
50   To observe Nature's works the Devil's way.

MEPHISTOPHELES. Let Nature do its will; what do I care!
    My word on it: Satan himself was there!
    Our methods—tumult, mad upheaval—get
    The best results; look round for proof!—But let

Me now speak plain: can we still offer you
No earthly joy? A panoramic view
Confronts you, far and wide you see unfurled
The glory of the kingdoms of this world (*Matt.* 4):
And can your discontentment still
Discern no pleasing prospect?

FAUST.   Yes!
A great thought has inspired me: guess
It if you can.

10   MEPHISTOPHELES. That I soon will.
In your place, I'd seek out some city for
My capital. One with a nookshotten core
Of streets where burghers munch, of Gothic gables,
Of poky markets selling vegetables—
Onions and cabbages and beet;
Benchfuls of fly-infested meat.
Come here at any time, you'll sense
The stink of ceaseless diligence.
Wide avenues and squares then raise
20   The social level of the place:
And finally long suburbs sprawl,
Impeded by no outer wall.
There would be traffic, loud and fast,
Such fun to watch! All bustling past,
And to and fro the scuttling slither,
The swarming ants, hither and thither.
And when I drove or rode, I'd be
Their cynosure for all to see:
A hundred thousand would revere me!

30   FAUST. All that, I fear, would fail to cheer me.
One likes a growing population,
Prospering, feeding, even taking
Their ease, acquiring education—
But they're all rebels in the making.

MEPHISTOPHELES. Then, somewhere suitable, to fit my state,
A grandiose pleasure-palace I'd create.
Forests and hills, wide meadows, open land,
Would be my garden, likewise very grand:
Green walls and velvet greensward, avenues
40   Straight as a die, precisely shaded views,
Rocky cascades in even steps descending,
And fountains in variety unending.
Here, a great noble jet; there, bordering it,
A thousand jetlets hiss and piss and spit.
I would have maisonettes built, and install
The most delightful women in them—all
My time I'd spend most cosily enstewed
In such companionable solitude.
And I say 'women' quite advisedly:
50   Charm in the singular's no charm to me.

FAUST. Babylonian debauch, modern vulgarity.

MEPHISTOPHELES. And what was your new project, may one ask?
Some bold and noble striving, I'll be bound;

Perhaps, since you've learnt to float above the ground,
A mission to the moon is our next task?

FAUST. Certainly not! This earthly sphere
Is room enough for high deeds; here
I still can achieve wonders. Never
Have I felt such great strength for bold endeavour.

MEPHISTOPHELES. So, fame is what you want? One sees you've been
Consorting with a heroine.

10 FAUST. I want to rule and to possess: what need
Have I of fame? What matters but the deed?

MEPHISTOPHELES. Poets will come nevertheless,
Your posthumous glory to profess;
Fools, kindling further foolishness.

FAUST. Mean spirit, you have no part nor lot
In any of man's longings: what
Can your embittered caustic mind
Know of the needs of humankind?

MEPHISTOPHELES. Well, tell me—I'll be governed by
20 Your will—what whim you now would satisfy.

FAUST. My eye fell, as I passed, on the high sea:
It surged and swelled, mounted up more and more,
Then checked, and spilt its waves tempestuously,
Venting its rage upon the flat, wide shore.
And this displeased me: as when pride's excess
And angry blood and passion unconfined,
Rising too high, fill with uneasiness
A free and just and equitable mind.
I thought it chance, and looked more closely: then
30 The tide stood still, it turned, rolled back again—
From its high point's proud goal the flood retreated.
And later, the whole process is repeated.

MEPHISTOPHELES [*ad spectatores*].
This is no news to me; I know that game,
For a hundred thousand years it's been the same.

FAUST [*continuing with passionate excitement*].
Landward it streams, and countless inlets fill;
Barren itself, it spreads its barren will;
It swells and swirls, its rolling waves expand
Over the dreary waste of dismal sand;
40 Breaker on breaker, all their power upheaved
And then withdrawn, and not a thing achieved!
I watch dismayed, almost despairingly,
This useless elemental energy!
And so my spirit dares new wings to span:
This I would fight, and conquer if I can.

And I can conquer it!—Flood as it may,
It slinks past all that rises in its way;
For all its gushing pride, a little hill
50 Denies it passage, and against its will
The least concavity lures it from its course.
At once my plan was made! My soul shall boast

An exquisite achievement: from our coast
I'll ban the lordly sea, I'll curb its force,
I'll set new limits to that watery plain
And drive it back into itself again.
I've worked out every detail, and I say:
This is my will, now dare to find a way!

*A sound of distant drums and martial music is heard from
behind the spectators, on the right.]*

MEPHISTOPHELES. Why, that's no problem!—Distant drums; do you hear?

10 FAUST. A sad sound to the wise; more war, I fear.

MEPHISTOPHELES. War or peace it may be, but the wise man
Turns both to his advantage if he can.
He waits for the right moment, till he sees it.
Now, Faust, your chance has come; be bold and seize it!

FAUST. Spare me this riddling rubbish and explain
Yourself! What's to be done? Just tell me plain.

MEPHISTOPHELES. On my way here I noticed, with distress,
Our friend the Emperor is in a mess.
You will recall, we entertained him well
20 And fooled him with false gold—why, he could sell
The whole world, he supposed. As a mere boy
He was elected to the throne;
And then, regrettably misguided
Of course, he very soon decided
To have it both ways: to enjoy
Both the imperial power and pleasures of his own.

FAUST. A great mistake. A ruler, to fulfil
His duty, which is to command, must find
Pleasure in the commanding. A high will
30 Dwells in his heart, yet none must know his mind.
He whispers it to intimates, and when
It's done, the world can wonder at it then.
That way, a lasting dignity allies
Itself to supreme power. Mere pleasures vulgarize.

MEPHISTOPHELES. That was not his way. Pleasure, endlessly,
Was what he sought; the Empire's anarchy
Is the result. Feuds between great or small,
Criss-crossing strife, brothers exiling, killing
40 Each other, castle against castle, all
The cities daggers-drawn, the guilds rebelling
Against the feudal lords, the bishops fighting
Chapter and parish, every man despiting
His fellow, throats cut in the church, no travellers
Or merchants safe from highway murderers.
And all men plucked up courage, for life now
Meant self-defence. Well, life went on somehow.

FAUST. Went on! Limped, fell, got to its feet, and then
Tripped up and fell head-over-heels again.

50 MEPHISTOPHELES. And no one did too badly; everyone
Tried to be someone; it was easily done.
Nonentities assumed sufficiency.

But the best and the strongest finally
Decided things had gone too far. They rose
In arms, and said: Let him be master who'll impose
Peace! This the Emperor cannot, will not do.
We shall elect another, who'll renew
The Empire, bring things back to life,
Protect us all from war and strife,
Remake the world and give us peace and justice too.

FAUST. Very religious.

10   MEPHISTOPHELES. Priests, indeed, they were;
They played a leading part in this affair,
Protecting their fat bellies. The insurrection
Increased: it had their holy benediction.
And so our Emperor, whom we entertained of late,
Comes here to fight the battle that may seal his fate.

FAUST. That's sad; he was a frank, good-natured man.

MEPHISTOPHELES. Come, while there's life there's hope; so let's do what we can!
This narrow gorge is trapping him: one bold
Rescue will rescue him a thousandfold
20   Who knows how soon his luck may turn?
And with his luck, his vassals will return.

[*They cross the lower mountain range and survey the disposition of the army in the valley. Drums and military music are heard from below.*]

MEPHISTOPHELES. A good position; he's quite well secured;
We'll join him, and his victory's assured.

FAUST. What help is ours supposed to be?
Fraud, sleight-of-hand, magical trickery!

MEPHISTOPHELES. Stratagems to win battles! You
Must keep your higher aims in view,
Your noble purpose. If we save
30   The Emperor's throne for him, restore his land,
Then you will kneel before him and receive
As your personal fief the wide sea-strand.

FAUST. Well, you have many talents, I don't doubt it;
Now win a battle too, and quick about it!

MEPHISTOPHELES. No, you will win it; this time, sir,
You're the commanding officer.

FAUST. Oh yes, that suits me very nicely,
My knowledge of war being nil precisely.

40   MEPHISTOPHELES. *Herr Feldmarschall!* Simply rely
On your general staff, and you'll get by.
I've smelt for some time there was war afoot,
And so my council has been put
On a war footing. Ancient human powers
From primal mountains; allies, now, of ours,

Fortunately.

FAUST.   What's that? I see armed men.
Have you stirred up the mountain people, then?

MEPHISTOPHELES. No, but like Peter Quince, I've brought a mere
Quintessence of the rabble here.

[*The* THREE MIGHTY MEN *enter* (2 *Sam.* 23:8).]

MEPHISTOPHELES. Here are my lads; as you can see,
Their age varies appreciably,
As do their clothes and armour. You shall be
Well served, I'll warrant, by all three.
[*ad spectatores*] Weapons, these days, and knightly gear
Are popular; these wretches here
10   Will also widen their appeal
By being more allegorical than real.

BUSTER [*young, lightly armed, colourfully dressed*].
If a man looks me in the eye,
I bash his face in till needs repairs.
Escape my fist? Just let him try!
I'll have him first by the short hairs.

BAGGER [*mature, well armed, richly dressed*].
Picking an empty quarrel's not
My style; why waste the day with words?
20   Be bold and grab the goods first; afterwards
It's time enough to ask what's what.

HUGGER [*middle-aged, heavily armed, without a cloak*].
That's not much profit either; when
You've gained wealth, it's soon lost again;
Life's current washes it away.
It's good to get, better to hold:
Let me take charge—I'm old and grey—
And then you'll keep it till you're old.

[*They descend together towards the valley.*]

ACT FIVE

OPEN COUNTRY

A WANDERER. There they are, so dark and strong,
Those old lindens, as before;
I have wandered for so long,
Now I find them here once more!
And the hut that sheltered me,
Tempest-tossed as I was then,
On the sand-dunes here I see:
This is the same place again!
And my hosts? That fine old couple
10   Rescued me with ready will:
They were pious gentle people—
Can I hope to find them still?
They were old at our first meeting.
Shall I knock or call?—My greeting
To you, if the gods still bless
You with your life of kindliness!

BAUCIS (*a very old little woman*).
Stranger dear, speak softly please,
Softly! My old husband, he's
20   Resting still. He needs the length
Of his nights, for short days' strength.

THE WANDERER. Dear old woman, is it true,
Can I still be thanking you
For my young life you and he
Long ago saved from the sea?
Baucis! You, who when death coldly
Kissed me, warmed my freezing blood?

[*The husband enters.*]

You, Philemon, who so boldly
30   Snatched my treasure from the flood?
Yours the hospitable fire,
Yours the bell with silver tone,
You, my rescuers from dire
Peril, you my help alone!
Now, to ease my heart's emotion,
I must look upon this shore;
I must kneel and pray once more,
Gazing on the boundless ocean.

[*He steps forward across the sand-dune.*]

40   PHILEMON [*to* BAUCIS].
Quickly now, let's lay the table
Here among the flowers and trees.
Let him go; he'll stare, unable
To believe the change he sees.

[*Standing by* THE WANDERER.]
Look! Your enemies of old,
The fierce foaming waves, have been

Turned into a park; behold
Now this paradisal scene!
I was not young enough to lend
My helping hands to this endeavour;
Soon my strength was at an end;
The sea was further off than ever.
Those wise lords, they sent bold slaves:
Dams and dikes built in a day
Stole the birthright of the waves
And usurped the ocean's sway.
Now green fields and gardens lie,
Woods and villages have grown
Up all round. But come, the sun
Will be setting by and by,
Let us eat. Those distant white
Sails seek haven for the night;
Now like nesting birds they know
Here's a port where they can go.
Thus it is; you must look far
Now to find the sea's blue shore,
For dense between, on wide new land,
New human habitations stand.

[The three sit at table in the little garden.]

BAUCIS.   You are silent? And no food
           Has refreshed you, stranger dear?

PHILEMON. Tell him about the wonders; you'd
           Like to talk, he'd like to hear.

BAUCIS.   Yes, the wonders. I'm still worried
           By strange doings we have seen.
           Things unnaturally hurried;
           Things not as they should have been.

PHILEMON. Can the Emperor sin? He named him
           Feudal lord of all the coast;
           Even a herald, marching past
           With his trumpet-call, proclaimed him.
           It began here near the dune,
           That first foothold on the flood;
           There were tents and huts. But soon
           In green fields a palace stood.

BAUCIS.   Slaves toiled vainly: blow by blow,
           Pick and shovel made no way.
           Then we saw the night-flames glow—
           And a dam stood there next day.
           They used human sacrifice:
           Fire ran down, like rivers burning.
           All night long we heard the cries—
           A canal was built by morning.
           He is godless, for he sorely
           Wants our hut, our clump of trees.
           As a neighbour he's too lordly;
           We must serve him, if you please!

PHILEMON. Yet a fine new house he's found
           For us on the polder-ground.

BAUCIS.   I'd not trust that soil for long.
             Stay up here where you belong!

PHILEMON. Come, let's watch the sun's last ray,
             When our chapel bell we've tolled.
             Let us kneel there, let us pray,
             Trusting our God, as of old.

[*A large ornamental park, with a long straight canal.*
FAUST in extreme old age, walking about pensively.
LYNCEUS THE WATCHMAN speaks through a megaphone.]

10   LYNCEUS.   The sun sinks, the last ships appear,
             Gaily they pass the harbour bar,
             Soon a tall vessel will be here
             In the canal; how merry are
             Those fluttering pennants! Each one plays
             From a proud standing mast; the crew
             Are sharing the good fortune too
             That greets you in your latter days.

[*The chapel bell sounds from the sand-dune.*]

FAUST [*starting up angrily*].
20   Damned bell! A treacherous wound that flies
             As from a sniper's shot behind me!
             Out there my endless kingdom lies,
             But this vexation at my back,
             These teasing envious sounds remind me
             My great estate's not pure! That line
             Of linden-trees, that little shack,
             That crumbling chapel, are not mine.
             On that green place I may not tread
             Another's shadow falls like dread;
30   It irks my feet, my eyes, my ear—
             How can I get away from here!

LYNCEUS THE WATCHMAN [*as above*].
             Now, in the evening breeze, all hail
             To this fine ship with swelling sail!
             How swift it glides, its load how high—
             Sacks, boxes, piled against the sky!

[*A splendid boat appears, richly loaded with a variety of*
products from distant lands. Enter MEPHISTOPHELES and
THE THREE MIGHTY MEN.]

40   CHORUS.   Welcome ashore!
             We're back again!
             Long live the master,
             Say his men!

[*They land; the cargo is brought ashore.*]

MEPHISTOPHELES. We have done well and had good sport;
             We hope my lord will be content.
             We'd only two ships when we went,
             With twenty now we're back in port.
             Our cargo richly testifies
50   To our great deeds that won this prize.
             The ocean sets one's notions free:

Who's plagued by scruple out at sea?
To catch a fish, to catch a ship,
The only way is grab and grip;
And once three ships have come one's way,
A fourth is easy grappling-prey.
Then guess what chance a fifth will stand!
For might is right, by sea or land.
Not *how* but *how much*—that's what's counted!
What seaman does not take for granted
10   The undivided trinity
Of war and trade and piracy?

THE THREE MIGHTY MEN. No thanks to meet us,
No word to greet us!
Our master thinks
Our cargo stinks.
His face expresses
Great displeasure;
He does not like
This princely treasure.

20   MEPHISTOPHELES. There's no more for you
On the house.
You took your cut,
So what's the grouse?

THE THREE. That's a mere penny
For our pains:
We ask fair shares
Of all the gains!

MEPHISTOPHELES. Go up there first
And set out all
The valuables
30   Hall by hall.
He'll see the richest
Show on earth;
Then he'll work out
Just what it's worth,
Decide he can
Afford a treat,
And order a feast-day
For the fleet.

Tomorrow the pretty birds we'll see;
40   They're my responsibility.

[The cargo is removed.]

MEPHISTOPHELES [*to* FAUST].
Why these dark looks, this frowning brow?
Sublime good fortune greets you now:
By your high wisdom, the sea-shore
And sea are reconciled once more;
Now from the land in easy motion
The ships glide swiftly to the ocean;
And thus, here in this royal place,
50   The whole world lies in your embrace!
Your kingdom started on this spot;
The first shed stood here, did it not?

Here the first shallow trench was tried
Where now the plashing oars are plied.
Your lofty plan, our industry,
Have made you lord of land and sea.
From here—

FAUST.   *Here*! That damned word again,
The theme and burden of my pain!
You are no fool: I must tell you
It cuts my very heart in two,
I'll not bear it another day!
Yet as I say it, even I
Feel shame. The old couple must give way!
I chose that linden clump as my
Retreat: those few trees not my own
Spoil the whole world that is my throne.
From branch to branch I planned to build
Great platforms, to look far afield,
From panoramic points to gaze
At all I've done; as one surveys
From an all-mastering elevation
A masterpiece of man's creation.
I'd see it all as I have planned:
Man's gain of habitable land.

This is the sharpest torment: what
A rich man feels he has not got!
That linden-scent, that chapel-chime
Haunt me like some grim funeral-time.
My will, my sovereign command
Is broken on that mound of sand!
How shall I cure my mental hell
That rages at that little bell!

MEPHISTOPHELES. Indeed, such matter for distress
Must turn your life to bitterness.
These cursèd tinkling sounds we hear
Must stink in every noble ear.
Ding-donging, tintinnabulating,
Clear evening skies obnubilating:
Every event of life it blights,
From that first bath to our last rites—
As if life were some dream-like thing
That fades away from dong to ding!

FAUST.   Their stubbornness, their opposition
Ruins my finest acquisition;
And in fierce agony I must
Grow weary now of being just.

MEPHISTOPHELES. Why scruple then at this late hour?
Are you not—a colonial power?

FAUST.   Well, do it! Clear them from my path!—
A fine new cottage, as you know,
I've built, where the old folk can go.

MEPHISTOPHELES. We'll lift them up and whisk them to it;
A moment's work, they'll scarcely know it.

They'll suffer it with a good grace
And settle down in their new place.

[*At his shrill whistle,* THE THREE MIGHTY MEN *appear.*]

Come, we have orders from my lord;
Tomorrow there'll be a feast on board.

THE THREE. We've had a poor reception here;
A feast's an excellent idea. [*Exeunt.*]

MEPHISTOPHELES [*ad spectators*].
The same old story! No doubt you
10   Have heard of Naboth's vineyard too. (1 *Kgs.* 21)

DEEP NIGHT

LYNCEUS THE WATCHMAN [*on the castle tower, singing*].
A watchman by calling,
Far-sighted by birth,
From this tower, my dwelling,
I gaze at the earth:

At the earth near and far,
At the world far and near,
At the moon and the stars,
20   At the woods and the deer.

A beauty eternal
In all things I see,
And the world and myself
Are both pleasing to me.

Oh blest are these eyes,
All they've seen and can tell:
Let it be as it may—
They have loved it so well!

[*A pause.*]

30   But I keep my watch so high,
Alas, not only for delight!
What dread terror of the night
Spreads its threat across the sky?
Fiery sparks are scattering, spraying
Through the twin-dark linden-trees:
Higher still the flames are playing,
Fanned to heat by their own breeze!
Now the hut's ablaze all through,
That was moist and mossy green;
40   Too late now for rescue—who
Can bring help to such a scene?
Smoke will choke the good old couple,
At their hearth so carefully
Kept and tended, poor old people,
What a dreadful tragedy!
Flames lick up, black mossy beams
Now are turned to burning red:

How grim this wild inferno seems!
Can they escape it? Have they fled?
Tongues of fearful lightning rise
Through those leaves and branches tall;
Dried-up boughs burn flickerwise;
Charred and breaking, soon they fall.
Cursèd eyes, why must I see?
Take your gift away from me!—
By their downward-crashing weight
10   Now the little chapel's crushed;
Snaking pointed flames have rushed
Up to crown the tree-tops' fate.
Hollow trunks in fiery showing
To their very roots are glowing.

[*A long pause; singing.*]

Something lovely to behold
Has vanished like an old tale told.

FAUST [*on the balcony, looking towards the sand-dunes*].
            From overhead, what song of woe?
20   Its words and music came too slow.
            My watchman wails: and inwardly
            The impatient deed now vexes me.
            What if the linden-trees are gone,
            Their trunks half-charred, a direful sight—
            I'll quickly build a watch-tower on
            That place, and scan the infinite!
            I see the new house over there,
            That soon will shelter that old pair;
            They'll praise my generous patronage
30   And pass a peaceable old age.

MEPHISTOPHELES and THE THREE [*from below*].
            We're back, sir, with due promptitude;
            Regrettably, they misconstrued
            Our meaning, and some force was needed.
            We knocked and banged, but were not heeded.
            We rattled on, and banged some more,
            Till there it lay, the rotten door.
            We threatened them and made a din:
            They would not budge, or ask us in,
            And as is common in such cases
40   They just sat on with stolid faces.
            On your behalf, our zeal not lacking,
            We grabbed them then and sent them packing.
            They didn't linger long—the pair
            Dropped dead of terror then and there.
            A stranger, lurking with them, drew
            His sword and was soon dealt with too.
            The fight was brief and violent;
            Some coals were scattered, and up went
50   Some straw; the merry blazing fire
            Is now a triple funeral pyre.

FAUST. And this you claim to have done for me?
            I said exchange, not robbery!

Deaf savages! I curse this deed;
Now share my curse, your folly's meed!

THE OTHERS [IN CHORUS]. The moral's plain, hear it who can:
Never resist the powerful man.
Don't put up a bold fight, or you
Risk house and home, and your life too. [*Exeunt.*]

FAUST [*on the balcony*].
The stars have hid their gleam and glow,
The fire sinks and glimmers low;
A breeze still fans its embers free
And blows the reek across to me.
A rash command, too soon obeyed!—
What comes now, like a hovering shade?

MIDNIGHT

[*Enter* FOUR GREY WOMEN.]

THE FIRST. My name is Want.
THE SECOND.   My name is Debt.
THE THIRD. My name is Care.
THE FOURTH.   My name is Need.
THREE OF THEM. The door will not open, we'll never get in.
    This is a rich man's house, there's no way in.
WANT. I am a shadow there.
DEBT.   I am as nothing there.
NEED. They pay no heed to me, for they need nothing there.
CARE. You are locked out, sisters, you cannot stay.
    But through his keyhole Care finds a way.

[CARE *vanishes.*]

WANT. Come then, my grey sisters, for you must be gone.
DEBT. I'll follow you closely, sister, lead on!
NEED. Need follows you, sister, as close as a breath.
ALL THREE. The dark clouds are drifting, the stars disappearing:
    From far off, from far off, another is nearing!
    Our brother is coming; he comes—brother Death.

[*Exeunt.*]

FAUST [*in the palace*].
I saw four come, I only saw three go.
What their speech meant I do not know.
They talked of *debt,* and then another word
That almost rhymed—could it be *death* I heard?
A dark and hollow sound, a ghostly sigh.
I have not broken through to freedom yet.
I must clear magic from my path, forget
All magic conjurations—for then I
Would be confronting Nature all alone:
Man's life worth while, man standing on his own!

So it was once, before I probed the gloom
And dared to curse myself, with words of doom
That cursed the world. The air is swarming now
With ghosts we would avoid if we knew how.

How logical and clear the daylight seems
Till the night weaves us in its web of dreams!
As we return from dewy fields, dusk falls
And birds of mischief croak their ominous calls.
All round us lurks this superstition's snare;
Some haunting, half-seen thing cries out Beware!
We shrink back in alarm, and are alone.
Doors creak, and no one enters.

[*In sudden alarm.*]

                                                        Is someone
There at the door?
CARE.   You ask, need I reply?
FAUST. And who are you?
CARE.   I am here, here am I.
FAUST. Go away!
CARE.   I am here where I should be.
FAUST [*at first angry, then calmer, to himself*].
I must take care to use no sorcery.

CARE.   Though no human ear can hear me,
            Yet the echoing heart must fear me;
            In an ever-changed disguise
            All men's lives I tyrannize.
            On the roads and on the sea
            Anxiously they ride with me;
            Never looked for, always there,
            Cursed and flattered. I am Care:
            Have I never crossed your path?

FAUST. I merely raced across the earth,
    Seized by the hair each passing joy,
    Discarded all that did not satisfy;
    What slipped my grasp, I let it go again.
    I have merely desired, achieved, and then
    Desired some other thing. Thus I have stormed
    Through life; at first with pride and violence,
    But now less rashly, with more sober sense.
    I've seen enough of this terrestrial sphere.
    There is no view to the Beyond from here:
    A fool will seek it, peer with mortal eyes
    And dream of human life above the skies!
    Let him stand fast in this world, and look round
    With courage: here so much is to be found!
    Why must he wander into timelessness?
    What his mind grasps, he may possess.
    Thus let him travel all his earthly day:
    Though spirits haunt him, let him walk his way,
    Let both his pain and joy be in his forward stride—
    Each moment leave him still unsatisfied!

CARE.   When a man is in my keeping,
            All his world is dead or sleeping;
            Everlasting dusk descending,
            Sun not moving, dark not ending.
            Though each outward sense be whole,
            Night has nested in his soul;
            Riches stand around him staling,

      Unpossessed and unavailing;
      Gladness, sadness are mere whim,
      Plenty cannot nourish him,
      He delays both joy and pain
      Till the day has passed again,
      And on time-to-come intent
      Comes to no accomplishment.

FAUST. Stop! You'll not put that blight on me!
    I will not listen to such stuff.
10   Leave me! Your wretched litany
    Can drive wise men to madness soon enough.

CARE. Shall he come or shall he go?
     He can't choose, he does not know.
     In the middle of the road,
     See, he staggers, tremble-toed!
     Wanders deeper in the maze,
     Sees the whole worlds crookedways,
     Burdening himself and others;
     Still he breathes, yet chokes and smothers—
20   Not quite choked, yet life-bereft,
     Stubborn, though with hope still left.
     Such a ceaseless downward course,
     Bitter *may not, must* by force,
     Now released, now re-pursued,
     Restless sleep and tasteless food,
     Binds him in a static state,
     Makes him hell's initiate.

FAUST. Horrible phantoms! Thus you still conspire
    Again against mankind and yet again;
30   Even indifferent days you turn into a dire
    Chaotic nexus of entangling pain.
    Demons, I know, are hard to exorcize,
    The spirit-bond is loath to separate:
    But though the creeping power of Care be great,
    This power I will never recognize!

CARE. Suffer it then; for as I go
     I leave a curse where I have passed.
     Men live their lives in blindness: so
     Shall even Faust be blinded at the last!

40   [*She breathes on him. Exit.*]

FAUST [*blinded*].
    Night seems to close upon me deeper still,
    But in my inmost soul a bright light shines.
    I hasten to complete my great designs:
    My words alone can work my mastering will.
    Rise from your sleep, my servants, every man!
    Give visible success to my bold plan!
    Set to work now with shovel and with spade:
    I have marked it all out, let it be made!
50   With a well-ordered project and with hard
    Toil we shall win supreme reward;
    Until the edifice of this achievement stands,
    One mind shall move a thousand hands.

THE GREAT FORECOURT OF THE PALACE

[Torches, MEPHISTOPHELES *as overseer leading a gang of* LEMURS.*]*

MEPHISTOPHELES. Come now, my lemur-goblins, patched-
    Up semi-skeletons,
    With mouldering sinews still attached
    To move your rattling bones!

LEMURS [*in chorus*].
    We came at once, sir, when you called;
    Is there—we did half hear of it—
10   A plot of land here to be sold,
    And shall we get our share of it?

    Here are the chains, here are the posts
    To measure out the site.
    Why did you summon us poor ghosts?
    We can't remember quite.

MEPHISTOPHELES. There's no need for these mysteries;
    Just use yourselves as measuring-rods!
    The tallest of you can lie down lengthwise,
    The rest stand round and cut away the sods.
20   A rectangle of earth dug deep,
    A good old-fashioned place to sleep!
    From palace to this narrow house descending—
    That always was the stupid story's ending.

LEMURS [*digging with mocking gestures*].
        In youth when I did love, did love
        Methought 'twas very sweet,
        And night and day to music gay
        I danced with nimble feet.

        But Age with his crutch and cunning clutch
        Has come to trip me now.
30   By a grave I stumbled, and in I tumbled;
        They'd left it open somehow.

FAUST [*comes out of the palace, groping at the doorpost*].
    The clash of spades: how it delights my heart!
    These are my many workmen; here they toil,
    The alienated earth to reconcile,
    To keep the ocean and the land apart,
    To rule the unruly waves once more.

MEPHISTOPHELES [*aside*].
40   And yet it's us you're working for
    With all your foolish dams and dikes;
    Neptune, the water-devil, likes
    To think of the great feast there'll be
    When they collapse. Do what you will, my friend,
    You all are doomed! They are in league with me,
    The elements, and shall destroy you in the end.

FAUST.   Overseer!

MEPHISTOPHELES. Sir!

FAUST.   I need more workers; bring
50   Them to me by the hundred! Use persuasion,
    Cajole or bully them, try everything,
    Inducements, money, force! This excavation

Must go ahead; the ditch I've now begun—
I must know daily how much has been done.

MEPHISTOPHELES [*sotto voce*].
    The digging has gone well today;
    No ditch or dike, but dust to dust, they say.

FAUST. A swamp surrounds the mountains' base;
    It poisons all I have achieved till now.
    I'll drain it too; that rotten place
    Shall be my last great project. I see how
    To give those millions a new living-space:
    They'll not be safe, but active, free at least.
    I see green fields, so fertile: man and beast
    At once shall settle that new pleasant earth,
    Bastioned by great embankments that will rise
    About them, by bold labour brought to birth.
    Here there shall be an inland paradise:
    Outside, the sea, as high as it can reach,
    May rage and gnaw; and yet a common will,
    Should it intrude, will act to close the breach.
    Yes! to this vision I am wedded still,
    And this as wisdom's final word I teach:
    Only that man earns freedom, merits life,
    Who must reconquer both in constant daily strife.
    In such a place, by danger still surrounded,
    Youth, manhood, age, their brave new world have founded.
    I long to see that multitude, and stand
    With a free people on free land!
    Then to the moment I might say:
    Beautiful moment, do not pass away!
    Till many ages shall have passed
    This record of my earthly life shall last.
    And in anticipation of such bliss
    What moment could give me greater joy than this?

      [FAUST *sinks back, the* LEMURS *seize him and lay him on the ground.*]

MEPHISTOPHELES. Poor fool! Unpleasured and unsatisfied,
    Still whoring after changeful fantasies,
    This last, poor, empty moment he would seize,
    Content with nothing else beside.
    How he resisted me! But in the end
    Time wins; so here you lie, my senile friend.
    The clock has stopped—

CHORUS.   Has stopped! Like midnight it is stilled.
    The dock-hands fall.

MEPHISTOPHELES. They fall. All is fulfilled.*

CHORUS. All's over now.

MEPHISTOPHELES.   Over! A stupid word!
    Why 'over'? What can be
    'Over' is just not there; it's all the same to me!
    Why bother to go on creating?
    Making, then endlessly annihilating!
    'Over and past!' What's that supposed to mean?
    It's no more than if it had never been,
    Yet it goes bumbling round as if it were.
    The Eternal Void is what I'd much prefer.

10

20

30

40

50

QUESTIONS

1. What four guesses did Mephistopheles make about Faust's goal?

2. What does Faust say is his goal?

3. Why does Faust find Baucis and Philemon annoying?

4. What are Faust's initial and final steps to secure their land?

5. How does Faust feel after he gets Baucis and Philemon's land?

6. Why does Faust persist in his project?

ECONOMY FROM *WALDEN*

Henry David Thoreau (1818–1862)

When I wrote the following pages, or rather the bulk of them, I lived alone, in the woods, a mile from any neighbour, in a house which I had built myself, on the shore of Walden Pond, in Concord, Massachusetts, and earned my living by the labour of my hands only. I lived there two years and two months. At present I am a sojourner in civilised life again.

I should not obtrude my affairs so much on the notice of my readers if very particular inquiries had not been made by my townsmen concerning my mode of life, which some would call impertinent, though they do not appear to me at all impertinent, but, considering the circumstances, very natural and pertinent. Some have asked what I got to eat; if I did not feel lonesome; if I was not afraid; and the like. Others have been curious to learn what portion of my income I devoted to charitable purposes; and some, who have large families, how many poor children I maintained. I will therefore ask those of my readers who feel no particular interest in me to pardon me if I undertake to answer some of these questions in this book. In most books, the I, or first person, is omitted; in this it will be retained; that, in respect to egotism, is the main difference. We commonly do not remember that it is, after all, always the first person that is speaking. I should not talk so much about myself if there were anybody else whom I knew as well. Unfortunately, I am confined to this theme by the narrowness of my experience. Moreover, I, on my side, require of every writer, first or last, a simple and sincere account of his own life, and not merely what he has heard of other men's lives; some such account as he would send to his kindred from a distant land; for if he has lived sincerely, it must have been in a distant land to me. Perhaps these pages are more particularly addressed to poor students. As for the rest of my readers, they will accept such portions as apply to them. I trust that none will stretch the seams in putting on the coat, for it may do good service to him whom it fits.

I would fain say something, not so much concerning the Chinese and Sandwich Islanders as you who read these pages, who are said to live in New England; something about your condition, especially your outward condition or circumstances in this world, in this town, what it is, whether it is necessary that it be as bad as it is, whether it cannot be improved as well as not. I have travelled a good deal in Concord: and everywhere, in shops, and offices, and fields, the inhabitants have appeared to me to be doing penance in a thousand remarkable ways. What I have heard of Brahmins sitting exposed to four fires and looking in the face of the sun; or hanging suspended, with their heads downward, over flames; or looking at the heavens over their shoulders, "until it becomes impossible for them to resume their natural position, while from the twist of the neck nothing but liquids can pass into the stomach"; or dwelling, chained for life, at the foot of a tree; or measuring with their bodies, like caterpillars, the breadth of vast empires; or standing on one leg on the tops of pillars—even these forms of conscious penance are hardly more incredible and astonishing than the scenes which I daily witness. The twelve labours of Hercules were trifling in comparison with those which my neighbours have undertaken; for they were only twelve, and had an end; but I could never see that these men slew or captured any monster or finished any labour. They have no friend Iolaus to burn with a hot iron the root of the hydra's head, but as soon as one head is crushed, two spring up.

I see young men, my townsmen, whose misfortune it is to have inherited farms, houses, barns, cattle, and farming tools; for these are more easily acquired than got rid of. Better if they had been born in the open pasture and suckled by a wolf, that they might have seen with clearer eyes what field they were called to labour in. Who made them serfs of the soil? Why should they eat their sixty acres, when man is condemned to eat only his peck of dirt? Why should they begin digging their graves as soon as they are born? They have got to live a man's life, pushing all these things before them, and get on as well as they can. How many a poor immortal soul have I met well-nigh crushed and smothered under its load, creeping down the road of life, pushing before it a barn seventy-five feet by forty, its Augean stables never cleansed, and one hundred acres of land, tillage, mowing, pasture, and wool-lot! The portionless, who struggle with no such unnecessary inherited encumbrances, find it labour enough to subdue and cultivate a few cubic feet of flesh.

But men labour under a mistake. The better part of the man is soon ploughed into the soil for compost. By a seeming fate, commonly called necessity, they are employed, as it says in an old book, laying up treasures which moth and rust will corrupt and thieves break through and steal. It is a fool's life, as they will find when they get to the end of it, if not before. It is said that Deucalion and Pyrrha created men by throwing stones over their heads behind them:—

> "Inde genus durum sumus, experiensque laborum, Et documenta damus qua simus origine nati."

Or, as Raleigh rhymes it in his sonorous way:—

> "From thence our kind hard-hearted, is, enduring pain and care, Approving that our bodies of a stony nature are."

So much for a blind obedience to a blundering oracle, throwing the stones over their heads behind them, and not seeing where they fell.

Most men, even in this comparatively free country, through mere ignorance and mistake, are so occupied with the factitious cares and superfluously course labours of life that its finer fruits cannot be plucked by them. Their fingers, from excessive toil, are too clumsy and tremble too much for that. Actually, the labouring man has not leisure for a true integrity day by day; he cannot afford to sustain the manliest relations to men; his labour would be depreci-ated in the market. He has no time to be anything but a machine. How can he remember well his ignorance—which his growth requires—who has so often to use his knowledge? We should feed and clothe him gratuitously sometimes, and recruit him with our cordials, before we judge of him. The finest qualities of our nature, like the bloom on fruits, can be preserved only by the most delicate handling. Yet we do not treat ourselves nor one another thus tenderly.

Some of you, we all know, are poor, find it hard to live, are sometimes, as it were, gasping for breath. I have no doubt that some of you who read this book are unable to pay for all the dinners which you have actually eaten, or for the coats and shoes which are fast wearing or already worn out, and have come to this page to spend borrowed or stolen time, robbing your creditors of an hour. It is very evident what mean and sneaking lives many of you live, for my sight has been whetted by experience; always on the limits, trying to get into business and trying to get out of debt, a very ancient slough, called by the Latins *as alienum*, another's brass, for some of their coins were made of brass; still living, and dying, and buried by this other's brass; always promising to pay, promising to pay, tomorrow, and dying today, insolvent; seeking to curry favor, to get custom, by how many modes, only not state-prison offenses: lying, flattering, voting, contracting yourselves into a nutshell of civility, or dilating into an atmosphere of thin and vaporous generosity, that you may persuade your neighbour to let you make his shoes, or his hat, or his coat, or his carriage, or import his groceries for him; making yourself sick, that you may lay up something against a sick day, something to be tucked away in an old chest, or in a stocking behind the plastering, or, more safely, in the brick bank; no matter where, no matter how much or how little.

I sometimes wonder that we can be so frivolous, I may almost say, as to attend to the gross but somewhat foreign form of servitude called Negro Slavery, there are so many keen and subtle masters that enslave both north and south. It is hard to have a southern overseer; it is worse to have a northern one; but worst of all when you are the slave-driver yourself. Talk of a divinity in man! Look at the teamster on the highway, wending to market by day or night; does any divinity stir within him? His highest duty to fodder and water his horses! What is his destiny to him compared with the shipping interests? Does not he drive for Squire Make-a-stir? How godlike, how immortal, is he? See how he cowers and sneaks, how vaguely all the day he fears, not being immortal nor divine, but the slave and prisoner of his own opinion of himself, a fame won by his own deeds. Public opinion is a weak tyrant compared with our own private opinion.

What a man thinks of himself, that it is which determines, or rather indicates, his fate. Self-emancipation even in the West Indian provinces of the fancy and imagination,—what Wilber-force is there to bring that about? Think, also, of the ladies of the land weaving toilet cushions against the last day, not to betray too green an interest in their fates! As if you could kill time without injuring eternity.

The mass of men lead lives of quiet desperation. What is called resignation is confirmed desperation. From the desperate city you go into the desperate country, and have to console yourself with the bravery of minks and muskrats. A stereotyped but unconscious despair is concealed even under what are called the games and amusements of mankind. There is no play in them, for this comes after work. But it is a characteristic of wisdom not to do desperate things.

When we consider what, to use the words of the catechism, is the chief end of man, and what are the true necessaries and means of life, it appears as if men had deliberately chosen the common mode of living because they preferred it to any other. Yet they honestly think there is no choice left. But alert and healthy natures remember that the sun rose clear. It is never too late to give up our prejudices. No way of thinking or doing, however ancient, can be trusted without proof. What everybody echoes or in silence passes by as true today may turn out to be falsehood tomorrow, mere smoke of opinion, which some had trusted for a cloud that would sprinkle fertilising rain on their fields. What old people say you cannot do you try and find that you can. Old deeds for old people, and new deeds for new. Old people did not know enough once, perchance, to fetch fuel to keep the fire agoing; new people put a little dry wood under a pot, and are whirled around the globe with the speed of birds, in a way to kill old people, as the phrase is. Age is no better, hardly so well, qualified for an instructor as youth, for it has not profited so much as it has lost. One may almost doubt if the wisest man has learned anything of absolute value by living. Practically, the old have no very important advice to give the young, their own experience has been so partial, and their lives have been such miserable failures, for private reasons, as they must believe; and it may be that they have some faith left which belies that experience, and they are only less young than they were. I have lived some thirty years on this planet, and I have yet to hear the first syllable of valuable or even earnest advice from my seniors. They have told me nothing, and probably cannot tell me anything, to the purpose. Here is life, an experiment to a great extent untried by me; but it does not avail me that they have tried it. If I have any experience which I think valuable, I am sure to reflect that this my Mentors said nothing about.

One farmer says to me, "You cannot live on vegetable food solely, for it furnishes nothing to make bones with"; and so he religiously devotes a part of his day to supplying his system with the raw material of bones; walking all the while he talks behind his oxen, which, with vegetable-made bones, jerk him and his lumbering plough along in spite of every obstacle. Some things are really necessaries of life in some circles, the most helpless and diseased, which in others are luxuries merely, and in others still are entirely unknown.

The whole ground of human life seems to some to have been gone over by their predecessors, both the heights and the valleys, and all things to have been cared for. According to Evelyn, "the wise Solomon prescribed ordinances for the very distances of trees; and the Roman prætors have decided how often you may go into your neighbour's land to gather the acorns which fall on it without trespass, and what share belongs to that neighbour." Hippocrates has even left directions how we should cut our nails; that is, even with the ends of the fingers, neither shorter nor longer. Undoubtedly the very tedium and ennui which presumes to have exhausted the variety and the joys of life are as old as Adam. But man's capacities have never been measured; nor are we to judge for what he can do by any precedents, so little has been tried. Whatever have been thy failures hitherto, "be not afflicted, my child, for who shall assign to thee what thou hast left undone?"

We might try our lives by a thousand simple tests; as, for instance, that the same sun which ripens my beans illumines at once a system of earths like ours. If I had remembered this it would have prevented some mistakes. This was not the light in which I hoed them. The stars are the apexes of what wonderful triangles! What distant and different beings in the various mansions of the universe are contemplating the same one at the same moment! Nature and human life are as various as our several constitutions. Who shall say what prospect life offers to another? Could a great miracle take place then for us to look through each other's eyes for an instant? We should live in all the ages of the world in an hour; ay, in all the worlds of the ages. History, Poetry, Mythology!—I know of no reading of another's experience so startling and informing as this would be.

The greater part of what my neighbours call good I believe in my soul to be bad, and if I repent of anything, it is very likely to be my good behaviour. What demon possessed me that I behaved so well? You may say the wisest thing you can, old man,—you who have lived seventy years, not without honour of a kind,—I hear an irresistible voice which invites me away from all that. One generation abandons the enterprises of another like stranded vessels.

I think that we may safely trust a good deal more than we do. We may waive just so much care of ourselves as we honestly bestow elsewhere. Nature is as well adapted to our weakness as to our strength. The incessant anxiety and strain of some is a well-nigh incurable form of disease. We are made to exaggerate the importance of what work we do; and yet how much is not done by us! or, what if we had been taken sick? How vigilant we are! determined not to live by faith if we can avoid it; all the day long on the alert, at night we unwillingly say our prayers and commit ourselves to uncertainties. So thoroughly and sincerely are we compelled to live, reverencing our life, and denying the possibility of change. This is the only way, we say; but there are as many ways as there can be drawn radii from one centre. All change is a miracle to contemplate; but it is a miracle which is taking place every instant. Confucius said, "To know that we know what we know, and that we do not know what we do not know, that is true knowledge." When one man has reduced a fact of the imagination to be a fact to his understanding, I foresee that all men will at length establish their lives on that basis.

Let us consider for a moment what most of the trouble and anxiety which I have referred to is about, and how much it is necessary that we be troubled, or at least, careful. It would be some advantage to live a primitive and frontier life, though in the midst of an outward civilisation, if only to learn what are the gross necessaries of life and what methods have been taken to obtain them; or even to look over the old day-books of the merchants, to see what it was that the men most commonly bought at the stores, what they stored, that is, what are the grossest groceries. For the improvements of ages have had but little influence on the essential laws of man's existence: as our skeletons, probably, are not to be distinguished from those of our ancestors.

By the words, *necessary of life,* I mean whatever, of all that man obtains by his own exertions, has been from the first, or from long use has become, so important to human life that few, if any, whether from savageness, or poverty, or philosophy, ever attempt to do without it. To many creatures there is in its sense but one necessary of life—Food. To the bison of the prairie it is a few inches of palatable grass, with water to drink; unless he seeks the Shelter of the forest or the mountain's shadow. None of the brute creation requires more than Food and Shelter. The necessaries of life for man in this climate may, accurately enough, be distributed under the several heads of Food, Shelter, Clothing, and Fuel; for not till we have secured these are we prepared to entertain the true problems of life with freedom and a prospect of success. Man has invented, not only houses, but clothes and cooked food; and possibly from the accidental discovery of the warmth of fire, and the consequent use of it, at first a luxury, arose the present necessity to sit by it. We observe cats and dogs acquiring the same second nature. By proper Shelter and Clothing we legitimately retain our own internal heat; but with an excess of these, or of Fuel, that is, with an external heat greater than our own internal, may not cookery properly be said to begin? Darwin, the naturalist, says of the inhabitants of Tierra del Fuego, that while his own party, who were well clothed and sitting close to a fire, were far from too warm, these naked savages, who were farther off, were observed, to his great surprise, "to be streaming with perspiration at undergoing such a roasting." So, we are told, the New Hollander goes naked with impunity, while the European shivers in his clothes. Is it impossible to combine the hardiness of these savages with the intellectualness of the civilised man? According to Liebeg, man's body is a stove, and food the fuel which keeps up the internal combustion in the lungs. In cold weather we eat more, in warm less. The animal heat is the result of a slow combustion, and disease and death take place when this is too rapid; or for want of fuel, or from some defect in the draught, the fire goes out. Of course the vital heat is not to be confounded with fire; but so much for analogy. It appears, therefore, from the above list, that the expression, *animal life,* is nearly synonymous with the expression, *animal heat;* for while Food may be regarded as the Fuel which keeps up the fire within us—and Fuel serves only to prepare that Food or to increase the warmth of our bodies by addition from without—Shelter and Clothing also serve only to retain the heat thus generated and absorbed.

The grand necessity, then, for our bodies, is to keep warm, to keep the vital heat in us. What pains we accordingly take, not only with our Food, and Clothing, and Shelter, but with our beds, which are our nightclothes, robbing the nests and breasts of birds to prepare this shelter within a shelter, as the mole has its bed of grass and leaves at the end of its burrow! The poor man is wont to complain that this is a cold world; and to cold, no less physical than social, we refer directly a great part of our ails. The summer, in some climates, makes possible to man a sort of Elysian life. Fuel, except to cook his Food, is then unnecessary; the sun is his fire, and many of the fruits are sufficiently cooked by its rays; while Food generally is more various, and more easily obtained, and Clothing and Shelter are wholly or half unnecessary. At the present day, and in this country, as I find by my own experience, a few implements, a knife, an axe, a spade, a wheelbarrow, &c., and for the studious, lamplight, stationery, and access to a few books, rank next to necessaries, and can all be obtained at a trifling cost. Yet some, not wise, go to the other side of the globe, to barbarous and unhealthy regions, and devote themselves to trade for ten to twenty years, in order that they may live—that is, keep comfortably warm—and die in New England at least. The luxuriously rich are not simply kept comfortably warm, but unnaturally hot; as I implied before, they are cooked, of course *à la mode.*

Most of the luxuries, and many of the socalled comforts of life, are not only not indispensable, but positive hindrances to the elevation of mankind. With respect to luxuries and comforts, the wisest have ever levied a more simple and meagre life than the poor. The ancient philosophers, Chinese, Hindoo, Persian, and Greek, were a class that which none has been poorer in outward riches, none so rich in inward. We know not much about them. It is remarkable that we know so much of them as we do. The same is true of the more modern reformers and benefactors of their race. None can be an impartial or wise observer of human life but from the vantage ground of what we should call voluntary poverty. Of a life of luxury the fruit is luxury, whether in agriculture, or commerce, or literature, or art. There are nowadays professors of philosophy, but not philosophers. Yet it is admirable to profess because it was once admirable to live. To be a philosopher is not merely to have subtle thoughts, nor even to found a school, but so to love wisdom as to live according to its dictates, a life of simplicity, independence, magnanimity, and trust. It is to solve some of the problems of life, not only theoretically, but practically. The success of great scholars and thinkers is commonly a courtier-like success, not kingly, not manly. They make shift to live merely by conformity, practically as their fathers did, and are in no sense the progenitors of a nobler race of men. But why do men degenerate ever? What makes families run out? What is the nature of the luxury which enervates and destroys nations? Are we sure that there is none of it in our own lives? The philosopher is in advance of his age even in the outward form of his life. He is not fed, sheltered, clothed, warmed, like his contemporaries. How can a man be a philosopher and not maintain his vital heat by better methods than other men?

When a man is warmed by the several modes which I have described, what does he want next? Surely not more warmth of the same kind, as more and richer food, larger and more splendid houses, finer and more abundant clothing, more numerous, incessant, and hotter fires, and the like. When he has obtained those things which are necessary to life, there is another alternative than to obtain the superfluities; and that is, to adventure on life now, his vacation from humbler toil having commenced. The soil, it appears, is suited to the seed, for it has sent its radical downward, and it may now send its shoot upward also with confidence. Why has man rooted himself thus firmly in the earth, but that he may rise in the same proportion into the heavens above?—for the nobler plants are valued for the fruit they bear at last in the air and light, far from the ground, and are not treated like the humbler esculents, which, though they may be biennials, are cultivated only till they have perfected

their root, and often cut down at top for this purpose, so that most would not know them in their flowering season.

I do not mean to prescribe rules to strong and valiant natures, who will mind their own affairs whether in heaven or hell, and perchance build more magnificently and spend more lavishly than the richest, without ever impoverishing themselves, not knowing how they live,—if, indeed, there are any such, as has been dreamed; nor to those who find their encouragement and inspiration in precisely the present condition of things, and cherish it with the fondness and enthusiasm of lovers,—and, to some extent, I reckon myself in this number; I do not speak to those who are well employed, in whatever circumstances, and they know whether they are well employed or not;—but mainly to the mass of men who are discontented, and idly complaining of the hardness of their lot or of the times, when they might improve them. There are some who complain most energetically and inconsolably of any, because they are, as they say, doing their duty. I also have in my mind that seemingly wealthy, but most terribly impoverished class of all, who have accumulated dross, but know not how to use it, or get rid of it, and thus have forged their own golden or silver fetters.

If I should attempt to tell how I have desired to spend my life in years past, it would probably surprise those of my readers who are somewhat acquainted with its actual history; it would certainly astonish those who know nothing about it. I will only hint at some of the enterprises which I have cherished.

In any weather, at any hour of the day or night, I have been anxious to improve the nick of time, and notch it on my stick too; to stand on the meeting of two eternities, the past and future, which is precisely the present moment; to toe that line. You will pardon some obscurities, for there are more secrets in my trade than in most men's, and yet not voluntarily kept, but inseparable from its very nature. I would gladly tell all that I know about it, and never paint "No Admittance" on my gate.

I long ago lost a hound, a bay horse, and a turtledove, and am still on their trail. Many are the travellers I have spoken concerning them, describing their tracks and what calls they answered to. I have met one or two who had heard the hound, and the tramp of the horse, and even seen the dove disappear behind a cloud, and they seemed as anxious to recover them as if they had lost them themselves.

To anticipate, not the sunrise and the dawn merely, but, if possible, Nature herself! How many mornings, summer and winter, before yet any neighbour was stirring about his business, have I been about mine! No doubt, many of my townsmen have met me returning from this enterprise, farmers starting for Boston in the twilight, or woodchoppers going to their work. It is true, I never assisted the sun materially in his rising, but, doubt not, it was of the last importance only to be present at it.

So many autumn, ay, and winter days, spent outside the town, trying to hear what was in the wind, to hear and carry it express! I well-nigh sunk all my capital in it, and lost my own breath into the bargain, running in the face of it. If it had concerned either of the political parties, depend upon it, it would have appeared in the *Gazette* with the earliest intelligence. At other times watching from the observatory of some cliff or tree, to telegraph any new arrival; or waiting at evening on the hill-tops, for the sky to fall, that I might catch something, though I never caught much, and that, manna-wise, would dissolve again in the sun.

For a long time I was reporter to a journal, of no very wide circulation, whose editor has never yet seen fit to print the bulk of my contributions, and, as is too common with writers, I got only my labour for my pains. However, in this case my pains were their own reward.

For many years I was self-appointed inspector of snow storms and rain storms, and did my duty faithfully; surveyor if not of highways, then of forest paths and all across-lot routes, keeping them open, and ravines bridged and passable at all seasons, where the public heel had testified to their utility.

I have looked after the wild stock of the town, which gave a faithful herdsman a good deal of trouble by leaping fences; and I have had an eye to the unfrequented nooks and corners of the farm, though I did not always know whether Jonas or Solomon worked in a particular field today—that was none of my business. I have watered the red huckleberry, the sand cherry and the nettle tree, the red pine and the black ash, the white grape and the yellow violet, which might have withered else in dry season.

In short, I went on thus for a long time, I may say it without boasting, faithfully minding my business, till it became more and more evident that my townsmen would not after all admit me into the list of town officers, nor make my place a sinecure with a moderate allowance. My accounts, which I can swear to have kept faithfully, I have, indeed, never got audited, still less accepted, still less paid and settled. However, I have not set my heart on that.

Not long since, a strolling Indian went to sell baskets at the house of a well-known lawyer in my neighbourhood. "Do you wish to buy any baskets?" he asked. "No, we do not want any," was the reply. "What!" exclaimed the Indian, as he went out the gate, "do you mean to starve us?" Having seen his industrious white neighbours so well off,—that the lawyer had only to weave arguments, and by some magic wealth and standing followed,— he had said to himself: I will go into business, I will weave baskets; it is a thing which I can do. Thinking that when he had made the baskets he would have done his part, and then it would be the white man's to buy them. He had not discovered that it was necessary for him to make it worth the other's while to buy them, or at least make him think that it was so, or to make something else which it would be worth his while to buy. I too had woven a kind of basket of delicate texture, but I had not made it worth any one's while to buy them. Yet not the less, in my case, did I think it worth my while to weave them, and instead of studying how to make it worth men's while to buy baskets, I studied rather how to avoid the necessity of selling them. The life which men praise and regard as successful is but one kind. Why should we exaggerate any one kind at the expense of the others?

Finding that my fellow-citizens were not likely to offer me any room in the court-house, or any curacy or living anywhere else, but I must shift for myself, I turned my face more exclusively than ever to the woods, where I was better known. I was determined to go into business at once, and not wait to acquire the usual capital, using such slender means as I had already got. My purpose in going to Walden Pond was not to live cheaply nor to live dearly there, but to transact some private business with the fewest obstacles; to be hindered from accomplishing which, for want of a little commonsense, a little enterprise, and business talent, appeared not so bad as foolish.

I have always endeavoured to acquire strict business habits; they are indispensable to every man. If your trade is with the Celestial Empire, then some small counting-house on the coast, in some Salem harbor, will be fixture enough. You will export such articles as the country affords, purely native products, much ice and pine timber and a little granite, always in native bottoms. These will be good ventures. To oversee all the details yourself in person; be at once pilot and captain, and owner and underwriter; to buy and sell and keep the accounts; to read every letter received, and write and read every letter sent; to superintend the discharge of papers night and day; to be upon many parts of the coast almost at the same time;—often the richest freight will be discharged upon a Jersey shore;—to be your own telegraph, unweariedly sweeping the horizon, speaking all passing vessels bound coast-wise; to keep up a steady despatch of commodities, for the supply of such a distant and exorbitant market; to keep yourself informed of the state of the markets, prospects of war and peace everywhere, and anticipate the tendencies of trade and civilisation,—taking advantage of the results of all exploring expeditions, using new passages and all improvements in navigation;—charts to be studied, the position of reefs and new lights and buoys to be ascertained, and ever, and ever, the logarithmic tables to be corrected, for by the error of some calculator the vessel often splits upon a rock that should have reached a friendly pier,—

there is the untold fate of La Perouse;—universal science to be kept pace with, studying the lives of all great discoverers and navigators, great adventurers and merchants, from Hanno and the Phœnicians down to our day; in fine, account of stock to be taken from time to time, to know how you stand. It is a labour to task the faculties of a man,—such problems of profit and loss, of interest, of tare and tret, and gauging of all kinds in it, as demand a universal knowledge.

I have thought that Walden Pond would be a good place for business, not solely on account of the railroad and the ice trade; it offers advantages which it may not be good policy to divulge; it is a good post and a good foundation. No Neva marshes to be filled; though you must everywhere build on piles of your own driving. It is said that a flood-tide, with a westerly wind, and ice in the Neva, would sweep St. Petersburg from the face of the earth.

***

For more than five years I maintained myself thus solely by the labour of my hands, and I found, that by working about six weeks in a year, I could meet all the expenses of living. The whole of my winters, as well as most of my summers, I had free and clear for study. I have thoroughly tried school-keeping, and found that my expenses were in proportion, or rather out of proportion, to my income, for I was obliged to dress and train, not to say think and believe, accordingly, and I lost my time into the bargain. As I did not teach for the good of my fellowmen, but simply for a livelihood, this was a failure. I have tried trade; but I found that it would take ten years to get under way in that, and that then I should probably be on my way to the devil. I was actually afraid that I might by that time be doing what is called a good business. When formerly I was looking about to see what I could do for a living, some sad experience in conforming to the wishes of friends being fresh in my mind to tax my ingenuity, I thought often and seriously of picking huckleberries; that surely I could do, and its small profits might suffice,—for my greatest skill has been to want but little,—so little capital is required, so little distraction from my wonted moods, I foolishly thought. While my acquaintances went unhesitatingly into trade or the professions, I contemplated this occupation as most like theirs; ranging the hills all summer to pick the berries which came in my way, and thereafter carelessly dispose of them; so, to keep the flocks of Admetus. I also dreamed that I might gather the wild herbs, or carry evergreens to such villagers as loved to be reminded of the wood, even to the city, by hay-cart loads. But I have since learned that trade curses everything it handles; and though you trade in messages from heaven, the whole curse of trade attaches to the business.

As I preferred some things to others, and especially valued my freedom, as I could fare hard and yet succeed well, I did not wish to spend my time in earning rich carpets or other fine furniture, or delicate cookery, or a house in the Grecian or the Gothic style just yet. If there are any to whom it is no interruption to acquire these things, and who know how to use them when acquired, I relinquish to them the pursuit. Some are "industrious," and appear to love labour for its own sake, or perhaps because it keeps them out of worse mischief; to such I have at present nothing to say. Those who would not know what to do with more leisure than they now enjoy, I might advise to work twice as hard as they do,—work till they pay for themselves, and get their free papers. For myself I found that the occupation of a day-labourer was the most independent of any, especially as it required only thirty or forty days in a year to support one. The laborer's day ends with the going down of the sun, and he is then free to devote himself to his chosen pursuit, independent of his labour; but his employer, who speculates from month to month, has no respite from one end of the year to the other.

In short, I am convinced, both by faith and experience, that to maintain one's self on this earth is not a hardship but a pastime, if we will live simply and wisely; as the pursuits of the simpler nations are still the sports of the most artificial. It is not necessary that a man should earn his living by the sweat of his brow, unless he sweats easier than I do.

One young man of my acquaintance, who has inherited some acres, told me that he thought he should live as I did, *if he had the means.* I would not have any one adopt *my* mode of living on any account; for, beside that before he has fairly learned it I may have found out another for myself, I desire that there may be as many different persons in the world as possible; but I would have each one be very careful to find out and pursue *his* own way, and not his father's or his mother's or his neighbour's instead. The youth may build or plant or sail, only let him not be hindered from doing that which he tells me he would like to do. It is by a mathematical point only that we are wise, as the sailor or the fugitive slave keeps the pole-star in his eyes; but that is sufficient guidance for all our life. We may not arrive at our port within a calculable period, but we would preserve the true course.

Undoubtedly, in this case, what is true for one is truer still for a thousand, as a large house is not proportionally more expensive than a small one, since one roof may cover, one cellar underlie, and one wall separate several apartments. But for my part, I preferred the solitary dwelling. Moreover, it will commonly be cheaper to build the whole yourself than to convince another of the advantage of the common wall; and when you have done this, the common partition, to be much cheaper, must be a thin one, and that other may prove a bad neighbour, and also not keep his side in repair. The only cooperation which is commonly possible is exceedingly partial and superficial; and what little true cooperation there is, is as if it were not, being a harmony inaudible to men. If a man has faith he will cooperate with equal faith everywhere; if he has not faith, he will continue to live like the rest of the world, whatever company he is joined to. To cooperate, in the highest as well as the lowest sense, means *to get our living together.* I heard it proposed lately that two young men should travel together over the world, the one without money, earning his means as he went, before the mast and behind the plough, the other carrying of a bill of exchange in his pocket. It was easy to see that they could not long be companions or cooperate, since one would not *operate* at all.

They would part at the first interesting crisis in their adventures. Above all, as I have implied, the man who goes alone can start today; but he who travels with another must wait till that other is ready, and it may be a long time before they get off.

***

I went to the woods because I wished to live deliberately, to front only the essential facts of life, and see if I could not learn what it had to teach, and not, when I came to die, discover that I had not lived. I did not wish to live what was not life, living is so dear; nor did I wish to practise resignation, unless it was quite necessary. I wanted to live deep and suck out all the marrow of life, to live so sturdily and Spartan-like as to put to rout all that was not life, to cut a broad swath and shave close, to drive life into a corner, and reduce it to its lowest terms, and, if it proved to be mean, why then to get the whole and genuine meanness of it, and publish its meanness to the world; or if it were sublime, to know it by experience, and be able to give a true account of it in my next excursion. For most men, it appears to me, are in a strange uncertainty about it, whether it is of the devil or of God, and have *somewhat hastily* concluded that it is the chief end of man here to "glorify God and enjoy Him forever."

Still we live meanly, like ants; though the fable tells us that we were long ago changed into men; like pygmies we fight with cranes; it is error upon error, and clout upon clout, and our best virtue has for its occasion a superfluous and evitable wretchedness. Our life is frittered away by detail. An honest man has hardly need to count more than his ten fingers, or in extreme cases he may add his ten toes, and lump the rest. Simplicity, simplicity, simplicity! I say, let your affairs be as two or three, and not a hundred or a thousand; instead of a million count half-a-dozen, and keep your accounts on your thumbnail. In the midst of this chopping sea of civilised life, such are the clouds and storms and quicksands and thousand-and-one items to be allowed for, that a man has to live, if he would not founder and go to the bottom and not make his port at all,

by dead reckoning, and he must be a great calculator indeed who succeeds. Simplify, simplify. Instead of three meals a-day, if it be necessary eat but one; instead of hundred dishes, five; and reduce other things in proportion. Our life is like a German Confederacy, made up of petty states, with its boundary forever fluctuating, so that even a German cannot tell you how it is bounded at any moment. The nation itself, with all its so-called internal improvements, which, by the way, are all external and superficial, is just such an unwieldy and overgrown establishment, cluttered with furniture and tripped up by its own traps, ruined by luxury and heedless expense, by want of calculation and a worthy aim, as the million households in the land; and the only cure for it as for them is in a rigid economy, a stern and more than Spartan simplicity of life and elevation of purpose. It lives too fast. Men think that it is essential that the *Nation* have commerce, and export ice, and talk through a telegraph, and ride thirty miles an hour, without a doubt, whether *they* do or not; but whether we should live like baboons or like men, is a little uncertain. If we do not get out sleepers, and forge rails, and devote days and nights to the work, but go to tinkering upon our *lives* to improve *them*, who will build railroads? And if railroads are not built, how shall we get to heaven in season? But if we stay at home and mind our business, who will want railroads? We do not ride on the railroad; it rides upon us. Did you ever think what those sleepers are that underlie the railroad? Each one is a man, an Irishman, or a Yankee man. The rails are laid on them, and they are covered with sand, and the cars run smoothly over them. They are sound sleepers, I assure you. And every few years a new lot is laid down and run over; so that, if some have the pleasure of riding on a rail, others have the misfortune to be ridden upon. And when they run over a man that is walking in his sleep, a supernumarary sleeper in the wrong position, and wake him up, they suddenly stop the cars, and make a hue and cry about it, as if this were an exception. I am glad to know that it takes a gang of men for every five miles to keep the sleepers down and level in their beds as it is, for this is a sign that they may sometime get up again.

Why should we live with such hurry and waste of life? We are determined to be starved before we are hungry. Men say that a stitch in time saves nine, and so they take a thousand stitches today to save nine tomorrow. As for *work*, we haven't any of any consequence. We have the Saint Vitus' dance, and cannot possibly keep our heads still. If I should only give a few pulls at the parish bell-rope, as for a fire, that is, without setting the bell, there is hardly a man on his farm in the outskirts of Concord, notwithstanding that press of engagements which was his excuse so many times this morning, nor a boy, nor a woman, I might also say, but would forsake all and follow that sound, not mainly to save property from the flames, but, if we will confess the truth, much more to see it burn, since burn it must, and we, be it known, did not set it on fire,—or to see it put out, and have a hand in it, if that is done as handsomely; yes, even if it were the parish church itself. Hardly a man takes a half-hour's nap after dinner, but when he wakes he holds up his head and asks, "What's the news?" as if the rest of mankind had stood his sentinels. Some give directions to be waked every half-hour, doubtless for no other purpose; and then to pay for it, they tell what they have dreamed. After a night's sleep the news is as indispensable as the breakfast. "Pray, tell me anything new that has happened to a man anywhere on this globe,"— and he reads it over his coffee and rolls, that a man has had his eyes gouged out this morning on the Wichita River; never dreaming the while that he lives in the dark unfathomed mammoth cave of this world, and has but the rudiment of an eye himself.

For my part, I could easily do without the post office. I think that there are very few important communications made through it. To speak critically, I never received more than one or two letters in my life—I wrote this some years ago—that were worth the postage. The pennypost is commonly, an institution through which you seriously offer a man that penny for his thoughts which is so often safely offered in jest. And I am sure that I never read any memorable news in a newspaper. If we read of one man robbed, or murdered, or killed by accident, or one house burned, or one vessel wrecked, or one steamboat blow-up, or one cow run over on the Western Railroad, or one mad dog killed, or one lot of grasshoppers in the winter,—we never need read of another. One is enough. If you are acquainted with the principle, what do you care for a myriad instances and applications? To a philosopher all *news*, as it is called, is gossip, and they who edit and read it are old women over their tea. Yet not a few are greedy after this gossip. There was such a rush, as I hear, the other day at one of the offices to learn the foreign news by the last arrival, that several large squares of plate glass belonging to the establishment were broken by the pressure,—news which I seriously think a ready wit might write a twelvemonth or twelve years beforehand with sufficient accuracy. As for Spain, for instance, if you know how to throw in Don Carlos and the Infanta, and Don Pedro and Seville and Granada, from time to time in the right proportions,—they may have changed the names a little since I saw the papers,—and serve up a bullfight when other entertainments fail, it will be true to the letter, and give us as good an idea of the exact state or ruin of things in Spain as the most succinct and lucid reports under this head in the newspapers: and as for England, almost the last significant scrap of news from that quarter was the Revolution of 1649; and if you have learned the history of her crops for an average year, you never need attend to that thing again, unless your speculations are of a merely pecuniary character. If one may judge who rarely looks into the newspapers, nothing new does ever happen in foreign parts, a French Revolution not excepted.

What news! how much more important to know what that is which was never old! "Kieou-he-yu (great dignitary of the state of Wei) sent a man to Khoung-tseu to know his news. Khoung-tseu caused the messenger to be seated near him, and questioned him in these terms: What is your master doing? The messenger answered with respect: My master desires to diminish the number of his faults, but he cannot come to the end of them. The messenger being gone, the philosopher remarked: What a worthy messenger! What a worthy messenger!" The preacher, instead of vexing the ears of drowsy farmers on their day of rest at the end of the week,—for Sunday is the fit conclusion of an illspent week, and not the fresh and brave beginning of a new one,—with this one other draggletale of a sermon, should shout with thundering voice,—"Pause! Avast! Why so seeming fast, but deadly slow?"

Shams and delusions are esteemed for soundest truths, while reality is fabulous. If men would steadily observe realities only, and not allow themselves to be deluded, life, to compare it with such things as we know, would be like a fairy tale and the Arabian Nights' Entertainments. If we respected only what is inevitable and has a right to be, music and poetry would resound along the streets. When we are unhurried and wise, we perceive that only great and worthy things have any permanent and absolute existence,—that petty fears and petty pleasures are but the shadow of the reality. This is always exhilarating and sublime. By closing the eyes and slumbering, and consenting to be deceived by shows, men establish and confirm their daily life of routine and habit everywhere, which still is built on purely illusory foundations. Children, who play life, discern its true law and relations more clearly than men, who fail to live it worthily, but who think that they are wiser by experience, that is, by failure. I have read in a Hindoo book, that "there was a king's son, who, being expelled in infancy from his native city, was brought up by a forester, and, growing up to maturity in that state, imagined himself to belong to the barbarous race with which he lived. One of his father's ministers having discovered him, revealed to him what he was, and the misconception of his character was removed, and he knew himself to be a prince. So soul," continues the Hindoo philosopher, "from the cir-

cumstances in which it is placed, mistakes its own character, until the truth is revealed to it by some holy teacher, and then it knows itself to be *Brahme*." I perceive that we inhabitants of New England live this mean life that we do because our vision does not penetrate the surface of things. We think that that is which *appears* to be. If a man should walk through this town and see only the reality, where, think you, would the "Mill dam" go to? If he should give us an account of the realities he beheld there, we should not recognise the place in his description. Look at a meetinghouse, or a courthouse, or a jail, or a shop, or a dwelling-house, and say what that thing really is before a true gaze, and they would all go to pieces in your account of them. Men esteem truth remote, in the outskirts of the system, behind the farthest star, before Adam and after the last man. In eternity there is indeed something true and sublime. But all these times and places and occasions are now and here. God himself culminates in the present moment, and will never be more divine in the lapse of all the ages. And we are enabled to apprehend at all what a sublime and noble only by the perpetual instilling and drenching of the reality that surrounds us. The universe constantly and obediently answers to our conceptions; whether we travel fast or slow, the track is laid for us. Let us spend our lives in conceiving then. The poet or the artist never yet had so fair and noble a design but some of his posterity at least could accomplish it.

Let us spend one day as deliberately as Nature, and not to be thrown off the track by every nutshell and mosquito's wing that falls on the rails. Let us rise early and fast, or break fast, gently and without perturbation; let company come and let company go, let the bells ring and the children cry,—determined to make a day of it. Why should we knock under and go with the stream? Let us not be upset and overwhelmed in that terrible rapid and whirlpool called a dinner, situated in the meridian shallows. Weather this danger and you are safe, for the rest of the way is down hill. With unrelaxed nerves, with morning vigour, sail by it, looking another way, tied to the mast like Ulysses. If the engine whistles, let it whistle till it is hoarse for its pains. If the bell rings, why should we run? We will consider what kind of music they are like. Let us settle ourselves, and work and wedge our feet downward through the mud and slush of opinion, and prejudice, and tradition, and delusion, and appearance, that alluvion which covers the globe, through Paris and London, through New York and Boston and Concord, through church and state, through poetry and philosophy and religion, till we come to a hard bottom and rocks in place, which we can call *reality*, and say, This is, and no mistake; and then begin, having a *point d'appui*, below freshet and frost and fire, a place where you might found a wall or a state, or set a lamp-post safely, or perhaps a gauge, not a Nilometer, but a Realometer, that future ages might know how deep a freshet of shams and appearances had gathered from time to time. If you stand right fronting and face to face to a fact, you will see the sun glimmer on both its surfaces, as if it were a cimeter, and feel its sweet edge dividing you through the heart and marrow, and so you will happily conclude your mortal career. Be it life or death, we crave only reality. If we are really dying, let us hear the rattle in our throats and feel cold in the extremities; if we are alive, let us go about our business.

Time is but the stream I go a-fishing in. I drank at it; but while I drank I see the sandy bottom and detect how shallow it is. Its thin current slides away, but eternity remains. I would drink deeper; fish in the sky, whose bottom is pebbly with stars. I cannot count one. I know not the first letter of the alphabet. I have always been regretting that I was not as wise as the day I was born. The intellect is a cleaver; it discerns and rifts its way into the secret of things. I do not wish to be any more busy with my hands than is necessary. My head is hands and feet. I feel all my best faculties concentrated in it. My instinct tells me that my head is an organ for burrowing, as some creatures use their snout and forepaws, and with it I would mine and burrow my way through these hills. I think that the richest vein is somewhere hereabouts; so by the divining rod and thin rising vapours I judge; and here I will begin to mine....

***

CONCLUSION

To the sick the doctors wisely recommend a change of air and scenery. Thank Heaven, here is not all the world. The buck-eye does not grow in New England, and the mocking-bird is rarely heard here. The wild goose is more of a cosmopolite than we; he breaks his fast in Canada, takes a luncheon in the Ohio, and plumes himself for the night in a southern bayou. Even the bison, to some extent, keeps pace with the season, cropping the pastures of the Colorado only till a greener and sweeter grass awaits him by the Yellowstone. Yet we think that if rail-fences are pulled down, and stone walls piled up on our farms, bounds are henceforth set to our lives and our fates decided. If you are chosen town-clerk, forsooth, you cannot go to Tierra del Fuego this summer: but you may go to the land of infernal fire nevertheless. The universe is wider than our views of it.

Yet we should oftener look over the tafferel of our craft, like curious passengers, and not make the voyage like stupid sailors picking oakum. The other side of the globe is but the home of our correspondent. Our voyaging is only great circle-sailing, and the doctors prescribe for diseases of the skin merely. One hastens to Southern Africa to chase the giraffe, but surely that is not the game he would be after. How long, pray, would a man hunt giraffes if he could? Snipes and woodcocks also may afford rare sport, but I trust it would be nobler game to shoot one's self.

> "Direct your eye right inward, and you'll find
> A thousand regions in your mind
> Yet discovered. Travel them, and be
> Expert in home-cosmography."

What does Africa—what does the West stand for? Is not our own interior white on the chart, black though it may prove, like the coast, when discovered? Is it the source of the Nile, or the Niger, or the Mississippi, or a North-West Passage around this continent, that we would find? Are these the problems which most concern mankind? Is Franklin the only man who is lost, that his wife should be so earnest to find him? Does Mr. Grinnell know where he himself is? Be rather the Mungo Park, the Louis and Clark and Frobisher, of your own streams and oceans; explore your own higher latitudes—with shiploads of preserved meats to support you, if they be necessary, and pile the empty cans sky-high for a sign. Were preserved meats invented to preserve meat merely? Nay, be a Columbus to whole new continents and worlds within you, opening new channels, not of trade, but of thought. Every man is the lord of a realm beside which the earthly empire of the Czar is but a petty state, a hammock left by the ice. Yet some can be patriotic who have no *self*-respect, and sacrifice the greater to the less. They love the soil which makes their graves, but have no sympathy with the spirit which may still animate their clay. Patriotism is a maggot in their heads. What was the meaning of that South-Sea Exploring Expedition, with all its parade and expense, but an indirect recognition of the fact that there are continents and seas in the moral world, to which every man is an isthmus or an inlet, yet unexplored by him, but that it is easier to sail many thousand miles through cold and storm and cannibals, in a government ship, with five hundred men and boys to assist one, than it is to explore the private sea, the Atlantic and Pacific Ocean of one's being alone.—

"Erret, et extremos alter acrutetur Iberos.
Plus habet hic vitæ, plus habet ille viæ."

Let them wander and scrutinise the outlandish Australians:
I have more of God, they have more of the road.

It is not worth the while to go around the world to count the cats in Zanzibar. Yet do this even till you can do better, and you may perhaps find some "Symmes' Hole," by which to get at the inside at last. England and France, Spain and Portugal, Gold Coast and Slave Coast, all front on this private sea; but no bark from them has ventured out of sight of land, though it is without doubt the direct way to India. If you would learn to speak all tongues and conform to the customs of all nations, if you would travel farther than all travellers, be naturalised in all climes, and cause the Sphinx to dash her head against a stone, even obey the precept of the old philosopher, and Explore thyself.

Herein are demanded the eye and the nerve. Only the defeated and deserters go to the wars, cowards that run away and enlist. Start now on that farthest western way, which does not pause at the Mississippi or the Pacific, nor conduct toward a worn-out China or Japan, but leads on direct a tangent to this sphere, summer and winter, day and night, sun down, moon down, and at last earth down too.

It is said that Mirabeau took to highway robbery "to ascertain what degree of resolution was necessary in order to place one's self in formal opposition to the most sacred laws of society." He declared that "a soldier who fights in the ranks does not require half so much courage as a foot-pad,"—"that honour and religion have never stood in the way of a well-considered and a firm resolve." This was manly, as the world goes; and yet it was idle, if not desperate. A saner man would have found himself often enough "in formal opposition" to what are deemed "the most sacred laws of society," through obedience to yet more sacred laws, and so have tested his resolution without going out of his way. It is not for a man to put himself in such an attitude to society, but to maintain himself in whatever attitude he finds himself through obedience to the laws of his being, which will never be one of opposition to a just government, if he should chance to meet with such.

I left the woods for as good a reason as I went there. Perhaps it seemed to me that I had several more lives to live, and could not spare any more time for that one. It is remarkable how easily and insensibly we fall into a particular route, and make a beaten track for ourselves. I had not lived there a week before my feet wore a path from my door to the pond-side; and though it is five or six years since I tried it, it is still quite distinct. It is true I fear that others may have fallen into it, and so helped to keep it open. The surface of the earth is soft and impressible by the feet of men; and so with the paths which the mind travels. How worn and dusty, then, must be the highways of the world—how deep the ruts of tradition and conformity! I did not wish to take a cabin passage, but rather to go before the mast and on the deck of the world, for there I could best see the moonlight amid the mountains. I do not wish to go below now.

I learned this, at least, by my experiment: that if one advances confidently in the direction of his dreams, and endeavors to live the life which he has imagined, he will meet with a success unexpected in common hours. He will put some things behind, will pass an invisible boundary; new, universal, and more liberal laws will begin to establish themselves around and within him; or the old laws be expanded, and interpreted in his favor in a more liberal sense, and he will live with the license of a higher order of beings. In proportion as he simplifies his life, the laws of the universe will appear less complex, and solitude will not be solitude, nor poverty poverty, nor weakness weakness. If you have built castles in the air, your work need not be lost; that is where they should be. Now put the foundations under them. ♦

Questions

1. Why does Thoreau say that most men are desperate?

2. Why does he think that age does not lead to knowledge?

3. What does Thoreau think people really need?

4. What does Thoreau say about luxuries?

5. What mistake does the basket-selling Indian make?

6. How much time does Thoreau have to spend working for money to meet his annual expenses?

7. What does Thoreau admonish us to do?

8. What kind of knowledge and exploration does Thoreau suggest we pursue?

THE WORLD IS TOO MUCH WITH US

William Wordsworth (1770–1850)

The world is too much with us; late and soon,
Getting and spending, we lay waste our
    powers;
Little we see in Nature that is ours;
We have given our hearts away, a sordid boon!
This Sea that bares her bosom to the moon,
The winds that will be howling at all hours,
And are up-gathered now like sleeping flowers,
For this, for everything, we are out of tune;
It moves us not—Great God! I'd rather be
A Pagan suckled in a creed outworn;[1]
So might I, standing on this pleasant lea,[2]
Have glimpses that would make me less forlorn;
Have sight of Proteus[3] rising from the sea;
Or hear old Triton[4] blow his wreathed horn.

ENDNOTES

1. Brought up in an outdated religion.
2. Meadow.
3. Greek sea god capable of taking many shapes.
4. Another sea god, often depicted as trumpeting on a shell.

QUESTION

1. What does Wordsworth suggest is the price people have paid for being part of a money economy?

III

Foundations of a Commercial Society

Introduction: Don't Know Much About History

Most of us accept the notion that every discipline has its primary principles—fundamentals that become the heart of practice and performance. For example, most of us accept that the articles of faith that are central to religious belief is an orthodoxy honored by even the most doggedly reformed among us. Also, the social contract requires that we accept, as a foundation, the legal and social groundwork that serves as the stabilizing force of our respective societies and even civilization itself. Even in the abstract, what we adopt as fundamental to the physics and the metaphysics of living become the foundations upon which our personal and collective histories unfold.

Fundamentals that were popular in their time may no longer be of any use to us. And ideas that were unpopular in their time may have been resurrected and adopted by contemporary audiences. Still, we reject as much as we adopt. We sift through history as if we were panning for ideas of gold—collecting the nuggets while rejecting the sand. We take these nuggets with us to the "market." We convert them into a "currency of fundamentals" that serves the many purposes of our lives.

Artists, such as musicians and composers, carry this currency around with them in the form of musical notions, which a Mozart or a Mahler may convert into a "Jupiter Symphony" or a "Resurrection Symphony." Scientists, such as astronomers and physicists, carry

currency that takes the shape of mathematical formulas, which a Halley or a Heisenberg may convert into a "comet theory" or an "uncertainty theory."

But when we get to the practice of *business*, which nuggets do we turn into the "currency of fundamentals" that are central to our business world? Have some fundamentals been lost among the "sifted" sands? Can we recover them for our own present and future uses? Do we even know ourselves and our world well enough to determine which fundamentals are firmly entrenched and which have been lost?

If it is true that *Homo Faber*, the creative human maker of things, has largely passed into history, and that *Homo Economicus*, the money-chasing human consumer, is the present and future incarnation to whom we have become heirs, then we might dismiss most of the fundamentals of business and accept only those that are most obvious— production and consumption. We would then be positioned to live from moment to moment, grasping and ingesting what we see as crucial to profit and appetite, respectively; evolving into undifferentiated practitioners of business and careless consumers of products and services. Such a destiny strikes most of us as incomplete and unsatisfactory.

Reading some of the classical ideas on the subject of business can help us think about alternative destinies.

Plato, who was intellectually informed and nurtured by the mental colossus, Socrates, spent much of his life thinking about a perfectible, potential state of affairs that might arise from an agreement to create the perfect society and the most reasonable population. He wastes no time in telling us why the state must "have a hand" in idealizing the world. There is profit in injustice, he tells us. If business is primarily about profit, then it follows that injustice will be a natural result from business practice. We are, after all, dependent on one another. If business, profit, and injustice are an interconnected mechanism for facilitating interdependency, what kind of lives can we be expected to lead?

But, remember, Plato is an idealist. He expects this perfect society to work ethically, not only functionally. He explains that specialization, division of labor, and an attention to needs rather than wants are essential to the smooth conduct of society. The first two of these ideas become the bedrock of modern production societies.

The concept of wants and needs (not needs alone, as Plato prefers) is the backbone of business. Most of us think that we know the difference between the two, but modern commerce so often blurs the distinction that we become confused. Our confusion may serve the purposes of many business practitioners and, in fact, may serve the general economy, though it may not serve our "real" needs.

Aristotle handles the issues of wants and needs by painting for us the "art of acquisition," which depicts a scenario with two very different views—one is angled toward what he calls the art of household management, the other toward the art of making money. The former is honorable; the latter is not. Is Aristotle suggesting that businesses are obligated to draw for us a clear picture of the difference between wants and needs?

Business and government are inexorably linked. In most countries, they are tied together philosophically as well as legislatively. But the tandem relationship has not always been a comfortable one. We are reminded, when reading the thoughts of Confucius, as interpreted in an excerpt by Chen Huan-Chang, that this relationship has passed through many ports over the past several thousand years.

Confucius is adamant about how government and business ought to behave toward one another. He sees business as an outgrowth of the natural tendencies and actions of the people. The term *natural* refers to human nature (though this is different from the Platonic and Aristotelian views of nature). If men and women are possessed of a specific nature, which has been born out of economic wants, then they cannot easily dispossess themselves of it. A contemporary way of stating this might be as follows: "we are what we are." Though Confucius is sympathetic to human nature, he also believes that government is possessed of a certain nature as well. Out of this tension of natures comes mutual obligations—governments should be prepared to follow the natural economic inclinations of their people, and people should be prepared to accept the leadership and regulations of their governments. Governments should obligate themselves to the idea of abundant production—especially where there is desire for wealth. And people should be prepared to commit themselves to this idea of production.

A quick, unscientific poll might indicate that Adam Smith is referred to as often by marketers and managers as by economists and financiers. Respect for his masterpiece, *An Inquiry into the Nature and Causes of the Wealth of Nations*, is typical among those who favor free markets.

Smith's antecedents should come to mind while reading some of his thoughts. His understanding of specialization and division of labor seems like "the next chapter" of Plato, while his feelings about government relations to citizens and business seem like "a deeper reading" of Confucius.

The capitalist ideal of freedom to have anything and everything is believed by many to be an unalterable tendency that needs no dogma or creed to justify its existence. Yet we do proffer justifications, such as those of a public nature related to requirements of growing economies, to ensure security and progress, or those of a private nature related to the requirements of the evolving "soul," to provide creative, actualizing opportunities for achievement and success. Choose almost any justification and at its foundation you will find a subterranean pool of overheated desire where the steam clouds our ability to see alternative uses for freedom. There, you will discover that the nation's educational purpose and cultural drive is to galvanize and guide young men and women, through years of commercial indoctrination, toward the uses of business activity without the effects of dissonant counterpoint that might retard the growth of domestic output and personal accumulation of wealth.

It is thought by many that Adam Smith's so-called invisible hand may have something to do with this phenomenon. Because Smith's invisible hand often serves as an explanation for how the public good is assured by the self-absorbed, individualistic pursuit of business interests, many capitalists are relieved to discover that self-advancing, solipsistic business aims do not hurt "the home country." In fact, a cursory reading of Smith's invisible hand passage might cause some to believe that any personal engagement in commerce does not require even a rudimentary moral understanding—as long as the laws are obeyed.

But this is an incomplete, and even mistaken, reading of Smith. A more thorough reading of Smith's *An Inquiry into the Nature and Causes of the Wealth of Nations* reveals that he, like most eighteenth-century English scholars, is committed to virtue as an end of all activities.

About twenty years prior to the publication of *Wealth of Nations,* Smith published *Theory of Moral Sentiments* (excerpt not included in this textbook). Here too, during a period when his economic tenets are not wholly formulated, it is clear that he believes that self-advancing aims, untenderized by self-improving sentiments, are harmful to any society. Though he argues on the side of individualism, he lays out a well-organized argument for virtue, governed by the personal practice of proper purpose, prudent planning, and benevolent behavior. To those who see in Smith's later evocation of the invisible hand a secular defense of excessive and inexcusably individualistic behavior, *Theory of Moral Sentiments* should provide a soothing anodyne whose Platonic ingredients of justice and magnanimity provide relief from the potentially infectious nature of self-interest. In fact, Smith argues

that self-interest and justice are directly related. His position is not, as some have accused, a secularized "all gods dead, all things permitted" program. Rather it is a moral desideratum that warns that, even though each individual is an agent of his or her own self-interest, he or she is also subject to larger, universal principles. Like the classical stoics, each individual agent is required to behave with "that perfect rectitude which [constitutes] the essence of virtue." Smith asks each then, in the practice of commerce and all quotidian affairs, "to live consistently, to live according to nature, and to obey those laws and directions which nature or the author of nature [has] prescribed for our conducts."

To ignore Smith's wider and deeper message regarding the nature of self-interest, is to alter his vision of the economic human, who he believes is assisted by an abstract invisible hand. The social actions of the invisible hand are governed by the same Platonic principles of justice that assist all good people.

In *Wealth of Nations*, Adam Smith explains the concept of division of labor by meticulously laying out the various operations in the production of something as simple as a pin. With a factory setting serving as a laboratory, most of us could see such operations for ourselves. Leonard Read, writing in *I Pencil*, asks that we look at the operations in the production of a pencil that take us out of the single laboratory and into multiple settings. Begin with the cedar tree and the various machines employed to cut and convert the tree into logs—in fact, think of all the gears in all the machines and what it took to create "saws, axes, motors."

Read also asks us to consider the elements of distribution and the necessity of constructing "flat cars and rails and railroad engines . . . ." And he has not yet even asked us to look into the operations (think of Smith's idea of the division of labor) once inside the pencil factory. To manufacture something as seemingly rudimentary as a pencil demands, if we are to be wholly conscious in the matter, then we accept its real complexities and the enormity of individual effort—from beginning to end—that really goes into the creation of something as convenient and necessary as a pencil.

To condemn vice and ridicule folly is the vocation of many eighteenth-century English and Continental poets, essayists, and novelists. Bernard Mandeville, a Dutch émigré physician living in the Augustan England of Dryden, Pope, and Defoe, is the author of an early eighteenth-century satire of such biting, acidulous wit, that in 1723, it was declared a "public nuisance" by the Grand Jury of Middlesex and was the subject of many critical attacks. In *The Fable of the Bees: or Private Vices, Publick Benefits*, Mandeville draws his pen against the licentious doctrine that private vices are public benefits. Years before Adam Smith explains how private vice can actuate public good (a notion still nurtured, romanced, and advanced by contemporary capitalists and business school professors), Mandeville protrays the modern, commercial city by describing it as a beehive addicted to vice. Editor and author, Philip Harth describes the population of the hive in this way:

> The lawyers in this kingdom bilk their clients, the physicians are only interested in extorting fees from patients whom they cannot cure . . . . the merchants defraud their customers, the customers accept bribes, and the ministers of the crown, rob the public treasury. Finally, the entire population, without exception, gratify their pride and indulge their appetite for glory.

Yet Mandeville demonstrates that the happiness of the hive depends on these vices, most of which engage the activities of business and profit:

> Thus every Part was full of vice, Yet the whole Mass a Paradice; . . . And lavish of their Wealth and Lives, The Balance of all other Hives. Such were the Blessings of that State; Their Crimes conspired to make 'em Great.

Mandeville's excoriation of those who would criticize commercial behavior, antedates Smith's *Wealth of Nations*, but it rests upon similar logic for its expression. Smith, however, does not draw nearly as baleful a conclusion from what seems to be a well-accepted economic explanation of affairs. This is explained in orderly fashion by Philip Harth, who writes:

The explanation for this paradox [that Vice and Paradice are coincident] is that full employment, which is the basis of national prosperity, and a brisk trade, which is necessary to its continuance, are the immediate consequence of immorality. The commission of crime, for example, is responsible for keeping whole multitudes at work, lawyers, gaolers, turnkeys, sergeants, bailiffs, tipstaffs, locksmiths and all those Officers that squeeze a Living out of Tears. As for the vices of luxury, avarice, prodigality, pride, envy, and vanity displayed by the more respectable members of the community, these promote trade by creating wants which it is the business of merchants, tradesmen, and manufacturers to supply.

Adam Smith has read Mandeville and is familiar with his carping cadences. He does not proclaim the late eighteenth century free of vice, but while condemning it, projects an invisible hand into the kingdom that will transform private vice into public virtue. Yes, says Smith, the world is a messy place, but there is no crisis! The axiom of Voltaire's Pangloss holds true—all is for the best in this best of possible worlds. The kingdom does not profit from private vice; rather, the invisible hand rotates, replaces, and reinstates some of the game pieces. The game goes on. People evolve and learn from their mistakes.

The contemporary mind may have difficulty with the Augustan (i.e., religious) belief that all things will work out in the end, but even Mandeville, in the midst of his satire, expresses hope for a "human" hive: It might still buzz with subanthropoid values and diminished moral capacity, but at least it is productive. He says:

> Those, that remain'd grown, temp'rate, strive not how to spend; but how to live.

Mandeville knows that, for some, the use of commerce to serve an intense desire to spend and get grows stale. The oldest classical, philosophical question once again arises—how are we to live our lives? How am I to manage? How is this hive to manage? And perhaps, the responses to these questions are mistaken or premature. Still, even in a hive, a few bees must pause to reconsider their flight paths.

Ralph Waldo Emerson is known as one of the most important writers of the American Transcendental movement of the nineteenth century. Transcendentalism, along with its perhaps more famous counterpart, Romanticism, grew out of a discontent with industrialization and modernism. Disciples of transcendentalism sought to lead Americans toward simpler, less material lives rather than trying to uncouple them from business enterprises. Emerson's life was a busy one, full of "speechifying" and travel. Still, he lived modestly and remained more interested in learning than in making a profit.

In his essay "Wealth," Emerson seeks to strike a balance between humankind's self-interested nature and its religious, transcendental nature. The essay's title alone might suggest that wealth is the *ne plus ultra* of all things, but a careful reading clarifies Emerson's intent. Business, he tells us, exists because by nature, we want things and business produces these things. Such desire is not open to argument. We seek wealth—that is what we do. Wealth confers so many opportunities, and in a young America—better yet, in a young world—growth and wealth move along parallel paths. But our religious natures must not be repressed. Wealth must serve *only* as a means to an end: a spiritual, transcendental end. We must not seek out wealth until we know how to animate our lives through it. Education is critical to understanding how to engage in this "animating" process. Once engaged, we are in a transcendental mood.

It seems odd, at first, to think of John Ruskin, a man of considerable inherited wealth, as having any pressing reason to study and write about the subject of money. A preeminent historian of art, architecture, and aesthetics in nineteenth-century England, he does not usually come to mind as one who might give much thought to the social, intellectual, and moral currents of commerce and cash. However, Ruskin is Emerson's "thoroughly-related" man and is on the scent of every vagary and vanity (including his own) of the day. When he publishes essays on wealth in *The Cornhill Magazine* and later publishes them as a book *Unto the Last* (1862), he intrigues readers as much with the range of his thoughts as he irritates them with the substance of his views. He is suspicious of motives and morals in the relationship between business practitioners and wealth, which annoys many of his moneyed friends and readers. While his views on art and architecture are, by the closing decade of the century, considered nearly infallible, his economic views are often thought of as products of an overzealous and overworked mind.

Still, Ruskin's analogy between the circulation of "blood in the natural body" and the circulation of "wealth in a nation" is a good one. Such a characterization recalls philosophic veins that reach back several centuries to the Socratic idea of a healthy city—a city founded on the economic principles of basic needs and necessary wants—contrasted with a fevered city—founded on the economic principles of infinite wants and uncontained growth. Ruskin reaches again—this time across the Atlantic—to borrow and integrate the Emersonian idea that the body is a manifestation of "a celestial sphere" in the mind—that the circulation of high moral thinking in the body of an economic individual is fundamental to the social health of that larger body we call an economic society.

Ruskin understands that those who accumulate great wealth do so most often by their claim over the labor of others (a central idea of English Fabianism). Such a claim generates inequalities and, for Ruskin, causes those who are wealthy to favor the continuation, and even magnification, of such inequalities. Such a state of economic disequilibrium sets the stage for power imbalance. These are dangerous irregularities—social and economic disjunctions, according to Ruskin—that cannot produce healthy consequences for a nation.

Whereas Emerson argues for a historical synthesis of self and community interest through *capital* reinvestment, Ruskin argues for a historical synthesis of sense and sensibility toward wealth through moral reassessment.

At the close of the nineteenth century, Russell Conwell, a noted American theologian, begins to address the issue of wealth and the Christian faith. His timing is no accident. Rural Americans are migrating to cities to seek out factory employment and to make their claims on wealth. At the same time, many of them are puzzled and conflicted over how to navigate their financial lives. After all, they are a religious, churchgoing people, and they are accustomed to a doctrine that condemns the pursuit of wealth. Conwell argues for the pursuit of wealth and points out that it is not antagonistic to Christian doctrine. In doing so, he asserts a strong Emersonian logic and says that it is wealth that builds churches and pays its pastors while, at the same time, ensuring a commitment to honesty rarely seen among the impoverished. This is Emerson's argument, too.

However, Conwell is committed to his Christian faith in a way that Emerson was not. In fact, Emerson left his position as church pastor in great part because he was troubled by doctrine. Conwell seems untroubled. He points out that difficulties with wealth disappear when the correct interpretation of doctrine is applied. The objection to wealth is not, says Conwell, the wealth itself—rather, it is the hoarding of wealth and the failure to relinquish it to causes greater than the self. This observation matches the spirit of Emerson. In bringing Emersonianism back to faith, Conwell ties the secular to the religious and invites not just American Christians, but all Americans, to the twentieth-century race for riches.

Ayn Rand, as philosopher and novelist, is a modern phenomenon. Few philosophers have platformed their views through the use of novels more successfully than Rand. Though Albert Camus and Jean-Paul Sartre have been notable in this packaging of philosophy through fiction, neither of them can be said to have written novels supportive of an ideology that has, and continues, to hold the world under its spell; that ideology is *capitalism*, of course.

Capitalism, for Rand, is the only reasonable and natural economic ideology humankind has ever produced. Inherent in capitalism are all those issues, technical and nontechnical, that pertain to factors of production and consumption. The personal philosophy that makes capitalism so perfectly logical and workable is one that Rand calls *objectivism*. This philosophy asks for no faith in the metaphysical, nor does it require subjugation to ascetic self-denial or subversion of intuitive logic. Rather, it holds us to a set of historic, enlightenment ideals: reason as supreme, objective reality as unassailable (there is a difference between sense as measurable truth [a table, for example] and nonsense as unmeasurable "truth" [God, for example]), self-interest as rational, and *laissez-faire* politics as ineradicable. Rand is an empiricist for the twenty-first century—a believer in what evidence can support. And the evidence, she believes, is objective and true—that capitalism is not God's way for fallen man. It is man's way for fallen God.

Rand explains that capitalism, despite all criticism, has won the war against paradoxical arguments. For example, she says that capitalism is often thought of as the institutionalization of:

1. selfishness—yet it is the only system that encourages voluntary cooperation;

2. greed—yet no other economic system better lifts the poor toward ever-increasing standards of living; and

3. cruelty—yet it is more progressive than any other economic ideology.

This background helps to make sense of Rand's attitude toward money and wealth. She is careful, in the text of *Atlas Shrugged*, to respond to both, the theological axiom regarding cupidity (the love of money is the root of all evil) and the popular corruption of that axiom (money is the root of all evil). Rand, a progressive thinker in conservative cloth, assertively confronts the problem. To oppose money, she says, is to oppose what is human—the power to imagine and create, to produce and distribute, to trade and prosper. All creativity is a product of the mind. Where such products improve well-being and conspire to augment creativity by sharing—one creative mind with another—often money is the natural and objective consequence of such sharing. To criticize money or affection for money is to berate the very mind of a human—such criticism is self-destructive and counterintuitive.

Where Aristotle sees money as a means of exchange of the most primary, or necessary, things, Rand sees it as the foundation for the production of all useful things, primary or secondary. And as money is the foundation for production, it is the foundation for consumption, too.

Karl Marx has more facets to his legacy than most. Some think of him strictly as a political economist, while others see him as a sociologist and even a psychologist. Some see him only as a revolutionary philosopher. He is all of these things and more. That he has multiple personas may indicate the magnitude of his importance.

Marx's "Capitalist Production," extracted from the voluminous *Das Kapital*, contributes a different perspective to the goods produced by business for general consumption. Marx introduces important economic terms and, after defining them, asks us to think about what they mean to us. We are asked to judge the phenomenon of use value as it is transformed and overwhelmed by exchange value. We are shown the relationship of our human productive powers to the value of the things we produce. Marx demands no less than that we think deeply about the nature of goods and the business world that sets in motion all the processes by which these goods are created and valued. These ideas are crucial to his idea of a communist state. Many of his ideas are still meaningful.

If Emerson suggests that our religious nature could be displaced easily by the rush to business and wealth, then R. H. Tawney's *Religion and the Rise of Capitalism* outlines and explains the historical course of events that has led to such a condition. His emphasis is on the Catholic period, especially from the twelfth to the sixteenth centuries.

Tawney portrays a cornered Catholic Church in "The Social Organism," from *Religion and the Rise of Capitalism*. Against the rising tide of economic human and a changing economic environment in which the church was losing some of its central authority, how were church leaders to deal with the unregulated practice of business? According to Tawney, church leaders were in a difficult position. Because they believed that the astonishing growth of business would lead to the infinite expansion of appetites and to the unleashing of predatory instincts, it seemed that the

church was obligated to do something to inhibit the expression of certain behaviors. However, they also feared that time was not on their side and that the spiritual would eventually be extinguished by the material. Tawney illuminates for us this encounter between "God and Mammon" in which the failures of the church give rise to some of the features we now recognize in capitalism.

If the Medieval Catholic Church is caught between the exigencies of religion and materialism, then the early and evolving American Protestant Church is equally entrapped in the dialectics of acceptable and unacceptable materialism. The opposition between the requirements of salvation and the realities of commercial culture is still a dialectical quagmire in the seventeenth- and eighteenth-century Protestant colonies. The concluding centuries of "the 1000 Catholic Years" have propelled the problem forward without actually arriving at the desired synthesis, although the Protestant Reformation has helped to plot a navigational path that suggests an ultimate terminus where wealth is recognized, in Calvinist terms, as a sign of "elect" status.

Nominally, one must work productively to gain wealth. In doing so, one contributes to the progressive requirements of the new world, which is in desperate need of basic civilization. As one works to reformulate a primitive yet promising environment into a "city on the hill," one accumulates personal wealth. This wealth becomes a sign that the "producer/citizen" has been "divinely elected" to occupy a place in paradise over the term of his eternal existence that follows his earthly one. The actual symbolic value is not clarified, however, by wealth or material abundance alone; rather, it is qualified by the security of knowing, really knowing, that an eternal existence in heaven is now a near-guarantee.

Thus, the Catholic equation, which sought to find a synthesis between materialism and spiritualism that would not endanger salvation, is, at long last, successfully constructed in the Protestant world. It is formulated as work in the name of family, community, and society that results in wealth, which in turn signifies election, by God, to an eternal Christian heaven. Still, the question of acceptable versus unacceptable wealth seeks an answer.

The answer is found in community "sumptuary" laws, which prohibit ostentatious display of wealth. Some consumption, or wealth, therefore, is available for display. Anything in excess, however, invalidates the "eternality" contract. Such Protestant restraint of excessive materialism becomes the soup stock of the future America into which are poured the constituent flavors of business society: Jeffersonian agrarianism; Hamiltonian industrialism; and, most flavorful of all (in Protestant terms), Lockean moderation.

Max Weber's *The Protestant Ethic and the Spirit of Capitalism* tells this story. Weber explains how work is properly dignified to serve as the foundation for eternity and as the justification for material wealth and even acquisitiveness, both cornerstones of the modern capitalist society. "What God demands," declares Weber, "is not labour [sic] in itself, but rational labor in a calling." Work and its concomitant, wealth, now become endowed with a moral component. Failing to follow this calling is tantamount to surrendering one's opportunity to be "God's steward." This sets the stage for a theological blessing on the pursuit of wealth, according to Weber, because:

> . . . in conformity with the Old Testament and in analogy to the ethical valuation of good works, asceticism looked upon the pursuit of wealth as an end in itself as highly reprehensible; but the attainment of it as a fruit of labour [sic] in a calling was a sign of God's blessing . . . the surest and most evident proof of rebirth and genuine faith . . . [This] must have been the most powerful conceivable lever for the expansion of that attitude toward life which we have here called the spirit of capitalism.

Combine the sumptuary attitude, which limits consumption, and combine it with acquisitive activity and the result is "accumulation of capital through compulsion to save." A modern "religious-inspired," documented creed cannot be far off now.

The Acquisitive Society finds Tawney once again illustrating a classical conflict. In this case, it is between business and social purpose.

If business grants as fundamental the right to pursue profits, then at what point do those rights become secondary to greater social needs? Tawney's examples suggest that contemporary business does not see the larger social purpose as primary at all. In fact, he condemns the world of business for generating an "acquisitive society" and compares it, in platonic fashion, to the more ideal "functional society." Tawney asks us to think of business as more than just the production of profits and the satisfaction of demands.

In 1868, after earning a considerable fortune at a young age, Andrew Carnegie decided to retire from business and to devote his life to more philanthropic pursuits. Though he did not retire and, in fact, went on to earn many millions of dollars, he never "gave up the ghost" of philanthropic ideas.

In *The Gospel of Wealth*, Carnegie demonstrates a way for administrating wealth. He accepts as fundamental the requirement that wealth, which is given to the few, should be redistributed to the many. It is important to remember that he supports capitalism and sees its skewed distribution of wealth as one of a number of problems associated with it. These problems are resolved as those who profit from capitalism embrace philanthropic actions. You may ask yourself several questions as you read Carnegie: At what level of wealth should this distribution begin? Should this distribution be required by law? Is there a difference between those who are philanthropic and those who are not? Carnegie does not answer all of these questions, though he does, at least, remind us in Emersonian fashion that the wealth produced by business is just a means to an end and that the end should not be further self-advancement.

John D. Rockefeller, Jr., learned something from some of the questionable motives and moves for personal power made by his more famous father, John D. Rockefeller. He also asks us to look at how business best serves the needs of society. However, he sees that the needs of business do not intersect with the needs of the greater community until the needs of individual stakeholders are met. If all stakeholders work to serve the needs of other stakeholders, then everybody benefits. This platonic idea of interdependency should, Rockefeller asserts, be the rule for all of us. When we look out for the needs of others, he intimates, the predator becomes the lonely exception. Rockefeller's "industrial creed" might serve as a roadmap for the possible evolution of business.

The urgent needs of the community do not seem to concern Nobel laureate Milton Friedman. Free competition requires us to engage in legal and forthright business activity. It does not, Friedman maintains, require social responsibility. It is enough of a responsibility for a business to achieve profitability.

When Friedman justifies his position, we can hear the influence of Adam Smith and other proponents of the free market system. But we cannot ignore Friedman's invitation to argue the point when he says that the concept of corporate social responsibility actually "undermines the very foundations of our free society." Freidman demands that businesses be left alone to do what they do best—make money for their shareholders. He is not opposed to the notion that businesses adapt their strategies and tactics in order to stay within the boundaries of law and moral custom. However, he is mortified by the idea of governments regulating what ought to be free markets.

Markets can work very well as self-regulating entities—which we can see from reading *The Shuchu Kiyaku* by Seika Fugiwara. As early as 1605, Fugiwara says that people can discern for themselves that personal conduct is crucial to wealth. Merchants looking "to make a quick profit will get less return than the merchant trying to make a profit in the long run." In economic affairs where voluntary cooperation is essential, we learn that the *quid pro quo* makes sense—that as we wish to do well, we should see to it that our business partners do well, too.

We might infer from Fugiwara that government is not the essential regulator for this kind of behavior. "All creatures," says Fugiwara, "between Heaven and Hell share the same outlook and the same heart."

Which ideas are fundamental to the business world and which are fundamental to us when we navigate our way through it? The following selections provide some answers. ♦

FROM *THE REPUBLIC*

Plato (428–349 BC)

. . . [M]en practise it [justice] against the grain, for lack of power to do wrong. How true that is, we shall best see if we imagine two men, one just, the other unjust, given full licence to do whatever they like, and then follow them to observe where each will be led by his desires. We shall catch the just man taking the same road as the unjust; he will be moved by self-interest, the end which it is natural to every creature to pursue as good, until forcibly turned aside by law and custom to respect the principle of equality.

Now, the easiest way to give them that complete liberty of action would be to imagine them possessed of the talisman found by Gyges, the ancestor of the famous Lydian. The story tells how he was a shepherd in the King's service. One day there was a great storm, and the ground where his flock was feeding was rent by an earthquake. Astonished at the sight, he went down into the chasm and saw, among other wonders of which the story tells, a brazen horse, hollow, with windows in its sides. Peering in, he saw a dead body, which seemed to be of more than human size. It was naked save for a gold ring, which he took from the finger and made his way out. When the shepherds met, as they did every month, to send an account to the King of the state of his flocks, Gyges came wearing the ring. As he was sitting with the others, he happened to turn the bezel of the ring inside his hand. At once he became invisible, and his companions, to his surprise, began to speak of him as if he had left them. Then, as he was fingering the ring, he turned the bezel outwards and became visible again. With that, he set about testing the ring to see if it really had this power, and always with the same result: according as he turned the bezel inside or out he vanished and reappeared. After this discovery he contrived to be one of the messengers sent to the court. There he seduced the Queen, and with her help murdered the King and seized the throne.

Now suppose there were two such magic rings, and one were given to the just man, the other to the unjust. No one, it is commonly believed, would have such iron strength of mind as to stand fast in doing right or keep his hands off other men's goods, when he could go to the market-place and fearlessly help himself to anything he wanted, enter houses and sleep with any woman he chose, set prisoners free and kill men at his pleasure, and in a word go about among men with the powers of a god. He would behave no better than the other; both would take the same course. Surely this would be strong proof that men do right only under compulsion; no individual thinks of it as good for him personally, since he does wrong whenever he finds he has the power. Every man believes that wrongdoing pays him personally much better, and, according to this theory, that is the truth. Granted full licence to do as he liked, people would think him a miserable fool if they found him refusing to wrong his neighbours or to touch their belongings, though in public they would keep up a pretence of praising his conduct, for fear of being wronged themselves. So much for that.

RUDIMENTS OF SOCIAL ORGANIZATION

My notion is, said I, that a state comes into existence because no individual is self-sufficing; we all have many needs. But perhaps you can suggest some different origin for the foundation of a community?

No, I agree with you.

So, having all these needs, we call in one another's help to satisfy our various requirements; and when we have collected a number of helpers and associates to live together in one place, we call that settlement a state.

Yes.

So if one man gives another what he has to give in exchange for what he can get, it is because each finds that to do so is for his own advantage.

Certainly.

Very well, said I. Now let us build up our imaginary state from the beginning. Apparently, it will owe its existence to our needs, the first and greatest need being the provision of food to keep us alive. Next we shall want a house; and thirdly, such things as clothing.

True.

How will our state be able to supply all these demands? We shall need at least one man to be a farmer, another a builder, and a third a weaver. Will that do, or shall we add a shoemaker and one or two more to provide for our personal wants?

By all means.

The minimum state, then, will consist of four or five men.

Apparently.

Now here is a further point. Is each one of them to bring the product of his work into a common stock? Should our one farmer, for example, provide food enough for four people and spend the whole of his working time in producing corn, so as to share with the rest; or should he take no notice of them and spend only a quarter of his time on growing just enough corn for himself, and divide the other three-quarters between building his house, weaving his clothes, and making his shoes, so as to save the trouble of sharing with others and attend himself to all his own concerns?

The first plan might be the easier, replied Adeimantus.

That may very well be so, said I; for, as you spoke, it occurred to me, for one thing, that no two people are born exactly alike. There are innate differences which fit them for different occupations.

I agree.

And will a man do better working at many trades, or keeping to one only?

Keeping to one.

And there is another point: obviously work may be ruined, if you let the right time go by. The workman must wait upon the work; it will not wait upon his leisure and allow itself to be done in a spare moment. So the conclusion is that more things will be produced and the work be more easily and better done, when every man is set free from all other occupations to do, at the right time, the one thing for which he is naturally fitted.

That is certainly true.

We shall need more than four citizens, then, to supply all those necessaries we mentioned. You see, Adeimantus, if the farmer is to have a good plough and spade and other tools, he will not make them himself. No more will the builder and weaver and shoemaker make all the many implements they need. So quite a number of carpenters and smiths and other craftsmen must be enlisted. Our miniature state is beginning to grow.

It is.

Still, it will not be very large, even when we have added cowherds and shepherds to provide the farmers with oxen for the plough, and the builders as well as the farmers with draught-animals, and the weavers and shoemakers with wool and leather.

No; but it will not be so very small either.

And yet, again, it will be next to impossible to plant our city in a territory where it will need no imports. So there will have to be still another set of people, to fetch what it needs from other countries.

There will.

Moreover, if these agents take with them nothing that those other countries require in exchange, they will return as empty-handed as they went. So, besides everything wanted for consumption at home, we must produce enough goods of the right kind for the foreigners whom we depend on to supply us. That will mean increasing the number of farmers and craftsmen.

Yes.

And then, there are these agents who are to import and export all kinds of goods—merchants, as we call them. We must have them; and if they are to do business overseas, we shall need quite a number of ship-owners and others who know about that branch of trading.

We shall.

Again, in the city itself how are the various sets of producers to exchange their products? That was our object, you will remember, in forming a community and so laying the foundation of our state.

Obviously, they must buy and sell.

That will mean having a market-place, and a currency to serve as a token for purposes of exchange.

Certainly.

Now suppose a farmer, or an artisan, brings some of his produce to market at a time when no one is there who wants to exchange with him. Is he to sit there idle, when he might be at work?

No, he replied; there are people who have seen an opening here for their services. In well-ordered communities they are generally men not strong enough to be of use in any other occupation. They have to stay where they are in the market-place and take goods for money from those who want to sell, and money for goods from those who want to buy.

That, then, is the reason why our city must include a class of shopkeepers—so we call these people who sit still in the marketplace to buy and sell, in contrast with merchants who travel to other countries.

Quite so.

There are also the services of yet another class, who have the physical strength for heavy work, though on intellectual grounds they are hardly worth including in our society—hired labourers, as we call them, because they sell the use of their strength for wages. They will go to make up our population.

Yes.

Well, Adeimantus, has our state now grown to its full size?

Perhaps.

Then, where in it shall we find justice or injustice? If they have come in with one of the elements we have been considering, can you say with which one?

I have no idea, Socrates; unless it be somewhere in their dealings with one another.

You may be right, I answered. Anyhow, it is a question which we shall have to face.

Let us begin, then, with a picture of our citizens' manner of life, with the provision we have made for them. They will be producing corn and wine, and making clothes and shoes. When they have built their houses, they will mostly work without their coats or shoes in summer, and in winter be well shod and

clothed. For their food, they will prepare flour and barley-meal for kneading and baking, and set out a grand spread of loaves and cakes on rushes or fresh leaves. Then they will lie on beds of myrtle-boughs and bryony and make merry with their children, drinking their wine after the feast with garlands on their heads and singing the praises of the gods. So they will live pleasantly together; and a prudent fear of poverty or war will keep them from begetting children beyond their means.

Here Glaucon interrupted me: You seem to expect your citizens to feast on dry bread.

True, I said; I forgot that they will have something to give it a relish, salt, no doubt, and olives, and cheese, and country stews of roots and vegetables. And for dessert we will give them figs and peas and beans; and they shall roast myrtle-berries and acorns at the fire, while they sip their wine. Leading such a healthy life in peace, they will naturally come to a good old age, and leave their children to live after them in the same manner.

That is just the sort of provender you would supply, Socrates, if you were founding a community of pigs.

Well, how are they to live, then, Glaucon?

With the ordinary comforts. Let them lie on couches and dine off tables on such dishes and sweets as we have nowadays.

Ah, I see, said I; we are to study the growth, not just of a state, but of a luxurious one. Well, there may be no harm in that; the consideration of luxury may help us to discover how justice and injustice take root in society. The community I have described seems to me the ideal one, in sound health as it were: but if you want to see one suffering from inflammation, there is nothing to hinder us. So some people, it seems, will not be satisfied to live in this simple way; they must have couches and tables and furniture of all sorts; and delicacies too, perfumes, unguents, courtesans, sweet-meats, all in plentiful variety. And besides, we must not limit ourselves now to those bare necessaries of house and clothes and shoes; we shall have to set going the arts of embroidery and painting, and collect rich materials, like gold and ivory.

Yes.

Then we must once more enlarge our community. The healthy one will not be big enough now; it must be swollen up with a whole multitude of callings not ministering to any bare necessity: hunters and fishermen, for instance; artists in sculpture, painting, and music; poets with their attendant train of professional reciters, actors, dancers, producers; and makers of all sorts of household gear, including everything for women's adornment. And we shall want more servants: children's nurses and attendants, lady's maids, barbers, cooks and confectioners. And then swineherds—there was no need for them in our original state, but we shall want them now; and a great quantity of sheep and cattle too, if people are going to live on meat.

Of course.

And with this manner of life physicians will be in much greater request.

No doubt.

The country, too, which was large enough to support the original inhabitants, will now be too small. If we are to have enough pasture and plough land, we shall have to cut off a slice of our neighbours' territory; and if they too are not content with necessaries, but give themselves up to getting unlimited wealth, they will want a slice of ours.

That is inevitable, Socrates.

So the next thing will be, Glaucon, that we shall be at war.

No doubt. ♦

QUESTIONS

1. What is the story of the ring of Gyges?

2. What is the common opinion about what anyone would do with the power conferred by the ring?

3. According to Plato, what are people's needs?

4. Why does Plato think that the division of labor is so important?

5. What is the role of the merchant and how does money contribute to that role?

6. What type of state is fevered and swollen for Plato?

7. To what does the development of a taste for luxury lead?

FROM *THE POLITICS*

Aristotle (384–322 BC)

Of the art of acquisition then there is one kind which is natural and is a part of the management of a household. Either we must suppose the necessaries of life to exist previously, or the art of household management must provide a store of them for the common use of the family or state. They are the elements of true wealth; for the amount of property which is needed for a good life is not unlimited, although Solon in one of his poems says that

> "No bound to riches has been fixed for man."

But there is a boundary fixed, just as there is in the arts; for the instruments of any art are never unlimited, either in number or size, and wealth may be defined as a number of instruments to be used in a household or in a state. And so we see that there is a natural art of acquisition which is practised by managers of households and by statesmen, and what is the reason of this.

There is another variety of the art of acquisition which is commonly and rightly called the art of making money, and has in fact suggested the notion that wealth and property have no limit. Being nearly connected with the preceding, it is often identified with it. But though they are not very different, neither are they the same. The kind already described is given by nature, the other is gained by experience and art.

Let us begin our discussion of the question with the following considerations:—

Of everything which we possess there are two uses: both belonging to the thing as such, but not in the same manner, for one is the proper, and the other the improper or secondary use of it. For example, a shoe is used for wear, and is used for exchange; both are uses of the shoe. He who gives a shoe in exchange for money or food to him who wants one, does indeed use the shoe as a shoe, but this is not its proper or primary purpose, for a shoe is not made to be an object of barter. The same may be said of all possessions, for the art of exchange extends to all of them, and it arises at first in a natural manner from the circumstance that some have too little, others too much. Hence we may infer that retail trade is not a natural part of the art of money-making; had it been so, men would have ceased to exchange when they had enough. And in the first community, which is the family, this art is obviously of no use, but only begins to be useful when the society increases. For the members of the family originally had all things in common; in a more divided state of society they still shared in many things, but they were different things which they had to give in exchange for what they wanted, a kind of barter which is still practised among barbarous nations who exchange with one another the necessaries of life and nothing more; giving and receiving wine, for example, in exchange for corn and the like. This sort of barter is not part of the money-making art and is not contrary to nature, but is needed for the satisfaction of men's natural wants. The other or more complex form of exchange grew out of the simpler. When the inhabitants of one country became more dependent on those of another, and they imported what they needed, and exported the surplus, money necessarily came into use. For the various necessaries of life are not easily carried about, and hence men agreed to employ in their dealings with each other something which was intrinsically useful and easily applicable to the purposes of life, for example, iron, silver, and the like. Of this the value was at first measured by size and weight, but in process of time they put a stamp upon it, to save the trouble of weighing and to mark the value.

When the use of coin had once been discovered, out of the barter of necessary articles arose the other art of money-making, namely, retail trade; which was at first probably a simple matter, but became more complicated as soon as men learned by experience whence and by what exchanges the greatest profit might be made. Originating in the use of coin, the art of money-making is generally thought to be chiefly concerned with it, and to be the art which produces wealth and money; having to consider how they may be accumulated. Indeed, wealth is assumed by many to be only a quantity of coin, because the art of money-making and retail trade are concerned with coin. Others maintain that coined money is a mere sham, a thing not natural, but conventional only, which would have no value or use for any of the purposes of daily life if another commodity were substituted by the users. And, indeed, he who is rich in coin may often be in want of necessary food. But how can that be wealth of which a man may have a great abundance and yet perish with hunger, like Midas in the fable, whose insatiable prayer turned everything that was set before him into gold?

Men seek after a better notion of wealth and of the art of making money than the mere acquisition of coin, and they are right. For natural wealth and the natural art of money-making are a different thing; in their true form they are part of the management of a household; whereas retail trade is the art of producing wealth, not in every way, but by exchange. And it seems to be concerned with coin; for coin is the beginning of exchange and the measure or limit of it. And there is no bound to the wealth which springs from this art of money-making. As in the art of medicine there is no limit to the pursuit of health, and as in the other arts there is no limit to the pursuit of their several ends, for they aim at accomplishing their ends to the uttermost (but of the means there is a limit, for the end is always the limit), so, too, in this art of money-making there is no limit of the end, which is wealth of the spurious kind, and the acquisition of money. But the art of household management has a limit; the unlimited acquisition of money is not its business. And, therefore, in one point of view, all wealth must have a limit; nevertheless, as a matter of fact, we find the opposite to be the case; for all money-makers increase their hoard of coin without limit. The source of the confusion is the near connexion between the two kinds of money-making; either, the instrument [i.e. wealth] is the same, although the use is different, and so they pass into one another; for

each is a use of the same property, but with a difference; accumulation is the end in the one case, but there is a further end in the other. Hence some persons are led to believe that making money is the object of household management, and the whole idea of their lives is that they ought either to increase their money without limit, or at any rate not to lose it. The origin of this disposition in men is that they are intent upon living only, and not upon living well; and, as their desires are unlimited, they also desire that the means of gratifying them should be without limit. Even those who aim at a good life seek the means of obtaining bodily pleasures; and, since the enjoyment of these appears to depend on property, they are absorbed in making money: and so there arises the second species of money-making. For, as their enjoyment is in excess, they seek an art which produces the excess of enjoyment; and, if they are not able to supply their pleasures by the art of making-money, they try other arts, using in turn every faculty in a manner contrary to nature. The quality of courage, for example, is not intended to make money, but to inspire confidence; neither is this the aim of the general's or of the physician's art; but the one aims at victory and the other at health. Nevertheless, some men turn every quality or art into a means of making money; this they conceive to be the end, and to the promotion of the end all things must contribute.

Thus, then, we have considered the art of money-making, which is unnecessary, and why men want it; and also the necessary art of money-making, which we have seen to be different from the other, and to be a natural part of the art of managing a household, concerned with the provision of food, not however, like the former kind, unlimited, but having a limit.

And we have found the answer to our original question, Whether the art of money-making is the business of the manager of a household and of the statesman or not their business?—viz. that it is an art which is presupposed by them. For political science does not make men, but takes them from nature and uses them; and nature provides them with food from the element of earth, air, or sea. At this stage begins the duty of the manager of a household, who has to order the things which nature supplies;—he may be compared to the weaver who has not to make but to use wool, and to know what sort of wool is good and serviceable or bad and unserviceable. Were this otherwise, it would be difficult to see why the art of money-making is a part of the management of a household and the art of medicine not; for surely the members of a household must have health just as they must have life or any other necessary. And as from one point of view the master of the house and the ruler of the state have to consider about health, from another point of view not they but the physician; so in one way the art of household management, in another way the subordinate art, has to consider about money. But, strictly speaking, as I have already said, the means of life must be provided beforehand by nature; for the business of nature is to furnish food to that which is born, and the food of the offspring always remains over in the parent. Wherefore the art of making money out of fruits and animals is always natural.

Of the two sorts of money-making one, as I have just said, is a part of household management, the other is retail trade: the former necessary and honourable, the latter a kind of exchange which is justly censured; for it is unnatural, and a mode by which men gain from one another. The most hated sort, and with the greatest reason, is usury, which makes a gain out of money itself, and not from the natural use of it. For money was intended to be used in exchange, but not to increase at interest. And this term usury [rókos], which means the birth of money from money, is applied to the breeding of money because the offspring resembles the parent. Wherefore of all modes of making money this is the most unnatural.

Enough has been said about the theory of money-making; we will now proceed to the practical part. The discussion of such matters is not unworthy of philosophy, but to be engaged in them practically is illiberal and irksome. The useful parts of money-making are, first, the knowledge of livestock,—which are most profitable, and where, and how,—as, for example, what sort of horses or sheep or oxen or any other animals are most likely to give a return. A

man ought to know which of these pay better than others, and which pay best in particular places, for some do better in one place and some in another. Secondly, husbandry, which may be either tillage or planting, and the keeping of bees and of fish, or fowl, or of any animals which may be useful to man. These are the divisions of the true or proper art of money-making and come first. Of the other, which consists in exchange, the first and most important division is commerce (of which there are three kinds—commerce by sea, commerce by land, selling in shops—these again differing as they are safer or more profitable), the second is usury, the third, service for hire—of this, one kind is employed in the mechanical arts, the other in unskilled and bodily labour. There is still a third sort of money-making intermediate between this and the first or natural mode which is partly natural, but is also concerned with exchange of the fruits and other products of the earth. Some of these latter, although they bear no fruit, are nevertheless profitable; for example, wood and minerals. The art of mining, by which minerals are obtained, has many branches, for there are various kinds of things dug out of the earth. Of the several divisions of money-making I now speak generally; a minute consideration of them might be useful in practice, but it would be tiresome to dwell upon them at greater length now.

Those occupations are most truly arts in which there is the least element of chance; they are the meanest in which the body is most deteriorated, the most servile in which there is the greatest use of the body, and the most illiberal in which there is the least need of excellence.

Works have been written upon these subjects by various persons; for example, by Chares the Parian, and Apollodorus the Lemnian, who have treated of Tillage and Planting, while others have treated of other branches; any one who cares for such matters may refer to their writings. It would be well also to collect the scattered stories of the ways in which individuals have succeeded in amassing a fortune; for all this is useful to persons who value the art of making money. There is the anecdote of Thales the Milesian and his financial device, which involves a principle of universal application, but is attributed to him on account of his reputation for wisdom. He was reproached for his poverty, which was supposed to show that philosophy was of no use. According to the story, he knew by his skill in the stars while it was yet winter that there would be a great harvest of olives in the coming year; so, having a little money, he gave deposits for the use of all the olive-presses in Chios and Miletus, which he hired at a low price because no one bid against him. When the harvest-time came, and many wanted them all at once and of a sudden, he let them out at any rate which he pleased, and made a quantity of money. Thus he showed the world that philosophers can easily be rich if they like, but that their ambition is of another sort. He is supposed to have given a striking proof of his wisdom, but, as I was saying, his device for getting money is of universal application, and is nothing but the creation of a monopoly. It is an art often practised by cities when they are in want of money; they make a monopoly of provisions.

There was a man of Sicily, who, having money deposited with him, bought up all the iron from the iron mines; afterwards, when the merchants from their various markets came to buy, he was the only seller, and without much increasing the price he gained 200 percent. Which when Dionysius heard, he told him that he might take away his money, but that he must not remain at Syracuse, for he thought that the man had discovered a way of making money which was injurious to his own interests. He had the same idea as Thales; they both contrived to create a monopoly for themselves. And statesmen ought to know these things; for a state is often as much in want of money and of such devices for obtaining it as a household,

or even more so; hence some public men devote themselves entirely to finance.

Of household management we have seen that there are three parts—one is the rule of a master over slaves, which has been discussed already, another of a father, and the third of a husband. A husband and father rules over wife and children, both free, but the rule differs, the rule over his children being a royal, over his wife a constitutional rule. For although there may be exceptions to the order of nature, the male is by nature fitter for command than the female, just as the elder and full-grown is superior to the younger and more immature. But in most constitutional states the citizens rule and are ruled by turns, for the idea of constitutional state implies that the natures of the citizens are equal, and do not differ at all. Nevertheless, when one rules and the other is ruled we endeavour to create a difference of outward forms and names and titles of respect, which may be illustrated by the saying of Amasis about his foot-pan. The relation of the male to the female is of this kind, but there the inequality is permanent. The rule of a father over his children is royal, for his receives both love and the respect due to age, exercising a kind of royal power. And therefore Homer has appropriately called Zeus 'father of Gods and men,' because he is the king of them all. For a king is the natural superior of his subjects, but he should be the same kin or kind with them, and such is the relation of elder and younger, of father and son.

Thus it is clear that household management attends more to men than to the acquisition of inanimate things, and to human excellence more than to the excellence of property which we call wealth, and to the virtue of freemen more than to the virtue of slaves. ♦

QUESTIONS

1. According to Aristotle, what are the two kinds of arts of acquisition?

2. What are the two kinds of value that goods can offer people?

3. Which art of acquisition is bounded by need and which is unbounded?

4. What is usury and why is it problematic?

LAISSEZ-FAIRE POLICY FROM *THE ECONOMIC PRINCIPLES OF CONFUCIUS AND HIS SCHOOL*

Chen Huan-Chang (1881–1933)

By the word *laissez-faire*, we do not mean to imply that Confucianism leaves every thing wholly unregulated. It simply indicates that the Confucian socialism depends not upon any revolutionary force, but upon the development of the natural course of things; that human nature can be developed to perfection, and that there is no need of too many artificial laws to restrain it and to retard its progress, except in special cases. Universal equality, universal opportunity, and economic freedom are the most important doctrines of Confucius. The class system, monopoly, and the tariff, are the object of his condemnation. According to the true Confucian theory, a full chance is given to the people for their natural development. This is the way to realize Confucian socialism. On the one hand, we find that Confucianism is in favor of social legislation; on the other, we find also that it is in favor of the *laissez-faire* policy. They are both advantageous. Confucianism is the golden mean, and it never goes to extremes. What is fitted to the time or condition is the best. In a word, the Confucian social legislation is by means of moral, rather than governmental laws.

For the exact statement of the *laissez-faire* policy, we find a general economic principle given by Confucius himself. When Tzu-chang, his pupil, asks Confucius about the art of government, he enumerates for him the five excellent things. The first of them is "bounteousness without any cost." Tzu-chang asks again: "What is meant by bounteousness without any cost?" "Follow what is the profit of the people, and profit them," answers Confucius; "is this not bounteousness without any cost?" This statement is most general and comprehensive, and needs no particular explanation.

In the *Many Dewdrops of the Spring and Autumn*, Tung Chung-shu also expresses the principle of the *laissez-fire* policy as follows: "If a sage governs a state, he must follow the nature of heaven and earth, and the personal interest of the senses of man." This is the general policy of leading the economic life of the people in the natural way.

Among all the Confucians, Ssu-ma Chien is the one who advocates the *laissez-faire* policy most strongly. His theory is based on human wants. He says:

> Before the time of Shen Nung (2287 B.K. or 2838 B.C.), I do not know; but since the dynasties of Yü and Hsia, told of by the Canons of *Poetry and History*, the ear and eye want to exhaust the fineness of sound and beauty; the mouth wants to exhaust the taste of meat; the body wants to be easy and pleasant; and the mind wants to be proud of the glory of power and ability. These economic wants have produced a general habit and have fixed the nature of the people for a very long time. Even though we should persuade them from door after door with a fine speech, we cannot change their habits. Therefore, the best policy is to follow the economic activities of man; the second is to lead them on profitably; the third is to teach them; the fourth is to regulate them; and the worst is to fight with them.

This is the basis of his theory. In a word, economic wants or self-interest, is the foundation upon which economic policy is based.

Then he comes to the process of production and says:

> Society depends upon the farmer for the supply of food; upon the miner for the development of the mine; upon the artisan for the manufacturing of goods; and upon the merchant for the exchange of them. Has this natural process anything to do with either political action, or religious teaching, or special order and meeting? It is simply

Reprinted from *The Economic Principles of Confucius and His School* (1938), Harper Collins Publishers, Inc.

that everyone respectively employs his own ability, and exhausts his own energy, in order to get what he wants. Therefore, when the commodity is cheap, it calls forth demand, and raises its price; and when it is dear, it calls forth supply, and lowers its price. Everyone respectively encourages his own occupation, and enjoys his own work. Such a natural thing is like the water drifting to the low place through day and night without any cessation. There is no one to call for it especially, but it comes itself; there is no one to demand it especially, but the people offer it themselves. Is it not the result of the natural law and the proof of the natural course?

The reason he is in favor of the *laissez-faire* policy is because he is afraid that the natural process of production would be interrupted if it were interfered with by the government. He quotes the four following sentences from the *Book of Chou*: "If there were no farmer, society would be in want of food; no artisan, it would be in want of business; no merchant, the three kinds of money [copper, silver, and gold] would disappear; no miner, wealth would be exhausted and insufficient."

He emphasizes the last sentence by saying that, if wealth were exhausted and insufficient, the natural resources of the mountains and marshes could not be developed. By this he points out the importance of capital. Then he concludes this quotation with the following remarks:

These four branches of production are the sources of the economic life of the people. When the sources are great, the people are rich; and when the sources are small, they are poor. Such sources are the causes for the enrichment, both of the state and of private families.

Here he means that there should be large production. If production be large, the sources of wealth are great, and it is good not only for the private families, but for the public as a whole. Therefore, the natural process of production should be left free, because it will bring great sources of wealth to society.

In regard to distribution, he says: "The reason why there are the rich and the poor is not by reason of taking something from the one and giving it to the other. It is simply that the clever get more than sufficient, and the stupid get less than they need." Thus, the division of the people into rich and poor is merely the result of free competition.

After describing the different lives of rich men, and the various economic conditions of great cities, he continues as follows:

Among the common people generally, if a man's wealth is tenfold, the people respect him; if one hundredfold, they fear him; if one thousandfold, they serve him; and if ten thousandfold, they enslave themselves to him. It is the nature of things. Generally, if one wishes to acquire wealth from a poor condition, to be a farmer is not so good as to be an artisan; to be an artisan is not so good as to be a merchant; and to make embroidery is not so good as to speculate in the market. This means that the commercial and industrial occupations are the resorts of the poor.

According to this statement, Ssu-ma Chien admits that there is an inequality of wealth on account of free competition, yet he points out that the employment of the poor depends upon the rich.

Through the ages of Spring and Autumn and of Warring States to the beginning of the Han dynasty, the economic condition of China was very dynamic, and great capitalists were numerous. Great capitalists would control whole provinces; smaller ones, whole districts; and still smaller ones, whole towns. Their wealth was accumulated by different occupations, such as agriculture, animal-breeding, mining, manufacture, trade and commerce. Since there had been a great amount of production and of accumulation, Ssu-ma Chien believed in the *laissez-faire* policy.

However, he does not go to the extreme. In conclusion, he says:

When wealth is not confined to any certain occupation, goods have no permanent owners. They go to the efficient as all the trains come to the central station, and dissolve from the grasp of the inefficient as the tiles fall from the roof to the ground. A millionaire is equal to the prince of a feudal state, and a billionaire even enjoys the same pleasure as a king. Are they not the so-called titleless lords? No.

At the very end of the whole chapter, he puts this negative answer for the withdrawal of his former statements. In fact, on the one hand, he likes large production, so that he thinks free competition is worth while; on the other hand, he hates unequal distribution, so that he employs sarcasm against the rich. To enlarge production and to equalize distribution is his final aim. Therefore, in his conclusion, he comes to the common point of the Confucians.

Taking Chinese history as a whole, we may say that the Chinese have enjoyed a great deal of economic freedom. Except for a few laws regulating consumption for social reasons, the people really do what they please. The fundamental cause is that, since the Chinese Empire is very large and its government is monarchical in form, it is impossible for the government to interfere closely with the economic life of the people. Therefore, although there are some laws respecting economic life, the people need not come in touch with them at all. In fact, the commercial community of the Chinese is governed by custom rather than by law.

III. DIVISIONS OF ECONOMICS

For the divisions of economics in the Confucian school, there is no passage more comprehensive than that in the "Great Learning." It reads: "There is a great principle for the increase of wealth: those who produce it should be many; and those who consume it, few. Those who create it should be rapid; and those who use it, slow. Then wealth will always be sufficient." According to this great principle, there are only two things, namely, production and consumption. While the terms *many* and *few* refer to the number of men, the terms *rapid* and *slow* refer to the process of production and consumption. This is a most comprehensive principle covering the whole field of economics.

This great principle makes production and consumption equal in rank, but recommends that production should be over and above consumption. This is quite correct. If production were just equal to consumption, there could be not only no increase of production, but also no increase of consumption. The only means of extending consumption, is to produce wealth over and above the limit of consumption. This is the way to accumulate capital, and to make wealth always sufficient. Such terms as *many* and *few*, *rapid* and *slow*, are only comparative expressions. They mean that the consumers should be fewer than the producers, and the using of wealth slower than the creation of it. This does not mean that the consumers should be so few as to check the producers, and the using of wealth so slow as to block its creation. Should it mean this, it would be not only inadvisable, but also impossible.

This great principle holds true not only in ancient times, but also today. As the words *many* and *few* refer to the number of men, their meaning is self-evident, and needs no explanation. The word *rapid*, however, has great significance. It includes all the improvements in economic life. In short, all those things which can quicken the process of creating wealth are embraced. Therefore, time-saving machines, transportation and communication, the money and banking system, business organizations, etc., all are included in the principle that those who create wealth should be rapid. Hence, this sentence covers not only production, but also exchange and distribution.

According to Professor J. B. Clark, exchange is only a part of production, because it produces either form utility, or place utility, or time utility. Distribution is intimately linked with production, because distribution to each member is according to the amount he has contributed to the product. Indeed, production continues up to the time when consumption begins. Therefore, the "Great Learning" in dividing economics into two parts, instead of four, covers the whole ground. ♦

QUESTIONS

1. How does Chen suggest that the Confucian ideal balances regulation of economic activity with individual freedom of action?

2. What does it mean to govern the economy in "the natural way"?

3. Do human wants or human needs drive economic actions, according to Chen?

4. What is the relationship among the production, distribution, and consumption of wealth?

From *An Inquiry into the Nature and Causes of the Wealth of Nations*

Adam Smith (1723–1790)

OF RESTRAINTS UPON THE IMPORTATION FROM FOREIGN COUNTRIES OF SUCH GOODS AS CAN BE PRODUCED AT HOME.

By restraining, either by high duties or by absolute prohibitions, the importation of such goods from foreign countries as can be produced at home, the monopoly of the home market is more or less secured to the domestic industry employed in producing them. Thus the prohibition of importing either live cattle or salt provisions from foreign countries secures to the graziers of Great Britain the monopoly of the home market for butcher's meat. The high duties upon the importation of corn, which in times of moderate plenty amount to a prohibition, give a like advantage to the growers of that commodity. The prohibition of the importation of foreign woollens is equally favourable to the woollen manufacturers. The silk manufacture, though altogether employed upon foreign materials, has lately obtained the same advantage. The linen manufacture has not yet obtained it, but is making great strides towards it. Many other sorts of manufacturers have, in the same manner, obtained in Great Britain, either altogether or very dearly, a monopoly against their countrymen. The variety of goods of which the importation into Great Britain is prohibited, either absolutely, or under certain circumstances, greatly exceeds what can easily be suspected by those who are not well acquainted with the laws of the customs.

That this monopoly of the home market frequently gives great encouragement to that particular species of industry which enjoys it, and frequently turns towards that employment a greater share of both the labour and stock of the society than would otherwise have gone to it, cannot be doubted. But whether it tends either to increase the general industry of the society, or to give it the most advantageous direction, is not, perhaps, altogether so evident.

The general industry of the society never can exceed what the capital of the society can employ. As the number of workmen that can be kept in employment by any particular person must bear a certain proportion to his capital, so the number of those that can be continually employed by all the members of a great society must bear a certain proportion to the whole capital of that society, and never can exceed that proportion. No regulation of commerce can increase the quantity of industry in any society beyond what its capital can maintain. It can only divert a part of it into a direction into which it might not otherwise have gone; and it is by no means certain that this artificial direction is likely to be more advantageous to the society than that into which it would have gone of its own accord.

Every individual is continually exerting himself to find out the most advantageous employment for whatever capital he can command. It is his own advantage, indeed, and not that of the society, which he has in view. But the study of his one advantage naturally, or rather necessarily, leads him to prefer that employment which is most advantageous to the society.

First, every individual endeavours to employ his capital as near home as he can, and consequently as much as he can in the support of domestic industry; provided always that he can thereby obtain the ordinary, or not a great deal less than the ordinary profits of stock.

Thus, upon equal or nearly equal profits, every wholesale merchant naturally prefers the home trade to the foreign trade of consumption, and the foreign trade of consumption to the carrying trade. In the home trade his capital is never so long out of his sight as it frequently is in the foreign trade of consumption.

He can know better the character and situation of the persons whom he trusts, and if he should happen to be deceived, he knows better the laws of the country from which he must seek redress. In the carrying trade, the capital of the merchant is, as it were, divided between two foreign countries and no part of it is ever necessarily brought home, or placed under his own immediate view and command. The capital which an Amsterdam merchant employs in carrying corn from Konnigsberg to Lisbon, and fruit and wine from Lisbon to Konnigsberg, must generally be the one-half of it at Konnigsberg and the other half at Lisbon. No part of it need ever come to Amsterdam. The natural residence of such a merchant should either be at Konnigsberg or Lisbon, and it can only be some very particular circumstances which can make him prefer the residence of Amsterdam. The uneasiness, however, which he feels at being separated so far from his capital generally determines him to bring part both of the Konnigsberg goods which he destines for the market of Lisbon, and of the Lisbon goods which he destines for that of Konnigsberg, to Amsterdam: and though this necessarily subjects him to a double charge of loading and unloading, as well as to the payment of some duties and customs, yet for the sake of having some part of his capital always under his own view and command, he willingly submits to this extraordinary charge; and it is in this manner that every country which has any considerable share of the carrying trade becomes always the emporium, or general market, for the goods of all the different countries whose trade it carries on. The merchant, in order to save a second loading and unloading, endeavours always to sell in the home market as much of the goods of all those different countries as he can, and thus, so far as he can, to convert his carrying trade into a foreign trade of consumption. A merchant, in the same manner, who is engaged in the foreign trade of consumption, when he collects goods for foreign markets, will always be glad, upon equal or nearly equal profits, to sell as great a part of them at home as he can. He saves himself the risk and trouble of exportation, when, so far as he can, he thus converts his foreign trade of consumption into a home trade. Home is in this manner the center, if I may say so, round which the capitals of the inhabitants of every country are continually circulating, and towards which they are always tending, though by particular causes they may sometimes be driven off and repelled from it towards more distant employment. But a capital employed in the home trade, it has already been shown, necessarily puts into motion a greater quantity of domestic industry, and gives revenue and employment to a greater number of the inhabitants of the country, than an equal capital employed in the foreign trade of consumption: and one employed in the foreign trade of consumption has the same advantage over an equal capital employed in the carrying trade. Upon equal, or only nearly equal profits, therefore, every individual naturally inclines to employ his capital in the manner in which it is likely to afford the greatest support to domestic industry, and to give revenue and employment to the greatest number of people of his own country.

Secondly, every individual who employs his capital in the support of domestic industry, necessarily endeavours so to direct that industry that its produce may be of the greatest possible value.

The produce of industry is what it adds to the subject or materials upon which it is employed. In proportion as the value of this produce is great or small, so will likewise be the profits of the employer. But it is only for the sake of profit that any man employs a capital in the support of industry; and he will always, therefore, endeavour to employ it in the support of that industry of which the produce is likely to be of the greatest value, or to exchange for the greatest quantity either of money or of other goods.

But the annual revenue of every society is always precisely equal to the exchangeable value of the whole annual produce of its industry, or rather is precisely the same thing with that exchangeable value. As every individual, therefore, endeavours as much as he can both to employ his capital in the support of domestic industry, and so to direct that industry that its produce may be of the greatest value; every individual necessarily labours to render the annual revenue of the society as great as he can. He generally, indeed, neither intends to promote the public interest, nor knows how much he is promoting it. By preferring the support of domestic to that of foreign industry, he intends only his own security; and by directing that industry in such a manner as its produce may be of the greatest value, he intends only his own gain, and he is in this, as in many other cases, led by an invisible hand to promote an end which was no part of his intention. Nor is it always the worse for the society that it was no part of it. By pursuing his own interest he frequently promotes that of the society more effectually than when he really intends to promote it. I have never known much good done by those who affected to trade for the public good. It is an affectation, indeed, not very common among merchants, and very few words need be employed in dissuading them from it.

What is the species of domestic industry which his capital can employ, and of which the produce is likely to be of the greatest value, every individual, it is evident, can, in his local situation, judge much better than any statesman or lawgiver can do for him. The statesman who should attempt to direct private people in what manner they ought to employ their capitals would not only load himself with a most unnecessary attention, but assume an authority which could safely be trusted, not only to no single person, but to no council or senate whatever, and which would nowhere be so dangerous as in the hands of a man who had folly and presumption enough to fancy himself fit to exercise it.

To give the monopoly of the home market to the produce of domestic industry, in any particular art or manufacture, is in some measure to direct private people in what manner they ought to employ their capitals, and must, in almost all cases, be either a useless or a hurtful regulation. If the produce of domestic can be brought there as cheap as that of foreign industry, the regulation is evidently useless. If it cannot, it must generally be hurtful. It is the maxim of every prudent master of a family never to attempt to make at home what it will cost him more to make than to buy. The tailor does not attempt to make his own shoes, but buys them from the shoemaker. The shoemaker does not attempt to make his own clothes, but employs a tailor. The farmer attempts to make neither the one nor the other, but employs those different artificers. All of them find it for their interest to employ their whole industry in a way in which they have some advantage over their neighbours, and to purchase with a part of its produce, or what is the same thing, with the price of a part of it, whatever else they have occasion for.

What is prudence in the conduct of every private family can scarce be folly in that of a great kingdom. If a foreign country can supply us with a commodity cheaper than we ourselves can make it, better buy it of them with some part of the produce of our own industry employed in a way in which we have some advantage. The general industry of the country, being always in proportion to the capital which employs it, will not thereby be diminished, no more than that of the above mentioned artificers; but only left to find out the way in which it can be employed with the greatest advantage. It is certainly not employed to the greatest advantage when it is thus directed towards an object which it can buy cheaper than it can make. The value of its annual produce is certainly more or less diminished when it is thus turned away from producing commodities evidently of more value than the commodity which it is directed to produce. According to the supposition, that commodity could be purchased from foreign countries cheaper than it can be made at home. It could, therefore, have been purchased with a part only of the commodities, or, what is the same thing, with a part only of the price of the commodities, which the industry employed by an equal capital would have produced at home, had it been left to follow its natural course. The industry of the country, therefore, is thus turned away from a more to a less advantageous employment, and the exchangeable value of its annual produce, instead of being increased, according to the intention of the lawgiver, must necessarily be diminished by every such regulation.

By means of such regulations, indeed, a particular manufacture may sometimes be acquired sooner than it could have been otherwise, and after a certain time may be made at home as cheap or cheaper than in the foreign country. But though the industry of the society may be thus carried with advantage into a particular channel sooner than it could have been otherwise, it will by no means follow that the sum total, either of its industry, or of its revenue, can ever be augmented by any such regulation. The industry of the society can augment only in proportion as its capital augments, and its capital can augment only in proportion to what can be gradually saved out of its revenue. But the immediate effect of every such regulation is to diminish its revenue, and what diminishes its revenue is certainly not very likely to augment its capital faster than it would have augmented of its own accord had both capital and industry been left to find out their natural employments.

Though for want of such regulations the society should never acquire the proposed manufacture, it would not, upon that account, necessarily be the poorer in any one period of its duration. In every period of its duration its whole capital and industry might still have been employed, though upon different objects, in the manner that was most advantageous at the time. In every period its revenue might have been the greatest which its capital could afford, and both capital and revenue might have been augmented with the greatest possible rapidity.

The natural advantages which one country has over another in producing particular commodities are sometimes so great that it is acknowledged by all the world to be in vain to struggle with them. By means of glasses, hotbeds, and hot walls, very good grapes can be raised in Scotland, and very good wine too can be made of them at about thirty times the expense for which at least equally good can be brought from foreign countries. Would it be a reasonable law to prohibit the importation of all foreign wines merely to encourage the making of claret and burgundy in Scotland? But if there would be a manifest absurdity in turning towards any employment thirty times more of the capital and industry of the country than would be necessary to purchase from foreign countries an equal quantity of the commodities wanted, there must be an absurdity, though not altogether so glaring, yet exactly of the same kind, in turning towards any such employment a thirtieth, or even a three-hundredth, part more of either. Whether the advantages which one country has over another be natural or acquired is in this respect of no consequence. As long as the one country has those advantages, and the other wants them, it will always be more advantageous for the latter rather to buy of the former than to make. It is an acquired advantage only, which one artificer has over his neighbour, who exercises another trade; and yet they both find it more advantageous to buy of one another than to make what does not belong to their particular trades. ◆

QUESTIONS

1. Why does Smith suggest that merchants prefer to employ their capital as close to home as possible?

2. What is the invisible hand and what does it do?

3. What is the proper role for governments in directing the economy of a country and its trade? Why?

I, Pencil

Leonard E. Read (1898–1983)

I am a lead pencil—the ordinary wooden pencil familiar to all boys and girls and adults who can read and write.

Writing is both my vocation and my avocation; that's all I do.

You may wonder why I should write a genealogy. Well, to begin with, my story is interesting. And, next, I am a mystery—more so than a tree or a sunset or even a flash of lightning. But, sadly, I am taken for granted by those who use me, as if I were a mere incident and without background. This supercilious attitude relegates me to the level of the commonplace. This is a species of the grievous error in which mankind cannot too long persist without peril. For, as a wise man observed, "We are perishing for want of wonder, not for want of wonders."

I, Pencil, simple though I appear to be, merit your wonder and awe, a claim I shall attempt to prove. In fact, if you can understand me—no, that's too much to ask of anyone—if you can become aware of the miraculousness which I symbolize, you can help save the freedom mankind is so unhappily losing. I have a profound lesson to teach. And I can teach this lesson better than can an automobile or an airplane or a mechanical dishwasher because—well, because I am seemingly so simple.

Simple? Yet, *not a single person on the face of this earth knows how to make me.* This sounds fantastic, doesn't it? Especially when it is realized that there are about one and one-half billion of my kind produced in the U.S.A. each year.

Pick me up and look me over. What do you see? Not much meets the eye—there's some wood, lacquer, the printed labeling, graphite lead, a bit of metal, and an eraser.

Just as you cannot trace your family tree back very far, so is it impossible for me to name and explain all my antecedents. But I would like to suggest enough of them to impress upon you the richness and complexity of my background.

My family tree begins with what in fact is a tree, a cedar of straight grain that grows in Northern California and Oregon. Now contemplate all the saws and trucks and rope and the countless other gear used in harvesting and carting the cedar logs to the railroad siding. Think of all the persons and the numberless skills that went into their fabrication: the mining of ore, the making of steel and its refinement into saws, axes, motors; the growing of hemp and bringing it through all the stages to heavy and strong rope; the logging camps with their beds and mess halls, the cookery and the raising of all the foods. Why, untold thousands of persons had a hand in every cup of coffee the loggers drink!

The logs are shipped to a mill in San Leandro, California. Can you imagine the individuals who make flat cars and rails and railroad engines and who construct and install the communication systems incidental thereto? These legions are among my antecedents.

Consider the millwork in San Leandro. The cedar logs are cut into small, pencil-length slats less than one-fourth of an inch in thickness. These are kiln dried and then tinted for the same reason women put rouge on their faces. People prefer that I look pretty, not a pallid white. The slats are waxed and kiln dried again. How many skills went into the making of the tint and the kilns, into supplying the heat, the light and power, the belts, motors, and all the other things a mill requires? Sweepers in the mill among my ancestors? Yes, and included are the men who poured the concrete for the dam of a Pacific Gas & Electric Company hydroplant which supplies the mill's power!

Don't overlook the ancestors present and distant who have a hand in transporting sixty carloads of slats across the nation from California to Wilkes-Barre!

COMPLICATED MACHINERY

Once in the pencil factory—$4,000,000 in machinery and building, all capital accumulated by thrifty and saving parents of mine—

each slat is given eight grooves by a complex machine, after which another machine lays leads in every other slat, applies glue, and places another slat atop—a lead sandwich, so to speak. Seven brothers and I are mechanically carved from this "wood-clinched" sandwich.

My "lead" itself—it contains no lead at all—is complex. The graphite is mined in Ceylon. Consider these miners and those who make their many tools and the makers of the paper sacks in which the graphite is shipped and those who make the string that ties the sacks and those who put them aboard ships and those who make the ships. Even the lighthouse keepers along the way assisted in my birth—and the harbor pilots.

The graphite is mixed with clay from Mississippi in which ammonium hydroxide is used in the refining process. Then wetting agents are added such as sulfonated tallow—animal fats chemically reacted with sulfuric acid. After passing through numerous machines, the mixture finally appears as endless extrusions—as from a sausage grinder—cut to size, dried, and baked for several hours at 1,850 degrees Fahrenheit. To increase their strength and smoothness the leads are then treated with a hot mixture which includes candelilla wax from Mexico, paraffin wax, and hydrogenated natural fats.

My cedar receives six coats of lacquer. Do you know all of the ingredients of lacquer? Who would think that the growers of castor beans and the refiners of castor oil are a part of it? They are. Why, even the processes by which the lacquer is made a beautiful yellow involves the skills of more persons than one can enumerate!

Observe the labeling. That's a film formed by applying heat to carbon black mixed with resins. How do you make resins and what, pray, is carbon black?

My bit of metal—the ferrule—is brass. Think of all the persons who mine zinc and copper and those who have the skills to make shiny sheet brass from these products of nature. Those black rings on my ferrule are black nickel. What is black nickel and how is it applied? The complete story of why the center of my ferrule has no black nickel on it would take pages to explain.

Then there's my crowning glory, inelegantly referred to in the trade as "the plug," the part man uses to erase the errors he makes with me. An ingredient called "factice" is what does the erasing. It is a rubber-like product made by reacting rape seed oil from the Dutch East Indies with sulfur chloride. Rubber, contrary to the common notion, is only for binding purposes. Then, too, there are numerous vulcanizing and accelerating agents. The pumice comes from Italy; and the pigment which gives "the plug" its color is cadmium sulfide.

Does anyone wish to challenge my earlier assertion that no single person on the face of this earth knows how to make me?

No One Knows

Actually, millions of human beings have had a hand in my creation, no one of whom even knows more than a very few of the others. Now, you may say that I go too far in relating the picker of a coffee berry in far off Brazil and food growers elsewhere to my creation; that this is an extreme position. I shall stand by my claim. There isn't a single person in all these millions, including the president of the pencil company, who contributes more than a tiny, infinitesimal bit of know-how. From the standpoint of know-how the only difference between the miner of graphite in Ceylon and the logger in Oregon is in the *type* of know-how. Neither the miner nor the logger can be dispensed with, any more than can the chemist at the factory or the worker in the oil field—paraffin being a by-product of petroleum.

Here is an astounding fact: Neither the worker in the oil field nor the chemist nor the digger of graphite or clay nor any who mans or makes the ships or trains or trucks nor the one who runs the machine that does the knurling on my bit of metal nor the president of the company performs his singular task because he wants me. Each one wants me less, perhaps, than does a child in the first grade. Indeed, there are some among this vast multitude who never saw a pencil nor would they know how to use one. Their motivation is other than me. Perhaps it is something like this: Each of these millions sees that he can thus exchange his tiny know-how for the goods and services he needs or wants. I may or may not be among these items.

There is a fact still more astounding: The absence of a master mind, of anyone dictating or forcibly directing these countless actions which bring me into being. No trace of such a person can be found. Instead, we find the Invisible Hand at work. This is the mystery to which I earlier referred. ♦

QUESTIONS

1. Why does Read think that the existence of a pencil is miraculous?

2. What does Read mean when he says that no one person knows how to make a pencil?

3. Why do so many people contribute to the making of a pencil if almost none of them actually wants a pencil?

4. Who, according to Read, coordinates all the many steps needed to make a pencil?

FROM *THE FABLE OF THE BEES*

Bernard Mandeville (1670–1733)

THE PREFACE

Laws and Government are to the Political Bodies of Civil Societies, what the Vital Spirits and Life itself are to the Natural Bodies of Animated Creatures; and as those that study the Anatomy of Dead Carkasses may see, that the chief Organs and nicest Springs more immediately required to continue the Motion of our Machine, are not hard Bones, strong Muscles and Nerves, nor the smooth white Skin that so beautifully covers them, but small trifling Films and little Pipes that are either overlook'd, or else seem inconsiderable to Vulgar Eyes; so they that examine into the Nature of Man, abstract from Art and Education, may observe, that what renders him a Sociable Animal, consists not in his desire of Company, good Nature, Pity, Affability, and other Graces of a fair Outside; but that his vilest and most hateful Qualities are the most necessary Accomplishments to fit him for the largest, and according to the World, the happiest and most flourishing Societies.

The following Fable, in which what I have said is set forth at large was printed above eight Years ago[1] in a Six-penny Pamphlet call'd, *The grumbling Hive; or Knaves turn'd Honest*; and being soon after Pyrated, cry'd about the Streets in a Half-penny Sheet. Since the first publishing of it I have met with several that either wilfully or ignorantly mistaking the Design, would have it, that the Scope of it was a Satyr upon Virtue and Morality, and the whole wrote for the Encouragement of Vice. This made me resolve, whenever it should be reprinted, some way or other to inform the Reader of the real Intent this little Poem was wrote with. I do not dignify these few loose Lines with the Name of Poem, that I would have the Reader expect any Poetry in them, but barely because they are Rhime, and I am in reallity puzled what name to give them; for they are neither Heroick nor Pastoral, Satyr, Burlesque nor Heroicomick; to be a Tale they want Probability, and the whole is rather too long for a Fable. All I can say of them is, that they are a Story told in Dogrel, which without the least design of being witty, I have endeavour'd to do in as easy and familiar a Manner as I was able: The Reader shall be welcome to call them what he pleases. 'Twas said of *Montagne*, that he was pretty well vers'd in the Defects of Mankind, but unacquainted with the Excellencies of Humane Nature: If I fare no worse, I shall think my self well used.

What Country soever in the Universe is to be understood by the Bee-Hive represented here, it is evident from what is said of the Laws and Constitution of it, the Glory, Wealth, Power and Industry of its Inhabitants, that it must be a large, rich and warlike Nation that is happily governed by a limited Monarchy. The Satyr therefore to be met with in the following Lines upon the several Professions and Callings, and almost every Degree and Station of People was not made to injure and point to particular Persons, but only to shew the Vileness of the Ingredients that all together compose the wholesome Mixture of a well order'd Society; in order to extol the wonderful Power of Political Wisdom, by the help of which so beautiful a Machine is rais'd from the most contemptible Branches. For the main design of the Fable, (as it is breefly explain'd in the Moral) is to shew the Impossibility of enjoying all the most elegant Comforts of Life that are to be met with in an industrious, wealthy and powerful Nation, and at the same time be bless'd with all the Virtue and Innocence that can be wish'd for in a Golden Age; from thence to expose the Unreasonableness and Folly of those, that desirous of being an opulent and flourishing People, and wonderfully greedy after all the Benefits they can receive as such, are yet always murmuring at and exclaiming against those Vices and Inconveniencies, that from the beginning of the World to this present Day, have been inseparable from all Kingdoms and States that ever were fam'd for Strength, Riches and Politeness at the same time.

To do this, I first slightly touch upon some of the Faults and Corruptions the several Professions and Callings are generally charg'd with. After that I shew that those very Vices of every Particular Person by skilful Management were made subservient to the Grandeur and worldly Happiness of the whole. Lastly, by setting forth what of necessity must be the consequence of general Honesty and Virtue and National Temperance, Innocence and Content, I demonstrate that if Mankind could be cured of the Failings they are Naturally guilty of they would cease to be capable of being rais'd into such vast, potent and polite Societies, as they have been under the several great Commonwealths and Monarchies that have flourish'd since the Creation.

If you ask me why I have done all this, *cui bono*? And what Good these Notions will produce; truly besides the Reader's Diversion, I believe none at all; but if I was ask'd what Naturally ought to be expected from 'em, I wou'd answer, That in the first Place the People, who continually find Fault with others, by reading them, would be taught to look at home, and examining their own Consciences, be made asham'd of always railing at what they are more or less guilty of themselves; and that in the next, those who are so fond of the Ease and Comforts, and reap all the Benefits that are the Consequence of a great and flourishing Nation, would learn more patiently to submit to those Inconveniencies, which no Government upon Earth can remedy, when they should see the Impossibility of enjoying any great share of the first, without partaking likewise of the latter.

This I say ought naturally to be expected from the publishing of these Notions, if People were to be made better by any thing that could be said to them; but Mankind having for so many Ages remain'd still the same, notwithstanding the many instructive and elaborate Writings, by which their Amendment has been endeavour'd, I am not so vain as to hope for better success from so inconsiderable a Trifle.

Having allow'd the small Advantage this little Whim is likely to produce, I think my self oblig'd to shew, that it cannot be prejudicial to any; for what is published, if it does no good, ought at least to do no harm: In order to this I have made some Explanatory Notes, to which the Reader will find himself refer'd in those Passages that seem to be most liable to Exceptions.

The Censorious that never saw the *Grumbling Hive*, will tell me, that whatever I may talk of the Fable, it not taking up a Tenth part of the Book, was only contriv'd to introduce the *Remark*s; that instead of clearing up the doubtful or obscure Places, I have only pitch'd upon such as I had a Mind to expatiate upon; and that far from striving to extenuate the Errors committed before I have made Bad worse, and shewn my self a more bare-fac'd Champion for Vice, in the rambling Digressions, than I had done in the Fable itself.

I shall spend no time in answering these Accusations; where Men are prejudic'd, the best Apologies are lost; and I know that those who think it Criminal to suppose a necessity of Vice in any Case whatever, will never be reconcil'd to any part of the Performance; but if this be thoroughly examin'd all the Offence it can give, must result from the wrong Inferences that may perhaps be drawn from it, and which I desire no body to make. When I assert, that Vices are inseparable from great and potent Societies, and that it is impossible their Wealth and Grandeur should subsist without, I do not say that the particular Members of them who are guilty of any, should not be continually reprov'd, or not be punish'd for them when they grow into Crimes.

There are, I believe, few People in *London*, of those that are at any time forc'd to go a foot, but what could wish the Streets of it much cleaner than generally they are; whilst they regard nothing but their own Cloaths and private Conveniency; but when once they come to consider, that what offends them is the result of the Plenty, great Traffick and Opulency of that mighty City, if they have any Concern in its Welfare, they will hardly ever wish to see the Streets of it less dirty. For if we mind the Materials of all sorts that must supply such an infinite number of Trades and Handicrafts, as are always going forward; the vast quantity of Victuals, Drink and Fewel that are daily consum'd in it, and the Waste and Superfluities that must be produc'd from them; the multitudes of

Horses and other Cattle that are always daw-bing the Streets, the Carts, Coaches and more heavy Carriages that are perpetually wearing and breaking the Pavement of them, and above all the numberless swarms of People that are continually harrassing and trampling through every part of them. If, I say, we mind all these, we shall find that every Moment must produce new Filth, and considering how far distant the great Streets are from the River side, what Cost and Care soever be bestow'd to remove the Nastiness almost as fast as 'tis made, it is impossible *London* should be more cleanly before it is less flourishing. Now would I ask if a good Citizen, in consideration of what has been said, might not assert, that dirty Streets are a necessary Evil inseparable from the Felicity of *London* without being the least hindrance to the cleaning of Shoes, or sweeping of Streets, and consequently without any Prejudice either to the *Blackguard*[2] or the Scavingers.

But if, without any regard to the Interest or Happiness of the City, the Question was put, What Place I thought most pleasant to walk in? No body can doubt but before the stinking Streets of *London*, I would esteem a fragrant Garden, or a shady Grove in the Country. In the same manner, if laying aside all worldly Greatness and Vain Glory, I should be ask'd where I thought it was most probable that Men might enjoy true Happiness, I would prefer a small peaceable Society, in which Men neither envy'd nor esteem'd by Neighbours, should be contented to live upon the Natural Product of the Spot they inhabit, to a vast multitude abounding in Wealth and Power, that should always be conquering others by their Arms Abroad, and debauching themselves by Foreign Luxury at Home.[3]

Thus much I had said to the Reader in the First Edition; and have added nothing by way of Preface in the Second. But since that, a violent Out-cry has been made against the Book, exactly answering the Expectation I always had of the Justice, the Wisdom, the Charity, and Fair-dealing of those whose Goodwill I despair'd of. It has been presented by the Grand-Jury, and condemn'd by thousands who never saw a word of it. It has been preach'd against before my Lord Mayor; and an utter Refutation of it is

daily expected from a Reverend Divine, who has call'd me Names in the Advertisements, and threatened to answer me in two Months time for above five Months together.[4] What I have to say for my self, the Reader will see in my Vindication at the end of the Book, where he will likewise find the Grand-Jury's Presentment, and a Letter to the Right Honourable Lord C. which is very Rhetorical beyond Argument or Connexion. The Author shews a fine Talent for Invectives, and great Sagacity in discovering Atheism, where others can find none. He is zealous against wicked Books, points at the Fable of the Bees, and is very angry with the Author: he bestows four strong Epithets on the Enormity of his Guilt, and by several elegant Innuendo's to the Multitude, as the Danger there is in suffering such Authors to live, and the Vengeance of Heaven upon a whole Nation, very charitably recommends him to their Care.

Considering the length of this Epistle, and that it is not wholly levell'd at me only, I thought at first to have made some Extracts from it of what related to my self; but finding, on a nearer Enquiry, that what concern'd me was so blended and interwoven with what did not, I was oblig'd to trouble the Reader with it entire; not without Hopes that, prolix as it is, the Extravagancy of it will be entertaining to those who have perused the Treatise it condemns with so much Horror.

A Spacious Hive well stock'd with Bees,
That lived in Luxury and Ease;
And yet as fam'd for Laws and Arms,
As yielding large and early Swarms;
Was counted the great Nursery
Of Sciences and Industry.
No Bees had better Government,
More Fickleness, or less Content.
They were not Slaves to Tyranny,
Nor ruled by wild Democracy;
But Kings, that could not wrong, because
Their Power was circumscrib'd by Laws.

These Insects lived like Men, and all
Our Actions they perform'd in small:
They did whatever's done in Town,
And what belongs to Sword, or Gown:
Tho' th' Artful Works, by nimble Slight
Of minute Limbs, 'scaped Human Sight;
Yet we've no Engines, Labourers,
Ships, Castles, Arms, Artificers,

Craft, Science, Shop, or Instrument;
But they had an Equivalent:
Which, since their Language is unknown,
Must be call'd, as we do our own.
As grant, that among other Things
They wanted Dice, yet they had Kings;
And those had Guards; from whence we may
Justly conclude, they had some Play;
Unless a Regiment be shewn
10   Of Soldiers, that make us of none.

Vast Numbers thronged the fruitful Hive;
Yet those vast Numbers made 'em thrive;
Millions endeavouring to supply
Each other's Lust and Vanity;
Whilst other Millions were employ'd,
To see their Handy-works destroy'd;
They furnish'd half the Universe;
Yet had more Work than Labourers.
Some with vast Stocks, and little Pains
20   Jump'd into Business of great Gains;
And some were damn'd to Sythes and Spades,
And all those hard laborious Trades;
Where willing Wretches daily sweat,
And wear out Strength and Limbs to eat:
(A.) Whilst others follow'd Mysteries,
To which few Folks bind 'Prentices;
That want no Stock, but that of Brass,
And may set up without a Cross;⁵
As Sharpers, Parasites, Pimps, Players,
30   Pick-Pockets, Coiners, Quacks, Sooth-Sayers,
And all those, that, in Enmity
With down-right Working, cunningly
Convert to their own Use the Labour
Of their good-natur'd heedless Neighbour.
(B.) These were called Knaves; but, bar the Name,
The grave Industrious were the Same.
All Trades and Places knew some Cheat,
No Calling was without Deceit.

The Lawyers, of whose Art the Basis
40   Was raising Feuds and splitting Cases,
Opposed all Registers, that Cheats
Might make more Work with dipt Estates;⁶
As were't unlawful, that one's own,
Without a Law-Suit, should be known.
They kept off Hearings wilfully,
To finger the refreshing Fee;
And to defend a wicked Cause,
Examin'd and survey'd the Laws;
As Burglars Shops and Houses do;
50   To find out where they'd best break through.

Physicians valued Fame and Wealth
Above the drooping Patient's Health,
Or their own Skill: The greatest Part
Study'd, instead of Rules of Art,
Grave pensive Looks, and dull Behaviour;

To gain th' Apothecary's Favour,
The Praise of Mid-wives, Priests and all,
That served at Birth, or Funeral;
To bear with th' ever-talking Tribe,
And hear my Lady's Aunt prescribe;   60
With formal Smile, and kind How d'ye,
To fawn on all the Family;
And, which of all the greatest Curse is,
T' endure th' Impertinence of Nurses.

Among the many Priests of *Jove*,
Hir'd to draw Blessings from Above,
Some few were learn'd and eloquent,
But Thousands hot and ignorant:
Yet all past Muster, that could hide
Their Sloth, Lust, Avarice and Pride;   70
For which they were as famed, as Taylors
For Cabbage; or for Brandy, Sailors:
Some meagre look'd, and meanly clad
Would mystically pray for Bread,
Meaning by that an ample Store,
Yet lit'rally receiv'd no more;
And, whilst these holy Drudges starv'd,
The lazy Ones, for which they serv'd,
Indulg'd their Ease, with all the Graces
Of Health and Plenty in their Faces.   80

(C.) The Soldiers, that were forced to fight,
If they survived, got Honour by't;
Tho' some, that shunn'd the bloody Fray,
Had Limbs shot off, that ran away:
Some valiant Gen'rals fought the Foe;
Others took Bribes to let them go:
Some ventur'd always, where 'twas warm;
Lost now a Leg, and then an Arm;
Till quite disabled, and put by,
They lived on half their Salary;   90
Whilst others never came in Play,
And staid at Home for Double Pay.

Their Kings were serv'd; but Knavishly
Cheated by their own Ministry;
Many, that for their Welfare slaved,
Robbing the very Crown they saved:
Pensions were small, and they lived high,
Yet boasted of their Honesty.
Calling, whene'er they strain'd their Right,
The slipp'ry Trick a Perquisite;   100
And, when Folks understood their Cant,
They chang'd that for Emolument;
Unwilling to be short, or plain,
In any thing concerning Gain:
(D.) For there was not a Bee, but would
Get more, I won't say, that he should;
But than he dared to let them know,
(E.) That pay'd for't; as your Gamesters do,
That, tho' at fair Play, ne'er will own
Before the Losers what they've won.   110

But who can all their Frauds repeat!
The very Stuff, which in the Street
They sold for Dirt t'enrich the Ground,
Was often by the Buyers found
Sophisticated with a Quarter
Of Good-for-nothing, Stones and Mortar;
Tho' Flail had little Cause to mutter,
Who sold the other Salt for Butter.

Justice her self, famed for fair Dealing,
10 By Blindness had not lost her Feeling;
Her Left Hand, which the Scales should hold,
Had often dropt 'em, bribed with Gold;
And, tho' she seem'd impartial,
Where Punishment was corporal,
Pretended to a reg'lar Course,
In Murther, and all Crimes of Force;
Tho' some, first Pillory'd for Cheating,
Were hang'd in Hemp of their own beating;
Yet, it was thought, the Sword she bore
20 Check'd but the Desp'rate and the Poor;
That, urged by mere Necessity,
Were tied up to the wretched Tree
For Crimes, which not deserv'd that Fate,
But to secure the Rich, and Great.

Thus every Part was full of Vice,
Yet the whole Mass a Paradice;
Flatter'd in Peace, and fear'd in Wars
They were th' Esteem of Foreigners,
And lavish of their Wealth and Lives,
30 The Ballance of all other Hives.
Such were the Blessings of that State;
Their Crimes conspired to make 'em Great;
(F.) And Vertue, who from Politicks
Had learn'd a Thousand cunning Tricks,
Was, by their happy Influence,
Made Friends with Vice: And ever since
(G.) The Worst of all the Multitude
Did something for the common Good.

This was the State's Craft, that maintain'd
40 The Whole, of which each Part complain'd:
This, as in Musick Harmony,
Made Jarrings in the Main agree;
(H.) Parties directly opposite
Assist each oth'r, as 'twere for Spight;
And Temp'rance with Sobriety
Serve Drunkenness and Gluttony.

(I.) The Root of evil Avarice,
That damn'd ill-natur'd baneful Vice,
Was Slave to Prodigality,
50 (K.) That Noble Sin; (L.) whilst Luxury
Employ'd a Million of the Poor,
(M.) And odious Pride a Million more.
(N.) Envy it self, and Vanity
Were Ministers of Industry;

Their darling Folly, Fickleness
In Diet, Furniture, and Dress,
That strange ridic'lous Vice, was made
The very Wheel, that turn'd the Trade.
Their Laws and Cloaths were equally
Objects of Mutability;   60
For, what was well done for a Time,
In half a Year became a Crime;
Yet whilst they alter'd thus their Laws,
Still finding and correcting Flaws,
They mended by Inconstancy
Faults, which no Prudence could foresee.

Thus Vice nursed Ingenuity,
Which join'd with Time, and Industry
Had carry'd Life's Conveniencies,
(O.) It's real Pleasures, Comforts, Ease,   70
(P.) To such a Height, the very Poor
Lived better than the Rich before;
And nothing could be added more:

How vain is Mortal Happiness!
Had they but known the Bounds of Bliss;
And, that Perfection here below
Is more, than Gods can well bestow,
The grumbling Brutes had been content
With Ministers and Government.
But they, at every ill Success,   80
Like Creatures lost without Redress,
Cursed Politicians, Armies, Fleets,
Whilst every one cry'd, Damn the Cheats,
And would, tho' Conscious of his own,
In Others barb'rously bear none.

One, that had got a Princely Store,
By cheating Master, King, and Poor,
Dared cry aloud; The Land must sink
For all it's Fraud; And whom d'ye think
The Sermonizing Rascal chid?   90
A Glover that sold Lamb for Kid.

The least Thing was not done amiss,
Or cross'd the Publick Business;
But all the Rogues cry'd brazenly,
Good Gods, had we but Honesty!
Merc'ry smiled at th'Impudence;
And Others call'd it want of Sence,
Always to rail at what they loved:
But Jove, with Indignation moved,
At last in Anger swore, he'd rid   100
The bawling Hive of Fraud, and did.
The very Moment it departs,
And Honesty fills all their Hearts;
There shews 'em, like th' Instructive Tree,
Those Crimes, which they're ashamed to see;
Which now in Silence they confess,
By Blushing at their Uglyness;
Like Children, that would hide their Faults,

And by their Colour own their Thoughts;
Imag'ning, when they're look'd upon,
That Others see, what they have done.

But, Oh ye Gods! What Consternation,
How vast and sudden was th'Alteration!
In half an Hour, the Nation round,
Meat fell a Penny in the Pound.
The Mask Hypocrisie's flung down,
From the great Statesman to the Clown'
10 And some, in borrow'd Looks well known,
Appear'd like Strangers in their own.
The Bar was silent from that Day;
For now the willing Debtors pay,
Ev'n what's by Creditors forgot;
Who quitted them, that had it not.
Those, that were in the Wrong, stood mute,
And dropt the patch'd vexatious Suit.
On which, since nothing less can thrive,
Than Lawyers in an honest Hive,
20 All, except those, that got enough,
With Ink-horns by their Sides troop'd off.

Justice hang'd some, set others free;
And, after Goal delivery,
Her Presence be'ng no more requir'd,
With all her Train, and Pomp retir'd.
First march'd some Smiths, with Locks and
Grates,
Fetters, and Doors with Iron-Plates;
Next Goalers, Turnkeys, and Assistants:
30 Before the Goddess, at some distance,
Her chief and faithful Minister
Squire Catch,[7] the Laws great Finisher,
Bore not th' imaginary Sword,
But his own Tools, an Ax and Cord:
Then on a Cloud the Hood-wink'd fair
Justice her self was push'd by Air:
About her Chariot, and behind,
Were Sergeants, Bums of every kind,[8]
Tip-staffs, and all those Officers,
40 That squeeze a Living out of Tears.
Tho' Physick lived, whilst Folks were ill,
None would prescribe, but Bees of Skill;
Which, through the Hive dispers'd so wide,
That none of 'em had need to ride,
Waved vain Disputes; and strove to free
The Patients of their Misery;
Left Drugs in cheating Countries grown,
And used the Product of their own,
Knowing the Gods sent no Disease
50 To Nations without Remedies.

Their Clergy rouz'd from Laziness,
Laid not their Charge on Journey-Bees;[9]
But serv'd themselves, exempt from Vice,
The Gods with Pray'r and Sacrifice;

All those, that were unfit, or knew,
Their Service might be spared, withdrew:
Nor was there Business for so many,
(If th' Honest stand in need of any.)
Few only with the High-Priest staid,
To whom the rest Obedience paid: 60
Himself, employ'd in holy Cares,
Resign'd to others State-Affairs:
He chased no Starv'ling from his Door,
Nor pinch'd the Wages of the Poor;
But at his House the Hungry's fed,
The Hireling finds unmeasur'd Bread,
The needy Trav'ler Board and Bed.

Among the King's great Ministers,
And all th' inferiour Officers
The Change was great; (Q.) for frugally   70
They now lived on their Salary.
That a poor Bee should Ten times come,
To ask his Due, a trifling Sum,
And by some well-hir'd Clerk be made,
To give a Crown, or ne'er be paid;
Would now be call'd a down-right Cheat,
Tho' formerly a Perquisite.
All Places; managed first by Three,
Who watch'd each other's Knavery,
And often for a Fellow-feeling,   80
Promoted one another's Stealing;
Are happily supply'd by one;
By which some Thousands more are gone.

(R.) No Honour now could be content,
To live, and owe for what was spent.
Liv'ries in Brokers Shops are hung,
They part with Coaches for a Song;
Sell stately Horses by whole Sets;
And Country-Houses to pay Debts.

Vain Cost is shunn'd as much as Fraud;   90
They have no Forces kept Abroad;
Laugh at th' Esteem of Foreigners,
And empty Glory got by Wars;
They fight but for their Country's Sake,
When Right or Liberty's at Stake.

Now mind the glorious Hive, and see,
How Honesty and Trade agree:
The Shew is gone, it thins apace;
And looks with quite another Face,
For 'twas not only that they went,   100
By whom vast Sums were Yearly spent;
But Multitudes, that lived on them,
Were daily forc'd to do the Same.
In vain to other Trades they'd fly,
All were o're-stock'd accordingly.

The Price of Land, and Houses falls;
Mirac'lous Palaces, whose Walls,
Like those of *Thebes*, were raised by Play,

Are to be lett; whilst the once gay,
Well-seated Houshold Gods would be
More pleased t'expire in Flames, than see
The mean Inscription on the Door
Smile at the lofty Ones they bore.
The Building Trade is quite destroy'd,
Artificers are not employ'd;
(S.) No Limner for his Art is famed;
Stone-cutters, Carvers are not named.

10   Those, that remain'd, grown temp'rate, strive,
Not how to spend; but how to live;
And, when they paid their Tavern Score,
Resolv'd to enter it no more:
No Vintners Jilt in all the Hive
Could wear now Cloth of Gold and thrive;
Nor *Torcol* such vast Sums advance,
For *Burgundy* and *Ortelans*;
The Courtier's gone, that with his Miss
Supp'd at his House on *Christmass* Peas;
20   Spending as much in Two Hours stay,
As keeps a Troop of Horse a Day.

    The haughty *Chloe*, to live Great,
Had made her (T.) Husband rob the State:
But now she sells her Furniture,
Which th' *Indies* had been ransack'd for;
Contracts th' expensive Bill of Fare,
And wears her strong Suit a whole Year:
The slight and fickle Age is past;
And Cloaths, as well as Fashions last.
30   Weavers that join'd rich Silk with Plate,
And all the Trades subordinate,
Are gone. Still Peace and Plenty reign,
And every Thing is cheap, tho' plain:
Kind Nature, free from Gard'ners Force,
Allows all Fruits in her own Course;
But Rarities cannot be had,
Where Pains to get 'em are not paid.

    As Pride and Luxury decrease,
So by degrees they leave the Seas.
40   Not Merchants now; but Companies
Remove whole Manufacturies.
All Arts and Crafts neglected lie;
(V.) Content the Bane of Industry,
Makes 'em admire their homely Store,
And neither seek, nor covet more.

    So few in the vast Hive remain;
The Hundredth part they can't maintain
Against th' Insults of numerous Foes;
Whom yet they valiantly oppose:
50   Till some well-fenced Retreat is found;
And here they die, or stand their Ground.
No Hireling in their Armies known;
But bravely fighting for their own,
Their Courage and Integrity

At last were crown'd with Victory.
They triumph'd not without their Cost;
For many Thousand Bees were lost.
Hard'ned with Toils, and Exercise
They counted Ease it self a Vice;
Which so improved their Temperance;   60
That, to avoid Extravagance,
They flew into a hollow Tree,
Blest with Content and Honesty.

THE MORAL

Then leave Complaints: Fools only strive
(X.) To make a Great an honest Hive.
(Y.) T' enjoy the World's conveniencies,
Be famed in War, yet live in Ease
Without great Vices, is a vain
Eutopia seated in the Brain.   70
Fraud, Luxury, and Pride must live
Whilst we the Benefits receive.
Hunger's a dreadful Plague, no doubt,
Yet who digests or thrives without?
Do we not owe the Growth of Wine
To the dry shabby crooked Vine?
Which, whilst its Shutes neglected stood,
Choak'd other Plants, and ran to Wood;
But blest us with its Noble Fruit;
As soon as it was tied, and cut: 80
So Vice is beneficial found,
When it's by Justice lopt, and bound;
Nay, where the People would be great,
As necessary to the State
As Hunger is to make 'em eat.
Bare Vertue can't make Nations live
In Splendour; they, that would revive
A Golden Age, must be as free,
For Acorns, as for Honesty.
Finis ◆   90

ENDNOTES

1. In 1714.

2. A shoeblack.—Ed.

3. The remainder of 'The Preface' was added in 1724.—Ed.

4. William Hendley, author of *A Defence of the Charity Schools* (1724).—Ed.

5. Without a groat to their name.—Ed.

6. Mortgaged estates.—Ed.

7. Jack Ketch, the proverbial hangman.—Ed.   100

8. Bailiffs.—Ed.

9. Curates.—Ed.

QUESTIONS

1. According to Mandeville, which is the most important source of benefits to society: the best virtues of individual human beings or their worst vices?

2. Are members in the hive happy with their situations?

3. How do individuals do well in the economy of the hive?

4. What leads to general decreases in prosperity?

WEALTH FROM *ESSAYS AND JOURNALS*

Ralph Waldo Emerson (1803–1882)

Who shall tell what did befall,
Far away in time, when once,
Over the lifeless ball,
Hung idle stars and suns?
What god the element obeyed?
Wings of what wind the lichen bore,
Wafting the puny seeds of power,
Which, lodged in rock, the rock abrade?
And well the primal pioneer
10　Knew the strong task to it assigned,
Patient through Heaven's enormous year
To build in matter home for mind.
From air the creeping centuries drew
The matted thicket low and wide,
This must the leaves of ages strew
The granite slab to clothe and hide,
Ere wheat can wave its golden pride.
What smiths, and in what furnace, rolled
In dizzy æons dim and mute
20　The reeling brain can ill compute
Copper and iron, lead, and gold?
What oldest star the fame can save
Of races perishing to pave
The planet with a floor of lime?
Dust is their pyramid and mole:
Who saw what ferns and palms were pressed
Under the tumbling mountain's breast,
In the safe herbal of the coal?
But when the quarried means were piled,
30　All is waste and worthless, till
Arrives the wise selecting will,
And, out of slime and chaos, Wit
Draws the threads of fair and fit.
Then temples rose, and towns, and marts,
The shop of toil, the hall of arts;
Then flew the sail across the seas
To feed the North from tropic trees;
The storm-wind wove, the torrent span,
Where they were bid the rivers ran;
40　New slaves fulfilled the poet's dream,
Galvanic wire, strong-shouldered steam.
Then docks were built, and crops were stored,
And ingots added to the hoard.
But, though light-headed man forget,
Remembering Matter pays her debt:
Still, through her motes and masses, draw
Electric thrills and ties of Law,
Which bind the strengths of Nature wild
To the conscience of a child.

As soon as a stranger is introduced into any company, one of the first questions which all wish to have answered, is, How does that man get his living? And with reason. He is no whole man until he knows how to earn a blameless livelihood. Society is barbarous until every industrious man can get his living without dishonest customs.

Every man is a consumer, and ought to be a producer. He fails to make his place good in the world unless he not only pays his debt but also adds something to the common wealth. Nor can he do justice to his genius without making some larger demand on the world than a bard subsistence. He is by constitution expensive, and needs to be rich.

Wealth has its source in applications of the mind to nature, from the rudest strokes of spade and axe up to the last secrets of art. Intimate ties subsist between thought and all production, because a better order is equivalent to vast amounts of brute labor. The forces and the resistances are nature's, but the mind acts in bringing things from where they abound to where they are wanted; in wise combining; in directing the practice of the useful arts, and in the creation of finer values by fine art, by eloquence, by song, or the reproductions of memory. Wealth is in applications of mind to nature; and the art of getting rich consists not in industry, much less in saving, but in a better order, in timeless, in being at the right spot. One man has stronger arms or longer legs; another sees by the course of streams and growth of markets where land will be wanted, makes a clearing to the river, goes to sleep and wakes up rich. Steam is no stronger now than it was a hundred years ago; but is put to better use. A clever fellow was acquainted with the expansive force of steam; he also saw the wealth of wheat and grass rotting in Michigan. Then he cunningly screws on the steam-pipe to the wheat-crop. Puff now, O Steam! The steam puffs and expands as before, but this time it is dragging all Michigan at its back to hungry New York and hungry England. Coal lay in ledges under the ground since the Flood, until a laborer with pick and windlass brings it to the surface. We may well call it black diamonds. Every basket is power and civilization.

For coal is a portable climate. It carries the heat of the tropics to Labrador and the polar circle; and it is the means of transporting itself whithersoever it is wanted. Watt and Stephenson whispered in the ear of mankind their secret, that a *half ounce of coal could draw two tons a mile*, and coal carries coal, by rail and by boat, to make Canada as warm as Calcutta; and with its comfort brings its industrial power.

When the farmer's peaches are taken from under the tree and carried into town, they have a new look and a hundredfold value over the fruit which grew on the same bough and lies fulsomely on the ground. The craft of the merchant is this bringing a thing from where it abounds to where it is costly.

Wealth begins in a tight roof that keeps the rain and wind out; in a good pump that yields you plenty of sweet water; in two suits of clothes, so to change your dress when you are wet; in dry sticks to burn, in a good double-wick lamp, and three meals; in a horse or a locomotive to cross the land, in a boat to cross the sea; in tools to work with, in books to read; and so in giving on all sides by tools and auxiliaries the greatest possible extension to our powers; as if it added feet and hands and eyes and blood, length to the day, and knowledge and good will.

Wealth begins with these articles of necessity. And here we must recite the iron law which nature thunders in these northern climates. First she requires that each man should feed himself. If happily his fathers have left him no inheritance, he must go to work, and by making his wants less or his gains more, he must draw himself out of that state of pain and insult in which she forces the beggar to lie. She gives him no rest until this is done; she starves, taunts and torments him, takes away warmth, laughter, sleep, friends and daylight, until he has fought his way to his own loaf. Then, less peremptorily but still with sting enough, she urges him to the acquisition of such things as belong to him. Every warehouse and shop-window, every fruit-tree, every thought of every hour opens a new want to him which it concerns his power and dignity to gratify. It is of no use to argue the wants down: the philosophers have laid the greatness of man in making his wants few, but will a man content himself with a hut and a handful of dried pease? He is born to be rich. He is thoroughly related; and is tempted out by his appetites and fancies to the conquest of this and that piece of nature, until he finds his wellbeing in the use of his planet, and of more planets than his own. Wealth requires, besides the crust of bread and the roof—the freedom of the city, the freedom of the earth, travelling, machinery, the benefits of science, music and fine arts, the best culture and the best company. He is the rich man who can avail himself of all men's faculties. He is the richest man who knows how to draw a benefit from the labors of the greatest number of men, of men in distant countries and in past times. The same correspondence that is between thirst in the stomach and water in the spring, exists between the whole of man and the whole of nature. The elements offer their service to him. The sea, washing the equator and the poles, offers its perilous aid and the power and empire that follow it—day by day to his craft and audacity. "Beware of me," it says, "but if you can hold me, I am the key to all the lands." Fire offers, on its side, an equal power. Fire, steam, lightning, gravity, ledges of rock, mines of iron, lead, quicksilver, tin and gold; forests of all woods; fruits of all climates; animals of all habits; the powers of tillage; the fabrics of his chemic laboratory; the webs of his loom; the masculine draught of his loco-motive; the talismans of the machine-shop; all grand and subtile things, minerals, gases, ethers, passions, war, trade, government—are his natural playmates, and according to the excellence of the machinery in each human being is his attraction for the instruments he is to employ. The world is his tool-chest, and he is successful, or his education is carried on just so far, as is the marriage of his faculties with nature, or the degree in which he takes up things into himself.

The strong race is strong on these terms. The Saxons are the merchants of the world; now, for a thousand years, the leading race, and by nothing more than their quality of personal independence, and in its special modification, pecuniary independence. No reliance for bread and games on the government; no clanship, no patriarchal style of living by the revenues of a chief, no marrying-on, no system of clientship suits them; but every man must pay his scot. The English are prosperous and peaceable, with their habit of considering that every man must take care of himself and has himself to thank if he do not maintain and improve his position in society.

The subject of economy mixes itself with morals, inasmuch as it is a peremptory point of virtue that a man's independence be secured. Poverty demoralizes. A man in debt is so far a slave, and Wall Street thinks it easy for a *millionaire* to be a man of his word, a man of honor, but that in failing circumstances no man can be relied on to keep his integrity. And when one observes in the hotels and palaces of our Atlantic capitals the habit of expense, the riot of the senses, the absence of bonds, clanship, fellow-feeling of any kind—he feels that when a man or a woman is driven to the wall, the chances of integrity are frightfully diminished; as if virtue were coming to be a luxury which few could afford, or, as Burke said, "at a market almost too high for humanity." He may fix his inventory of necessities and of enjoyments on what scale he pleases, but if he wishes the power and privilege of thought, the chalking out his own career and having society on his own terms, he must bring his wants within his proper power to satisfy.

The manly part is to do with might and main what you can do. The world is full of tops who never did anything and who had persuaded beauties and men of genius to wear their fop livery; and these will deliver the fop opinion, that it is not respectable to be seen earning a living; that it is much more respectable to spend without earning; and this doctrine of the snake will come also from the elect sons of light; for wise men are not wise at all hours, and will speak five times from their taste or their humor, to once from their reason. The brave workman, who might betray his feeling of it in his manners, if he do not succumb in his practice, must replace the grace or elegance forfeited, by the merit of the work done. No matter whether he makes shoes, or statutes, or laws. It is the privilege of any human work which is well done to invest the doer with a certain haughtiness. He can well afford not to conciliate, whose faithful work will answer for him. The mechanic at his bench carries a quiet heart and assured manners, and deals on even terms with men of any condition. The artist has made his picture so true that it disconcerts criticism. The statue is so beautiful that it contracts no stain from the market, but makes the market a silent gallery for itself. The case of the young lawyer was pitiful to disgust—a paltry matter of buttons or tweezercases; but the determined youth saw in it an aperture to insert his dangerous wedges, made the insignificance of the thing forgotten, and gave fame by his sense and energy to the name and affairs of the Tittleton snuffbox factory.

Society in large towns is babyish, and wealth is made a toy. The life of pleasure is so ostentatious that the shallow observer must believe that this is the agreed best use of wealth, and whatever is pretended, it ends in cosseting. But if this were the main use of surplus capital, it would bring us to barricades, burned towns and tomahawks, presently. Men of sense esteem wealth to be the assimilation of nature to themselves, the converting of the sap and juices of the planet to the incarnation and nutriment of their design. Power is what they want, not candy—power to execute their design, power to give legs and feet form and actuality to their thought; which, to a clear-sighted man, appears the end for which the universe exists, and all its resources might be well applied. Columbus thinks that the sphere is a problem for practical navigation as well as for closet geometry, and looks on all kings and peoples as cowardly landsmen until they dare fit him out. Few men on the planet have more truly belonged to it. But he was forced to leave much of his map blank. His successors inherited his map, and inherited his fury to complete it.

So the men of the mine, telegraph, mill, map and survey—the monomaniacs who talk up their project in marts and offices and entreat men to subscribe—how did our factories get built? how did North America get netted with iron rails, except by the importunity of these orators who dragged all the prudent men in? Is party the madness of many for the gain of a few? This *speculative* genius is the madness of a few for the gain of the world. The projectors are sacrificed, but the public is the gainer. Each of these idealists, working after his thought, would make it tyrannical, if he could. He is met and antagonized by other speculators as hot as he. The equilibrium is preserved by these counteractions, as one tree keeps down another in the forest, that it may not absorb all the sap in the ground. And the supply in nature of railroad-presidents, cooper-miners, grand-junctioners, smoke-burners, fire-annihilators, etc., is limited by the same law which keeps the proportion in the supply of carbon, of alum, and of hydrogen.

To be rich is to have a ticket of admission to the master-works and chief men of each race. It is to have the sea, by voyaging; to visit the mountains, Niagara, the Nile, the desert, Rome, Paris, Constantinople; to see galleries, libraries, arsenals, manufactories. The reader of Humboldt's Cosmos follows the marches of a man whose eyes, ears and mind are armed by all the science, art and implements which mankind have anywhere accumulated, and who is using these to add to the stock. So it is with Denon, Beckford, Belzoni, Wilkinson, Layard, Kane, Lepsius and Livingstone. "The rich man," says Saadi, "is everywhere expected and at home." The rich take up something more of the world into man's life. They include the country as well as the town, the ocean-side, the White Hills, the Far West and the old European homesteads of man, in their notion of available material. The world is his who has money to go over it. He arrives at the seashore and a sumptuous ship has floored and carpeted for him the stormy Atlantic, and made it a luxurious hotel, amid the horrors of tempests. The Persians say, "'Tis the same to him who wears a shoe, as if the whole earth were covered with leather."

Kings are said to have long arms, but every man should have long arms, and should pluck his living, his instruments, his power and his knowing, from the sun, moon and stars. Is not there the demand to be rich legitimate? Yet I have never seen a rich man. I have never seen a rich man as rich as all men ought to be or with an adequate command of nature. The pulpit and the press have many commonplaces denouncing the thirst for wealth; but if men should take these moralists at their word and leave off aiming to be rich, the moralists would rush to rekindle at all hazards this love of power in the people, lest civilization should be undone. Men are urged by their ideas to acquire the command over nature. Ages derive a culture from the wealth of Roman Cæsars, Leo Tenths, magnificent Kings of France, Grand Dukes of Tuscany, Dukes of Devonshire, Townleys, Vernons and Peels, in England; or whatever great proprietors. It is the interest of all men that there should be Vaticans and Louvres full of noble works of art; British Museums and French Gardens of Plants, Philadelphia Academies of Natural History, Bodleian, Ambrosian, Royal, Congressional Libraries. It is the interest of all that there should be Exploring Expeditions; Captain Cooks to voyage round the world, Rosses, Franklins, Richardsons and Kanes, to find the magnetic and the geographic poles. We are all richer for the measurement of a degree of latitude on the earth's surface. Our navigation is safer for the chart. How intimately our knowledge of the system of the Universe rests on that!—and a true economy in a state or an individual will forget its frugality in behalf of claims like these.

Whilst it is each man's interest that not only ease and convenience of living, but also wealth or surplus product should exist somewhere, it need not be in his hands. Often it is very undesirable to him. Goethe said well, "No body should be rich but those who understand it." Some men are born to own, and can animate all their possessions. Others cannot: their owning is not graceful; seems to be a compromise of their character; they seem to steal their own dividends. They should own who can administer, not they who hoard and conceal; not they who, the greater proprietors they are, are only the greater beggars, but they whose work carves out work for more, opens a path for all. For he is the rich man in whom the people are rich, and he is the poor man in whom the people are poor; and how to give all access to the masterpieces of art and nature, is the problem of civilization. The socialism of our day has done good service in setting men on thinking how certain civilizing benefits, now only enjoyed by the opulent, can be enjoyed by all. For example, the providing to each man the means and apparatus of science and of the arts. There are many articles good for occasional use, for few man are able to own. Every man wishes to see the ring of Saturn, the satellites and belts of Jupiter and Mars, the mountains and craters in the moon; yet how few can buy a telescope! and of those, scarcely one would like the trouble of keeping it in order and exhibiting it. So of electrical and chemical apparatus, and many the like things. Every man may have occasion to consult books which he does not care to possess, such as cyclopaedias, dictionaries, tables, charts, maps and other public documents; pictures also of birds, beasts, fishes, shells, trees, flowers, whose names he desires to know.

There is a refining influence from the arts of Design on a prepared mind which is as positive as that of music, and not to be supplied from any other resource. But pictures, engravings, statues and casts, beside their first cost, entail expenses, as of galleries and keepers for the exhibition; and the use which any man can make of them is rare, and their value too is much enhanced by the numbers of men who can share their enjoyment. In the Greek cities it was reckoned profane that any person should pretend a property in a work of art, which belonged to all who could behold it. I think sometimes, could I only have music on my own terms; could I live in a great city and know where I could go whenever I wished the ablution and inundation of musical waves—that were a bath and a medicine.

If properties of this kind were owned by states, towns and lyceums, they would draw the bonds of neighborhood closer. A town would exist to an intellectual purpose. In Europe, where the feudal forms secure the permanence of wealth in certain families, those families buy and preserve these things and lay them open to the public. But in America, where democratic institutions divide every estate into small portions after a few years, the public should step into the place of these proprietors, and provide this culture and inspiration for the citizens.

Man was born to be rich, or inevitably grows rich by the use of his faculties; by the union of thought with nature. Property is an intellectual production. The game requires coolness, right reasoning, promptness and patience in the players. Cultivated labor drives out brute labor. An infinite number of shrewd men, in infinite years, have arrived at certain best and shortest ways of doing, and this accumulated skill in arts, cultures, harvesting, curings, manufactures, navigators, exchanges, constitutes the worth of our world today.

Commerce is a game of skill, which every man cannot play, which few men can play well. The right merchant is one who has the just average of faculties we call *common-sense*; a man of a strong affinity for facts, who makes up his decision on what he has seen. He is thoroughly persuaded of the truths of arithmetic. There is always a reason, *in the man*, for his good or bad fortune, and so in making money. Men talk as if there were some magic about this, and believe in magic, in all parts of life. He knows that all goes on the old road, pound for pound, cent for cent—for every effect a perfect cause—and that good luck is another name for tenacity of purpose. He insures himself in every transaction, and likes small and sure gains. Probity and closeness to the facts are the basis, but the masters of the art add a certain long arithmetic. The problem is to combine many and remote operations with the accuracy and adherence to the facts which is easy in near and small transactions; so to arrive at gigantic results, without any compromise of safety. Napoleon was fond of telling the story of the Marseilles banker who said to his visitor, surprised at the contrast between the splendor of the banker's chateau and hospitality and the meanness of the counting-room in which he had seen him—"Young man, you are too young to understand how masses are formed; the true and only power, whether composed of money, water or men; it is all alike; a mass is an immense centre of motion, but it must be begun, it must be kept up"—and he might have added that the way in which it must be begun and kept up is by obedience to the law of particles.

Success consists in close appliance to the laws of the world, and since those laws are intellectual and moral, an intellectual and moral obedience. Political Economy is as good a book wherein to read the life of man and the ascendancy of laws over all private and hostile influences, as any Bible which has come down to us.

Money is representative, and follows the nature and fortunes of the owner. The coin is a delicate meter of civil, social and moral changes. The farmer is covetous of his dollar, and with reason. It is no waif to him. He knows how many strokes of labor it represents. His bones ache with the days' work that earned it. He knows how much land it represents—how much rain, frost and sunshine. He knows that, in the dollar, he gives you so much discretion and patience, so much hoeing and threshing. Try to lift his dollar; you must lift all that weight. In the city, where money follows the skit of a pen or a lucky rise in exchange, it comes to be looked on as light. I wish the farmer held it dearer, and would spend it only for real bread; force for force.

The farmer's dollar is heavy and the clerk's is light and nimble; leaps out of his pocket; jumps on to card and faro-tables; but still more curious is its susceptibility to metaphysical changes. It is the finest barometer of social storms, and announces revolutions.

Every step of civil advancement makes every man's dollar worth more. In California, the country where it grew—what would it buy? A few years since, it would buy a shanty, dysentery, hunger, bad company and crime. There are wide countries, like Siberia, where it would buy little else today than some petty mitigation of suffering. In Rome it will buy beauty and magnificence. Forty years ago, a dollar would not buy much in Boston. Now it will buy a great deal more in our old towns, thanks to railroads, telegraphs, steamers, and the contemporaneous growth of New York and the whole country. Yet there are many goods appertaining to a capital city which are not yet purchasable here, no, not with a mountain of dollars. A dollar in Florida is not worth a dollar in Massachusetts. A dollar is not value, but representative of value, and, at last, of moral values. A dollar is rated for the corn it will buy, or to speak strictly, not for the corn or house-room, but for Athenian corn, and Roman house-room—for the wit, probity and power which we eat bread and dwell in houses to share and exert. Wealth is mental; wealth is moral. The value of a dollar is, to buy just things; a dollar goes on increasing in value with all the genius and all the virtue of the world. A dollar in a university is worth more than a dollar in a jail; in a temperate, schooled, law-abiding community than in some sink of crime, where dice, knives and arsenic are in constant play.

The Bank-Note Detector is a useful publication. But the current dollar, silver or paper, is itself the detector of the right and wrong where it circulates. Is it not instantly enhanced by the increase of equity? If a trader refuses to sell his vote, or adheres to some odious right, he makes so much more equity in Massachusetts; and every acre in the state is more worth, in the hour of his action. If you take out of State Street the ten honestest merchants and put in ten roguish persons controlling the same amount of capital, the rates of insurance will indicate it; the soundness of banks will show it; the highways will be less secure; the schools will feel it, the children will bring home their little dose of the poison; the judge will sit less firmly on the bench, and his decisions be less upright; he has lost so much support and constraint, which all need; and the pulpit will betray it, in a laxer rule of life. An apple-tree, if you take out every day for a number of days a load of loam and put in a load of sand about its roots, will find it out. An apple-tree is a stupid kind of creature, but if this treatment be pursued for a short time I think it would begin to mistrust something. And if you should take out of the powerful class engaged in trade a hundred good men and put in a hundred bad, or what is just the same thing, introduce a demoralizing institution, would not the dollar, which is not much stupider than an apple-tree, presently find it out? The value of a dollar is social, as it is created by society. Every man who removes into this city with any purchasable talent or skill in him, gives to every man's labour in the city a new worth. If a talent is anywhere born into the world, the community of nations is enriched; and much more with a new degree of probity. The expense of crime, one of the prin-

cipal charges of every nation, is so far stopped. In Europe, crime is observed to increase or abate with the price of bread. If the Rothschilds at Paris do not accept bills, the people at Manchester, at Paisley, at Birmingham are forced into the highway, and landlords are shot down in Ireland. The police-records attest it. The vibrations are presently felt in New York, New Orleans and Chicago. Not much otherwise the economical power touches the masses through the political lords. Rothschild refuses the Russian loan, and there is peace and the harvests are saved. He takes it, and there is war and an agitation through a large portion of mankind, with every hideous result, ending in revolution and a new order.

Wealth brings with it its own checks and balances. The basis of political economy is non-interference. The only safe rule is found in the self-adjusting meter of demand and supply. Do not legislate. Meddle, and you snap the sinews with your sumptuary laws. Give no bounties, make equal laws, secure life and property, and you need not give alms. Open the doors of opportunity to talent and virtue and they will do themselves justice, and property will not be in bad hands. In a free and just commonwealth, property rushes from the idle and imbecile to the industrious brave and persevering.

The laws of nature play through trade, as a toy-battery exhibits the effects of electricity. The level of the sea is not more surely kept than is the equilibrium of value in society by the demand and supply; and artifice or legislation punishes itself by reactions, gluts and bankruptcies. The sublime laws play indifferently through atoms and galaxies. Whoever knows what happens in the getting and spending of a loaf of bread and a pint of beer, that no wishing will change the rigorous limits of pints and penny loaves; that for all that is consumed so much less remains in the basket and pot, but what is gone out of these is not wasted, but well spent, if it nourish his body and enable him to finish his task—know all of political economy that the budgets of empires can teach him. The interest of petty economy is this symbolization of the great economy; the way in which a house and a private man's methods tally with the solar system and the laws of give and take, throughout nature; and however wary we are of the falsehoods and petty tricks which we suicidally play off on each other, every man has a certain satisfaction whenever his dealing touches on the inevitable facts; when he sees that things themselves dictate the price, as they always tend to do, and, in large manufacturers, are seen to do. Your paper is not fine or coarse enough—is too heavy, or too thin. The manufacturer says he will furnish you with just that thickness or thinness you want; the pattern is quite indifferent to him; here is his schedule—any variety of paper, as cheaper or dearer, with the prices annexed. A pound of paper costs so much, and you may have it made up in any pattern you fancy.

There is in all our dealings a self-regulation that supersedes chaffering. You will rent a house, but must have it cheap. The owner can reduce the rent, but so he incapacitates himself from making proper repairs, and the tenant gets not the house he would have, but a worse one; besides that, a relation a little injurious is established between landlord and tenant. You dismiss your laborer, saying, "Patrick, I shall send for you as soon as I cannot do without you." Patrick goes off contented, for he knows that the weeds will grow with the potatoes, the vines must be planted, next week, and however unwilling you may be, the cantaloupes, crook-necks and cucumbers will send for him. Who but must wish that all labor and value should stand on the same simple and surly market? If it is the best of its kind, it will. We must have joiner, locksmith, planter, priest, poet, doctor, cook, weaver, ostler, each in turn, through the year.

If a St. Michael's pear sells for a shilling, it costs a shilling to raise it. If, in Boston, the best securities offer twelve per cent for money, they have just six per cent of insecurity. You may not see that the fine pear costs you a shilling, but it costs the community so much more. The shilling represents the number of enemies the pear has, and the amount of risk in ripening it. The price of coal shows the narrowness of the coal-field, and a compulsory confinement of the miners to a certain district. All salaries are reckoned on contingent as well as on actual service. "If the wind were always southwest by west,"

said the skipper, "women might take ships to sea." One might say that all things are of one price; that nothing is cheap or dear, and that the apparent disparities that strike us are only a shopman's trick of concealing the damage in your bargain. A youth coming into the city from his native New Hampshire farm, with its hard fare still fresh in his remembrance, boards at a first-class hotel, and believes he must somehow have outwitted Dr. Franklin and Malthus, for luxuries are cheap. But he pays for the one convenience of a better dinner, by the loss of some of the richest social and educational advantages. He has lost what guards! what incentives! He will perhaps find by and by that he left the Muses at the door of the hotel, and found the Furies inside. Money often costs too much, and power and pleasure are not cheap. The ancient poet said, "The gods sell all things at a fair price."

There is an example of the compensations in the commercial history of this country. When the European wars threw the carrying trade of the world, from 1800 to 1812, into American bottoms, a seizure was now and then made of an American ship. Of course the loss was serious to the owner, but the country was indemnified; for we charged threepence a pound for carrying cotton, sixpence for tobacco, and so on; which paid for the risk and loss, and brought into the country an immense prosperity, early marriages, private wealth, the building of cities and of states; and after the war was over, we received compensation over and above, by treaty, for all the seizures. Well, the Americans grew rich and great. But the pay-day comes round. Britain, France and Germany, which our extraordinary profits had impoverished, send out, attracted by the fame of our advantages, first their thousands, then their millions of poor people, to share the crop. At first we employ them, and increase our prosperity; but in the artificial system of society and of protected labor, which we also have adopted and enlarged, there come presently checks and stoppages. Then we refuse to employ these poor men. But they will not be so answered. They go into the poor-rates, and though we refuse wages, we must now pay the same amount in the form of taxes. Again, it turns out that the largest proportion of crimes are committed by foreigners. The cost of the crime and the expense of courts and of prisons we must bear, and the standing army of preventive police we must pay. The cost of education of the posterity of this great colony, I will not compute. But the gross amount of these costs will begin to pay back what we thought was a net gain from our transatlantic customers of 1800. It is vain to refuse this payment. We cannot get rid of these people, and we cannot get rid of their will to be supported. That has become an inevitable element of our politics; and, for their votes, each of the dominant parties courts and assists them to get it executed. Moreover, we have to pay, not what would have contented them at home, but what they have learned to think necessary here; so that opinion, fancy and all manner of moral considerations complicate the problem.

There are few measures of economy which will bear to be named without disgust; for the subject is tender and we may easily have too much of it, and therein resembles the hideous animalcules of which our bodies are built up— which, offensive in the particular, yet compose valuable and effective masses. Our nature and genius force us to respect ends whilst we use means. We must use the means, and yet, in our most accurate using somehow screen and cloak them, as we can only give them any beauty by a reflection of the glory of the end. That is the good head, which serves the end and commands the means. The rabble are corrupted by their means; the means are too strong for them, and they desert their end.

1.   The first of these measures is that each man's expense must proceed from his character. As long as your genius buys, the investment is safe, though you spend like a monarch. Nature arms each man with some faculty which enables him to do easily some feat impossible to any other, and thus makes him necessary to society. This native determination guides his labor and his spending. He wants an equipment of means and tools proper to his talent. And to save on this point were to neutralize the special strength and helpfulness of each mind. Do your work, respecting the excellence of the work, and not its acceptableness.

This is so much economy that, rightly read, it is the sum of economy. Profligacy consists not in spending years of time or chests of money— but in spending them off the line of your career. The crime which bankrupts men and states is job-work—declining from your main design, to serve a turn here or there. Nothing is beneath you, if it is in the direction of your life; nothing is great or desirable if it is off from that. I think we are entitled here to draw a straight line and say that society can never prosper but must always be bankrupt, until every man does that which he was created to do.

Spend for your expense, and retrench the expense which is not yours. Allston the painter was wont to say that he built a plain house, and filled it with plain furniture, because he would hold out no bribe to any to visit him who had not similar tastes to his own. We are sympathetic, and, like children, want everything we see. But it is a large stride to independence, when a man, in the discovery of his proper talent, has sunk the necessity for false expenses. As the betrothed maiden by one secure affection is relieved from a system of slaveries—the daily inculcated necessity of pleasing all—so the man who has found what he can do, can spend on that and leave all other spending. Montaigne said, "When he was a younger brother, he went brave in dress and equipage, but afterward his chateau and farms might answer for him." Let a man who belongs to the class of nobles, those namely who have found out that they can do something, relieve himself of all vague squandering on objects not his. Let the realist not mind appearances. Let him delegate to others the costly courtesies and decorations of social life. The virtues are economists, but some of the vices are also. Thus, next to humility, I have noticed that pride is a pretty good husband. A good pride is, as I reckon it, worth from five hundred to fifteen hundred a year. Pride is handsome, economical; pride eradicates so many vices, letting none subsist but itself, that it seems as if it were a great gain to exchange vanity for pride. Pride can go without domestics, without fine clothes, can live in a house with two rooms, can eat potato, purslain, beans, lyed corn, can work on the soil, can travel afoot, can talk with poor men, or sit silent well contented in fine saloons. But vanity costs money, labor, horses, men, women, health and peace, and is still nothing at last; a long way leading nowhere. Only one drawback; proud people are intolerably selfish, and the vain are gentle and giving.

Art is a jealous mistress, and if a man have a genius for painting, poetry, music, architecture or philosophy, he makes a bad husband and an ill provide, and should be wise in season and not fetter himself with duties which will embitter his days and spoil him for his proper work. We had in this region, twenty years ago, among our educated men, a sort of Arcadian fanaticism, a passionate desire to go upon the land and unite farming to intellectual pursuits. Many effected their purpose and made the experiment, and some became downright ploughmen; but all were cured of their faith that scholarship and practical farming (I mean, with one's own hands) could be united.

With brow bent, with firm intent, the pale scholar leaves his desk to draw a freer breath and get a juster statement of his thought, in the garden-walk. He stoops to pull up a purslain or a dock that is choking the young corn, and finds there are two; close behind the last is a third; he reaches out his hand to a fourth, behind that are four thousand and one. He is heated and untuned, and by and by wakes up from his idiot dream of chickweed and red-root, to remember his morning though, and to find that with his adamantine purposes he has been duped by a dandelion. A garden is like those pernicious machineries we read of every month in the newspapers, which catch a man's coat-skirt or his hand and draw in his arm, his leg and his whole body to irresistible destruction. In an evil hour he pulled down his wall and added a field to his homestead. No land is bad, but land is worse. If a man own land, the land owns him. Now let him leave home, if he dare. Every tree and graft, every hill of melons, row of corn, or quickset hedge; all he has done and all he means to do, stand in his way like duns, when he would go out of his gate. The devotion to these vines and trees he finds poisonous. Long free walks, a circuit of miles, free his brain and serve his body. Long marches are no hardship to him. He believes his composes

easily on the hills. But this pottering in a few square yards of garden is dispiriting and drivelling. The smell of the plants had drugged him and robbed him of energy. He finds a catalepsy in his bones. He grows peevish and poorspirited. The genius of reading and of gardening are antagonistic, like resinous and vitreous electricity. One is concentrative in sparks and shocks; the other is diffuse strength; so that each disqualifies its workman for the other's duties.

An engraver, whose hands must be of an exquisite delicacy of stroke, should not lay stone walls. Sir David Brewster gives exact instructions for microscopic observation: "Lie down on your back, and hold the single lens and object over your eye," etc., etc. How much more the seeker of abstract truth, who needs periods of isolation and rapt concentration and almost a going out of the body to think!

2.   Spend after your genius, *and by system.* Nature goes by rule, not by sallies and saltations. There must be system in the economies. Saving and unexpensiveness will not keep the most pathetic family from ruin, nor will bigger incomes make free spending safe. The secret of success lies never in the amount of money, but in the relation of income to outgo; as, after expense has been fixed at a certain point, then new and steady rills of income, though never so small, being added, wealth begins. But in ordinary, as means increase, spending increases faster, so that large incomes, in England and elsewhere, are found not to help matters—the eating quality of debt does not relax its voracity. When the cholera is in the potato, what is the use of planting larger crops? In England, the richest country in the universe, I was assured by shrewd observers that great lords and ladies had no more guineas to give away than other people; that liberality with money is as rare and as immediately famous a virtue as it is here. Want is a growing giant whom the coat of Have was never large enough to cover. I remember in Warwickshire to have been shown a fair manor, still in the same name as in Shakespeare's time. The rent-roll I was told is some fourteen thousand pounds a year; but when the second son of the late proprietor was

born, the father was perplexed how to provide for him. The eldest son must inherit the manor; what to do with this supernumerary? He was advised to breed him for the Church and to settle him in the rectorship which was in the gift of the family; which was done. It is a general rule in that country that bigger incomes do not help anybody. It is commonly observed that a sudden wealth, like a prize drawn in a lottery or a large bequest to a poor family, does not permanently enrich. They have served no apprenticeship to wealth, and with the rapid wealth come rapid claims which they do not know how to deny, and the treasure is quickly dissipated.

A system must be in every economy, or the best single expedients are of no avail. A farm is a good thing when it begins and ends with itself, and does not need a salary or a shop to eke it out. Thus, the cattle are a main link in the chain-ring. If the non-conformist or æsthetic farmer leaves out the cattle and does not also leave out the want which the cattle must supply, he must fill the gap by begging or stealing. When men now alive were born, the farm yielded everything that was consumed on it. The farm yielded no money, and the farmer got on without. If he fell sick, his neighbors came into his aid; each gave a day's work, or a half day; or lent his yoke of oxen, or his horse, and kept his work even; hoed his potatoes, mowed his hay, reaped his rye; well knowing that no man could afford to hire labor without selling his land. In autumn a farmer could sell an ox or a hog and get a little money to pay taxes withal. Now, the farmer buys almost all he consumes— tinware, cloth, sugar, tea, coffee, fish, coal, railroad tickets and newspapers.

A master in each art is required, because the practice is never with still or dead subjects, but they change in your hand. You think farm buildings and broad acres a solid property; but its value is flowing like water. It requires as much watching as if you were decanting wine from a cask. The farmer knows what to do with it, stops every leak, turns all the streamlets to one reservoir and decants wine; but a blunderhead comes out of Cornhill, tries his hand, and it all leaks away. So is it with granite streets or timber townships as with fruit or flowers. Nor

is any investment so permanent that it can be allowed to remain without incessant watching, as the history of each attempt to lock up an inheritance through two generations for an unborn inheritor may show.

When Mr. Cockayne takes a cottage in the country, and will keep his cow, he thinks a cow is a creature that is fed on hay and gives a pail of milk twice a day. But the cow that he buys gives milk for three months; then her bag dries up. What to do with a dry cow? who will buy her? Perhaps he bought also a yoke of oxen to do his work; but they get blown and lame. What to do with blown and lame oxen? The farmer fats his after the spring when work is done, and kills them in the fall. But how can Cockayne, who has no pastures, and leaves his cottage daily in the cars at business hours, be bothered with fatting and killing oxen? He plants trees; but there must be crops, to keep the trees in ploughed land. What shall be the crops? He will have nothing to do with trees, but will have grass. After a year or two the grass must be turned up and ploughed; now what crops? Credulous Cockayne!

3. Help comes in the custom of the country, and the rule of *Impera parendo*. The rule is not to dictate nor to insist on carrying out each of your schemes by ignorant willfulness, but to learn practically the secret spoken from all nature, that things themselves refuse to be mismanaged, and will show to the watchful their own law. Nobody need stir hand or foot. The custom of the country will do it all. I know not how to build or to plant; neither how to buy wood, nor what to do with the house-lot, the field, or the wood-lot, when bought. Never fear; it is all settled how it shall be, long beforehand, in the custom of the country—whether to sand or whether to clay it, when to plough, and how to dress, whether to grass or to corn; and you cannot help or hinder it. Nature has her own best mode of doing each thing, and she has somewhere told it plainly, if we will keep our eyes and ears open. If not, she will not be slow in undeceiving us when we prefer our own way to hers. How often we must remember the art of the surgeon, which, in replacing the broken bone, contents itself with releasing

the parts from false position; they fly into place by the action of the muscles. On this art of nature all our arts rely.

Of the two eminent engineers in the recent construction of railways in England, Mr. Brunel went straight from terminus to terminus, through mountains, over streams, crossing highways, cutting ducal estates in two, and shooting through this man's cellar and that man's attic window, and so arriving at his end, at great pleasure to geometers, but with cost to his company. Mr. Stephenson on the contrary, believing that the river knows the way, followed his valley as implicitly as our Western Railroad follows the Westfield River, and turned out to be the safest and cheapest engineer. We say the cows laid out Boston. Well, there are worse surveyors. Every pedestrian in our pastures has frequent occasion to thank the cows for cutting the best path through the thicket and over the hills; and travellers and Indians know the value of the buffalo-trail, which is sure to be the easiest possible pass through the ridge.

When a citizen fresh from Dock Square or Milk Street comes out and buys land in the country, his first thought is to a fine outlook from his windows; his library must command a western view; a sunset every day, bathing the shoulder of Blue Hills, Wachusett, and the peaks of Monadnoc and Uncanoonuc. What, thirty acres, and all this magnificence for fifteen hundred dollars! It would be cheap at fifty thousand. He proceeds at once, his eyes dim with tears of joy, to fix the spot for his cornerstone. But the man who is to level the ground thinks it will take many hundred loads of gravel to fill the hollow to the road. The stone-mason who should build the well thinks he shall have to dig forty feet; the baker doubts he shall never like to drive up to the door; the practical neighbor cavils at the position of the barn; and the citizen comes to know that his predecessor the farmer built the house in the right spot for the sun and wind, the spring, and water-drainage, and the convenience to the pasture, the garden, the field and the road. So Dock Square yields the point, and things have their own way. Use has made the farmer wise, and the foolish citizen learns to take his counsel. From step to step he comes at last to surrender at discretion. The farmer affects to take his orders; but the citizen says, You may ask me as often as you will, and in what ingenious forms, for an opinion concerning the mode of building my wall, or sinking my well, or laying out my acre, but the ball will rebound to you. These are matters on which I neither know nor need to know anything. These are questions which you and not I shall answer.

Not less, within doors, a system settles itself paramount and tyrannical over master and mistress, servant and child, cousin and acquaintance. 'Tis in vain that genius or virtue or energy of character strive and cry against it. This is fate. And 'tis very well that the poor husband reads in a book of a new way of living, and resolves to adopt it at home: let him go home and try it, if he dare.

4.   Another point of economy is to look for seed of the same kind as you sow, and not to hope to buy one kind with another kind. Friendship buys friendship; justice, justice; military merit, military success. Good husbandry finds wife, children and household. The good merchant, large gains, ships, stocks and money. The good poet, fame and literary credit; but not either, the other. Yet there is commonly a confusion of expectations on these points. Hotspur lives for the moment, praises himself for it, and despises Furlong, that he does not. Hotspur of course is poor, and Furlong a good provider. The odd circumstance is that Hotspur thinks it is a superiority in himself, this improvidence, which ought to be rewarded with Furlong's land.

I have not at all completed my design. But we must not leave the topic without casting one glance into the interior recesses. It is a doctrine of philosophy that man is a being of degrees; that there is nothing in the world which is not repeated in his body, his body being a sort of miniature or summary of the world; then that there is nothing in his body which is not repeated as in a celestial sphere in his mind; then, there is nothing in his brain which is not repeated in a higher sphere in his moral system.

5.   Now these things are so in nature. All things ascend, and the royal rule of economy

is that it should ascend also, or, whatever we do must always have a higher aim. Thus it is a maxim that money is another kind of blood, *Pecunia alter sanguis*; or, the estate of a man is only a larger kind of body, and admits of regimen analogous to his bodily circulations. So there is no maxim of the merchant which does not admit of an extended sense, e.g., "Best use of money is to pay debts': "Every business by itself"; "Best time is present time'" "The right investment is in tools of your trade"; and the like. The counting-room maxims liberally expounded are laws of the universe. The merchant's economy is a coarse symbol of the soul's economy. It is to spend for power and not for pleasure. It is to invest income; that is to say, to take up particulars into generals; days into integral eras—literary, emotive, practical—of its life, and still to ascend in its investment. The merchant has but one rule, *absorb and invest*; he is to be capitalist; the scraps and fillings must be gathered back into the crucible; the gas and smoke must be burnt, and earnings must not go to increase expense, but to capital again. Well, the man must be capitalist. Will he spend his income, or will he invest? His body and every organ is under the same law. His body is a jar in which the liquor of life is stored. Will he spend for pleasure? The way to ruin is short and facile. Will he not spend but hoard for power? It passes through the sacred fermentations, by that law of nature whereby everything climbs to higher platforms, and bodily vigor becomes mental and moral vigor. The bread he eats is first strength and animal spirits: it becomes, in higher laboratories, imaginary and thoughtful; and in still higher results, courage and endurance. This is the right compound interest; this is capital doubled, quadrupled, centupled; man raised to his highest power.

The true thrift is always to spend on the higher plane; to invest and invest, with keener avarice, that he may spend in spiritual creation and not in augmenting animal existence. Nor is the man enriched, in repeating the old experiments of animal sensation; nor unless through new powers and ascending pleasures he knows himself by the actual experience of higher good to be already on the way to the highest. ♦

QUESTIONS

1. What does Emerson mean by "Matter pays her debt"?

2. What is the essence of the business of the merchant?

3. What is the connection between economics and morality?

4. What does Emerson believe the single-mindedness of the entrepreneur creates?

5. What does Emerson think to be economic laws? What happens if people transgress them?

6. What does the price of a product reflect?

7. According to Emerson, what are the five measures of an economy?

THE VEINS OF WEALTH FROM *UNTO THIS LAST AND OTHER ESSAYS ON ART AND POLITICAL ECONOMY*

John Ruskin (1819–1900)

The answer which would be made by an ordinary political economist to the statements contained in the preceding paper [that political economy is unrealistic because it ignores the social bonds among people], is in few words as follows:—

"It is indeed true that certain advantages of a general nature may be obtained by the development of social affections. But political economists never professed, nor profess, to take advantages of a general nature into consideration. Our science is simply the science of getting rich. So far from being a fallacious or visionary one, it is found by experience to be practically effective. Persons who follow its precepts do actually become rich, and persons who disobey them become poor. Every capitalist of Europe has acquired his fortune by following the known laws of our science, and increases his capital daily by an adherence to them. It is vain to bring forward tricks of logic, against the force of accomplished facts. Every man of business knows by experience how money is made, and how it is lost."

Pardon me. Men of business do indeed know how they themselves made their money, or how, on occasion, they lost it. Playing a long-practised game, they are familiar with the chances of its cards, and can rightly explain their losses and gains. But they neither know who keeps the bank of the gambling-house, nor what other games may be played with the same cards, nor what other losses and gains, far away among the dark streets, are essentially, though invisibly, dependent on theirs in the lighted rooms. They have learned a few, and only a few, of the laws of mercantile economy; but not one of those of political economy.

Primarily, which is very notable and curious, I observe that men of business rarely know the meaning of the word "rich." At least if they know, they do not in their reasonings allow for the fact, that it is a relative word, implying its opposite "poor" as positively as the word "north" implies its opposite "south." Men nearly always speak and write as if riches were absolute, and it were possible, by following certain scientific precepts, for everybody to be rich. Whereas riches are a power like that of electricity, acting only through inequalities or negations of itself. The force of the guinea you have in your pocket depends wholly on the default of a guinea in your neighbour's pocket. If he did not want it, it would be of no use to you; the degree of power it possesses depends accurately upon the need or desire he has for it,—and the art of making yourself rich, in the ordinary mercantile economist's sense, is therefore equally and necessarily the art of keeping your neighbour poor.

I would not contend in this matter (and rarely in any matter), for the acceptance of terms. But I wish the reader clearly and deeply to understand the difference between the two economies, to which the terms "Political" and "Mercantile" might not unadvisably be attached.

Political economy (the economy of a state, or of citizens) consists simply in the production, preservation, and distribution, at fittest time and place, of useful or pleasurable things. The farmer who cuts his hay at the right time; the ship-wright who drives his bolts well home in sound wood; the builder who lays good bricks in well-tempered mortar; the housewife who takes care of her furniture in the parlour, and guards against all waste in her kitchen; and the singer who rightly disciplines, and never overstrains her voice: are all political economists in the true and final sense; adding continually to the riches and well-being of the nation to which they belong.

But mercantile economy, the economy of "merces" or of "pay," signifies the accumulation, in the hands of individuals, of legal or moral claim upon, or power over, the labour of others; every such claim implying precisely as much poverty or debt on one side, as it implies riches or right on the other.

It does not, therefore, necessarily involve an addition to the actual property, or well-being, of the State in which it exists. But since this commercial wealth, or power over labour, is nearly always convertible at once into real property, while real property is not always convertible at once into power over labour, the idea of riches among active men in civilized nations, generally refers to commercial wealth; and in estimating their possessions, they rather calculate the value of their horses and fields by the number of guineas they could get for them, than the value of their guineas by the number of horses and fields they could buy with them.

There is, however, another reason for this habit of mind; namely, that an accumulation of real property is of little use to its owner, unless, together with it, he has commercial power over labour. Thus, suppose any person to be put in possession of a large estate of fruitful land, with rich beds of gold in its gravel, countless herds of cattle in its pastures; houses, and gardens, and storehouses full of useful stores; but suppose, after all, that he could get no servants? In order that he may be able to have servants, some one in his neighbourhood must be poor, and in want of his gold—or his corn. Assume that no one is in want of either, and that no servants are to be had. He must, therefore, bake his own bread, make his own clothes, plough his own ground, and shepherd his own flocks. His gold will be as useful to him as any other yellow pebbles on his estate. His stores must rot, for he cannot consume them. He can eat no more than another man could eat, and wear no more than another man could wear. He must lead a life of severe and common labour to procure even ordinary comforts; he will be ultimately unable to keep either houses in repair, or fields in cultivation; and forced to content himself with a poor man's portion of cottage and garden, in the midst of a desert of waste land, trampled by wild cattle, and

encumbered by ruins of palaces, which he will hardly mock at himself by calling "his own."

The most covetous of mankind would, with small exultation, I presume, accept riches of this kind on these terms. What is really desired, under the name of riches, is essentially, power over men; in its simplest sense, the power of obtaining for our own advantage the labour of servant, tradesman, and artist; in wider sense, authority of directing large masses of the nation to various ends (good, trivial or hurtful, according to the mind of the rich person). And this power of wealth of course is greater or less in direct proportion to the poverty of the men over whom it is exercised, and in inverse proportion to the number of persons who are as rich as ourselves, and who are ready to give the same price for an article of which the supply is limited. If the musician is poor, he will sing for small pay, as long as there is only one person who can pay him; but if there be two or three, he will sing for the one who offers him most. And thus the power of the riches of the patron (always imperfect and doubtful, as we shall see presently, even when most authoritative) depends first on the poverty of the artist, and then on the limitation of the number of equally wealthy persons, who also want seats at the concert. So that, as above stated, the art of becoming "rich," in the common sense, is not absolutely nor finally the art of accumulating much money for ourselves, but also of contriving that our neighbours shall have less. In accurate terms, it is "the art of establishing the maximum inequality in our own favour."

Now the establishment of such inequality cannot be shown in the abstract to be either advantageous or disadvantageous to the body of the nation. The rash and absurd assumption that such inequalities are necessarily advantageous, lies at the root of most of the popular fallacies on the subject of political economy. For the eternal and inevitable law in this matter is, that the beneficialness of the inequality depends, first, on the methods by which it was accomplished, and, secondly, on the purposes to which it is applied. Inequalities of wealth, unjustly established, have assuredly injured the nation in which they exist during their establishment; and, unjustly directed, injure it yet more during their existence. But inequalities of wealth justly established, benefit the nation in the course of their establishment; and, nobly used, aid it yet more by their existence. That is to say, among every active and well-governed people, the various strength of individuals, tested by full exertion and specially applied to various need, issues in unequal, but harmonious results, receiving reward or authority according to its class and service;[1] while, in the inactive or ill-governed nation, the gradations of decay and the victories of treason work out also their own rugged system of subjection and success; and substitute, for the melodious inequalities of concurrent power, the iniquitous dominances and depressions of guilt and misfortune.

Thus the circulation of wealth in a nation resembles that of the blood in the natural body. There is one quickness of the current which comes of cheerful emotion or wholesome exercise; and another which comes of shame or of fever. There is a flush of the body which is full of warmth and life; and another which will pass in to putrefaction.

The analogy will hold, down even to minute particulars. For as diseased local determination of the blood involves depression of the general health of the system, all morbid local action of riches will be found ultimately to involve a weakening of the resources of the body politic.

The mode in which this is produced may be at once understood by examining one or two instances of the development of wealth in the simplest possible circumstances.

Suppose two sailors cast away on an uninhabited coast, and obliged to maintain themselves there by their own labour for a series of years.

If they both kept their health, and worked steadily, and in amity with each other, they might build themselves a convenient house, and in time come to possess a certain quantity of cultivated land, together with various stores laid up for future use. All these things would be real riches or property; and, supposing the men both to have worked equally hard, they would each have right to equal share or use of it. Their political economy would consist merely in careful preservation and just division of these possessions. Perhaps, however,

after some time one or other might be dissatisfied with the results of their common farming; and they might in consequence agree to divide the land they had brought under the spade into equal shares, so that each might thenceforward work in his own field and live by it. Suppose that after this arrangement had been made, one of them were to fall ill, and be unable to work on his land at a critical time—say of sowing or harvest.

He would naturally ask the other to sow or reap for him.

Then his companion might say, with perfect justice, "I will do this additional work for you; but if I do it, you must promise to do as much for me at another time. I will count how many hours I spend on your ground, and you shall give me a written promise to work for the same number of hours on mine, whenever I need your help, and you are able to give it."

Suppose the disabled man's sickness to continue, and that under various circumstances, for several years, requiring the help of the other, he on each occasion gave a written pledge to work, as soon as he was able, at his companion's orders, for the same number of hours which the other had given up to him. What will the positions of the two men be when the invalid is able to resume work?

Considered as a "Polis," or state, they will be poorer than they would have been otherwise: poorer by the withdrawal of what the sick man's labour would have produced in the interval. His friend may perhaps have toiled with an energy quickened by the enlarged need, but in the end his own land and property must have suffered by the withdrawal of so much of his time and thought from them; and the united property of the two men will be certainly less than it would have been if both had remained in health and activity.

But the relations in which they stand to each other are also widely altered. The sick man has not only pledged his labour for some years, but will probably have exhausted his own share of the accumulated stores, and will be in consequence for some time dependent on the other for food, which he can only "pay" or reward him for by yet more deeply pledging his own labour.

Supposing the written promises to be held entirely valid (among civilized nations their validity is secured by legal measures[2]), the person who had hitherto worked for both might now, if he chose, rest altogether, and pass his time in idleness, not only forcing his companion to redeem all the engagements he had already entered into, but exacting from him pledges for further labour, to an arbitrary amount, for what food he had to advance to him.

There might not, from first to last, be the least illegality (in the ordinary sense of the word) in the arrangement; but if a stranger arrived on the coast at this advanced epoch of their political economy, he would find one man commercially Rich; the other commercially Poor. He would see, perhaps with no small surprise, one passing his days in idleness; the other labouring for both, and living sparely, in the hope of recovering his independence, at some distant period.

This is, of course, an example of one only out of many ways in which inequality of possession may be established between different persons, giving rise to the Mercantile forms of Riches and Poverty. In the instance before us, one of the men might from the first have deliberately chosen to be idle, and to put his life in pawn for present ease; or he might have mismanaged his land, and been compelled to have recourse to his neighbour for food and help, pledging his future labour for it. But what I want the reader to note especially is the fact, common to a large number of typical cases of this kind, that the establishment of the mercantile wealth which consists in a claim upon labour, signifies a political diminution of the real wealth which consists in substantial possessions.

Take another example, more consistent with the ordinary course of affairs of trade. Suppose that three men, instead of two, formed the little isolated republic, and found themselves obliged to separate in order to farm different pieces of land at some distance from each other along the coast; each estate furnishing a distinct kind of produce, and each more or less in need of the material raised on the other. Suppose that the third man, in order to save the time of all three, undertakes simply to superintend the transference of commodities from one farm to the other; on condition of receiving some sufficiently remunerative share of every parcel of goods conveyed, or of some other parcel received in exchange for it.

If this carrier or messenger always brings to each estate, from the other, what is chiefly wanted, at the right time, the operations of the two farmers will go on prosperously, and the largest possible result in produce, or wealth, will be attained by the little community. But suppose no intercourse between the landowners is possible, except through the travelling agent; and that, after a time, this agent, watching the course of each man's agriculture, keeps back the articles with which he has been entrusted until there comes a period of extreme necessity for them, on one side or other, and then exacts in exchange for them all that the distressed farmer can spare of other kinds of produce; it is easy to see that by ingeniously watching his opportunities, he might possess himself regularly of the greater part of the superfluous produce of the two estates, and at last, in some year of severest trial or scarcity, purchase both for himself, and maintain the former proprietors thenceforward as his labourers or his servants.

This would be a case of commercial wealth acquired on the exactest principles of modern political economy. But more distinctly even than in the former instance, it is manifest in this that the wealth of the State, or of the three men considered as a society, is collectively less than it would have been had the merchant been content with juster profit. The operations of the two agriculturists have been cramped to the utmost; and the continual limitations of the supply of things they wanted at critical times, together with the failure of courage consequent on the prolongation of a struggle for mere existence, without any sense of permanent gain, must have seriously diminished the effective results of their labour; and the stores finally accumulated in the merchant's hands will not in anywise be of equivalent value to those which, had his dealings been honest, would have filled at once the granaries of the farmers and his own.

The whole question, therefore, respecting not only the advantage, but even the quantity, of national wealth, resolves itself finally into one of abstract justice. It is impossible to conclude, of any given mass of acquired wealth, merely by the fact of its existence, whether it signifies good or evil to the nation in the midst of which it exists. Its real value depends on the moral sign attached to it, just as sternly as that of a mathematical quantity depends on the algebraical sign attached to it. Any given accumulation of commercial wealth may be indicative, on the one hand, of faithful industries, progressive energies, and productive ingenuities; or, on the other, it may be indicative of mortal luxury, merciless tyranny, ruinous chicane. Some treasures are heavy with human tears, as an ill-stored harvest with untimely rain; and some gold is brighter in sunshine than it is in substance.

And these are not, observe, merely moral or pathetic attributes of riches, which the seeker of riches may, if he chooses, despise; they are literally and sternly, material attributes of riches, depreciating or exalting, incalculably, the monetary signification of the sum in question. One mass of money is the outcome of action which has created,—another, of action which has annihilated,—ten times as much in the gathering of it; such and such strong hands have been paralyzed, as if they had been numbed by nightshade: so many strong men's courage broken, so many productive operations hindered; this and the other false direction given to labour, and lying image of prosperity set up, on Dura plains dug into seven-times-heated furnaces. That which seems to be wealth may in verity be only the gilded index of far reaching ruin; a wrecker's handful of coin gleaned from the beach to which he has beguiled an argosy; a camp-follower's bundle of rags unwrapped from the breasts of goodly soldiers dead; the purchase-pieces of potter's fields, wherein shall be buried together the citizen and the stranger.

And therefore, the idea that directions can be given for the gaining of wealth, irrespectively of the consideration of its moral sources, or that any general and technical law of purchase and gain can be set down for national practice, is perhaps the most insolently futile of all that ever beguiled men through their vices. So far as I know, there is not in history record of anything

so disgraceful to the human intellect as the modern idea that the commercial text, "Buy in the cheapest market and sell in the dearest," represents, or under any circumstances could represent, an available principle of national economy. Buy in the cheapest market?—yes; but what made your market cheap? Charcoal may be cheap among your roof timbers after a fire, and bricks may be cheap in your streets after an earthquake; but fire and earthquake may not therefore be national benefits. Sell in the dearest?—yes, truly; but what made your market dear? You sold your bread well today; was it to a dying man who gave his last coin for it, and will never need bread more, or to a rich man who tomorrow will buy your farm over your head; or to a soldier on his way to pillage the bank in which you have put your fortune?

None of these things you can know. One thing only you can know, namely, whether this dealing of yours is a just and faithful one, which is all you need concern yourself about respecting it; sure thus to have done your own part in bringing about ultimately in the world a state of things which will not issue in pillage or in death. And thus every question concerning these things merges itself ultimately in the great question of justice, which, the ground being thus far cleared for it, I will enter upon in the next paper, leaving only, in this, three final points for the reader's consideration.

It has been shown that the chief value and virtue of money consists in its having power over human beings; that, without this power, large material possessions are useless, and to any person possessing such power, comparatively unnecessary. But power over human beings is attainable by other means than by money. As I said a few pages back, the money power is always imperfect and doubtful; there are many things which cannot be reached with it, others which cannot be retained by it. Many joys may be given to men which cannot be bought for gold, and many fidelities found in them which cannot be rewarded with it.

Trite enough,—the reader thinks. Yes: but it is not so trite,—I wish it were,—that in this moral power, quite inscrutable and immeasurable though it be, there is a monetary value just as real as that represented by more ponderous currencies. A man's hand may be full of invisible gold, and the wave of it, or the grasp, shall do more than another's with a shower of bullion. This invisible gold, also, does not necessarily diminish in spending. Political economists will do well some day to take heed of it, though they cannot take measure.

But farther. Since the essence of wealth consists in its authority over men, if the apparent or nominal wealth fail in this power, it fails in essence; in fact, ceases to be wealth at all. It does not appear lately in England, that our authority over men is absolute. The servants show some disposition to rush riotously upstairs, under an impression that their wages are not regularly paid. We should augur ill of any gentleman's property to whom this happened every other day in his drawing-room.

So also, the power of our wealth seems limited as respects the comfort of the servants, no less than their quietude. The persons in the kitchen appear to be ill dressed, squalid, half-starved. One cannot help imagining that the riches of the establishment must be of a very theoretical and documentary character.

Finally, since the essence of wealth consists in power over men, will it not follow that the nobler and the more in number the persons are over whom it has power, the greater the wealth? Perhaps it may even appear after some consideration, that the persons themselves *are* the wealth—that these pieces of gold with which we are in the habit of guiding them, are, in fact, nothing more than a kind of Byzantine harness or trappings, very glittering and beautiful in barbaric sight, wherewith we bridle the creatures; but that if these same living creatures could be guided without the fretting and jingling of the Byzants in their mouths and ears, they might themselves be more valuable than their bridles. In fact, it may be discovered that the true veins of wealth are purple—and not in Rock, but in Flesh—perhaps even that the final outcome and consummation of all wealth is in the producing as many as possible full-breathed, bright-eyed, and happy-hearted human creatures. Our modern wealth, I think, has rather a tendency the other way;—most political economists appearing to consider multitudes of human creatures not conducive to wealth, or at best conducive to it only by remaining in a dim-eyed and narrow-chested state of being.

Nevertheless, it is open, I repeat, to serious question, which I leave to the reader's pondering, whether, among national manufactures, that of Souls of a good quality may not at last turn out a quite leadingly lucrative one? Nay, in some far-away and yet undreamt-of hour, I can even imagine that England may cast all thoughts of possessive wealth back to the barbaric nations among whom they first arose; and that, while the sands of the Indus and adamant of Golconda may yet stiffen the housings of the charger, and flash from the turban of the slave, she, as a Christian mother, may at last attain to the virtues and the treasures of a Heathen one, and be able to lead forth her Sons, saying,—

"These are MY Jewels." ♦

ENDNOTES

1. I have been naturally asked several times, with respect to the sentence in the first of these papers, "the bad workmen unemployed," "But what are you to do with your bad unemployed workmen?" Well, it seems to me the question might have occurred to you before. Your housemaid's place is vacant—you give twenty pounds a year—two girls come for it, one neatly dressed, the other dirtily; one with good recommendations, the other with none. You do not, under these circumstances, usually ask the dirty one if she will come for fifteen pounds, or twelve; and, on her consenting, take her instead of the well-recommended one. Still less do you try to beat both down by making them bid against each other, till you can hire both, one at twelve pounds a year, and the other at eight. You simply take the one fittest for the place, and send away the other, not perhaps concerning yourself quite as much as you should with the question which you now impatiently put to me, "What is to become of her?" For all that I advise you to do, is to deal with workmen as with servants; and verily the question is of weight:

"Your bad workman, idler, and rogue—what are you to do with him?"

We will consider of this presently: remember that the administration of a complete system of national commerce and industry cannot be explained in full detail within the space of twelve pages. Meantime, consider whether, there being confessedly some difficulty in dealing with rogues and idlers, it may not be advisable to produce as few of them as possible. If you examine into the history of rogues, you will find they are as truly manufactured articles as anything else, and it is just because our present system of political economy gives so large a stimulus to that manufacture that you may know it to be a false one. We had better seek for a system which will develop honest men, than for one which will deal cunningly with vagabonds. Let us reform our schools, and we shall find little reform needed in our prisons.

2. The disputes which exist respecting the real nature of money arise more from the disputants examining its functions on different sides, than from any real dissent in their opinions. All money, properly so called, is an acknowledgment of debt; but as such, it may either be considered to represent the labour and property of the creditor, or the idleness and penury of the debtor. The intricacy of the question has been much increased by the (hitherto necessary) use of marketable commodities, such as gold, silver, salt, shells, &c., to give intrinsic value or security to currency; but the final and best definition of money is that it is a documentary promise ratified and guaranteed by the nation to give or find a certain quantity of labor on demand. A man's labour for a day is a better standard of value than a measure of any produce, because no produce ever maintains a consistent rate of productibility.

QUESTIONS

1. According to Ruskin, why is *rich* a relative term?

2. What is needed for a person's riches to be useful?

3. What do people really want in trying to get rich?

FROM *ACRES OF DIAMONDS*

Russell H. Conwell (1843–1925)

Now then, I say again that the opportunity to get rich, to attain unto great wealth, is here in Philadelphia now, within the reach of almost every man and woman who hears me speak tonight, and I mean just what I say. I have not come to this platform even under these circumstances to recite something to you. I have come to tell you what in God's sight I believe to be the truth, and if the years of life have been of any value to me in the attainment of common sense, I know I am right; that the men and women sitting here, who found it difficult perhaps to buy a ticket to this lecture or gathering tonight, have within their reach "acres of diamonds," opportunities to get largely wealthy. There never was a place on earth more adapted than the city of Philadelphia today, and never in the history of the world did a poor man without capital have such an opportunity to get rich quickly and honestly as he has now in our city. I say it is the truth, and I want you to accept it as such; for if you think I have come to simply recite something, then I would better not be here. I have no time to waste in any such talk, but to say the things I believe, and unless some of you get richer for what I am saying tonight my time is wasted.

I say that you ought to get rich, and it is your duty to get rich. How many of my pious brethren say to me, "Do you, a Christian minister, spend your time going up and down the country advising young people to get rich, to get money?" "Yes, of course I do." They say, "Isn't that awful! Why don't you preach the gospel instead of preaching about man's making money?" "Because to make money honestly is to preach the gospel." That is the reason. The men who get rich may be the most honest men you find in the community.

"Oh," but says some young man here tonight, "I have been told all my life that if a person has money he is very dishonest and dishonorable and mean and contemptible." My friend, that is the reason why you have none, you can do more good with it than you could without it. Money printed your Bible, money builds your churches, money sends your missionaries, and money pays your preachers, and you would not have many of them, either, if you did not pay them. I am always willing that my church should raise my salary, because the church that pays the largest salary always raises it the easiest. You never knew an exception to it in your life. The man who gets the largest salary can do the most good with the power that is furnished to him. Of course he can if his spirit be right to use it for what it is given to him.

I say, then, you ought to have money. If you can honestly attain unto riches in Philadelphia, it is your Christian and godly duty to do so. It is an awful mistake of these pious people to think you must be awfully poor in order to be pious.

Some men say, "Don't you sympathize with the poor people?" Of course I do, or else I would not have been lecturing these years. I won't give in but what I sympathize with the poor, but the number of poor who are to be sympathized with is very small. To sympathize with a man whom God has punished for his sins, thus to help him when God would still continue a just punishment, is to do wrong, no doubt about it, and we do that more than we help those who are deserving. While we should sympathize with God's poor—that is, those who cannot help themselves—let us remember there is not a poor person in the United States who was not made poor by his own shortcomings, or by the shortcomings of someone else. It is all wrong to be poor, anyhow. Let us give in to that argument and pass that to one side.

A gentleman gets up back there, and says, "Don't you think there are some things in this world that are better than money?" Of course I do, but I am talking about money now. Of course there are some things higher than money. Oh yes, I know by the grave that has left me standing alone that there are some things in this world that are higher and sweeter and purer than money. Well do I know there are some things higher and grander than gold. Love is the grandest thing on God's earth, but fortunate the lover who has plenty of money. Money is power, money is force, money will do good as well as harm. In the hands of good men and women it could accomplish, and it has accomplished, good.

I hate to leave that behind me. I heard a man get up in a prayer-meeting in our city and thank the Lord he was "one of God's poor." Well, I wonder what his wife thinks about that? She earns all the money that comes into that house, and he smokes a part of that on the veranda. I don't want to see any more of the Lord's poor of that kind, and I don't believe the Lord does. And yet there are some people who think in order to be pious you must be awfully poor and awfully dirty. That does not follow at all. While we sympathize with the poor, let us not teach a doctrine like that.

Yet the age is prejudiced against advising a Christian man (or, as a Jew would say, a godly man) from attaining unto wealth. The prejudice is so universal and the years are far enough back, I think, for me to safely mention that years ago up at Temple University there was a young man in our theological school who thought he was the only pious student in that department. He came into my office one evening and sat down by my desk, and said to me: "Mr. President, I think it is my duty sir, to come in and labor with you." "What has happened now?" Said he, "I heard you say at the Academy, at the Peirce School commencement, that you thought it was an honorable ambition for a young man to desire to have wealth, and that you thought it made him temperate, made him anxious to have a good name, and made him industrious. You spoke about man's ambition to have money helping to make him a good man. Sir, I have come to tell you the Holy Bible says that 'money is the root of all evil.'"

I told him I had never seen it in the Bible, and advised him to go out into the chapel and get the Bible, and show me the place. So out he went for the Bible, and soon he stalked into my office with the Bible open, with all the bigoted pride of the narrow sectarian, or of one who founds his Christianity on some misinterpretation of Scripture. He flung the Bible down on my desk, and fairly squealed into my ear: "There it is, Mr. President; you can read it for yourself." I said to him: "Well, young man, you will learn when you get a little older that you cannot trust another denomination to read the Bible for you. You belong to another denomination. You are taught in the theological school, however, that emphasis is exegesis. Now, will you take that Bible and read it yourself, and give the proper emphasis to it?"

He took the Bible, and proudly read, "'The love of money is the root of all evil.'"

Then he had it right, and when one does quote aright from that same old Book he quotes the absolute truth. I have lived through fifty years of the mightiest battle that old Book has ever fought, and I have lived to see its banners flying free; for never in the history of this world did the great minds of earth so universally agree that the Bible is true—all true—as they do at this very hour.

So I say that when he quoted right, of course he quoted the absolute truth. "The love of money is the root of all evil." He who tries to attain unto it too quickly, or dishonestly, will fall into many snares, no doubt about that. The love of money. What is that? It is making an idol of money, and idolatry pure and simple everywhere is condemned by the Holy Scriptures and by man's common sense. The man that worships the dollar instead of thinking of the purposes for which it ought to be used, the man who idolizes simply money, the miser that hoards his money in the cellar, or hides it in his stocking, or refuses to invest it where it will do the world good, that man who hugs the dollar until the eagle squeals has in him the root of all evil.

QUESTIONS

1. What did Conwell think of the claim that money was the root of all evil?

2. If not money, then what is the root of evil?

3. Why did Conwell think it was one's duty to be rich?

4. According to Conwell, why are people poor?

FROM ATLAS SHRUGGED

Ayn Rand (1905–1982)

"So you think that money is the root of all evil?" said Francisco d'Anconia. "Have you ever asked what is the root of money? Money is a tool of exchange, which can't exist unless there are goods produced and men able to produce them. Money is the material shape of the principle that men who wish to deal with one another must deal by trade and give value for value. Money is not the tool of the moochers, who claim your product by tears, or of the looters, who take it from you by force. Money is made possible only by the men who produce. Is this what you consider evil?

"When you accept money in payment for your effort, you do so only on the conviction that you will exchange it for the product of the effort of others. It is not the moochers or the looters who give value to money. Not an ocean of tears nor all the guns in the world can transform these pieces of paper in your wallet into the bread you will need to survive tomorrow. Those pieces of paper, which should have been gold, are a token of honor—your claim upon the energy of the men who produce. Your wallet is your statement of hope that somewhere in the world around you there are men who will not default on that moral principle which is the root of money. Is this what you consider evil?

"Have you ever looked for the root of production? Take a look at an electric generator and dare tell Yourself that it was created by the muscular effort of unthinking brutes. Try to grow a seed of wheat without the knowledge left to you by men who had to discover it for the first time. Try to obtain your food by means of nothing but physical motions—and you'll learn that man's mind is the root of all the goods produced and of all the wealth that has ever existed on earth.

"But you say that money is made by the strong at the expense of the weak? What strength do you mean? It is not the strength of guns or muscles. Wealth is the product of man's capacity to think. Then is money made by the man who invents a motor at the expense of those who did not invent it? Is money made by the intelligent at the expense of the fools? By the able at the expense of the incompetent? By the ambitious at the expense of the lazy? Money is made before it can be looted or mooched—made by the effort of every honest man, each to the extent of his ability. An honest man is one who knows that he can't consume more than he has produced.

"To trade by means of money is the code of the men of good will. Money rests on the axiom that every man is the owner of his mind and his effort. Money allows no power to prescribe the value of your effort except the voluntary choice of the man who is willing to trade you his effort in return. Money permits you to obtain for your goods and your labor that which they are worth to the men who buy them, but no more. Money permits no deals except those to mutual benefit by the unforced judgment of the traders. Money demands of you the recognition that men must work for their own benefit, not for their own injury, for their gain, not their loss—the recognition that they are not beasts of burden, born to carry the weight of your misery—that you must offer them values, not wounds—that the common bond among men is not the exchange of suffering, but the exchanger of goods. Money demands that you sell, not your weakness to men's stupidity, but your talent to their reason; it demands that you buy, not the shoddiest they offer, but the best that your money can find. And when men live by trade—with reason, not force, as their final arbiter—it is the best product that wins, the best performance, the man of best judgment and highest ability—and the degree of a man's productiveness is the degree of his reward. This is the code of existence whose tool and symbol is money. Is this what you consider evil?

"But money is only a tool. It will take you wherever you wish, but it will not replace you as the driver. It will give you the means for the satisfaction of your desires, but it will not provide you with desires. Money is the scourge of the men who attempt to reverse the law of causality—the men who seek to replace the mind by seizing the products of the mind.

"Money will not purchase happiness for the man who has no concept of what he wants: money will not give him a code of values, if he's evaded the knowledge of what to value, and it will not provide him with a purpose, if he's evaded the choice of what to seek. Money will not buy intelligence for the fool, or admiration for the coward or respect for the incompetent. The man who attempts to purchase the brains of his superiors to serve him, with his money replacing his judgment, ends up by becoming the victim of his inferiors. The men of intelligence desert him, but the cheats and the frauds come flocking to him, drawn by a law which he has not discovered: that no man may be smaller than his money. Is this the reason why you call it evil?

"Only the man who does not need it, is fit to inherit wealth—the man who would make his own fortune no matter where he started. If an heir is equal to his money, it serves him; if not, it destroys him. But you look on and you cry that money corrupted him. Did it? Or did he corrupt his money? Do not envy a worthless heir; his wealth is not yours and you would have done no better with it. Do not think that it should have been distributed among you, loading the world with fifty parasites instead of one, would not bring back the dead virtue which was the fortune. Money is a living power that dies without its root. Money will not serve the mind that cannot match it. Is this the reason why you call it evil?

"Money is your means of survival. The verdict you pronounce upon the source of your livelihood is the verdict you pronounce upon your life. If the source is corrupt, you have damned your own existence. Did you get your money by fraud? By pandering to men's vices or men's stupidity? By catering to fools, in the hope of getting more than your ability deserves? By lowering your standards? By doing work you despise for purchasers you scorn? If so, then your money will not give you a moment's or a penny's worth of joy. Then all the things you buy will become, not a tribute to

you, but a reproach; not an achievement, but a reminder of shame. Then you'll scream that money is evil. Evil, because it would not pinch-hit for your self-respect? Evil, because it would not let you enjoy your depravity? Is this the root of your hatred of money?

"Money will always remain an effect and refuse to replace you as the cause. Money is the product of virtue, but it will not give you virtue and it will not redeem your vices. Money will not give you the unearned, neither in matter nor in spirit. Is this the root of your hatred of money?

"Or did you say it's the love of money that's the root of all evil? To love a thing is to know and love its nature. To love money is to know and love the fact that money is the creation of the best power within you, and your passkey to trade your effort for the effort of the best among men. It's the person who would sell his soul for a nickel, who is loudest in proclaiming his hatred of money—and he has good reason to hate it. The lovers of money are willing to work for it. They know they are able to deserve it.

"Let me give you a tip on a clue to men's characters: the man who damns money has obtained it dishonorably; the man who respects it has earned it.

"Run for your life from any man who tells you that money is evil. That sentence is the leper's bell of an approaching looter. So long as men live together on earth and need means to deal with one another—their only substitute, if they abandon money, is the muzzle of a gun.

"But money demands of you the highest virtues, if you wish to make it or to keep it. Men who have no courage, pride or self-esteem, men who have no moral sense of their right to their money and are not willing to defend it as they defend their life, men who apologize for being rich—will not remain rich for long. They are the natural bait for the swarms of looters that stay under rocks for centuries, but come crawling out at the first smell of a man who begs to be forgiven for the guilt of owning wealth. They will hasten to relieve him of the guilt—and of his life, as he deserves.

"Then you will see the rise of the men of the double standard—the men who live by force, yet count on those who live by trade to create the value of their looted money—the men who are the hitchhikers of virtue. In a moral society, these are the criminals, and the statutes are written to Protect you against them. But when a society establishes criminals-by-right and looters-by-law—men who use force to seize the wealth of disarmed victims—then money becomes its creators' avenger. Such looters believe it safe to rob defenseless men, once they've passed a law to disarm them. But their loot becomes the magnet for other looters, who get it from them as they got it. Then the race goes, not to the ablest at production, but to those most ruthless at brutality. When force is the standard, the murderer wins over the pickpocket. And then that society vanishes, in a spread of ruins and slaughter.

"Do you wish to know whether that day is coming? Watch money. Money is the barometer of a society's virtue. When you see that trading is done, not by consent, but by compulsion—when you see that in order to produce, you need to obtain permission from men who produce nothing—when you see that money is flowing to those who deal, not in goods, but in favors—when you see that men get richer by graft and by pull than by work, and your laws don't protect you against them, but protect them against you—when you see corruption being rewarded and honesty becoming a self-sacrifice—you may know that your society is doomed. Money is so noble a medium that it does not compete with guns and it does not make terms with brutality. It will not permit a country to survive as half-property, half-loot.

"Whenever destroyers appear among men, they start by destroying money, for money is men's protection and the base of a moral existence. Destroyers seize gold and leave to its owners a counterfeit pile of paper. This kills all objective standards and delivers men into the arbitrary power of an arbitrary setter of values. Gold was an objective value, art equivalent of wealth produced. Paper is a mortgage on wealth that does not exist, backed by a gun aimed at those who are expected to Produce it. Paper is a check drawn by legal looters upon an account which is not theirs: upon the virtue of the victims. Watch for the day when it bounces, marked: 'Account overdrawn.'

"When you have made evil the means of survival, do not expect men to remain good. Do not expect them to stay moral and lose their lives for the purpose of becoming the fodder of the immoral. Do not expect them to produce, when production is punished and looting rewarded. Do not ask, 'Who is destroying the world?' You are.

"You stand in the midst of the greatest achievements of the greatest productive civilization and you wonder why it's crumbling around you, while you're damning its life-blood—money. You look upon money as the savages did before you, and you wonder why the jungle is creeping back to the edge of your cities. Throughout men's history, money was always seized by looters of one brand or another, whose names changed, but whose method remained the same: to seize wealth by force and to keep the products bound, demeaned, defamed, deprived of honor. That phrase about the evil of money, which you mouth with such righteous recklessness, comes from a time when wealth was produced by the labor of slaves—slaves who repeated the motions once discovered by somebody's mind and left unimproved for centuries. So long as production was ruled by force, and wealth was obtained by conquest, there was little to conquer. Yet through all the centuries of stagnation and starvation, men exalted the looters, as aristocrats of the sword, as aristocrats of birth, as aristocrats of the bureau, and despised the producers, as slaves, as traders, as shopkeepers—as industrialists.

"To the glory of mankind, there was, for the first and only time in history, a country of money—and I have no higher, more reverent tribute to pay to America, for this means: a country of reason, justice, freedom, production, achievement. For the first time, man's mind and money were set free, and there were no fortunes-by-conquest, but only fortunes-by-work, and instead of swordsmen and slaves, there appeared the real maker of wealth, the greatest worker, the highest type of human being—the self-made man—the American industrialist.

"If you ask me to name the proudest distinction of Americans, I would choose—because it contains all the others—the fact that they were the people who created the phrase 'to make money.' No other language or nation had ever used these words before; men had always thought of wealth as a static quantity—to be seized, begged, inherited, shared, looted or obtained as a favor. Americans were the first to understand that wealth has to be created. The words 'to make money' hold the essence of human morality.

10   "Yet these were the words for which Americans were denounced by the rotted cultures of the looters' continents. Now the looters' credo has brought you to regard your proudest achievements as a hallmark of shame, your prosperity as guilt, your greatest men, the industrialist, as blackguards, and your magnificent factories as the product and property of muscular labor, the labor of whip-driven slaves, like the pyramids of Egypt. The rotter who simpers that he sees no difference between 60 the power of the dollar and the power of the whip, ought to learn the difference on his own hide—as, I think, he will.

    "Until and unless you discover that money is the root of all good, you ask for your own destruction. When money ceases to be the tool by which men deal with one another, then men become the tools of men. Blood, whips and guns—or dollar. Take your choice—there is no other—and your time is running out." ◆ 70

QUESTIONS

1. What did Rand think money indicated about a society?

2. What sole alternative to money did Rand say could order society?

3. What is the root of evil for Rand?

4. Who does Rand think is the best type of person, and why?

SELECTION FROM: *THE BUSINESS GUIDE*

J. L. Nichols (1851–1895) self-published Naperville, Ill 1893

TEACHING BUSINESS TO LADIES

Teaching Wives and Daughters the Ways of Business.

Women are too frequently ridiculed because of their ignorance of business matters. How can they understand business and business methods, if they have never had an opportunity to learn and transact business? Every husband should teach his wife some of the more important ways of business. He should interest her in his financial affairs, and show her some of the business forms and business documents which form a part of his business transactions. It is a great advantage for a wife to be familiar with her husband's business, as she is liable to be called upon at any time to settle his estate.

How many burdens are annually thrust upon widows, and at what a disadvantage they are in managing the business affairs of the family! Then why not make the path straighter and smoother by beginning now, by teaching your wives and daughters practical business methods?

For family instruction we would suggest the following rules:

1. *Assist your wife or daughter in drawing up notes, and teach her not only the correct form, but give her some of the laws bearing upon the legal relations of both debtor and creditor.*

2. *Make various endorsements upon the notes which have been thus written for copy. Write a note for each endorsement and explain it. This is a very easy and simple lesson and can be mastered in a very few evenings.*

3. *Teach the forms of receipts. Write receipts for rent, for money paid on account, for money to be paid a third party, etc. This will be found a very interesting exercise.*

4. *Checks and drafts will form the same interesting exercise.*

5. *The next step will be to secure a few blank forms of notes, checks, drafts, deeds, leases, etc., and any husband will be surprised what progress his wife will make in a few lessons in filling out these business documents.*

6. *If you carry out this plan your wife or daughter will become interested in your business, and will understand the different forms of paper and will soon be able to give you considerable assistance as well as safe counsel.*

How to Teach Business to Children.

Give your sons and daughters some familiarity with the customs of the business world. Let them learn while young how to transact the ordinary forms of business. It is probably best to give them opportunities for earning a little money and try and teach them its value in disposing of same.

It is best to buy them a little account book, and make them have an account of all the money they receive, and the disposition they make of it. Teach them how to make such entries, and always insist upon their keeping a correct record of all the money they receive, and to give an account of the money they pay out, and always show a correct itemized account.

In this way they may receive a degree of benefit which will insure their business success during life. This learned early in life will always produce an abiding and substantial benefit, and no doubt give birth to many practical ideas of business.

Capitalist Production from *Das Kapital*

Karl Marx (1818–1883)

Section 1.—The Two Factors of a Commodity: Use-Value and Value (The Substance of Value and the Magnitude of Value).

The wealth of those societies in which the capitalist mode of production prevails, presents itself as "an immense accumulation of commodities," its unit being a single commodity. Our investigation must therefore begin with the analysis of a commodity.

A commodity is, in the first place, an object outside us, a thing that by its properties satisfies human wants of some sort or another. The nature of such wants, whether, for instance, they spring from the stomach or from fancy, makes no difference. Neither are we here concerned to know how the object satisfies these wants, whether directly as means of subsistence, or indirectly as means of production.

Every useful thing, as iron, paper, &c., may be looked at from the two points of view of quality and quantity. It is an assemblage of many properties, and may therefore be of use in various ways. To discover the various use of things is the work of history. So also is the establishment of socially-recognized standards of measure for the quantities of these useful objects. The diversity of these measures has its origin partly in the diverse nature of the objects to be measured, partly in convention.

The utility of a thing makes it a use-value. But this utility is not a thing of air. Being limited by the physical properties of the commodity, it has no existence apart from that commodity. A commodity, such as iron, corn, or a diamond, is therefore, so far as it is a material thing, a use-value, something useful. This property of a commodity is independent of the amount of labour required to appropriate its useful qualities. When treating of use-value, we always assume to be dealing with definite quantities, such as dozens of watches, yards of linen, or tons of iron. The use-values of commodities furnish the material for a special study, that of the commercial knowledge of commodities.

Use-values become a reality only by use or consumption: they also constitute the substance of all wealth, whatever may be the social form of that wealth. In the form of society we are about to consider, they are, in addition, the material depositories of exchange value.

Exchange value, at first sight, presents itself as a quantitative relation as the proportion in which values in use of one sort are exchanged for those of another sort, a relation constantly changing with time and place. Hence exchange value appears to be something accidental and purely relative, and consequently an intrinsic value, *i.e.*, an exchange value that is inseparably connected with, inherent in commodities, seems a contradiction in terms. Let us consider the matter a little more closely.

A given commodity, *e.g.*, a quarter of wheat is exchanged for x blacking, y silk, or z gold, &c.—in short, for other commodities in the most different proportions. Instead of one exchange value, the wheat has, therefore, a great many. But since x blacking, y silk, or z gold, &c., each represent the exchange value of one quarter of wheat, x blacking, y silk, z gold, &c., must as exchange values be replaceable by each other, or equal to each other. Therefore, first: the valid exchange values of a given commodity express something equal; secondly, exchange value, generally, is only the mode of expression, the phenomenal form, of something contained in it, yet distinguishable from it.

Let us take two commodities, *e.g.*, corn and iron. The proportions in which they are exchangeable, whatever those proportions may be, can always be represented by an equation in which a given quantity of corn is equated to some quantity of iron: *e.g.*, 1 quarter corn = x cwt. iron. What does this equation tell us? It tells us that in two different things—in 1 quarter of corn and x cwt. of iron, there exists in equal quantities something common to both. The two things must therefore be equal to a third, which in itself is neither the one nor the other. Each of them, so far as it is exchange value, must therefore be reducible to this third.

A simple geometrical illustration will make this clear. In order to calculate and compare the areas of rectilinear figures, we decompose them into triangles. But the area of the triangle itself is expressed by something totally different from its visible figure, namely, by half the product of the base into the altitude. In the same way the exchange values of commodities must be capable of being expressed in terms of something common to them all, of which thing they represent a greater or less quantity.

This common "something" cannot be either a geometrical, a chemical, or any other natural property of commodities. Such properties claim our attention only in so far as they affect the utility of those commodities, make them use-values. But the exchange of commodities is evidently an act characterised by a total abstraction from use-value. Then one use-value is just as good as another, provided only it be present in sufficient quantity. Or, as old Barbon says, "one sort of wares are as good as another, if the values be equal. There is no difference or distinction in things of equal value. . . . A hundred pounds' worth of lead or iron, is of as great value as one hundred pounds' worth of silver or gold." As use-values, commodities are, above all, of different qualities, but as exchange values they are merely different quantities, and consequently do not contain an atom of use-value.

If then we leave out of consideration the use-value of commodities, they have only one common property left, that of being products of labour. But even the product of labour itself has undergone a change in our hands. If we make abstraction from its use-value, we make abstraction at the same time from the material elements and shapes that make the product a use-value; we see in it no longer a table, a house, yarn, or any other useful thing. Its existence as a material thing is put out of sight. Neither can it any longer be regarded as the product of the labour of the joiner, the mason, the spinner, or of any other definite kind of productive labour. Along with the useful quali-

ties of the products themselves, we put out of sight both the useful character of the various kinds of labour embodied in them, and the concrete forms of that labour; there is nothing left but what is common to them all; all are reduced to one and the same sort of labour, human labour in the abstract.

Let us now consider the residue of each of these products; it consists of the same unsubstantial reality in each, a mere congelation of homogeneous human labour, of labour-power expended without regard to the mode of its expenditure. All that these things now tell us is, that human labour-power has been expended in their production, that human labor is embodied in them. When looked at as crystals of this social substance, common to them all, they are—Values.

We have seen that when commodities are exchanged, their exchange value manifests itself as something totally independent of their use-value. But if we abstract from their use-value, there remains their Value as defined above. Therefore, the common substance that manifests itself in the exchange value of commodities, whenever they are exchanged, is their value. The progress of our investigation will show that exchange value is the only form in which the value of commodities can manifest itself or be expressed. For the present, however, we have to consider the nature of value independently of this, its form.

A use-value, or useful article, therefore, has value only because human labour in the abstract has been embodied or materialised in it. How, then, is the magnitude of this value to be measured? Plainly, by the quantity of the value-creating substance, the labour, contained in the article. The quantity of labour, however, is measured by its duration, and labour-time in its turn finds its standard in weeks, days, and hours.

Some people might think that if the value of a commodity is determined by the quantity of labour spent on it, the more idle and unskillful the labourer, the more valuable would his commodity be, because more time would be required in its production. The labour, however, that forms the substance of value, is homogeneous human labour, expenditure of one uniform labour-power. The total labour-power of society, which is embodied in the sum total of the values of all commodities produced by that society, counts here as one homogeneous mass of human labour-power, composed though it be of innumerable individual units. Each of these units is the same as any other, so far as it has the character of the average labour-power of society, and takes effect as such; that is, so far as it requires for producing a commodity, no more time than is needed on an average, no more than is socially necessary. The labour-time socially necessary is that required to produce an article under the normal conditions of production, and with the average degree of skill and intensity prevalent at the time. The introduction of power looms into England probably reduced by one half the labour required to weave a given quantity of yarn into cloth. The hand-loom weavers, as a matter of fact, continued to require the same time as before; but for all that, the product of one hour of their labour represented after the change only half an hour's social labour, and consequently fell to one-half its former value.

We see then that that which determines the magnitude of the value of any article is the amount of labour socially necessary, or the labour-time socially necessary for its production. Each individual commodity, in this connexion, is to be considered as an average sample of its class. Commodities, therefore, in which equal quantities of labour are embodied, or which can be produced in the same time, have the same value. The value of one commodity is to the value of any other, as the labour-time necessary for the production of the one is to that necessary for the production of the other. "As values, all commodities are only definite masses of congealed labour-time."

The value of a commodity would therefore remain constant, if the labour-time required for its production also remained constant. But the latter changes with every variation in the productiveness of labour. This productiveness is determined by various circumstances, amongst others, by the average amount of skill of the workmen, the state of science, and the degree of its practical application, the social organisation of production, the extent and capabilities of the means of production, and by physical

conditions. For example, the same amount of labour in favourable seasons is embodied in 8 bushels of corn, and in unfavourable, only in four. The same labour extracts from rich mines more metal than from poor mines. Diamonds are of very rare occurrence on the earth's surface, and hence their discovery costs, on an average, a great deal of labour-time. Consequently much labour is represented in a small compass. Jacob doubts whether gold has ever been paid for at its full value. This applies still more to diamonds. According to Eschwege, the total produce of the Brazilian diamond mines for the eighty years, ending in 1823, had not realised the price of one-and-a-half years' average produce of the sugar and coffee plantations of the same country, although the diamonds cost much more labour, and therefore represented more value. With richer mines, the same quantity of labour would embody itself in more diamonds and their value would fall. If we could succeed at a small expenditure of labour, in converting carbon into diamonds, their value might fall below that of bricks. In general, the greater the productiveness of labour, the less is the labour-time required for the production of an article, the less is the amount of labour crystallised in that article, and the less is its value; and *vice versa*, the less the productiveness of labour, the greater is the labour-time required for the production of an article, and the greater is its value. The value of a commodity, therefore, varies directly as the quantity, and inversely as the productiveness, of the labour incorporated in it.

A thing can be a use-value, without having value. This is the case whenever its utility to man is not due to labour. Such are air, virgin soil, natural meadows, &c. A thing can be useful, and the product of human labour, without being a commodity. Whoever directly satisfies his wants with the produce of his own labour, creates, indeed, use-values, but not commodities. In order to produce the latter, he must not only produce use-values, but use-values for others, social use-values. Lastly, nothing can have value, without being an object of utility. If the thing is useless, so is the labour contained in it; the labour does not count as labour, and therefore creates no value. ◆

QUESTIONS

1. According to Marx, what are use-value and exchange-value?

2. What determines the value of a commodity? Why?

THE SOCIAL ORGANISM FROM RELIGION AND THE RISE OF CAPITALISM

R. H. Tawney (1880–1962)

We are asking these questions today. Men were asking the same questions, though in different language, throughout the sixteenth century. It is a commonplace that modern economic history begins with a series of revolutionary changes in the direction and organization of commerce, in finance, in prices, and in agriculture. To the new economic situation men brought a body of doctrine, law and tradition, hammered out during the preceding three centuries. Since the new forces were bewildering, and often shocking, to conservative consciences, moralists and religious teachers met them at first by a re-affirmation of the traditional doctrines, by which, it seemed, their excesses might be restrained and their abuses corrected. As the changed environment became, not a novelty, but an established fact, these doctrines had to be modified. As the effects of the Reformation developed, different Churches produced characteristic differences of social opinion.

But these were later developments, which only gradually became apparent. The new economic world was not accepted without a struggle. Apart from a few extremists, the first generation of reformers were rarely innovators in matters of social theory, and quoted Fathers and church councils, decretals and canon lawyers, in complete unconsciousness that changes in doctrine and church government involved any breach with what they had learned to regard as the moral tradition of Christendom. Hence the sixteenth century sees a collision, not only between different schools of religious thought, but between the changed economic environment and the accepted theory of society. To understand it, one must place oneself at the point from which it started. One must examine, however summarily, the historical background.

That background consisted of the body of social theory, stated and implicit, which was the legacy of the Middle Ages. The formal teaching was derived from the Bible, the works of the Fathers and Schoolmen, the canon law and its commentators, and had been popularized in sermons and religious manuals. The informal assumptions were those implicit in law, custom, and social institutions. Both were complex, and to speak of them as a unity is to sacrifice truth to convenience. It may be that the political historian is justified when he covers with a single phrase the five centuries or more to which tradition has assigned the title of the Middle Ages. For the student of economic conditions that suggestion of homogeneity is the first illusion to be discarded.

The mediaeval economic world was marked, it is true, by certain common characteristics. They sprang from the fact that on the west it was a closed system, that on the north it had so much elbow-room as was given by the Baltic and the rivers emptying themselves into it, and that on the east, where it was open, the apertures were concentrated along a comparatively short coast-line from Alexandria to the Black Sea, so that they were easily commanded by any naval power dominating the eastern Mediterranean, and easily cut by any military power which could squat across the trade routes before they reached the sea. While, however, these broad facts determined that the two main currents of trade should run from east to west and north to south, and that the most progressive economic life of the age should cluster in the regions from which these currents started and where they met, within this general economic framework there was the greatest variety of condition and development. The contours of economic civilization ran on different lines from those of subsequent centuries, but the contrast between mountain and valley was not less clearly marked. If the sites on which a complex economic structure rose were far removed from those of later generations, it flourished none the less where conditions favoured its growth. In spite of the ubiquity of manor and gild, there was as much difference between the life of a centre of capitalist industry, like fifteenth-century Flanders, or a centre of capitalist finance, like fifteenth-century Florence, and a pastoral society exporting raw materials and a little food, like mediaeval England, as there is between modern Lancashire or London and modern Denmark. To draw from English conditions a picture of a whole world stagnating in economic squalor, or basking in economic innocence, is as absurd as to reconstruct the economic life of Europe in the twentieth century from a study of the Shetland Islands or the Ukraine. The elements in the social theory of the Middle Ages were equally various, and equally changing. Even if the student confines himself to the body of doctrine which is definitely associated with religion, and takes as typical of it the *Summae* of the Schoolmen, he finds it in constant process of development. The economic teaching of St. Antonino in the fifteenth century, for example, was far more complex and realistic than that of St. Thomas in the thirteenth, and down to the very end of the Middle Ages the best-established and most characteristic parts of the system—for instance, the theory of prices and of usury—so far from being stationary, were steadily modified and elaborated.

There are, perhaps, four main attitudes which religious opinion may adopt toward the world of social institutions and economic relations. It may stand on one side in ascetic aloofness and regard them as in their very nature the sphere of unrighteousness, from which men *may* escape—from which, if they consider their souls, they *will* escape—but which they can conquer only by flight. It may take them for granted and ignore them, as matters of indifference belonging to a world with which religion has no concern; in all ages the prudence of looking problems boldly in the face and passing on has seemed too self-evident to require justification. It may throw itself into an agitation for some particular reform, for the removal of some crying scandal, for the promotion of some final revolution, which will inaugurate the reign of righteousness on earth. It may at once accept and criticize, tolerate and amend, welcome the gross world of human appetites, as the squalid scaffolding from amid which the life of the spirit must rise, and insist that this also is the material of the Kingdom of God. To such a temper, all activities divorced from religion are brutal or dead, but none are too mean to be beneath or too great to be above it, since all, in their different degrees, are touched with the spirit which permeates the whole. It finds its most sublime expression in the words of Piccarda: "Paradise is everywhere, though the grace of the highest good is not shed everywhere in the same degree."

Each of these attitudes meets us today. Each meets us in the thought of the Middle Ages, as differences of period and place and economic environment and personal temperament evoke it. In the early Middle Ages the ascetic temper predominates. Lanfranc, for example, who sees nothing in economic life but the struggle of wolves over carrion, thinks that men of business can hardly be saved, for they live by cheating and profiteering. It is monasticism, with its repudiation of the prizes and temptations of the secular world, which is *par excellence* the life of religion. As one phase of it succumbed to ease and affluence, another rose to restore the primitive austerity, and the return to evangelical poverty, preached by St. Francis but abandoned by many of his followers, was the note of the majority of movements for reform. As for indifferentism—what else, for all its communistic phrases, is Wyclif's teaching, that the "just man is already lord of all" and that "in this world God must serve the devil," but an anticipation of the doctrine of celestial happiness as the compensation of earthly misery, to which Hobbes gave a cynical immortality when he wrote that the persecuted, instead of rebelling, "must expect their reward in Heaven," and which Mr. and Mrs. Hammond have revealed as an opiate dulling both the pain and the agitation of the Industrial Revolution? If obscure sects like the Poor Men of Lyons are too unorthodox to be cited, the Friars are not, and it was not only Langland and that gentlemanly journalist, Froissart, who accused them—the phrase has a long history—of stirring up class hatred.

To select from so immense a sea of ideas about society and religion only the specimens that fit the meshes of one's own small net, and to label them "mediaeval thought," is to beg all questions. Ideas have a pedigree which, if realized, would often embarrass their exponents. The day has long since passed when it could be suggested that only one-half of modern Christianity has its roots in mediaeval religion. There is a mediaeval Puritanism and rationalism as well as a mediaeval Catholicism. In the field of ecclesiastical theory, as Mr. Manning has pointed out in his excellent book, Gregory VII and Boniface VIII have their true successors in Calvin and Knox. What is true of religion and political thought is equally true of economic and social doctrines. The social theories of Luther and Latimer, of Bucer and Bullinger, of sixteenth-century Anabaptists and seventeenth-century Levellers, of Puritans like Baxter, Anglicans like Laud, Baptists like Bunyan, Quakers like Bellers, are all the children of mediaeval parents. Like the Church to-day in regions which have not yet emerged from savagery, the Church of the earlier Middle Ages had been engaged in an immense missionary effort, in which, as it struggled with the surrounding barbarism, the work of conversion and of social construction had been almost indistinguishable. By the very nature of its task, as much as by the intention of its rulers, it had become the greatest of political institutions. For good or evil it aspired to be, not a sect, but a civilization, and, when its unity was shattered at the Reformation, the different Churches which emerged from it endeavoured, according to their different opportunities, to perpetuate the same tradition. Asceticism or renunciation, quietism or indifferentism, the zeal which does well to be angry, the temper which seeks a synthesis of the external order and the religion of the spirit—all alike, in one form or another, are represented in the religious thought and practice of the Middle Ages.

All are represented in it, but not all are equally representative of it. Of the four attitudes suggested above, it is the last which is most characteristic. The first fundamental assumption which is taken over by the sixteenth century is that the ultimate standard of human institutions and activities is religion. The archtectonics of the system had been worked out in the *Summae* of the Schoolmen. In sharp contrast to the modern temper, which takes the destination for granted, and is thrilled by the hum of the engine, mediaeval religious thought strains every interest and activity, by however arbitrary a compression, into the service of a single idea. The lines of its scheme run up and down, and, since purpose is universal and all-embracing, there is, at least in theory, no room for eccentric bodies which move in their own private orbit. That purpose is set by the divine plan of the universe. "The perfect happiness of man cannot be other than the vision of the divine essence."

Hence all activities fall within a single system, because all, though with different degrees of immediateness, are related to a single end, and derive their significance from it. The Church in its wider sense is the Christian Commonwealth, within which that end is to be realized; in its narrower sense it is the hierarchy divinely commissioned for its interpretation; in both it embraces the whole of life, and its authority is final. Though practice is perpetually at variance with theory, there is no absolute division between the inner and personal life, which is "the sphere of religion," and the practical interests, the external order, the impersonal mechanism, to which, if some modern teachers may be trusted, religion is irrelevant.

There is no absolute division, but there is a division of quality. There are—to use a modern phrase—degrees of reality. The distinctive feature of mediaeval thought is that contrasts which later were to be presented as irreconcilable antitheses appear in it as differences within a larger unity, and that the world of social organization, originating in physical necessities, passes by insensible gradations into that of the spirit. Man shares with other animals the necessity of maintaining and perpetuating his species; in addition, as a natural creature, he has what is peculiar to himself, an inclination to the life of the intellect and of society—"to know the truth about God and to live in communities." These activities, which form his life according to the law of nature, may be regarded, and sometimes are regarded, as indifferent or hostile to the life of the spirit. But the characteristic thought is different. It is that of a synthesis.

The contrast between nature and grace, between human appetites and interests and religion, is not absolute, but relative. It is a contrast of matter and the spirit informing it, of stages in a process, of preparation and fruition. Grace works on the unregenerate nature of man, not to destroy it, but to transform it. And what is true of the individual is true of society. An attempt is made to give it a new significance by relating it to the purpose of human life as known by revelation. In the words of a famous (or notorious) Bull: "The way of religion is to lead the things which are lower to the things which are higher through the things which are intermediate. According to the law of the universe all things are not reduced to order equally and immediately; but the lowest through the intermediate, the intermediate through the higher." Thus social institutions assume a character which may almost be called sacramental, for they are the outward and imperfect expression of a supreme spiritual reality. Ideally conceived, society is an organism of different grades, and human activities form a hierarchy of functions, which differ in kind and in significance, but each of which is of value on its own plane, provided that it is governed, however remotely, by the end which is common to all. Like the celestial order, of which it is the dim reflection, society is stable, because it is straining upwards:

> Anzi 'e formale ad esto beato esse
> Tenersi dentro alla divina voglia,
> Per ch' una fansi nostre voglie stresse.

Needless to say, metaphysics, however sublime, were not the daily food of the Middle Ages, any more than of to-day. The fifteenth century saw an outburst of commercial activity and of economic speculation, and by the middle of it all this teaching was becoming antiquated. Needless to say, also, general ideas cannot be kept in compartments, and the conviction of mediaeval thinkers that life has a divine purpose coloured the interpretation of common affairs, as it was coloured by physics in the eighteenth century and by the idea of evolution in the nineteenth. If the first legacy of the Middle Ages to the sixteenth century was the idea of religion as embracing all aspects of human life, the second and third flowed naturally from the working of that idea in the economic environment of the time. They may be called, respectively, the functional view of class organization, and the doctrine of economic ethics.

From the twelfth century to the sixteenth, from the work of Beckett's secretary in 1159 to the work of Henry VIII's chaplain in 1537, the analogy by which society is described—an analogy at once fundamental and commonplace—is the same. Invoked in every economic crisis to rebuke extortion and dissension with a high doctrine of social solidarity, it was not finally discarded till the rise of a theoretical individualism in England in the seventeenth century. It is that of the human body. The gross facts of the social order are accepted, in all their harshness and brutality. They are accepted with astonishing docility, and, except on rare occasions, there is no question of reconstruction. What they include is no trifle. It is nothing less than the whole edifice of feudal society—class privilege, class oppression, exploitation, serfdom. But these things cannot, it is thought, be treated as simply alien to religion, for religion is all-comprehensive. They must be given some ethical meaning, must be shown to be the expression of some larger plan. The meaning given them is simple. The facts of class status and inequality were rationalized in the Middle Ages by a functional theory of society, as the facts of competition were rationalized in the eighteenth by the theory of economic harmonies; and the former took the same delight in contemplating the moral purpose revealed in social organization, as the latter in proving that to the curious mechanism of human society a moral purpose was superfluous or disturbing. Society, like the human body, is an organism composed of different members. Each member has its own function, prayer, or defence, or merchandise, or tilling the soil. Each must receive the means suited to its station, and must claim no more. Within classes there must be equality; if one takes into his hand the living of two, his neighbour will go short. Between classes there must be inequality; for otherwise a class cannot perform its function, or—a strange thought to us—enjoy its rights. Peasants must not encroach on those above them. Lords must not despoil peasants. Craftsmen and merchants must receive what will maintain them in their calling, and no more.

As a rule of social policy, the doctrine was at once repressive and protective. "There is degree above degree, as reason is, and skill it is that men do their devoir thereas it is due. But certes, extortions and despite of your underlings is damnable." As a philosophy of society, it attempted to spiritualize the material by incorporating it in a divine universe, which should absorb and transform it. To that process of transmutation the life of mere money-making was recalcitrant, and hence, indeed, the stigma attached to it. For, in spite of the ingenuity of theorists, finance and trade, the essence of which seemed to be, not service but a mere *appetitus divitiarum infinitus,* were not easily interpreted in terms of social function. Comparatively late intruders in a world dominated by conceptions hammered out in a pre-commercial age, they were never fitted harmoniously into the mediaeval synthesis, and ultimately, when they grew to their full stature, were to contribute to its overthrow. But the property of the feudal lord, the labour of the peasant or the craftsman, even the ferocity of the warrior, were not dismissed as hostile or indifferent to the life of the spirit. Touched by the spear of Ithuriel, they were to be sublimated into service, vocation and chivalry, and the ritual which surrounded them was designed to emphasize that they had undergone a re-dedication at the hands of religion. Baptized by the Church, privilege and power became office and duty.

That the reconciliation was superficial, and that in attempting it the Church often degraded itself without raising the world, is as indisputable as that its tendency was to dignify material interests, by stamping them with the impress of a universal design. Gentlemen took hard tallages and oppressed the poor; but it was something that they should be told that their true function was "to defend God's law by power of the world." Craftsmen—the burden of endless sermons—worked deceitfully; but it was perhaps not wholly without value that they should pay even lip-service to the ideal of so conducting their trade, that the common people should not be defrauded by the evil ingenuity of those exercising the craft. If lord and peasant, merchant and artisan, burgess and villager, pressed each other hard, was it meaningless to meet their struggles with an assertion of universal solidarity, to which economic convenience and economic power must alike give way? "The health of the whole commonwealth will be assured and vigorous, if the higher members consider the lower and the lower answer in like manner the higher, so that each is in its turn a member of every other."

If the mediaeval moralist was often too naïve in expecting sound practice as the result of lofty principles alone, he was at least free from that not unfashionable form of credulity which expects it from their absence or from their opposite. To say that the men to whom such teaching was addressed went out to rob and cheat is to say no more than that they were men. Nor is it self-evident that they would have been more likely to be honest, if they had been informed, like some of their descendants, that competition was designed by Providence to provide an automatic substitute for honesty. Society was interpreted, in short, not as the expression of economic self-interest, but as held together by a system of mutual, though varying, obligations. Social well-being exists, it was thought, in so far as each class performs its functions and enjoys the rights proportioned thereto. "The Church is divided in these three parts, preachers, and defenders, and...labourers.... As she is our mother, so she is a body, and health of this body stands in this, that one part of her answer to another, after the same measure that Jesus Christ has ordained it.... Kindly man's hand helps his head, and his eye helps his foot, and his foot his body . . . and thus should it be in parts of the Church.... As divers parts of man served unkindly to man if one took the service of another and left his own proper work, so divers parts of the Church have proper works to serve God; and if one part leave his work that God has limited him and take work of another part, sinful wonder is in the Church.... Surely the Church shall never be whole before proportions of her parts be brought again by this heavenly leech and [by] medicine of men."

Speculation does not develop *in vacuo*. It echoes, however radical it is, the established order. Clearly this patriarchal doctrine is a softened reflection of the feudal land system. Not less clearly the Church's doctrine of economic ethics is the expression of the conditions of mediaeval industry. A religious philosophy, unless it is frankly to abandon nine-tenths of conduct to the powers of darkness, cannot admit the doctrine of a world of business and economic relations self-sufficient and divorced from ethics and religion. But the facts may be difficult to moralize, or they may be relatively easy. Over a great part of Europe in the later Middle Ages, the economic environment was less intractable than it had been in the days of the Empire or than it is to-day. In the great commercial centres there was sometimes, it is true, a capitalism as inhuman as any which the world has seen, and from time to time ferocious class wars between artisans and merchants. But outside them trade, industry, the money market, all that we call the economic system, was not a system, but a mass of individual trades and individual dealings. Pecuniary transactions were a fringe on a world of natural economy. There was little mobility or competition. There was very little large-scale organization. With some important exceptions, such as the textile workers of Flanders and Italy, who, in the fourteenth century, again and again rose in revolt, the mediaeval artisan, especially in backward countries like England, was a small master. The formation of temporary organizations, or "parliaments," of wage-earners, which goes on in London even before the end of the thirteenth century, and the growth of journeymen's associations in the later Middle Ages, are a proof that the conditions which produced modern trade unionism were not unknown. But even in a great city like Paris the 128 gilds which existed at the end of the thirteenth century appear to have included 5,000 masters, who employed not more than 6,000 to 7,000 journeymen. At Frankfurt-am-Main in 1387 actually not more than 750 to 800 journeymen are estimated to have been in the service of 1,554 masters.

In cities of this kind, with their freedom, their comparative peace, and their strong corporate feeling, large enough to be prolific of associations and small enough for each man to know his neighbour, an ethic of mutual aid was not wholly impossible, and it is in the light of such conditions that the most characteristic of mediaeval industrial institutions is to be interpreted. To suggest that anything like a majority of mediaeval workers were ever members of a craft gild is extravagant. In England, at any rate, more than nine-tenths were peasants, among whom, though friendly societies called gilds were common, there was naturally no question of craft organization. Even in the towns it is a question whether there was not a considerable population of casual workers—consider only the number of unskilled workers that must have been required as labourers by the craftsmen building a cathedral in the days before mechanical cranes—who were rarely organized in permanent societies. To invest the craft gilds with a halo of economic chivalry is not less inappropriate. They were, first and foremost, monopolists, and the cases in which their vested interests came into collision with the consumer were not a few. Wyclif, with his almost modern devotion to the conception of a unitary society over-riding particular interests for the common good, was naturally prejudiced against corporations, on the ground that they distracted social unity by the intrusion of sectarian cupidities and sinister ambitions; but there was probably from time to time more than a little justification for his complaint, that "all new fraternities or gilds made of men seem openly to run in this curse [against false conspiratours]," because "they conspire to bear up each other, yea in wrong, and oppress other men in their right by their wit and power." It is significant that the most striking of the projects of political and social reconstruction produced in Germany in the century before the Reformation proposed the complete abolition of gilds, as intolerably corrupt and tyrannical.

There are, however, monopolists and monopolists. An age in which combinations are not tempted to pay lip-service to religion may do well to remember that the characteristic, after all, of the mediaeval gild was that, if it sprang from economic needs, it claimed, at least, to subordinate them to social interests, as

conceived by men for whom the social and the spiritual were inextricably intertwined. "Tout ce petit monde antique," writes the historian of French gilds, "était fortement imbu des idées chrétiennes sur le juste salaire et le juste prix; sans doute il y avait alors, comme aujourd'hui, des cupidités et des convoitises; mais un règle puissante s'imposait à tous et d'une manière générale exigeait pour chacun le pain quotid-
ien promis par l'Evangile." The attempt to pre-serve a rough equality among "the good men of the mistery," to check economic egotism by insisting that every brother shall share his good fortune with another and stand by his neigh-bour in need, to resist the encroachments of a conscienceless money-power, to preserve pro-fessional standards of training and craftsman-ship, and to repress by a strict corporate discipline the natural appetite of each to snatch
special advantages for himself to the injury of all—whether these things outweigh the evils of conservative methods and corporate exclu-siveness is a question which each student will answer in accordance with his own predilec-tions. What is clear, at least, is that both the rules of fraternities and the economic teaching of the Church were prompted by the problems of a common environment. Much that is now mechanical was then personal, intimate and
direct, and there was little room for organiza-tion on a scale too vast for the standards that are applied to individuals, or for the doctrine which silences scruples and closes all accounts with the final plea of economic expediency.

Such an environment, with its personal economic relations, was a not unfavourable field for a system of social ethics. And the Church, which brought to its task the tremen-dous claim to mediate between even the hum-
blest activity and the divine purpose, sought to supply it. True, its teaching was violated in practice, and violated grossly, in the very cita-del of Christendom which promulgated it. Contemporaries were under no illusion as to the reality of economic motives in the Age of Faith. They had only to look at Rome. From the middle of the thirteenth century a continuous wail arises against the iniquity of the Church, and its burden may be summed up in one word,
"avarice." At Rome, everything is for sale. What is followed is the gospel, not according to St. Mark, but according to the marks of silver.

> Cum ad papam veneris, habe pro constanti,
> Non est locus pauperi, soli favet danti.
>
> Papa, si rem tangimus, nomen habet a re,
> Quicquid habent alii, solus vult papare;
> Vel, si verbum gallicum vis apocopare,
> 'Payez payez,' dit le mot si vis impetrare.

The Papacy might denounce usurers, but, as the centre of the most highly organized administrative system of the age, receiving remittances from all over Europe, and receiv-ing them in money at a time when the revenue of other Governments still included personal services and payments in kind, it could not dis-pense with them. Dante put the Cahorsine money-lenders in hell, but a Pope gave them the title of "peculiar sons of the Roman Church." Grosstête rebuked the Lombard bankers, and a bishop of London expelled them, but papal protection brought them back. Archbishop Peckham, a few years later, had to implore Pope Nicholas III to withdraw a threat of excommunication, intended to compel him to pay the usurious interest demanded by Ital-ian money-lenders, though, as the archbishop justly observed, "by your Holiness's special mandate, it would be my duty to take strong measures against such lenders." The Papacy was, in a sense, the greatest financial institu-tion of the Middle Ages, and, as its fiscal sys-tem was elaborated, things became, not better, but worse. The abuses which were a trickle in the thirteenth century were a torrent in the fif-teenth. And the frailties of Rome, if exceptional in their notoriety, can hardly be regarded as unique. Priests, it is from time to time com-plained, engage in trade and take usury. Cathe-dral chapters lend money at high rates of interest. The profits of usury, like those of simony, should have been refused by church-men, as hateful to God; but a bishop of Paris, when consulted by a usurer as to the salvation of his soul, instead of urging restitution, rec-ommended him to dedicate his ill-gotten wealth to the building of Notre-Dame. "Thus," exclaimed St. Bernard, as he gazed at the glo-ries of Gothic architecture, "wealth is drawn up by ropes of wealth, thus money bringeth money. . . . O vanity of vanities, yet no more vain than insane! The Church is resplendent in her walls, beggarly in her poor. She clothes her stones in gold, and leaves her sons naked."

The picture is horrifying, and one must be grateful to those, like M. Luchaire and Mr. Coulton, who demolish romance. But the denunciation of vices implies that they are recognized as vicious; to ignore their condemnation is not less one-sided than to conceal their existence; and, when the halo has vanished from practice, it remains to ask what principles men valued and what standards they erected. The economic doctrines elaborated in the *Summae* of the Schoolmen, in which that question receives its most systematic answer, have not infrequently been dismissed as the fanciful extravagances of writers disqualified from throwing light on the affairs of this world by their morbid preoccupation with those of the next. In reality, whatever may be thought of their conclusions, both the occasion and the purpose of scholastic speculations upon economic questions were eminently practical. The movement which prompted them was the growth of trade, of town life, and of a commercial economy, in a world whose social categories were still those of the self-suffing village and the feudal hierarchy. The object of their authors was to solve the problems to which such developments gave rise. It was to reconcile the new contractual relations, which sprang from economic expansion, with the traditional morality expounded by the Church. Viewed by posterity as reactionaries, who dammed the currents of economic enterprise with an irrelevant appeal to Scripture and to the Fathers, in their own age they were the pioneers of a liberal intellectual movement. By lifting the weight of antiquated formulae, they cleared a space within the stiff framework of religious authority for new and mobile economic interests, and thus supplied an intellectual justification for developments which earlier generations would have condemned.

The mercantilist thought of later centuries owed a considerable debt to scholastic discussions of money, prices, and interest. But the specific contributions of mediaeval writers to the technique of economic theory were less signifi-

cant than their premises. Their fundamental assumptions, both of which were to leave a deep imprint on the social thought of the sixteenth and seventeenth centuries, were two: that economic interests are subordinate to the real business of life, which is salvation, and that economic conduct is one aspect of personal conduct, upon which, as on other parts of it, the rules of morality are binding. Material riches are necessary; they have a secondary importance, since without them men cannot support themselves and help one another; the wise ruler, as St. Thomas said, will consider in founding his State the natural resources of the country. But economic motives are suspect. Because they are powerful appetites, men fear them, but they are not mean enough to applaud them. Like other strong passions, what they need, it is thought, is not a clear field, but repression. There is no place in mediaeval theory for economic activity which is not related to a moral end, and to found a science of society upon the assumption that the appetite for economic gain is a constant and measurable force, to be accepted, like other natural forces, as an inevitable and self-evident *datum*, would have appeared to the mediaeval thinker as hardly less irrational or less immoral, than to make the premise of social philosophy the unrestrained operation of such necessary human attributes as pugnacity or the sexual instinct. The outer is ordained for the sake of the inner; economic goods are instrumental—*sicut quaedam adminicula, quibus adjuvamur ad tendendum in beatitudinem.* "It is lawful to desire temporal blessings, not putting them in the first place, as though setting up our rest in them, but regarding them as aids to blessedness, inasmuch as they support our corporal life and serve as instruments for acts of virtue." Riches, as St. Antonino says, exist for man, not man for riches.

At every turn, therefore, there are limits, restrictions, warnings against allowing economic interests to interfere with serious affairs. It is right for a man to seek such wealth as is necessary for a livelihood in his station. To seek more is not enterprise, but avarice, and avarice is a deadly sin. Trade is legitimate; the different resources of different countries show that it was intended by Providence. But it is a dangerous business. A man must be sure that he carries it on for the public benefit, and that the profits which he takes are no more than the wages of his labour. Private property is a necessary institution, at least in a fallen world; men work more and dispute less when goods are private, than when they are common. But it is to be tolerated as a concession to human frailty, not applauded as desirable in itself; the ideal—if only man's nature could rise to it—is communism. "Communis enim," wrote Gratian in his *Decretum*, "usus omnium, quae sunt in hoc mundo, omnibus hominibus esse debuit." At best, indeed, the estate is somewhat encumbered. It must be legitimately acquired. It must be in the largest possible number of hands. It must provide for the support of the poor. Its use must as far as practicable be common. Its owners must be ready to share it with those who need, even if they are not in actual destitution. Such were the conditions which commended themselves to an archbishop of the business capital of fifteenth-century Europe. There have been ages in which they would have been described, not as a justification of property, but as a revolutionary assault on it. For to defend the property of the peasant and small master is necessarily to attack that of the monopolist and usurer, which grows by devouring it.

The assumption on which all this body of doctrine rested was simple. It was that the danger of economic interests increased in direct proportion to the prominence of the pecuniary motives associated with them. Labour—the common lot of mankind—is necessary and honourable; trade is necessary, but perilous to the soul; finance, if not immoral, is at best sordid and at worst disreputable. This curious inversion of the social values of more enlightened ages is best revealed in mediaeval discussions of the ethics of commerce. The severely qualified tolerance extended to the trader was partly, no doubt, a literary convention derived from classical models; it was natural that Aquinas should laud the State which had small need of merchants because it could meet its needs from the produce of its own soil; had not the Philosopher himself praised aτ'ταρxεια? But it was a convention which coincided with a vital element in mediaeval social theory, and struck a responsive note in wide sections of mediaeval society. It is not disputed, of course, that trade is indispensable; the merchant supplements the deficiencies of one country with the abundance of another. If there were no private traders, argued Duns Scotus, whose indulgence was less carefully guarded, the governor would have to engage them. Their profits, therefore, are legitimate, and they may include, not only the livelihood appropriate to the trader's status, but payment for labour, skill and risk.

The defence, if adequate, was somewhat embarrassing. For why should a defence be required? The insistence that trade is not positively sinful conveys a hint that the practices of traders may be, at least, of dubious propriety. And so, in the eyes of most mediaeval thinkers, they are. *Summe periculosa est venditionis et emptionis negotiatio.* The explanation of that attitude lay partly in the facts of contemporary economic organization. The economy of the mediaeval borough—consider only its treatment of food supplies and prices—was one in which consumption held somewhat the same primacy in the public mind, as the undisputed arbiter of economic effort, as the nineteenth century attached to profits. The merchant pure and simple, though convenient to the Crown, for whom he collected taxes and provided loans, and to great establishments such as monasteries, whose wool he bought in bulk, enjoyed the double unpopularity of an alien and a parasite. The best practical commentary on the tepid indulgence extended by theorists to the trader is the network of restrictions with which mediaeval policy surrounded his activities, the recurrent storms of public indignation against him, and the ruthlessness with which boroughs suppressed the middleman who intervened between consumer and producer.

Apart, however, from the colour which it took from its environment, mediaeval social theory had reasons of its own for holding that business, as distinct from labour, required some special justification. The suspicion of economic motives had been one of the earliest elements in the social teaching of the Church, and was to survive till Calvinism endowed the life of economic enterprise with a new sanctification. In mediaeval philosophy the ascetic tradition, which condemned all commerce as the sphere of iniquity, was softened by a recognition of practical necessities, but it was not obliterated; and, if reluctant to condemn, it was insistent to warn. For it was of the essence of trade to drag into a position of solitary prominence the acquisitive appetites; and towards those appetites, which to most modern thinkers have seemed the one sure social dynamic, the attitude of the mediaeval theorist was that of one who holds a wolf by the ears. The craftsman labours for his living; he seeks what is sufficient to support him, and no more. The merchant aims not merely at livelihood, but at profit. The traditional distinction was expressed in the words of Gratian: "Whosoever buys a thing, not that he may sell it whole and unchanged, but that it may be a material for fashioning something, he is no merchant. But the man who buys it in order that he may gain by selling it again unchanged and as he bought it, that man is of the buyers and sellers who are cast forth from God's temple." By very definition a man who "buys in order that he may sell dearer," the trader is moved by an inhuman concentration on his own pecuniary interest, unsoftened by any tincture of public spirit or private charity. He turns what should be a means into an end, and his occupation, therefore, "is justly condemned, since, regarded in itself, it serves the lust of gain."

The dilemma presented by a form of enterprise at once perilous to the soul and essential to society was revealed in the solution most commonly propounded for it. It was to treat profits as a particular case of wages, with the qualification that gains in excess of a reasonable remuneration for the merchant's labour were, though not illegal, reprehensible as *turpe lucrum.* The condition of the trader's exoneration is that "he seeks gain, not as an end, but as the wages of his labour." Theoretically convenient, the doctrine was difficult of application, for evidently it implied the acceptance of what the sedate irony of Adam Smith was later to describe as "an affectation not very common among merchants." But the motives which prompted it were characteristic. The mediaeval theorist condemned as a sin precisely that effort to achieve a continuous and unlimited increase in material wealth which modern societies applaud as meritorious, and the vices for which he reserved his most merciless denunciations were the more refined and subtle of the economic virtues. "He who has enough to satisfy his wants," wrote a Schoolman of the fourteenth century, "and nevertheless ceaselessly labours to acquire riches, either in order to obtain a higher social position, or that subsequently he may have enough to live without labour, or that his sons may become men of wealth and importance—all such are incited by a damnable avarice, sensuality or pride." Two and a half centuries later, in the midst of a revolution in the economic and spiritual environment, Luther, in even more unmeasured language, was to say the same. The essence of the argument was that payment may properly be demanded by the craftsmen who make the goods, or by the merchants who transport them, for both labour in their vocation and serve the common need. The unpardonable sin is that of the speculator or the middleman, who snatches private gain by the exploitation of public necessities. The true descendant of the doctrines of Aquinas is the labour theory of value. The last of the Schoolmen was Karl Marx. ◆

QUESTIONS

1. What were the physical constraints on medieval trade and how was that trade controlled?

2. What are the four possible relationships between religious and economic attitudes, according to Tawney?

3. During the medieval and early modern times (that is up to the late sixteenth century), what was the fundamental assumption about economic and religious orders?

4. What metaphor of the economy does Tawney claim was then universal?

5. What later view of social cohesion replaces the medieval one and when?

6. What medieval notions persisted long into the sixteenth and seventeenth centuries, according to Tawney?

7. For medieval thinkers, what is the distinction between enterprise and avarice?

8. Why were medieval thinkers wary of trade and traders?

FROM *THE PROTESTANT ETHIC AND THE SPIRIT OF CAPITALISM*

Max Weber (1864–1920)

CHAPTER V

Asceticism and the Spirit of Capitalism

In order to understand the connection between the fundamental religious ideas of ascetic Protestantism and its maxims for everyday economic conduct, it is necessary to examine with especial care such writings as have evidently been derived from ministerial practice. For in a time in which the beyond meant everything, when the social position of the Christian depended upon his admission to the communion, the clergyman, through his ministry, Church discipline, and preaching, exercised an influence (as a glance at collections of *consilia, casus conscientiæ*, etc., shows) which we modern men are entirely unable to picture. In such a time the religious forces which express themselves through such channels are the decisive influences in the formation of national character.

For the purposes of this chapter, though by no means for all purposes, we can treat ascetic Protestantism as a single whole. But since that side of English Puritanism which was derived from Calvinism gives the most consistent religious basis for the idea of the calling, we shall, following our previous method, place one of its representatives at the centre of the discussion. Richard Baxter stands out above many other writers on Puritan ethics, both because of his eminently practical and realistic attitude, and, at the same time, because of the universal recognition accorded to his works, which have gone through many new editions and translations. He was a Presbyterian and an apologist of the Westminster Synod, but at the same time, like so many of the best spirits of his time, gradually grew away from the dogmas of pure Calvinism. At heart he opposed Cromwell's usurpation as he would any revolution. He was

unfavourable to the sects and the fanatical enthusiasm of the saints, but was very broad-minded about external peculiarities and objective towards his opponents. He sought his field of labour most especially in the practical promotion of the moral life through the Church. In the pursuit of this end, as one of the most successful ministers known to history, he placed his services at the disposal of the Parliamentary Government, of Cromwell, and of the Restoration, until he retired from office under the last, before St. Bartholomew's day. His *Christian Directory* is the most complete compendium of Puritan ethics, and is continually adjusted to the practical experiences of his own ministerial activity. In comparison we shall make use of Spener's *Theologische Bedenken*, as representative of German Pietism, Barclay's *Apology* for the Quakers, and some other representatives of ascetic ethics, which, however, in the interest of space, will be limited as far as possible.

Now, in glancing at Baxter's *Saints' Everlasting Rest*, or his *Christian Directory*, or similar works of others, one is struck at first glance by the emphasis placed, in the discussion of wealth and its acquisition, on the ebionitic elements of the New Testament. Wealth as such is a great danger; its temptations never end, and its pursuit is not only senseless as compared with the dominating importance of the Kingdom of God, but it is morally suspect. Here asceticism seems to have turned much more sharply against the acquisition of earthly goods than it did in Calvin, who saw no hindrance to the effectiveness of the clergy in their wealth, but rather a thoroughly desirable enhancement of their prestige. Hence he permitted them to employ their means profitably. Examples of the condemnation of the pursuit of money and goods may be gathered without end from Puritan writings, and may be contrasted with the late mediæval ethical literature, which was much more open-minded on this point.

Moreover, these doubts were meant with perfect seriousness; only it is necessary to examine them somewhat more closely in order to understand their true ethical significance and implications. The real moral objection is to relaxation in the security of possession, the enjoyment of wealth with the consequence of idleness and the temptations of the flesh, above all of distraction from the pursuit of a righteous life. In fact, it is only because possession involves this danger of relaxation that it is objectionable at all. For the saints' everlasting rest is in the next world; on earth man must, to be certain of his state of grace, "do the works of him who sent him, as long as it is yet day." Not leisure and enjoyment, but only activity serves to increase the glory of God, according to the definite manifestations of His will.

Waste of time is thus the first and in principle the deadliest of sins. The span of human life is infinitely short and precious to make sure of one's own election. Loss of time through sociability, idle talk, luxury, even more sleep than is necessary for health, six to at most eight hours, is worthy of absolute moral condemnation. It does not yet hold, with Franklin, that time is money, but the proposition is true in a certain spiritual sense. It is infinitely valuable because every hour lost is lost to labour for the glory of God. Thus inactive contemplation is also valueless, or even directly reprehensible if it is at the expense of one's daily work. For it is less pleasing to God than the active performance of His will in a calling. Besides, Sunday is provided for that, and, according to Baxter, it is always those who are not diligent in their callings, who have no time for God when the occasion demands it.

Accordingly, Baxter's principal work is dominated by the continually repeated, often almost passionate preaching of hard, continuous bodily or mental labour. It is due to a combination of two different motives. Labour is, on the one hand, an approved ascetic technique, as it always has been in the Western Church, in sharp contrast not only to the Orient but to almost all monastic rules the world over. It is in particular the specific defence against all those temptations which Puritanism united under the name of the unclean life, whose role for it was by no means small. The sexual asceticism of Puritanism differs only in degree, not in fundamental principle, from that of monasticism; and on account of the Puritan conception of marriage, its practical influence is more far-reaching than that of the latter. For sexual intercourse is permitted, even within marriage, only as the means willed by God for the increase of His glory according to the commandment, "Be fruitful and multiply." Along with a moderate vegetable diet and cold baths, the same prescription is given for all sexual temptations as is used against religious doubts and a sense of moral unworthiness: "Work hard in your calling." But the most important thing was that even beyond that labour came to be considered in itself the end of life, ordained as such by God. St. Paul's "He who will not work shall not eat" holds unconditionally for everyone. Unwillingness to work is symptomatic of the lack of grace.

Here the difference from the mediæval view-point becomes quite evident. Thomas Aquinas also gave an interpretation of that statement of St. Paul. But for him labour is only necessary *naturali ratione* for the maintenance of individual and community. Where this end is achieved, the precept ceases to have any meaning. Moreover, it holds only for the race, not for every individual. It does not apply to anyone who can live without labour on his possessions, and of course contemplation, as a spiritual form of action in the Kingdom of God, takes precedence over the commandment in its literal sense. Moreover, for the popular theology of the time, the highest form of monastic productivity lay in the increase of the *Thesaurus ecclesiæ* through prayer and chant.

Not only do these exceptions to the duty to labour naturally no longer hold for Baxter, but he holds most emphatically that wealth does not exempt anyone from the unconditional command. Even the wealthy shall not eat without working, for even though they do not need to labour to support their own needs, there is God's commandment which they, like the poor, must obey. For everyone without exception God's Providence has prepared a calling, which he should profess and in which he should labour. And this calling is not, as it was for the Lutheran, a fate to which he must submit and which he must make the best of, but God's commandment to the individual to work for the divine glory. This seemingly subtle difference had far-reaching psychological consequences, and became connected with a further development of the providential interpretation of the economic order which had begun in scholasticism.

The phenomenon of the division of labour and occupations in society had, among others, been interpreted by Thomas Aquinas, to whom we may most conveniently refer, as a direct consequence of the divine scheme of things. But the places assigned to each man in this cosmos follow *ex causis naturalibus* and are fortuitous (contingent in the Scholastic terminology). The differentiation of men into the classes and occupations established through historical development became for Luther, as we have seen, a direct result of the divine will. The perseverance of the individual in the place and within the limits which God had assigned to him was a religious duty. This was the more certainly the consequence since the relations of Lutheranism to the world were in general uncertain from the beginning and remained so. Ethical principles for the reform of the world could not be found in Luther's realm of ideas; in fact it never quite freed itself from Pauline indifference. Hence the world had to be accepted as it was, and this alone could be made a religious duty.

But in the Puritan view, the providential character of the play of private economic interests takes on a somewhat different emphasis. True to the Puritan tendency to pragmatic interpretations, the providential purpose of the division of labour is to be known by its fruits. On this point Baxter expresses himself in terms which more than once directly recall Adam Smith's well-known apotheosis of the division of labour. The specialization of occupations leads, since it makes the development of skill possible, to a quantitative and qualitative improvement in production, and thus serves the common good, which is identical with the good of the greatest possible number. So far,

the motivation is purely utilitarian, and is closely related to the customary view-point of much of the secular literature of the time.

But the characteristic Puritan element appears when Baxter sets at the head of his discussion the statement that "outside of a well-marked calling the accomplishments of a man are only casual and irregular, and he spends more time in idleness than at work," and when he concludes it as follows: "and he [the specialized worker] will carry out his work in order while another remains in constant confusion, and his business knows neither time nor place… therefore is a certain calling the best for everyone." Irregular work, which the ordinary labourer is often forced to accept, is often unavoidable, but always an unwelcome state of transition. A man without a calling thus lacks the systematic, methodical character which is, as we have seen, demanded by worldly asceticism.

The Quaker ethic also holds that a man's life in his calling is an exercise in ascetic virtue, a proof of his state of grace through his conscientiousness, which is expressed in the care and method with which he pursues his calling. What God demands is not labour in itself, but rational labour in a calling. In the Puritan concept of the calling the emphasis is always placed on this methodical character of worldly asceticism, not, as with Luther, on the acceptance of the lot which God has irretrievably assigned to man.

Hence the question whether anyone may combine several callings is answered in the affirmative, if it is useful for the common good or one's own, and not injurious to anyone, and if it does not lead to unfaithfulness in one of the callings. Even a change of calling is by no means regarded as objectionable, if it is not thoughtless and is made for the purpose of pursuing a calling more pleasing to God, which means, on general principles, one more useful.

It is true that the usefulness of a calling, and thus its favour in the sight of God, is measured primarily in moral terms, and thus in terms of the importance of the goods produced in it for the community. But a further, and, above all, in practice the most important, criterion is found in private profitableness. For if that God, whose hand the Puritan sees in all the occurrences of life, shows one of His elect a chance of profit, he must do it with a purpose. Hence the faithful Christian must follow the call by taking advantage of the opportunity. "If God show you a way in which you may lawfully get more than in another way (without wrong to your soul or to any other), if you refuse this, and choose the less gainful way, you cross one of the ends of your calling, and you refuse to be God's steward, and to accept His gifts and use them for Him when He requireth it: you may labour to be rich for God, though not for the flesh and sin."

Wealth is thus bad ethically only in so far as it is a temptation to idleness and sinful enjoyment of life, and its acquisition is bad only when it is with the purpose of later living merrily and without care. But as a performance of duty in a calling it is not only morally permissible, but actually enjoined. The parable of the servant who was rejected because he did not increase the talent which was entrusted to him seemed to say so directly. To wish to be poor was, it was often argued, the same as wishing to be unhealthy; it is objectionable as a glorification of works and derogatory to the glory of God. Especially begging, on the part of one able to work, is not the sin of slothfulness, but a violation of the duty of brotherly love according to the Apostle's own word.

The emphasis on the ascetic importance of a fixed calling provided an ethical justification of the modern specialized division of labour. In a similar way the providential interpretation of profit-making justified the activities of the business man. The superior indulgence of the *seigneur* and the parvenu ostentation of the *nouveau riche* are equally detestable to asceticism. But, on the other hand, it has the highest ethical appreciation of the sober, middle-class, self-made man. "God blesseth His trade" is a stock remark about those good men who had successfully followed the divine hints. The whole power of the God of the Old Testament, who rewards His people for their obedience in this life, necessarily exercised a similar influence on the Puritan who, following Baxter's advice, compared his own state of grace with that of the heroes of the Bible, and in the process interpreted the statements of the Scriptures as the articles of a book of statutes.

Of course, the words of the Old Testament were not entirely without ambiguity. We have seen that Luther first used the concept of the calling in the secular sense in translating a passage from Jesus Sirach. But the book of Jesus Sirach belongs, with the whole atmosphere expressed in it, to those parts of the broadened Old Testament with a distinctly traditionalistic tendency, in spite of Hellenistic influences. It is characteristic that down to the present day this book seems to enjoy a special favour among Lutheran German peasants, just as the Lutheran influence in large sections of German Pietism has been expressed by a preference for Jesus Sirach.

The Puritans repudiated the Apocrypha as not inspired, consistently with their sharp distinction between things divine and things of the flesh. But among the canonical books that of Job had all the more influence. On the one hand it contained a grand conception of the absolute sovereign majesty of God, beyond all human comprehension, which was closely related to that of Calvinism. With that, on the other hand, it combined the certainty which, though incidental for Calvin, came to be of great importance for Puritanism, that God would bless His own in this life—in the book of Job only—and also in the material sense. The Oriental quietism, which appears in several of the finest verses of the Psalms and in the Proverbs, was interpreted away, just as Baxter did with the traditionalistic tinge of the passage in the Ist Epistle to the Corinthians, so important for the idea of the calling.

But all the more emphasis was placed on those parts of the Old Testament which praise formal legality as a sign of conduct pleasing to God. They held the theory that the Mosaic Law had only lost its validity through Christ in so far as it contained ceremonial or purely historical precepts applying only to the Jewish people, but that otherwise it had always been valid as an expression of the natural law, and must hence be retained. This made it possible, on the one hand, to eliminate elements which could not be reconciled with modern life. But still, through its numerous related features, Old Testament morality was able to give a powerful impetus to that spirit of self-righteous and sober legality which was so characteristic of the worldly asceticism of this form of Protestantism.

Thus when authors, as was the case with several contemporaries as well as later writers, characterize the basic ethical tendency of Puritanism, especially in England, as English Hebraism they are, correctly understood, not wrong. It is necessary, however, not to think of Palestinian Judaism at the time of the writing of the Scriptures, but of Judaism as it became under the influence of many centuries of formalistic, legalistic, and Talmudic education. Even then one must be very careful in drawing parallels. The general tendency of the older Judaism toward a naive acceptance of life as such was far removed from the special characteristics of Puritanism. It was, however, just as far—and this ought not to be overlooked—from the economic ethics of mediæval and modern Judaism, in the traits which determined the positions of both in the development of the capitalistic ethos. The Jews stood on the side of the politically and speculatively oriented adventurous capitalism; their ethos was, in a word, that of pariah-capitalism. But Puritanism carried the ethos of the rational organization of capital and labour. It took over from the Jewish ethic only what was adapted to this purpose.

To analyse the effects on the character of peoples of the penetration of life with Old Testament norms—a tempting task which, however, has not yet satisfactorily been done even for Judaism—would be impossible within the limits of this sketch. In addition to the relationships already pointed out, it is important for the general inner attitude of the Puritans, above all, that the belief that they were God's chosen people saw in them a great renaissance. Even the kindly Baxter thanked God that he was born in England, and thus in the true Church, and nowhere else. This thankfulness for one's own perfection by the grace of God penetrated the attitude toward life of the Puritan middle class, and played its part in developing that formalistic, hard, correct character which was peculiar to the men of that heroic age of capitalism.

***

Although we cannot here enter upon a discussion of the influence of Puritanism in all these directions, we should call attention to the fact that the toleration of pleasure in cultural goods, which contributed to purely æsthetic or athletic enjoyment, certainly always ran up against one characteristic limitation: they must not cost anything. Man is only a trustee of the goods which have come to him through God's grace. He must, like the servant in the parable, give an account of every penny entrusted to him, and it is at least hazardous to spend any of it for a purpose which does not serve the glory of God but only one's own enjoyment. What person, who keeps his eyes open, has not met representatives of this view-point even in the present? The idea of a man's duty to his possessions, to which he subordinates himself as an obedient steward, or even as an acquisitive machine, bears with chilling weight on his life. The greater the possessions the heavier, if the ascetic attitude toward life stands the test, the feeling of responsibility for them, for holding them undiminished for the glory of God and increasing them by restless effort. The origin of this type of life also extends in certain roots, like so many aspects of the spirit of capitalism, back into the Middle Ages. But it was in the ethic of ascetic Protestantism that it first found a consistent ethical foundation. Its significance for the development of capitalism is obvious.

This worldly Protestant asceticism, as we may recapitulate up to this point, acted powerfully against the spontaneous enjoyment of possessions; it restricted consumption, especially of luxuries. On the other hand, it had the psychological effect of freeing the acquisition of goods from the inhibitions of traditionalistic ethics. It broke the bonds of the impulse of acquisition in that it not only legalized it, but (in the sense discussed) looked upon it as directly willed by God. The campaign against the temptations of the flesh, and the dependence on external things, was, as besides the Puritans the great Quaker apologist Barclay expressly says, not a struggle against the rational acquisition, but against the irrational use of wealth.

But this irrational use was exemplified in the outward forms of luxury which their code condemned as idolatry of the flesh, however natural they had appeared to the feudal mind. On the other hand, they approved the rational and utilitarian uses of wealth which were

willed by God for the needs of the individual
and the community. They did not wish to
impose mortification on the man of wealth, but
the use of his means for necessary and practical things. The idea of comfort characteristi-
cally limits the extent of ethically permissible
expenditures. It is naturally no accident that
the development of a manner of living consistent with that idea may be observed earliest and
most clearly among the most consistent representatives of this whole attitude toward life.
Over against the glitter and ostentation of feudal magnificence which, resting on an unsound
economic basis, prefers a sordid elegance to a
sober simplicity, they set the clean and solid
comfort of the middle-class home as an ideal.

On the side of the production of private
wealth, asceticism condemned both dishonesty
and impulsive avarice. What was condemned
as covetousness, Mammonism, etc., was the
pursuit of riches for their own sake. For wealth
in itself was a temptation. But here asceticism
was the power "which ever seeks the good but
ever creates evil"; what was evil in its sense was
possession and its temptations. For, in conformity with the Old Testament and in analogy to
the ethical valuation of good works, asceticism
looked upon the pursuit of wealth as an end in
itself as highly reprehensible; but the attainment of it as a fruit of labour in a calling was a
sign of God's blessing. And even more important: the religious valuation of restless, continuous, systematic work in a worldly calling, as
the highest means to asceticism, and at the
same time the surest and most evident proof of
rebirth and genuine faith, must have been the
most powerful conceivable lever for the expansion of that attitude toward life which we have
here called the spirit of capitalism.

When the limitation of consumption is combined with this release of acquisitive activity, the
inevitable practical result is obvious: accumulation of capital through ascetic compulsion to
save. The restraints which were imposed upon
the consumption of wealth naturally served to
increase it by making possible the productive
investment of capital. How strong this influence
was is not, unfortunately, susceptible of exact sta-
tistical demonstration. In New England the connection is so evident that it did not escape the eye

of so discerning a historian as Doyle. But also in
Holland, which was really only dominated by
strict Calvinism for seven years, the greater simplicity of life in the more seriously religious circles, in combination with great wealth, led to an
excessive propensity to accumulation.

That, furthermore, the tendency which has
existed everywhere and at all times, being
quite strong in Germany to-day, for middle-
class fortunes to be absorbed into the nobility,
was necessarily checked by the Puritan antipa-
thy to the feudal way of life, is evident. English
Mercantilist writers of the seventeenth century
attributed the superiority of Dutch capital to
English to the circumstance that newly
acquired wealth there did not regularly seek
investment in land. Also, since it is not simply
a question of the purchase of land, it did not
there seek to transfer itself to feudal habits of
life, and thereby to remove itself from the possibility of capitalistic investment. The high
esteem for agriculture as a peculiarly important branch of activity, also especially consistent with piety, which the Puritans shared,
applied (for instance in Baxter) not to the landlord, but to the yeoman and farmer, in the
eighteenth century not to the squire, but the
rational cultivator. Through the whole of English society in the time since the seventeenth
century goes the conflict between the squirear-
chy, the representatives of "merrie old England," and the Puritan circles of widely varying
social influence. Both elements, that of an
unspoiled naive joy of life, and of a strictly regulated, reserved self-control, and conventional
ethical conduct are even to-day combined to
form the English national character. Similarly,
the early history of the North American Colonies is dominated by the sharp contrast of the
adventurers, who wanted to set up plantations
with the labour of indentured servants, and
live as feudal lords, and the specifically middle-class outlook of the Puritans.

As far as the influence of the Puritan outlook extended, under all circumstances—and
this is, of course, much more important than the
mere encouragement of capital accumulation—
it favoured the development of a rational bourgeois economic life; it was the most important,
and above all the only consistent influence in

the development of that life. It stood at the cradle of the modern economic man.

To be sure, these Puritanical ideals tended to give way under excessive pressure from the temptations of wealth, as the Puritans themselves knew very well. With great regularity we find the most genuine adherents of Puritanism among the classes which were rising from a lowly status, the small bourgeois and farmers, while the *beati possidentes*, even among Quakers, are often found tending to repudiate the old ideals. It was the same fate which again and again befell the predecessor of this worldly asceticism, the monastic asceticism of the Middle Ages. In the latter case, when rational economic activity had worked out its full effects by strict regulation of conduct and limitation of consumption, the wealth accumulated either succumbed directly to the nobility, as in the time before the Reformation, or monastic discipline threatened to break down, and one of the numerous reformations became necessary.

In fact the whole history of monasticism is in a certain sense the history of a continual struggle with the problem of the secularizing influence of wealth. The same is true on a grand scale of the worldly asceticism of Puritanism. The great revival of Methodism, which preceded the expansion of English industry toward the end of the eighteenth century, may well be compared with such a monastic reform. We may hence quote here a passage from John Wesley himself which might well serve as a motto for everything which has been said above. For it shows that the leaders of these ascetic movements understood the seemingly paradoxical relationships which we have here analysed perfectly well, and in the same sense that we have given them. He wrote:

> I fear, wherever riches have increased, the essence of religion has decreased in the same proportion. Therefore I do not see how it is possible, in the nature of things, for any revival of true religion to continue long. For religion must necessarily produce both industry and frugality, and these cannot but produce riches. But as riches increase, so will pride, anger, and love of the world in all its branches. How then is it possible that Methodism, that is, a religion of the heart, though it flourishes now as a green bay tree, should continue in this state? For the Methodists in every place grow diligent and frugal; consequently they increase in goods. Hence they proportionately increase in pride, in anger, in the desire of the flesh, the desire of the eyes, and the pride of life. So, although the form of religion remains, the spirit is swiftly vanishing away. Is there no way to prevent this—this continual decay of pure religion? We ought not to prevent people from being diligent and frugal; *we must exhort all Christians to gain all they can, and to save all they can; that is, in effect, to grow rich.*

There follows the advice that those who gain all they can and save all they can should also give all they can, so that they will grow in grace and lay up a treasure in heaven. It is clear that Wesley here expresses, even in detail, just what we have been trying to point out.

***

One of the fundamental elements of the spirit of modern capitalism, and not only of that but of all modern culture: rational conduct on the basis of the idea of the calling, was born—that is what this discussion has sought to demonstrate—from the spirit of Christian asceticism. One has only to re-read the passage from Franklin, quoted at the beginning of this [reading selection], in order to see that the essential elements of the attitude which was there called the spirit of capitalism are the same as what we have just shown to be the content of the Puritan worldly asceticism, only without the religious basis, which by Franklin's time had died away. The idea that modern labour has an ascetic character is of course not new. Limitation to specialized work, with a renunciation of the Faustian universality of man which it involves, is a condition of any valuable work in the modern world; hence deeds and renunciation inevitably condition each other to-day. This fundamentally ascetic trait of middle-class life, if it attempts to be a way of life at all, and not simply the absence of any, was what Goethe wanted to teach, at the height of his wisdom, in the *Wanderjahren*, and in the end which he gave to the life of his *Faust*. For him the realization meant a renunciation, a departure from an age of full and beautiful humanity, which can no more be repeated in the course of our cultural development than can the flower of the Athenian culture of antiquity.

The Puritan wanted to work in a calling; we are forced to do so. For when asceticism was carried out of monastic cells into everyday life, and began to dominate worldly morality, it did its part in building the tremendous cosmos of the modern economic order. This order is now bound to the technical and economic conditions of machine production which to-day determine the lives of all the individuals who are born into this mechanism, not only those directly concerned with economic acquisition, with irresistible force. Perhaps it will so determine them until the last ton of fossilized coal is burnt. In Baxter's view the care for external goods should only lie on the shoulders of the "saint like a light cloak, which can be thrown aside at any moment." But fate decreed that the cloak should become an iron cage.

Since asceticism undertook to remodel the world and to work out its ideals in the world, material goods have gained an increasing and finally an inexorable power over the lives of men as at no previous period in history. To-day the spirit of religious asceticism—whether finally, who knows?—has escaped from the cage. But victorious capitalism, since it rests on mechani-

cal foundations, needs its support no longer. The rosy blush of its laughing heir, the Enlightenment, seems also to be irretrievably fading, and the idea of duty in one's calling prowls about in our lives like the ghost of dead religious beliefs. Where the fulfilment of the calling cannot directly be related to the highest spiritual and cultural values, or when, on the other hand, it need not be felt simply as economic compulsion, the individual generally abandons the attempt to justify it at all. In the field of its highest development, in the United States, the pursuit of wealth, stripped of its religious and ethical meaning, tends to become associated with purely mundane passions, which often actually give it the character of sport.

No one knows who will live in this cage in the future, or whether at the end of this tremendous development entirely new prophets will arise, or there will be a great rebirth of old ideas and ideals, or, if neither, mechanized petrification, embellished with a sort of convulsive self-importance. For of the last stage of this cultural development, it might well be truly said: "Specialists without spirit, sensualists without heart; this nullity imagines that it has attained a level of civilization never before achieved." ◆

QUESTIONS

1. According to Weber, what were traditional, modern, and contemporary attitudes toward wealth and work?

2. How does wealth result from Puritan attitudes?

3. Who should work, according to Puritanism?

4. What is meant by one's "calling" and how would he or she know what it is?

5. What does Weber mean by the iron cage in which "we" are trapped? What is its source?

FROM *THE ACQUISITIVE SOCIETY*

R. H. Tawney (1881–1962)

This doctrine has been qualified in practice by particular limitations to avert particular evils and to meet exceptional emergencies. But it is limited in special cases precisely because its general validity is regarded as beyond controversy, and, up to the eve of the present war, it was the working faith of modern economic civilization. What it implies is, that the foundation of society is found, not in functions, but in rights; that rights are not deducible from the discharge of functions, so that the acquisition of wealth and the enjoyment of property are contingent upon the performances of services, but that the individual enters the world equipped with rights to the free disposal of his property and the pursuit of his economic self-interest, and that these rights are anterior to, and independent of, any service which he may render. True, the service of society will, in fact, it is assumed, result from their exercise. But it is not the primary motive and criterion of industry, but a secondary consequence, which emerges incidentally through the exercise of rights, a consequence which is attained, indeed, in practice, but which is attained without being sought. It is not the end at which economic activity aims, or the standard by which it is judged, but a by-product, as coal-tar is a by-product of the manufacture of gas; whether that by-product appears or not, it is not proposed that the rights themselves should be abdicated. For they are regarded, not as a conditional trust, but as a property, which may, indeed, give way to the special exigencies of extraordinary emergencies, but which resumes its sway when the emergency is over, and in normal times is above discussion.

That conception is written large over the history of the nineteenth century, both in England and in America. The doctrine which it inherited was that property was held by an absolute right on an individual basis, and to this fundamental it added another, which can be traced in principle far back into history, but which grew to its full stature only after the rise of capitalist industry, that societies act both unfairly and unwisely when they limit opportunities of economic enterprise. Hence every attempt to impose obligations as a condition of the tenure of property or of the exercise of economic activity has been met by uncompromising resistance. The story of the struggle between humanitarian sentiment and the theory of property transmitted from the eighteenth century is familiar. No one has forgotten the opposition offered in the name of the rights of property to factory legislation, to housing reform, to interference with the adulteration of goods, even to the compulsory sanitation of private houses. "May I not do what I like with my own?" was the answer to the proposal to require a minimum standard of safety and sanitation from the owners of mills and houses. Even to this day, while an English urban landlord can cramp or distort the development of a whole city by withholding land except at fancy prices, English municipalities are without adequate powers of compulsory purchase, and must either pay through the nose or see thousands of their members overcrowded. The whole body of procedure by which they may acquire land, or indeed new powers of any kind, has been carefully designed by lawyers to protect owners of property against the possibility that their private rights may be subordinated to the public interest, because their rights are thought to be primary and absolute and public interests secondary and contingent.

No one needs to be reminded, again, of the influence of the same doctrine in the sphere of taxation. Thus the income tax was excused as a temporary measure, because the normal society was conceived to be one in which the individual spent his whole income for himself and owed no obligations to society on account of it. The death duties were denounced as robbery, because they implied that the right to benefit by inheritance was conditional upon a social sanction. The Budget of 1909 created a storm, not because the taxation of land was heavy—in amount the land-taxes were trifling—but because it was felt to involve the doctrine that property is not an absolute right, but that it may properly be accompanied by special obligations, a doctrine which, if carried to its logical conclusion, would destroy its sanctity by making ownership no longer absolute but conditional.

Such an implication seems intolerable to an influential body of public opinion, because it has been accustomed to regard the free disposal of property and the unlimited exploitation of economic opportunities, as rights which are absolute and unconditioned. On the whole, until recently, this opinion had few antagonists who could not be ignored. As a consequence the maintenance of property rights has not been seriously threatened even in those cases in which it is evident that no service is discharged, directly or indirectly, by their exercise. No one supposes, that the owner of urban land, performs *qua* owner, any function. He has a right of private taxation; that is all. But the private ownership of urban land is as secure today as it was a century ago; and Lord Hugh Cecil, in his interesting little book on Conservatism, declares that whether private property is mischievous or not, society cannot interfere with it, because to interfere with it is theft, and theft is wicked. No one supposes that it is for the public good that large areas of land should be used for parks and game. But our country gentlemen are still settled heavily upon their villages and still slay their thousands. No one can argue that a monopolist is impelled by "an invisible hand" to serve the public interest. But over a considerable field of industry competition, as the recent Report on Trusts shows, has been replaced by combination, and combinations are allowed the same unfettered freedom as individuals in the exploitation of economic opportunities. No one really believes that the production of coal depends upon the payment of mining royalties or that ships will not go to and fro unless ship-owners can earn fifty percent upon their capital. But coal mines, or rather the coal miner, still pay royalties, and ship-owners still make fortunes and are made Peers.

At the very moment when everybody is talking about the importance of increasing the output of wealth, the last question, apparently, which it occurs to any statesman to ask is why wealth should be squandered on futile activities, and in expenditure which is either disproportionate to service or made for no service at all. So inveterate, indeed, has become the practice of payment in virtue of property rights, without even the pretense of any service being rendered, that when, in a national emergency, it is proposed to extract oil from the ground, the Government actually proposes that every gallon shall pay a tax to landowners who never even suspected its existence, and the ingenuous proprietors are full of pained astonishment at any one questioning whether the nation is under moral obligation to endow them further. Such rights are, strictly speaking, privileges. For the definition of a privilege is a right to which no corresponding function is attached.

The enjoyment of property and the direction of industry are considered, in short, to require no social justification, because they are regarded as rights which stand by their own virtue, not functions to be judged by the success with which they contribute to a social purpose. Today that doctrine, if intellectually discredited, is still the practical foundation of social organization. How slowly it yields even to the most insistent demonstration of its inadequacy is shown by the attitude which the heads of the business world have adopted to the restrictions imposed on economic activity during the war. The control of railways, mines and shipping, the distribution of raw materials through a public department instead of through competing merchants, the regulation of prices, the attempts to check "profiteering"—the detailed application of these measures may have been effective or ineffective, wise or injudicious. It is evident, indeed, that some of them have been foolish, like the restriction of imports when the world has five years' destruction to repair, and that others, if sound in conception, have been questionable in their execution. If they were attacked on the ground that they obstruct the efficient performance of function—if the leaders of industry came forward and said generally, as some, to their honor, have:—"We accept your policy, but we will improve its execution; we desire payment for service and service only and will help the state to see that it pays for nothing else"—there might be controversy as to the facts, but there could be none as to the principle.

In reality, however, the gravamen of the charges brought against these restrictions appears generally to be precisely the opposite. They are denounced by most of their critics not because they limit the opportunity of service, but because they diminish the opportunity for gain, not because they prevent the trader enriching the community, but because they make it more difficult for him to enrich himself; not, in short, because they have failed to convert economic activity into a social function, but because they have come too near succeeding. If the financial adviser to the Coal Controller may be trusted, the shareholders in coal mines would appear to have done fairly well during the war. But the proposal to limit their profits to ½ per ton is described by Lord Gainford as "sheer robbery and confiscation." With some honorable exceptions, what is demanded is that in the future as in the past the directors of industry should be free to handle it as an enterprise conducted for their own convenience or advancement, instead of being compelled, as they have been partially compelled during the war, to subordinate it to a social purpose. For to admit that the criterion of commerce and industry is its success in discharging a social purpose is at once to turn property and economic activity from rights which are absolute into rights which are contingent and derivative, because it is to affirm that they are relative to functions and that they may justly be revoked when the functions are not performed. It is, in short, to imply that property and economic activity exist to promote the ends of society, whereas hitherto society has been regarded in the world of business as existing to promote them. To those who hold their position, not as functionaries, but by virtue of their success in making industry contribute to their own wealth and social influence, such a reversal of means and ends appears little less than a revolution. For it means that they must justify before a social tribunal rights which they have hitherto taken for granted as part of an order which is above criticism.

During the greater part of the nineteenth century the significance of the opposition between the two principles of individual rights and social functions was masked by the doctrine of the inevitable harmony between private interests and public good. Competition, it was argued, was an effective substitute for honesty. Today that subsidiary doctrine has fallen to pieces under criticism; few now would profess adherence to the compound of economic optimism and moral bankruptcy which led a nineteenth century economist to say: "Greed is held in check by greed, and the desire for gain sets limits to itself." The disposition to regard individual rights as the center and pivot of society is still, however, the most powerful element in political thought and the practical foundation of industrial organization. The laborious refutation of the doctrine that private and public interests are coincident, and that man's self-love is God's Providence, which was the excuse of the last century for its worship of economic egotism, has achieved, in fact, surprisingly small results. Economic egotism is still worshiped; and it is worshiped because that doctrine was not really the center of the position. It was an outwork, not the citadel, and now that the outwork has been captured, the citadel is still to win.

What gives its special quality and character, its toughness and cohesion, to the industrial system built up in the last century and a half, is not its exploded theory of economic harmonies. It is the doctrine that economic rights are anterior to, and independent of economic functions, that they stand by their own virtue, and need adduce no higher credentials. The practical result of it is that economic rights remain whether economic functions are performed or not. They remain today in a more menacing form than in the age of early industrialism. For those who control industry no longer compete but combine, and the rivalry between property in capital and property in land has long since ended. The basis of the New Conservatism appears to be a determination so to organize society, both by political and economic action, as to make it secure against every attempt to extinguish payments which are made, not for service, but because the owners possess a right to extract income without it. Hence the fusion of the two traditional parties, the proposed "strengthening" of the second chamber, the return to protection, the swift conversion of rival industrialists to the advantages of monopoly, and the attempts to buy off with concessions the more influential section of the working classes. Revolutions, as a long and bitter experience reveals, are apt to take their color from the régime which they overthrow. Is it any wonder that the creed which affirms the absolute rights of property should sometimes be met with a counter-affirmation of the absolute rights of labor, less anti-social, indeed, and inhuman, but almost as dogmatic, almost as intolerant and thoughtless as itself?

A society which aimed at making the acquisition of wealth contingent upon the discharge of social obligations, which sought to proportion remuneration to service and denied it to those by whom no service was performed, which inquired first not what men possess but what they can make or create or achieve, might be called a Functional Society, because in such a society the main subject of social emphasis would be the performance of functions. But such a society does not exist, even as a remote ideal, in the modern world, though something like it has hung, an unrealized theory, before men's minds in the past. Modern societies aim at protecting economic rights, while leaving economic functions, except in moments of abnormal emergency, to fulfil themselves. The motive which gives color and quality to their public institutions, to their policy and political thought, is not the attempt to secure the fulfilment of tasks undertaken for the public service, but to increase the opportunities open to individuals of attaining the objects which they conceive to be advantageous to themselves. If asked the end or criterion of social organization, they would give an answer reminiscent of the formula the greatest happiness of the greatest number. But to say that the end of social institutions is happiness, is to say that they have no common end at all. For happiness is individual, and to make happiness the object of society is to resolve society itself into the ambitions of numberless individuals, each directed towards the attainment of some personal purpose.

Such societies may be called Acquisitive Societies, because their whole tendency and interest and preoccupation is to promote the acquisition of wealth. The appeal of this conception must be powerful, for it has laid the whole modern world under its spell. Since England first revealed the possibilities of industrialism, it has gone from strength to strength, and as industrial civilization invades countries hitherto remote from it, as Russia and Japan and India and China are drawn into its orbit, each decade sees a fresh extension of its influence. The secret of its triumph is obvious. It is an invitation to men to use the powers with which they have been endowed by nature or society, by skill or energy or relentless egotism or mere good fortune, without inquiring whether there is any principle by which their exercise should be limited. It assumes the social organization which determines the opportunities which different classes shall in fact possess, and concentrates attention upon the right of those who possess or can acquire power to make the fullest use of it for their own self-advancement. By fixing men's minds, not upon the discharge of social obligations, which restricts their energy, because it defines the goal to which it should be directed, but upon the exercise of the right to pursue their own self-interest, it offers unlimited scope for the acquisition of riches, and therefore gives free play to one of the most powerful of human instincts. To the strong it promises unfettered freedom for the exercise of their strength; to the weak the hope that they too one day may be strong. Before the eyes of both it suspends a golden prize, which not all can attain, but for which each may strive, the enchanting vision of infinite expansion. It assures men that there are no ends other than their ends, no law other than their desires, no limit other than that which they think advisable. Thus it makes the individual the center of his own universe, and dissolves moral principles into a choice of expediences. And it immensely simplifies the problems of social life in complex communities. For it relieves them of the necessity of discriminating between different types of economic activity and different sources of wealth, between enterprise and avarice, energy and unscrupulous greed, property which is legitimate and property which is theft, the just enjoyment of the fruits of labor and the idle parasitism of birth or fortune, because it treats all economic activities as standing upon the same level, and suggests that excess or defect, waste or superfluity, require no conscious effort of the social will to avert them, but are corrected almost automatically by the mechanical play of economic forces.

Under the impulse of such ideas men do not become religious or wise or artistic; for religion and wisdom and art imply the acceptance of limitations. But they become powerful and rich. They inherit the earth and change the face of nature, if they do not possess their own souls; and they have that appearance of freedom which consists in the absence of obstacles between opportunities for self-advancement and those whom birth or wealth or talent or good fortune has placed in a position to seize them. It is not difficult either for individuals or for societies to achieve their object, if that object be sufficiently limited and immediate, and if they are not distracted from its pursuit by other considerations. The temper which dedicates itself to the cultivation of opportunities, and leaves obligations to take care of themselves, is set upon an object which is at once simple and practicable. The eighteenth century defined it. The twentieth century has very largely attained it. Or, if it has not attained it, it has at least grasped the possibilities of its attainment. The national output of wealth per head of population is estimated to have been approximately $200 in 1914. Unless mankind chooses to continue the sacrifice of prosperity to the ambitions and terrors of nationalism, it is possible that by the year 2000 it may be doubled. ♦

QUESTIONS

1. Why does Tawney distinguish between "rights" and "functions" of individual members of society?

2. What does Tawney mean when he says that in contemporary England and America, rights would more accurately be thought of as privileges?

3. Why would recognition of a social function of business threaten property rights?

4. According to Tawney, what is the appeal of industrial civilization?

5. Contrast a "Functional" and an "Acquisitive" society.

FROM *THE GOSPEL OF WEALTH*
Andrew Carnegie (1835–1919)

THE PROBLEM OF THE ADMINISTRATION OF WEALTH

The problem of our age is the proper administration of wealth, that the ties of brotherhood may still bind together the rich and poor in harmonious relationship. The conditions of human life have not only been changed, but revolutionized, within the past few hundred years. In former days there was little difference between the dwelling, dress, food, and environment of the chief and those of his retainers. The Indians are today where civilized man then was. When visiting the Sioux, I was led to the wigwam of the chief. It was like the others in external appearance, and even within the difference was trifling between it and those of the poorest of his braves. The contrast between the palace of the millionaire and the cottage of the laborer with us today measures the change which has come with civilization. This change, however, is not to be deplored, but welcomed as highly beneficial. It is well, nay, essential, for the progress of the race that the houses of some should be homes for all that is highest and best in literature and the arts, and for all the refinements of civilization, rather than that none should be so. Much better this great irregularity than universal squalor. Without wealth there can be no Maecenas. The "good old times" were not good old times. Neither master nor servant was as well situated then as to-day. A relapse to old conditions would be disastrous to both—not the least so to him who serves—and would sweep away civilization with it. But whether the change be for good or ill, it is upon us, beyond our power to alter, and, therefore, to be accepted and made the best of. It is a waste of time to criticize the inevitable.

It is easy to see how the change has come. One illustration will serve for almost every phase of the cause. In the manufacture of products we have the whole story. It applies to all combinations of human industry, as stimulated and enlarged by the inventions of this scientific age. Formerly, articles were manufactured at the domestic hearth, or in small shops which formed part of the household. The master and his apprentices worked side by side, the latter living with the master, and therefore subject to the same conditions. When these apprentices rose to be masters, there was little or no change in their mode of life, and they, in turn, educated succeeding apprentices in the same routine. There was, substantially, social equality, and even political equality, for those engaged in industrial pursuits had then little or no voice in the State.

The inevitable result of such a mode of manufacture was crude articles at high prices. Today the world obtains commodities of excellent quality at prices which even the preceding generation would have deemed incredible. In the commercial world similar causes have produced similar results, and the race is benefited thereby. The poor enjoy what the rich could not before afford. What were the luxuries have become the necessaries of life. The laborer has now more comforts than the farmer had a few generations ago. The farmer has more luxuries than the landlord had, and is more richly clad and better housed. The landlord has books and pictures rarer and appointments more artistic than the king could then obtain.

The price we pay for this salutary change is, no doubt, great. We assemble thousands of operatives in the factory, and in the mine, of whom the employer can know little or nothing, and to whom he is little better than a myth. All intercourse between them is at an end. Rigid castes are formed, and, as usual, mutual ignorance breeds mutual distrust. Each caste is without sympathy with the other, and ready to credit anything disparaging in regard to it. Under the law of competition, the employer of thousands is forced into the strictest economies, among which the rates paid to labor figure prominently, and often there is friction between the employer and the employed, between capital and labor, between rich and poor. Human society loses homogeneity.

The price which society pays for the law of competition, like the price it pays for cheap comforts and luxuries, is also great; but the advantages of this law are also greater still than its cost—for it is to this law that we owe our wonderful material development, which brings improved conditions in its train. But, whether the law be benign or not, we must say of it, as we say of the change in the conditions of men to which we have referred: It is here; we cannot evade it; no substitutes for it have been found; and while the law may be sometimes hard for the individual, it is best for the race, because it insures the survival of the fittest in every department. We accept and welcome, therefore, as conditions to which we must accommodate ourselves, great inequality of environment; the concentration of business, industrial and commercial, in the hands of a few; and the law of competition between these, as being not only beneficial, but essential to the future progress of the race. Having accepted these, it follows that there must be great scope for the exercise of special ability in the merchant and in the manufacturer who has to conduct affairs upon a great scale. That this talent for organization and management is rare among men is proved by the fact that it invariably secures enormous rewards for its possessor, no matter where or under what laws or conditions. The experienced in affairs always rate the MAN whose services can be obtained as a partner as not only the first consideration, but such as render the question of his capital scarcely worth considering: for able men soon create capital; in the hands of those without the special talent required, capital soon takes wings. Such men become interested in firms or corporations using millions; and, estimating only simple interest to be made upon the capital invested, it is inevitable that their income must exceed their expenditure and that they must, therefore, accumulate wealth. Nor is there any middle ground which such men can occupy, because the great manufacturing or commercial concern which does not earn at least interest upon its capital soon becomes bankrupt. It must either go forward or fall

behind; to stand still is impossible. It is a condition essential to its successful operation that it should be thus far profitable, and even that, in addition to interest on capital, it should make profit. It is a law, as certain as any of the others named, that men possessed of this peculiar talent for affairs, under the free play of economic forces must, of necessity, soon be in receipt of more revenue than can be judiciously expended upon themselves; and this law is as beneficial for the race as the others.

Objections to the foundations upon which society is based are not in order, because the condition of the race is better with these than it has been with any other which has been tried. Of the effect of any new substitutes proposed we cannot be sure. The Socialist or Anarchist who seeks to overturn present conditions is to be regarded as attacking the foundation upon which civilization itself rests, for civilization took its start from the day when the capable, industrious workman said to his incompetent and lazy fellow, "If thou dost not sow, thou shalt not reap," and thus ended primitive Communism by separating the drones from the bees. One who studies this subject will soon be brought face to face with the conclusion that upon the sacredness of property civilization itself depends—the right of the laborer to his hundred dollars in the savings-bank, and equally the legal right of the millionaire to his millions. Every man must be allowed "to sit under his own vine and fig-tree, with none to make afraid," if human society is to advance, or even to remain so far advanced as it is. To those who propose to substitute Communism for this intense Individualism, the answer therefore is: The race has tried that. All progress from that barbarous day to the present time has resulted from its displacement. Not evil, but good, has come to the race from the accumulation of wealth by those who have had the ability and energy to produce it. But even if we admit for a moment that it might be better for the race to discard its present foundation, Individualism,— that it is a nobler ideal that man should labor, not for himself alone, but in and for a brotherhood of his fellows, and share with them all in common, realizing Swedenborg's idea of heaven, where, as he says, the angels derive their happiness, not from laboring for self, but for each other,—even admit all this, and a sufficient answer is, This is not evolution, but revolution. It necessitates the changing of human nature itself—a work of eons, even if it were good to change it, which we cannot know.

It is not practicable in our day or in our age. Even if desirable theoretically, it belongs to another and long-succeeding sociological stratum. Our duty is with what is practicable now— with the next step possible in our day and generation. It is criminal to waste our energies in endeavoring to uproot, when all we can profitably accomplish is to bend the universal tree of humanity a little in the direction most favorable to the production of good fruit under existing circumstances. We might as well urge the destruction of the highest existing type of man because he failed to reach our ideal as to favor the destruction of Individualism, Private Property, the Law of Accumulation of Wealth, and the Law of Competition; for these are the highest result of human experience, the soil in which society, so far, has produced the best fruit. Unequally or unjustly, perhaps, as these laws sometimes operate, and imperfect as they appear to the Idealist, they are, nevertheless, like the highest type of man, the best and most valuable of all that humanity has yet accomplished.

We start, then, with a condition of affairs under which the best interests of the race are promoted, but which inevitably gives wealth to the few. Thus far, accepting conditions as they exist, the situation can be surveyed and pronounced good. The question then arises,— and if the foregoing be correct, it is the only question with which we have to deal,—What is the proper mode of administering wealth after the laws upon which civilization is founded have thrown it into the hands of the few? And it is of this great question that I believe I offer the true solution. It will be understood that fortunes are here spoken of, not moderate sums saved by many years of effort, the returns from which are required for the comfortable maintenance and education of families. This is not wealth, but only competence, which it should be the aim of all to acquire, and which it is for the best interests of society should be acquired.

There are but three modes in which surplus wealth can be disposed of. It can be left to the families of the decedents; or it can be bequeathed for public purposes; or, finally, it can be administered by its possessors during their lives. Under the first and second modes most of the wealth of the world that has reached the few has hitherto been applied. Let us in turn consider each of these modes. The first is the most injudicious. In monarchical countries, the estates and the greatest portion of the wealth are left to the first son, that the vanity of the parent may be gratified by the thought that his name and title are to descend unimpaired to succeeding generations. The condition of this class in Europe today teaches the failure of such hopes or ambitions. The successors have become impoverished through their follies, or from the fall in the value of land. Even in Great Britain the strict law of entail has been found inadequate to maintain an hereditary class. Its soil is rapidly passing into the hands of the stranger. Under republican institutions the division of property among the children is much fairer; but the question which forces itself upon thoughtful men in all lands is, Why should men leave great fortunes to their children? If this is done from affection, is it not misguided affection? Observation teaches that, generally speaking, it is not well for the children that they should be so burdened. Neither is it well for the State. Beyond providing for the wife and daughters moderate sources of income, and very moderate allowances indeed, if any, for the sons, men may well hesitate; for it is no longer questionable that great sums bequeathed often work more for the injury than for the good of the recipients. Wise men will soon conclude that, for the best interests of the members of their families, and of the State, such bequests are an improper use of their means.

It is not suggested that men who have failed to educate their sons to earn a livelihood shall cast them adrift in poverty. If any man has seen fit to rear his sons with a view to their living idle lives, or, what is highly commendable, has instilled in them the sentiment that they are in a position to labor for public ends without reference to pecuniary considerations, then, of course, the duty of the parent is to see that such are provided for in moderation. There are instances of millionaires' sons unspoiled by wealth, who, being rich, still perform great services to the community. Such are the very salt of the earth, as valuable as, unfortunately, they are rare. It is not the exception, however, but the rule, that men must regard; and, looking at the usual result of enormous sums conferred upon legatees, the thoughtful man must shortly say, "I would as soon leave to my son a curse as the almighty dollar," and admit to himself that it is not the welfare of the children, but family pride, which inspires these legacies.

As to the second mode, that of leaving wealth at death for public uses, it may be said that this is only a means for the disposal of wealth, provided a man is content to wait until he is dead before he becomes of much good in the world. Knowledge of the results of legacies bequeathed is not calculated to inspire the brightest hopes of much posthumous good being accomplished by them. The cases are not few in which the real object sought by the testator is not attained, nor are they few in which his real wishes are thwarted. In many cases the bequests are so used as to become only monuments of his folly. It is well to remember that it requires the exercise of not less ability than that which acquires it, to use wealth so as to be really beneficial to the community. Besides this, it may fairly be said that no man is to be extolled for doing what he cannot help doing, nor is he to be thanked by the community to which he only leaves wealth at death. Men who leave vast sums in this way may fairly be thought men who would not have left it at all had they been able to take it with them. The memories of such cannot be held in grateful remembrance, for there is no grace in their gifts. It is not to be wondered at that such bequests seem so generally to lack the blessing.

The growing disposition to tax more and more heavily large estates left at death is a cheering indication of the growth of a salutary change in public opinion. The State of Pennsylvania now takes—subject to some exceptions—one tenth of the property left by its citizens. The budget presented in the British Parliament the other day proposes to increase the death duties; and, most significant of all, the new tax is to be a graduated one. Of all forms of taxation this seems the wisest. Men who continue hoarding great sums all their lives, the proper use of which for public ends would work good to the community from which it chiefly came, should be made to feel that the community, in the form of the State, cannot thus be deprived of its proper share. By taxing estates heavily at death the State marks its condemnation of the selfish millionaire's unworthy life.

It is desirable that nations should go much further in this direction. Indeed, it is difficult to set bounds to the share of a rich man's estate which should go at his death to the public through the agency of the State, and by all means such taxes should be graduated, beginning at nothing upon moderate sums to dependents, and increasing rapidly as the amounts swell, until of the millionaire's hoard, as of Shylock's, at least

> The other half
> Comes to the privy coffer of the State.

This policy would work powerfully to induce the rich man to attend to the administration of wealth during his life, which is the end that society should always have in view, as being by far the most fruitful for the people. Nor need it be feared that this policy would sap the root of enterprise and render men less anxious to accumulate, for, to the class whose ambition it is to leave great fortunes and to be talked about after their death, it will attract even more attention, and, indeed, be a somewhat nobler ambition, to have enormous sums paid over to the State from their fortunes.

There remains, then, only one mode of using great fortunes; but in this we have the true antidote for the temporary unequal distribution of wealth, the reconciliation of the rich and the poor—a reign of harmony, another ideal, differing, indeed, from that of the Communist in requiring only the further evolution of existing conditions, not the total overthrow of our civilization. It is founded upon the present most intense Individualism, and the race is prepared to put it in practice by degrees whenever it pleases. Under its sway we shall have an ideal State, in which the surplus wealth of the few will become, in the best sense, the property of the many, because administered for the common good; and this wealth, passing through the hands of the few, can be made a much more potent force for the elevation of our race than if distributed in small sums to the people themselves. Even the poorest can be made to see this, and to agree that great sums gathered by some of their fellow-citizens and spent for public purposes, from which the masses reap the principal benefit, are more valuable to them than if scattered among themselves in trifling amounts through the course of many years.

If we consider the results which flow from the Cooper Institute, for instance, to the best portion of the race in New York not possessed of means, and compare these with those which would have ensued for the good of the masses from an equal sum distributed by Mr. Cooper in his lifetime in the form of wages, which is the highest form of distribution, being for work done and not for charity, we can form some estimate of the possibilities for the improvement of the race which lie embedded in the present law of the accumulation of wealth. Much of this sum, if distributed in small quantities among the people, would have been wasted in the indulgence of appetite, some of it in excess, and it may be doubted whether even the part put to the best use, that of adding to the comforts of the home, would have yielded results for the race, as a race, at all comparable to those which are flowing and are to flow from the Cooper Institute from generation to generation. Let the advocate of violent or radical change ponder well this thought.

We might even go so far as to take another instance—that of Mr. Tilden's bequest of five millions of dollars for a free library in the city of New York; but in referring to this one cannot help saying involuntarily: How much better if Mr. Tilden had devoted the last years of his own life to the proper administration of this immense sum; in which case neither legal contest nor any other cause of delay could have interfered with his aims. But let us assume that Mr. Tilden's millions finally became the means of giving to this city a noble public library, where the treasures of the world contained in books will be open to all forever, without money and without price. Considering the good of that part of the race which congregates in and around Manhattan Island, would its permanent benefit have been better promoted had these millions been allowed to circulate in small sums through the hands of the masses? Even the most strenuous advocate of Communism must entertain a doubt upon this subject. Most of those who think will probably entertain no doubt whatever.

Poor and restricted are our opportunities in this life, narrow our horizon, our best work most imperfect; but rich men should be thankful for one inestimable boon. They have it in their power during their lives to busy themselves in organizing benefactions from which the masses of their fellows will derive lasting advantage, and thus dignify their own lives. The highest life is probably to be reached, not by such imitation of the life of Christ as Count Tolstoi gives us, but, while animated by Christ's spirit, by recognizing the changed conditions of this age, and adopting modes of expressing this spirit suitable to the changed conditions under which we live, still laboring for the good of our fellows, which was the essence of his life and teaching, but laboring in a different manner.

This, then, is held to be the duty of the man of wealth: To set an example of modest, unostentatious living, shunning display or extravagance; to provide moderately for the legitimate wants of those dependent upon him; and, after doing so, to consider all surplus revenues which come to him simply as trust funds, which he is called upon to administer, and strictly bound as a matter of duty to administer in the manner which, in his judgment, is best calculated to produce the most beneficial results for the community—the man of wealth thus becoming the mere trustee and agent for his poorer brethren, bringing to their service his superior wisdom, experience, and ability to administer, doing for them better than they would or could do for themselves.

We are met here with the difficulty of determining what are moderate sums to leave to members of the family; what is modest, unostentatious living; what is the test of extravagance.

There must be different standards for different conditions. The answer is that it is as impossible to name exact amounts or actions as it is to define good manners, good taste, or the rules of propriety; but, nevertheless, these are verities, well known, although indefinable. Public sentiment is quick to know and to feel what offends these. So in the case of wealth. The rule in regard to good taste in dress of men or women applies here. Whatever makes one conspicuous offends the canon. If any family be chiefly known for display, for extravagance in home, table, or equipage, for enormous sums ostentatiously spent in any form upon itself—if these be its chief distinctions, we have no difficulty in estimating its nature or culture. So likewise in regard to the use or abuse of its surplus wealth, or to generous, free-handed cooperation in good public uses, or to unabated efforts to accumulate and hoard to the last, or whether they administer or bequeath. The verdict rests with the best and most enlightened public sentiment. The community will surely judge, and its judgments will not often be wrong.

The best uses to which surplus wealth can be put have already been indicated. Those who would administer wisely must, indeed, be wise; for one of the serious obstacles to the improvement of our race is indiscriminate charity. It were better for mankind that the millions of the rich were thrown into the sea than so spent as to encourage the slothful, the drunken, the unworthy. Of every thousand dollars spent in so-called charity today, it is probable that nine hundred and fifty dollars is unwisely spent—so spent, indeed, as to produce the very evils which it hopes to mitigate or cure. A well-known writer of philosophic books admitted the other day that he had given a quarter of a dollar to a man who approached him as he was coming to visit the house of his friend. He knew nothing of the habits of this beggar, knew not the use that would be made of this money, although he had every reason to suspect that it would be spent improperly. This man professed to be a disciple of Herbert Spencer; yet the quarter-dollar given that night will probably work more injury than all the money will do good which its thoughtless donor will

ever be able to give in true charity. He only gratified his own feelings, saved himself from annoyance—and this was probably one of the most selfish and very worst actions of his life, for in all respects he is most worthy.

In bestowing charity, the main consideration should be to help those who will help themselves; to provide part of the means by which those who desire to improve may do so; to give those who desire to rise the aids by which they may rise; to assist, but rarely or never to do all. Neither the individual nor the race is improved by almsgiving. Those worthy of assistance, except in rare cases, seldom require assistance. The really valuable men of the race never do, except in case of accident or sudden change. Every one has, of course, cases of individuals brought to his own knowledge where temporary assistance can do genuine good, and these he will not overlook. But the amount which can be wisely given by the individual for individuals is necessarily limited by his lack of knowledge of the circumstances connected with each. He is the only true reformer who is as careful and as anxious not to aid the unworthy as he is to aid the worthy, and, perhaps, even more so, for in almsgiving more injury is probably done by rewarding vice than by relieving virtue.

The rich man is thus almost restricted to following the examples of Peter Cooper, Enoch Pratt of Baltimore, Mr. Pratt of Brooklyn, Senator Stanford, and others, who know that the best means of benefiting the community is to place within its reach the ladders upon which the aspiring can rise—free libraries, parks, and means of recreation, by which men are helped in body and mind; works of art, certain to give pleasure and improve the public taste; and public institutions of various kinds, which will improve the general condition of the people; in this manner returning their surplus wealth to the mass of their fellows in the forms best calculated to do them lasting good.

Thus is the problem of rich and poor to be solved. The laws of accumulation will be left free, the laws of distribution free. Individualism will continue, but the millionaire will be but a trustee for the poor, entrusted for a season with a great part of the increased wealth of the community, but administering it for the community far better than it could or would have done for itself. The best minds will thus have reached a stage in the development of the race in which it is clearly seen that there is no mode of disposing of surplus wealth creditable to thoughtful and earnest men into whose hands it flows, save by using it year by year for the general good. This day already dawns. Men may die without incurring the pity of their fellows, still sharers in great business enterprises from which their capital cannot be or has not been withdrawn, and which is left chiefly at death for public uses; yet the day is not far distant when the man who dies leaving behind him millions of available wealth, which was free to him to administer during life, will pass away "unwept, unhonored, and unsung," no matter to what uses he leaves the dross which he cannot take with him. Of such as these the public verdict will then be: "The man who dies thus rich dies disgraced."

Such, in my opinion is the true gospel concerning wealth, obedience to which is destined some day to solve the problem of the rich and the poor, and to bring "Peace on earth, among men good will." ♦

QUESTIONS

1. According to Carnegie, why is it acceptable that industrial civilization leads to inequality and friction?

2. What does Carnegie mean by "wealth"?

3. What are the three ways that wealth can be disposed of? According to Carnegie, which is best and why?

Selection From: *The Business Guide*

J. L. Nichols (1851–1895) self-published Naperville, Ill 1893

My son, you shall have a home while I live. But I cannot deed you my farm. It is all I have to support me in my old age.

Teaching Business to Children

Do Not Give Away Your Property in Old Age.

Many persons, as they advance in years, make the fatal mistake of giving away their property, to children and then depend upon them for support.

How many old persons have gone to their graves broken-hearted and suffering for the necessaries of life, because they desired to help their children, and gave to them their property. If the weight of years become heavy and there is plenty of property, a portion may be safely divided among the children, but the major portion should always be held and controlled directly or indirectly by the old couple.

1. It will insure good care and plenty of the necessaries of life.
2. The devotion and love of children will never grow cold while there is something in store for them.

It was the writer's experience in his boyhood to board in a family where the father in his old age had bequeathed his entire property to his children. When the same was divided between them their aged father became a burden, and he was sent from daughter to son, as they had all obligated themselves to care in turn for their aged father. But he never entered the home of a son or daughter, where he was a welcome guest. In the family, where the writer boarded, when the aged father was with them, if there was a cup of coffee short in the morning, it was the old man's cup that was not filled; if meat or other food was short, it was the old man's plate that indicated the shortage; if the pie was somewhat deficient, it was the old man's piece that was cut in two, and he was compelled to sleep in a cold garret at night alone and deserted, and when the broken-hearted old man passed away, no doubt every child felt delight instead of sorrow in their hearts.

A man may have a farm or factory, or houses, and it may be necessary owing to his age to shift the burdens and cares of business to younger shoulders; the ownership, however, should never be changed, but the running and looking after the property may be delegated to some child or disinterested party.

A competent lawyer is always prepared to do such business.

Every man should make a will in favor of his wife, so that in her old age she shall not become dependent.

FROM *THE PERSONAL RELATION IN INDUSTRY*

John D. Rockefeller, Jr. (1874–1960)

COÖPERATION IN INDUSTRY

I

Today the world is passing through a period of reconstruction.

As we address ourselves to the grave problems which confront us, problems both national and international, we may look for success in their solution just in so far as we continue to be animated by the spirit of coöperation and brotherhood. The hope in the future lies in the perpetuation of this spirit, and unless increasingly it is made the foundation of the political, social, and industrial life of the world, there will not be permanent peace and good will among men, either nationally or internationally.

In no one of these spheres of human relations is the spirit of coöperation more essential than in industry, since industry touches almost every department of life. Moreover, there is no problem pressing more urgently upon the attention of the world to-day than the industrial problem, none more important, none more difficult of solution. There are pessimists who say that there is no solution short of revolution and the overturn of the existing social order.

Surely the nations which have shown themselves capable of such lofty sacrifice, which have given themselves so freely, gladly, unreservedly, during these past years of struggle, will bring to bear in the solution of this great problem powers of head and heart, not less wise and unselfish than those exhibited in dealing with the problems of the war; surely a way out of the impenetrable maze will be found.

Almost countless are the suggested solutions of the industrial problem, which have been brought forth since industry first began to be a problem. Most of these are impracticable; some are unjust; some are selfish and therefore unworthy; some have merit and should be carefully studied. None can be looked to as a panacea.

There are those who believe that legislation is the cure-all for every political, social, and industrial ill. Much can be done by legislation to prevent injustice and encourage right tendencies, but legislation of itself will never solve the industrial problem. Its solution can be brought about only by the introduction of a new spirit into the relationship between the parties to industry—the spirit of coöperation and brotherhood.

It is this theme, *coöperation in industry,* that I desire to develop.

We must ask ourselves at the outset certain fundamental questions:

First, what is the purpose of industry? Shall we cling to the conception of industry as an institution, primarily of private interest, which enables certain individuals to accumulate wealth, too often irrespective of the well-being, the health, and the happiness of those engaged in its production? Or shall we adopt the modern viewpoint and regard industry as being a form of social service, quite as much as a revenue-producing process?

Is it not true that any industry, to be permanently successful, must insure to labor adequately remunerative employment under proper working and living conditions, to capital a fair return upon the money invested, and to the community a useful service?

The soundest industrial policy is that which has constantly in mind the welfare of the employees as well as the making of profits, and which, when human considerations demand it, subordinates profits to welfare. Industrial relations are essentially human relations. It is therefore the duty of everyone entrusted with industrial leadership to do all in his power to improve the conditions under which men work and live. The day has passed when the conception of industry as chiefly a revenue-producing process can be maintained. To cling to such a conception is only to arouse antagonisms and to court trouble. In the light of the present every thoughtful man must concede that the purpose of industry is quite as much the advancement of social well-being as the production of wealth. It remains none the less true, however, that to be successful, industry must not only serve the community and the workers adequately, but must also realize a just return on capital invested.

Next we must ask ourselves, who are the parties to industry: The parties to industry are four in number: capital, management, labor, and the community.

I am, of course, well aware of the social theories and experiments that seek to merge capital and labor, either through ownership of capital by the state or by the workers themselves. But the difficulties that confront the realization of these plans are vast and the objection to many of them fundamental.

Under our present system, capital is represented by the stockholders, and is usually regarded as embracing management. Management is, however, an entirely separate and distinct party to industry; its function is essentially administrative. It comprises the executive officers who bring to industry technical skill and managerial experience. Labor consists of the employees. Labor, like capital, is an investor in industry, but labor's contribution, unlike that of capital, is not detachable from the one who makes it, since it is in the nature of physical effort and is a part of the worker's strength and life. Here the list usually ends.

The fourth party, namely, the community, whose interest is vital and in the last analysis controlling, is too often ignored. The community's right to representation in the control of industry and in the shaping of industrial policies is similar to that of the other parties. Were it not for the community's contribution, in maintaining law and order, in providing agencies of transportation and communication, in furnishing systems of money and credit and in rendering other services, all involving continuous outlays, the operation of capital, management, and labor would be enormously hampered, if not rendered wellnigh impossible. The community, furthermore, is the consumer of the product of industry, and the money which it pays for the product reimburses capital for its advances and ultimately provides the wages, salaries, and profits that are distributed among the other parties.

Finally we must inquire: what are the relations between the parties to industry? It is frequently maintained that the parties to industry must necessarily be hostile and antagonistic; that each must arm itself to wrest from the others its share of the product of their common toil. This is unthinkable; it is not true; the parties to industry are in reality not enemies, but partners; they have a common interest; no one can get on without the others. Labor must look to capital to supply the tools, machinery, and working capital, without which it cannot make its vital contribution to industry; and capital is equally powerless to turn a wheel in industry without labor. Management is essential to supply the directing force, while without the community as the consumer, the services of the other three parties would have no outlet. Just what the relative importance of the contribution made to the success of industry by the several factors is, and what their relative rewards should be, are debatable questions.

But, however views may differ on these questions, it is clear that the common interest cannot be advanced by the effort of any one party to dominate the others, arbitrarily to dictate the terms on which alone it will cooperate, or to threaten to withdraw if any attempt is made to thwart the enforcement of its will. Success is dependent upon the coöperation of all four. Partnership, not enmity, is the watchword.

II

If coöperation between the parties to industry is sound business and good social economics, why then is antagonism so often found in its stead? The answer is revealed in a survey of the development of industry. In the early days of industry, as we know, the functions of capital and management were not infrequently combined in the one individual, who was the employer. He in turn was in constant touch with his employees. Together they formed a vital part of the community. Personal relations were frequent and mutual confidence existed. When differences arose they were quickly adjusted. As industry developed, aggregations of capital larger than a single individual could provide were required. In answer to this demand, the corporation with its many stockholders was evolved. Countless workers took the place of the handful of employees of earlier days. Plants under a single management scattered all over the country superseded the single plant in a given community. Obviously, this development rendered impossible the personal relations which had existed in industry, and lessened the spirit of common interest and understanding. Thus the door was opened to suspicion and distrust; enmity crept in; antagonisms developed. Capital not infrequently used its power to enforce long hours and low wages; labor likewise retaliated with such strength as it had, and gradually the parties to industry came to view each other as enemies instead of as friends and to think of their interests as antagonistic rather than common.

Where men are strangers and have no contact, misunderstanding is apt to arise. On the other hand, where men meet frequently about a table, rub elbows, exchange views, and discuss matters of common interest, almost invariably it happens that the vast majority of their differences quickly disappear and friendly relations are established.

Several years ago I was one of a number of men who were asked two questions by a Commission appointed by the President of the United States to deal with certain labor difficulties.

The first was: "What do you regard as the underlying cause of industrial unrest?" The second: "What remedy do you suggest?"

I stated that in my judgment the chief cause of industrial unrest is that capital does not strive to look at questions at issue from labor's point of view, and labor does not seek to get capital's angle of vision. My answer to the second question was that when employers put themselves in the employee's place and the employees put themselves in the employer's place, the remedy for industrial unrest will have been found. In other words, when the principle adopted by both parties in interest is: "Do as you would be done by," there will be no industrial unrest, no industrial problem.

It is to be regretted that there are capitalists who regard labor as their legitimate prey, from whom they are justified in getting all they can for as little as may be. It is equally to be deplored that on the part of labor there is often a feeling that it is justified in wresting everything possible from capital. Where such attitudes have been assumed, a gulf has been opened between capital and labor which has continually widened. Thus the two forces have come to work against each other, each seeking solely to promote its own selfish ends. As a consequence have come all too frequently the strike, the lockout, and other incidents of industrial warfare.

A man, who recently devoted some months to studying the industrial problem and who came into contact with thousands in various industries throughout the United States, has said that it was obvious to him from the outset that the working men were seeking for something, which at first he thought to be higher wages. As his touch with them extended, he came to the conclusion, however, that not higher wages, but recognition as men, was what they really sought. What joy can there be in life, what interest can a man take in his work, what enthusiasm can he be expected to develop on behalf of his employer, when he is regarded as a number on a pay-roll, a cog in a wheel, a mere "hand"? Who would not earnestly seek to gain recognition of his manhood and the right to be heard and treated as a human being, not as a machine?

Then, too, as industry has become increasingly specialized, the workman of to-day, instead of following the product through from start to finish and being stimulated by the feeling that he is the sole creator of a useful article, as was more or less the case in early days, now devotes his energies for the most part to countless repetitions of a single act or process, which is but one of perhaps a hundred operations necessary to transform the raw material into the finished product. Thus the worker loses sight of the significance of the part he plays in industry and feels himself to be merely one of many cogs in a wheel. All the more, therefore, is it necessary that he should have contact with men engaged in other processes and fulfilling other functions in industry, that he may still realize he is a part, and a necessary, though it may be an inconspicuous, part of a great enterprise. In modern warfare, those who man the large guns find the range, not by training the gun on the object which they are seeking to reach, but in obedience to a mechanical formula which is worked out for them. Stationed behind a hill or mound, they seldom see the object at which their deadly fire is directed. One can readily imagine the sense of detachment and ineffectiveness which must come over these men. But when the airplane, circling overhead, gets into communication with the gunner beneath and describes the thing to be accomplished and the effectiveness of the shot, a new meaning comes into his life. In a second he has become a part of the great struggle. He knows that his efforts are counting, that he is helping to bring success to his comrades. There comes to him a new enthusiasm and interest in his work. The sense of isolation and detachment from the accomplishments of industry, which too often comes to the workers of to-day, can be overcome only by contact with the other contributing parties. In this way only can common purpose be kept alive, individual interests safeguarded, and the general welfare promoted.

While obviously under present conditions those who invest their capital in an industry, often numbered by the thousand, cannot have personal acquaintance with the thousands and tens of thousands of those who invest their labor, contact between those two parties in interest can and must be established, if not directly, then through their respective representatives. The resumption of such personal relations through frequent conferences and current meetings, held for the consideration of matters of common interest, such as terms of employment and working and living conditions, is essential in order to restore a spirit of mutual confidence, good will, and coöperation. Personal relations can be revived under modern conditions only through the adequate representation of the employees. Representation is a principle which is fundamentally just and vital to the successful conduct of industry. It means, broadly speaking, democracy through coöperation, as contrasted with autocracy.

It is not for me or anyone else to undertake to determine for industry at large what specific form representation shall take. Once having adopted the principle, it is obviously wise that the method to be employed should be left, in each specific instance, to be determined by the parties interested. If there is to be peace and goodwill between the several parties in industry, it will surely not be brought about by the enforcement upon unwilling groups of a method which in their judgment is not adapted to their peculiar needs. In this, as in all else, persuasion is an essential element in bringing about conviction.

With the developments in industry what they are to-day, there is sure to come a progressive evolution from the autocratic single control, whether by capital, management, labor, or the community, to some form of democratic coöperative control participated in by all four. The whole movement is evolutionary. That which is fundamental is the idea of coöperation, and that idea must find expression in those forms which will serve it best, with conditions, forces and times what they are.

In the United States, the coöperation in war service of labor, capital, management, and Government afforded a striking and most gratifying illustration of this tendency.

After all, the basic principles governing the relations between the parties to industry are as applicable in the successful conduct of industry to-day as in earlier times. The question which now confronts us is how to reestablish personal relations and coöperation in spite of changed conditions. The answer is not doubtful or questionable, but absolutely clear and unmistakable: it is, through adequate representation of the four parties in the councils of industry....

IV

...If the points which I have endeavored to make are sound, might not the four parties to industry subscribe to an Industrial Creed somewhat as follows:—

1. I believe that labor and capital are partners, not enemies; and that their interests are common, not opposed; and that neither can attain the fullest measure of prosperity

at the expense of the other, but only in association with the other.

2. I believe that the community is an essential party to industry and that it should have adequate representation with the other parties.

3. I believe that the purpose of industry is quite as much to advance social well-being as material prosperity; that in the pursuit of that purpose, the interests of the community should be carefully considered, the well-being of employees fully guarded, management adequately recognized, and capital justly compensated, and that failure in any of these particulars means loss to all four parties.

4. I believe that every man is entitled to an opportunity to earn a living, to fair wages, to reasonable hours of work and proper working conditions, to a decent home, to the opportunity to play, to learn, to worship and to love, as well as to toil, and that the responsibility rests as heavily upon industry as upon government or society, to see that these conditions and opportunities prevail.

5. I believe that diligence, initiative, and efficiency, wherever found, should be encouraged and adequately rewarded; that indolence, indifference, and restriction of production should be discountenanced; and that service is the only justification for the possession of power.

6. I believe that the provision of adequate means of uncovering grievances and promptly adjusting them is of fundamental importance to the successful conduct of industry.

7. I believe that the most potent measure in bringing about industrial harmony and prosperity is adequate representation of the parties in interest; that existing forms of representation should be carefully studied and availed of, in so far as they may be found to have merit and are adaptable to conditions peculiar to the various industries.

8. I believe that the most effective structure of representation is that which is built from the bottom up, which includes all employees, which starts with the election of representatives and the formation of joint committees in each industrial plant, proceeds to the formation of joint district councils and annual joint conferences in a single industrial corporation, and admits of extension to all corporations in the same industry, as well as to all industries in a community, in a nation, and in the various nations.

9. I believe that to "do unto others as you would that they should do unto you" is as sound business as it is good religion; that the application of right principles never fails to effect right relations; that "the letter killeth, but the spirit giveth life"; that forms are wholly secondary, while attitude and spirit are all important; and that only as the parties in industry are animated by the spirit of fair play, justice to all, and brotherhood, will any plan which they may mutually work out succeed.

10. I believe that that man renders the greatest social service who so coöperates in the organization of industry as to afford to the largest number of men the greatest opportunity for self-development and the enjoyment of those benefits which their united efforts add to the wealth of civilization.

V

In these days the selfish pursuit of personal ends at the expense of the group can and will no longer be tolerated. The reign of autocracy has passed. Men are rapidly coming to see that human life is of infinitely greater value than material wealth; that the health, happiness, and well-being of the individual, however humble, is not to be sacrificed to the selfish aggrandizement of the more fortunate or more powerful. Modern thought is placing less emphasis on material considerations. It is recognizing that the basis of national progress, whether industrial or social, is the health, efficiency, and spiritual development of the people. Never was there a more profound belief in human life than to-day. Whether men work with brain or brawn, they are human beings, and are much alike in their cravings, their aspirations, their hatreds, and their capacity for suffering and for enjoyment.

What is the attitude of the leaders in industry as they face this critical period of reconstruction? Is it that of the standpatters, who ignore the extraordinary changes which have come over the face of the civilized world and have taken place in the minds of men; who, arming themselves to the teeth, attempt stubbornly to resist the inevitable and invite open warfare with the other parties in industry, and who say:

"What has been and is, must continue to be; with our backs to the wall we will fight it out along the old lines or go down in defeat!"

Those who take such an attitude are willfully heedless of the fact that its certain outcome will be financial loss, general inconvenience and suffering, the development of bitterness and hatred, and in the end submission to far more drastic and radical conditions imposed by legislation, if not by force, than could now be amicably arrived at through mutual concession in friendly conference.

Or is their attitude one in which I myself profoundly believe, which takes cognizance of the inherent right and justice of the coöperative principle underlying the new order, which recognizes that mighty changes are inevitable, many of them desirable, and which does not wait until forced to adopt new methods, but takes the lead in calling together the parties to industry for a round-table conference to be held in a spirit of justice, fair play, and brotherhood, with a view to working out some plan of coöperation, which will insure to all those concerned adequate representation, will afford to labor a voice in the forming of industrial policy, and an opportunity to earn a fair wage under such conditions as shall leave time, not alone for food and sleep, but also for recreation and the development of the higher things of life?

Never was there such an opportunity as exists to-day for the industrial leader with clear vision and broad sympathy permanently to bridge the chasm that is daily gaping wider between the parties to industry, and to establish a solid foundation for industrial prosperity, social improvement, and national solidarity. Future generations will rise up and call those men blessed who have the courage of their convictions, a proper appreciation of the value of human life as contrasted with material gain, and who, imbued with the spirit of coöperation, will lay hold of the great opportunity for leadership which is open to them to-day.

In conclusion, let it be said that upon the heads of those leaders—it matters not to which of the four parties they belong—who refuse to reorganize their industrial households in the light of the modern spirit, will rest the responsibility for such radical and drastic measures as may later be forced upon industry, if the highest interests of all are not shortly considered and dealt with in a spirit of fairness.

Who, then, will dare to block the wheels of progress and to let pass the present opportunity of helping to usher in a new era of peace and prosperity throughout the world, brought about through coöperation in industry? ♦

QUESTIONS

1. According to Rockefeller, what is the purpose of business and industry?

2. Who are the parties to industrial production?

3. What did Rockefeller think was the alternative to recognizing the common interests among these parties?

4. What are the ten components of Rockefeller's industrial creed?

The Social Responsibility of
Business Is to Increase Its Profits

Milton Friedman (1912–2006)

When I hear businessmen speak eloquently about the "social responsibilities of business in a free-enterprise system," I am reminded of the wonderful line about the Frenchman who discovered at the age of 70 that he had been speaking prose all his life. The businessmen believe that they are defending free enterprise when they declaim that business is not concerned "merely" with profit but also with promoting desirable "social" ends; that business has a "social conscience" and takes seriously its responsibilities for providing employment, eliminating discrimination, avoiding pollution and whatever else may be the catchwords of the contemporary crop of reformers. In fact they are—or would be if they or anyone else took them seriously—preaching pure and unadulterated socialism. Businessmen who talk this way are unwitting puppets of the intellectual forces that have been undermining the basis of a free society these past decades.

The discussions of the "social responsibilities of business" are notable for their analytical looseness and lack of rigor. What does it mean to say that "business" has responsibilities? Only people can have responsibilities. A corporation is an artificial person and in this sense may have artificial responsibilities, but "business" as a whole cannot be said to have responsibilities, even in a vague sense. The first step toward clarity to examining the doctrine of the social responsibility of business is to ask precisely what it implies for whom.

Presumably, the individuals who are to be responsible are businessmen, which means individual proprietors or corporate executives. Most of the discussion of social responsibility is directed at corporations, so in what follows I shall mostly neglect the individual proprietors and speak of corporate executives.

In a free-enterprise, private-property system, a corporate executive is an employee of the owners of the business. He has direct responsibility to his employers. That responsibility is to conduct the business in accordance with their desires, which generally will be to make as much money as possible while conforming to the basic rules of the society, both those embodied in law and those embodied in ethical custom. Of course, in some cases his employers may have a different objective. A group of persons might establish a corporation for an eleemosynary purpose—for example, a hospital or a school. The manager of such a corporation will not have money profit as his objectives but the rendering of certain services.

In either case, the key point is that, in his capacity as a corporate executive, the manager is the agent of the individuals who own the corporation or establish the eleemosynary institution, and his primary responsibility is to them.

Needless to say, this does not mean that it is easy to judge how well he is performing his task. But at least the criterion of performance is straightforward, and the persons among whom a voluntary contractual arrangement exists are clearly defined.

Of course, the corporate executive is also a person in his own right. As a person, he may have many other responsibilities that he recognizes or assumes voluntarily—to his family, his conscience, his feelings of charity, his church, his clubs, his city, his country. He may feel impelled by these responsibilities to devote part of his income to causes he regards as worthy, to refuse to work for particular corporations, even to leave his job, for example, to join his country's armed forces. If we wish, we may refer to some of these responsibilities as "social responsibilities." But in these respects he is acting as a principal, not an agent; he is spending his own money or time or energy, not the money of his employers or the time or energy he has contracted to devote to their purposes. If these are "social responsibilities," they are the social responsibilities of individuals, not of business.

What does it mean to say that the corporate executive has a "social responsibility" in his capacity as businessman? If this statement is not pure rhetoric, it must mean that he is to act in some way that is not in the interest of his employers. For example, that he is to refrain from increasing the price of the product in order to contribute to the social objective of preventing inflation, even though a price increase would be in the best interests of the corporation. Or that he is to make expenditures on reducing pollution beyond the amount that is in the best interests of the corporation or that is required by law in order to contribute to the social objective of improving the environment. Or that, at the expense of corporate profits, he is to hire "hard-core" unemployed instead of better qualified available workmen to contribute to the social objective of reducing poverty.

In each of these cases, the corporate executive would be spending someone else's money for a general social interest. Insofar as his actions in accord with his "social responsibility" reduce returns to stockholders, he is spending their money. Insofar as his actions raise the price to customers', he is spending the customers' money. Insofar as his actions lower the wages of some employees, he is spending their money.

The stockholder or the customers or the employees could separately spend their own money on the particular action if they wished to do so. The executive is exercising distinct "social responsibility," rather than serving as an agent of the stockholders or the customers or the employees, only if he spends the money in a different way than they would have spent it.

But if he does this, he is in effect imposing taxes, on the one hand, and deciding how the tax proceeds shall be spent, on the other.

This process raises political questions on two levels: principle and consequences. On the level of political principle, the imposition of taxes and the expenditure of proceeds are governmental functions. We have established elaborate constitutional, parliamentary and judicial provisions to control these functions, to assume that taxes are imposed so far as possible in accordance with the preferences and desires of the public—after all, "taxation without representation" was one of the battle cries of the American Revolution. We have a system of checks and balances to separate the legislative function of imposing taxes and enacting expenditure from the executive function of collecting taxes and administering expenditure programs and from the judicial function of mediating disputes and interpreting the law.

Here the businessman—self-selected or appointed directly or indirectly by stockholders— is to be simultaneously legislator, executive and jurist. He is to decide whom to tax by how much and for what purpose, and he is to spend the proceeds—all this guided only by general exhortations from on high to restrain inflation, improve the environment, fight poverty and so on and on.

The whole justification for permitting the corporate executive to be selected by the stockholders is that the executive is an agent serving the interests of his principal. This justification disappears when the corporate executive imposes taxes and spends the proceeds for "social" purposes. He becomes in effect a public employee, a civil servant, even though he remains in name an employee of a private enterprise. On grounds of political principle, it is intolerable that such civil servants—insofar as their actions in the name of social responsibility are real and not just window-dressing— should be selected as they are now. If they are to be civil servants, then they must be elected through a political process. If they are to impose taxes and make expenditures to foster "social" objectives, then political machinery must be set up to make the assessment of taxes and to determine through a political process the objectives to be served.

This is the basic reason why the doctrine of "social responsibility" involves the acceptance of the socialist view that political mechanisms, not market mechanisms, are the appropriate way to determine the allocation of scarce resources to alternative uses.

On the grounds of consequences, can the corporate executive in fact discharge his alleged "social responsibilities"? On the one hand, suppose he could get away with spending the stockholders' or customers' or employees' money. How is he to know how to spend it? He

is told that he must contribute to fighting inflation. How is he to know what action of his will
contribute to that end? He is presumably an
expert in running his company—in producing a
product or selling it or financing it. But nothing
about his selection makes him an expert on
inflation. Will his holding down the price of his
product reduce inflationary pressure? Or, by
leaving more spending power in the hands of
his customers, simply divert it elsewhere? Or,
by forcing him to produce less because of the
lower price, will it simply contribute to short-
ages? Even if he could answer these questions,
how much cost is he justified in imposing on his
stockholders, customers and employees for this
social purpose? What is his appropriate share
and what is the appropriate share of others?

   And, whether he wants to or not, can he get
away with spending his stockholders', customers' or employees' money? Will not the stockholders fire him? (Either the present ones or
those who take over when his actions in the
name of social responsibility have reduced the
corporation's profits and the price of its stock.)
His customers and his employees can desert him
for other producers and employers less scrupulous in exercising their social responsibilities.

   This facet of "social responsibility" doctrine is brought into sharp relief when the doctrine is used to justify wage restraint by trade
unions. The conflict of interest is naked and
clear when union officials are asked to subordinate the interest of their members to some
more general purpose. If the union officials try
to enforce wage restraint, the consequence is
likely to be wildcat strikes, rank-and-file
revolts and the emergence of strong competitors for their jobs. We thus have the ironic phenomenon that union leaders—at least in the
U.S.—have objected to Government interference with the market far more consistently and
courageously than have business leaders.

   The difficulty of exercising "social responsibility" illustrates, of course, the great virtue
of private competitive enterprise—it forces
people to be responsible for their own actions
and makes it difficult for them to "exploit"
other people for either selfish or unselfish purposes. They can do good—but only at their
own expense.

Many a reader who has followed the argument this far may be tempted to remonstrate
that it is all well and good to speak of Government's having the responsibility to impose
taxes and determine expenditures for such
"social" purposes as controlling pollution or
training the hard-core unemployed, but that
the problems are too urgent to wait on the slow
course of political processes, that the exercise
of social responsibility by businessmen is a
quicker and surer way to solve pressing current problems.

   Aside from the question of fact—I share
Adam Smith's skepticism about the benefits
that can be expected from "those who affected
to trade for the public good"—this argument
must be rejected on grounds of principle. What
it amounts to is an assertion that those who
favor the taxes and expenditures in question
have failed to persuade a majority of their fellow citizens to be of like mind and that they are
seeking to attain by undemocratic procedures
what they cannot attain by democratic procedures. In a free society, it is hard for "evil" people to do "evil," especially since one man's
good is another's evil.

   I have, for simplicity, concentrated on the
special case of the corporate executive, except
only for the brief digression on trade unions.
But precisely the same argument applies to the
newer phenomenon of calling upon stockholders to require corporations to exercise social
responsibility (the recent G.M. crusade, for
example). In most of these cases, what is in
effect involved is some stockholders trying to
get other stockholders (or customers or
employees) to contribute against their will to
"social" causes favored by the activists. Insofar
as they succeed, they are again imposing taxes
and spending the proceeds.

   The situation of the individual proprietor is
somewhat different. If he acts to reduce the
returns of his enterprise in order to exercise his
"social responsibility," he is spending his own
money, not someone else's. If he wishes to spend
his money on such purposes, that is his right,
and I cannot see that there is any objection to his
doing so. In the process, he, too, may impose
costs on employees and customers. However,
because he is far less likely than a large corporation

or union to have monopolistic power, any such side effects will tend to be minor.

Of course, in practice the doctrine of social responsibility is frequently a cloak for actions that are justified on other grounds rather than a reason for those actions.

To illustrate, it may well be in the long-run interest of a corporation that is a major employer in a small community to devote resources to providing amenities to that community or to improving its government. That may make it easier to attract desirable employees, it may reduce the wage bill or lessen losses from pilferage and sabotage or have other worthwhile effects. Or it may be that, given the laws about the deductibility of corporate charitable contributions, the stockholders can contribute more to charities they favor by having the corporation make the gift than by doing it themselves, since they can in that way contribute an amount that would otherwise have been paid as corporate taxes.

In each of these—and many similar—cases, there is a strong temptation to rationalize these actions as an exercise of "social responsibility." In the present climate of opinion, with its widespread aversion to "capitalism," "profits," the "soulless corporation" and so on, this is one way for a corporation to generate goodwill as a byproduct of expenditures that are entirely justified in its own self-interest.

It would be inconsistent of me to call on corporate executives to refrain from this hypocritical window-dressing because it harms the foundations of a free society. That would be to call on them to exercise a "social responsibility"! If our institutions, and the attitudes of the public make it in their self-interest to cloak their actions in this way, I cannot summon much indignation to denounce them. At the same time, I can express admiration for those individual proprietors or owners of closely held corporations or stockholders of more broadly held corporations who disdain such tactics as approaching fraud.

Whether blameworthy or not, the use of the cloak of social responsibility, and the nonsense spoken in its name by influential and prestigious businessmen, does clearly harm the foundations of a free society. I have been impressed time and again by the schizophrenic character of many businessmen. They are capable of being extremely farsighted and clearheaded in matters that are internal to their businesses. They are incredibly shortsighted and muddle-headed in matters that are outside their businesses but affect the possible survival of business in general. The short-sightedness is strikingly exemplified in the calls from many businessmen for wage and price guidelines or controls or income policies. There is nothing that could do more in a brief period to destroy a market system and replace it by a centrally controlled system than effective governmental control of prices and wages.

The short-sightedness is also exemplified in speeches by businessmen on social responsibility. This may gain them kudos in the short run. But it helps to strengthen the already too prevalent view that the pursuit of profits is wicked and immoral and must be curbed and controlled by external forces. Once this view is adopted, the external forces that curb the market will not be the social consciences, however highly developed, of the pontificating executives; it will be the iron fist of Government bureaucrats. Here, as with price and wage controls, businessmen seem to me to reveal a suicidal impulse.

The political principle that underlies the market mechanism is unanimity. In an ideal free market resting on private property, no individual can coerce any other, all cooperation is voluntary, all parties to such cooperation benefit or they need not participate. There are no values, no "social" responsibilities in any sense other than the shared values and responsibilities of individuals. Society is a collection of individuals and of the various groups they voluntarily form.

The political principle that underlies the political mechanism is conformity. The individual must serve a more general social interest—whether that be determined by a church or a dictator or a majority. The individual may have a vote and say in what is to be done, but if he is overruled, he must conform. It is appropriate for some to require others to contribute to a general social purpose whether they wish to or not. Unfortunately, unanimity is not always feasible. There are some respects in which conformity appears unavoidable, so I do not see how one can avoid the use of the political mechanism altogether.

But the doctrine of "social responsibility" taken seriously would extend the scope of the political mechanism to every human activity. It does not differ in philosophy from the most explicitly collectivist doctrine. It differs only by professing to believe that collectivist ends can be attained without collectivist means. That is why, in my book "Capitalism and Freedom," I have called it a "fundamentally subversive doctrine" in a free society, and have said that in such a society, "there is one and only one social responsibility of business—to use its resources and engage in activities designed to increase its profits so long as it stays within the rules of the game, which is to say, engages in open and free competition without deception or fraud." ♦

QUESTIONS

1. According to Friedman, what is the purpose of the firm?

2. What is the manager's job and why does the manager have this obligation?

3. If the manager fails to maximize profits, what is he or she doing and where does the money come from?

4. What is Friedman's attitude toward corporate philanthropy as "window dressing"?

5. What limits are there to actions that are designed to maximize profits?

6. Why does Friedman think these limits exist?

THE SHUCHU KIYAKU*

Seika Fujiwara

Trade must be beneficial for both parties. We should not make money by making our trade partner worse off. If we do not share the profit with our trade partner, we may lose business opportunities in the long run. The profits will grow as long as we share them with our trade partner. Otherwise, they will decline. What is called profit is that which accrues through right conduct. Therefore, the merchant trying to make a quick profit will get less return than the merchant trying to make a profit in the long run.

Although Japan and foreign countries have different languages and cultures, the principle accorded by Heaven should be the same. We cannot justify cheating and looking down upon foreign trade partners by focusing on these differences and disregarding the commonalities. Even if they do not take cognizance of the principle accorded by Heaven, we should not tolerate our own ignorance of them. Even the dolphin honors trust and even the seagull manifests the ways of Heaven. Heaven will not tolerate deception, so we should not dishonor our own manners and customs. When we have an opportunity to meet a gentleman of virtue from another country, we should respect him as if he were our own father or teacher. We should try to learn from him what to do and what not to do according to his country's manners and customs, so as to practice them ourselves.

All creatures between Heaven and Earth share the same outlook and the same heart. Even more so do the people of the same country or those aboard the same boat. It behooves us to rescue those in trouble. We should not seek relief just for ourselves.

However grave a risk a storm at sea might pose, it is to be feared less than the risk that human greed poses. Of all the objects of human greed, wine and women are to be feared most. All of us always walking the same path should remind one another of this greatest risk. Thus it is well said, "fear is to tread the path amidst the temptation of lust and greed."

You should write about these particulars and consult them in your conduct of daily affairs.

*From the shuchu kiyaku as written for the Soan Suminokura family business by Seika Fugiwara in approximately 1605 AD and as reported in "The Confucian Roots of Business Kyosei" by Calvin M. Boardman and Hideaki Kiyoshi Kato, published in the *Journal of Business Ethics* (Volume 48, No. 4; December, 2003), pages 317 to 333.

QUESTIONS

1. Why does Fugiwara think it is important that an exchange benefit both parties?

2. What attitude should a businessperson adopt toward foreigners?

3. Why is greed dangerous?

IV

Marketing

Introduction: You Are Who You Think You Are; So Be Careful About Who You Think You Are

Marketing means different things to practitioners of the discipline. Some believe that it is primarily a matter of promoting products and services to potential customers. Others see it as creating new products and services to serve those customers, or creating innovative and efficient channels of distribution by which to make those products and services available in convenient and price-sensitive ways. Some live by a principle founded on the hard rock of intelligent pricing—price it right and build a customer base overnight. All of these meanings are relevant to the world of marketing. And you could add a hundred more meanings that would handily fit into the pocket of marketing.

Most contemporary definitions of marketing seem to fall squarely between the aspects of human nature and market evolution—that is, marketing grows out of our own personal natures and is given an impersonal external life that is propelled by forces that seem beyond our ability to control or even sometimes to understand. As an example, early proponents of materialism in late eighteenth-century and early nineteenth-century America agreed with Alexander Hamilton that man's nature is acquisitive—that we are naturally envious and that if we give free reign to our natural impulses, then our own self-interested efforts will serve public good and private ambition. Combined with science and its application to industrial progress, private ambition becomes economic entrepreneurialism. The fruits of such a combination result in products, services, employment, growth, and the shared belief that as our material wealth advances, so we are improved as a species by the same forces of nature that catalyzed commercial interest and the same markets that organized, almost magically, to develop, distribute, and promote products and services at prices we appreciate.

Today, we may too readily accept the simplistic, materialistic definitions of marketing dropped into textbooks by ivory-tower academics and slipped into marketing seminars by self-proclaimed marketing oracles. We learn little about marketing, or ourselves, when we exclusively adopt their old saws like "marketing is creating a customer and keeping that customer" or "marketing is finding a need and filling it." While marketing does both of these things, we, as practitioners, know that such definitions are "drops in the ocean."

Sun Tzu's *The Art of War* is considered one of the earliest and best texts ever written on the subject of strategy in times of conflict. Although Sun Tzu's work was composed more than 2500 years ago, during a time of civil strife in China, Sun Tzu manages to sound contemporary in his understanding of the politics of competition and combat. Despite the eastern Taoist "twist" to his observations regarding military operations, his conclusions are often in concert with modern western thinking on the subject of organizational marketing strategies and tactics. Current marketing principles emphasize a complete comprehension of the strengths, weaknesses, opportunities, and threats inherent in any introduction of the forces of "products and/or services" into the battlefield of competitive markets. Sun Tzu's view of staged combat—analyzing weak and strong organizational and competitive characteristics, planning for combat in a logical way, waging "war," and attacking by strategy and tactics—seems to many an obvious foundation for market planning in the twenty-first century.

In an age when commerce may be, as Sigmund Freud has suggested in *Civilization and Its Discontents,* a substitute or sublimation for war, we should not be surprised to find that competitive business strategies are influenced and informed by ancient thinking that has governed the logic and disposition of wars for empire these past three centuries. The question we might ask is this: If marketing warfare, an almost universal manifestation of the conflict resolution of antiquity, is a modern substitute for real, violent war, have we any reason to believe that marketing offers us anything more than the satisfaction of needs and wants through a higher, "civilized" barbarianism?

Cicero, a Roman statesman and eclectic philosopher whose speeches electrified and galvanized the governmental senate of his day, has much to say about us as practitioners of the art of marketing—even though business, as practiced during the Roman Empire, did not specifically hold places for professional marketers. He tells several stories, in parable fashion, so that we might be better able to consider the ethical questions that direct marketing. Certainly, marketing is designed to engage groups in the process of buying for the sake of individual profit to the seller. But what are the seller's responsibilities to the buyer? Isn't the buyer part of the larger republic? For that matter, isn't the seller also part of that same republic? What are the responsibilities, if any, that exist between individuals and the republic? Do these responsibilities transcend all efforts for private gain?

Must these responsibilities reflect a deeper accountability to people and all living things?

In early dialectical fashion, Cicero dispels notions regarding the balance between self-interest and the public interest. He never misses a beat in placing marketing at the doorstep of the public interest. His simple yet profound viewpoint stands in vivid contrast to the contemporary ethic of producing and selling goods and services based on the satisfaction of almost any desire, regardless of the public good. As a philosopher, Cicero is not at all in opposition to self-interest and gain. However, he says that we must not detach philosophic principles from self-interested strategies for profit. The difference between an educated and uneducated person is that the former sees no conflict between moral philosophy and marketing practice.

Feudal European societies were marked by the conflict between economic ambition and theological restraints. The advance of the mercantile class, with its tendency to profit at almost any cost, was viewed by the Catholic Church as a most dangerous social transformation. Cognizant of the impossible task of legislating against this new breed of economic thinking and activity, efforts to reform those in lockstep pursuit of wealth through the conduct of business became an ecumenical commonplace. The most outspoken and respected of the church reformers was St. Thomas Aquinas.

Thomist thinking, as portrayed in his treatise on cheating, taken from *The Summa Theologica,* is characterized by a strong analogical and biblical approach. Aquinas was speaking from the "bully pulpit" of his time and he was aware that his theological and secular references (Athens and Jerusalem) would resonate among his audience of learned readers. His astonishingly detailed approach to laying out a "fairness doctrine," with specific reference to those in the buying and selling game, is a glorious primer of do's and don'ts for a target audience that still viewed salvation as the most important objective. Though the church was ineffective as a consistent legislator of business, the work of St. Thomas Aquinas went a long way in laying the moral and legal foundations of marketing for modern regulatory thinking. In fact, each of his "objections" relates to these respective areas of the "marketing mix": pricing, product, promotion, and place (distribution).

Charles Darwin did not have business and marketing in mind when he wrote his seminal work *Origin of the Species.* The theory of natural selection was appropriated by social analysts in the years following the publication of Darwin's work, and it comes as no surprise to discover that Darwin was sympathetic to the use of his theory for thinking about the world of business and social affairs.

You should keep in mind that Herbert Spencer, an acclaimed social thinker who had corresponded with Darwin on numerous occasions, originated this concept of a social "survival of the fittest" independently and prior to Darwin's publication of *Origin of the Species.* Historical documentation serves not only as proof of this claim, but proves also that Darwin was aware of Spencer's ideas and concurred with some of them.

Social Darwinism, as popularly accepted, proffers a day-to-day world where the struggle for economic existence and primacy unfolds in some similar ways to Darwin's biological expression of natural selection. To Darwin's way of thinking, the biological adaptations that arise on an unconscious, randomized basis are transmuted into conscious, planned variations in a social setting. Though a species cannot, as Darwin explains, plan for its biological variations so that it might be in sympathy with the natural environment, a business can, through the insight of its marketers, plan its products, services, and even its overall structure by observing the marketplace as an environment and modifying itself for the present, the short-term future, and even in some cases a future as far out as twenty or thirty years. Marketers "naturally" select out what doesn't work from what does within a world of uncontrollable external variables. The call is to consciously adapt to these variables—culture, competition, technology, law, economic conditions, physical environment—and in the process set the stage for competitive advantage and potential market domination.

Natural selection is the subject of the lobster and squid selection from Theodore Dreiser's *The Financier.* Dreiser's eponymous antihero,

Frank Cowperwood, is attempting to understand how the world is organized. Cowperwood is just a boy and is given to first impressions. Watching the unfair and forced battle between the lobster and squid elucidates the unfairness of life for him. There is little room in this staged battle for the squid to adapt to the superior predator. For young Cowperwood, the implication is clear—some are prey and some are predators. Even beyond this, the battle between the two, at least on the human stage, is all planned out. The objective is clear—one must plan to be the predator for natural selection to work in one's favor; it is necessary to select for one's own natural advantage.

Dreiser, one of America's early realist novelists, takes a dim view of individualism in economic markets and reckons the "art of war" a strategic play for domination. Still, he recognizes that the "go-getters" of the world will do what it takes to "win the game"—whether it is to achieve higher revenue and profits, to create superior goods and services, or to outflank any competitors.

The terms *pecuniary emulation* and *conspicuous consumption* are commonplace to modern marketers. First introduced in Thorstein Veblen's *The Theory of the Leisure Class* in 1899, these terms refer to an important cause-and-effect phenomenon in the world of marketing. Veblen grants his readers a view into the sanctum *sanctorum* of buyer motivation. Without understanding what motivates people to buy, marketers are trapped in a selling orientation in which they are left to sell whatever they produce rather than to uncover what it is the marketplace wants or demands. Without a clear vision of buyer motivation, manufacturers are unable to research, develop, and produce the goods that are sent on to advertising for the creation of latent, unspoken, unregistered needs and wants (see John Kenneth Galbraith's selection for a discussion of the propriety of such desire generation).

It is especially interesting to know that Veblen's formulation for the standard of living, which he sees as a factor of pecuniary emulation and conspicuous consumption, was revolutionary for his time. In fact, the suggestion that we are human apes in the acquisitive mode, humans aping other humans in the case of acquisition, is not a favorable characterization. It was enough to make him suspect in certain academic arenas and, in conjunction with his unconventional and nonconforming behavior, enough to get him dismissed from several university professorial positions—although you might be hard-pressed to find the documented proof that his beliefs about consumer behavior had anything to do with such dismissals.

Veblen describes a society where marketing plays the dominant role in creating chronic dissatisfaction. Although he understands that such widespread and habitual dissatisfaction is the engine that ignites product output and wealth creation, he is also aware that it perpetuates a growing rejection of concern for and effort toward the construction of authentic personality. The luxury of chronic dissatisfaction is that marketing, through the distribution and promotion of products and services, and the general availability of nearly any status marker, makes it unnecessary for anyone to search for the deeper causes of dissatisfaction. Rather, there is always a quick fix available. Of even greater concern is the accelerating, narcoticlike dependency on accumulation to neutralize the dissatisfaction expressed by the habituated esteem "need" for placing a wider and wider interval between ourselves and those in our social group or class. The social and pecuniary logic of capitalism, as expressed by consumers, is, for Veblen, a predatory and "invidious distinction," at least to the degree that it precedes or usurps the opportunity to fully develop human intellect and personality; it holds out, instead, the seduction of "social class leaping"—gaining esteem through accumulating enough goods in a short enough span of time to move upward through the social classes.

The classical Athenian philosophers found something unsavory in the idea of distribution—moving products from where they are produced to where they are consumed. Although Socrates could see the purpose of merchants involved in such activity, he thought them blockheaded; Aristotle, ever the obdurate, opinionated advocate of needs-based production and consumption, could more easily justify slavery than he could the idea of merchant

distributors. To him, such people engaged in the commercial process complicated and devalued the high morality required of both producers and consumers by placing an unacceptably high value on money as the singular reward of commerce. By the twentieth century, however, classical and ultimately theological concerns aside, distribution had become one of the most critical components of need-satisfaction and want-creation—a primary driver of gross national product. Nobody, prior to 1920, knew this better than Albert Atwood.

Atwood is one of the early proponents of independent distribution—as critical to the "marketing mix" as it is to a more equalized sharing of goods for humankind. He is not unaware of the issues that ground the subject of distribution in a whirligig of producer complaints about costs, consumer complaints about prices, and regulatory concerns about secret agreements and trade restraints among all channel members—consumers excepted. Still, he sees what we now call *channel distribution* as essential to the standard of living. Even more, he recognizes what is the near-impossibility, given an evolving specialization of trade, for producers to act as distributors, too. And though there are instances of such integration, they are not very common. His essay is an exercise in marketing *realpolitik*, which, in the early twentieth century, was an attempt to "put to bed" an old and seemingly endless argument.

A "suspicious" character to marketers and economists alike is John Kenneth Galbraith. A contemporary economic thinker of the "liberal" persuasion, he generates many controversies regarding his unconventional assessment of the business world. Unlike most economic soothsayers of mid-twentieth-century America, however, he produced a marvelously popular and successful book in *The Affluent Society*. In this book, Galbraith says that "private affluence" has created "public squalor." He suggests that a dominant production culture, which he later refers to as an industrial order, has overwhelmed governmental spending on the essentials that create an improved environment. He is referring to the creation of an ideal environment with institutional structures—public spaces, roads and infrastructure, and so on—that would improve our collective lives and the state of the nation. This improvement, in turn, would make us better people and an economically richer people. Galbraith does not disagree with Andrew Carnegie in the matter of wealthy individuals contributing to the betterment of society, but he believes than a superheated emphasis on production and consumption generates a narrow field of vision, aimed too specifically on private affluence. He is distressed by a capitalist state that provides oligopolistic corporations with the opportunity to entrench production as a primary motive of modern society. This motive tends to support at least two things: (1) the notion that the goal is to maintain the "life" of the corporation, to simply keep it going—where even profit becomes less important than maintenance; and (2) the idea that ownership of the goods produced should be an individual goal—where even if the individual has no particular desire for the goods, he or she seeks them out anyway, disregarding even the law of diminishing marginal utility.

Galbraith writes of the "dependence effect" : Production of goods should not be determined by the needs of the industrial state. Rather, he says, production should be determined by authentic needs and wants generated in the marketplace.

A corporation that creates products and services for which there is no obvious interest must rely on advertising, or some form of promotion, to generate demand. This leaves advertising, a subset of marketing, with what Galbraith considers the untenable job of creating desire where it does not exist. Production, then, produces the demand it is designed to satisfy. This argument is rarely persuasive to those whose purpose is to generate revenue and profit with the assistance of advertising and promotions. Yet Galbraith's argument strikes at the heart of what may be the *raison d'etre* of all modern economies—to generate revenue and profit (and thus perpetuate themselves) and do so within all legal boundaries. That we can promote products and services employing all legal advertising and promotions may not be adequate justification. Galbraith takes to task contemporary marketing ideologies and asks us to reconsider previous notions about the subject of marketing.

Galbraith's 1966 Reith lecture is a broader argument about the power of this production environment, what he refers to as "The New Industrial State." There exists a tendency, he tells us, for a few corporations, in respective industrial sectors, to control pricing. This is the capitalist version of what some would see as state-controlled pricing in the socialist countries of the twentieth century. These oligopolistic corporations may be condemned for exerting so much control; however, in the end, through processes Galbraith explains, the final prices are not out of line with costs and expenses. These are not monopolistic prices, yet they are controlled prices for the purposes of planning—prices that "reflect generally the goals of those who guide the corporations" and allow these firms to grow over time, ensuring efficiency and effectiveness of output, as long as consumption can be similarly controlled. Galbraith also tells us that the capitalist state controls wages and prices. The net effect is that controlled economies are produced, and their goals, in the final analysis, are not all that different from those in planned economies.

Galbraith maintains that this all works when demand is also managed. This is the ligature between "The Affluent Society" and "The New Industrial State." The efficient argument here is that where corporations can manage demand, security can be provided to suppliers for "a reliable and predictable flow of orders which allows of planning." This security redounds to other stakeholders as well. To ensure this kind of security and planning, corporate marketers must control consumer behavior. Most consumer needs are served by a relatively small number of products, so to ensure continued stability to this industrial planning, marketers must emphasize the consumption of products whose origin of demand is psychological. This entails careful planning at all levels of marketing, including production, pricing, promotion, and distribution. Finally, persuasive management of demand generates a mass, compulsive response toward consumption. While some individuals (followers of Thoreau perhaps) may escape this control, Galbraith is convinced most will not. This "New Industrial State" becomes the basis of "The Affluent Society." ◆

FROM *THE ART OF WAR*

Sun Tzu (ca. 460–400 BC)

I. LAYING PLANS

1. Sun Tzu said: The art of war is of vital importance to the State.

2. It is a matter of life and death, a road either to safety or to ruin. Hence it is a subject of inquiry which can on no account be neglected.

3. The art of war, then, is governed by five constant factors, to be taken into account in one's deliberations, when seeking to determine the conditions obtaining in the field.

4. These are: (1) The Moral Law; (2) Heaven; (3) Earth; (4) The Commander; (5) Method and discipline.

5,6. *The Moral Law* causes the people to be in complete accord with their ruler, so that they will follow him regardless of their lives, undismayed by any danger.

7. *Heaven* signifies night and day, cold and heat, times and seasons.

8. *Earth* comprises distances, great and small; danger and security; open ground and narrow passes; the chances of life and death.

9. *The Commander* stands for the virtues of wisdom, sincerity, benevolence, courage and strictness.

   The five cardinal virtues of the Chinese are (1) humanity or benevolence; (2) uprightness of mind; (3) self-respect, self-control, or "proper feeling"; (4) wisdom; (5) sincerity or good faith.

10. *By Method and discipline* are to be understood the marshalling of the army in its proper subdivisions, the gradations of rank among the officers, the maintenance of roads by which supplies may reach the army, and the control of military expenditure.

11. These five heads should be familiar to every general: he who knows them will be victorious; he who knows them not will fail.

12. Therefore, in your deliberations, when seeking to determine the military conditions, let them be made the basis of a comparison, in this wise.

13. (1) Which of the two sovereigns is imbued with the Moral law?

    (2) Which of the two generals has most ability?

    (3) With whom lie the advantages derived from Heaven and Earth?

    (4) On which side is discipline most rigorously enforced?

    Tu Mu alludes to the remarkable story of Ts'ao Ts'ao (A.D. 155–220), who was such a strict disciplinarian that once, in accordance with his own severe regulations against injury to standing crops, he condemned himself to death for having allowed his horse to shy into a field of corn! However, in lieu of losing his head, he was persuaded to satisfy his sense of justice by cutting off his hair. "When you lay down a law, see that it is not disobeyed; if it is disobeyed, the offender must be put to death."

    (5) Which army is the stronger?

    (6) On which side are officers and men more highly trained?

    "Without constant practice, the officers will be nervous and undecided when mustering for battle; without constant practice, the general will be wavering and irresolute when the crisis is at hand."

    (7) In which army is there the greater constancy both in reward and punishment?

    That is, on which side is there the most absolute certainty that merit will be properly rewarded and misdeeds summarily punished?

14. By means of these seven considerations I can forecast victory or defeat.

15. The general that hearkens to my counsel and acts upon it, will conquer—let such a one be retained in command! The general that hearkens not to my counsel nor acts upon it, will suffer defeat—let such a one be dismissed!

16. While heeding the profit of my counsel, avail yourself also of any helpful circum-

stances over and beyond the ordinary rules.

17. According as circumstances are favourable, one should modify one's plans.

Sun Tzu as a practical soldier, cautions us here not to pin our faith to abstract principles; "for," as Chang Yü puts it, "while the main laws of strategy can be stated clearly enough for the benefit of all and sundry, you must be guided by the actions of the enemy in attempting to secure a favourable position in actual warfare." On the eve of the battle of Waterloo, Lord Uxbridge, commanding the cavalry, went to the Duke of Wellington in order to learn what his plans and calculations were for the morrow, because, as he explained, he might suddenly find himself Commander-in-chief and would be unable to frame new plans in a critical moment. The Duke listened quietly and then said: "Who will attack the first to-morrow—I or Bonaparte?" "Bonaparte," replied Lord Uxbridge. "Well," continued the Duke, "Bonaparte has not given me any idea of his projects; and as my plans will depend upon his, how can you expect me to tell you what mine are?"

18. All warfare is based on deception.

The truth of this pithy and profound saying will be admitted by every soldier. Wellington, great in so many military qualities, was especially distinguished by "the extraordinary skill with which he concealed his movements and deceived both friend and foe."

19. Hence, when able to attack, we must seem unable; when using our forces, we must seem inactive; when we are near, we must make the enemy believe we are far away: when far away, we must make him believe we are near.

20. Hold out baits to entice the enemy. Feign disorder and crush him.

21. If he is secure at all points, be prepared for him. If he is in superior strength, evade him.

22. If your opponent is of choleric temper, seek to irritate him. Pretend to be weak, that he may grow arrogant.

The good tactician plays with his adversary as a cat plays with a mouse, first feigning weakness and immobility, and then suddenly pouncing upon him.

23. If he is taking his ease, give him no rest. If his forces are united, separate them.

24. Attack him where he is unprepared, appear where you are not expected.

25. These military devices, leading to victory, must not be divulged beforehand.

26. Now the general who wins a battle makes many calculations in his temple ere the battle is fought. The general who loses a battle makes but few calculations beforehand. Thus do many calculations lead to victory, and few calculations to defeat: how much more no calculation at all! It is by attention to this point that I can foresee who is likely to win or lose.

II. WAGING WAR

"He who wishes to fight must first count the cost," which prepares us for the discovery that the subject of the chapter is not what we might expect from the title, but is primarily a consideration of ways and means.

1. Sun Tzu said: In the operations of war, where there are in the field a thousand swift chariots, as many heavy chariots, and a hundred thousand mail-clad soldiers, with provisions enough to carry them a thousand *li*,[1] the expenditure at home and at the front, including entertainment of guests, small items such as glue and paint, and sums spent on chariots and armour, will reach the total of a thousand ounces of silver per day. Such is the cost of raising an army of 100,000 men.

2. When you engage in actual fighting, if victory is long in coming, the men's weapons will grow dull and their ardour will be damped. If you lay siege to a town, you will exhaust your strength.

3. Again, if the campaign is protracted, the resources of the State will not be equal to the strain.

4. Now, when your weapons are dulled, your ardour damped, your strength exhausted and your treasure spent, other chieftains will spring up to take advantage of your extremity. Then no man, however wise, will be able to avert the consequences that must ensue.

5. Thus, though we have heard of stupid haste in war, cleverness has never been seen associated with long delays.

6. There is no instance of a country having benefited from prolonged warfare.

7. It is only one who is thoroughly acquainted with the evils of war that can thoroughly understand the profitable way of carrying it on.

That is, with rapidity. Only one who knows the disastrous effects of a long war can realise the supreme importance of rapidity in bringing it to a close.

8. The skilful soldier does not raise a second levy, neither are his supply-waggons loaded more than twice.

Once war is declared, he will not waste precious time in waiting for reinforcements, nor will he turn his army back for fresh supplies, but crosses the enemy's frontier without delay. This may seem an audacious policy to recommend, but with all great strategists, from Julius Caesar to Napoleon Bonaparte, the value of time—that is, being a little ahead of your opponent—has counted for more than either numerical superiority or the nicest calculations with regard to commissariat.

9. Bring war material with you from home, but forage on the enemy. Thus the army will have food enough for its needs.

10. Poverty of the State exchequer causes an army to be maintained by contributions from a distance. Contributing to maintain an army at a distance causes the people to be impoverished.

11. On the other hand, the proximity of an army causes prices to go up; and high prices cause the people's substance to be drained away.

12. When their substance is drained away, the peasantry will be afflicted by heavy exactions.

13, 14. With this loss of substance and exhaustion of strength, the homes of the people will be stripped bare, and three-tenths of their incomes will be dissipated; while government expenses for broken chariots, worn-out horses, breast-plates and helmets, bows and arrows, spears and shields, protective mantlets, draught-oxen and heavy waggons, will amount to four-tenths of its total revenue.

"The *people* being regarded as the essential part of the State, and *food* as the people's heaven, is it not right that those in authority should value and be careful of both?"

15. Hence a wise general makes a point of foraging on the enemy. One cartload of the enemy's provisions is equivalent to twenty of one's own, and likewise a single picul of his provender is equivalent to twenty from one's own store.

Because twenty cartloads will be consumed in the process of transporting one cartload to the front.

16. Now in order to kill the enemy, our men must be roused to anger; that there may be advantage from defeating the enemy, they must have their rewards.

"Rewards are necessary in order to make the soldiers see the advantage of beating the enemy; thus, when you capture spoils from the enemy, they must be used as rewards, so that all your men may have a keen desire to fight, each on his own account."

17. Therefore in chariot fighting, when ten or more chariots have been taken, those should be rewarded who took the first.

Our own flags should be substituted for those of the enemy, and the chariots mingled and used in conjunction with ours. The captured soldiers should be kindly treated and kept.

18. This is called, using the conquered foe to augment one's own strength.

19. In war, then, let your great object be victory, not lengthy campaigns.

"War is not a thing to be trifled with."

20. Thus it may be known that the leader of armies is the arbiter of the people's fate, the man on whom it depends whether the nation shall be in peace or in peril.

III. ATTACK BY STRATAGEM

1. Sun Tzu said: In the practical art of war, the best thing of all is to take the enemy's country whole and intact; to shatter and destroy it is not so good. So, too, it is better to capture an army entire than to destroy it, to capture a regiment, a detachment or a company entire than to destroy them.

2. Hence to fight and conquer in all your battles is not supreme excellence; supreme excellence consists in breaking the enemy's resistance without fighting.

3. Thus the highest form of generalship is to baulk the enemy's plans; the next best is to prevent the junction of the enemy's forces;

Isolating him from his allies. We must not forget that Sun Tzu in speaking of hostilities, always has in mind the numerous states or principalities into which the China of his day was split up.

the next in order is to attack the enemy's army in the field;

When he is already in full strength.

and the worst policy of all is to besiege walled cities.

4. The rule is, not to besiege walled cities if it can possibly be avoided.

The preparation of mantlets, movable shelters, and various implements of war, will take up three whole months; and the piling up of mounds over against the walls will take three months more.

5. The general, unable to control his irritation, will launch his men to the assault like swarming ants, with the result that one-third of his men are slain, while the town still remains untaken. Such are the disastrous effects of a siege.

6. Therefore the skilful leader subdues the enemy's troops without any fighting; he captures their cities without laying siege to them; he overthrows their kingdom without lengthy operations in the field.

7. With his forces intact he will dispute the mastery of the Empire, and thus, without losing a man, his triumph will be complete. This is the method of attacking by stratagem.

8. It is the rule in war, if our forces are ten to the enemy's one, to surround him; if five to one, to attack him; if twice as numerous, to divide our army into two.

"If our force is twice as numerous as that of the enemy, it should be split up into two divisions, one to meet the enemy in front, and one to fall upon his rear; if he replies to the frontal attack, he may be crushed from behind; if to the rearward attack, he may be crushed in front. This is what is meant by saying that 'one part may be used in the regular way, and the other for some special diversion.'"

9. If equally matched, we can offer battle;

"If attackers and attacked are equally matched in strength, only the able general will fight."

if slightly inferior in numbers, we can avoid the enemy; if quite unequal in every way, we can flee from him.

10. Hence, though an obstinate fight may be made by a small force, in the end it must be captured by the larger force.

11. Now the general is the bulwark of the State: if the bulwark is complete at all points, the State will be strong; if the bulwark is defective, the State will be weak.

12. There are three ways in which a ruler can bring misfortune upon his army:

13. (1) By commanding the army to advance or to retreat, being ignorant of the fact that it cannot obey. This is called hobbling the army.

"A kingdom should not be governed from without, an army should not be directed from within." Of course it is true that, during an engagement, or when in close touch with the enemy, the general should not be in the thick of his own troops, but a little distance apart. Otherwise, he will be liable to misjudge the position as a whole, and give wrong orders.

14. (2) By attempting to govern an army in the same way as he administers a kingdom, being ignorant of the conditions which obtain in an army. This causes restlessness in the soldiers' minds.

"The military sphere and the civil sphere are wholly distinct; you can't handle an army in kid gloves." And: "Humanity and justice are the principles on which to govern a state, but not an army; opportunism and flexibility, on the other hand, are military rather than civic virtues."

15. (3) By employing the officers of his army without discrimination,

That is, he is not careful to use the right man in the right place

through ignorance of the military principle of adaptation to circumstances. This shakes the confidence of the soldiers.

"If a general is ignorant of the principle of adaptability, he must not be entrusted with a position of authority." The skilful employer of men will employ the wise man, the brave man, the covetous man, and the stupid man. For the wise man delights in establishing his merit, the brave man likes to show his courage in action, the covetous man is quick at seizing advantages, and the stupid man has no fear of death."

16. But when the army is restless and distrustful, trouble is sure to come from the other feudal princes. This is simply bringing anarchy into the army, and flinging victory away.

17. Thus we may know that there are five essentials for victory:

(1) He will win who knows when to fight and when not to fight.

"If he can fight, he advances and takes the offensive; if he cannot fight, he retreats and remains on the defensive. He will invariably conquer who knows whether it is right to take the offensive or the defensive."

(2) He will win who knows how to handle both superior and inferior forces.

This is not merely the general's ability to estimate numbers correctly: "By applying the art of war, it is possible with a lesser force, to defeat a greater, and vice versa. The secret lies in an eye for locality, and in not letting the right moment slip. With a superior force, make for easy ground; with an inferior one, make for difficult ground."

(3) He will win whose army is animated by the same spirit throughout all its ranks.

(4) He will win who, prepared himself, waits to take the enemy unprepared.

(5) He will win who has military capacity and is not interfered with by the sovereign.

"It is the sovereign's function to give broad instructions, but to decide on battle is the function of the general." It is needless to dilate on the military disasters which have been caused by undue interference with operations in the field on the part of the home government. Napoleon undoubtedly owed much of his extraordinary success to the fact that he was not hampered by any central authority.

Victory lies in the knowledge of these five points.

18. Hence the saying: If you know the enemy and know yourself, you need not fear the result of a hundred battles. If you know yourself but not the enemy, for every victory gained you will also suffer a defeat. If you know neither the enemy nor yourself, you will succumb in every battle.

"Knowing the enemy enables you to take the offensive, knowing yourself enables you to stand on the defensive. Attack is the secret of defense; defense is the planning of an attack."

IV. TACTICAL DISPOSITIONS

1. Sun Tzu said: The good fighters of old first put themselves beyond the possibility of defeat, and then waited for an opportunity of defeating the enemy.

2. To secure ourselves against defeat lies in our own hands, but the opportunity of defeating the enemy is provided by the enemy himself.

3. Thus the good fighter is able to secure himself against defeat,

"By concealing the disposition of his troops, covering up his tracks and taking unremitting precautions" (Chang Yü).

but cannot make certain of defeating the enemy.

4. Hence the saying: One may *know* how to conquer without being able to *do* it.

5. Security against defeat implies defensive tactics; ability to defeat the enemy means taking the offensive.

6. Standing on the defensive indicates insufficient strength: attacking, a superabundance of strength.

7. The general who is skilled in defense hides in the most secret recesses of the earth; he who is skilled in attack flashes forth from the topmost heights of heaven. Thus on the one hand we have ability to protect ourselves; on the other, a victory that is complete.

8. To see victory only when it is within the ken of the common herd is not the acme of excellence.

9. Neither is it the acme of excellence if you fight and conquer and the whole Empire says, "Well done!"

True excellence being, "To plan secretly, to move surreptitiously, to fail the enemy's intentions and baulk his schemes, so that at last the day may be won without shedding a drop of blood."

10. To lift an autumn hair is no sign of great strength; to see sun and moon is no sign of sharp sight; to hear the noise of thunder is no sign of a quick ear.

Ho Shih gives as real instances of strength, sharp sight and quick hearing: Wu Huo, who could lift a tripod weighing 250 stone (350 lb.); Li Chu, who at a distance of a hundred paces could see objects no bigger than a mustard seed; and Shih K'uang, a blind musician who could hear the foot-steps of a mosquito.

11. What the ancients called a clever fighter is one who not only wins, but excels in winning with ease.

"He who only sees the obvious, wins his battles with difficulty; he who looks below the surface of things, wins with ease."

12. Hence his victories bring him neither reputation for wisdom nor credit for courage.

"Inasmuch as his victories are gained over circumstances that have not come to light, the world at large knows nothing of them, and he wins no reputation for wisdom; inasmuch as the hostile state submits before there has been any bloodshed, he receives no credit for courage."

13. He wins his battles by making no mistakes.

"He plans no superfluous marches, he devises no futile attacks. One who seeks to conquer by sheer strength, clever though he may be at winning pitched battles, is also liable on occasion to be vanquished; whereas he who can look into the future and discern conditions that are not yet manifest, will never make a blunder and therefore invariably win."

Making no mistakes is what establishes the certainty of victory, for it means conquering an enemy that is already defeated.

14. Hence the skilful fighter puts himself into a position which makes defeat impossible, and does not miss the moment for defeating the enemy.

15. Thus it is that in war the victorious strategist only seeks battle after the victory has been won, whereas he who is destined to defeat first fights and afterwards looks for victory.

"In warfare, first lay plans which will ensure victory, and then lead your army to battle; if you will not begin with stratagem but rely on brute strength alone, victory will no longer be assured."

16. The consummate leader cultivates the moral law, and strictly adheres to method and discipline; thus it is in his power to control success.

17. In respect of military method, we have, firstly, Measurement; secondly, Estimation of quantity; thirdly, Calculation; fourthly, Balancing of chances; fifthly, Victory.

18. Measurement owes its existence to Earth; Estimation of quantity to Measurement; Calculation to Estimation of quantity; Balancing of chances to Calculation; and Victory to Balancing of chances.

19. A victorious army opposed to a routed one, is as a pound's weight placed in the scale against a single grain.

20. The onrush of a conquering force is like the bursting of pent-up waters into a chasm a thousand fathoms deep. So much for tactical dispositions.

V. ENERGY

1. Sun Tzu said: The control of a large force is the same in principle as the control of a few men: it is merely a question of dividing up their numbers.

2. Fighting with a large army under your command is nowise different from fighting with a small one: it is merely a question of instituting signs and signals.

3. To ensure that your whole host may withstand the brunt of the enemy's attack and remain unshaken—this is effected by maneuvers direct and indirect.

"We must cause the enemy to regard our straightforward attack as one that is secretly designed, and vice versa."

4. That the impact of your army may be like a grindstone dashed against an egg—this is effected by the science of weak points and strong.

5. In all fighting, the direct method may be used for joining battle, but indirect methods will be needed in order to secure victory.

"Steadily develop indirect tactics, either by pounding the enemy's flanks or falling on his rear."

6. Indirect tactics, efficiently applied, are inexhaustible as Heaven and Earth, unending as the flow of rivers and streams; like the sun and moon, they end but to begin anew; like the four seasons, they pass away but to return once more.

7. There are not more than five musical notes, yet the combinations of these five give rise to more melodies than can ever be heard.

8. There are not more than five primary colours,

blue, yellow, red, white and black.

yet in combination they produce more hues than can ever be seen.

9. There are not more than five cardinal tastes,

sour, acrid, salt, sweet, bitter.

yet combinations of them yield more flavours than can ever be tasted.

10. In battle, there are not more than two methods of attack—the direct and the indirect; yet these two in combination give rise to an endless series of manoeuvres.

11. The direct and the indirect lead on to each other in turn. It is like moving in a circle—you never come to an end. Who can exhaust the possibilities of their combination?

12. The onset of troops is like the rush of a torrent which will even roll stones along in its course.

13. The quality of decision is like the well-timed swoop of a falcon which enables it to strike and destroy its victim.

14. Therefore the good fighter will be terrible in his onset, and prompt in his decision.

15. Energy may be likened to the bending of a crossbow; decision, to the releasing of the trigger.

16. Amid the turmoil and tumult of battle, there may be seeming disorder and yet no real disorder at all; amid confusion and chaos, your array may be without head or tail, yet it will be proof against defeat.

17. Simulated disorder postulates perfect discipline; simulated fear postulates courage; simulated weakness postulates strength.

"If you wish to feign confusion in order to lure the enemy on, you must first have perfect discipline; if you wish to display timidity in order to entrap the enemy, you must have extreme courage; if you wish to parade your weakness in order to make the enemy overconfident, you must have exceeding strength."

18. Hiding order beneath the cloak of disorder is simply a question of subdivision; concealing courage under a show of timidity presupposes a fund of latent energy; masking strength with weakness is to be effected by tactical dispositions.

Chang Yü relates the following anecdote of Kao Tsu, the first Han Emperor: Wishing to crush the Hsiung-nu, he sent out spies to report on their condition. But the Hsiung-nu, forewarned, carefully concealed all their able-bodied men and well-fed horses, and only allowed infirm soldiers and emaciated cattle to be seen. The result was that the spies one and all recommended the Emperor to deliver his attack. Lou Ching alone opposed them, saying: "When two countries go to war, they are naturally inclined to make an ostentatious display of their strength. Yet our spies have seen nothing but old age and infirmity. This is surely some *ruse* on the part of the enemy, and it would be unwise for us to attack." The Emperor, however, disregarding this advice, fell into the trap and found himself surrounded at Po-têng.

19. Thus one who is skilful at keeping the enemy on the move maintains deceitful appearances, according to which the enemy will act. He sacrifices something that the enemy may snatch at it.

In 341 B.C., the Ch'i State being at war with Wei, sent T'ien Chi and Sun Pin against the general P'ang Chüan, who happened to be a deadly personal enemy of the latter. Sun Pin said: "The Ch'i State has a reputation for cowardice, and therefore our adversary despises us. Let us turn this circumstance to account." Accordingly, when the army had crossed the border into Wei territory, he gave orders to show 100,000 fires on the first night, 50,000 on the next, and the night after only 20,000. P'ang Chüan pursued them hotly, saying to himself. "I knew these men of Ch'i were cowards: their numbers have already fallen away by more than half." In his retreat, Sun Pin came to a narrow defile, which he calculated that his pursuers would reach after dark. Here he had a tree stripped of its bark, and inscribed upon it the words: "Under this tree shall P'ang Chüan die." Then, as night began to fall, he placed a strong body of archers in ambush near by with orders to shoot directly they saw a light. Later on, P'ang Chüan arrived at the spot, and noticing the tree, struck a light in order to read what was written on it. His body was immediately riddled by a volley of arrows, and his whole army thrown into confusion. [The above is Tu Mu's version of the story; the *Shih Chi*, less dramatically but probably with more historical truth, makes P'ang Chüan cut his own throat with an exclamation of despair, after the rout of his army.]

20. By holding out baits, he keeps him on the march; then with a body of picked men he lies in wait for him.

21. The clever combatant looks to the effect of combined energy, and does not require too much from individuals.

"He first of all considers the power of his army in the bulk; afterwards he takes individual talent into account, and uses each man according to his capabilities. He does not demand perfection from the untalented."

Hence his ability to pick out the right men and to utilise combined energy.

22. When he utilises combined energy, his fighting men become as it were like unto rolling logs or stones. For it is the nature of a log or stone to remain motionless on level ground, and to move when on a slope; if four-cornered, to come to a standstill, but if round-shaped, to go rolling down.

23. Thus the energy developed by good fighting men is as the momentum of a round stone rolled down a mountain thousands of feet in height. So much on the subject of energy.

The chief lesson is the paramount importance in war of rapid evolutions and sudden rushes. "Great results can thus be achieved with small forces."

VI. WEAK POINTS AND STRONG

1. Sun Tzü said: Whoever is first in the field and awaits the coming of the enemy, will be fresh for the fight; whoever is second in the field and has to hasten to battle, will arrive exhausted.

2. Therefore the clever combatant imposes his will on the enemy, but does not allow the enemy's will to be imposed on him.

3. By holding out advantages to him, he can cause the enemy to approach of his own accord; or, by inflicting damage, he can make it impossible for the enemy to draw near.

In the first case, he will entice him with a bait; in the second, he will strike at some important point which the enemy will have to defend.

4. If the enemy is taking his ease, he can harass him; if well supplied with food, he can starve him out; if quietly encamped, he can force him to move.

5. Appear at points which the enemy must hasten to defend; march swiftly to places where you are not expected.

6. An army may march great distances without distress, if it marches through country where the enemy is not.

"Emerge from the void, strike at vulnerable points, shun places that are defended, attack in unexpected quarters."

7. You can be sure of succeeding in your attacks if you only attack places which are undefended. You can ensure the safety of your defense if you only hold positions that cannot be attacked.

"He who is skilled in attack flashes forth from the topmost heights of heaven, making it impossible for the enemy to guard against him. This being so, the places that I shall attack are precisely those that the enemy cannot defend . . . He who is skilled in defense hides in the most secret recesses of the earth, making it impossible for the enemy to estimate his whereabouts. This being so, the places that I shall hold are precisely those that the enemy cannot attack."

8. Hence that general is skilful in attack whose opponent does not know what to defend; and he is skilful in defense whose opponent does not know what to attack.

9. O divine art of sublety and secrecy! Through you we learn to be invisible, through you inaudible and hence we can hold the enemy's fate in our hands.

10. You may advance and be absolutely irresistible, if you make for the enemy's weak points; you may retire and be safe from pursuit if your movements are more rapid than those of the enemy.

11. If we wish to fight, the enemy can be forced to an engagement even though he be sheltered behind a high rampart and a deep ditch. All we need do is to attack some other place that he will be obliged to relieve.

"If the enemy is the invading party, we can cut his line of communications and occupy the roads by which he will have to return; if we are the invaders, we may direct our attack against the sovereign himself." It is clear that Sun Tzu was no believer in frontal attacks.

12. If we do not wish to fight, we can prevent the enemy from engaging us even though the lines of our encampment be merely traced out on the ground. All we need do is to throw something odd and unaccountable in his way.

Chu-ko Liang, who when occupying Yang-p'ing and about to be attacked by Ssu-ma I, suddenly struck his colours, stopped the beating of the drums, and flung open the city gates, showing only a few men engaged in sweeping and sprinkling the ground. This unexpected proceeding had the intended effect; for Ssu-ma, suspecting an ambush, actually drew off his army and retreated. What Sun Tzu is advocating here, therefore, is nothing more nor less than the timely use of "bluff."

13. By discovering the enemy's dispositions and remaining invisible ourselves, we can keep our forces concentrated, while the enemy's must be divided.

"If the enemy's dispositions are visible, we can make for him in one body; whereas, our own dispositions being kept secret, the enemy will be obliged to divide his forces in order to guard against attack from every quarter."

14. We can form a single united body, while the enemy must split up into fractions. Hence there will be a whole pitted against separate parts of a whole, which means that we shall be many to the enemy's few.

15. And if we are able thus to attack an inferior force with a superior one, our opponents will be in dire straits.

16. The spot where we intend to fight must not be made known; for then the enemy will have to prepare against a possible attack at several different points;

Sheridan once explained the reason of General Grant's victories by saying that "while his opponents were kept fully employed wondering what he was going to do, he was thinking most of what he was going to do himself."

and his forces being thus distributed in many directions, the numbers we shall have to face at any given point will be proportionately few.

17. For should the enemy strengthen his van, he will weaken his rear; should he strengthen his rear, he will weaken his van; should he strengthen his left, he will weaken his right; should he strengthen his right, he will weaken his left. If he sends reinforcements everywhere, he will everywhere be weak.

"A defensive war is apt to betray us into too frequent detachment. Those generals who have had but little experience attempt to protect every point, while those who are better acquainted with their profession, having only the capital object in view, guard against a decisive blow, and acquiesce in smaller misfortunes to avoid greater."

18. Numerical weakness comes from having to prepare against possible attacks; numerical strength, from compelling our adversary to make these preparations against us.

The highest generalship is "to compel the enemy to disperse his army, and then to concentrate superior force against each fraction in turn."

19. Knowing the place and the time of the coming battle, we may concentrate from the greatest distances in order to fight.

20. But if neither time nor place be known, then the left wing will be impotent to succour the right, the right equally impotent to succour the left, the van unable to relieve the rear, or

the rear to support the van. How much more so if the furthest portions of the army are anything under a hundred *li* apart, and even the nearest are separated by several *li*!

The mental picture we are required to draw is that of an army advancing towards a given rendezvous in separate columns, each of which has orders to be there on a fixed date. If the general allows the various detachments to proceed at haphazard, without precise instructions as to the time and place of meeting, the enemy will be able to annihilate the army in detail. "If we do not know the place where our opponents mean to concentrate or the day on which they will join battle, our unity will be forfeited through our preparations for defense, and the positions we hold will be insecure. Suddenly happening upon a powerful foe, we shall be brought to battle in a flurried condition, and no mutual support will be possible between wings, vanguard or rear, especially if there is any great distance between the foremost and hindmost divisions of the army."

21. Though according to my estimate the soldiers of Yueh exceed our own in number, that shall advantage them nothing in the matter of victory. I say then that victory can be achieved.

22. Though the enemy be stronger in numbers, we may prevent him from fighting. Scheme so as to discover his plans and the likelihood of their success.

23. Rouse him, and learn the principle of his activity or inactivity.

Chang Yü tells us that by noting the joy or anger shown by the enemy on being thus disturbed, we shall be able to conclude whether his policy is to lie low or the reverse. He instances the action of Chu-ko Liang, who sent the scornful present of a woman's head-dress to Ssu-ma I, in order to goad him out of his Fabian tactics. Force him to reveal himself, so as to find out his vulnerable spots.

24. Carefully compare the opposing army with your own, so that you may know where strength is superabundant and where it is deficient.

25. In making tactical dispositions, the highest pitch you can attain is to conceal them; conceal your dispositions, and you will be safe from the prying of the subtlest spies, from the machinations of the wisest brains.

26. How victory may be produced for them out of the enemy's own tactics—that is what the multitude cannot comprehend.

27. All men can see the tactics whereby I conquer, but what none can see is the strategy out of which victory is evolved.

28. Do not repeat the tactics which have gained you one victory, but let your methods be regulated by the infinite variety of circumstances.

"There is but one root-principle underlying victory, but the tactics which lead up to it are infinite in number." The rules of strategy are few and simple. They may be learned in a week. They may be taught by familiar illustrations or a dozen diagrams. But such knowledge will no more teach a man to lead an army like Napoleon than a knowledge of grammar will teach him to write like Gibbon.

29. Military tactics are like unto water; for water in its natural course runs away from high places and hastens downwards.

30. So in war, the way is to avoid what is strong and to strike at what is weak. Like water, taking the line of least resistance.

31. Water shapes its course according to the nature of the ground over which it flows; the soldier works out his victory in relation to the foe whom he is facing.

32. Therefore, just as water retains no constant shape, so in warfare there are no constant conditions. The five elements: Water, fire, wood, metal, earth, are not always equally predominant; the four seasons make way for each other in turn. There are short days and long; the moon has its periods of waning and waxing.

33. He who can modify his tactics in relation to his opponent and thereby succeed in winning, may be called a heaven-born captain. ◆

ENDNOTE

1. 2.78 modern *li* go to a mile. The length may have varied slightly since Sun Tzu's time.

Questions

1. What are the five constant factors of the art of war according to Sun Tzu? How might they be applied to business?

2. What are the roles that Sun Tzu lays out for change, flexibility, planning, span of control, deception, and winning without fighting?

3. What does Sun Tzu think about the importance of knowledge of the enemy and of oneself? How does this knowledge affect success?

4. What are the strengths of having combinations of alternatives?

5. Who is the enemy of the contemporary marketer?

FROM *DE OFFICIIS*

Cicero (106–43 BC)

IX

By way of illustrating this truth Plato introduces the familiar story of Gyges: Once upon a time the earth opened in consequence of heavy rains; Gyges went down into the chasm and saw, so the story goes, a horse of bronze; in its side was a door. On opening this door he saw the body of a dead man of enormous size with a gold ring upon his finger. He removed this and put it on his own hand and then repaired to an assembly of the shepherds, for he was a shepherd of the king. As often as he turned the bezel of the ring inwards toward the palm of his hand, he became invisible to everyone, while he himself saw everything; but as often as he turned it back to its proper position, he became visible again. And so, with the advantage which the ring gave him, he debauched the queen, and with her assistance he murdered his royal master and removed all those who he thought stood in his way, without anyone's being able to detect him in his crimes. Thus, by virtue of the ring, he shortly rose to be king of Lydia.

Now, suppose a wise man had just such a ring, he would not imagine that he was free to do wrong any more than if he did not have it; for good men aim to secure not secrecy but the right.

And yet on this point certain philosophers, who are not at all vicious but who are not very discerning, declare that the story related by Plato is fictitious and imaginary. As if he affirmed that it was actually true or even possible! But the force of the illustration of the ring is this: if nobody were to know or even to suspect the truth, when you do anything to gain riches or power or sovereignty or sensual gratification—if your act should be hidden for ever from the knowledge of gods and men, would you do it? The condition, they say, is impossible. Of course it is. But my question is, if that were possible which they declare to be impossible, what, pray, would one do? They press their point with right boorish obstinacy: they assert that it is impossible and insist upon it; they refuse to see the meaning of my words, "if possible." For when we ask what they would do, if they could escape detection, we are not asking whether they can escape detection; but we put them as it were upon the rack: should they answer that, if impunity were assured, they would do what was most to their selfish interest, that would be a confession that they are criminally minded; should they say that they would not do so, they would be granting that all things in and of themselves immoral should be avoided.

But let us now return to our theme.

X

Many cases oftentimes arise to perplex our minds with a specious appearance of expediency: the question raised in these cases is not whether moral rectitude is to be sacrificed to some considerable advantage (for that would of course be wrong), but whether the apparent advantage can be secured without moral wrong. When Brutus deposed his colleague Collatinus from the consular office, his treatment of him might have been thought unjust; for Collatinus had been his associate, and had helped him with word and deed in driving out the royal family. But when the leading men of the state had determined that all the kindred of Superbus and the very name of the Tarquins and every reminder of the monarchy should be obliterated, then the course that was expedient—namely, to serve the country's interests—was so pre-eminently right, that it was even Collatinus's own duty to acquiesce in its justice. And so expediency gained the day because of its moral rightness; for without moral rectitude there could have been no possible expediency.

Not so as in the case of the king who founded the city: it was the specious appearance of expediency that actuated him; and when he decided that it was more expedient for him to reign alone than to share the throne with another, he slew his brother. He threw to the winds his brotherly affection and his human feelings, to secure what seemed to him—but was not—expedient; and yet in defense of his deed he offered the excuse about his wall—a specious show of moral rectitude, neither reasonable nor adequate at all. He committed a crime, therefore, with due respect to him let me say so, be he Quirinus or Romulus.

And yet we are not required to sacrifice our own interests and surrender to others what we need for ourselves, but each one should consider his own interests, as far as he may without injury to his neighbour's. "When a man enters the foot-race," says Chrysippus with his usual aptness, "it is his duty to put forth all his strength and strive with all his might to win; but he ought never with his foot to trip, or with his hand to foul a competitor. Thus in the stadium of life, it is not unfair for anyone to seek to obtain what is needful for his own advantage, but he has no right to wrest it from his neighbour."

It is in the case of friendships, however, that men's conceptions of duty are most confused; for it is a breach of duty either to fail to do for a friend what one rightly can do, or to do for him what is not right. But for our guidance in all such cases we have a rule that is short and easy to master: apparent advantages—political preferment, riches, sensual pleasures, and the like—should never be preferred to the obligations of friendship. But an upright man will never for a friend's sake do anything in violation of his country's interests or his oath or his sacred honour, not even if he sits as judge in a friend's case; for he lays aside the role of friend when he assumes that of judge. Only so far will he make concessions to friendship, that he will prefer his friend's side to be the juster one and that he will set the time for presenting his case, as far as the laws will allow, to suit his friend's convenience. But when he comes to pronounce the verdict under oath, he should remember that he has God as his witness—that is, as I understand it, his own conscience, than which God himself has bestowed upon man nothing more divine. From this point of view it is a fine custom that we have inherited from our forefathers (if we were only true to it now), to appeal to the juror with this formula—"to do what he

can consistently with his sacred honour." This form of appeal is in keeping with what I said a moment ago would be morally right for a judge to concede to a friend. For supposing that we were bound to do everything that our friends desired, such relations would have to be accounted not friendships but conspiracies. But I am speaking here of ordinary friendships; for among men who are ideally wise and perfect such situations cannot arise.

They say that Damon and Phintias, of the Pythagorean school, enjoyed such ideally perfect friendship, that when the tyrant Dionysius had appointed a day for the execution of one of them, and the one who had been condemned to death requested a few days' respite for the purpose of putting his loved ones in the care of friends, the other became surety for his appearance, with the understanding that if his friend did not return, he himself should be put to death. And when the friend returned on the day appointed, the tyrant in admiration for their faithfulness begged that they would enroll him as a third partner in their friendship.

Well then, when we are weighing what seems to be expedient in friendship against what is morally right, let apparent expediency be disregarded and moral rectitude prevail; and when in friendship requests are submitted that are not morally right, let conscience and scrupulous regard for the right take precedence of the obligations of friendship. In this way we shall arrive at a proper choice between conflicting duties—the subject of this part of our investigation.

XI

Through a specious appearance of expediency wrong is very often committed in transactions between state and state, as by our own country in the destruction of Corinth. A more cruel wrong was perpetrated by the Athenians in decreeing that the Aeginetans, whose strength lay in their navy, should have their thumbs cut off. This seemed to be expedient; for Aegina was too grave a menace, as it was close to the Piraeus. But no cruelty can be expedient; for cruelty is most abhorrent to human nature, whose lead we ought to follow. They, too, do wrong who would debar foreigners from enjoying the advantages of their city and would exclude them from its borders, as was done by Pennus in the time of our fathers, and in recent times by Papius. It may not be right, of course, for one who is not a citizen to exercise the rights and privileges of citizenship; and the law on this point was secured by two of our wisest consuls, Crassus and Scaevola. Still, to debar foreigners from enjoying the advantages of the city is altogether contrary to the laws of humanity.

There are splendid examples in history where the apparent expediency of the state has been set at naught out of regard for moral rectitude. Our own country has many instances to offer throughout her history, and especially in the Second Punic War, when news came of the disaster at Cannae, Rome displayed a loftier courage than ever she did in success; never a trace of faint-heartedness, never a mention of making terms. The influence of moral right is so potent, that it eclipses the specious appearance of expediency.

When the Athenians could in no way stem the tide of the Persian invasion and determined to abandon their city, bestow their wives and children in safety at Troezen, embark upon their ships, and fight on the sea for the freedom of Greece, a man named Cyrsilus proposed that they should stay at home and open the gates of their city to Xerxes. They stoned him to death for it. And yet he was working for what he thought was expediency; but it was not—not at all, for it clashed with moral rectitude.

After the victorious close of that war with Persia, Themistocles announced in the Assembly that he had a plan for the welfare of the state, but that it was not politic to let it be generally known. He requested the people to appoint someone with whom he might discuss it. They appointed Aristides. Themistocles confided to him that the Spartan fleet, which had been hauled up on shore at Gytheum, could be secretly set on fire; this done, the Spartan power would inevitably be crushed. When Aristides heard the plan, he came into the Assembly amid the eager expectation of all and reported that the plan proposed by Themistocles was in the highest degree expedient, but anything but morally right. The result

was that the Athenians concluded that what was not morally right was likewise not expedient, and at the instance of Aristides they rejected the whole proposition without even listening to it. Their attitude was better than ours; for we let pirates go scot free, while we make our allies pay tribute.

XII

Let it be set down as an established principle, then, that what is morally wrong can never be expedient—not even when one secures by means of it that which one thinks expedient; for the mere act of thinking a course expedient, when it is morally wrong, is demoralizing. But, as I said above, cases often arise in which expediency may seem to clash with moral rectitude; and so we should examine carefully and see whether their conflict is inevitable or whether they may be reconciled. The following are problems of this sort: suppose, for example, a time of dearth and famine at Rhodes, with provisions at fabulous prices; and suppose that an honest man has imported a large cargo of grain from Alexandria and that to his certain knowledge also several other importers have set sail from Alexandria, and that on the voyage he has sighted their vessels laden with grain and bound for Rhodes; is he to report the fact to the Rhodians or is he to keep his own counsel and sell his own stock at the highest market price? I am assuming the case of a virtuous, upright man, and I am raising the question how a man would think and reason who would not conceal the facts from the Rhodians if he thought that it was immoral to do so, but who might be in doubt whether such silence would really be immoral.

In deciding cases of this kind Diogenes of Babylonia, a great and highly esteemed Stoic, consistently holds one view; his pupil Antipater, a most profound scholar, holds another. According to Antipater all the facts should be disclosed, that the buyer may not be uninformed of any detail that the seller knows; according to Diogenes the seller should declare any defects in his wares, in so far as such a course is prescribed by the common law of the land; but for the rest, since he has goods to sell, he may try to sell them to the best possible advantage, provided he is guilty of no mis–representation.

"I have imported my stock," Diogenes's merchant will say; "I have offered it for sale; I sell at a price no higher than my competitors— perhaps even lower, when the market is over-stocked. Who is wronged?"

"What say you?" comes Antipater's argument on the other side; "it is your duty to consider the interests of your fellow-men and to serve society; you were brought into the world under these conditions and have these inborn principles which you are in duty bound to obey and follow, that your interest shall be the interest of the community and conversely that the interest of the community shall be your interest as well; will you, in view of all these facts, conceal from your fellow-men what relief in plenteous supplies is close at hand for them?"

"It is one thing to conceal," Diogenes will perhaps reply; "not to reveal is quite a different thing. At this present moment I am not con-cealing from you, even if I am not revealing to you, the nature of the gods or the highest good; and to know these secrets would be of more advantage to you than to know that the price of wheat was down. But I am under no obliga-tion to tell you everything that it may be to your interest to be told."

"Yea," Antipater will say, "but you are, as you must admit, if you will only bethink you of the bonds of fellowship forged by Nature and existing between man and man."

"I do not forget them," the other will reply; "but do you mean to say that those bonds of fellowship are such that there is no such thing as private property? If that is the case, we should not sell anything at all, but freely give everything away."

XIII

In this whole discussion, you see, no one says, "However wrong morally this or that may be, still, since it is expedient, I will do it"; but the one side asserts that a given act is expedient, without being morally wrong, while the other insists that the act should not be done, because it is morally wrong.

Suppose again that an honest man is offer-ing a house for sale on account of certain unde-sirable features of which he himself is aware but which nobody else knows; suppose it is unsanitary, but has the reputation of being healthful; suppose it is not generally known that vermin are to be found in all the bedrooms; suppose, finally, that it is built of unsound tim-ber and likely to collapse, but that no one knows about it except the owner; if the vendor does not tell the purchaser these facts but sells him the house for far more than he could reasonably have expected to get for it, I ask whether his transaction is unjust or dishonourable.

"Yes," says Antipater, "it is; for to allow a purchaser to be hasty in closing a deal and through mistaken judgment to incur a very serious loss, if this is not refusing 'to set a man right when he has lost his way' (a crime which at Athens is prohibited on pain of public exe-cration), what is? It is even worse than refusing to set a man on his way: it is deliberately lead-ing a man astray."

"Can you say," answers Diogenes, "that he compelled you to purchase, when he did not even advise it? He advertised for sale what he did not like; you bought what you did like. If people are not considered guilty of swindling when they place upon their placards FOR SALE: A FINE VILLA, WELL BUILT, even when it is nei-ther good nor properly built, still less guilty are they who say nothing in praise of their house. For where the purchaser may exercise his own judgment, what fraud can there be on the part of the vendor? But if, again, not all that is expressly stated has to be made good, do you think a man is bound to make good what has not been said? What, pray, would be more stu-pid than for a vendor to recount all the faults in the article he is offering for sale? And what would be so absurd as for an auctioneer to cry, at the owner's bidding, 'Here is an unsanitary house for sale'?"

In this way, then, in certain doubtful cases moral rectitude is defended on the one side, while on the other side the case of expediency is so presented as to make it appear not only morally right to do what seems expedient, but even morally wrong not to do it. This is the contradiction that seems often to arise between the expedient and the morally right. But I must give my decision in these two cases; for I did not propound them merely to raise the questions, but to offer a solution. I think, then, that it was the duty of that grain-dealer not to keep back the facts from the Rhodians, and of this vendor of the house to deal in the same way with his purchaser. The fact is that merely holding one's peace about a thing does not constitute concealment, but concealment consists in trying for your own profit to keep others from finding out something that you know, when it is for their interest to know it. And who fails to discern what manner of concealment that is and what sort of person would be guilty of it? At all events he would be no candid or sincere or straightforward or upright or honest man, but rather one who is shifty, sly, artful, shrewd, underhand, cunning, one grown old in fraud and subtlety. Is it not inexpedient to subject oneself to all these terms of reproach and many more besides? ♦

QUESTIONS

1. What does Cicero think a wise person would do with the power of the ring of Gyges?

2. What does Cicero think of the relationship between what is morally right and what is expedient?

3. What is the difference for Cicero between friendship and conspiracy?

4. What does Cicero think is the right course of action for the ship captain who arrives at Rhodes?

5. How does Cicero define concealment?

OF CHEATING, WHICH IS COMMITTED IN BUYING AND SELLING FROM *THE SUMMA THEOLOGICA*

Thomas Aquinas (1225–1274)

We must now consider those sins which relate to voluntary commutations. First, we shall consider cheating, which is committed in buying and selling: secondly, we shall consider usury, which occurs in loans. In connection with the other voluntary commutations no special kind of sin is to be found distinct from rapine and theft.

Under the first head there are four points of inquiry: (1) Of unjust sales as regards the price; namely, whether it is lawful to sell a thing for more than its worth? (2) Of unjust sales on the part of the thing sold. (3) Whether the seller is bound to reveal a fault in the thing sold? (4) Whether it is lawful in trading to sell a thing at a higher price than was paid for it?

FIRST ARTICLE.

Whether It Is Lawful to Sell a Thing for More Than Its Worth?

We proceed thus to the First Article:—

Objection I. It would seem that it is lawful to sell a thing for more than its worth. In the commutations of human life, civil laws determine that which is just. Now according to these laws it is just for buyer and seller to deceive one another (Cod., IV., xliv., *De Rescind. Vend.* 8, 15): and this occurs by the seller selling a thing for more than its worth, and the buyer buying a thing for less than its worth. Therefore it is lawful to sell a thing for more than its worth.

Obj. 2. Further, That which is common to all would seem to be natural and not sinful. Now Augustine relates that the saying of a certain jester was accepted by all, *You wish to buy for a song and to sell at a premium*, which agrees with the saying of Prov. xx. 14, *It is naught, it is naught, saith every buyer: and when he is gone away, then he will boast.* Therefore it is lawful to sell a thing for more than its worth.

Obj. 3. Further, It does not seem unlawful if that which honesty demands be done by mutual agreement. Now, according to the Philosopher (*Ethic.* viii. 13), in the friendship which is based on utility, the amount of the recompense for a favour received should depend on the utility accruing to the receiver: and this utility sometimes is worth more than the thing given, for instance if the receiver be in great need of that thing, whether for the purpose of avoiding a danger, or of deriving some particular benefit. Therefore, in contracts of buying and selling, it is lawful to give a thing in return for more than its worth.

On the contrary, It is written (Matth. vii. 12): *All things . . . whatsoever you would that men should do to you, do you also to them.* But no man wishes to buy a thing for more than its worth. Therefore no man should sell a thing to another man for more than its worth.

I answer that, It is altogether sinful to have recourse to deceit in order to sell a thing for more than its just price, because this is to deceive one's neighbour so as to injure him. Hence Tully says (*De Offic.* iii. 15): *Contracts should be entirely free from double-dealing; the seller must not impose upon the bidder, nor the buyer upon one that bids against him.*

But, apart from fraud, we may speak of buying and selling in two ways. First, as considered in themselves, and from this point of view, buying and selling seem to be established for the common advantage of both parties, one of whom requires that which belongs to the other, and vice versa, as the Philosopher states (*Polit.* i. 3). Now whatever is established for the common advantage, should not be more of a burden to one party than to another, and consequently all contracts between them should observe equality of thing and thing. Again, the quality of a thing that comes into human use is measured by the price given for it, for which purpose money was invented, as stated in *Ethic.* v. 5.

Therefore if either the price exceed the quantity of the thing's worth, or, conversely, the thing exceed the price, there is no longer the equality of justice: and consequently, to sell a thing for more than its worth, or to buy it for less than its worth, is in itself unjust and unlawful.

Secondly we may speak of buying and selling, considered as accidentally tending to the advantage of one party, and to the disadvantage of the other: for instance, when a man has great need of a certain thing, while another man will suffer if he be without it. In such a case the just price will depend not only on the thing sold, but on the loss which the sale brings on the seller. And thus it will be lawful to sell a thing for more than it is worth in itself, though the price paid be not more than it is worth to the owner. Yet if the one man derive a great advantage by becoming possessed of the other man's property, and the seller be not at a loss through being without that thing, the latter ought not to raise the price, because the advantage accruing to the buyer, is not due to the seller, but to a circumstance affecting the buyer. Now no man should sell what is not his, though he may charge for the loss he suffers.

On the other hand if a man find that he derives great advantage from something he has bought, he may, of his own accord, pay the seller something over and above: and this pertains to his honesty.

Reply Obj. 1. As stated above (I.–II., Q. XCVI., A. 2) human law is given to the people among whom there are many lacking virtue, and it is not given to the virtuous alone. Hence human law was unable to forbid all that is contrary to virtue; and it suffices for it to prohibit whatever is destructive of human intercourse, while it treats other matters as though they were lawful, not by approving of them, but by not punishing them. Accordingly, if without employing deceit the seller disposes of his goods for more than their worth, or the buyer obtain them for less than their worth, the law looks upon this as licit, and provides no punishment for so doing, unless the excess be too great, because then even human law demands restitution to be made, for instance if a man be deceived in regard of more than half the amount of the just price of a thing.

On the other hand the Divine law leaves nothing unpunished that is contrary to virtue. Hence, according to the Divine law, it is reckoned unlawful if the equality of justice be not observed in buying and selling: and he who has received more than he ought must make compensation to him that has suffered loss, if the loss be considerable. I add this condition, because the just price of things is not fixed with mathematical precision, but depends on a kind of estimate, so that a slight addition or subtraction would not seem to destroy the equality of justice.

Reply Obj. 2. As Augustine says (*ibid.*) *this jester, either by looking into himself or by his experience of others, thought that all men are inclined to wish to buy for a song and sell at a premium. But since in reality this is wicked, it is in every man's power to acquire that justice whereby he may resist and overcome this inclination.* And then he gives the example of a man who gave the just price for a book to a man who through ignorance asked a low price for it. Hence it is evident that this common desire is not from nature but from vice, wherefore it is common to many who walk along the broad road of sin.

Reply Obj. 3. In commutative justice we consider chiefly real equality. On the other hand, in friendship based on utility we consider equality of usefulness, so that the recompense should depend on the usefulness accruing, whereas in buying it should be equal to the thing bought.

SECOND ARTICLE.

Whether a Sale Is Rendered Unlawful Through a Fault in the Thing Sold?

We proceed thus to the Second Article:—

Objection I. It would seem that a sale is not rendered unjust and unlawful through a fault in the thing sold. For less account should be taken of the other parts of a thing than of what belongs to its substance. Yet the sale of a thing does not seem to be rendered unlawful through a fault in its substance: for instance, if a man sell instead of the real metal, silver or gold produced by some chemical process, which is adapted to all the human uses for which silver and gold are necessary, for instance in the making of vessels and the like. Much less therefore will it be an unlawful sale if the thing be defective in other ways.

Obj. 2. Further, Any fault in the thing, affecting the quantity, would seem chiefly to be opposed to justice which consists in equality. Now quantity is known by being measured: and the measures of things that come into human use are not fixed, but in some places are greater, in others less, as the Philosopher states (*Ethic.* v. 7). Therefore just as it is impossible to avoid defects on the part of the thing sold, it seems that a sale is not rendered unlawful through the thing sold being defective.

Obj. 3. Further, the thing sold is rendered defective by lacking a fitting quality. But in order to know the quality of a thing, much knowledge is required that is lacking in most buyers. Therefore a sale is not rendered unlawful by a fault (in the thing sold).

On the contrary, Ambrose says (*De Offic.* iii. II): *It is manifestly a rule of justice that a good man should not depart from the truth, nor inflict an unjust injury on anyone, nor have any connection with fraud.*

I answer that, A threefold fault may be found pertaining to the thing which is sold. One, in respect of the thing's substance: and if the seller be aware of a fault in the thing he is selling, he is guilty of a fraudulent sale, so that the sale is rendered unlawful. Hence we find it written against certain people (Isa. i. 22), *Thy silver is turned into dross, thy wine is mingled with water:* because that which is mixed is defective in its substance.

Another defect is in respect of quantity which is known by being measured: wherefore if anyone knowingly make use of a faulty measure in selling, he is guilty of fraud, and the sale is illicit. Hence it is written (Deut. xxv. 13, 14): *Thou shalt not have divers weights in thy bag, a greater and a less: neither shall there be in thy house a greater bushel and a less,* and further on (*verse* 16): *For the Lord … abhorreth him that doth these things, and He hateth all injustice.*

A third defect is on the part of the quality, for instance, if a man sell an unhealthy animal as being a healthy one: and if anyone do this knowingly he is guilty of a fraudulent sale, and the sale, in consequence, is illicit.

In all these cases not only is the man guilty of a fraudulent sale, but he is also bound to restitution. But if any of the foregoing defects be in the thing sold, and he knows nothing about this, the seller does not sin, because he does that which is unjust materially, nor is his deed unjust, as shown above (Q. LIX., A. 2). Nevertheless he is bound to compensate the buyer, when the defect comes to his knowledge. Moreover what has been said of the seller applies equally to the buyer. For sometimes it happens that the seller thinks his goods to be specifically of lower value, as when a man sells gold instead of copper, and then if the buyer be aware of this, he buys it unjustly and is bound to restitution: and the same applies to a defect in quantity as to a defect in quality.

Reply Obj. I. Gold and silver are costly not only on account of the usefulness of the vessels and other like things made from them, but also on account of the excellence and purity of their substance. Hence if the gold or silver produced by alchemists has not the true specific nature of gold and silver, the sale thereof is fraudulent and unjust, especially as real gold and silver can produce certain results by their natural action, which the counterfeit gold and silver of alchemists cannot produce. Thus the true metal has the property of making people joyful, and is helpful medicinally against certain maladies. Moreover real gold can be employed more frequently, and lasts longer in its condition of purity than counterfeit gold. If however real gold were to be produced by alchemy, it would not be unlawful to sell it for the genuine article, for nothing prevents art from employing certain natural causes for the production of natural and true effects, as Augustine says (*De Trin.* iii. 8) of things produced by the art of the demons.

Reply Obj. 2. The measures of saleable commodities must needs be different in different places, on account of the difference of supply: because where there is greater abundance, the measures are wont to be larger. However in each place those who govern the state must determine the just measures of things saleable, with due consideration for the conditions of place and time. Hence it is not lawful to disregard such measures as are established by public authority or custom.

Reply Obj. 3. As Augustine says (*De Civ. Dei* xi. 16) the price of things saleable does not depend on their degree of nature, since at times a horse fetches a higher price than a slave; but it depends on their usefulness to man. Hence it is not necessary for the seller or buyer to be cognizant of the hidden qualities of the thing sold, but only of such as render the thing adapted to man's use, for instance, that the horse be strong, run well and so forth. Such qualities the seller and buyer can easily discover.

Third Article.

Whether the Seller Is Bound to State the Defects of the Thing Sold?

We proceed thus to the Third Article:—

Objection I. It would seem that the seller is not bound to state the defects of the thing sold. Since the seller does not bind the buyer to buy, he would seem to leave it to him to judge of the goods offered for sale. Now judgment about a thing and knowledge of that thing belong to the same person. Therefore it does not seem imputable to the seller if the buyer be deceived in his judgment, and be hurried into buying a thing without carefully inquiring into its condition.

Obj. 2. Further, It seems foolish for anyone to do what prevents him carrying out his work. But if a man states the defects of the goods he has for sale, he prevents their sale: wherefore Tully (*De Offic.* iii. 13) pictures a man as saying: *Could anything be more absurd than for a public crier, instructed by the owner, to cry: 'I offer this unhealthy house for sale'?* Therefore the seller is not bound to state the defects of the thing sold.

Obj. 3. Further, Man needs more to know the road of virtue than to know the faults of things offered for sale. Now one is not bound to offer advice to all or to tell them the truth about matters pertaining to virtue, though one should not tell anyone what is false. Much less therefore is a seller bound to tell the faults of what he offers for sale, as though he were counselling the buyer.

Obj. 4. Further, If one were bound to tell the faults of what one offers for sale, this would only be in order to lower the price. Now sometimes the price would be lowered for some other reason, without any defect in the thing sold: for instance, if the seller carry wheat to a place where wheat fetches a high price, knowing that many will come after him carrying wheat; because if the buyers knew this they would give a lower price. But apparently the seller need not give the buyer this information. Therefore, in like manner, neither need he tell him the faults of the goods he is selling.

On the contrary, Ambrose says (*De Offic.* iii. 10): *In all contracts the defects of the saleable commodity must be stated; and unless the seller make them known, although the buyer has already acquired a right to them, the contract is voided on account of the fraudulent action.*

I answer that, It is always unlawful to give anyone an occasion of danger or loss, although a man need not always give another the help or counsel which would be for his advantage in any way; but only in certain fixed cases, for instance when someone is subject to him, or when he is the only one who can assist him. Now the seller who offers goods for sale, gives the buyer an occasion of loss or danger, by the very fact that he offers him defective goods, if such defect may occasion loss or danger to the buyer:—loss, if, by reason of this defect, the goods are of less value, and he takes nothing off the price on that account:—danger, if this defect either hinder the use of the goods or render it hurtful, for instance, if a man sells a lame for a fleet horse, a tottering house for a safe one, rotten or poisonous food for wholesome. Wherefore if such like defects be hidden, and the seller does not make them known, the sale will be illicit and fraudulent, and the seller will be bound to compensation for the loss incurred.

On the other hand, if the defect be manifest, for instance if a horse have but one eye, or if the goods though useless to the buyer, be useful to someone else, provided the seller take as much as he ought from the price, he is not bound to state the defect of the goods, since perhaps on account of that defect the buyer might want him to allow a greater rebate than he need. Wherefore the seller may look to his own indemnity, by withholding the defect of the goods.

Reply Obj. 1. Judgment cannot be pronounced save on what is manifest: for *a man judges of what he knows* (*Ethic.* i. 3). Hence if the defects of the goods offered for sale be hidden, judgment of them is not sufficiently left with the buyer unless such defects be made known to him. The case would be different if the defects were manifest.

Reply Obj. 2. There is no need to publish beforehand by the public crier the defects of the goods one is offering for sale, because if he were to begin by announcing its defects, the bidders would be frightened to buy, through ignorance of other qualities that might render the thing good and serviceable. Such defect ought to be stated to each individual that offers to buy: and then he will be able to compare the various points one with the other, the good with the bad: for nothing prevents that which is defective in one respect being useful in many others.

Reply Obj. 3. Although a man is not bound strictly speaking to tell everyone the truth about matters pertaining to virtue, yet he is so bound in a case when, unless he tells the truth, his conduct would endanger another man in detriment to virtue: and so it is in this case.

Reply Obj. 4. The defect in a thing makes it of less value now than it seems to be: but in the case cited, the goods are expected to be of less value at a future time, on account of the arrival of other merchants, which was not foreseen by the buyers. Wherefore the seller, since he sells his goods at the price actually offered him, does not seem to act contrary to justice through not stating what is going to happen. If however he were to do so, or if he lowered his price, it would be exceedingly virtuous on his part: although he does not seem to be bound to do this as a debt of justice.

FOURTH ARTICLE.

Whether, In Trading, It Is Lawful to Sell a Thing at a Higher Price Than What Was Paid For It?

We proceed thus to the Fourth Article:—

Objection I. It would seem that it is not lawful, in trading, to sell a thing for a higher price than we paid for it. For Chrysostom says on Matth. xxi. 12: *He that buys a thing in order that he may sell it, entire and unchanged, at a profit, is the trader who is cast out of God's temple.* Cassiodorus speaks in the same sense in his commentary on Ps. lxx. 15, *Because I have not known learning,* or *trading* according to another version: *What is trade,* says he, *but buying at a cheap price with the purpose of retailing at a higher price?* and he adds: *Such were the tradesmen whom Our Lord cast out of the temple.* Now no man is cast out of the temple except for a sin. Therefore suchlike trading is sinful.

Obj. 2. Further, It is contrary to justice to sell goods at a higher price than their worth, or to buy them for less than their value, as shown above (A. I). Now if you sell a thing for a higher price than you paid for it, you must either have bought it for less than its value, or sell it for more than its value. Therefore this cannot be done without sin.

Obj. 3. Further, Jerome says (*Ep. ad. Nepot.* lii.): *Shun, as you would the plague, a cleric who from being poor has become wealthy, or who, from being a nobody has become a celebrity.* Now trading would not seem to be forbidden to clerics except on account of its sinfulness. Therefore it is a sin in trading, to buy at a low price and to sell at a higher price.

On the contrary, Augustine commenting on Ps. lxx. 15, *Because I have not known learning,* says: *The greedy tradesman blasphemes over his losses; he lies and perjures himself over the price of his wares. But these are vices of the man, not of the craft, which can be exercised without these vices.* Therefore trading is not in itself unlawful.

I answer that, A tradesman is one whose business consists in the exchange of things. According to the Philosopher (*Polit.* i. 3), exchange of things is twofold; one, natural as it were, and necessary, whereby one commodity is exchanged for another, or money taken in exchange for a commodity, in order to satisfy the needs of life. Such like trading, properly speaking, does not belong to tradesmen, but rather to housekeepers or civil servants who have to provide the household or the state with the necessaries of life. The other kind of exchange is either that of money for money, or of any commodity for money, not on account of the necessities of life, but for profit, and this kind of exchange, properly speaking, regards tradesmen, according to the Philosopher (*Polit.* i. 3). The former kind of exchange is commendable because it supplies a natural need: but the latter is justly deserving of blame, because, considering in itself, it satisfies the greed for gain, which knows no limit and tends to infinity. Hence trading, considered in itself, has a certain debasement attaching thereto, in so far as, by its very nature, it does not imply a virtuous or necessary end. Nevertheless gain which is the end of trading, though not implying, by its nature, anything virtuous or necessary, does not, in itself, connote anything sinful or contrary to virtue: wherefore nothing prevents gain from being directed to some necessary or even virtuous end, and thus trading becomes lawful. Thus, for instance, a man may intend the moderate gain which he seeks to acquire by trading for the upkeep of his household, or for the assistance of the needy: or again, a man may take to trade for some public advantage, for instance, lest his country lack the necessaries of life, and seek gain, not as an end, but as payment for his labour.

Reply Obj. I. The saying of Chrysostom refers to the trading which seeks gain as a last end. This is especially the case where a man sells something at a higher price without its undergoing any change. For if he sells at a higher price something that has changed for the better, he would seem to receive the reward of his labour. Nevertheless the gain itself may be lawfully intended, not as a last end, but for the sake of some other end which is necessary or virtuous, as stated above.

Reply Obj. 2. Not everyone that sells at a higher price than he bought is a tradesman, but only he who buys that he may sell at a profit. If, on the contrary, he buys not for sale but for possession, and afterwards, for some reason wishes to sell, it is not a trade transaction even if he sell at a profit. For he may lawfully do this, either because he has bettered the thing, or because the value of the thing has changed with the change of place or time, or on account of the danger he incurs in transferring the thing from one place to another, or again in having it carried by another. In this sense neither buying nor selling is unjust.

Reply Obj. 3. Clerics should abstain not only from things that are evil in themselves, but even from those that have an appearance of evil. This happens in trading, both because it is directed to worldly gain, which clerics should despise, and because trading is open to so many vices, since *a merchant is hardly free from sins of the lips* (Ecclus. xxvi. 28). There is also another reason, because trading engages the mind too much with worldly cares, and consequently withdraws it from spiritual cares; wherefore the Apostle says (2 Tim. ii. 4): *No man being a soldier to God entangleth himself with secular businesses.* Nevertheless it is lawful for clerics to engage in the first mentioned kind of exchange, which is directed to supply the necessaries of life, either by buying or by selling. ♦

QUESTIONS

1. What is the main issue in each of the four articles?

2. Does Aquinas think that human law and divine law are the same?

3. Why does Aquinas think that the main principle in pricing an object is to sell it for no more or less than it is truly worth?

4. What must someone who unknowingly sells a defective product do?

5. When can a defect be simply ignored by the seller?

6. Under what circumstances must a person help another?

7. According to Aquinas, what four reasons clearly justify profits?

8. What additional five reasons does Aquinas give for justifying profits?

SELECTION FROM: *THE BUSINESS GUIDE*

J. L. Nichols (1851–1895) self-published Naperville, Ill 1893

The early home of Abraham Lincoln, who was known as "Honest Abe."

HONESTY

No legacy is so rich as HONESTY.—*Shakespere.*

He who freely praises what he means to purchase, and he who enumerates the faults of what he means to sell, may set up a partnership with Honesty!—*Lavater.*

What is becoming, is honest, and whatever is honest must always be becoming.—*Cicero.*

Nothing more completely baffles one who is full of trick and duplicity himself, than straight-forward and simple integrity in another.—*Colton.*

Truth and honesty show themselves in various ways. They characterize the men of just dealing, the faithful men of business, the men who will not deceive you to their own advantage. Honesty gives full measure, just weights, true samples, full service, and a strict fulfilment of every engagement.

The truth of the good old maxim, "Honesty is the best policy," is fully demonstrated every day of our life; and uprightness and integrity are found as successful in business as in everything else. As Hugh Miller's worthy uncle used to advise him, "In all your dealings give your neighbor the cast of the bank—good measure, heaped up, and running over,—and you will not lose by it in the end." Truth is the essence of principle, integrity and independence, and every man needs it. Absolute veracity is more needed today than at any former period in our history.

Remember that honesty rises above fortune and above kings; by that alone, and not by the splendor of riches or of titles in glory acquired, that glory which it will be your happiness and pride to transmit unspotted to your posterity. Honesty is greatness itself; dishonesty never made a man great, and never will. Rather be and continue poor, while others around grow rich by fraud and disloyalty, rather be without place or power, while others beg their way upward; rather bear the pain of disappointed hopes, while others win their way by flattery, and forego the gracious pressure of the hand for which others cringe and crawl. Wrap yourself in the cloak of virtue, and seek your bread with an honest hand, and if you grow gray in this cause, with unsoiled honor bless God, and rejoice.

"The honest man, though e'er so poor,
Is king of men for all that."

SELECTION FROM: *THE BUSINESS GUIDE*

J. L. Nichols (1851–1895) self-published Naperville, Ill 1893

RAPID METHODS
FOR MARKING GOODS

Those who buy largely can best appreciate the value of a quick and rapid method for calculating the per cent, of profits desired.

If you wish to calculate the per cent on a single article, the following table will be an excellent method. If you desire to sell an article at any of the following per cents, say the article costs 70 cents, and you wish to make

10 per cent. divide by 10, multiply by 11 = 77.
20 per cent. divide by 10, multiply by 12 = 84.
25 per cent. multiply by 10, divide by 8 = 87½.
30 per cent. divide by 10, multiply by 13 = 91.
33½ per cent. add ½ of itself = 93 ½.
33½ per cent. divide by 3, multiply by 4 = 93½.
50 per cent. add ½ of itself = $1.03.

NATURAL SELECTION FROM
THE ORIGIN OF SPECIES

Charles Darwin (1809–1882)

Natural Selection—its power compared with man's selection—its power on characters of trifling importance—its power at all ages and on both sexes—Sexual Selection—On the generality of intercrosses between individuals of the same species—Circumstances favourable and unfavourable to the results of Natural Selection, namely, intercrossing, isolation, number of individuals—Slow action—Extinction caused by Natural Selection—Divergence of Character, related to the diversity of inhabitants of any small area, and to naturalisation—Action of Natural Selection, through Divergence of Character, and Extinction, and on the descendants from a common parent—Explains the grouping of all organic beings—Advance in organization—Low forms preserved—Convergence of character—Indefinite multiplication of species—Summary.

How will the struggle for existence, briefly discussed [earlier] . . . , act in regard to variation? Can the principle of selection, which we have seen is so potent in the hands of man, apply under nature? I think we shall see that it can act most efficiently. Let the endless number of slight variations and individual differences occurring in our domestic productions, and, in a lesser degree, in those under nature, be borne in mind; as well as the strength of the hereditary tendency. Under domestication, it may be truly said that the whole organization becomes in some degree plastic. But the variability, which we almost universally meet with in our domestic productions, is not directly produced, as Hooker and Asa Gray have well remarked, by man; he can neither originate varieties, nor prevent their occurrence; he can only preserve and accumulate such as do occur. Unintentionally he exposes organic beings to new and changing conditions of life, and variability ensues; but similar changes of conditions might and do occur under nature. Let it also be borne in mind how infinitely complex and close-fitting are the mutual relations of all organic beings to each other and to their physical conditions of life; and consequently what infinitely varied diversities of structure might be of use to each being under changing conditions of life. Can it, then, be thought improbable, seeing that variations useful to man have undoubtedly occurred, that other variations useful in some way to each being in the great and complex battle of life, should occur in the course of many succes-

sive generations? If such do occur, can we doubt (remembering that many more individuals are born than can possibly survive) that individuals having any advantage, however slight, over others, would have the best chance of surviving and of procreating their kind? On the other hand, we may feel sure that any variation in the least degree injurious would be rigidly destroyed. This preservation of favourable individual differences and variations, and the destruction of those which are injurious, I have called Natural Selection, or the Survival of the Fittest. Variations neither useful nor injurious would not be affected by natural selection, and would be left either a fluctuating element, as perhaps we see in certain polymorphic species, or would ultimately become fixed, owing to the nature of the organism and the nature of the conditions.

Several writers have misapprehended or objected to the term Natural Selection. Some have even imagined that natural selection induces variability, whereas it implies only the preservation of such variations as arise and are beneficial to the being under its conditions of life. No one objects to agriculturists speaking of the potent effects of man's selection; and in this case the individual differences given by nature, which man for some object selects, must of necessity first occur. Others have objected that the term selection implies conscious choice in the animals which become modified; and it has even been urged that, as plants have no volition, natural selection is not applicable to them! In the literal sense of the word, no doubt, natural selection is a false term; but who ever objected to chemists speaking of the elective affinities of the various elements?—and yet an acid cannot strictly be said to elect the base with which it in preference combines. It has been said that I speak of natural selection as an active power or Deity; but who objects to an author speaking of the attraction of gravity as ruling the movements of the planets? Every one knows what is meant and is implied by such metaphorical expressions; and they are almost necessary for brevity. So again it is difficult to avoid personifying the word Nature; but I mean by Nature, only the aggregate action and product of many natural laws, and by laws the sequence of events as ascertained by us. With a little familiarity such superficial objections will be forgotten.

We shall best understand the probable course of natural selection by taking the case of a country undergoing some slight physical change, for instance, of climate. The proportional numbers of its inhabitants will almost immediately undergo a change, and some species will probably become extinct. We may conclude, from what we have seen of the intimate and complex manner in which the inhabitants of each country are bound together, that any change in the numerical proportions of the inhabitants, independently of the change of climate itself, would seriously affect the others. If the country were open on its borders, new forms would certainly immigrate, and this would likewise seriously disturb the relations of some of the former inhabitants. Let it be remembered how powerful the influence of a single introduced tree or mammal has been shown to be. But in the case of an island, or of a country partly surrounded by barriers, into which new and better adapted forms could not freely enter, we should then have places in the economy of nature which would assuredly be better filled up, if some of the original inhabitants were in some manner modified; for, had the area been open to immigration, these same places would have been seized on by intruders. In such cases, slight modifications, which in any way favoured the individuals of any species, by better adapting them to their altered conditions, would tend to be preserved; and natural selection would have free scope for the work of improvement.

We have good reason to believe, as shown [earlier] . . . , that changes in the conditions of life give a tendency to increased variability; and in the foregoing cases the conditions have changed, and this would manifestly be favourable to natural selection, by affording a better chance of the occurrence of profitable variations. Unless such occur, natural selection can do nothing. Under the term of "variations," it must never be forgotten that mere individual differences are included. As man can produce a great result with his domestic animals and plants by adding up in any given direction individual differences, so could natural selection, but far more easily from having incomparably longer time for action. Nor do I believe that any great physical change, as of climate, or any unusual degree of isolation to check immigration, is necessary in order that new and unoccupied places should be left, for natural selection to fill up by improving some of the varying inhabitants. For as all the inhabitants of each country are struggling together with nicely balanced forces, extremely slight modifications in the structure or habits of one species would often give it an advantage over others; and still further modifications of the same kind would often still further increase the advantage, as long as the species continued under the same conditions of life and profited by similar means of subsistence and defense. No country can be named in which all the native inhabitants are now so perfectly adapted to each other and to the physical conditions under which they live, that none of them could be still better adapted or improved; for in all countries, the natives have been so far conquered by naturalised productions, that they have allowed some foreigners to take firm possession of the land. And as foreigners have thus in every country beaten some of the natives, we may safely conclude that the natives might have been modified with advantage, so as to have better resisted the intruders.

As man can produce, and certainly has produced, a great result by his methodical and unconscious means of selection, what may not natural selection effect? Man can act only on external and visible characters: Nature if I may be allowed to personify the natural preservation or survival of the fittest, cares nothing for appearances, except in so far as they are useful to any being. She can act on every internal organ, on every shade of constitutional difference, on the whole machinery of life. Man selects only for his own good: Nature only for that of the being which she tends. Every selected character is fully exercised by her, as is implied by the fact of their selection. Man keeps the natives of many climates in the same country; he seldom exercises each selected character in some peculiar and fitting manner; he feeds a long and a short beaked pigeon on the same food; he does not exercise a long-backed or long-legged quadruped in any peculiar manner; he exposes sheep with long and short wool to the same climate. He does not allow the most vigorous males to struggle for the females. He does not rigidly destroy all inferior animals, but protects during each varying season, as far as lies in his power, all his productions. He often begins his selection by some half-monstrous form; or at least by some modification prominent enough to catch the eye or to be plainly useful to him. Under nature, the slightest differences of structure or constitution may well turn the nicely-balanced scale in the struggle for life, and so be preserved. How fleeting are the wishes and efforts of man! how short his time! and consequently how poor will be his results, compared with those accumulated by Nature during whole geological periods! Can we wonder, then, that Nature's productions should be far "truer" in character than man's productions; that they should be infinitely better adapted to the most complex conditions of life, and should plainly bear the stamp of far higher workmanship?

It may metaphorically be said that natural selection is daily and hourly scrutinising, throughout the world, the slightest variations; rejecting those that are bad, preserving and adding up all that are good; silently and insensibly working, *whenever and wherever opportunity offers,* at the improvement of each organic being in relation to its organic and inorganic conditions of life. We see nothing of these slow changes in progress, until the hand of time has marked the lapse of ages, and then so imperfect is our view into long-past geological ages, that we see only that the forms of life are now different from what they formerly were. ♦

QUESTIONS

1. What is Darwin's concept of survival of the fittest?

2. How might the concept of survival of the fittest apply to business?

3. What is the role of "extremely slight modifications" in biology and in business?

4. What constitutes the environment for contemporary business?

FROM *THE FINANCIER*

Theodore Dreiser (1871–1945)

Frank Cowperwood, even at ten, was a natural-born leader. At the day school he attended, and later at the Central High School, he was looked upon as one whose common sense could unquestionably be trusted in all cases. He was a sturdy youth, courageous and defiant. From the very start of his life, he wanted to know about economics and politics. He cared nothing for books. He was a clean, stocky, shapely boy, with a bright, clean-cut, incisive face; large, clear, gray eyes; a wide forehead; short, bristly, dark-brown hair. He had an incisive, quick-motioned, self-sufficient manner, and was forever asking questions with a keen desire for an intelligent reply. He never had an ache or pain, ate his food with gusto, and ruled his brothers with a rod of iron. "Come on, Joe!" "Hurry, Ed!" These commands were issued in no rough but always a sure way, and Joe and Ed came. They looked up to Frank from the first as a master, and what he had to say was listened to eagerly.

He was forever pondering, pondering—one fact astonishing him quite as much as another—for he could not figure out how this thing he had come into—this life—was organized. How did all these people get into the world? What were they doing here? Who started things, anyhow? His mother told him the story of Adam and Eve, but he didn't believe it. There was a fish-market not so very far from his home, and there, on his way to see his father at the bank, or conducting his brothers on after-school expeditions, he liked to look at a certain tank in front of one store where were kept odd specimens of sea-life brought in by the Delaware Bay fishermen. He saw once there a sea-horse—just a queer little sea-animal that looked somewhat like a horse—and another time he saw an electric eel which Benjamin Franklin's discovery had explained. One day he saw a squid and a lobster put in the tank, and in connection with them was witness to a tragedy which stayed with him all his life and cleared things up considerably intellectually. The lobster, it appeared from the talk of the idle bystanders, was offered no food, as the squid was considered his rightful prey. He lay at the bottom of the clear glass tank on the yellow sand, apparently seeing, nothing—you could not tell in which way his beady, black buttons of eyes were looking—but apparently they were never off the body of the squid. The latter, pale and waxy in texture, looking very much like pork fat or jade, moved about in torpedo fashion; but his movements were apparently never out of the eyes of his enemy, for by degrees small portions of his body began to disappear, snapped off by the relentless claws of his pursuer. The lobster would leap like a catapult to where the squid was apparently idly dreaming, and the squid, very alert, would dart away, shooting out at the same time a cloud of ink, behind which it would disappear. It was not always completely successful, however. Small portions of its body or its tail were frequently left in the claws of the monster below. Fascinated by the drama, young Cowperwood came daily to watch.

One morning he stood in front of the tank, his nose almost pressed to the glass. Only a portion of the squid remained, and his ink-bag was emptier than ever. In the corner of the tank sat the lobster, poised apparently for action.

The boy stayed as long as he could, the bitter struggle fascinating him. Now, maybe, or in an hour or a day, the squid might die, slain by the lobster, and the lobster would eat him. He looked again at the greenish-copperish engine of destruction in the corner and wondered when this would be. To-night, maybe. He would come back to-night.

He returned that night, and lo! the expected had happened. There was a little crowd around the tank. The lobster was in the corner. Before him was the squid cut in two and partially devoured.

"He got him at last," observed one bystander. "I was standing right here an hour ago, and up he leaped and grabbed him. The squid was too tired. He wasn't quick enough. He did back up, but that lobster he calculated on his doing that. He's been figuring on his movements for a long time now. He got him to-day."

Frank only stared. Too bad he had missed this. The least touch of sorrow for the squid came to him as he stared at it slain. Then he gazed at the victor.

"That's the way it has to be, I guess," he commented to himself. "That squid wasn't quick enough." He figured it out.

"The squid couldn't kill the lobster—he had no weapon. The lobster could kill the squid—he was heavily armed. There was nothing for the squid to feed on; the lobster had the squid as prey. What was the result to be? What else could it be? He didn't have a chance," he concluded finally, as he trotted on homeward.

The incident made a great impression on him. It answered in a rough way that riddle which had been annoying him so much in the past: "How is life organized?" Things lived on each other—that was it. Lobsters lived on squids and other things. What lived on lobsters? Men, of course! Sure, that was it! And what lived on men? he asked himself. Was it other men? Wild animals lived on men. And there were Indians and cannibals. And some men were killed by storms and accidents. He wasn't so sure about men living on men; but men did kill each other. How about wars and street fights and mobs? He had seen a mob once. It attacked the *Public Ledger* building as he was coming home from school. His father had explained why. It was about the slaves.

That was it! Sure, men lived on men. Look at the slaves. They were men. That's what all this excitement was about these days. Men killing other men—negroes.

He went on home quite pleased with himself at his solution.

"Mother!" he exclaimed, as he entered the house, "he finally got him!"

"Got who? What got what?" she inquired in amazement. "Go wash your hands."

"Why, that lobster got that squid I was telling you and pa about the other day."

"Well, that's too bad. What makes you take any interest in such things? Run, wash your hands."

"Well, you don't often see anything like that. I never did."

He went out in the back yard, where there was a hydrant and a post with a little table on it, and on that a shining tin-pan and a bucket of water. Here he washed his face and hands.

"Say, papa," he said to his father, later, "you know that squid?"

"Yes."

"Well, he's dead. The lobster got him."

His father continued reading. "Well, that's too bad," he said, indifferently.

But for days and weeks Frank thought of this and of the life he was tossed into, for he was already pondering on what he should be in this world, and how he should get along. From seeing his father count money, he was sure that he would like banking; and Third Street, where his father's office was, seemed to him the cleanest, most fascinating street in the world. ◆

QUESTIONS

1. Why is Frank Cowperwood so surprised by how society is organized?

2. How is life in the tank that contains the squid and the lobster organized?

3. Is organization in the tank natural?

4. In what way did seeing the scene played out between the lobster and the squid help clarify the order of things for Frank?

Pecuniary Emulation and Conspicuous Consumption from *Theory of the Leisure Class*

Thorstein Veblen (1857–1929)

In the sequence of cultural evolution the emergence of a leisure class coincides with the beginning of ownership. This is necessarily the case, for these two institutions result from the same set of economic forces. In the inchoate phase of their development they are but different aspects of the same general facts of social structure.

It is as elements of social structure—conventional facts—that leisure and ownership are matters of interest for the purpose in hand. An habitual neglect of work does not constitute a leisure class; neither does the mechanical fact of use and consumption constitute ownership. The present inquiry, therefore, is not concerned with the beginning of indolence, nor with the beginning of the appropriation of useful articles to individual consumption. The point in question is the origin and nature of a conventional leisure class on the one hand and the beginnings of individual ownership as a conventional right or equitable claim on the other hand.

The early differentiation out of which the distinction between a leisure and a working class arises is a division maintained between men's and women's work in the lower stages of barbarism. Likewise the earliest form of ownership is an ownership of the women by the able-bodied men of the community. The facts may be expressed in more general terms, and truer to the import of the barbarian theory of life, by saying that it is an ownership of the woman by the man.

There was undoubtedly some appropriation of useful articles before the custom of appropriating women arose. The usages of existing archaic communities in which there is no ownership of women is warrant for such a view. In all communities the members, both male and female, habitually appropriate to their individual use a variety of useful things; but these useful things are not thought of as owned by the person who appropriates and consumes them. The habitual appropriation and consumption of certain slight personal effects goes on without raising the question of ownership; that is to say, the question of a conventional, equitable claim to extraneous things.

The ownership of women begins in the lower barbarian stages of culture, apparently with the seizure of female captives. The original reason for the seizure and appropriation of women seems to have been their usefulness as trophies. The practice of seizing women from the enemy as trophies, gave rise to a form of ownership-marriage, resulting in a household with a male head. This was followed by an extension of slavery to other captives and inferiors, besides women, and by an extension of ownership-marriage to other women than those seized from the enemy. The outcome of emulation under the circumstances of a predatory life, therefore, has been on the one hand a form of marriage resting on coercion, and on the other hand the custom of ownership. The two institutions are not distinguishable in the initial phase of their development; both arise from the desire of the successful men to put their prowess in evidence by exhibiting some durable results of their exploits. Both also minister to that propensity for mastery which pervades all predatory communities. From the ownership of women the concept of ownership extends itself to include the products of their industry, and so there arises the ownership of things as well as of persons.

In this way a consistent system of property in goods is gradually installed. And although in the latest stages of the development, the serviceability of goods for consumption has come to be the most obtrusive element of their value, still, wealth has by no means yet lost its utility as a honorific evidence of the owner's prepotence.

Wherever the institution of private property is found, even in a slightly developed form, the economic process bears the character of a struggle between men for the possession of goods. It has been customary in economic theory, and especially among those economists who adhere with least faltering to the body of modernized classical doctrines, to construe this struggle for wealth as being substantially a struggle for subsistence. Such is, no doubt, its character in large part during the earlier and less efficient phases of industry. Such is also its character in all cases where the "niggardliness of nature" is so strict as to afford but a scanty livelihood to the community in return for strenuous and unremitting application to the business of getting the means of subsistence. But in all progressing communities an advance is presently made beyond this early stage of technological development. Industrial efficiency is presently carried to such a pitch as to afford something appreciably more than a bare livelihood to those engaged in the industrial process. It has not been unusual for economic theory to speak of the further struggle for wealth on this new industrial basis as a competition for an increase of the comforts of life,—primarily for an increase of the physical comforts which the consumption of goods affords.

The end of acquisition and accumulation is conventionally held to be the consumption of the goods accumulated—whether it is consumption directly by the owner of the goods or by the household attached to him and for this purpose identified with him in theory. This is at least felt to be the economically legitimate end of acquisition, which alone it is incumbent on the theory to take account of. Such consumption may of course be conceived to serve the consumer's physical wants—his physical comfort—or his so-called higher wants—spiritual, aesthetic, intellectual, or what not; the latter class of wants being served indirectly by an expenditure of goods, after the fashion familiar to all economic readers.

But it is only when taken in a sense far removed from its naïve meaning that consumption of goods can be said to afford the incentive from which accumulation invariably proceeds. The motive that lies at the root of ownership is emulation; and the same motive of emulation continues active in the further development of the institution to which it has given rise and in the development of all those

features of the social structure which this institution of ownership touches. The possession of wealth confers honour; it is an invidious distinction. Nothing equally cogent can be said for the consumption of goods, nor for any other conceivable incentive to acquisition, and especially not for any incentive to the accumulation of wealth.

It is of course not to be overlooked that in a community where nearly all goods are private property the necessity of earning a livelihood is a powerful and ever-present incentive for the poorer members of the community. The need of subsistence and of an increase of physical comfort may for a time be the dominant motive of acquisition for those classes who are habitually employed at manual labour, whose subsistence is on a precarious footing, who possess little and ordinarily accumulate little; but it will appear in the course of the discussion that even in the case of these impecunious classes the predominance of the motive of physical want is not so decided as has sometimes been assumed. On the other hand, so far as regards those members and classes of the community who are chiefly concerned in the accumulation of wealth, the incentive of subsistence or of physical comfort never plays a considerable part. Ownership began and grew into a human institution on grounds unrelated to the subsistence minimum. The dominant incentive was from the outset the invidious distinction attaching to wealth, and, save temporarily and by exception, no other motive has usurped the primacy at any later stage of the development.

Property set out with being booty held as trophies of the successful raid. So long as the group had departed but little from the primitive communal organization, and so long as it still stood in close contact with other hostile groups, the utility of things or persons owned lay chiefly in an invidious comparison between their possessor and the enemy from whom they were taken. The habit of distinguishing between the interests of the individual and those of the group to which he belongs is apparently a later growth. Invidious comparison between the possessor of the honorific booty and his less successful neighbours within the group was no doubt present early as an element of the utility of the things possessed, though this was not at the outset the chief element of their value. The man's prowess was still primarily the group's prowess, and the possessor of the booty felt himself to be primarily the keeper of the honour of his group. This appreciation of exploit from the communal point of view is met with also at later stages of social growth, especially as regards the laurels of war.

But so soon as the custom of individual ownership begins to gain consistency, the point of view taken in making the invidious comparison on which private property rests will begin to change. Indeed, the one change is but the reflex of the other. The initial phase of ownership, the phase of acquisition by naïve seizure and conversion, begins to pass into the subsequent stage of an incipient organization of industry on the basis of private property (in slaves); the horde develops into a more or less self-sufficing industrial community; possessions then come to be valued not so much as evidence of successful foray, but rather as evidence of the prepotence of the possessor of these goods over other individuals within the community. The invidious comparison now becomes primarily a comparison of the owner with the other members of the group. Property is still of the nature of trophy, but, with the cultural advance, it becomes more and more a trophy of successes scored in the game of ownership carried on between the members of the group under the quasi-peaceable methods of nomadic life.

Gradually, as industrial activity further displaces predatory activity in the community's everyday life and in men's habits of thought, accumulated property more and more replaces trophies of predatory exploit as the conventional exponent of prepotence and success. With the growth of settled industry, therefore, the possession of wealth gains in relative importance and effectiveness as a customary basis of repute and esteem. Not that esteem ceases to be awarded on the basis of other, more direct evidence of prowess; not that successful predatory aggression or warlike exploit ceases to call out the approval and admiration of the crowd, or to stir the envy of the less successful competitors; but the opportunities for gaining distinction by means of this direct manifesta-

tion of superior force grow less available both in scope and frequency. At the same time opportunities for industrial aggression, and for the accumulation of property by the quasi-peaceable methods of nomadic industry, increase in scope and availability. And it is even more to the point that property now becomes the most easily recognised evidence of a reputable degree of success as distinguished from heroic or signal achievement. It therefore becomes the conventional basis of esteem. Its possession in some amount becomes necessary in order to any reputable standing in the community. It becomes indispensable to accumulate, to acquire property, in order to retain one's good name. When accumulated goods have in this way once become the accepted badge of efficiency, the possession of wealth presently assumes the character of an independent and definitive basis of esteem. The possession of goods, whether acquired aggressively by one's own exertion or passively by transmission through inheritance from others, becomes a conventional basis of reputability. The possession of wealth, which was at the outset valued simply as an evidence of efficiency, becomes, in popular apprehension, itself a meritorious act. Wealth is now itself intrinsically honourable and confers honour on its possessor. By a further refinement, wealth acquired passively by transmission from ancestors or other antecedents presently becomes even more honorific than wealth acquired by the possessor's own effort; but this distinction belongs at a later stage in the evolution of the pecuniary culture and will be spoken of in its place.

Prowess and exploit may still remain the basis of award of the highest popular esteem, although the possession of wealth has become the basis of common place reputability and of a blameless social standing. The predatory instinct and the consequent approbation of predatory efficiency are deeply ingrained in the habits of thought of those peoples who have passed under the discipline of a protracted predatory culture. According to popular award, the highest honours within human reach may, even yet, be those gained by an unfolding of extraordinary predatory efficiency in war, or by a quasi-predatory efficiency in statecraft; but for the purposes of a commonplace decent standing in the community these means of repute have been replaced by the acquisition and accumulation of goods. In order to stand well in the eyes of the community, it is necessary to come up to a certain, somewhat indefinite, conventional standard of wealth; just as in the earlier predatory stage it is necessary for the barbarian man to come up to the tribe's standard of physical endurance, cunning, and skill at arms. A certain standard of wealth in the one case, and of prowess in the other, is a necessary condition of reputability, and anything in excess of this normal amount is meritorious.

Those members of the community who fall short of this, somewhat indefinite, normal degree of prowess or of property suffer in the esteem of their fellow-men; and consequently they suffer also in their own esteem, since the usual basis of self-respect is the respect accorded by one's neighbours. Only individuals with an aberrant temperament can in the long run retain their self-esteem in the face of the disesteem of their fellows. Apparent exceptions to the rule are met with, especially among people with strong religious convictions. But these apparent exceptions are scarcely real exceptions, since such persons commonly fall back on the putative approbation of some supernatural witness of their deeds.

So soon as the possession of property becomes the basis of popular esteem, therefore, it becomes also a requisite to that complacency which we call self-respect. In any community where goods are held in severalty it is necessary, in order to his own peace of mind, that an individual should possess as large a portion of goods as others with whom he is accustomed to class himself; and it is extremely gratifying to possess something more than others. But as fast as a person makes new acquisitions, and becomes accustomed to the resulting new standard of wealth, the new standard forthwith ceases to afford appreciably greater satisfaction than the earlier standard did. The tendency in any case is constantly to make the present pecuniary standard the point of departure for a fresh increase of wealth; and this in turn gives rise to a new standard of sufficiency and a new pecuniary classification of one's self

as compared with one's neighbours. So far as concerns the present question, the end sought by accumulation is to rank high in comparison with the rest of the community in point of pecuniary strength. So long as the comparison is distinctly unfavourable to himself, the normal, average individual will live in chronic dissatisfaction with his present lot; and when he has reached what may be called the normal pecuniary standard of the community, or of his class in the community, this chronic dissatisfaction will give place to a restless straining to place a wider and ever-widening pecuniary interval between himself and this average standard. The invidious comparison can never become so favourable to the individual making it that he would not gladly rate himself still higher relatively to his competitors in the struggle for pecuniary reputability.

In the nature of the case, the desire for wealth can scarcely be satiated in any individual instance, and evidently a satiation of the average or general desire for wealth is out of the question. However widely, or equally, or "fairly," it may be distributed, no general increase of the community's wealth can make any approach to satiating this need, the ground of which is the desire of every one to excel every one else in the accumulation of goods. If, as is sometimes assumed, the incentive to accumulation were the want of subsistence or of physical comfort, then the aggregate economic wants of a community might conceivably be satisfied at some point in the advance of industrial efficiency; but since the struggle is substantially a race for reputability on the basis of an invidious comparison, no approach to a definitive attainment is possible.

What has just been said must not be taken to mean that there are no other incentives to acquisition and accumulation than this desire to excel in pecuniary standing and so gain the esteem and envy of one's fellow-men. The desire for added comfort and security from want is present as a motive at every stage of the process of accumulation in a modern industrial community; although the standard of sufficiency in these respects is in turn greatly affected by the habit of pecuniary emulation. To a great extent this emulation shapes the methods and selects the objects of expenditure for personal comfort and decent livelihood.

Besides this, the power conferred by wealth also affords a motive to accumulation. That propensity for purposeful activity and that repugnance to all futility of effort which belong to man by virtue of his character as an agent do not desert him when he emerges from the naïve communal culture where the dominant note of life is the unanalyzed and undifferentiated solidarity of the individual with the group with which his life is bound up. When he enters upon the predatory stage, where self-seeking in the narrower sense becomes the dominant note, this propensity goes with him still, as the pervasive trait that shapes his scheme of life. The propensity for achievement and the repugnance to futility remain the underlying economic motive. The propensity changes only in the form of its expression and in the proximate objects to which it directs the man's activity. Under the régime of individual ownership the most available means of visibly achieving a purpose is that afforded by the acquisition and accumulation of goods; and as the self-regarding antithesis between man and man reaches fuller consciousness, the propensity for achievement—the instinct of workmanship—tends more and more to shape itself into a straining to excel others in pecuniary achievement. Relative success, tested by an invidious pecuniary comparison with other men, becomes the conventional end of action. The currently accepted legitimate end of effort becomes the achievement of a favourable comparison with other men; and therefore the repugnance to futility to a good extent coalesces with the incentive of emulation. It acts to accentuate the struggle for pecuniary reputability by visiting with a sharper disapproval all shortcoming and all evidence of shortcoming in point of pecuniary success. Purposeful effort comes to mean, primarily, effort directed to or resulting in a more creditable showing of accumulated wealth. Among the motives which lead men to accumulate wealth, the primacy, both in scope and intensity, therefore, continues to belong to this motive of pecuniary emulation.

In making use of the term "invidious," it may perhaps be unnecessary to remark, there is no intention to extol or depreciate, or to commend or deplore any of the phenomena which the word is used to characterise. The term is used in a technical sense as describing a comparison of persons with a view to rating and grading them in respect of relative worth or value—in an aesthetic or moral sense—and so awarding and defining the relative degrees of complacency with which they may legitimately be contemplated by themselves and by others. An invidious comparison is a process of valuation of persons in respect of worth.

CONSPICUOUS CONSUMPTION

In what has been said of the evolution of the vicarious leisure class and its differentiation from the general body of the working classes, reference has been made to a further division of labour,—that between different servant classes. One portion of the servant class, chiefly those persons whose occupation is vicarious leisure, come to undertake a new, subsidiary range of duties—the vicarious consumption of goods. The most obvious form in which this consumption occurs is seen in the wearing of liveries and the occupation of spacious servants' quarters. Another, scarcely less obtrusive or less effective form of vicarious consumption, and a much more widely prevalent one, is the consumption of food, clothing, dwelling, and furniture by the lady and the rest of the domestic establishment.

But already at a point in economic evolution far antedating the emergence of the lady, specialized consumption of goods as an evidence of pecuniary strength had begun to work out in a more or less elaborate system. The beginning of a differentiation in consumption even antedates the appearance of anything that can fairly be called pecuniary strength. It is traceable back to the initial phase of predatory culture, and there is even a suggestion that an incipient differentiation in this respect lies back of the beginnings of the predatory life. This most primitive differentiation in the consumption of goods is like the later differentiation with which we are all so intimately familiar, in that it is largely of a ceremonial character, but unlike the latter it does not rest on a difference in accumulated wealth. The utility of consumption as an evidence of wealth is to be classed as a derivative growth. It is an adaptation to a new end, by a selective process, of a distinction previously existing and well established in men's habits of thought.

In the earlier phases of the predatory culture the only economic differentiation is a broad distinction between an honourable superior class made up of the able-bodied men on the one side, and a base inferior class of laboring women on the other. According to the ideal scheme of life in force at that time it is the office of the men to consume what the women produce. Such consumption as falls to the women is merely incidental to their work; it is a means to their continued labour, and not a consumption directed to their own comfort and fullness of life. Unproductive consumption of goods is honourable, primarily as a mark of prowess and a perquisite of human dignity; secondarily it becomes substantially honourable in itself, especially the consumption of the more desirable things. The consumption of choice articles of food, and frequently also of rare articles of adornment, becomes tabu to the women and children; and if there is a base (servile) class of men, the tabu holds also for them. With a further advance in culture this tabu may change into simple custom of a more or less rigorous character; but whatever be the theoretical basis of the distinction which is maintained, whether it be a tabu or a larger conventionality, the features of the conventional scheme of consumption do not change easily. When the quasi-peaceable stage of industry is reached, with its fundamental institution of chattel slavery, the general principle, more or less rigorously applied, is that the base, industrious class should consume only what may be necessary to their subsistence. In the nature of things, luxuries and the comforts of life belong to the leisure class. Under the tabu, certain victuals, and more particularly certain beverages, are strictly reserved for the use of the superior class.

The ceremonial differentiation of the dietary is best seen in the use of intoxicating beverages and narcotics. If these articles of consumption are costly, they are felt to be noble and honorific. Therefore the base classes, primarily the women, practise an enforced continence with respect to these stimulants, except in countries where they are obtainable at a very low cost. From archaic times down through all the length of the patriarchal regime it has been the office of the women to prepare and administer these luxuries, and it has been the perquisite of the men of gentle birth and breeding to consume them. Drunkenness and the other pathological consequences of the free use of stimulants therefore tend in their turn to become honorific, as being a mark, at the second remove, of the superior status of those who are able to afford the indulgence. Infirmities induced by over-indulgence are among some peoples freely recognised as manly attributes. It has even happened that the name for certain diseased conditions of the body arising from such an origin has passed into everyday speech as a synonym for "noble" or "gentle." It is only at a relatively early stage of culture that the symptoms of expensive vice are conventionally accepted as marks of a superior status, and so tend to become virtues and command the deference of the community; but the reputability that attaches to certain expensive vices long retains so much of its force as to appreciably lessen the disapprobation visited upon the men of the wealthy or noble class for any excessive indulgence. The same invidious distinction adds force to the current disapproval of any indulgence of this kind on the part of women, minors, and inferiors. This invidious traditional distinction has not lost its force even among the more advanced peoples of today. Where the example set by the leisure class retains its imperative force in the regulation of the conventionalities, it is observable that the women still in great measure practise the same traditional continence with regard to stimulants.

This characterization of the greater continence in the use of stimulants practiced by the women of the reputable classes may seem an excessive refinement of logic at the expense of common sense. But facts within easy reach of any one who cares to know them go to say that the greater abstinence of women is in some part due to an imperative conventionality; and this conventionality is, in a general way, strongest where the patriarchal tradition—the tradition that the woman is a chattel—has retained its hold in greatest vigour. In a sense which has been greatly qualified in scope and rigour, but which has by no means lost its meaning even yet, this tradition says that the woman, being a chattel, should consume only what is necessary to her sustenance,—except so far as her further consumption contributes to the comfort or the good repute of her master. The consumption of luxuries, in the true sense, is a consumption directed to the comfort of the consumer himself, and is, therefore, a mark of the master. Any such consumption by others can take place only on a basis of sufferance. In communities where the popular habits of thought have been profoundly shaped by the patriarchal tradition we may accordingly look for survivals of the tabu on luxuries at least to the extent of a conventional deprecation of their use by the unfree and dependent class. This is more particularly true as regards certain luxuries, the use of which by the dependent class would detract sensibly from the comfort or pleasure of their masters, or which are held to be of doubtful legitimacy on other grounds. In the apprehension of the great conservative middle class of Western civilization the use of these various stimulants is obnoxious to at least one, if not both, of these objections; and it is a fact too significant to be passed over that it is precisely among these middle classes of the Germanic culture, with their strong surviving sense of the patriarchal proprieties, that the women are to the greatest extent subject to a qualified tabu on narcotics and alcoholic beverages. With many qualifications—with more qualifications as the patriarchal tradition has gradually weakened—the general rule is felt to be right and binding that women should consume only for the benefit of their masters. The objection of course presents itself that expenditure on women's dress and household paraphernalia is an obvious exception to this rule; but it will appear [below] . . . that this exception is much more obvious than substantial.

During the earlier stages of economic development, consumption of goods without stint, especially consumption of the better grades of goods,—ideally all consumption in excess of the subsistence minimum, pertains normally to the leisure class. This restriction tends to disappear, at least formally, after the later peaceable stage has been reached, with private ownership of goods and an industrial system based on wage labour or on the petty household economy. But during the earlier quasi-peaceable stage, when so many of the traditions through which the institution of a leisure class has affected the economic life of later times were taking form and consistency, this principle has had the force of a conventional law. It has served as the norm to which consumption has tended to conform, and any appreciable departure from it is to be regarded as an aberrant form, sure to be eliminated sooner or later in the further course of development.

The quasi-peaceable gentleman of leisure, then, not only consumes of the staff of life beyond the minimum required for subsistence and physical efficiency, but his consumption also undergoes a specialization as regards the quality of the goods consumed. He consumes freely and of the best, in food, drink, narcotics, shelter, services, ornaments, apparel, weapons and accoutrements, amusements, amulets, and idols or divinities. In the process of gradual amelioration which takes place in the articles of his consumption, the motive principle and the proximate aim of innovation is no doubt the higher efficiency of the improved and more elaborate products for personal comfort and well-being. But that does not remain the sole purpose of their consumption. The canon of reputability is at hand and seizes upon such innovations as are, according to its standard, fit to survive. Since the consumption of these more excellent goods is an evidence of wealth, it becomes honorific; and conversely, the failure to consume in due quantity and quality becomes a mark of inferiority and demerit.

This growth of punctilious discrimination as to qualitative excellence in eating, drinking, etc., presently affects not only the manner of life, but also the training and intellectual activity of the gentleman of leisure. He is no longer simply the successful, aggressive male,—the man of strength, resource, and intrepidity. In order to avoid stultification he must also cultivate his tastes, for it now becomes incumbent on him to discriminate with some nicety between the noble and the ignoble in consumable goods. He becomes a connoisseur in creditable viands of various degrees of merit, in manly beverages and trinkets, in seemly apparel and architecture, in weapons, games, dancers, and the narcotics. This cultivation of the aesthetic faculty requires time and application, and the demands made upon the gentleman in this direction therefore tend to change his life of leisure into a more or less arduous application to the business of learning how to live a life of ostensible leisure in a becoming way. Closely related to the requirement that the gentleman must consume freely and of the right kind of goods, there is the requirement that he must know how to consume them in a seemly manner. His life of leisure must be conducted in due form. Hence arise good manners.... High-bred manners and ways of living are items of conformity to the norm of conspicuous leisure and conspicuous consumption.

Conspicuous consumption of valuable goods is a means of reputability to the gentleman of leisure. As wealth accumulates on his hands, his own unaided effort will not avail to sufficiently put his opulence in evidence by this method. The aid of friends and competitors is therefore brought in by resorting to the giving of valuable presents and expensive feasts and entertainments. Presents and feasts had probably another origin than that of naïve ostentation, but they acquired their utility for this purpose very early, and they have retained that character to the present; so that their utility in this respect has now long been the substantial ground on which these usages rest. Costly entertainments, such as the potlatch or the ball, are peculiarly adapted to serve this end. The competitor with whom the entertainer wishes to institute a comparison is, by this method, made to serve as a means to the end. He consumes vicariously for his host at the same time that he is a witness to the consumption of that excess of good things which his host is unable to dispose of single-handed, and he is also made to witness his host's facility in etiquette.

In the giving of costly entertainments other motives, of a more genial kind, are of course also present. The custom of festive gatherings probably originated in motives of conviviality and religion; these motives are also present in the later development, but they do not continue to be the sole motives. The latter-day leisure-class festivities and entertainments may continue in some slight degree to serve the religious need and in a higher degree the needs of recreation and conviviality, but they also serve an invidious purpose; and they serve it none the less effectually for having a colourable non-invidious ground in these more avowable motives. But the economic effect of these social amenities is not therefore lessened, either in the vicarious consumption of goods or in the exhibition of difficult and costly achievements in etiquette.

As wealth accumulates, the leisure class develops further in function and structure, and there arises a differentiation within the class. There is a more or less elaborate system of rank and grades. This differentiation is furthered by the inheritance of wealth and the consequent inheritance of gentility. With the inheritance of gentility goes the inheritance of obligatory leisure; and gentility of a sufficient potency to entail a life of leisure may be inherited without the complement of wealth required to maintain a dignified leisure. Gentle blood may be transmitted without goods enough to afford a reputably free consumption at one's ease. Hence results a class of impecunious gentlemen of leisure, incidentally referred to already. These half-caste gentlemen of leisure fall into a system of hierarchical gradations. Those who stand near the higher and the highest grades of the wealthy leisure class, in point of birth, or in point of wealth, or both, outrank the remoter-born and the pecuniarily weaker. These lower grades, especially the impecunious, or marginal, gentlemen of leisure, affiliate themselves by a system of dependence or fealty to the great ones; by so doing they gain an increment of repute, or of the means with which to lead a life of leisure, from their patron. They become his courtiers or retainers, servants; and being fed and countenanced by their patron they are indices of his rank and vicarious consumers of his superfluous wealth. Many of these affiliated gentlemen of leisure are at the same time lesser men of substance in their own right; so that some of them are scarcely at all, others only partially, to be rated as vicarious consumers. So many of them, however, as make up the retainers and hangers-on of the patron may be classed as vicarious consumers without qualification. Many of these again, and also many of the other aristocracy of less degree, have in turn attached to their persons a more or less comprehensive group of vicarious consumers in the persons of their wives and children, their servants, retainers, etc.

Throughout this graduated scheme of vicarious leisure and vicarious consumption the rule holds that these offices must be performed in some such manner, or under some such circumstance or insignia, as shall point plainly to the master to whom this leisure or consumption pertains, and to whom therefore the resulting increment of good repute of right inures. The consumption and leisure executed by these persons for their master or patron represents an investment on his part with a view to an increase of good fame. As regards feasts and largesses this is obvious enough, and the imputation of repute to the host or patron here takes place immediately, on the ground of common notoriety. Where leisure and consumption is performed vicariously by henchmen and retainers, imputation of the resulting repute to the patron is effected by their residing near his person so that it may be plain to all men from what source they draw. As the group whose good esteem is to be secured in this way grows larger, more patent means are required to indicate the imputation of merit for the leisure performed, and to this end uniforms, badges, and liveries come into vogue. The wearing of uniforms or liveries implies a considerable degree of dependence, and may even be said to be a mark of servitude, real or ostensible. The wearers of uniforms and liveries may be roughly divided into two classes—the free and the servile, or the noble and the ignoble. The services performed by them are likewise divisible into noble and ignoble. Of course the distinction is not observed with strict consistency in practice; the less debasing of the base services and the less honorific of the noble functions are not infrequently merged in the same person. But the general distinction is not on that account to be overlooked. What may add some perplexity is the fact that this fundamental distinction between noble and ignoble, which rests on the nature of the ostensible service performed, is traversed by a secondary distinction into honorific and humiliating, resting on the rank of the person for whom the service is performed or whose livery is worn. So, those offices which are by right the proper employment of the leisure class are noble; such are government, fighting, hunting, the care of arms and accoutrements, and the like,—in short, those which may be classed as ostensibly predatory employments. On the other hand, those employments which properly fall to the industrious class are ignoble; such as handicraft or other productive labour, menial services, and the like. But a base service performed for a person of very high degree may become a very honorific office; as for instance the office of a Maid of Honour or of a Lady in Waiting to the Queen, or the King's Master of the Horse or his Keeper of the Hounds. The two offices last named suggest a principle of some general bearing. Whenever, as in these cases, the menial service in question has to do directly with the primary leisure employments of fighting and hunting, it easily acquires a reflected honorific character. In this way great honour may come to attach to an employment which in its own nature belongs to the baser sort.

***

It is for this class to determine, in general outline, what scheme of life the community shall accept as decent or honorific; and it is their office by precept and example to set forth this scheme of social salvation in its highest, ideal form. But the higher leisure class can exercise this quasi-sacerdotal office only under certain material limitations. The class cannot at discretion effect a sudden revolution or reversal of the popular habits of thought with respect to any of these ceremonial requirements. It takes time for any change to permeate the mass and change the habitual attitude of the people; and especially it takes time to change the habits of those classes that are socially more remote from the radiant body. The process is slower where the mobility of the population is less or where the intervals between the several classes are wider and more abrupt. But if time be allowed, the scope of the discretion of the leisure class as regards questions of form and detail in the community's scheme of life is large; while as regards the substantial principles of reputability, the changes which it can effect lie within a narrow margin of tolerance. Its example and precept carries the force of prescription for all classes below it; but in working out the precepts which are handed down as governing the form and method of reputability—in shaping the usages and the spiritual attitude of the lower classes—this authoritative prescription constantly works under the selective guidance of the canon of conspicuous waste, tempered in varying degree by the instinct of workmanship. To these norms is to be added another broad principle of human nature—the predatory animus—which in point of generality and of psychological content lies between the two just named. The effect of the latter in shaping the accepted scheme of life is yet to be discussed.

The canon of reputability, then, must adapt itself to the economic circumstances, the traditions, and the degree of spiritual maturity of the particular class whose scheme of life it is to regulate. It is especially to be noted that however high its authority and however true to the fundamental requirements of reputability it may have been at its inception, a specific formal observance can under no circumstances maintain itself in force if with the lapse of time or on its transmission to a lower pecuniary class it is found to run counter to the ultimate ground of decency among civilised peoples, namely, serviceability for the purpose of an invidious comparison in pecuniary success.

It is evident that these canons of expenditure have much to say in determining the standard of living for any community and for any class. It is no less evident that the standard of living which prevails at any time or at any given social altitude will in its turn have much to say as to the forms which honorific expenditure will take, and as to the degree to which this "higher" need will dominate a people's consumption. In this respect the control exerted by the accepted standard of living is chiefly of a negative character; it acts almost solely to prevent recession from a scale of conspicuous expenditure that has once become habitual.

A standard of living is of the nature of habit. It is an habitual scale and method of responding to given stimuli. The difficulty in the way of receding from an accustomed standard is the difficulty of breaking a habit that has once been formed. The relative facility with which an advance in the standard is made means that the life process is a process of unfolding activity and that it will readily unfold in a new direction whenever and wherever the resistance to self-expression decreases. But when the habit of expression along such a given line of low resistance has once been formed, the discharge will seek the accustomed outlet even after a change has taken place in the environment whereby the external resistance has appreciably risen. That heightened facility of expression in a given direction which is called habit may offset a considerable increase in the resistance offered by external circumstances to the unfolding of life in the given direction. As between the various habits, or habitual modes and directions of expression, which go to make up an individual's standard of living, there is an appreciable difference in point of persistence under counteracting circumstances and in point of the degree of imperativeness with which the discharge seeks a given direction.

That is to say, in the language of current economic theory, while men are reluctant to retrench their expenditures in any direction, they are more reluctant to retrench in some directions than in others; so that while any accustomed consumption is reluctantly given up, there are certain lines of consumption which are given up with relatively extreme reluctance. The articles or forms of consumption to which the consumer clings with the greatest tenacity are commonly the so-called necessaries of life, or the subsistence minimum. The subsistence minimum is of course not a rigidly determined allowance of goods, definite and invariable in kind and quantity; but for the purpose in hand it may be taken to comprise a certain, more or less definite, aggregate of consumption required for the maintenance of life. This minimum, it may be assumed, is ordinarily

given up last in case of a progressive retrenchment of expenditure. That is to say, in a general
way, the most ancient and ingrained of the habits which govern the individual's life—those
habits that touch his existence as an organism—
are the most persistent and imperative. Beyond
these come the higher wants—later-formed
habits of the individual or the race—in a somewhat irregular and by no means invariable gra-
dation. Some of these higher wants, as for
instance the habitual use of certain stimulants,
or the need of salvation (in the eschatological
sense), or of good repute, may in some cases
take precedence of the lower or more elementary wants. In general, the longer the habituation, the more unbroken the habit, and the more
nearly it coincides with previous habitual forms
of the life process, the more persistently will the
given habit assert itself. The habit will be
stronger if the particular traits of human nature
which its action involves, or the particular aptitudes that find exercise in it, are traits or aptitudes that are already largely and profoundly
concerned in the life process or that are intimately bound up with the life history of the
particular racial stock.

The varying degrees of ease with which
different habits are formed by different persons, as well as the varying degrees of reluctance with which different habits are given up,
goes to say that the formation of specific habits
is not a matter of length of habituation simply.
Inherited aptitudes and traits of temperament
count for quite as much as length of habituation in deciding what range of habits will come
to dominate any individual's scheme of life.
And the prevalent type of transmitted aptitudes, or in other words the type of temperament belonging to the dominant ethnic element
in any community, will go far to decide what
will be the scope and form of expression of the
community's habitual life process. How greatly
the transmitted idiosyncracies of aptitude may
count in the way of a rapid and definitive formation of habit in individuals is illustrated by
the extreme facility with which an all-dominat-
ing habit of alcoholism is sometimes formed;
or in the similar facility and the similarly inevitable formation of a habit of devout observ-
ances in the case of persons gifted with a

special aptitude in that direction. Much the
same meaning attaches to that peculiar facility
of habituation to a specific human environment that is called romantic love.

Men differ in respect of transmitted aptitudes, or in respect of the relative facility with
which they unfold their life activity in particular directions; and the habits which coincide
with or proceed upon a relatively strong specific aptitude or a relatively great specific facility of expression become of great consequence
to the man's well-being. The part played by
this element of aptitude in determining the
relative tenacity of the several habits which
constitute the standard of living goes to explain
the extreme reluctance with which men give
up any habitual expenditure in the way of conspicuous consumption. The aptitudes or propensities to which a habit of this kind is to be
referred as its ground are those aptitudes
whose exercise is comprised in emulation; and
the propensity for emulation—for invidious
comparison—is of ancient growth and is a per-
vading trait of human nature. It is easily called
into vigorous activity in any new form, and it
asserts itself with great insistence under any
form under which it has once found habitual
expression. When the individual has once
formed the habit of seeking expression in a
given line of honorific expenditure,—when a
given set of stimuli have come to be habitually
responded to in activity of a given kind and
direction under the guidance of these alert and
deep-reaching propensities of emulation,—it is
with extreme reluctance that such an habitual
expenditure is given up. And on the other
hand, whenever an accession of pecuniary
strength puts the individual in a position to
unfold his life process in larger scope and with
additional reach, the ancient propensities of
the race will assert themselves in determining
the direction which the new unfolding of life is
to take. And those propensities which are
already actively in the field under some related
form of expression, which are aided by the
pointed suggestions afforded by a current
accredited scheme of life, and for the exercise
of which the material means and opportunities
are readily available,—these will especially
have much to say in shaping the form and

direction in which the new accession to the individual's aggregate force will assert itself. That is to say, in concrete terms, in any community where conspicuous consumption is an element of the scheme of life, an increase in an individual's ability to pay is likely to take the form of an expenditure for some accredited line of conspicuous consumption.

With the exception of the instinct of self preservation, the propensity for emulation is probably the strongest and most alert and persistent of the economic motives proper. In an industrial community this propensity for emulation expresses itself in pecuniary emulation; and this, so far as regards the Western civilised communities of the present, is virtually equivalent to saying that it expresses itself in some form of conspicuous waste. The need of conspicuous waste, therefore, stands ready to absorb any increase in the community's industrial efficiency or output of goods, after the most elementary physical wants have been provided for. Where this result does not follow, under modern conditions, the reason for the discrepancy is commonly to be sought in a rate of increase in the individual's wealth too rapid for the habit of expenditure to keep abreast of it; or it may be that the individual in question defers the conspicuous consumption of the increment to a later date—ordinarily with a view to heightening the spectacular effect of the aggregate expenditure contemplated. As increased industrial efficiency makes it possible to procure the means of livelihood with less labour, the energies of the industrious members of the community are bent to the compassing of a higher result in conspicuous expenditure, rather than slackening to a more comfortable pace. The strain is not lightened as industrial efficiency increases and makes a lighter strain possible, but the increment of output is turned to use to meet this want, which is indefinitely expansible, after the manner commonly imputed in economic theory to higher or spiritual wants. It is owing chiefly to the presence of this element in the standard of living that J. S. Mill was able to say that "hitherto it is questionable if all the mechanical inventions yet made have lightened the day's toil of any human being."

The accepted standard of expenditure in the community or in the class to which a person belongs largely determines what his standard of living will be. It does this directly by commending itself to his common sense as right and good, through his habitually contemplating it and assimilating the scheme of life in which it belongs; but it does so also indirectly through popular insistence on conformity to the accepted scale of expenditure as a matter of propriety, under pain of disesteem and ostracism. To accept and practise the standard of living which is in vogue is both agreeable and expedient, commonly to the point of being indispensable to personal comfort and to success in life. The standard of living of any class, so far as concerns the element of conspicuous waste, is commonly as high as the earning capacity of the class will permit—with a constant tendency to go higher. The effect upon the serious activities of men is therefore to direct them with great singleness of purpose to the largest possible acquisition of wealth, and to discountenance work that brings no pecuniary gain. At the same time the effect on consumption is to concentrate it upon the lines which are most patent to the observers whose good opinion is sought; while the inclinations and aptitudes whose exercise does not involve a honorific expenditure of time or substance tend to fall into abeyance through disuse.

Through this discrimination in favour of visible consumption it has come about that the domestic life of most classes is relatively shabby, as compared with the éclat of that overt portion of their life that is carried on before the eyes of observers. As a secondary consequence of the same discrimination, people habitually screen their private life from observation. So far as concerns that portion of their consumption that may without blame be carried on in secret, they withdraw from all contact with their neighbours. Hence the exclusiveness of people, as regards their domestic life, in most of the industrially developed communities; and hence, by remoter derivation, the habit of privacy and reserve that is so large a feature in the code of proprieties of the better classes in all communities. The low birthrate of the classes upon whom the requirements of reputable expenditure fall with great urgency is likewise traceable to the exigencies of a standard of living based on conspicuous waste. The conspicuous consumption, and the consequent increased expense, required in the reputable maintenance of a child is very considerable and acts as a powerful deterrent. It is probably the most effectual of the Malthusian prudential checks.

The effect of this factor of the standard of living, both in the way of retrenchment in the obscurer elements of consumption that go to physical comfort and maintenance, and also in the paucity or absence of children, is perhaps seen at its best among the classes given to scholarly pursuits. Because of a presumed superiority and scarcity of the gifts and attainments that characterise their life, these classes are by convention subsumed under a higher social grade than their pecuniary grade should warrant. The scale of decent expenditure in their case is pitched correspondingly high, and it consequently leaves an exceptionally narrow margin disposable for the other ends of life. By force of circumstances, their own habitual sense of what is good and right in these matters, as well as the expectations of the community in the way of pecuniary decency among the learned, are excessively high—as measured by the prevalent degree of opulence and earning capacity of the class, relatively to the non-scholarly classes whose social equals they nominally are. In any modern community where there is no priestly monopoly of these occupations, the people of scholarly pursuits are unavoidably thrown into contact with classes that are pecuniarily their superiors. The high standard of pecuniary decency in force among these superior classes is transfused among the scholarly classes with but little mitigation of its rigour; and as a consequence there is no class of the community that spends a larger proportion of its substance in conspicuous waste than these. ♦

QUESTIONS

1. What does Veblen mean by the "leisure class"?

2. According to Veblen, what was the first private property?

3. Why do people want to acquire goods, according to Veblen?

4. What does Veblen indicate as the more conventional view about the desire for acquisition?

5. How is self-esteem connected to direct and vicarious consumption of goods?

6. What are some examples of vicarious consumption?

From *The Middleman*

Albert W. Atwood (1880–1955)

Twenty-two different delivery wagons from as many different grocery stores stood in front of a large New York City apartment house one day. George W. Perkins, whose prominent part in the formation and direction of several of our great industrial combinations is well known, heard of these twenty-two wagons and remembered the incident. The next time he spoke on the subject of combinations and trusts, which was before the Senate Committee on Interstate Commerce, he drove home his argument with that very illustration of the economic waste involved in many of the present methods of bridging the gap between producer and consumer.

The question of the high cost of living has been discussed until it has become tiresome, but the subject is one which must remain engrossing until it is solved. While the fact is ascribed to many causes, the man on the street points most insistently to the trust and the middleman. Let us lay aside trusts for the present and examine the Middleman.

Even the most superficial observation at once reveals an astonishing discrepancy between what the producer receives for his products and what the ultimate consumer pays for them. Many figures on this subject are haphazard, it is true, but there are enough reliable data to establish beyond a doubt the fact that present facilities for bridging the gap between producer and consumer are an expensive makeshift, without orderly plan or system. Grapes which sell for forty cents a basket in the city have been known to return the grower but seven cents. A ten-cent bottle of milk in New York returns the dairyman about three cents. The difference between what the wholesaler pays for creamery butter and what you and I pay is 17¼ per cent., on cheese it is 27 per cent., on eggs 56½ per cent., and on poultry 25 per cent. On food products as a whole, in New York City and other large cities in the Empire State, the producer is receiving only about 40 per cent. of the retail price. "That is absurd," says the New York State Food Investigating Commission; "he should receive from 60 to 70 per cent."

Not long ago when sentencing several dealers in live poultry to jail for combining in restraint of trade, the judge said: "Between the farm and the kitchen a chicken has six separate profits fastened on it. Six separate profits must be paid when a chicken is bought over the retailers' counter. Is it any wonder that the poor are getting poorer?"

Fresh, abundant, and cheap food can only be had by encouraging production. The present excessive cost for transportation, storage, selling, and delivery, that is, for all the various processes of distribution which the so-called Middleman performs, simply discourages the producer. Under present conditions the near-by sources of food supplies for many of the great cities are dormant or drying up. New York gets its fresh vegetables from the most distant points; Buffalo is fed very largely from the West; Albany does not receive one-quarter of her butter, eggs, chicken, or veal from the excellent farm lands around that city. The final absurdity is reached when far better apples than those which cost five cents each at the fruit stand, rot on the ground within a hundred miles of a great city, as the writer has seen them do.

Clearly there is a tremendous amount of waste in this whole process. New York City's annual food supply, which costs $350,000,000 at the terminals, rises to $500,000,000 when the consumer gets it. Each inhabitant of the city pays his share of this $150,000,000. Either the profits are excessive or else the flow of food supplies from producer to consumer is hindered and stopped by inexpressibly poor facilities. Is the Middleman fattening upon the consumer? Should every wholesaler, jobber, dealer, commission man and retailer go to jail?

What light, for example, do certain recent doings of a picturesque and spectacular, if not almost hysterical nature, throw upon the subject? A clergyman in one city and a mayor in another attracted an astonishing amount of attention some months ago by opening markets and selling food products at less than the retail store prices. Mayor Shank, of Indianapolis, and the Rev. Madison C. Peters, of New York, both declare that the middleman, that is, the retailer, as much as any of the other agencies engaged in the distribution of food products, is the party responsible for high prices. Mayor Shank sold fruit, vegetables, and poultry at far lower prices than the scale prevailing elsewhere in his city. The reverend gentleman in New York sold potatoes at several cents a pound below prevailing prices.

These extra-vocational activities of mayor and clergyman, petty as they were, are nevertheless incidents in a mighty train of events connected with the protest against high living costs. Not long afterward, a Housewives' League in New York City undertook to show women how to buy food cheaply. Then there were meat boycotts and riots in many cities. Coöperative stores have been started in suburbs of New York City. Markets are being formed for the despised push-cart peddlers. The organization of large municipal markets has been urged. "More terminal markets!" is one cry, and it is pointed out that because of poor handling and defective arrangements for the reception and distribution of food there is an unnecessary damage each year of $75,000,000 to eggs and poultry.

Railroads and steamship lines are being blamed for affording inadequate terminal facilities as compared with those of such model cities as Hamburg. The express companies come in for their share of censure, and the Parcel Post is expected to lower living costs. Fruit growers of the Northwest have formed selling agencies to wipe out the Middleman. In Pittsburgh, Buffalo, Cleveland, and Chicago federated marketing clubs of consumers have been organized. Consumers' coöperative buying societies are springing up everywhere, in the army and navy, and among postal clerks. Village improvement societies are studying the question. Then there are those who think the lack of roads in the country districts is mainly responsible. There are a thousand and one explanations and proffered remedies. The air is surcharged with bitterness against the Middleman. The one fact which men have firmly fixed in their minds is this: *Of the sum which consumers of this country pay for agricultural products less than one-half goes to the farmer.*

But what does this bewildering medley of fact and fancy, protests hysterical and protests well considered, passing incident and significant tendency, all go to prove, if it proves anything? Does it prove that the Middleman is fattening upon the consumer? Look about you. Are the little grocers and butchers growing rich? There are 11,000 grocers in New York City and the State Food Investigating Commission says that high operating costs make their elimination inevitable. "He is now slowly wearing out." Of the 33⅓ per cent. which this class of stores adds to the wholesale price, less than 5 per cent. is profit. Referring even to wholesalers and jobbers, the report of the commission declares that no class is making an undue profit, whereas the smaller dealers are "merely making wages."

What, then, do these attempts to solve the problem of high living costs prove? Well, they prove there are indispensable functions which some one must perform. They prove that distribution is costly, no matter how you arrange it. They prove that as civilization grows more complex the cost of getting an article to the consumer in the shape he wants it is proportionately greater than the cost of the article itself. *It is possible by some artificial or mechanical change of plan to do away with the shipper, the commission merchant, the jobber and the retailer, but it is impossible to do away with the services they perform.* We can eliminate the Middleman, but it has been well said that if we do so there will be sore hands, aching backs, and tired heads after he is gone.

Let us return for a moment to the activities of Mayor Shank and the Rev. Mr. Peters, but let us not jump at conclusions. These men had free advertising, free rent, and abnormal "goodwill" to begin with. They had practically no clerk hire, extended no credit, delivered no goods, cashed no checks for customers, accumulated no bad debts and paid no taxes or insurance. A prominent jurist of New York City complained recently that he paid $1.80 for a basket of potatoes. But the learned judge neglected to tell his interviewer that his residence is on Fifth Avenue, and that any grocery store, to be near that thoroughfare, must pay an enormous rent, which can only be gotten back by charging the consumer proportionately large prices.

Let us be quite honest about this matter. The retailer not only has to pay high rents to be near your home, but he has to light, heat, and man his store from daylight to late at night so that you can go to him at any time of day that may please your fancy. He maintains expensive teams, or else pays wages to delivery boys, and buys carts. He sends solicitors to your door to learn what groceries you wish for the day. He will deliver to you a five-cent package of matches at any time of day. He sends you your articles carefully done up in nice packages and carefully wrapped. It is a costly process.

The delivery charge for the average grocery, or corner store, averages nearly one-half the total expenses for the establishment and adds from 10 to 15 per cent. to the cost to the consumer. The fancy packages add from 50 to 100 per cent. to the cost of the goods, and the public seems unable to withstand the bombardment of advertising by the large firms dealing in package goods. Then, again, the telephone has greatly increased the expense of doing business, while it has often lowered the quality of goods received by the housekeeper. With telephone at her elbow she does not take the trouble to prepare a list of her needs in advance, give one order and have it sent up with a minimum of expense in delivery, but sends in three or four separate orders a day.

There are few if any facilities for storage of food in the modern city apartment, so that the meals are of the hand-to-mouth variety, and this tendency is further emphasized by the increasing number of women who go out to work, and who, upon their return, find it necessary to prepare hasty meals. Their purchases, especially of meats, are of the chop and steak variety, which can be quickly cooked, and there is a decline in the use of the cheaper but equally nutritious stew meats.

For all these comforts, conveniences, and luxuries, performed as they are by the Middleman, the consumer must pay. "It is about time for him to stop playing the part of a man with a grievance," says Mr. Holmes of the Department of Agriculture. "Nearly all the grievances that can be corrected at all can be corrected by himself. He can buy with greater economy through co-operative efforts, and by paying cash, and also with greater economy in forms, preparations, and varieties of things." If consumers are willing to go to market instead of expecting the market to come to them, if they are willing to carry the purchases home, and even wrap and tie the bundles themselves, then they may fairly claim the profit which now goes to the Middleman.

Let the women buy as their mothers used to do. Let them send their own crock to the grocer's for lard, and bring back for 65 cents what will cost them $1 in a can which they will throw away, or ruin in the opening. Let them buy their crackers from a box by weight and they will get sixty to the pound, instead of about forty in a pretty package for the same money. Instead of buying package oats at the rate of one-half cent per ounce, let them buy in bulk and get 10 cents' worth for 7 cents. Instead of buying sliced bacon in a glass jar, let them buy a "side" and cut it as wanted at half price.

But will women buy as their mothers did in these days when their interests have become so much greater and more diversified? Have they the time? As for fancy packages, probably they are more sanitary than the old barrel. Milk in bottles is more expensive than in the old tin can, but who wishes to return to the dirty can? *The waste of many delivery wagons, expensive locations, and extension of credit are the natural results of competition!* Ordering by telephone and by means of servants are merely time-saving devices, and, while they cost a great deal of money, this is a time-saving age.

The consumer demands far more than formerly, and the Middleman is supplying the want. Greater demands mean greater cost which the consumer must pay. But why, you may ask, cannot the producer himself perform some of these middle functions? Why can he not reach the consumer directly? In many cases this is possible, but there is no sweeping panacea in that direction.

An acquaintance of the writer's has a dairy farm near Washington, D.C. He would be glad to sell directly to the consumer, and if he could do so without increase of expense he could probably afford to sell the richest of milk and cream to consumers at lower prices than they now pay for an inferior product. But there is no way by which the dairy farmer can have his empty receptacles returned if he sells direct to the householder. Then in order to get trade of a desirable class he would have to advertise extensively, have a distinctive mark for his product, and put the milk into expensive bottles. This is too much for a single farmer to do. He prefers to sell to middlemen even though he knows the consumer pays as much again for the milk.

My acquaintance already spends much money in producing milk, without entering upon the still larger expenditures necessary to reach the consumer directly. The health authorities of the District of Columbia have adopted new and strict regulations. They require from each dairy a veritable bill of particulars. There are regulations as to whether the cows shall be on wood floors or cement floors. Frequent examinations and reports are the rule. This all takes more capital, even though it raises the standard of the product. My friend, in order to be abreast of the best methods of dairy farming, has actually taken away from the Department of Agriculture the best expert to be had, a graduate of an important agricultural college. This man was obtainable only by paying a large salary, the expense of which must be spread over many quarts of milk and pounds of butter. All this makes for cleaner, better milk and butter, but it makes their cost so much the more.

But suppose our dairy friend were in close co-operation with a hundred other dairymen, or suppose his business were a hundred times as great as it is, and his capital in proportion. Would he not then be able to reach the consumer more directly and with an appreciable saving in costs? Undoubtedly, as has been shown many times. Experts who have investigated food conditions in New York City declare that if there were 200 great food stores for the entire city, instead of 20,000 small stores as at present, there could be effected a saving in retail prices of $60,000,000 a year. Perhaps the consumer would not get all the saving, but the possibility is there. The books of a few of the big department food stores show that their cost of operation is about half that of the small retailer.

Mr. Perkins was right when he pointed to the wastefulness of twenty-two grocery stores catering to one apartment house. Those who have purchased in small shops and in great department stores need no argument to prove the economy of large-scale business. Of course the mere fact that a corporation is large does not prove it efficient. We are learning daily that mere size does not mean efficiency. It may merely indicate the possession of special privileges or the employment of predatory and piratical methods. But up to a certain point there is efficiency and saving in doing things on a large scale, a fact which the investigations of experts and daily, common knowledge and experience, as well as the theories of economists, prove beyond question. A distinguished economist recently enumerated thirteen distinct economies which might follow combination and concentration.

To many men, however, these economies mean nothing. Their belief in the blessings of competition is so fixed that it cannot be dislodged. They lose the substance in grasping for the shadow. They think that two telephone companies or two gas companies covering the same field are better than one. They refuse to see that almost invariably the public is inconvenienced by poor service and that it pays the excessive cost of construction, operation and upkeep. Generally it does not pay profits, for there are seldom any. They do not see the waste involved in a half-dozen concerns all attempting to cover the same territory and offering the same service. Gradually, however, the consumer is beginning to see that he pays for all this duplication and that a great part of his trouble arises from this fact. *Whenever two salesmen are paid for doing an amount of work one could easily do, when two delivery wagons or teams are kept where one would be sufficient, the consumer pays.*

Why then should not we, the consumers, urge with every means in our power the formation of combinations, co-operative arrangements, and agreements? But do you realize that the moment men begin to make agreements they must employ a lawyer to see that they do not violate the Sherman Anti-Trust

Law? It is all very well, for example, to point to the citrus-fruit growers who by agreement and co-operation among themselves have wonderfully improved the handling of their product in the great cities. No doubt they are within the law, but there are hundreds of associations and agreements not so widely different in their purposes, the members of which do not know whether they are within or without the law.

The average citizen has no idea to how great an extent mere associations or agreements in contradistinction to formal trusts have been held responsible for the high cost of living. In 1911 there were forty-four cases either decided or pending under the Sherman Law, all of which had to do with alleged efforts to control the prices of commodities. No less than 107 suits have been brought under this law, and the great majority have been directed at mere trade agreements, associations, and pools of business men.

The range of these prosecutions has been astonishing. The mammoth steel, oil and tobacco trusts were sued, but so also were the kindling-wood, plumbers' and bill-posters' trusts, the existence of which was never before hinted at outside the comic papers, and now the Horseshoe Trust is threatened. Go over the list of suits brought under the Sherman Law. *It reveals the striking fact, not generally known, or heretofore anywhere emphasized, that the Law has been directed not so much against the great, formal, single trusts as against individuals and moderate-sized and even small concerns in agreement one with another.* Besides the plumbers, bill-posters, and kindling-wood dealers, there have been grocers, a dozen associations of lumber dealers, coffee merchants, moving-picture men, wire manufacturers, wall-paper manufacturers, milk dealers, egg and butter dealers, meat dealers, cotton operators, manufacturers of enamel ware, a score of steamship lines, railroads in agreement as to rates, railroads in agreement as to the production of soft coal, railroads in agreement as to the production of hard coal, railroads in agreement as to the use of a terminal station, hide and rendering companies, magazines, manufacturers of lamps, and companies controlling towing facilities on the Great Lakes. Many of these associations were formed to fight a great trust which was attempting to monopolize the field. Now absurd as it may seem to invoke the mighty engine of the Sherman Law against the petty dealers in kindling wood, there is involved in suits such as these a principle of vital importance to the nation.

Most of the suits which have been pushed to a termination have spelled victory for the Government, and the defendants have been compelled to give up old practices. Many combinations have agreed to change their ways merely on threat of a suit, although the most expensive lawyers were on their side. What the Department of Justice has attacked are the agreements among numerous concerns, in no way connected by stock ownership, but all desirous in some way of regulating the expensive and wasteful competition previously existing among themselves.

In almost every case, either where a suit has been fought to successful conclusion, or where the trust has come down like Davy Crockett's coon, the point at issue had to do with methods of selling goods. It is unnecessary to go into details here, but suffice it to say that many methods of reducing or destroying competition have been stopped by the enforcement of the Sherman Law.

But the present method of attacking combinations which work against the public welfare is most unsatisfactory. To the Attorney-General is left the discretion of bringing suit. So wide is the range which the suits already brought have taken, and so unlimited is the discretion of the Attorney-General as to what trade agreements he may attack that no business man can tell from day to day when he may be haled into court. At best regulation by lawsuit is sporadic and unfair. There is room for too much favoritism. One Attorney-General may be high-minded and wholly devoted to the public interest, but another may not. Regulation by lawsuit will not suffice. The country is too open to the evil of shifting policies. There is involved in this method no well-ordered or scientific system of regulating combinations.

. . . The testimony given before the [United States Senate Committee on Interstate Commerce held last winter] . . . cannot be neglected by any serious thinker upon our present day economic problems. Perhaps the most striking feature in all this mass of testimony is the bewilderment of the business men; and by this term is meant the really constructive factors in our industrial life and not the speculators or the parasites. These men declare that they are in a quandary. They cannot tell whether or not they are violating the law. No matter how honest their intentions, at any moment they may be charged with crime. Naturally they are afraid to extend their business.

This is no slight matter, and the accuracy of the statement is confirmed by other testimony. One of the distinguished lawyers in the country with large experience as a legal adviser of corporations, declares that he is unable to advise his clients with any degree of assurance. Where one concern may be haled before a court and another with apparently similar organization and methods is untouched, no wonder there is unrest and uncertainty.

But this is far from being the only objection to the one hundred and seven law suits. The country is fairly honeycombed with trade agreements—with informal trusts—if you will have it that way. Practically all business is carried on by means of trade agreements, more or less strong, and the business is usually prosperous where the agreements are strongest. Business men say they cannot prosper without these agreements. Cutthroat competition will ruin them. They must associate one with another. But what are they to do with the terror of the Sherman Law with them by day and by night?

Moreover, where the Department of Justice has broken up one old agreement, there are hundreds which it has not reached. Samuel Untermeyer, the corporation lawyer, has gone so far as to assert that not one in a thousand has been touched. It is true that many of the old-style agreements have gone,—those that were made hard and fast in writing. Since the Sherman Law has been so extensively enforced most of these have become as dead as the old pool arrangements of two or three decades ago. There are safes in New York stuffed with the written evidences of these "conspiracies," and with "big" men's signatures attached to them. These agreements are no longer in effect, but

how about the associations for the betterment of trade, the dinner and luncheon clubs, the reunions and general understandings, the gentlemen's agreements, and the telephone messages?

In one of his campaign speeches Governor Woodrow Wilson remarked that the trial of the meat packers had developed some very interesting things. "We found out," he said, "that you did not have to form a great combination, that all you had to do was to be polite, that all that the meat packers did was to meet without forming a legal or illegal union of any kind, and consult together as to what price they would like to have meat sell at. Then a very nice young gentleman, whom they employed for the purpose as their secretary and spokesman, would write a very prettily phrased letter to all of them suggesting that perhaps it was desirable to quote meat at such and such a price and they felt bound by the etiquette of perfect gentlemen to observe that price. That is all."

There are undoubtedly dangers and evils lurking in the trusts, but much greater are the evils and dangers in the many forms of trade agreements, for they are vastly more numerous. At present the public has no protection against secret agreements except an occasional long drawn out lawsuit. But these suits with their revelations of the inside history and methods of American combinations show conclusively the remarkable similarity of many of these combinations to the long discarded pools of twenty and thirty years ago, and demonstrate beyond a doubt that combination through agreement or pool arrangements, where there is no merging of ownership or ownership interest of one concern in the other, is a persistent feature of modern industrial life. If further proof of this were required we need only look to Germany where combination and concentration has reached an even higher degree than in this country. (An Austrian Consul reported to his government that fifty men controlled the finances and industries of Germany solely through the form of cartels and syndicates, in other words through trade agreements.)

It is hopeless, then, absolutely to forbid business men, or any other class of men, to agree. The more intelligent and efficient a man is the more likely he is to reach an understanding with others engaged in the same profession or trade. Try it on yourself. How would you like to be haled to court just because you had agreed on some detail of business policy with other men? The Congressmen who so suspiciously questioned prominent business men who appeared before them as to just how far these and other business men were in the habit of agreeing among themselves went out from the committee rooms and reached understandings with other Congressmen as to pending legislation.

The Sherman Law, strictly construed, would prevent an association of merchants from exchanging information valuable to every member. It has been held to be unlawful for a number of mills to have a common selling agent. Associations of farmers having for their purpose more systematic marketing of their products have been threatened with the terrors of the law. It is probably unlawful for fire insurance companies to maintain a common survey office to report upon the construction of buildings and the hazards, physical and moral, involved in insuring them. Coal and ice dealers, who, in order to lessen the costs of delivery, have divided the territory, have been branded as criminals. The purpose of all these agreements is the elimination of waste. If they are not allowed the cost of doing business is increased, and in the long run the consumer pays.

It is human nature, and especially modern human nature, to reach understandings, or agreements, with our fellow men. But when these understandings adversely affect the lives of countless other fellow men what is to be done about it? Publicity is the thesis of these articles. We have seen that the tendency in large affairs is toward publicity. Why not allow business men to make agreements, provided, however, that these agreements, to be legal, be filed publicly with some government body? One thing is certain, that great benefits would follow from the mere publicity given to the filing of these instruments.

It may be objected that to permit business men to file trade agreements would merely be licensing them to raise their prices to the already overburdened consumer. But do these men not get together now and exact all they can? How much better it would be if their agreements, now wholly secret, were made public? For if all these agreements are made public they cannot exist very long unless they are legitimate and needful. In any industry the weak member, who is living on credit, who is reckless, and has nothing to lose, is the one who cuts prices to the bone and forces the others to follow. No one wants ruinous competition. In the case of one of the combinations now under attack by the government it is admitted in the government's own papers that before the combination was formed goods were being sold below cost, so ruinous was the competition. Such competition must necessarily result in agreement or in monopoly. In cases such as these, agreements of a certain nature are needful and reasonable. But if business men feel they must put a brake upon the laws of ruinous competition, let them do so openly and present their agreements to the government for inspection and supervision.

But would it not be possible for men to continue to form secret agreements in addition to those submitted to the government for proper publicity and reasonable supervision? Such a thing is conceivable, but the great present motive for doing it would be gone. Any study of the corporation and economic history of this country will show that the chief motive for pools and agreements has been to prevent ruinous competition which is necessarily wasteful and expensive. But the Sherman Law does not recognize the legality of agreements even to this end. If such necessary agreements were legalized, there would be little motive for forming other agreements; and moreover, a strong Federal Commission on Interstate Trade would be able to ferret out such secret compacts as might be made, a task which is beyond the powers of the Attorney-General.

It may be suggested that this body would be overwhelmed with agreements. But these agreements are now in force. The public would not suffer more if they were made openly. There are less than 500 corporations doing a business of $5,000,000, and a vast number of combinations of various descriptions are purely local. These could be cared for by state and city. Certainly if the Federal Government set the pace by requiring complete publicity in regard to all interstate agreements, the states and cities would follow its examples in regard to combinations within their own borders. Meanwhile the Commission would be passing judgment upon them.

It is secrecy which works for evil. If business men form a pool or syndicate which is not unfair to the public then it can stand the light of day. If it is harmful, the publicity attending the filing of details would so arouse public opinion, even if there were no supervisory power to operate against it, that the agreement would soon become void. The force of public opinion would work more or less automatically to keep trade agreements within wholesome lines.

Even under the present haphazard method of regulating combinations by law suit the element of publicity has proven of great value. The mere threat of the Department of Justice to sue certain combinations after investigating their practices and telling the public through the newspapers of the essential features of such practices has served in several instances to end the evil practices. The electric-lamp pool did not carry its case to the highest courts after the fact that its members discriminated against buyers had been brought to the light in the lower courts. It is further reported that the photographic supply trust, against which no suit at all has yet been brought, has agreed to give up its practice of forcing customers to buy all or none of their supplies from it. Publicity brought about this result.

Publicity is a sharp sword that cuts deep. In a great city where the dealers in food products were supposed to have an agreement to keep up prices, a semi-public body saw to it that for a period of time the prices of all foodstuffs were regularly published in the newspapers. The result was a sudden drop in prices on the part of the dealers.

The problem of cheap production of manufactured goods has, broadly speaking, been solved. Improvements in farm machinery and better methods in farming tend toward cheaper production of agricultural products. The problem of to-day is to secure cheaper distribution of these products to the consumers. It cannot be solved by throwing hindrances and obstacles in the way of the producers. On the contrary, every consideration of policy and good sense demands that they be permitted to eliminate all possible waste and duplication of service.

The trust problem is a big one. Men are afraid of it. They tremble before it. Many believe combinations must increase and wax greater and greater. But many of the greatest combinations in this country have waxed mighty, not because of natural advantages or increased efficiency but because of special privileges or because of predatory or piratical methods.

If competitors were permitted to make reasonable trade arrangements in regard to prices and output, the same to be supervised by a competent public body, "it could no longer be claimed," says Samuel Untermeyer, "that the trust, with its attendant evils of stock watering, closing of factories, oppression of competitors, and the many other attendant wrongs of permanent combination, is the only alternative. The temporary character of these agreements, the fact that each party continues to operate his own plant independently of the others, and gets exclusively the benefit of his own economies and superior management, and that competition on prices between the parties may be resumed at the expiration of the agreement, all assure the use of the most modern methods and the continued effort to cheapen production and to improve the quality of the product."

Many of the trusts have been defeated in the courts where the Sherman Law was invoked against them, and many have made overtures to the Government to give up methods which were piratical and predatory and re-establish fair play and open markets. These overtures came after the Government had given the fullest publicity to the unfair methods. But the Department of Justice can reach only a fraction of these combinations, for, as a rule, a lawsuit requires years to settle. This objection is serious, if not fatal.

Publicity must be applied by a commission, and it will then be found that as wrongful methods of competition disappear before the light, in which they cannot thrive, much of the dreaded tendency toward the concentration, consolidation, and centralization of our industries will dissolve into thin air. ◆

Questions

1. According to Atwood, why are retail prices for food products so much higher than those paid to the producer?

2. What are the various services provided by the middleman?

CONTROL OF PRICES AND PEOPLE FROM
THE NEW INDUSTRIAL STATE

John Kenneth Galbraith (1908–2006)

. . . I have sought to show that modern and highly technical processes of production lead, inevitably, to planning by producers. The enemy of the market is not ideology but technology. And so planning extensively replaces the market as the force determining what the economy does. The principal planning instrument is the modern large corporation. Within broad limits, it determines what the consumer shall have and at what price he shall have it. And it foresees the need for, and arranges the necessary supply of, capital, machinery, and materials.

The business-man or entrepreneur has been regarded as subordinate to the market since Adam and as a matter of settled doctrine since Adam Smith. The modern large corporation is the direct descendant of the entrepreneur. This has kept us from seeing it in its new role. Had the corporation been an outgrowth of the state which we associate with planning, we would not be in doubt. . . . [T]he modern corporation has moved into a much closer association with the state than most of us imagine. And its planning activities are extensively, and indeed systematically, supplemented by those of the state.

But first I must speak of the regulation of prices in the modern economy and the means by which public behaviour is accommodated to plan. For here we encounter some of the more entrenched folk myths of our time, including a certain vested interest in error on the part of both economists and businessmen. If one takes faith in the market away from the economist, he is perilously barren of belief. His situation is much like that of a theologian who is suddenly faced not only with the thought that God is dead but that the world He made does not exist. And the large corporate enterprise needs the concept of the market, in the language of the late [sic] James Bond, as a cover for authority. The corporation has great influence over our lives and our beliefs. But market theory holds that in all of its behaviour it is subordinate to market influences. It is merely an automaton responding to these influences. This is most convenient.

Control of prices is an intrinsic feature of all planning. In the modern industrial state it is made necessary by the heavy commitment of capital and time required by advanced technology. It is made urgent by the special vagaries of the market for highly technical products. In the formally planned economies, that of the Soviet Union for example, price control is a forthright function of the state although there has been some tendency, in recent times, to allow some power over prices to devolve on the socialist firm. In the western-type economies comprehensive systems of price control have come about by evolution and adaptation to circumstance. Nobody willed them. But, unlike the Victorian Empire, they are no accidental product of a fit of absentmindedness. They were required by circumstance.

The power to set minimum industrial prices exists whenever a small number of firms share a market. The innocent at the universities have long been taught that small numbers—oligopoly as it is known—accord to sellers the same power in imperfect form that has anciently been associated with monopoly. The principal difference is the imperfect nature of this monopoly power. It does not allow of the exploitation of the consumer in quite such efficient fashion as was possible under the patents of monopoly accorded by Elizabeth to her favourites or by John D. Rockefeller to himself.

But, in fact, oligopoly is combined, in one of the more disconcerting contradictions of economic theory, with efficient production, expansive output, and prices that are generally thought rather favourable to the public. The consequences of oligopoly are greatly condemned in principle and greatly approved in practice. Professor Paul Samuelson, the most distinguished of my generation of economists, warns in his famous textbook that "To reduce imperfections of competition [by which he mean markets consisting of small numbers of large firms or oligopoly], a nation must struggle perpetually and must ever maintain vigilance." Since the American economy, as we have seen, is dominated by a very small number of very large firms the struggle has obviously been a losing one. Indeed, it has been lost. But what is the result? The result, as Professor Samuelson agrees, is that the economy functions well and cannot fail to continue to do so. Man-hour efficiency in the United States, he concludes, "can hardly help but grow at the rate of three per cent or more, even if we do not rouse ourselves." A similar conflict between the inefficiency of oligopoly, and the efficiency of an economy composed thereof, is present in every well-regarded textbook. Professor Samuelson would say—and indeed says—that technology and associated capital use are what improve efficiency. But these, we have seen, are what require that there be planning and associated price control.

REASON FOR PRICE CONTROLS

And here is the answer: prices in the modern economy are controlled not for the purposes of monopolistic exploitation of the market; they are controlled for purposes of planning. This comes about as an effortless consequence of the development of that economy. Modern industrial planning both requires and rewards great size. This means, in turn, that a comparatively small number of large firms will share in producing the typical product. Each, as a matter of ordinary prudence, will act with full consideration of its own needs and of the common need. Each must have control of its own prices. Each will recognize this to be the common requirement. Each will forswear any action, and notably any sanguinary or competitive price-cutting, which would be prejudicial to the common interest in price control. The control is neither difficult to achieve nor to maintain. Moreover, one firm's prices are another firm's costs. Stability in prices means stability in costs. This complex of controlled prices and costs not only makes possible long-term contracts but is generally useful in

providing the stable platform that industrial planning requires.

The fact of control is far more important than the precise price level at which it exists. In 1964 in the United States the big automobile companies had profits on sales ranging from five per cent. to over ten per cent. There was security against collapse of prices and earnings for firms with profits at either level. Planning was possible at either level of return. All firms could function. But none could have functioned had the price of a standard model automobile fluctuated, depending on whim and reaction to the current novelties, from $1,750 (600 [British pounds]) to $3,500 (1,200 [British pounds]) with steel, glass, plastics, paint, tyres, sub-assemblies, and labour moving over a similar range. However, the level of prices is not unimportant. And, from time to time, in response to major changes in cost—often when the renegotiation of a wage contract provides a common signal to all firms in the industry— prices must be changed. The prices so established will reflect generally the goals of those who guide the enterprise—the decision-making organization. Security of earnings will be a prime objective. This is necessary, we have seen, for autonomy—for freedom from interference by shareholders and creditors.

A further important goal will be the growth of the firm. As I will later urge, this is almost certainly more important than maximum profits. The professional managers and technicians who direct and guide the modern firm do not themselves get the profits. These accrue mainly to shareholders. But the managers and technicians do get the benefits of the expansion. This brings the prestige that is associated with a larger firm and which is associated with growth as such. And, as a very practical matter, it opens up new executive jobs, new opportunities for promotion, and better excuses for higher pay. Prices, accordingly, will be set with a view to attracting customers and expanding sales. In contrast with prices that are set to maximize profits, these offer no grounds, in the short run or long, for complaint by the consumer. When price control is put in the context of planning, the contradiction between monopolistic exploitation and the efficiency of the modern economy is resolved. That is a remarkable advantage of reality, it has, by its nature, this internal consistency.

I cannot refrain from mentioning one practical consequence of this argument. It concerns punitive action against monopoly—that of the Monopolies Commission in Britain and of the anti-trust laws in the United States. It must already have occurred to many that there is a remarkable discrimination in the way such legislation is now applied. A great corporation wielding vast power over its markets is substantially immune. It does not appear to misuse the power; accordingly it is left alone. And in any case to declare the big corporations illegal is, in effect, to declare the modern economy illegal. But if two small firms seek to unite, this corporate matrimony will be meticulously scrutinized. And, very possibly, it will be forbidden. This may be so even though the merged firm is miniscule in size or market power as compared with the giant that is already a giant.

ANTI-MONOPOLY LAWS AS A CHARADE

The explanation is that the modern anti-monopoly and anti-trust laws are a charade. Their function is not to prevent exploitation of the public. If great size and market power led to that our case would already be hopeless. The function is to persuade people in general and British socialists and American liberals in particular, that the market is still extant. And it persuades them that the state is still vigilant in protecting the market. This is accomplished by bringing the force of law to bear on the ambitions of firms that seek to become larger (and possibly more effective as planning units) while exempting those that already are large.

The French, German, and Japanese either do not have or do not enforce such laws. That is because they are not impelled similarly to worship at the altar of the market. They quietly accept the logic of planning and its requirements in size, and there is no indication that they suffer in consequence.

When prices for a particular product are set by a few large firms, along the lines and for the purposes I have indicated, there is little danger of price-cutting. This part of the control is secure. There does remain a danger of uncontrolled price increases.

In particular, when a few large firms bargain with a strong union, conflict can be avoided by acceding to union demands. And there is not much incentive to resist: There is a common understanding among the firms that all will raise their prices to compensate for such a settlement. If demand is strong enough to keep the economy near full employment, it will be strong enough to make such price increases feasible. It will be comparatively unelastic. The price increases, in turn, set in motion demands for further wage increases. Thus, the familiar upward spiral of wages and prices increases. This too is prejudicial to planning. The individual firm cannot prevent such price increases; they are beyond the control of the planning unit.

So here, increasingly, we follow the practice of the formally planned economies. We rely on the state to set maximum wages and prices. In the United States, as in Britain, the government does this with great caution, circumspection, and diffidence, somewhat in the manner of a Victorian spinster viewing an erotic statue. Such action is held to be unnatural and exceptional. Economists accord it—the guideposts in the United States, the wage and price freezes here in Britain—little or no acceptance as established economic policy. Unions say it interferes with free collective bargaining. Business-men say it interferes with their natural freedom of decision on prices. Economists say that it interferes with the market. What everyone opposes in principle, all advanced industrial countries end up by doing in practice. The answer once more is clear. In a market economy, such wage and price ceilings would be unnecessary. But they are an indispensable counterpart of economic planning and of the minimum price control that already exists.

This price and wage setting by the state could be dispensed with by having such a shortage of demand that it would be impossible for firms to raise prices and unions to raise wages. That is to say, we could have it by rehabilitating the market for labour and industrial products. This would require a shortage of jobs, a scarcity of demand. It would not then be possible to raise wages in response to prices or prices in response to wages. But that would mean unemployment or greater uncertainty of employment and, an important but much neglected factor, uncertainty in planning of production by producers. Despite everyone's affection for the market, not many want these results. So we have the maximum price and wage controls, and seek only to avert our eyes from it so far as possible. It would be simpler were we to recognize that we have planning and that this control is an indispensable aspect. The graves of Smith, Mill, Jevons, and Marshall would convulse slightly but soon subside. Their undeviating apostles and disciples who, biologically speaking, are still alive would suffer more. But many of them, one trusts, have already learned to live with their own irrelevance.

KEY TO THE MANAGEMENT OF DEMAND

Let me now say a word about the management of what people buy at the controlled prices. The key to the management of demand is effective control of, or sufficient influence on, the purchases of final consumers. The latter includes both private individuals and the state. If these purchases are under effective control, there will then be a comparatively reliable demand throughout the system for raw materials, parts, machinery, and other items going into the ultimate product. If the demand for its automobiles is reliable, an automobile firm can accord its suppliers the security of long-term contracts for their planning. And, even in the absence of such contracts, there will still be a reliable and predictable flow of orders which allows of planning. Although the techniques for management of government purchases are very different from those for management of the consumer, it makes the same contribution to planning by prime and sub-contractors. How are individual consumers managed? As so often, change in modern industrial society has made possible what change requires. The need to control consumer behaviour arises

from the exigencies of planning. Planning, in turn, is made necessary by extensive use of advanced technology, the capital this requires, and the related sophistication of organization. This is an efficient way of producing goods; the result is a very large volume of production.

As a further consequence, in the economically advanced countries goods that serve elementary physical sensation—that prevent hunger, protect against cold, provide shelter, suppress pain—come to comprise a small and diminishing part of what people consume. Only a few goods serve needs that are made known to the individual by the palpable discomfort or pain that is experienced in their absence. Most are enjoyed because of some mental or aesthetic response to their possession or use. They give the individual a sense of personal achievement; they accord him a feeling of equality with his neighbour; they divert his mind from thought or its absence; they promote or satisfy sexual aspiration; or they promise social acceptability; or they enhance his subjective feeling of health, well-being, and orderly peristalsis; or they are thought to contribute to personal beauty; or they are otherwise psychologically rewarding.

Thus it comes about that, as the industrial system develops to where it has need for planning and the management of the consumer that this requires, we find it serving wants which are psychological in origin. These are admirably subject to appeal to the psyche. Hence they can be managed. A man whose stomach is totally empty cannot be persuaded that his need is for entertainment. Physical discomfort will tell him he needs food more. A man who is very cold will have a nearly absolute preference for what makes him warm. But psychic reactions have no such internal anchor; since they exist in the mind, they are subject to what influences the mind. Though a hungry man cannot be persuaded as between bread and a circus, a well-nourished man can. And he can be persuaded as between different circuses and different foods.

By giving a man a ration card or distributing to him the specific commodities he is to consume, the individual can be required to consume in accordance with plan. But this is an onerous form of control and it is ill-adapted to differences in personality. In advanced industrial societies, it is considered acceptable only in times of great stress or for the very poor. Even the formally planned economies—the Soviet Union and the eastern-European states—regard the ration card as a manifestation of failure. It is easier and, if less precise, still sufficient to manage by persuasion rather than by [fiat]. . . .

Although advertising will be thought of as the central feature of this persuasion, and is certainly important, it is but a part of a much larger apparatus for the management of demand. Nor does this consist, alone, in devising a sales strategy for a particular product. It often means devising a product, or features of a product, around which a sales strategy can be built. Product design, model change, packaging, and even performance reflect the need to provide what are called strong selling points. They are as much a part of the process of demand management as the advertising campaign. The first step in this process, generally speaking, is to recruit a loyal or automatic corps of customers. This is known in the trade as building customer loyalty and brand recognition. To the extent that it is successful, it means that the firm has a stable body of custom which is secure against any large-scale defection. To say that consumers are loyal is to say that they do not exercise choice. And being made thus more reliable and predictable, they are successfully incorporated in the planning of the firm.

A purely defensive strategy will not, however, suffice. In line with the goals of its directing organization, the firm will want to expand sales. And such effort is necessary to hold a given position. Out of this effort, from firms that are fully able to play the game, comes a crude equilibrating process which accords to each participant a reasonably reliable share of the market. It works, very roughly, as follows.

When a firm is enjoying steady patronage by its existing customers and recruiting new ones at what seems a satisfactory rate, the existing strategy for consumer management—advertising, selling methods, product design—will be considered satisfactory. The firm will

not quarrel with success. If sales are stationary or slipping, this calls for a change in selling methods—in advertising, product design, or even in the product itself. Testing and experiment are possible. And, sooner or later, a formula providing a suitable response is obtained. This will lead, in turn, to countering action by firms that are then failing to make gains.

This process of action and response belongs to the field of knowledge which has come in modern times to be called game theory. It leads to a rough but controlled equilibrium between the firms that have the resources to play it. Each may win for a time or lose for a time but the game will be played out within a narrow range of gain or loss. Market shares will remain comparatively constant over a long period of time. Firms that do not have the resources to play—particularly to stand the very large cost of advertising, sales force, product design and redesign, as in the case of the smaller motor manufacturers—will disappear. And the firms that can play the game will, on occasion, find customers adamant in their resistance to a particular product. As in the case of the Ford Motor Company's Edsel a few years ago no response can be obtained at tolerable cost by any strategy that can be devised. But the size and product diversification of the mature corporation allow the firm to accept an occasional such failure without hazard.

Nevertheless, it is the everyday assumption of those who engage in this management that if sales of a product are slipping, a new selling formula can be found that will correct the situation. By and large, this assumption is justified. Means can almost always be found to keep exercise of consumer discretion within safe limits.

Management of the consumer on the scale just outlined requires that there be some means for comprehensive, repetitive, and compelling communications between the managers of demand and those who are managed. It must be possible to win the attention of those who are being managed for considerable periods of time without great effort on their part. It should reach people in all spectrums of intelligence; no one should be barred by illiteracy or unwillingness to read, or a negative score in an intelligence test. Such a means of mass communication was not needed when the wants of the masses were anchored primarily in physical need. The masses could not then be persuaded. Most of their income went for basic foods and shelter. The wants of a well-to-do minority could then be managed. But since this minority was generally literate, or sought to seem so, they could be reached selectively by newspapers and magazines. With mass affluence, and therewith the need to manage people at levels of literacy, education, and intelligence, these no longer served.

Technology, once again, solved the problems that it created. Coincidentally with rising mass incomes came first radio, and then television. These, in their capacity to hold effortless interest and their accessibility over the entire cultural spectrum, their independence of any educational qualification, were admirably suited to mass persuasion. Television was especially serviceable. Not since the invention of speech itself has any medium of communication shown such adaptability in accommodating itself to the entire spectrum of intellectual capacity. There is an insistent tendency among social scientists to think of any institution which, as in the United States, features singing commercials, shows the human intestinal tract in full or impaired operation, equates effortless elimination of human whiskers with the greatest happiness of man, and implies that exceptional but antiseptic and wholesome seduction is associated with a particular make of automobile, as inherently trivial. This is a great mistake. The modern industrial system is profoundly dependent on such art. What is called progress makes it increasingly so.

The management of demand, as here to be seen, is in all respects an admirably subtle arrangement in social design. It works not on the individual but on the mass. An individual of will and determination can, in principle, contract out from under its influence. This being so, no case for individual compulsion in the purchase of any product can be established. To all who object there is a natural answer: you are at liberty to leave! Yet there is no danger that enough people will ever assert this choice to impair the management of mass behaviour.

I have not completed this aspect of planning. It embraces the problem of managing not only the purchases of the individual but also those of the state. And I have been talking so far of the demand for individual products. There is also the matter of aggregate demand. It does not greatly profit an automobile company or a soap manufacturer to have a loyal and reliable corps of customers if they lack the purchasing power with which to buy. This purchasing power must be regulated, and thus insured, if planning is to be secure. And no single firm, however powerful, can insure stability in this total flow of purchasing power.

We saw earlier in this lecture that where price and wage control are beyond the planning powers of the firm, the state steps in. This is a pattern. The state similarly steps in to stabilize aggregate purchasing power. And it supplements the planning of the corporation in other important ways. . . . ◆

QUESTIONS

1. According to Galbraith, why do corporations want to control demand?

2. How and at what level do the managers of large corporations maintain prices?

3. Why does Galbraith think that managers care about the growth of their firms?

4. What allows for demand to be managed?

5. How is demand managed for most goods in an advanced economy?

V

ACCOUNTING

INTRODUCTION: WHEN YOU ADD, YOU SUBTRACT

Among the Jewish people, there is a living tradition of ancient beliefs based on the *Five Books of Moses*, the *Sayings of the Fathers*, the *Talmud* and other theological, philosophical, and legal tracts. This tradition holds that money is just a means of exchange for things and that both money and things should serve ends that are bigger than ourselves. At a "physical" level, sustenance and charity would be considered proper ends for money and things. At a more "spiritual" level, meditation and prayer would be considered proper and sanctified ends.

Jewish thinking about commerce and the community of humankind has always recognized the problematic nature of money—that money, the thing itself, can cause us to focus on "improper" and artificially created wants while ignoring our more "proper" spiritual needs and community obligations. This "old" problem has inspired philosopher Jacob Needleman to give new voice to this concern in his book, *Money and the Meaning of Life*. He declares that "ours is a society that has given material wealth first priority in our common life" and that because of this unbalanced emphasis, we live in a perpetual hell where "we are barred from receiving what we truly need because of the value we give to what we merely want." When we spend too much time on our own accounts, adding up accumulated money and things, we subtract from the deeper purposes of life and become ironically impov-

erished in meaning and joy. But if we spend *no* time on our accounts, then the means to achieving *any* end remain unachieved. Such a failure leaves us in a wretched state of limbo where we may serve neither "physical" nor "spiritual" purposes.

Therefore, we are interested in the study of accounting and how it affects us, the firm, and the public. The better we understand its technical nature and its larger concerns, the more alert we become to the need for preparing our own personal balance sheets for assessing the meaning of our individual lives.

A. C. Littleton provides some historical perspective on the subject of bookkeeping. His reach is impressive, and it begins with the Babylonians and Egyptians, whose media for computation and entries were the clay tablet and papyrus. He tells us that the Greek and Roman contributions to bookkeeping were more in the way of mathematical progression. Though he finds no evidence of double-entry bookkeeping in any of their accounting media, these same artifacts tell us much about ancient cultures. In this cultural realm, Littleton's reach extends to the demographic transformations and the economic shifts that served as evolving antecedents to the eventual development of double-entry bookkeeping in the late Middle Ages. Double-entry bookkeeping became the Copernican center of accounting from the European Renaissance to the our present age of global markets. And as with the heliocentric theory of Copernicus, the significance of double-entry bookkeeping escaped serious notice until someone found a way to canonize it. Thus, Luca Pacioli played Galileo to the merchants of Venice, and the rest of the Mediterranean world of commerce.

This study begins in earnest with what has become known as the first published accounting book, written in Venice during the late fifteenth century, by Luca Pacioli. At this time, Venice was the center of commerce in the civilized world, and the business procedures developed and practiced there most often became standardized wherever trade was transacted. Pacioli documented the proper accounting methods for those transactions.

Pacioli clarifies the need for an ordering of a firm's, or an individual's, assets in order of liquidity. He suggests the proper role of accounting for ownership of those assets, and he records the use of debits and credits in the accounting of business transactions. Reflecting his role as a monk and the role of the Catholic Church in the world of business, he presents terms that should be written into financial statements and acknowledges the place of the church in business negotiations. Pacioli, true to his calling and his time, admonishes those who practice accounting to "begin their business with the name of God at the beginning of every book and have His holy name in their minds."

At the time of Pacioli's writing, business was becoming a more common activity for people, and church leaders were concerned about where such a prevailing money orientation was going to lead humanity. Pacioli's invocation of God's name was a reminder that the chapter "Particulars of Reckonings and Their Recordings" from his *Treatise* is as much about reckonings in the spiritual world as it is about reckonings in the material world.

Ihara Saikaku, a seventeenth-century Japanese writer, is probably better known as a poet than a composer of short stories, though in the 1680s and 1690s, he wrote powerful tales of money and seduction. His preoccupation with the subject of money sets him apart from other Japanese writers of his generation. James Buchan, contemporary author of *Frozen Desire: The Meaning of Money*, has written:

> Saikaku is more fascinated by money even than Defoe: there is more coined money in his stories than in any others. . . . We learn down to the last copper mon how much it costs a girl to rent her working costume for the night, how much, in the rigid monetary stratification of the licensed quarters, it costs a man to visit the highest rank of girl in Kyoto (five hundred and fifty-one momme of silver with tips); even, at one point, the capital cost of loving such a woman (five hundred kamme of silver).

Buchan goes on to say, speaking of Saikaku's epoch, that the "introduction of money has also demolished the ethical basis of society." This may be so; Saikaku's writing recognizes the importance of money as a categorizer of one's social and even moral class. But Saikaku is not demoralized by the presence and power of money. He demystifies it and even disempowers it by following it. For him, money's meaning is tied strictly to character. The more one is in control of money, specifically through entering cash flow into a ledger, the more controlled is one's life. This has moral implications. To control and monitor the flow of money is to demonstrate that one controls one's own life—it cannot be controlled by a mon or a kamme.

The section called "The Tycoon of All Tenants" in Saikaku's *The Eternal Storehouse of Japan* introduces readers to Fuji-ichi, a millionaire who knows "his own mind" and for whom this is the "basis of his success." His books are in perfect order in the same way that his life is in perfect order. It is "his ambition to serve as a model for others in the management of everyday affairs." He gives "the closest attention to even the smallest of details." In so doing, he pays special attention to costs because he believes that frugality is critical to getting rich. Make the lowering of costs a critical accounting function, and this will have an impact on wealth production.

The subject of ethics is about the systemization of moral thinking. To be ethical is to be committed to a moral program without deviation and without self-deception. It requires an orderliness of mind and a perfect sense of emotional and intellectual balance. It also requires excellent managerial skills and the ability to see beyond cultural norms. If a culture is saturated in money, then to monitor money as carefully as does Fuji-ichi might suggest the kind of preoccupation that, following Buchan's assertion, demolishes "the ethical basis of society." But Fuji-ichi is an "accountant." For him, orderly books demand an orderly mind. An orderly mind loves an ordered society. Ethics requires order. Thus, Fuji-ichi scrutinizes the flow of cash in the same way he scrutinizes the flow of his life. He manages his affairs with ordered brilliance. He gives close attention to the smallest details of every aspect of his life. Money interest and counting fixation aside, he is a moral miracle—the bedrock of healthy, commercial society. If "the love of money is the root of all evil," then we can always trust Fuji-ichi to be a good man. Why? It is because he loves to count money, not to marshal it for narcissistic or nefarious purposes. For him, adding does not subtract from life; adding does what it should do—it adds to life. In Saikaku's characterological lexicon, it is the accountant whose ethical foundation is unassailable.

By the time Daniel Defoe, an eighteenth-century writer known as one of the earliest novelists in the English language (*Moll Flanders* and *Robinson Crusoe*), offers his practical advice on the subject of keeping a business, the capitalist world is deep in its own development of infrastructure. No longer at serious odds with theological streams of thought, cultural currents have transported it upstream, where it has been received without far-reaching dispute. Though free markets are largely nascent and undeveloped, free market thinking is already a defacto reality. Land, labor, and capital are for sale. There are mercantile entrepreneurs aplenty. Capitalism is thriving, but it is a still developing ideology. It will have to wait for another fifty years or so for Adam Smith's *The Wealth of Nations* to establish it as the ideological and political status quo. But shopkeepers and tradespeople are their own accountants and manage their own cash flow and their own souls; they are uninterested in dogma—a reminder that the modern age is not far off. Their interest is in their books.

Daniel Defoe exudes what to most modern readers seems a most unexpected delight in exposing business practitioners to accounting principles in *The Compleat English Tradesman*, a practical, nuts-and-bolts guide to running a business. In its time, it was the most comprehensive business compendium available in the English language, and it is readable in a way that anyone, with just the right amount of common sense, can benefit from its generally useful and friendly counsel.

Like Pacioli before him, Defoe extols the virtues of order and balance. To this, he adds the necessity of exactitude. He is a rationalist, but he is not prepared to present good empiric bookkeeping advice without tying it to an ethical and religious end. God, theology, and business, if not bedfellows, are friendly acquaintances for Defoe. And salvation is now as dependent on financial success as it was once dependent on classical and religious virtue. "A tradesman's books," intones Defoe, "like a Christian conscience, should always be kept clean and neat; and he that is not careful of both, will give but a sad account of himself either to God or man." That a tradesperson may interpret this as he or she pleases is a reminder that the market orientation, which church leaders feared might lead the business practitioner to Hell, is, by this time, not always antithetical to theological preconceptions. London may be a kind of hell to combatants in the early phases of competition, but it is not a literal Hell. And eternality, though still a meaningful consideration, is not as pressing an issue to the competent, Christian accountant as are matters of practicality in the mortal sphere where he must "keep his books in such a posture, that if he should be snatched away by death, his distressed widow and fatherless family may know what is left for them, and may know where to look for it. . . ."

On balance, accounting principles have now found an honored and permanent place. ♦

THE ANTECEDENTS OF DOUBLE-ENTRY

A. C. Littleton (1886–1974)

As most readers will at once perceive, it will be unnecessary [here] . . . to consider the direct parental antecedents of double-entry. That was done three years ago in an accounting classic of matchless spirit by Professor Hatfield ["An Historical Defense of Bookkeeping"]. Rather, it is proposed to follow the genealogy of bookkeeping back beyond those parental ancestors whose respectability was so ably proved at the time. The purpose here will be to trace out those blood-lines of pre-parental inheritance which finally converged at a certain time and place, there to confer certain characteristics upon the offspring. If respectability of sire and dam constitutes "presumptive evidence" of respectability of offspring, as Professor Hatfield phrased it, surely, respectability in still earlier forbears will still further assure the acceptance of our subject in polite circles.

In trying to perceive the forces which produced double-entry, two questions, it seems to me, must be answered in the process. First, what were the antecedent elements out of which double-entry finally evolved? We need an answer to this question, I think, so that we may better appreciate how closely accounting has been, and still is, related to several collateral fields. Second, what surrounding conditions were necessary to give vitality to these antecedent elements? We need an answer to this question in order to perceive that accounting owes more to the evolutionary forces of society than to particular genius, either in our own times or earlier.

The antecedents of double-entry—those factors which in time became so interwoven as to render double-entry inevitable—are all familiar quantities; some of them are very old and some are very obvious, but all of them are, in the writer's opinion, indispensable. They are given below in a rough sort of sequence.

The *art of writing* is an indispensable antecedent, since bookkeeping is before all else a record; *arithmetic* is essential also, since bookkeeping is a sequence of simple computations, even though they are cast into certain forms; *private property,* since bookkeeping is concerned only with recording the facts about property and property rights; *money,* (i.e., a money economy) since bookkeeping is useless except as it reduces all transactions in properties or property rights to a common denominator; *credit,* (i.e., incompleted transactions) since there would be little impulse to make any record whatever if all transactions were completed and closed on the spot; *commerce,* since a merely local trade would never have created enough pressure (volume of business) to stimulate men to coordinate various ideas into a system; *capital,* since without capital, commerce would be trivial, and credit would be inconceivable.

We can recognize these elements as essential to the formation of double-entry; had any of them failed to appear, the appearance of double-entry would have been problematical. If either property or capital were not present, there would be nothing for records to record. Without money, trade would be only barter; without credit, each transaction would be closed at the time; without commerce, the need for financial records would not extend beyond governmental taxes. If either writing or arithmetic were absent, the "vehicle" of bookkeeping would not exist. All of these items are antecedent elements to bookkeeping; we could not dispense with any of them and expect to see double-entry remain.

But indispensable though they are, even these elements could not produce bookkeeping by merely appearing together historically. All of them were present in some form throughout the era of ancient history, but the ancient civilizations failed to produce double-entry.

Writing, for example, is as old as civilization itself. Babylonian mortgages impressed in cuneiform characters upon clay tablets, and Egyptian tax collections painted in hieroglyphics upon papyrus can still be read after 4,000 years. But there was in none of this writing any sign of double-entry bookkeeping; for book-keeping is more than a writing, although always written.

Arithmetic as we understand it—the easy and systematic manipulation of number symbols—did not exist in the ancient world, although the Greeks had made great advances in geometry. Numbers could be expressed by the use of letters of the alphabet, it is true, but arithmetical manipulations, even addition and subtraction, were very difficult to perform. The lack of an easy means of computation must have been as strong a deterrent to financial record-making at this time as its later appearance was a favorable factor.

Property is an indispensable antecedent to bookkeeping, of course; for without the right to possess, enjoy, and dispose of articles of property there would be little reason indeed to "keep books." But property rights under the ancient civilizations were not of the kind to inspire other conditions necessary to book-keeping. Property acquired by conquest or obtained from slave labor, is likely to be expended in lavish display or in further wars—in any case unproductively. The highest conceivable need for bookkeeping under these conditions would be satisfied with a sort of "stores accounting," which would merely tell what property was available. The accounting of the Egyptians extended no further than that; and the financial records of the Roman head of a family were little better—hardly more than receipts and disbursements.

Even the addition of the factor, *money*, to the art of writing and to private property could not produce double-entry bookkeeping. These three factors made possible a written record of private properties which could be expressed in a common denominator. But the incentive to convert a possibility into an actuality was lacking.

Credit there was too, such as was extended by the ancient moneychangers. But this offered little incentive to systematic record-making. Loans for the most part were based upon pledged valuables as in modern pawn broker-age; money was not loaned commercially but against necessity—for consumption rather than for production. Indeed, lending could

hardly be called a credit transaction until far into the Middle Ages. A loan upon pledged property was to the lender practically a completed transaction. If the borrower never reappeared to redeem his property, it was his loss, not the lender's worry. There was little need here for records.

Nor was the *commerce* that existed in the ancient world the kind to stimulate such a thing as bookkeeping. The Phoenicians were great traders along the coast of the eastern Mediterranean 3,500 years ago, and they may have given us the basis of our alphabet of twenty-six letters, but they did not give us double-entry. Barter needed no bookkeeping.

The antecedent of double-entry which we designate commerce is not just trading exchange; it must be an extensive commerce in order to produce the pressure of a great volume of trade. This sort did not exist in the era of ancient history. The demand for trade goods was small because populations were relatively small and largely self-sufficing; because they consisted of many slaves, serfs, and poor artisans with low purchasing power, and but few persons of wealth. Besides this the supply of trade goods was very limited and the means of transportation inadequate. The commerce which was required to foster the formulation of double-entry was a large-scale and *profitable* commerce, for a profitable commerce alone creates a fund of capital which can be reemployed productively and thus give rise to additional capital in turn.

Here, in the opinion of the writer, is the principal explanation of why the ancient world did not produce bookkeeping. It did not have the conception of productive business capital; it lived throughout its era in an agricultural stage of development where there was no occasion to consider capital as a factor in production. This stage was to be followed long afterward by an era of handicraft and of commerce, and still later by an industrial era. These later stages were better suited to the development of bookkeeping, but neither of them had been reached when the doors closed upon ancient history.

There was *capital*, in the sense of wealth, in the ancient world, but the mere existence of wealth does not inevitably give rise to the other conditions essential to the formation of double-entry. It is not wealth in marble palaces and secret hoards which creates conditions favorable to the appearance of a coordinate system of financial records, but wealth in the form of merchandise and ships—wealth which is active, turning over, ever changing in the processes of producing more. Wealth in that form creates questions and doubts and hopes, and men, in striving to find answers to these questions, slowly evolve methods of record to serve their needs. In other words, wealth in the ancient world was not possessed of the energy to become "capital" in a sense to make it an antecedent of double-entry.

In fact all of these elements which we here accept as indispensable antecedents of double-entry bookkeeping, were already present in the ancient civilizations in recognizable form. Yet they failed to produce then what the same elements later did produce—bookkeeping. Why later? The answer lies, I think, in the historical characteristics of the next period—in the differences in outlook and background, in the differences in men's aspirations and interests, and in the differences in the quantity of the wants and the quality of the ideas of the times.

Let us look at these same elements in their new setting of medieval conditions between the years 1200 and 1500—more than eight hundred years after the crumbling of the Roman Empire brought an end to ancient history. They are the same elements, yet different.

Reading and writing, formerly the prized possession of a few scholars, were now more common among the traders and bankers of Venice than anywhere else outside of the monasteries. Scholars had long been able to write, but traders could now, for the first time, write down what trade would need to have written. *Property rights,* which in an earlier day had meant little to a slave population, now were freely enjoyed by freemen. In the prosperous city-republics of Italy, there existed the most stable governments of ten centuries; private ownership of property was widely diffused and amply protected. These oases of stable government proved an advantage in another respect, for they gave *money* a significance as a

medium of exchange it had never known before, and thus hastened the day of a money economy.

So, it is evident that even these very ancient institutions of money, property, and the art of writing, took on a new vitality in the new surroundings. But in the other items in the list of antecedents to bookkeeping, even greater changes appear. *Commerce, capital, credit,* and *arithmetic,* all partake of the spirit of the Renaissance which surrounded them; they seem animated by a new life in comparison with that seen in ancient history. Of these, commerce attracts first attention, because the others are not a little influenced by it.

Because ancient civilizations lived, for the most part, in an agricultural stage of economic development, with large slave or serf classes which had no purchasing power, barter was the usual method of exchange, and traders were hardly more than "peddlers." Compare with this the great and growing trade of Venice and other cities of the medieval period. Venice alone had 300 ships on the Mediterranean and 32,000 traders in the Near East. Northern Italy was populated by a nation of traders rather than by agricultural serfs and landed nobility. Crusaders and camp followers, returning from the luxurious East to their own crude countryside, and no longer satisfied with the old style of living, were largely responsible for the great expansion of trade which followed the Crusades, and the Venetians were strategically located in the natural path of that trade. On the one hand, a hardy, growing population in Europe developing a taste for distant products, and, on the other hand, a source of abundant supply of the products of eastern climates and handicraft now known and become accessible. The foreign trade which developed out of those conditions was something the ancient world had never seen, and something which had far-reaching consequences.

The transportation of numerous armies of crusaders between 1096 and 1272, as well as supplying them with necessities and equipment, was a profitable business. And when to these sources is added the trade in commodities which the Crusades so largely stimulated, and which for centuries flowed through the cities of Northern Italy, it is obvious that *capital* will accumulate rapidly in the cities most concerned, and having accumulated, will seek employment.

The wealth of the ancient civilizations was stagnant in the form of palaces rather than active in the form of ships. But in the city-republics of Italy, between the years 1200 and 1500, the wealth was urged into productiveness. Trading was the vocation of large and small; the wealthy owned their own ships and ventured their capital in goods to fill them; those in more moderate circumstances went adventuring as active partners upon the capital of silent partners. Others chose the safer road of lending money upon the security of the ships themselves, or of lending to various governments. Here was the beginning of real *credit* transactions.

These loans to the government marked the beginning of investment banking—the participation of many individuals in one loan. As early as 1178 the merchants of Genoa advanced funds to the government upon the security of the public revenues and the profits from military expeditions. This financing later developed into the famous Bank of St. George. The Bank of Venice had a similar origin, when in 1171 the merchants were given transferable book credits for gold advanced to the government. The size of some of the early deals is staggering to contemplate. For example, in 1307 the merchants acting as a group loaned the Republic of Florence seven million gold florins ($15,000,000), and a little later (1340) loaned nearly $4,000,000 to King Edward III of England. This stands in graphic contrast with credit in more ancient times, when loans were largely for consumption and usually based upon pledged valuables as security.

With the accumulation of capital seeking employment, it is not surprising that the great merchant houses of the day added a rudimentary sort of commercial banking to their activities. Indeed, it soon became practically a necessity, for the sums often involved in trade were too large to be risked unnecessarily on unprotected roads. Even before the year 1200, bills of exchange had made their appearance, and in the next century their use spread so rapidly that the bankers became important enough to have a duly organized guild to regulate many of their practices.

By 1230 Florentine and other bankers had representatives scattered over the whole of Europe who, among other activities, collected most of the papal revenues, remitting usually by bills of exchange through branch offices of their banking houses. How extensive these scattered connections had become by the next century, may be judged from the example of the firm of Peruzzi, which had no less than sixteen branch houses at this time, and one hundred and thirty agents looking after its interests. Much of the firm's activity was trading, of course, but along with this it carried on banking operations, for the two were seldom separated as early as this. By 1338 there were eighty houses in Florence alone conducting a banking business, and by the end of that century there were fully one hundred and twenty.

All through this period of 300 years, *arithmetic* had been quietly playing its appointed part along with the other antecedents of bookkeeping. The ancient world had been greatly handicapped by inability to make computations easily; the literal symbols used for numbers by the Greeks, and the even more faulty system used by the Romans, did not lend themselves readily to calculations. But in the Middle Ages Europe began to learn arithmetic from the Arabs and this condition was in the way of being remedied.

There is small doubt that Italian traders knew the essentials of early commercial arithmetic before the material appeared in Europe in manuscripts; their contacts with the Arabs of Northern Africa and in Constantinople would indicate this. And in 1202 Arabic numerals and methods of computation were introduced into Europe in book form by Leonardo of Pisa. This book had chapters on addition, subtraction, prices of goods, barter, partnership, and the like, and would be of interest to merchants because of this type of contents as well as because it made use of the new system of ten numerals, including a zero.

Such a system lent itself naturally to computations and had already been applied by the Arabs to a great number of arithmetical problems of trade. This knowledge the Italians acquired early in this period, and it seems very probable that it opened the way for systematizing the record-keeping made necessary by bills of exchange, as nothing else could have done. This connection would not be easy to prove to the satisfaction of a critical historian, however, and no attempt is made here to go into the argument.

Arabic numerals were used for a long time by Italian merchants along with the Roman system, for the one did not replace the other. It seemed that the rules of the bankers' guild prescribed Roman numerals for ledger records, and thus forced the older system of enumeration to remain in use after a better had appeared. The idea prevailed for a long time that Roman numerals made fraudulent alterations more difficult. This was an important consideration even as early as the Middle Ages, as is shown by the requirement of the guild in the 13th century that members must keep records and must open them to surprise inspections by guild agents. Illegibility was severely censured, as were, of course, inaccuracies and falsifications (Staley, "The Guilds of Florence"). Were not these 13th century "inspecting agents" of the bankers' guild the forerunners of auditors?

It is evident from all this that the circumstances surrounding commerce, capital, and credit in the Middle Ages were very different from those which surrounded the same elements in the period of ancient history. And it must become increasingly evident that these surroundings so changed the size and extent of commerce, and the purposes for which capital and credit were employed, that these elements could now become the vitalized antecedents of bookkeeping where before they could not. Together with medieval arithmetic, they now lead directly to the development of double-entry.

The elements of double-entry bookkeeping appear early in this same 300-year period, and the formation of the system is complete before 1500. By 1211 evidences are found of cross entries between the accounts of clients in the records of a Florentine banker. Records of the stewards to the local authorities of Genoa of

1278 show no trace of double entry; but the books of Rinerio and Bolda Fini (1297) have accounts with persons as well as things, and the records of the stewards to the local authorities of Genoa of 1340 now appear in quite complete double-entry. The ledgers of Soranzo Bros. (1406–1434) are particularly complete trading records, with nominal accounts closed into Profit and Loss, and thence into capital in the regular way. Here is tangible evidence of a practical kind that bookkeeping was actually developing now that conditions were right. In another generation (i.e., by 1494) double-entry had been fully explained in a printed book (Pacioli). So well were the fundamentals of double-entry established by the end of the century that they have needed no change since that time.

But the story of antecedents is not yet quite finished. Professor Hatfield spoke very convincingly in that earlier paper concerning double-entry's parentage and immediate associates; and we have sketched here its earlier ancestral antecedents to show that blueblood from ancient time runs in its veins. It would seem only fitting, therefore, before leaving the subject, to inquire briefly concerning the progeny of double-entry as well as the ancestors, parents, and associates. The embodiment of all this ancestral heritage is now some 500 years old—old enough to be judged by its successors as well as by its forbears.

Let us change the figure of speech and draw a metaphor from the nurseryman's practice among his fruit trees. He grafts the buds taken from one strain of cherry tree on the hardy root stock of another strain, and thus produces a tree which combines the hardy life of the parent root and the engaging characteristics of the engrafted stock.

The hardy root stock you will recognize at once is double-entry bookkeeping. What buds have been grafted onto that root, and what has the combination produced? Here is just a suggestion; there is time for no more.

One of the buds grafted on the parent stock has been the philosophy of economics. From this younger discipline, bookkeeping acquires a body of concepts and a language which has been invaluable in producing a new hybrid of far greater value to business than the parent alone. From this source came our concepts of cost and of income, for example, and the distinction between current and fixed capital. Another engrafted bud has been secured from the science of law in the form of the limited liability, joint stock corporation. From this source comes the distinction between initial capital and reinvested profits, the concept of permanent capital investment and dividends only out of profits. A third bud has been grafted on to the hardy root from the art of business management. From this source come certain practical necessities of the executive, such as the periodicity of financial statements, with all that implies in the way of valuation, accruals, depreciation, etc., and such practical necessities of management and cost accounting, budgeting, and the like.

Each of these three graftings has changed the fruits of the parent stem and where for nearly 500 years men saw merely bookkeeping—financial records leading at best to little more than a calculation of profits—they now see accounting—a scientific procedure of inestimable value to society through the service it performs in facilitating sound business management.

We have reason, therefore, to be proud of double-entry—though we should at all times carry our pride with humility. We have reason to feel that double-entry lacks nothing in either remote ancestors or in parents and associates. Few indeed are the other institutions which were so soundly established in their beginning that they have continued for 500 years as little altered in their essentials as double-entry. We have reason to be proud too of the results of uniting bookkeeping and other disciplines—in other words of accounting. Accounting has had a large part in the world of affairs recently and it bids fair to continue to give increasing service. But just as the accounting of today is clearly a product of historical evolution, influenced by many men and many forces, so the accounting of tomorrow will be but a continuation of that evolution, influenced still by all of the circumstances which may surround it. ◆

Questions

1. According to Littleton, what in general allows for the emergence of vigorous commerce?

2. What are the specific material and linguistic requirements of the emergence of double-entry bookkeeping?

3. Explain why accounting emerged at the time that it did in northern Italy.

Particulars of Reckonings and Their Recording from *Ancient Double Entry Bookkeeping: Luca Pacioli's Treatise*

Luca Pacioli (1445–1517)

Chapter 1.

Things that Are Necessary to the Good Merchant and the Method of Keeping a Ledger with Its Journal, in Venice and Elsewhere.

In order that the subjects of His Illustrious Highness, the most honorable and magnanimous Duke of Urbino (D.U.D.S.—*Docis Urbini Domini Serenissimi*), may have all the rules that a good merchant needs, I decided to compile . . . a special treatise which is much needed. I have compiled it for this purpose only, *i.e.*, that they (the subjects) may whenever necessary find in it everything with regard to accounts and their keeping. And thereby I wish to give them enough rules to enable them to keep all their accounts and books in an orderly way. For, as we know, there are three things needed by any one who wishes to carry on business carefully. The most important of these is cash or any equivalent, according to that saying, *Unum aliquid necessarium est substantia.* Without this, business can hardly be carried on.

It has happened that many without capital of their own but whose credit was good, carried on big transactions and by means of their credit, which they faithfully kept, became very wealthy. We became acquainted with many of these throughout Italy. In the great republics nothing was considered superior to the word of the good merchant, and oaths were taken on the word of a good merchant. On this confidence rested the faith they had in the trustworthiness of an upright merchant. And this is not strange, because, according to the Christian religion, we are saved by faith, and without it, it is impossible to please God.

The second thing necessary in business is to be a good bookkeeper and ready mathematician. . . .

The third and last thing is to arrange all the transactions in such a systematic way that one may understand each one of them at a glance, *i.e.*, by the debit (*debito*—owed to) and credit (*credito*—owed by) method. This is very essential to merchants, because, without making the entries systematically it would be impossible to conduct their business, for they would have no rest and their minds would always be troubled. For this purpose I have written this treatise, in which, step by step, the method is given of making all sorts of entries. Although one cannot write out every essential detail for all cases, nevertheless a careful mind will be able, from what is given, to make the application to any particular case.

This treatise will adopt the system used in Venice, which is certainly to be recommended above all the others, for by means of this, one can find his way in any other. We shall divide this treatise in two principal parts. The one we shall call the Inventory, and the other, Disposition (arrangement). We shall talk first of the one and then of the other. . . .

He who wants to know how to keep a ledger and its journal in due order must pay strict attention to what I shall say. To understand the procedure well, we will take the case of one who is just starting in business, and tell how he must proceed in keeping his accounts and books so that at a glance he may find each thing in its place. For, if he does not put each thing in its own place, he will find himself in great trouble and confusion as to all his affairs, according to the familiar saying, *Ubi non est ordo, ibi est confusio* (Where there is no order, there is confusion). In order to give a perfect model to every merchant, we will divide the whole system, as we have said, in two principal parts, and we will arrange these so clearly that one can get good results from them. First, we will describe what the inventory is and how to make it.

CHAPTER **2.**

First Part of this Treatise, Which Is Called Inventory— What Inventory Is, and How to Make It.

First, we must assume that every action is determined by the end in view, and in order to pursue this end properly, we must use every effort. The purpose of every merchant is to make a lawful and reasonable profit so as to keep up his business. Therefore, the merchants should begin their business with the name of God at the beginning of every book and have His holy name in their minds. To begin with, the merchant must make his inventory (*inventario*) in this way: He must always put down on a sheet of paper or in a separate book whatever he has in this world, personal property or real estate, beginning with the things that are most valuable and most likely to be lost, such as cash, jewels, silver, etc., for the real estate, such as houses, lands, lakes, meadows, ponds, etc., cannot be lost as personal property. Then all the other things must be put down one after another. In the said inventory give always first the day, the year, the place and your name. This whole inventory must be completed in one day, otherwise there will be trouble in the future in the management of the business.

As an example for you, I will give you, now, an idea as to how the inventory is to be made, so that you may use it as a guide in any particular case.

CHAPTER **3.**

Example of an Inventory with all Its Formal Requirements.

In the name of God, November 8th, 1493, Venice.

The following is the inventory of myself, N. N., of Venice, Street of the Holy Apostles.

I have written down systematically, or had written by Mr. So-and-So, this inventory of all my property, personal and real, what is owed to me (*debiti*), and what is owed by me (*crediti*), of which I on this said day find myself possessed in this world.

First Item: First I find myself possessed in cash, in gold and coin of so many ducats, of which so many are Venetian, and so many gold Hungarian; of so many large florins made up of Papal, Siennese and Florentine, etc. The rest consists of many different kinds of silver and copper coins, *i.e., troni, marcelli,* papal and royal *carlini* and Florentine *grossi,* and Milanese *testoni,* etc.

Second Item: I also possess, in set and unset jewels, so-and-so-many pieces, among which are many *balassi* set in gold, rings weighing so-and-so-many ounces, carats, grains, etc., per piece or in bulk, etc., which you can express in any manner you wish. There are so-and-so-many sapphires set on clamps for women; they weigh so much. And there are so-and-so-many rubies, unset, weighing so much. The rest consists of unpolished pointed diamonds, etc. Here you may give such descriptions and weight as you desire.

Third Item: I have clothes of many kinds; so many of such kind; and so many of such-and-such kind, etc., describing their condition, colors, linings, styles, etc.

Fourth Item: I have several kinds of silverware, as cups, basins, rammi, cosileri, piromi, etc. Here describe all the different kinds one by one, etc., and weigh each kind diligently. Keep an account of pieces and weights, and of the alloy, whether the Venetian or the one used at Ragusa, etc. Also mention the stamp or mark that they might have.

Fifth Item: I have so much *massaria dei lini*—that is, bed sheets, table cloths, shirts, handkerchiefs, etc., so many of each. Of the bed sheets, so many are made three-piece sheets, and so many are three and one-half, etc., mentioning whether the linen is Padua linen or some other kind, new or used; length so many *braccia*, etc.; so many shirts, etc.; table clothes of so many threads; so many big handkerchiefs and so many small, mentioning whether new or used, giving the different kind in your own way.

Sixth Item: I have so many feather beds and their respective pillows, mentioning whether the feathers are new or used, whether the pillow-cases are new or used, etc., which altogether or one by one weigh so much, marked with my mark or with some other mark, as the custom is.

Seventh Item: I have at home or in the store so much goods of different kinds: First, so many cases of ginger *michino,* weighing so many pounds, marked with such-and-such mark, and so on, describing each kind of said goods with all their marks that you might possibly give and with all the possible accuracy as to weight, number, measurement, etc.

Eighth Item: I have so many cases of ginger *bellidi,* etc., and so many sacks of pepper, long pepper or round pepper, depending on what it is; so many packages of cinnamon, etc., that weigh so much; so many packages of cloves, etc., that weigh so much, with *fusti polvere* and *cappelletti* or without, etc., and so many pieces of *verzini* weighing so much, and so much sandalwood, red or white, weighing so much, and so on, entering one item after another.

Ninth Item: I have so many skins for coverings, that is, so many white kids and so many *albertoni* or *marchiani,* etc., so many of such-and-such kind, etc., so many fox skins, so many tanned and so many raw, so many chamois skins tanned, and so many raw.

Tenth Item: I have so many fine skins, *fore armenti, dossi varii, zebelini,* etc., so many of such-and-such kind, and so many of such-and-such kind—defining diligently and truthfully

each time so that truth will always guide you, etc., distinguishing the things that ought to be entered by pieces from those that ought to be entered by weight, and those that ought to be entered by measurement, because in these three ways business is conducted everywhere; certain things are reckoned by the bushel, others by the hundreds, others by the pound, others by the ounce, others by number, others by a *conto* (by single numbers) as leather goods or skins, others by the piece, as precious stones and fine pearls, etc.; so you will make a notation of each thing. These examples will serve as a guide for all the rest, etc.

Eleventh Item: I have in real estate: first, a house with so many stories, so many rooms, court yard, wells, garden, etc., situated in St. Apostle Street over the Canal, etc., adjoining such-and-such parties, etc., giving the names of the boundary line properties, making reference to the oldest and most reliable deeds, if there are any; and so, if you have more houses in different localities, you will enter them in a similar way.

Twelfth Item: I have so many pieces of land under cultivation (fields or *staiore* or *panora*) etc., entering them by the name according to the usage of the country where you are, saying where they are situated, etc., as, for instance, a field of so many *tavole,* or *canne,* or *pertiche,* or *bevolche,* etc., situated in such-and-such town in the Province of Padua or somewhere else, adjoining the land of so-and-so, giving all the boundary lines and referring to deeds or the description from the recorder's office, for which land you pay taxes in such-and-such municipality, which are worked by so-and-so with a yearly income of so much, and so on; you will enter all your possessions, etc., cattle, etc.

Thirteenth Item: I have in deposit with the Camera de l'Impresti (a bank), or with another bank in Venice, so many ducats; or with the parish of Canareggio, etc., or part in one parish and part in another giving the names under which they have been deposited, mentioning the book or the bank, the number of the page where your account is, and the name of the clerk who keeps said book, so that you can easily find your account when you go to get money, because in such offices they must keep very many accounts on account of the big crowd that sometimes goes there, and you must also see that dates are put down precisely so that you know when everything falls due and what the per cent is.

Fourteenth Item: I have so many debtors (*debitori*): one is so-and-so, who owes me (*me dee dare*—shall give me) so many ducats, and so on, giving the names of each one, putting down all annotations as to the names, their family names, and how much they owe you (*te debbono dore*—shall have to give you) and why; also whether there are any written papers or notarial instruments. In total I have so many ducats to collect, you will say, of good money, if the money is due from good people, otherwise you will say of bad money.

Fifteenth Item: I am debtor in total to the extent of so many ducats, etc. I owe so many to so-and-so. Here mention your creditors (*creditori*) one by one, writing down whether there are any documents or writings or instruments; if possible, mention the persons present when the debt was incurred, the reason, the time and the place, for any case that might arise in court or out of court.

CHAPTER 4.

Very Useful Admonition and Good Advice to the Good Merchant.

And so, as we have said, you shall enter diligently every thing that you have, whether personal property or real estate, one by one, even if there were ten thousand items, putting down the condition and nature, whether deposited or loaned, etc. You will have to mention each thing in proper order in the said Inventory with all marks, names, surnames—as far as possible—for things are never too clear to a merchant on account of the different things that may happen in business, as anybody in business knows. Right is the proverb which says: More bridges are necessary to make a good merchant than a lawyer can make. Who is the person that can count all the things that can happen to a merchant—on the sea, on land, in times of peace and abundance and times of war and famine, in times of health or pestilence? In these crises he must know what to do, in the marketplaces and in the fairs which are held now in one place and now in another. For this reason it is right to say that the merchant is like a rooster, which of all the animals (*animale*) is the most alert and in winter and summer keeps his night vigils and never rests. And they say of the nightingale that it sings throughout the whole night; however, this may be in the summer during the hot weather, but not during the winter, as experience shows. Also it is said that the head of the merchant has a hundred eyes, and still they are not sufficient for all he has to say or to do. These things are told by people who have had experience in them, such as the Venetians, Florentines, Genoans, Neapolitans, Milanese, people of Ancona, Brescia, Bragama, Aquila, Sienna, Lucca, Perugia, Urbino, Forosempronio, Cagli, Ugubio, Castello, Brogo, Fuligno, Pisa, Bologna, Ferrara, Mantua, Verona, Vincenza, Padua, Trani, Lecce, Bitonto, which are among the first cities of Italy and have the first place in commerce—especially the cities of Venice and Florence, which adopt rules that respond to any need. And well say the municipal laws: *Vigilantibus et non dormientibus jura subveniunt*—which means, The law helps those that are awake, not those that sleep. So in the divine functions of the Holy Church they sing that God promised the crown to the watchful ones, and this was the instruction that Virgil gave to Dante as to his son, in Canto 24 of the Inferno, where he exhorts him to the work by which one can reach the hill of virtue: Now, my son, it behooves that you quit your laziness, said my master, for he who lies on feathers or under covers will never amount to anything. Whoever spends his life in this way, he said, will leave on this earth the same trace as the smoke in the air or foam on the water, etc.; and another Italian poet admonishes us in the same way, saying: Work should not seem to you strange, for Mars never granted a victory to those that spent their time resting. And it is also very good to quote that sage who said to the lazy man to take the ant as an example; and the Apostle Paul says that no one will be worthy of the crown except he who shall fight valiantly for it.

I wanted to bring in these reminders for your own good, so that the daily care about your business would not seem heavy to you, especially the writing down everything and putting down every day everything that happens to you, as we shall unfold in the next chapters. But above all, remember God and your neighbor; never forget to attend to religious meditation every morning, for through this you will never lose your way, and by being charitable, you will not lose your riches, as the poet says: *Nec caritas, nec Missa minuit iter,* etc. And to this our Savior exhorts us in the book of St. Matthew, when he says: *Primum quaerite regulum dei, et haec omnia adiicietur vobis,* which means: Seek you, Christians, first the kingdom of God and then the other temporal and spiritual things you will easily obtain, because your Heavenly Father knows very well your needs, etc.

And this I hope will be sufficient as an instruction for you to make the Inventory, etc., and to do other things well.

Chapter 5.

Second Principal Part of this Treatise Named Disposition (Arrangement)— What Is Understood by it—What It Consists of in Business, and the Three Principal Books of the Merchant.

Comes now the second principal part of this treatise, which is called disposition, and of this I have to talk more at length than of the first part, in order to make it very clear. I will divide it in two parts. We shall call the one, *Corpo overo monte de sutto el trafico;* the other, *Corpor overo monte de botega* (Commerce in general, and Your store in particular).

First, we shall speak of commerce in general and its requirements. Immediately after the Inventory, you need three books to make the work proper and easy. One is called Memorandum (*Memoriale*), the second Journal (*Giornale*), and the third Ledger (*Quaderno*). Many, on account of their small business, use only the last two, that is, the journal and the ledger.

We shall speak about the first—that is, of the memorandum book, and thereafter of the other two, about their makeup, and how they should be kept. First of all, we will give the definition of the memorandum book.

Chapter 6.

Of the First Book, Which Is Called Memorandum Book (Memoriale), or Scrap Book (*Squarta Loglio*), or Blotter (*Vachetta*). What Is Understood by It and How Entries Should Be Made in It and by Whom.

The memorandum book, or, according to others, scrap book or blotter, is a book in which the merchant shall put down all his transactions, small or big, as they take place, day by day, hour by hour. In this book he will put down in detail everything that he sells or buys, and every other transaction without leaving out a job; who, what, when, where, mentioning everything to make it fully as clear as I have already said in talking about the Inventory, so that there is no necessity of saying it over again in detail. Many are accustomed to enter their inventory in this book, but it is not wise to let people see and know what you possess. It is not wise to enter all your personal property and real property in this book. This book is kept on account of volume of business, and in it entries should be made in the absence of the owner by his servants, or his women if there are any, for a big merchant never keeps his assistants idle; they are now here, now there, and at times both he and they are out, some at the market place and some attending a fair, leaving perhaps at home only the servants or the women who, perhaps, can barely write. These latter, in order not to send customers away, must sell, collect or buy, according to the orders left by the boss or owner, and they, as well as they can, must enter every transaction in this memorandum book, naming simply the money and weights which they know; they should note the various kinds of money that they may collect or take in or that they may give in exchange. As far as this book is concerned, it is not as important to transfer to standards the various kinds of coin handled as it is with the journal and ledger, as we will see hereafter.

The bookkeeper will put everything in order before he transcribes a transaction in the journal. In this way, when the owner comes back he will see all the transactions, and he may put them in a better order if he thinks necessary. Therefore, this book is very necessary to those who have a big business. It would be too much trouble to put down in a beautiful and orderly way every transaction immediately after it takes place, in books which are authentic and kept neat with care. You must make a mark on the cover of this book, as well as on all the others, so that you can distinguish them when, in the process of the business, the book is filled or has served for a certain period of time and you take another book. You must take another book when the first one has been used entirely, yet many are accustomed in different localities to balance annually these books although they are not full; and they do likewise

with the other books not yet mentioned, as you will see hereafter.

On the second book you should put another mark different from the first, so that at any time you can trace your transaction easily. For this purpose we use the date. Among true Christians there is the good custom to mark their first books with that glorious sign from which every enemy of the spiritual flees and before which all the inferno spirits justly tremble—that is, the holy cross, by which in our tender years we begin to learn to read. The books that follow, you may mark in alphabetical order, calling A the second, and B the third, etc. So that we call the first books with the Cross, or Memorandum with Cross, and the second Memorandum A, Journal A, Ledger A. The pages of each of these books ought to be marked for several reasons known to the merchant, although many say that this is not necessary for the Journal and Memorandum books. The transactions are entered day by day, one under the other, in such way that it may be easy to trace them. This would be all right if all the transactions of one day would not take more than one page; but, as we have seen, for many of the bigger merchants, not one, but several pages have to be used in one day. If some one would wish to do something crooked, he could tear out one of the pages and this fraud could not be discovered, as far as the dates are concerned, for the days would follow properly one after the other, and yet the fraud may have been committed. Therefore, for this and other reasons, it is always good to number and mark each single page in all the books of the merchants; the books kept in the house or kept in the store.

CHAPTER 7.

Of the Manner in Which in Many Places Mercantile Books are Authenticated, Why and by Whom.

All these books, according to the good customs of several countries where I have been, should be taken and shown to a certain mercantile officer such as the Consuls in the City of Perosa employ, and to him you should state that those

are the books in which you intend to write down, or somebody else write down for you, all your transactions in an orderly way; and also state in what kind of money the transactions therein should be entered—that is, whether in *lire di Picioli*, or in *lire di Grossi*, or in *ducats* and *lire*, etc., or in *florins* and *denari*, or in ounces, *tari*, *grani*, *denari*, etc. The good merchant should put down these things always on the first page of his book, and if afterwards the handwriting should be done by somebody else than the one stated at the beginning of the book, this should be recorded at the office of the said officer. The clerk should mention all this in the records of the said officer—that is, on such and such a day you presented such and such books, marked with such and such mark, which books are named, one so-and-so, the other so-and-so, etc.; of which books one has so many pages, another so many, etc., which books you said would be kept by you or by so-and-so; but that it may be that in said Memorandum Book or Scrap Book or Blotter, some person of your family might enter said transaction, as explained before. In this case, the said clerk shall write down on the first page of your books, in his own handwriting, the name of the said officer, and will attest to the truth of everything and shall attach the seal of that office to make the books authentic for any case in court when they might be produced.

This custom ought to be commended exceedingly; also the places where the custom is followed. Many keep their books in duplicate. They show one to the buyer and one to the seller, and this is very bad, because in this way they commit perjury. By presenting books to the said officer, one cannot easily lie or defraud. These books, after they have been carefully marked and authenticated, shall be kept in the name of God in your own place, and you are then ready to start your business. But first you shall enter in an orderly way in your Journal all the different items of the Inventory in the way that I will tell you later. But first you must understand how entries should be made in this Memorandum Book.

CHAPTER 8.

How Entries Should be Made in the Said Memorandum Book, and Examples of the Same.

We have said already, if you will remember, that any one in your family can make entries in the said Memorandum Book, or Scrap Book or Blotter. Therefore, it cannot be fully stated how the entries should be made, because some members of your family will understand and some will not. But the common custom is this: Let us say, for instance, that you bought several pieces of cloth—for instance, 20 white *bresciani*, at 12 ducats apiece. It will be enough simply to make the entry in this way: On this day we have or I have bought from Mr. Filippo d'Rufoni of Brescia, 20 pieces of white *bresciani*. These goods are at Mr. Stefano Tagliapietra's place; one piece is so long, according to the agreement, and paid for at so many ducats, etc., marked with such and such number, etc. You mention whether the cloth is *a trelici*, or *a la piana*, wide or narrow, fine or medium, whether the Bergamo kind, or Vincenza, or Verona, or Padua, or Florence, or Mantua. Also you have to state here whether the transaction was made through a broker and whether it was made in cash entirely or part only in cash and part on time, stating the time, or whether it was part in cash and part in trade. In this case you must specify the things that were given in exchange, number, weight, measurement, and the price of the bushel or of the piece, or of the pound, etc., or whether the transaction was all by payment on time, stating the time when the payment should be made, whether on *Galia de Barutto*, or on *Galia de Fiandra*, or on the return day of a ship, or on the date of some fair, or other festivity, as for instance, on the next harvest day or on next Easter, or on next Christmas, or on Resurrection day or Carnival day, etc., according to what was understood in the transaction. Finally, I must say that in this memorandum book nothing should be omitted. If it were possible, it should be noted what many others had said during the transaction because, as we have said about the Inventory, the merchant never can be too plain.

CHAPTER 9.

Of Nine Ways in Which the Merchant Usually Buys, and the Goods Which It Is More or Less Necessary to Buy on Time.

Since we are talking about buying, you must know that usually you can make your purchase in nine ways—that is: either in cash or on time; or by exchanging something, which is usually called a trade; or partly in cash and partly on time; or partly in cash and partly by trading and partly on time; or by draft (*assegnatione de ditta*); or partly by draft and partly on time, or partly by draft and partly by trading. In these nine ways it is customary to make purchases. If you would make your purchases in some other way you must state in your memorandum book with precision the way that you have made the purchase, or have somebody else do it for you, and you will do well.

You buy on time usually when you buy *guati* or oats, wines, salt, remnants from a butcher shop, and fats. In these cases, the seller promises to the buyer to give all the *guati* that he will have in that season. The butcher will sell you and promises to give you all the hearts, skins, fat, etc., that he will have during that year. This kind for so much a pound, that kind for so much a pound, etc., and similarly for the fat of beef, of mutton, etc.; the black skins of mutton at so much apiece; and the white mutton skins, etc., and so with the oats, or *guati*; you must specify the price for each bushel or other measure and the kind of oats as is the custom at Chiusi de Perugia. In buying *guati* you must see whether they are of our city San Sepolero, or Mercatello, or Sant' Angelo, or Citta de Costello, or Forli, etc.

In this memorandum book, whether kept by you or by others, you must mention every single point. You state the things in a simple way as they happened, and then the skillful bookkeeper, after four or five days, or eight days, may enter all these transactions from the said memorandum book into the Journal, day by day; with this difference, though, that it is not necessary for him to put down in the Journal all the long lines of words that were used in the memorandum book, because it is sufficient to put them down in an abridged way, and besides, references should always be made from one book to the other. Those that are used to keeping these three books in the way we have said never must enter one thing in the Journal if they have not first entered it in the memorandum book. This will be enough as to the arrangement of the said memorandum book, whether it is kept by you or others. Remember that there are as many ways to buy as to sell; therefore, I need not explain the ways of selling, because you knowing of the ways of buying can understand the selling.

CHAPTER 10.

The Second Important Mercantile Book Which Is Called Journal; What It Is, and How It Should Be Kept in an Orderly Way.

The second common mercantile book is called the Journal (*Giornale*) which, as we have said, must have the same mark that is on the memorandum book and the pages marked as we have said in talking of the memorandum book.

Always at the beginning of each page you must put down the date, and then, one after another, enter all the different items of your inventory.

In this Journal, which is your private book, you may fully state all that you own in personal or real property, always making reference to the inventory papers which you or others may have written and which are kept in some box, or chest, or *filza*, or *mazzo*, or pouch, as is customary and as is usually done with letters and other instruments of writing.

The different items entered in the said Journal ought to be entered there in a neater and more systematic way, not too many or too few words, as I will show in the few following examples. But first of all you must know that there are two words or expressions (*termini*) necessary in the keeping of a Journal, used according to the custom of the great City of Venice, and of these I will now speak.

CHAPTER 11.

The Two Expressions Used in the Journal, Especially in Venice, the One Called "Per," and the Other "A," and What Is Understood by Them.

As we have said, there are two expressions (*termini*) used in the said Journal; the one is called "per," and the other is called "a," each of which has a meaning of its own. "Per" indicates the debtor (*debitore*) one or more as the case may be, and "a." creditor (*creditore*), one or more as the case may be. Never is any item entered in the Journal which also is to be entered in the Ledger, without preceding it by one of the two expressions. At the beginning of each entry, we always provide "per," because, first, the debtor must be given, and immediately after the creditor, the one separated from the other by two little slanting parallels (*virgolette*), thus, //, as the example below will show.

CHAPTER 12.

How the Entry Should be Made into the Journal by Means of the Debit and the Credit, With Many Examples. The Two Other Expressions Used in the Ledger, the One Called "Cash," and the Other "Capital," and What Should be Understood by Them.

With the name of God you shall begin to enter into your Journal the first item of your Inventory, that is, the quantity of cash that you possess, and in order to know how to enter this Inventory into the Ledger and Journal, you must make use of the two other expressions (*termini*); the one called "cash" (*cassa*) and the other "capital" (*cavedale*). By cash is understood your property or pocketbook (*borscia:* from *bursa,* or bag); by capital is understood the entire amount of what you now possess.

This capital must always be placed as creditor (*creditore*) in all the principal mercantile Ledgers and Journals and the cash always debtor. Never at any time in the management of your business may cash be creditor, but only debtor unless it balances. For if, in balancing your book, you find that cash is in the credit, it would denote a mistake in the book, as I will remind you hereafter at its proper place. Now this entry ought to be made in the Journal, and ought to be arranged in this way:

Example of Making an Entry in the Journal.

FIRST. November 8, MCCCCLXXXXIII in Venice.

Line 1

Credit 2

Line to the debit.

Per cash // A—Capital of myself so and so, etc. In cash I have at present, in gold and coin, silver and copper of different coinage as it appears in the first sheet of the Inventory in cash, etc., in total so many gold ducats and so many silver ducats. All this is our Venetian money; that is counting 24 *grossi* per ducat and 32 *picioli* per *grosso* in gold is worth:

L_____ (*Lire*), S_____ (*Soldi*), G_____ (*Grossi*), P_____ (*Picioli*).

For the second item you shall say this way:

Second. Per mounted and unmounted precious stones of several kinds //. A capital ditto for so many mounted *belassi*, etc., weighing, etc., and so many sapphires, etc., and rubies and diamonds, etc., as the said Inventory shows to which, according to current prices I give these values: *Belassi* worth, etc.; and so you shall state a price for each kind in total that are worth so many ducats. Their value is:

L_____, S_____, G_____, P_____

After you have once named the day, the debtor and the creditor, you may say for brevity—if you don't make any other entry in between: On the day ditto, per ditto, // a ditto.

Third. Per silver //. A ditto—by which capital is understood—for several kinds of silver which at present I possess—that is, wash basins so many, so many coppers, so many cups, so many *pironi*, and so many *cosilier*, etc., weighing in total so much. Their value is:

L_____, S_____, G_____, P_____

You shall give all the details in entering these items for everything as you have them in the Inventory, giving to each thing a customary price. Make the prices rather higher than lower; for instance, if it seems to you that they are worth 20, you put down 24, so that you can make a larger profit; and so you will enter everything, putting down for each thing its weight, number, value, etc.

Fourth. Per woolen clothes //. A ditto, for so many clothes of such and such color, etc., of such and such style, etc., lined, etc., new or used, etc., for myself or for my wife or for my children, I give the total value, according to the current price, so many ducats. And for cloaks, so many of such and such color, etc., and so on, for all the other clothes:

L_____, S_____, G_____, P_____

Fifth. Per linen //. A ditto, for so many bed sheets, etc., and put down their number and value as the Inventory shows:

L_____, S_____, G_____, P_____

Sixth. Per feather beds //. A ditto, etc., for so many feathers—and here put down all that the Inventory shows, number and value:

L_____, S_____, G_____, P_____

Seventh. Per ginger //. A ditto, for so many packages, etc., giving all the details that are contained in the Inventory, number, value, according to common prices, etc., so many ducats:

L_____, S_____, G_____, P_____

In this way you can continue to enter all the other items, making a separate entry for each different lot, and as we have said before, giving the current prices, number, marks, weights, as the Inventory shows. Indicate only one kind of money, to which you reduce the estimated values. In the column for the amounts, only one kind of money should appear, as it would not be proper to have appear in this column different kinds of money.

You shall close each entry in the Journal by drawing a line from the end of the last word of your descriptive narrative (explanation) up to the column of the figures. You shall do the same in the Memorandum book, and as you transfer an entry into the Journal from the Memorandum book, you shall draw a single diagonal line (*una sola riga a traverso*) through it in this way /; this will show that this item has been entered (*posta*) in the Journal.

If you should not draw this line through the entry, you shall check off (*lanciarai*) the first letter of the beginning of the entry, or the last letter, as we have done at the beginning of this; or otherwise you shall use some other sign by which you will understand that the said item has been transferred into the Journal. Although you may use many various and diverse expressions or marks, nevertheless you must try to use the common ones which are used by the other merchants, so that it will not look as if you would deviate from the usual mercantile custom.

CHAPTER 13.

Third and Last Principal Mercantile Book Called the Ledger. How It Is to Be Kept. Its Alphabet (Index), and How This Can Be Kept Single and Double.

After you have made all your entries in the Journal in an orderly way, you must transfer them to the third book, called Ledger (*Quaderno Grande, i.e.,* big book). This Ledger contains usually twice as many pages as the Journal. In it there must be an alphabet or repertory or *"trovarello"* (finding key) according to some; the Florentines call it *"Stratto."* In this index you shall write down all the debtors and creditors in the order of their initial letter, together with the number of their respective pages. You shall put the names that begin with A in the A page, etc.

This Ledger, as we have said before, must bear the same sign or mark that is on the Journal and Memorandum book; its Pages should be numbered; and at the top at the right margin as well as at the left margin, you shall put down the date. On the first Page you shall enter cash as debtor. As in the Journal, so in the Ledger, cash should be entered on the first page. It is customary to reserve the whole of the first Page to cash, and not to enter anything else either under the debit (in dare) or the credit (in havere). This because the cash entries are more numerous than all others on account of almost continuously paying out and receiving money; therefore, it needs much space. This Ledger must be ruled, and should have as many lines as there are kinds of money that you want to enter. If you enter lire, soldi, denari and picioli, you shall draw four lines, and in front of lire you shall draw another line in order to put in the number of the pages of the Ledger debit and credit entries. Before these lines you shall draw two more lines wherein to mark the dates as you go on, as you have seen in the other books, so that you may find each item quickly. This book shall also bear the sign of the cross as the others.

* * *

Things Which Should Be Entered in the Books of the Merchants.

Of all the cash that you might have, if it is your own—that is, that you might have earned at different times in the past, or which might have been bequeathed to you by your dead relatives or given you as a gift from some Prince, you shall make yourself creditor (*creditore te medesima*), and make cash debitor. As to all jewelry or goods which might be your own—that is, that you may have got through business or that might have been left you through a will or given to you as a present, you must value them in cash and make as many accounts as there are things and make each debitor by saying: For so many, etc., of which I find myself possessed on this day, so many *denari*, posted credit entry at such and such page; and then you make creditor your account (*tuo conto*), that is yourself (*medesimo*), with the amount of each of these entries. But remember these entries should not be for less than ten ducats each, as small things of little value are not entered in the Ledger.

Of the real property that you might own, as houses, lands, stores you make the cash debitor and estimate their value at your discretion in cash, and you make creditor yourself or your personal account (*tuo sopradette conto*). Then you make debitor an account of that special property by giving the value, as I have said above, and make yourself creditor because, as I have told you, all entries must have three things: The date, the value in cash, and the reason.

If you should buy merchandise or anything else, partly for cash and partly on time, you shall make that special merchandise debitor, and make a creditor of the party from whom you bought it on time and under the conditions that you might have agreed upon; as, for instance, one-third in cash and the rest in six months. After this you will have to make another entry—that is, make a debitor of the party from whom you bought it for the amount of the cash that you have given him for that one-third, and make creditor cash or the bank which might have paid that much for you.

If you should sell any merchandise or anything else, you should proceed as above with the exception that you should proceed in the opposite way—that is, where I told you that when you bought you should make the merchandise debitor, when you sell you will have to make your merchandise a creditor and charge the cash account if it is sold for cash, or charge the bank that might have promised the payment. And if you make a sale on time, you will have to charge the party to whom you sold it on time, and if you make the sale partly for cash and partly on time, you shall proceed as I have shown you in explaining about the buying.

If you should give merchandise in exchange, for instance, let us say I have sold 1,000 pounds of English wool in exchange for pepper—that is,

for 2,000 pounds of pepper—I ask, how shall we make this entry in the Ledger? You shall do as follows: Estimate what the value of the pepper is, at your discretion, in cash. Now let us say that you estimated 12 ducats per hundred; the 2,000 pounds would be worth 240 ducats. Therefore, you shall make the wool a creditor with 240 ducats, for which amount you have sold it. This is the manner that you should follow in all the trade entries. If you have received 2,000 pounds of pepper valued at 240 ducats, you shall make the pepper a debitor and say: Said pepper debitor on this day, see page, etc., etc.

If you should loan cash to some of your friends, you shall charge the friend to whom you have given it and credit cash. If you should borrow cash from some friend, you will have to debit cash and credit your friend.

If you have received 8 or 10 or 20 ducats in order to insure a ship or a galley, or anything else, you should credit the account "ship insurance," and explain all about it—how, when and where, and how much per cent.; and shall charge the cash account.

If anybody should send you any goods with instructions to sell them or exchange them on commission, I say that you have to charge in the Ledger that special merchandise belonging to so and so with the freight, or duty, or for storage, and credit the cash account. You shall credit the cash for all cash that you have to pay on account of goods: for instance, cash paid for transportation or duty, or brokerage, etc., and charge the account of that special goods for that which you have paid in money.

Things Which Should Be Recorded in a Record Book (*Recordanze*) of the Merchant.

All the house and store goods that you may find yourself possessed of—these should be put down in order—that is, all the things made of iron by itself, leaving space enough to make additions if necessary; also leaving room to mark in the margin the things that might be lost or sold or given as presents or spoiled. But I don't mean small things of little value.

Make a record of all the brass things separately, as I have said, and then a record of the tin things, and then the wooden things, and

copper things, and then the silver things and gold things, always leaving enough space between each class so that you may add something if necessary, and to put down a memorandum of any object that might be missing.

All sureties or obligations or promises of payment that you might make for some friend, explaining clearly everything.

All goods or other things that might be left with you in custody, or that you might borrow from some friend, as well as all the things that other friends of yours might borrow from you.

All conditional transactions—that is, purchases and sales, as, for instance, a contract that you shall send me by the next ship coming from England, so many *cantara* of *woll di li mistri,* on condition that it is good; and when I receive it I will pay you so much per *cantara* or by the hundred, or otherwise; I will send you in exchange so many *cantara* of cotton.

All houses, lands, stores or jewels that you might rent at so many ducats and so many lire per year. And when you collect the rent, then that money should be entered in the Ledger, as I have told you.

If you should lend some jewels, silver or gold vase to some friend, say, for instance, for eight or fifteen days, things like this should not be entered in the Ledger, but should be recorded in this record book, because in a few days, you will get them back. In the same way, if somebody should lend you something like the things mentioned, you should not make any entry in the Ledger, but put down a little memorandum in the record book, because in a short time you will have to give it back. . . .

How *Lire, Soldi, Denari* and *Picioli,* etc., should be written down as abbreviations.

Lire; Soldi; Denari; Picioli; Libbre; Once; Danarpesi; Grani; Carati; Ducati; Florin larghi. ◆

NOTE

The words in parentheses are the authors, as also the punctuation and paragraphing, as the original is extremely deficient in these. The words in italics are copied exact from the original.

HOW THE DEBIT (LEDGER) ENTRIES ARE MADE.

MCCCCLXXXXIII. Lodovico, son of Piero Forestani, shall give on the 14th day of November, 1493, L 44, S 1, D 8, for cash loaned, posted cash shall have at page 2:

L 44, S 1, D 8

And on the 18th ditto, L 18, S 11, D 6, which we promised to pay for him to Martino, son of Piero Foraboschi at his pleasure, posted said shall have at page 2:

L 18, S 11, D 6

Cash in hands of Simone, son of Alessio Bombeni, shall give on Nov. 14, 1493, for L 62, S 13, D 2, for Francesco, son of Antonio Cavalcanti, page 2:

L 62, S 13, D 6

Martino, son of Piero Foraboschi, shall give on Nov. 20, 1493, for L 18, S 11, D 6, taken by him in cash, posted Cash at page 2:

L 18, S 11, D 6

Francesco, son of Antonio Cavalcanti, shall give, on Nov. 12, 1493, L 20, S 4, D 2, which he promised to pay to us at our pleasure for Lodovico, son of Pietro Forestani; page 2:

L 20, S 4, D 2

HOW THE CREDIT (LEDGER) ENTRIES ARE MADE.

MCCCCLXXXXIII. Lodovico, son of Piero Forestani, shall have, on Nov. 22, 1493, for L 20, S 4, D 2, for part payment. And for him Francesco, son of Antonio Cavalcanti, promised to pay it to us at our pleasure; posted shall give at page 2:

L 20, S 4, D 2

Cash in hands of Simone, son of Alessio Bombeni, shall have, on Nov. 14, 1493, for L 44, S 1, D 8, from Lodovico Pietro Forestani, L 44, S 1, D 8; and on Nov. 22, 1493, L 18, S 11, D 6, to Martino, son of Piero Forbaschi, page 2:

L 18, S 11, D 6

Martino, son of Piero Foraboschi, shall have on Nov. 18, 1493, for L 18, S 11, D 6, which we promised to pay him at his pleasure for Lodovico, son of Pietro Forestani; posted shall give entry at p. 8:

L 44, S 1, D 8

Francesco, son of Antonio Cavalcanti, shall have on Nov. 14, 1493, for L 62, S 13, D 6, which he brought himself in cash; posted cash shall give at page 2:

L 62, S 13, D 6

QUESTIONS

1. According to Pacioli, what are the requirements of business?

2. What are the four main elements of a good recordkeeping system for business?

3. What animal should the merchant emulate and why?

Selection from: *The Business Guide*

J. L. Nichols (1851–1895) self-published Naperville, Ill 1893

CASH BOOK.

1891			Cash Rec'd		Cash Paid	
May	2	Received for 500 bush. Corn..................	200	00		
"	5	Paid Hired Man............................ ..			20	00
"	6	Paid Interest........ ...			150	40
"	10	Received for 22 Hogs.......................	208	90		
"	12	Paid for Groceries........................			11	90
"	15	Received for 20 doz. Eggs.................	2	00		
"	19	Received for One Cow......	20	00		
"	23	Paid for Coal.			16	00
"	27	Paid for Lumber...........			102	65
June	1	Received for Butter.......................	9	25		
"	2	Received one Load of Hay............	6	30		
"	10	Balance Cash on Hand...			145	50
		NOTE :—To find the balance in cash add up the amount received and subtract from that the amount paid out and the result will always equal the cash on hand.	446	45	446	45

How to Keep Accounts

Rules for Keeping Accounts.

The following are suggested as simple forms for keeping accounts for the use of those whose business or taste does not require a more elaborate form of book-keeping:—

Always charge or "debit" a person for what he may get, "credit" him for what you receive from him. The word, "To," prefixed to an entry, indicates a debit, and the word "By," a credit.

The books necessary are two, called Day Book and Ledger. In the Day Book should be entered, in diary form, every transaction as it occurs, using as simple and concise wording as possible to express all the facts.

Accounts may be opened with "Cash," "Stock," "Merchandise," "Bills Payable," "Bills Receivable," "Interest," "Profit and Loss," "Expense," etc.; and the farmer may open accounts with each field of his farm, as "Field No. 1," "Field No. 2," "Orchard," "Meadow," etc., charging each field with the amount of labor and material expended upon it, and crediting it with its products. He may also keep an account with his own cows, pigs, fowls, etc., and thus at any time tell at a glance the profits or losses of each department of his business.

THE ETERNAL STOREHOUSE OF JAPAN [NIPPON EITAIGURA]

Ihara Saikaku (1642–1693)

THE TYCOON OF ALL TENANTS

"This is to certify that the person named Fuji-ichi, tenant in a house belonging to Hishiya Chozaemon, is to my certain knowledge the possessor of one thousand *kamme* in silver . . ."

Such would be the form of testimonial when Fuji-ichi sought new lodgings. It was his proud claim that in the whole wide world there was no millionaire quite like himself. For although he was worth a thousand *kamme*, he lived in a rented house no more than four yards wide. In this way he became the talk of Kyoto. However, one day he accepted a house as surety for a loan of thirty-eight *kamme*; in the course of time, as the interest mounted, the surety itself became forfeit; and for the first time Fuji-ichi became a property owner. He was much vexed at this. Up to now he had achieved distinction as "the millionaire in lodgings," but now that he had a house of his own, he was commonplace as his money in itself was mere dust by comparison with what lay in the strong rooms of the foremost merchants of Kyoto.

Fuji-ichi was a clever man, and his substantial fortune was amassed in his own lifetime. But first and foremost he was a man who knew his own mind, and this was the basis of his success. In addition to carrying on his regular business, he kept a separate ledger, bound from odd scraps of paper, in which, as he sat all day in his shop, pen in hand, he entered a variety of chance information. As the clerks from the money exchanges passed by he noted down the market ratio of copper and gold; he inquired about the current quotations of the rice brokers; he sought information from druggists' and haberdashers' assistants on the state of the market at Nagasaki; for the latest news on the prices of ginned cotton, salt, and saké, he noted the various days on which the liyoto dealers received dispatches from the Edo branch shops. Every day a thousand things were entered in his book, and people came to Fuji-ichi if they were ever in doubt. He became a valuable asset to the citizens of Kyoto.

Invariably his dress consisted of an unlined vest next to his skin, and on top of that a cotton kimono, stuffed on occasion with three times the usual amount of padding. He never put on more than one layer of kimono. It was he who first started the wearing of detachable cuffs on the sleeves—a device which was both fashionable and economical. His socks were of deerskin and his clogs were fitted with high leather soles, but even so he was careful not to walk too quickly along the hard main roads. Throughout life his only silk garments were of pongee, dyed plain dark blue. There was one, it is true, which he had dyed a persistently undisguisable seaweed brown, but this was a youthful error of judgment, and he was to regret it for the next twenty years. For his ceremonial dress he had no settled crests, being content with a three-barred circle or a small conventional whirl, but even during the summer airing time he was careful to keep them from direct contact with the floor. His pantaloons were of hemp, and his starched jacket of an even tougher variety of the same cloth, so that they remained correctly creased no matter how many times he wore them.

When there was a funeral procession which his whole ward was obliged to join, he followed it perforce to the cemetery, but coming back he hung behind the others and, on the path across the moor at Rokuhara, he and his apprentices pulled up sour herbs by the roots.

"Dried in the shade," he explained, "they make excellent stomach medicine."

He never passed by anything which might be of use. Even if he stumbled he used the opportunity to pick up stones for fire-lighters, and tucked them in his sleeve. The head of a household, if he is to keep the smoke rising steadily from his kitchen, must pay attention to a thousand things like this.

Fuji-ichi was not a miser by nature. It was merely his ambition to serve as a model for others in the management of everyday affairs. Even in the days before he made his money he never had the New Year rice cakes prepared in his own lodgings. He considered that to bother over the various utensils, and to hire a man to pound the rice, was too much trouble at such a busy time of the year; so he placed an order with the rice-cake dealer in front of the Great Buddha. However, with his intuitive grasp of good business, he insisted on paying by weight—so much per pound. Early one morning, two days before the New Year, a porter from the cake-maker, hurrying about his rounds, arrived before Fuji-ichi's shop and, setting down his load, shouted for someone to receive the order. The newly pounded cakes, invitingly arrayed, were as fresh and warm as spring itself. The master, pretending not to hear, continued his calculations on the abacus, and the cake-man, who begrudged every moment at this busy time of the year, shouted again and again. At length a young clerk, anxious to demonstrate his businesslike approach, checked the weight of the cakes on the large scales with a show of great precision, and sent the man away.

About two hours later Fuji-ichi said: "Has anyone taken in the cakes which arrived just now?"

"The man gave them to me and left long ago," said the clerk.

"Useless fellow!" cried Fuji-ichi. "I expect people in my service to have more sense! Don't you realize that you took them in before they had cooled off?"

He weighed them again, and to everyone's astonishment their weight had decreased. Not one of the cakes had been eaten, and the clerk stood gazing at them in open-mouthed amazement.

It was the early summer of the following year. The local people from the neighborhood of the Eastern Temple had gathered the first crop of eggplants in wicker baskets and brought them to town for sale. "Eat young egg-plants and live seventy-five days longer" goes the saying, and they are very popular. The price was fixed at two coppers for one egg-plant, or three coppers for two, which meant that everybody bought two.

But Fuji-ichi bought only one, at two coppers, because—as he said—"With the one copper I now have in pocket I can buy any number of larger ones when the crop is fully grown."

That was the way he kept his wits about him, and he seldom made a mistake.

In an empty space in his grounds he planted an assortment of useful trees and flowers such as willow, holly, laurel, peach, iris, and bead-beans. This he did as an education for his only daughter. Morning-glory started to grow of its own accord along the reed fence, but Fuji-ichi said that if it was a question of beauty such short-lived things were a loss, and in their place he planted runner-beans, whose flowers he thought an equally fine sight. Nothing delighted him more than watching over his daughter. When the young girl grew into womanhood he had a marriage screen constructed for her, and since he considered that one decorated with views of Kyoto would make her restless to visit the places she had not yet seen, and that illustrations of "The Tale of Genji" or "The Tales of Ise" might engender frivolous thoughts, he had the screen painted with busy scenes of the silver and copper mines at Tada. He composed Instructional Verses on the subject of economy and made his daughter recite them aloud. Instead of sending her to a girls' temple school, he taught her how to write himself, and by the time he had reached the end of his syllabus, he had made her the most finished and accomplished girl in Kyoto. Imitating her father in his thrifty ways, after the age of eight she spilt no more ink on her sleeves, played no longer with dolls at the Doll Festival, nor joined in the dancing at Bon. Every day she combed her own hair and bound it in a simple bun. She never sought others' help in her private affairs. She mastered the art of stretching silk padding and learned to fit it perfectly to the length and breadth of each garment. Since young girls can do all this if properly disciplined, it is a mistake to leave them to do as they please.

Once, on the evening of the seventh day of the New Year, some neighbors asked leave to send their sons to Fuji-ichi's house to seek advice on how to become millionaires. Lighting the lamp in the sitting room, Fuji-ichi set his daughter to wait, bidding her let him know when she heard a noise at the private door from the street. The young girl, doing as she was told with charming grace, first carefully lowered the wick in the lamp. Then, when she heard the voices of the visitors, she raised the wick again and retired to the scullery. By the time the three guests had seated themselves the grinding of an earthenware mortar could be heard from the kitchen, and the sound fell with pleasant promise on their ears. They speculated on what was in store for them.

"Pickled whaleskin soup?" hazarded the first.

"No. As this is our first visit of the year, it ought to be rice-cake gruel," said the second.

The third listened carefully for some time, and then confidently announced that it was noodle soup. Visitors always go through this amusing performance. Fuji-ichi then entered and talked to the three of them on the requisites for success.

"Why is it that today is called the Day of the Seven Herbs?" one asked him.

"That was the beginning of economy in the Age of the Gods: it was to teach us the ingredients of a cheap stew."

"Why do we leave a salted bream hanging before the God of the Kitchen Range until the sixth moon?" asked another.

"That is so that when you look at it at meal times you may get the feeling of having eaten fish without actually doing so."

Finally he was asked the reason for using thick chopsticks at the New Year.

"That is so that when they become soiled they can be scraped white again, and in this way one pair will last the whole year."

"As a general rule," concluded Fuji-ichi, "give the closest attention to even the smallest details. Well now, you have kindly talked with me from early evening, and it is high time that refreshments were served. But not to provide refreshments is one way of becoming a millionaire. The noise of the mortar which you heard when you first arrived was the pounding of starch for the covers of the Account Book." ◆

Translated By G. W. Sargent

QUESTIONS

1. According to Saikaku's character Fuji-ichi, what traits should a businessperson possess if he or she wishes to do well financially?

2. What was the point of the story about the young men who visited Fuji-ichi?

FROM *THE COMPLEAT ENGLISH TRADESMAN*

Daniel Defoe (1660–1731)

CHAP. XXXI.

*Of the tradesman's keeping his books, and cast-
ing up his shop. A remarkable story of a man
keeping his accounts in a large business, without being able to write. The necessity of exact
bookkeeping. Of balancing the cash-book. Cautions on this head necessary to be observed.
Exact bookkeeping indicates a man is determined to thrive, if possible; as negligence in this
respect denotes the contrary. The credit a man
gains in the former case, even though he proves
unfortunate. Numberless lawsuits preventable
by exact bookkeeping. Next to taking care of his
soul, a tradesman should take care of his books.
The comfort of so doing in case of sudden ill-
ness, &c.*

It was an ancient and laudable custom with
tradesmen in England, once a year to balance
their accounts of stock, and of profit and loss;
by which means they could always tell whether
they went backwards or forwards in the world;
and this is called casting up shop; and indeed
this is so necessary a thing to be done, that it is
always to me a bad sign when it is omitted, and
looks as if the tradesman was afraid of entering
into a close examination of his affairs.

As casting up his shop is of great importance to a tradesman, so he must cast up his
books too, or else it carries a very ominous face
with it.

Now, in order to do this effectually once a
year, it is needful the tradesman should keep
his books always in order; his day-book duly
posted, his cash duly balanced, and every one's
accounts always fit for a view; he that delights
in his trade, will delight in his books; and, as I
have already laid it down for a rule, that he
who will thrive must diligently attend his shop
or warehouse, and take up his delight there, so
I say now, he must also diligently keep his
books, or else he will never know whether he
thrives or not.

Exact keeping his books is one essential
part of a tradesman's prosperity; the books are
the register of his estate, the index of his stock;

all the tradesman has in the world must be
found in these three articles, or some of them;—

Goods in the shop; money in cash; debts
abroad.

The shop will at any time show the first of
these upon a small stop to cast it up; the cash-
chest and bill-box will show the second at
demand; and the ledger, when posted, will
show the last; so that a tradesman can at any
time, at a week's notice, cast up all these three;
and then examine his accounts to take the balance, which is a real trying what he is worth in
the world.

It cannot be satisfactory to any tradesman
to let his books go unsettled, and uncast up; for
then he knows nothing of himself, or of his circumstances in the world; the books can tell
him at any time what his condition is, and will
satisfy him what is the condition of his debts
abroad.

In order to his regular keeping his books,
several things may be said very useful for the
tradesman to consider:—

1. Everything done in the whole circumfer-
   ence of his trade must be set down in a
   book, except the retail trade; and this is
   clear, if the goods are not in bulk, then the
   money is in cash, and so the substance will
   be always found either there, or somewhere else; for if it is neither in the shop,
   nor in the cash, nor in the books, it must be
   stolen or lost.

2. As everything done must be set down in
   the books, so it should be done at the very
   time of it; all goods sold must be entered
   into the books before they are sent out of
   the house; goods sent away, and not
   entered, are goods lost; and he that does
   not keep an exact account of what goes out
   and comes in, can never swear to his books,
   or prove his debts, if occasion calls for it.

That tradesman who keeps no books, may
depend upon it he will ere long keep no trade,
unless he resolves also to give no credit; he

that gives no trust, and takes no trust, either by wholesale or retail, and keeps his cash all himself, may indeed go on without keeping any book at all, and has nothing to do, when he would know his estate, but to cast up his shop and his cash, and see how much they amount to, and that is his whole and neat estate; for, as he owes nothing, so nobody is in debt to him, and his estate is in his shop; but I suppose the tradesman who trades wholly thus, is not yet born.

A tradesman's books, like a Christian's conscience, should always be kept clean and neat; and he that is not careful of both, will give but a sad account of himself either to God or man.

I heard of a tradesman indeed that could not write, and yet he supplied the defect with so many ingenious knacks of his own, to secure the account of what people owed him, and was so exact in doing it, and then took such care to have but very short accounts with anybody, that he brought this method to be every way an equivalent to writing; and, he was often told, with half the study and application that those things cost him, he might have learned to write, and keep books too; he made notches upon sticks for all the middling sums, and scored with chalk for lesser things; he had drawers for every particular customer's name, which his memory supplied; for he knew every particular drawer, though he had a great many, as well as if their faces had been painted upon them; he had innumerable figures to signify what he would have written, if he could; and his shelves and boxes always put people in mind of the Egyptian hieroglyphics, and nobody understood anything of them but himself.

It was an odd thing to see him, when a country chap came up to settle accounts with him; he would go to a drawer directly, among such a number as was amazing; in that drawer was nothing but little pieces of split sticks, like laths with chalk marks on them, all as unintelligible as the signs of the zodiac to an old schoolmistress who teaches the hornbook; every stick had notches on one side for single pounds, on the other side for tens of pounds, and so higher; and the length and breadth also

had its signification, and the colour too; for they were painted in some places with one colour, and in some places with another; by which he knew what goods had been delivered for the money; and his way of casting up was very remarkable; for he knew nothing of figures, but he kept six spoons in a place on purpose, near his counter, which he took out when he had occasion to cast up any sum, and laying the spoons on a row before him, he counted upon them thus:—

One, two, three, and another; one odd spoon, and t'other.

By this he told up to six; if he had any occasion to tell any further he began again, as we do after the number ten in our ordinary numeration; and by this method, and running them up very thick, he would count any number under thirty-six, which was six spoons of six spoons; and then by the strength of his head he could number as many more as he pleased, multiplying them always by sixes, but never higher.

This tradesman was indeed a country shopkeeper, but he was so considerable a dealer that he became mayor of the place which he lived in; and his posterity have been very considerable traders there ever since, and they show their great grandfather's six counting spoons and his hieroglyphics to this day.

After some time, the old tradesman bred up two of his sons to his business, and the young men, having learned to write, brought books into the counting-house, things their father had never used before; but the old man kept to his old method for all that, and would cast up a sum, and make up an account, with his spoons and his drawers, as soon as they could with their pen and ink, if it was not too full of small articles; and that he had always avoided in his business.

However, this evidently shows the necessity of book-keeping to a tradesman; and the very nature of the thing evidences also, that it must be done with the greatest exactness. He that does not keep his books exactly, and so as that he may depend upon them for charging his debtors, had better keep no books at all; but, like my shopkeeper, score and notch everything; for as books well kept make business regular, easy, and certain, so books neglected turn all into confusion, and leave the tradesman in a wood, which he can never get out of without damage and loss. If ever his dealers know that his books are ill kept, they play upon him, and impose horrid forgeries and falsities upon him; whatever he omits they catch at, and leave it out; whatever they put upon him, he is bound to yield to; so that, in short, as books well kept are the security of a tradesman's estate, and the ascertaining of his debts, so books ill kept will assist every knavish customer and chapman to cheat and deceive him.

Some men keep a due and exact entry or journal of all they sell, or perhaps of all they buy or sell, but are utterly remiss in posting it forward to a ledger; that is to say, to another book, where every parcel is carried to the debtor's particular account; likewise they keep another book, where they enter all the money they receive; but, as above, never keeping any account of debtor and creditor for the man, there it stands in the cash-book; and both these books must be ransacked over for the particulars, as well of goods sold, as of the money received, when this customer comes to have his account made up; and as the goods are certainly entered when sold or sent away, and the money is certainly entered when it is received, this they think is sufficient, and all the rest superfluous.

I doubt not such tradesmen often suffer as much by their negligent book-keeping, as might, if their business is considerable, pay for a book-keeper; for what is such a man's case, when his customer, suppose a country dealer, comes to town, which perhaps he does once a year (as is the custom of other tradesman) and desires to have his account made up? The London tradesman goes to his books, and first he rummages his day-book back for the whole year, and takes out the foot of all the parcels sent to his chapman, and they make the debtor side of the account; then he takes his cash-book, if it deserves that name; and there he takes out all the sums of money which the chapman has sent up, or bills which he has received, and these make the creditor side of the account; and so the balance is drawn out; and this man thinks himself a mighty good accountant, that he keeps his books exactly; and so perhaps he does, as far as he keeps them at all; that is to say, he never sends a parcel away to his customer but he enters it down; and never receives a bill from him, but he sets it down when the money is paid; but now take this man and his chap together, as they are making up this account, he will find, that if his chapman has kept his accounts exactly, he will be able to do himself justice on the credit side of his account, if the tradesman has, as he well may, overlooked any sum he has paid him; but if, in the confusion of mixed articles, he has erred on the other hand, the latter, though he as easily finds it out as he did the other, perhaps is not honest enough to do him justice on that side, but takes the account as it is given him, pays the balance, and takes a receipt in full. And perhaps this is never discovered till some years after, that the tradesman dies; when a person expert at accounts, and employed by the executors, finds himself obliged to draw out a ledger from the other two books, which the shopkeeper ought to have done; and though it is demanded by the executors, and proof offered to be made, the man who could take such an advantage, will be very likely to keep his hold, and plead his receipt in full, and possibly, if six years are elapsed, the statute of limitations, in bar of any proceedings upon such a demand. And as several other such mistakes might also happen, a tradesman's family may be in very great suffering by his negligence; so that if he did not know how to keep a ledger himself, he had better have hired a book-keeper to have come once a week, or once a month, to have posted his day-book for him.

The like misfortune attends the not balancing his cash; without which a tradesman can never be thoroughly satisfied either of his own not committing mistakes, or of any people cheating him.

What I call balancing his cash-book, is, first, the casting up, daily, or weekly, or monthly, his receipts and payments, and then seeing what money is left in hand, or, as the usual expression of the tradesman is, that money is in cash; secondly, the examining his money, telling it over, and seeing how much he has; and then seeing if it agrees with the balance of his book, that what is, and what should be, correspond.

And here let me give tradesmen a caution or two.

1. Never sit down satisfied with an error in the cash; that is to say, with a difference between the money really in the cash, and the balance in the book; for if they do not agree, there must be a mistake somewhere; for if his money does not come right, he must have paid something that is not set down, and that is to be supposed as bad as if it were lost; or he must have somebody about him that can find the way to his money besides himself, and if so, what is the difference between that and having a gang of thieves about him? and how can he ever pretend to know anything of his affairs, that does not know which way his money goes?

2. A tradesman, endeavouring to balance his cash, should no more be satisfied if he finds more in cash than by the balance of his cash ought to be there, than if he finds less; for how does he know but some money has been recovered that is not entered? and if so, whether the whole of that money be put into the cash? Let us, to make this clear, suppose a case: thus.

My cash-book being cast up for the last month, I find by the foot of the leaf there is cash remaining in hand to balance, 176*l*. 10s. 6d.

To see if all things are right, I go and tell my money over; and there, to my surprise, I find 194*l*. 10s. 6d. in cash; so that I have 18*l* there more than I should have: now, far from being pleased, that I have more money by me than I should have, my inquiry is plain, How comes this to pass?

Perhaps I puzzle my head a great while about it; but, not being able to find it out, I sit down easy and satisfied, and say, Well, I don't much concern myself about it, 'tis better to be so than 18*l*. missing: I cannot tell where it lies; but let it lie where it will, here's the money to make up the mistake when it appears.

But how foolish is this? how ill-grounded the satisfaction? and how weak am I, to argue thus, and please myself with the delusion? For some months after it appears, perhaps, that whereas there was 38*l*. entered, received of Mr. Bernard Keith, the figure three was mistaken, and set down for a figure of five; for the firm received was 58*l*. so that, instead of having 18*l* more in cash than there ought to be, I have forty shillings wanting in my cash; which my son or my apprentice stole from me when they put in the money, and made the mistake of the figures to puzzle the book, that it might be some time before it should be discovered.

The keeping of a cash-book is one of the nicest parts of a tradesman's business, because there is always the bag and the book to be brought together; and if they do not exactly speak the same language, even to a farthing, there must be some omission; and how big or how little that omission may be, who knows? or how shall it be known, but by casting and recasting up, and telling over and over again the money?

I knew indeed a strong-water-man, who drove a very considerable trade; but, being an illiterate tradesman, never balanced his cash-books for many years, nor scarce posted his other books, and indeed hardly understood how to do it; but, knowing his trade was exceeding profitable, and keeping his money all himself, he was easy, and grew rich apace, in spite of the most unjustifiable, and indeed the most intolerable negligence; but though this man grew rich in spite of indolence, and a neglect of his book, yet when he died, two things appeared, which no tradesman in his wits would desire should be said of him.

I. The servants, falling out, and maliciously accusing one another, had, as it appeared by the affidavits of several of them, wronged him of several considerable sums of money, which they received, and never brought into the books; and others, of sums which they brought into the books, but never brought into the cash; and others, of sums which they took ready money in the shop, and never set down, either the goods in the day-book, or the money in the cash-book; and it was thought, though he was so rich as not to feel it to his hurt, yet that he lost three or four hundred pounds a year in that manner, for the two or three last years of his life; but his widow and son, who came after him, having the discovery made to them, took better measures afterwards.

II. He never did or could know what he was worth; for the accounts in his books were never made up; nor, when he came to die, could his executors make up any man's account, so as to be able to prove the particulars, and make a just demand of their debt; but found a prodigious number of small sums of money paid by the debtors, as by receipts in their books, and on their files, some by himself, and some by his man, which were never brought to account, or brought into cash: and his man's answer being still, that he gave all to the master, they could not tell how to charge him by the master's account, because several sums, which the master himself received, were omitted being entered in the same manner; so that all was confusion and neglect: and though the man died rich, as I said, it was in spite of that management that would have made any but himself poor.

Exact book-keeping is to me a certain indication of a man whose heart is in his business, and who intends to thrive; he that cares not whether his books are kept well or no, seems to me one that does not much care whether he thrives or no; or else, befog in desperate circumstances, knows it, and that he cannot thrive; and so matters not which way it goes.

It is true, the neglect of his books is private and secret, and is seldom known to anybody but the tradesman himself; at least till he comes to break, and be a bankrupt; and then you frequently hear them exclaim against him upon that very account. Break, says one of the assigns! how should he but break? Why, he kept no books; why, he has not posted his cash-book for I know not how many months; nor posted his day-book and journal at all, except here and there an account that he perhaps wanted to know the balance of; and as for balancing his cash, I don't see anything of that

done, I know not how long; why, this fellow could never tell how he went on, or how things stood with him; I wonder he did not break a long time ago.

Now this man's case was this; he knew how to keep his books well enough perhaps, and could write well enough; and if you look into his first five or six years of trade, you find all his accounts well kept, the journal duly posted, the cash monthly balanced; but the poor man found after, that things went wrong, that all went downhill; and he hated to look into his books. As a profligate never looks into his conscience, because he can see nothing there but what terrifies and affrights him, makes him uneasy and melancholy; so a sinking tradesman cares not to look into his books, because the prospect there is dark and melancholy. What signifies the account to me, says he? I can see nothing in the books but debts that I cannot pay; and debtors that will never pay me: I can see nothing there but how I have trusted my estate away like a fool, and how I am to be ruined for my easiness, and being a sot. This makes him throw them away, and hardly post things enough to make up when folks call to pay; or if he does post such accounts as he has money to receive from them. that is all; and the rest lie at random, till, as I say, the assignees come to reproach him with his negligence.

But let me here advise tradesmen to keep a perfect acquaintance with their books, though things are bad and discouraging; it keeps them in full knowledge of what they are doing, and how they really stand; and it brings them sometimes to the just reflections on their circumstances which they ought to make; and so to stop in time . . . before they are surprised and torn to pieces by violence.

And, at the worst, if his creditors find his books punctually kept to the last, it will be a credit to him, and they will see he was fit for business; and that it was not probably owing to his negligence, at least that way, that he failed: and I have known cases where that very thing has recommended a tradesman so much to his creditors, that, after the ruin of his fortunes, some or other of them have taken him into partnership, or into employment, only because they knew him to be qualified for business, and for keeping books in particular.

I doubt not that many a tradesman has miscarried by the mistakes and neglect of his books; for the losses that men suffer on that account are not easily set down; besides, his exactness in this respect may prevent him numberless lawsuits, quarrels, and contentions, while he lives; and, if he dies, may free his family and executors from many more; for many a debt has been lost, many an account been perplexed by the debtor, many a sum of money been actually paid over again, especially after a tradesman's death, for want of keeping his books carefully and exactly when he was alive; by which negligence, if he has not been ruined when he was living, his widow and children have been ruined after his decease; though perhaps, had justice been done, he had left them in good circumstances, and with sufficient to support them.

Next to being prepared for death, with respect to heaven and his soul, a tradesman should be always in a state of preparation for death, with respect to his books; it is in vain that he calls for a scrivener or lawyer, and makes a will, when he finds a sudden summons sent him for the grave, and calls his friends about him to divide and settle his estate: if his business is in confusion below stairs, his books out of order, and his accounts unsettled, to what purpose does he give his estate among his relations, when nobody knows where to find it?

As then the minister exhorts us to take care of our souls and make our peace with heaven, while we are in a state of health, and while life has not threatening enemies about it, no diseases, no fevers attending; so let me second that advice to the tradesman, always to keep his books in such a posture, that if he should be snatched away by death, his distressed widow and fatherless family may know what is left for them, and may know where to look for it: he may depend upon it, that what he owes to any,

they will come fast enough for, and his widow and executrix will be pulled to pieces for it, if she cannot and does not speedily pay it; why then should he not put her in a condition to have justice done her and her children, and to know how and of whom to seek for his just debts, that she may be able to pay others, and secure the remainder for herself and her children? I must confess, a tradesman not to leave his books in order, when he dies, argues him to be either,

1. A very bad Christian, who had few or no thoughts of death upon him, or that considered nothing of its frequent coming unexpected and sudden, without warning: or,

2. A very unnatural relation, without the affections of a father or husband, or even of a friend; that should rather leave what he had to be swallowed up by strangers, than leave his family and friends in a condition to find and to recover it.

Again, it is the same case as in matters religious, with respect to the doing this in time, and while health and strength remain; for, as we say very well, and with great reason, that the work of eternity should not be left to the last moments; that a death-bed is no place. and a sick languishing body no condition, and the last breath no time, for repentance; so I may add, neither are these the place, the condition, or the time, to make up our worldly accounts; there is no posting the books on a death-bed, or balancing the cash-book in a high fever. Can the tradesman tell you where his effects lie, and to whom he has lent or trusted sums of money, or large quantities of goods, when he is delirious and light-headed? All these things must be done in time, and the tradesman should take care that his books should always do this for him; and then he has nothing to do but to make his will, and dispose of what he has; and for the rest he refers them to his books, to know where everything is to be had. ♦

QUESTIONS

1. What is "casting up shop," according to Defoe, and why is it important?

2. According to Defoe, how should an error in the books be dealt with?

3. What are three reasons to keep perfect acquaintance with one's books?

SELECTION FROM: *THE BUSINESS GUIDE*

J. L. Nichols (1851–1895) self-published Naperville, Ill 1893

HOW TO DETECT ERRORS IN A TRIAL BALANCE

No rule or set of rules can be given for *the certain* detection of all errors in a Trial Balance, save a careful review of the entire work. If the errors are few the following rules may be of service:

1. If the error be exactly $1, $100, $1000, etc., the mistake is very likely to be found in the additions either in the Ledger accounts or in the Trial Balance.

2. If the error is a large amount, see that all the amounts have been entered in the Trial Balance.

3. If an amount has been omitted in posting, the Trial Balance will be just that amount of Balance. Look for that amount in Journal or other books.

4. The Cash Balance can never be on the credit side. The balance of Bills Receivable should never be on the credit side, nor the balance of Bills Payable on the debit side of the account.

5. If the amount has been posted on the wrong side of the Ledger the Trial Balance will be just twice that amount out of balance. Look for half that amount through the books.

6. If the error is divisible by 9, it is very likely that the mistake was made by a transposition of figures as, 345 posted 453 makes an error of 108, which is divisible by 9, again 753 posted 735 makes an error of 18, also divisible by 9. Errors of transposition are the most difficult to find.

7. If the error is in the dollar column or cents column only, the columns on the left need not be re-added.

8. If the above rules fail, only a careful review of the entire work, checking each entry, will determine where the mistake has been made.

VI

FINANCE

INTRODUCTION: PUTTING IT ALL TOGETHER, BIT BY BIT

Alfred Sloan provides a framework for thinking about the foundations of finance when he writes in *My Life with General Motors* that "General Motors is a growth company" and that growth is marked by periods of "expansion, contraction, and stabilization." He states further that this growth can be analyzed by "looking at the financial record of the business—how the funds were supplied or secured, and how they were used from the beginning to the present."

We can understand Sloan's observations better by giving them some metaphoric dimension and by imagining that we are individual corporations—that each of us is a "General Motors" of sorts and that growth is an important issue. Now, let us think of "expansion" as that period of time when we are in school accumulating the intellectual funds of knowledge necessary for initiating our own personal operations. And let us add the time when we enter into the business world accumulating the funds of expertise and material wealth necessary for investing in a family and its required operations. "Stabilization" might refer to that period when we feel secure, and no new investments in personal or family operations are necessary for optimum living. All is going marvelously well. Finally, we go through "contraction" as our family shrinks, we move from unlimited income to fixed income, and we find that to get the best value

from our present funds and to maintain operations, we must do without certain amenities. Were we to review the record of these three growth periods and to analyze how we paid for them, we would get a complete history of how we managed the financial resources of our own lives. This would be, in a narrow way, the study of finance.

In a broader sense, however, finance is concerned with the efficient management of financial resources in an operational and market environment of risk and return. Applied to the corporate world common to a company like General Motors, the ideology of financial management holds that by efficiently managing a firm's resources, individuals may determine those investments that yield the greatest return given the company's mission, seek the source of funds at the lowest cost with which to finance the acquisition of those investments, and manage the cash flows within the firm for the uses and the sources of those funds. A firm's financial managers gain access to capital markets, both debt and equity, where both may be necessary for the appropriate funds. Understanding how these markets work is essential to financial managers who, along with everyone else associated with a firm, should fully comprehend the tradeoffs between the risk faced by a firm and the returns required and potentially earned commensurate with that risk.

Though financial issues are more complex today than they were two or three hundred years ago, the foundations of financial thinking have not changed much. Three primary issues maintain their place in the study of finance and make their way into this chapter's selection of financial readings: return/profit/ interest as compensation for risk/time/effort, tradeoffs regarding the use of debt in the financing of a business, and the function and use of capital markets in the efficient allocation of financial resources. Discussions of money and credit were nothing out of the ordinary during the late Middle Ages. In fact, the Catholic schoolmen, prior to the Reformation, engaged in such discussions with some regularity. That tradition is continued and extended to include the related subject of "coinage," by Dudley North, a wealthy Tory member of Parliament in late seventeenth-century England.

North writes like a man who knows the value of money—and he should. He earned a great deal of it without a formal education and then turned it into significant political power. Prior to North's political elevation, he had been treasurer of the Turkey company, a Constantinople-based merchant corporation. So this much should not surprise us: North recognizes the need for standardized coinage and the easy, fluid transfer of money from one locale to another—all for the sake of facilitating trade and finance. Today, we may take for granted the nearly unassailable rate standardization for currencies such as the dollar, the yen, the yuan, and the euro, but a glance at North's "Discourse" shows us that such stability of currency and exchange did not always exist.

Who would ever give a thought to the possibility of silver and gold coins being melted down, or having their edges clipped to alter their weight and ultimately their shape? Why would anyone do that? North points out what, for the seventeenth-century tradesman or financier, would be only too obvious—if there were no laws to outlaw such "evils," then there would be no reason, except for those well-informed in the matter, to refrain from it. Additionally, if coinage were not set at different values, there would be no reason to abstain from changing its form, as long as it remained gold or silver, both of which possess value regardless of form.

Marco Polo is known as the first European to march across Asia on a 1275 trade mission to China—the kingdom of Kublai Khan. In his autobiography, *The Travels of Marco Polo*, he details his observations with the precision of a careful cartographer, creating for readers a wonderfully realized map of medieval Chinese culture. Especially colorful and illuminating are his encyclopedic descriptions of the essentials of Chinese commerce. For example, Polo's entry for a Chinese "mint," with its complete assaying of the process of money production, is an epiphany of sorts, revealing a highly evolved money culture without religious or moral impositions and without the European/ Latinate warnings that link cupidity with evil. He refers to this Chinese "art of producing money" as a kind of "alchemy." For Marco Polo to praise the Chinese system of currency production is meaningful in itself—especially considering that the Italians of his era had developed a sophisticated currency system of their own, in addition to harboring some of the most advanced institutions for trade in the Mediterranean.

These Chinese journeys of Marco Polo constitute the construction of a metaphoric bridge between two worlds, laying a foundation for material exchange and building a fraternity of commercial and financial interests between two regions that has lasted for many centuries.

A survey of older European literature reveals what appears to be a systematic and crudely drawn attempt to associate Jews with the practice of usury, or lending at excessive interest. Perhaps the most famous of all European literary usurers is Shakespeare's Shylock, from *The Merchant of Venice*. Shylock's usurious practices seem to be the natural result of his predatory predilections. However, Shakespeare's characterization of Shylock stands in clear contrast to the historical Jewish attitude toward usury expressed by the twelfth-century Jewish philosopher Moses Maimonides. It is obvious, Maimonides says, that usury takes place in the conduct of personal business. However, its practice must be carefully examined and limited. Usury is not allowed, he says, as a legal or moral return to money. His source for such restrictions is the *Five Books of Moses*—and though his codification is an interpretation, he takes few liberties when dealing with commerce and money. He understands that the foundation upon which Jews transact business is the difference between survival and extinction. Finance is a very serious matter.

Maimonides demonstrates an understanding of how illegal and immoral types of financial transactions can never, despite appearances, serve the growth of individuals or the community. He understands the concept of tradeoffs and is at great pains to explain how important *fairness* is in the conduct of our daily dealings. The rules he outlines regarding the borrowing and lending of money, particularly when interest, or usury, is involved, clarify the deep respect held by Jewish tradition for individual integrity and community growth.

The traditional Catholic attitude toward the proper use of interest in financial transactions is represented in *The Summa Theologica* of St. Thomas Aquinas. We can see the influence of Maimonides in his position on usury, and we can appreciate the reasonable structuring of his arguments against certain kinds of debt. Just like Maimonides, Aquinas cites special conditions wherein usury might be considered legal, especially when some good comes from the usury. But he is careful to elucidate the many ways that borrowing and lending could be harmful to both individual and community. He is not unaware of the contradictions that lard the practice of a usurious Catholic Church and its more resplendent ideals, and he knows how careful he must be in stating a financial doctrine acceptable to his superiors. In the end, he finds a way to "slice the bread without cutting his fingers."

The traditional Protestant attitude toward financial matters stresses, among other things, the importance of the relationship between industriousness and time management on the one hand, and between frugality and freedom from debt on the other. A serious interest in these areas is vital to dedicated Protestants in colonial America, who believe in the eternal hopefulness of an afterlife. Such persons recognize that the way to wealth has a bearing on the way to heaven—that personal profits and wealth are signs of having been chosen for divine salvation. Obviously, the subject of finance has the attention of these people and, few colonial American authors write more seriously on this issue than Benjamin Franklin.

Franklin, one of the wealthiest American colonists, is also one of the earliest exponents of the doctrine of self-reliance. In "The Way to Wealth" from *The Works of Benjamin Franklin*, he says that wealth can be attained through skillful management of time and resources and a self-reliant attitude. Franklin is opposed to debt where one is unable to make payments and believes that financing for growth should come from present cash where allowable. In truth, however, he can find no serious argument against borrowing money as long as in doing so, it does not adversely affect wealth and integrity. These positions, fortified by the copious use of homilies, apply to conduct in the home as well as in the workplace. Franklin's tendency to see the impact that financial decisions have on our virtue is much in keeping with mainstream, practical concerns during the Age of Reason. That he is a deist may distance him a bit from the theistic relationship between wealth (earned through labor or finance) and Calvinist election to heaven. But he can hardly be unaware of the idea.

The time Francis Bacon spent in prison, around the turn of the seventeenth century, may have marvelously concentrated his faculties. One cannot help but wonder if it was during this very short time that he was transformed from a bourgeois swindler into a moral and scientific philosopher with an acute sense of the dangers inherent in the acquisition of power, privilege, and place. He seems to have become a sincere counselor in his advocacy of "caring" mercantilism.

Bacon conflates the issue of "riches" and "usury" while admonishing readers to be cautious in their relationships to money. He knows how easily our affections are turned to cash and the creation of its offspring—more cash—

through the instruments of borrowing and lending, or finance. Bacon is equally suspicious of parsimony—radical individualism turned to greed—on the grounds that it mutates the human character. Nonetheless, he attempts to find in usury—that most hated species of parsimony—the germ of practical and tolerable finance. In his search, he begins to lay the foundation for the separation of usury from its theological underpinnings and from its association with predatory forms of commerce. Even as he finds a justifiable place in society for some types of borrowing and lending at interest, he remains adamantly opposed to the practice without strict rules and/or regulations. His argument for a more common or decent type of usury without the "bite" is, however, based on philosophy rather than religion. He is, after all, a believer in early Enlightenment virtues, and the lessons he has learned remind us that we can coexist with financial principles as long as we never exist for them.

John Stuart Mill is often thought of as one of the fathers of utilitarianism, a philosophy of action that has transformed ethical thinking. But he is also considered one of the preeminent economists of the nineteenth century, and his landmark book *Principles of Political Economy* expands our understanding of interest, or profit, and includes a complete discussion of compensation for risk, time, and managerial talents used to increase wealth.

Mill justifies the returns of everyone who makes funds available for the creation of a business and its returns. He is not unaware of the religious restrictions that exist in relationship to borrowing and lending. But he is a committed atheist and no religious doctrine can muddy the clear water of his thinking. Investors abstain from the use of their money, for one or another purpose, and devote it to the growth of a business: they deserve a return. When measured against the investor's risk and "assiduity of skill," equilibrium is attained only through a justifiable return on the investment. The variability of profit in industry must have seemed a deep question in mid-nineteenth-century England. Why are some business ventures more profitable than others? Mill explains the factors that create such disparities: risk, barriers to entry, and natural monopolies (which he explains without prejudice or bitterness). Such answers were available in his time, but they did not exist in a readable form within the substance of an impressively complete disquisition on the subject of political economics until Mill wrote about them.

The tulip bulb craze of the sixteenth century exposes an early and somewhat persistent suspicion about the market system: It works well, but not always perfectly. This axiom is of no little importance to financial managers whose attention is often focused on specific markets. Charles Mackay documents the history of this "tulipomania" in *Extraordinary Popular Delusions and the Madness of Crowds*. The story develops along the lines of a financial morality play and causes us to ponder the use of markets for the efficient allocation of capital, goods, and labor. Mackay gives us reason to consider the fundamental value of goods with respect to market value and the use of capital markets to provide, and efficiently allocate, financial resources to and from the firm.

Joseph De La Vega introduces into the financial vocabulary two words: *bulls* and *bears*. He regards both as species of speculators who occupy a "gambling hell." The bulls, he says, fear absolutely nothing and "always desire a rise in the price of shares." The bears "ruled by fear, trepidation, and nervousness . . . always begin operations with sales." These terms today may be stripped of some of their cachet, but we generally understand bull markets as "buy" markets and bear markets as "sell" markets. Investors will tell you, however, that cleverness in investing can easily "neuter" the bulls and the bears.

Although the selection from John Maynard Keynes is brief, he is an important figure in economic thinking and in business markets. He has suggested that bad economic times require government intervention. More specifically, he tells us that, during such times, governments should borrow money and spend that money to stimulate economic growth. The debt incurred from such a tactic ought to be paid back after economies have regained their momentum. Keynes's *The General Theory of Employment, Interest, and Money* is, in some ways, as controversial today as it was when it was introduced in the 1930s. He offers a reassuring thought about risk in investing: "that of a genuine change in the news *over the near future* . . . ." Keynes tells us that as we are looking at news about our investments only in the near term, and that these investments are "reasonably safe" and that we should not lose much sleep over them. Some might say this reassurance is not so reassuring! This selection is also an early statement of what modern finance practitioners call an efficient market. Such a market is one that quickly and accurately absorbs information into stock prices, and Keynes describes such a market in this selection.

Ultimately, finance is about growth. Familiarity with the world of finance helps us to plan for our personal passage through periods of "expansion, contraction, and stabilization" because *our* stories, like the General Motors story, are also about growth. ♦

A Discourse of Coyned Money

Sir Dudley North (1641–1691)

. . . Gold and Silver for their scarcity, have obtained in small quantities, to equal in value far greater quantities of other Metals, &c. And farther, from their easie Removal, and convenient Custody, have also obtained to be the common Measure in the World between Man and Man in their dealings, as well for Land, Houses, &c., as for Goods and other Necessaries.

For the greater Improvement of this Convenience, and to remove some Difficulties, which would be very troublesome, about knowing quantities and qualities in common and ordinary dealing: Princes and States have made it a matter of Public concern, to ascertain the Allay,[1] and to determine the Weights, *viz.* the quantities of certain Pieces, which we call Coyn, or Money; and such being distinguish'd by Stamps, and Inscriptions, it is made difficult, and highly Penal to Counterfeit them.

By this means the Trade of the World is made easie, and all the numerous species of several Commodities have a common Measure. Besides the Gold and Silver being thus coyned into Money, and so become more useful for Commerce than in the Log or Block, hath in all places, except in *England* since the free Coynage, reasonably obtained a greater value than it had before: And that not only above the real charge of making it so, but is become a State-Revenue (except as before) tho' not very great. Whereas if Silver coyned and uncoyned bore the same rate, as it doth with us in England, where it is coyned at the Charge of the Public, it will be lyable frequently to be melted down, as I shall shew anon.

Money being thus the Common Measure of Buying and Selling, every body who hath any thing to sell, and cannot procure Chapmen for it, is presently apt to think, that want of Money in the Kingdom, or Country is the cause why his Goods do not go off; and so, want of Money, is the common Cry; which is a great mistake, as shall be shewn. I grant all stop in Trade proceeds from some cause; but it is not from the want of specifick Money, there being other Reasons for it; as will appear by the following Discourse.

No Man is richer for having his Estate all in Money, Plate, &c. lying by him, but on the contrary, he is for that reason the poorer. That man is richest, whose Estate is in a growing condition, either in Land at Farm, Money at Interest, or Goods in Trade: If any man, out of an humour, should turn all his Estate into Money, and keep it dead, he would soon be sensible of Poverty growing upon him, whilst he is eating out of the quick stock.

But to examine the matter closer, what do these People want, who cry out for Money? I will begin with the Beggar; he wants, and importunes for Money: What would he do with it if he had it? buy Bread, &c. Then in truth it is not Money, but Bread, and other Necessaries for Life that he wants. Well then; the Farmer complains, for the want of Money; surely it is not for the Beggar's Reason, to sustain Life, or pay Debts; but he thinks that were more Money in the Country, he should have a Price for his Goods. Then it seems Money is, not his want, but a Price for his Corn, and Cattel, which he would sell, but cannot. If it be askt, if the want of Money be not, what then is the reason, why he cannot get a price? I answer, it must proceed from one of these three Causes.

1. Either there is too much Corn and Cattel in the Country, so that most who come to Market have need of selling, as he hath, and few of buying: Or, 2. There wants the usual vent abroad, by Transportation, as in time of War, when Trade is unsafe, or not permitted. Or, 3. The Consumption fails, as when men by reason of Poverty, do not spend so much in their Houses as formerly they did; wherefore it is not the increase of specifick Money, which would at all advance the Farmer's Goods, but the removal of any of these three Causes, which do truly keep down the Market.

The Merchant and Shop-keeper want Money in the same manner, that is, they want a Vent for the Goods they deal in, by reason that the Markets fail, as they will always upon any cause, like what I have hinted. Now to consider what is the true source of Riches, or in the common Phrase, plenty of Money, we must look a little back, into the nature and steps of Trade.

Commerce and Trade, as hath been said, first springs from the Labour of Man, but as the Stock increases, it dilates more and more. If you suppose a Country to have nothing in it but the Land itself, and the Inhabitants; it is plain that at first, the People have only the Fruits of the Earth, and Metals raised from the Bowels of it, to Trade withal, either by carrying out into Foreign Parts, or by selling to such as will come to buy of them, whereby they may be supplyed with the Goods of other Countries wanted there.

In process of time, if the People apply themselves industriously, they will not only be supplied, but advance to a great overplus of Foreign Goods, which improv'd, will enlarge their Trade. Thus the English Nation will sell unto the French, Spaniards, Turk, &c. not only the product of their own Country, as Cloath, Tin, Lead, &c. but also what they purchase of others, as Sugar, Pepper, Callicoes, &c. still buying where Goods are produc'd, and cheap, and transporting them to Places where they are wanted, making great advantage thereby.

In this course of Trade, Gold and Silver are in no sort different from other Commodities, but are taken from them who have Plenty, and carried to them who want, or desire them, with as good profit as other Merchandises. So that an active prudent Nation growth rich, and the sluggish Drones grow poor; and there cannot be any Policy other than this, which being introduc'd and practis'd, shall avail to increase Trade and Riches.

But this Proposition, as single[2] and plain as it is, is seldom so well understood, as to pass with the generality of Mankind; but they think by force of Laws, to retain in their Country all the Gold and Silver which Trade brings in; and thereby expect to grow rich immediately: All which is a profound Fallacy, and hath been a Remora,[3] whereby the growing Wealth of many Countries have been obstructed.

The Case will more plainly appear, if it be put of a single Merchant, or if you please to come nearer the point, of a City or County only.

Let a Law be made, and what is more, be observ'd, that no Man whatsoever shall carry any Money out of a particular Town, County, or Division, with liberty to carry Goods of any sort: so that all the Money which every one brings with him, must be left behind, and none be carried out.

The consequence of this would be, that such Town, or County were cut off from the rest of the Nation; and no Man would dare to come to Market with his Money there; because he must buy, whether he likes, or not: and on the other side, the People of that place could not go to other Markets as Buyers, but only as Sellers, being not permitted to carry any Money out with them.

Now would not such a Constitution as this, soon bring a Town or County to a miserable Condition, with respect to their Neighbors, who have free Commerce, whereby the Industrious gain from the slothful and luxurious part of Mankind? The Case is the same, if you extend your thought from a particular Nation, and the several Divisions, and Cities, with the Inhabitants in them, to the whole World, and the several Nations, and Governments in it. And a Nation restrained in its Trade, of which Gold and Silver is a principal, if not an essential Branch, would suffer, and grow poor, as a particular place within a Country, as I have discoursed. A Nation in the World, as to Trade, is in all respects like a City in a Kingdom, or Family in a City.

Now since the Increase of Trade is to be esteem'd the only cause that Wealth and Money increase, I will add some farther Considerations upon that subject.

The main spur to Trade, or rather to Industry and Ingenuity, is the exorbitant Appetites of Men, which they will take pains to gratifie, and so be disposed to work, when nothing else will incline them to it; for did Men content themselves with bare Necessaries, we should have a poor World.

The Glutton works hard to purchase Delicacies, wherewith to gorge himself; the Gamester, for Money to venture at Play; the

Miser, to hoard; and so others. Now in their pursuit of those Appetites, other Men less exorbitant are benefitted; and tho' it may be thought few profit by the Miser, yet it will be found otherwise, if we consider, that besides the humour of every Generation, to dissipate what another had collected, there is benefit from the very Person of a covetous Man; for if he labours with his own hands, his Labour is very beneficial to them who imploy him; if he doth not work, but profit by the Work of others, then those he sets on work have benefit by their being employed.

Countries which have sumptuary Laws, are generally poor; for when Men by those Laws are confin'd to narrower Expence than otherwise they would be, they are at the same time discouraged from the Industry and Ingenuity which they would have imployed in obtaining wherewithal to support them, in the full latitude of Expence they desire.

It is possible Families may be supported by such means, but then the growth of Wealth in the Nation is hindered; for that never thrives better, then when Riches are tost from hand to hand. The meaner sort seeing their Fellows become rich, and great, are spurr'd up to imitate their Industry. A Tradesman sees his Neighbour keep a Coach, presently all his Endeavors is at work to do the like, and many times is beggered by it; however the extraordinary Application he made, to support his Vanity, was beneficial to the Public, tho' not enough to answer his false Measures as to himself. It will be objected, That the Home Trade signifies nothing to the enriching a Nation, and that the increase of Wealth comes out of Forreign Trade.

I answer, That what is commonly understood by Wealth, *viz.* Plenty, Bravery, Gallantry, &c. cannot be maintained without Forreign Trade. Nor in truth, can Forreign Trade subsist without the Home Trade, both being connected together.

I have toucht upon these matters concerning Trade, and Riches in general, because I conceive a true Notion of them, will correct many common Errors, and more especially conduce to the Proposition I chiefly aim to prove; which is, that Gold and Silver, and, out of them, Money are nothing but the Weights and Meas-

ures, by which Traffic is more conveniently carried on, then could be done without them: and also a proper Fund for a surplusage of Stock to be deposited in.

In confirmation of this, we may take Notice, That Nations which are very poor, have scarce any Money, and in the beginnings of Trade have often made use of something else; as Sueden hath used Copper, and the Plantations, Sugar and Tobacco, but not without great Inconveniences; and still[4] as Wealth hath increas'd, Gold and Silver hath been introduc'd, and drove out the others, as now almost in the Plantations it hath done.

It is not necessary absolutely to have a Mint for the making Money plenty, tho' it be very expedient; and a just benefit is lost by the want of it, where there is none; for it hath been observed, that where no Mints were, Trade hath not wanted a full supply of Money; because if it be wanted, the Coyn of other Princes will become currant, as in *Ireland*, and the *Plantations*; so also in *Turky*, where the Money of the Country is so minute, that it is inconvenient for great Payments; and therefore the Turkish Dominions are supplied by almost all the Coyns of Christendom, the same being currant there.

But a Country which useth Forreign Coyns, hath great disadvantage from it; because they pay strangers, for what, had they a Mint of their own, they might make themselves. For Coyned Money, as was said, is more worth than Uncoyned Silver of the same weight and allay; that is, you may buy more Uncoyned Silver, of the same fineness with the Money, than the Money weighs; which advantage the Stranger hath for the Coynage.

If it be said, That the contrary sometimes happens, and coyned Money shall be current for less than Bullion shall sell for. I answer, That where-ever this happens, the Coyned Money being undervalued, shall be melted down into Bullion, for the immediate Gain that is had from it.

Thus it appears, that if you have no Mint whereby to increase your Money, yet if you are a rich People, and have Trade, you cannot want Specifick Coyn, to serve your occasions in dealing.

The next thing to be shewed is, That if your Trade pours in never so much Money upon you, you have no more advantage by the being of it Money, then you should have were it in Logs, or Blocks; save only that Money is much better for Transportation than Logs are.

For when Money grows up to a greater quantity than Commerce requires, it comes to be of no greater value, than uncoyned Silver, and will occasionally be melted down again.

Then let not the care of Specifick Money torment us so much; for a people that are rich cannot want it, and if they make none, they will be supplied with the Coyn of other Nations; and if never so much be brought from abroad, or never so much coyned at home, all that is more than what the Commerce of the Nation requires, is but Bullion, and will be treated as such; and coyned Money, like wrought Plate at Second hand, shall sell but for the Intrinsick.

I call to witness the vast Sums that have been coyned in *England,* since the free Coynage was set up; What is become of it all? No body believes it to be in the Nation, and it cannot well be all transported, the Penalties for so doing being so great. The case is plain, it being exported, as I verily believe little of it is, the Melting-Pot devours all.

The rather, because that Practice is so easie, profitable, and safe from all possibility of being detected, as every one knows it is. And I know no intelligent Man who doubts, but the New Money goes this way.

Silver and Gold, like other Commodities, have their ebbings and flowings: Upon the arrival of Quantities from *Spain,* the Mint commonly gives the best price; that is, coyned Silver, for uncoyned Silver, weight for weight. Wherefore is it carried into the *Tower,* and coyned? not long after there will come a demand for Bullion, to be Exported again: If there is none, but all happens to be in Coyn, What then? Melt it down again; there's no loss in it, for the Coyning cost the Owners nothing.

Thus the Nation hath been abused, and made to pay for the twisting of straw, for Asses to eat. If the Merchant were made to pay the price of the Coynage, he would not have sent his Silver to the *Tower* without Consideration;

and coyned Money would always keep a value above uncoyned Silver: which is now so far from being the case, that many times it is considerably under, and generally the King of *Spain's* Coyn here is worth One penny *per* Ounce more than our New Money.

This Nation, for many Years last past, hath groaned, and still groans under the abuse of clipt Money, which with respect to their Wisdom, is a great mistake; and the *Irish* whom we ridicule so much, when in Peace, would not be so gulled, but weighed their (Pieces of Eight) Cobbs, as they call them, Piece by Piece; this Errour springs from the same Source with the rest, and needs no other Cure then will soon result from Noncurrency. Whereof I shall set down my thoughts.

There is great fear, that if clipt Money be not taken, there will be no Money at all. I am certain, that so long as clipt Money is taken, there will be little other: And is it not strange, that scarce any Nation, or People in the whole World, take diminisht Money by Tale;[5] but the *English?*

What is the reason that a New Half-crown-piece, if it hath the least snip taken from the edge, will not pass; whereas an Old Half-crown clipt to the very quick, and not intrinsically worth Eighteen Pence, shall be currant?

I know no reason, why a Man should take the one, more than the other; I am sure, that if New Money should pass clipt, there would soon be enough served so. And I do not in the least doubt, unless the currency of clipt Money be stopt, it will not be very long before every individual piece of the Old Coynes be clipt.

And if this be not remedied, for fear of the Evil now, how will it be born hereafter, when it will be worse? Surely at length it will become insupportable, and remedy itself as Groats[6] have done; but let them look out, in whose time it shall happen; we are all shoving the Evil-Day as far off as may be, but it will certainly come at last.

I do not think the great Evil is so hard to be remedied, nor so chargeable as some have judged; but if rightly managed, it may be done with no intolerable loss, some there will be, and considerable; but when I reflect where it will fall, I cannot think it grievous.

The general Opinion is, That it cannot be done otherwise, then by calling in of all the Old Money, and changing of it, for doing which the whole Nation must contribute by a general Tax; but I do not approve of this way, for several Reasons.

For it will be a matter of great trouble, and will require many hands to execute, who will expect, and deserve good pay; which will add to the Evil, and increase the Charge of the Work; and the Trust of it, is also very great, and may be vastly abused.

Now before I give any Opinion for the doing this thing, let some estimate be made of the loss, wherein I will not undertake to compute the Total, but only how the same may fall out in One Hundred Pound: There may be found in it Ten Pound of good New Money, then rests Ninety Pound; and of that I will suppose half to be clipt Money, and half good; so there will be but Five and Forty, in One Hundred Pounds, whereupon there will be any loss; and that will not surely be above a Third part: so I allow 15 *l. per Cent.* for the loss by clipt Money, which is with the most, and in such Computes, it is safest to err on that side.

Now in case it should be thought fit, that the King should in all the Receipts of the Public Revenue, forbid the taking of clipt Coyn, unless the Subject were content to pay it by weight at 5 *s.* 2 *d. per* Ounce, every Piece being cut in Two (which must be especially and effectually secured to be done), I grant it would be a great surprize, but no great cause of Complaint when nothing is required, but that the Public Revenue may be paid in lawful *English* Money.

And those who are to make Payments, must either find good Money, or clip in two their cropt Money, and part with it on such terms; by this Example it would likewise be found, that in a short time, all Men would refuse clipt Money in common Payment.

Now let us consider, where the loss would light, which I have estimated to be about 15 *per Cent.*

We are apt to make Over-estimates of the Quantities of current Money; for we see it often, and know it not again; and are not willing to consider how very a little time it stays in a place; and altho' every one desires to have it,

yet none, or very few care for keeping it, but they are forthwith contriving to dispose it; knowing that from all the Money that lies dead, no benefit is to be expected, but it is a certain loss.

The Merchant and Gentleman keep their Money for the most part, with Goldsmiths, and Scriveners; and they, instead of having Ten Thousand Pounds in Cash by them, as their Accounts shew they should have, of other Mens ready Money, to be paid at sight, have seldom One Thousand in Specie; but depend upon a course of Trade, whereby Money comes in as fast as it is taken out: Wherefore I conclude, that the Specific Money of this Nation is far less than the common Opinion makes.

Now suppose all the loss by clipt Money should happen and fall where the Cash is, it would be severe in very few Places. It could do no great harm to Hoards of Money; because those who intend to keep Money, will be sure to lay up that which is good. It would not signifie much to the poor Man, for he many times hath none; and for the most part, if he hath any, it is very little, seldom Five Shillings at a time. The Farmer is supposed to pay his Landlord, as fast as he gets Money; so it is not likely he should be catcht with much: Wherefore it will light chiefly upon Trading Men, who may sometimes be found with Hundreds by them; and frequently not with many Pounds. Those who happen to have such great Cashes at such time would sustain loss.

In short, clipt Money is an Evil, that the longer it is born with, the harder will the Cure be. And if the Loss therein be lain on the Public (as the Common Project is) the Inconveniences are (as hath been shewed), very great; but in the other way of Cure it is not such a terrible Grievance, as most Men have imagined it would be.

So to conclude, when these Reasons, which have been hastily and confusedly set down, are duly considered, I doubt not but we shall joyn in one uniform Sentiment: That Laws to hamper Trade, whether Foreign, or Domestick, relating to Money, or other Merchandises, are not Ingredients to make a People Rich, and abounding in Money, and Stock. But if Peace be procured, easie Justice maintained, the Navigation not clogg'd, the Industrious encouraged, by indulging them in the participation of Honours, and Imployments in the Government, according to their Wealth and Characters, the Stock of the Nation will increase, and consequently Gold and Silver abound, Interest be easie, and Money cannot be wanting.

POSTSCRIPT

Upon farther Consideration, of the Foregoing Matters, I think fit to add the following Notes.

When a Nation is grown Rich, Gold, Silver, Jewels, and every thing useful, or desirable, (as I have already said) will be plentiful; and the Fruits of the Earth will purchase more of them, than before, when People were poorer: As a fat Oxe in former Ages, was not sold for more Shillings, than now Pounds. The like takes place in Labourers Wages, and every thing whatever; which confirms the Universal Maxim I have built upon, *viz.* That Plenty of any thing makes it cheap.

Therefore Gold and Silver being now plentiful, a Man hath much more of it for his labour, for his Corn, for his Cattle, &c. then could be had Five Hundred Years ago, when, as must be owned, there was not near so much by many parts as now.

Notwithstanding this, I find many, who seem willing to allow, that this Nation at present, abounds with Gold and Silver, in Plate and Bullion; but are yet of Opinion, That coyned Money is wanted to carry on the Trade, and that were there more Specifick Money, Trade would increase, and we should have better Markets for every thing.

That this is a great Error, I think the foregoing Papers makes out: but to clear it a little farther, let it be considered, that Money is a Manufacture of Bullion wrought in the Mint. Now if the Materials are ready, and the Workmen also, 'tis absurd to say, the Manufacture is wanted.

For instance: Have you Corn, and do you want Meal? Carry the Corn to the Mill, and grind it. Yes; but I want Meal, because others will not carry their Corn; and I have none: say you so; then buy Corn of them, and carry it to the Mill your self. This is exactly the Case of Money. A very rich Man hath much Plate, for Honour and Show; whereupon a Poorer Man thinks, if it were coyned into Money, the Public, and his self among the rest, would be the better for it; but he is utterly mistaken; unless at the same time you oblige the rich Man to squander his new coyn'd Money away.

For if he lays it up, I am sure the matter is not mended: if he commutes it for Diamonds, Pearl, &c. the Case is still the same; it is but changed from one hand to another: and it may be the Money is dispatcht to the *Indies* to pay for those Jewels: then if he buys Land, it is no more than changing the hand, and regarding all Persons, except the Dealers only, the Case is still the same. Money will always have an Owner, and never goeth a Beggar for Entertainment, but must be purchast for valuable consideration in *solido*.

If the use of Plate were prohibited, then it were a sumptuary Law, and, as such, would be a vast hindrance to the Riches and Trade of the Nation: for now seeing every Man hath Plate in his House, the Nation is possest of a solid Fund, consisting in those Metals, which all the World desire, and would willingly draw from us; and this in far greater measure than would be, if Men were not allowed that liberty. For the poor Tradesman, out of an ambition to have a Piece of Plate upon his Cupboard, works harder to purchase it, than he would do if that humour were restrained as I have said elsewhere.

There is required for carrying on the Trade of the Nation, a determinate Sum of Specifick Money, which varies, and is sometimes more, sometimes less, as the Circumstances we are in requires. War time calls for more Money than time of Peace, because every one desires to keep some by him, to use upon Emergiences; not thinking it prudent to rely upon Moneys currant in dealing, as they do in times of Peace, when Payments are more certain.

This ebbing and flowing of Money, supplies and accommodates itself, without any aid of Politicians. For when Money grows scarce, and begins to be hoarded, then forthwith the Mint works, till the occasion be filled up again. And on the other side, when Peace brings out the Hoards, and Money abounds, the Mint not only ceaseth, but the overplus of Money will be presently melted down, either to supply the Home Trade, or for Transportation.

Thus the Buckets work alternately, when Money is scarce, Bullion is coyn'd; when Bullion is scarce, Money is melted. I do not allow that both should be scarce at one and the same time; for that is a state of Poverty, and will not be, till we are exhausted, which is besides my subject.

Some have fancied, that if by a Law the Ounce of Silver were restrained to 5 *s*. value, in all dealings, and at the *Tower* the same were coyned into 5 *s*. 4 *d*. or 5 *s*. 6 *d*. per Ounce, all the Plate in *England* would soon be coyned. The answer to this, in short is: That the Principle they build upon is impossible. How can any Law hinder me from giving another Man, what I please for his Goods? The Law may be evaded a thousand ways. As be it so: I must not give, nor he receive above 5 *s*. per Ounce for Silver; I may pay him 5 *s*. and present him with 4 *d*. or 6 *d*. more; I may give him Goods in barter, at such, or greater profit; and so by other contrivances, *ad Infinitum*.

But put case it took effect, and by that means all the Silver in *England* were coyned into Money; What then? would any one spend more in Cloaths, Equipages, Housekeeping, &c. then is done? I believe not; but rather the contrary: For the Gentry and Commonalty being nipt in their delight of seeing Plate, &c. in their Houses, would in all probability be dampt in all other Expences: Wherefore if this could be done, as I affirm it cannot, yet instead of procuring the desired effect, it would bring on all the Mischiefs of a sumptuary Law.

Whenever the Money is made lighter, or baser in allay (which is the same thing), the effect is, that immediately the price of Bullion answers. So that in reality you change the Name, but not the thing: and whatever the difference is, the Tenant and Debtor hath it in his favor; for Rent and Debts will be paid less, by just so much as the intrinsick value is less, then what was to be paid before.

For example: One who before received for Rent or Debt, 3 *l*. 2 *s*. could with it buy twelve Ounces, or a Pound of Sterling Silver; but if the Crown-piece be worse in value than now it is, by 3 *d*. I do averr, you shall not be able to buy a Pound of such Silver under 3 *l*. 5 *s*. but either directly, or indirectly it shall cost so much.

But then it is said, we will buy an Ounce for 5 *s*. because 'tis the Price set by the Parliament, and no body shall dare to sell for more. I answer, If they cannot sell it for more, they may coyn it; And then what Fool will sell an Ounce of Silver for 5 *s*. when he may coyn it into 5 *s*. 5 *d*.?

Thus we may labour to hedge in the Cuckow, but in vain; for no People ever yet grew rich by Policies; but it is Peace, Industry, and Freedom that brings Trade and Wealth, and nothing else. ◆

ENDNOTES

1. Alloy.
2. Particular.
3. A let, or obstacle.
4. To this time, till now.
5. Reckoning, numerical account.
6. Pieces valued at 4 pence.

QUESTIONS

1. According to North, what is the role of the government in coining money?

2. When coins were made of silver and gold, what happened if the purchasing power of money was not nearly equivalent with the value of the metal contained in the coins?

3. What happened when gold and silver became more plentiful?

4. What is clipt (clipped) money and why is it a problem?

5. What does North identify as the main factor in creating wealth in a community? What drives this activity?

FROM *THE TRAVELS OF MARCO POLO*

Marco Polo (1254–1324)

OF THE KIND OF PAPER MONEY ISSUED BY THE GREAT KHAN
AND MADE TO PASS CURRENT THROUGHOUT HIS DOMINIONS

In this city of Kanbalu is the mint of the Great Khan, who may truly be said to possess the secret of the alchemists, as he has the art of producing money by the following process.

He causes the bark to be stripped from those mulberry trees the leaves of which are used for feeding silk-worms, and takes from it that thin inner rind which lies between the coarser bark and the wood of the tree. This being steeped, and afterwards pounded in a mortar, until reduced to a pulp, is made into paper, resembling, in substance, that which is manufactured from cotton, but quite black. When ready for use, he has it cut into pieces of money of different sizes, nearly square, but somewhat longer than they are wide. Of these, the smallest pass for a half tournois; the next size for a Venetian silver groat; others for two, five, and ten groats; others for one, two, three, and as far as ten bezants of gold. The coinage of this paper money is authenticated with as much form and ceremony as if it were actually of pure gold or silver; for to each note a number of officers, specially appointed, not only subscribe their names, but affix their seals also. When this has been regularly done by the whole of them, the principal officer, appointed by his Majesty, having dipped into vermilion the royal seal committed to his custody, stamps with it the piece of paper, so that the form of the seal tinged with the vermilion remains impressed upon it. In this way it receives full authenticity as current money, and the act of counterfeiting it is punished as a capital offence.

When thus coined in large quantities, this paper currency is circulated in every part of the Great Khan's dominions; nor dares any person, at the peril of his life, refuse to accept it in payment. All his subjects receive it without hesitation, because, wherever their business may call them, they can dispose of it again in the purchase of merchandise they may require; such as pearls, jewels, gold, or silver. With it, in short, every article may be procured.[1]

Several times in the course of the year, large caravans of merchants arrive with such articles as have just been mentioned, together with gold tissues, which they lay before the Great Khan. He thereupon calls together twelve experienced and skilful persons, selected for this purpose, whom he commands to examine the articles with great care, and to fix the value at which they should be purchased. Upon the sum at which they have been thus conscientiously appraised he allows a reasonable profit, and immediately pays for them with this paper. To this the owners can have no objection, because, as has been observed, it answers the purpose of their own disbursements; and even though they should be inhabitants of a country where this kind of money is not current, they invest the amount in other articles of merchandise suited to their own markets.

When any persons happen to be possessed of paper money which from long use has become damaged, they carry it to the mint, where, upon the payment of only three percent, they receive fresh notes in exchange. Should any be desirous of procuring gold or silver for the purposes of manufacture, such as of drinking-cups, girdles, or other articles wrought of these metals, they in like manner apply to the mint, and for their paper obtain the bullion they require.

All his Majesty's armies are paid with this currency, which is to them of the same value as if it were gold or silver. Upon these grounds, it may certainly be affirmed that the Great Khan has a more extensive command of treasure than any other sovereign in the universe. ◆

ENDNOTE

1. "Early in the ninth century, bills of exchange came into use; and from the middle of the twelfth century paper money became quite common, and is still in general use all over China, notes being issued in some places for amounts less even than a shilling." Giles, *The Civilization of China*.

QUESTIONS

1. Describe the production of paper money in China, as described by Marco Polo.

2. Why do you suppose anyone would accept this first paper money?

3. Paper money may have been legal tender only within China, but why were foreign merchants willing to accept this money?

4. What crimes does Marco Polo associate with paper money in China? What is the penalty for committing these crimes?

5. Why does Marco Polo liken the use of paper money to alchemy?

Lender and Borrower from *The Code of Maimonides*

Moses ben Maimonides (1135–1204)

Malveh Veloveh Perek 4 (Lender and Borrower Chapter 4)

1. NESHECH (biting interest) and MARBIT (interest) are one, as was written: "Do not give him your money with NESHECH and do not put forth your food at MARBIT" (Leviticus 25:37). As it further says "NESHECH: from money, NESHECH from food, NESHECH from any substance that will accrue" (Deuteronomy 23:20). And why would it be called NESHECH?[1] Because it bites. It causes grief to one's colleague and consumes his flesh. Why were two terms used (in the Torah)? To pass on it with two "nos" (to make this violation twofold in its severity).

2. Just as it is forbidden to lend with an interest, it is forbidden to borrow an interest bearing loan as stated: "Do not offer interest to your brother" (Deuteronomy 23:20). From what was heard (the oral tradition), they learned that this is a warning to the borrower, meaning, you shall not pay interest to your brother. In addition, it is forbidden to engage as a broker between a borrower and a lender if interest is involved. Any guarantor, writer (scribe), or witness who is involved, transgresses a negative commandment[2] as Exodus 22:24 states: "Do not lay interest upon him." This is a warning for the witnesses, the guarantor and the scribe. Thus, we learn that a person who offers an interest bearing loan violates six prohibitions: "Do not behave as a creditor toward him," "Do not give him your money with biting interest," "Do not put forth your food at interest," "Do not take biting interest from him" (Leviticus 25:36), "Do not lay interest upon him," and "Do not place a stumbling block in front of the blind" (Leviticus 19:14).

The one who borrows at interest violates two prohibitions: "Do not offer interest to your brother" and "Do not place a stumbling block in front of the blind."

The guarantor, the witnesses, and the like violate only the prohibition: "Do not lay biting interest upon him." Any middleman (broker) who connects between the lender and the borrower or assists one of them or instructs one of them transgresses the commandment: "Do not place a stumbling block in front of the blind" (Leviticus 19:14).

Malveh Veloveh Perek 5 (Lender and Borrower Chapter 5)

1. The gentile and the resident alien, one may lend money to and borrow money from with interest, as written: "Do not offer interest to your brother" (Deuteronomy 23:20). We deduce: To your brother is prohibited, but to everybody else ("rest of the world") it is permitted. It is a positive commandment (Mitzvah) to charge interest from a gentile, as it states: "You may offer interest to a gentile" (Deuteronomy 23:21). The oral tradition teaches that this is a positive commandment and a scriptural law. . . .

5. It is forbidden for a Jew to entrust his money to a gentile with the intention of subsequent lending of the money at interest to a Jew. If a gentile loans an interest bearing loan to a Jew, it is forbidden for another Jew to serve as a guarantor. The rationale is that according to the gentiles' laws, the lender may demand payment from the guarantor first. Then after paying this debt, the guarantor will demand payment for the interest that he was obligated to the gentile. Thus, if the gentile makes a commitment to not demand payment from the guarantor first, it is permitted. . . .

7. It is an obligation (Mitzvah) to prioritize the lending of interest free money to a Jew before lending money to a gentile at interest.

8. It is forbidden for a person to invest his money in a venture where he does not bear an equal share of the profits and the losses. If his

share in the profit is greater than his share in the potential loss it is considered the shade of interest,[3] and the man is considered wicked. If a person invests in a venture, the profits and the losses are divided according to the laws governing the business or venture. A person who invests his money in a manner where his share in the profit is smaller than his share in the potential loss is considered pious (or righteous). . . .

11. It is forbidden to pay interest ahead or after its due time. What is implied? If a man pays his interest early, this is considered to be gifts or bribes in the anticipation of receiving further loans. If he took a loan and returned the debt, and then sent the lender a gift for the idle money in his possession, this is considered to be as paying delayed interest. If one transgresses to do this it is a shade of interest.

12. If a man who borrowed money from a colleague who did not usually greet him first, it is forbidden for the borrower to start greeting the lender first. Needless to say, it is forbidden for him to publicly praise the lender or go to his house often. As it is written: "All types of interest" (Deuteronomy 23:20), meaning, even words are forbidden.

13. Similarly, it is forbidden for the borrower to teach the lender Scripture or Talmud while the loan is outstanding, if the borrower did not previously engage in these, as implied by the phrase: "All types of interest."

14. There are practices that are permitted even though they resemble interest. What is the reason? A person may purchase a note from a colleague for less than its face value without any worry. A person may give a colleague a small amount so that he will lend to a third party 100 times that amount. The reason being is that the Torah forbade only interest that is given to the lender by the borrower.

Similarly, a person may tell a colleague: "Here is an amount of money. Tell that man to give me a loan." This is permitted, because he gave him a commission only for making the loan referral. ◆

ENDNOTES

1. After this point, the words "Neshech" and "interest" are used interchangeably.

2. *Commandment* here is used as a translation for mitzvah. This is not to be confused with commandment as in the Ten Commandments, but rather means a precept or moral duty.

3. Literally, "interest dust."

QUESTIONS

1. What are the conditions under which Jews were allowed to lend money at interest?

2. If interest were wrongly charged, what could be done about it?

3. Could a gift legally substitute for money paid as interest?

4. What possibilities do all partners to a business have to accept under Jewish economic laws?

Of the Sin of Usury
From *The Summa Theologica*

Thomas Aquinas (1225–1274)

We must now consider the sin of usury, which is committed in loans: and under this head there are four points of inquiry: (1) Whether it is a sin to take money as a price for money lent, which is to receive usury? (2) Whether it is lawful to lend money for any other kind of consideration, by way of payment for the loan? (3) Whether a man is bound to restore just gains derived from money taken in usury? (4) Whether it is lawful to borrow money under a condition of usury?

First Article.

Whether It Is a Sin to Take Usury for Money Lent?

We proceed thus to the First Article:—

Objection 1. It would seem that it is not a sin to take usury for money lent. For no man sins through following the example of Christ. But Our Lord said of Himself (Luke xix.23): *At My coming I might have exacted it,* i.e. the money lent, *with usury.* Therefore it is not a sin to take usury for lending money.

Obj. 2. Further, According to Ps. xviii. 8, *The law of the Lord is unspotted,* because, to wit, it forbids sin. Now usury of a kind is allowed in the Divine law, according to Deut. xxiii. 19, 20. *Thou shalt not fenerate to thy brother money, nor corn, nor any other thing, but to the stranger:* nay more, it is even promised as a reward for the observance of the Law, according to Deut. xxviii. 12: *Thou shalt fenerate to many nations, and shalt not borrow of any one.* Therefore it is not a sin to take usury.

Obj. 3. Further, In human affairs justice is determined by civil laws. Now civil law allows usury to be taken. Therefore it seems to be lawful.

Obj. 4. Further, The counsels are not binding under sin. But, among other counsels we find (Luke vi. 35): *Lend, hoping for nothing thereby.* Therefore it is not a sin to take usury.

Obj. 5. Further, It does not seem to be in itself sinful to accept a price for doing what one is not bound to do. But one who has money is not bound in every case to lend it to his neighbour. Therefore it is lawful for him sometimes to accept a price for lending it.

Obj. 6. Further, Silver made into coins does not differ specifically from silver made into a vessel. But it is lawful to accept a price for the loan of a silver vessel. Therefore it is also lawful to accept a price for the loan of a silver coin. Therefore usury is not in itself a sin.

Obj. 7. Further, Anyone may lawfully accept a thing which its owner freely gives him. Now he who accepts the loan, freely gives the usury. Therefore he who lends may lawfully take the usury.

On the contrary, It is written (Exod. xxii. 25): *If thou lend money to any of thy people that is poor, that dwelleth with thee, thou shalt not be hard upon them as an extortioner, nor oppress them with usuries.*

I answer that, To take usury for money lent is unjust in itself, because this is to sell what does not exist, and this evidently leads to inequality which is contrary to justice.

In order to make this evident, we must observe that there are certain things the use of which consists in their consumption: thus we consume wine when we use it for drink, and we consume wheat when we use it for food. Wherefore in suchlike things the use of the thing must not be reckoned apart from the thing itself, and whoever is granted the use of the thing, is granted the thing itself; and for this reason, to lend things of this kind is to transfer the ownership. Accordingly if a man wanted to sell wine separately from the use of the wine, he would be selling the same thing twice, or he would be selling what does not exist, wherefore he would evidently commit a sin of injustice. In like manner he commits an injustice who lends wine or wheat, and asks for double payment, viz. one, the return of the thing in equal measure, the other, the price of the use, which is called usury.

On the other hand there are things the use of which does not consist in their consumption: thus to use a house is to dwell in it, not to destroy it. Wherefore in such things both may be granted: for instance, one man may hand over to another the ownership of his house while reserving to himself the use of it for a time, or vice versa, he may grant the use of the house, while retaining the ownership. For this reason a man may lawfully make a charge for the use of his house, and, besides this, revendicate the house from the person to whom he has granted its use, as happens in renting and letting a house.

Now money, according to the Philosopher (*Ethic.* v. 5; *Polit.* i. 3) was invented chiefly for the purpose of exchange: and consequently the proper and principal use of money is its consumption or alienation whereby it is sunk in exchange. Hence it is by its very nature unlawful to take payment for the use of money lent, which payment is known as usury: and just as a man is bound to restore other ill-gotten goods, so is he bound to restore the money which he has taken in usury.

Reply Obj. 1. In this passage usury must be taken figuratively for the increase of spiritual goods which God exacts from us, for He wishes us ever to advance in the goods which we receive from Him: and this is for our own profit not for His.

Reply Obj. 2. The Jews were forbidden to take usury from their brethren, i.e. from other Jews. By this we are given to understand that to take usury from any man is evil simply, because we ought to treat every man as our neighbour and brother, especially in the state of the Gospel, whereto all are called. Hence it is said without any distinction in Ps. xiv. 5: *He that hath not put out his money to usury,* and (Ezech. xviii. 8): *Who hath not taken usury.* They were permitted, however, to take usury from foreigners, not as though it were lawful, but in order to avoid a greater evil, lest, to wit, through avarice to which they were prone according to Is. lvi. II, they should take usury from the Jews who were worshippers of God.

Where we find it promised to them as a reward, *Thou shalt fenerate to many nations,* etc., fenerating is to be taken in a broad sense for lending, as in Ecclus. xxix. 10, where we read: *Many have refused to fenerate, not out of wickedness,* i.e. they would not lend. Accordingly the Jews are promised in reward an abundance of wealth, so that they would be able to lend to others.

Reply Obj. 3. Human laws leave certain things unpunished, on account of the condition of those who are imperfect, and who would be deprived of many advantages, if all sins were strictly forbidden and punishments appointed for them. Wherefore human law has permitted usury, not that it looks upon usury as harmonizing with justice, but lest the advantage of many should be hindered. Hence it is that in civil law it is stated that *those things according to natural reason and civil law which are consumed by being used, do not admit of usufruct,* and that *the senate did not (nor could it) appoint a usufruct to such things, but established a quasi-usufruct,* namely by permitting usury. Moreover the Philosopher, led by natural reason, says (*Polit.* i. 3) that *to make money by usury is exceedingly unnatural.*

Reply Obj. 4. A man is not always bound to lend, and for this reason it is placed among the counsels. Yet it is a matter of precept not to seek profit by lending: although it may be called a matter of counsel in comparison with the maxims of the Pharisees, who deemed some kinds of usury to be lawful, just as love of one's enemies is a matter of counsel. Or again, He speaks here not of the hope of usurious gain, but of the hope which is put in man. For we ought not to lend or do any good deed through hope in man, but only through hope in God.

Reply Obj. 5. He that is not bound to lend, may accept repayment for what he has done, but he must not exact more. Now he is repaid according to equality of justice if he is repaid as much as he lent. Wherefore if he exacts more for the usufruct of a thing which has no other use but the consumption of its substance, he exacts a price of something non-existent: and so his exaction is unjust.

Reply Obj. 6. The principal use of a silver vessel is not its consumption, and so one may lawfully sell its use while retaining one's ownership of it. On the other hand the principal use of silver money is sinking it in exchange, so that it is not lawful to sell its use and at the same time expect the restitution of the amount lent. It must be observed, however, that the secondary use of silver vessels may be an exchange, and such use may not be lawfully sold. In like manner there may be some secondary use of silver money; for instance, a man might lend coins for show, or to be used as security.

Reply Obj. 7. He who gives usury does not give it voluntarily simply, but under a certain necessity, in so far as he needs to borrow money which the owner is unwilling to lend without usury.

SECOND ARTICLE.

Whether it is lawful to ask for any other kind of consideration for money lent?

We proceed thus to the Second Article:—

Objection 1. It would seem that one may ask for some other kind of consideration for money lent. For everyone may lawfully seek to indemnify himself. Now sometimes a man suffers loss through lending money. Therefore he may lawfully ask for or even exact something else besides the money lent.

Obj. 2. Further, As stated in *Ethic.* v. 5 one is in duty bound by a point of honour, to repay anyone who has done us a favour. Now to lend money to one who is in straits is to do him a favour for which he should be grateful. Therefore the recipient of a loan, is bound by a natural debt to repay something. Now it does not seem unlawful to bind oneself to an obligation of the natural law. Therefore it is not unlawful, in lending money to anyone, to demand some sort of compensation as a condition of the loan.

Obj. 3. Further, Just as there is real remuneration, so is there verbal remuneration, and remuneration by service, as a gloss says on Isa. xxxiii. 15, *Blessed is he that shaketh his hands from all bribes.* Now it is lawful to accept service or praise from one to whom one has lent money.

Therefore in like manner it is lawful to accept any other kind of remuneration.

Obj. 4. Further, Seemingly the relation of gift to gift is the same as of loan to loan. But it is lawful to accept money for money given. Therefore it is lawful to accept repayment by loan in return for a loan granted.

Obj. 5. Further, The lender, by transferring his ownership of a sum of money removes the money further from himself than he who entrusts it to a merchant or craftsman. Now it is lawful to receive interest for money entrusted to a merchant or craftsman. Therefore it is also lawful to receive interest for money lent.

Obj. 6. Further, A man may accept a pledge for money lent, the use of which pledge he might sell for a price: as when a man mortgages his land or the house wherein he dwells. Therefore it is lawful to receive interest for money lent.

Obj. 7. Further, It sometimes happens that a man raises the price of his goods under guise of loan, or buys another's goods at a low figure; or raises his price through delay in being paid, and lowers his price that he may be paid the sooner. Now in all these cases there seems to be payment for a loan of money: nor does it appear to be manifestly illicit. Therefore it seems to be lawful to expect or exact some consideration for money lent.

On the contrary, Among other conditions requisite in a just man it is stated (Ezech. xviii. 17) that he *hath not taken usury and increase.*

I answer that, According to the Philosopher (*Ethic.* iv. I), a thing is reckoned as money *if its value can be measured by money.* Consequently, just as it is a sin against justice, to take money, by tacit or express agreement, in return for lending money or anything else that is consumed by being used, so also is it a like sin, by tacit or express agreement to receive anything whose price can be measured by money. Yet there would be no sin in receiving something of the kind, not as exacting it, nor yet as though it were due on account of some agreement tacit or expressed, but as a gratuity: since, even before lending the money, one could accept a gratuity, nor is one in a worse condition through lending.

On the other hand it is lawful to exact compensation for a loan, in respect of such things as are not appreciated by a measure of money, for instance, benevolence, and love for the lender, and so forth.

Reply Obj. 1. A lender may without sin enter an agreement with the borrower for compensation for the loss he incurs of something he ought to have, for this is not to sell the use of money but to avoid a loss. It may also happen that the borrower avoids a greater loss than the lender incurs, wherefore the borrower may repay the lender with what he has gained. But the lender cannot enter an agreement for compensation, through the fact that he makes no profit out of his money: because he must not sell that which he has not yet and may be prevented in many ways from having.

Reply Obj. 2. Repayment for a favour may be made in two ways. In one way, as a debt of justice; and to such a debt a man may be bound by a fixed contract: and its amount is measured according to the favour received. Wherefore the borrower of money or any such thing the use of which is its consumption is not bound to repay more than he received in loan: and consequently it is against justice if he be obliged to pay back more. In another way a man's obligation to repayment for favour received is based on a debt of friendship, and the nature of this debt depends more on the feeling with which the favour was conferred than on the greatness of the favour itself. This debt does not carry with it a civil obligation, involving a kind of necessity that would exclude the spontaneous nature of such a repayment.

Reply Obj. 3. If a man were, in return for money lent, as though there had been an agreement tacit or expressed, to expect or exact repayment in the shape of some remuneration of service or words, it would be the same as if he expected or exacted some real remuneration, because both can be priced at a money value, as may be seen in the case of those who offer for hire the labour which they exercise by work or by tongue. If on the other hand the remuneration by service or words be given not as an obligation, but as a favour, which is not to be appreciated at a money value, it is lawful to take, exact, and expect it.

Reply Obj. 4. Money cannot be sold for a greater sum than the amount lent, which has to be paid back: nor should the loan be made with a demand or expectation of aught else but of a feeling of benevolence which cannot be priced at a pecuniary value, and which can be the basis of a spontaneous loan. Now the obligation to lend in return at some future time is repugnant to such a feeling, because again an obligation of this kind has its pecuniary value. Consequently it is lawful for the lender to borrow something else at the same time, but it is unlawful for him to bind the borrower to grant him a loan at some future time.

Reply Obj. 5. He who lends money transfers the ownership of the money to the borrower. Hence the borrower holds the money at his own risk and is bound to pay it all back: wherefore the lender must not exact more. On the other hand he that entrusts his money to a merchant or craftsman so as to form a kind of society, does not transfer the ownership of his money to them, for it remains his, so that at his risk the merchant speculates with it, or the craftsman uses it for his craft, and consequently he may lawfully demand as something belonging to him, part of the profits derived from his money.

Reply Obj. 6. If a man in return for money lent to him pledges something that can be valued at a price, the lender must allow for the use of that thing towards the repayment of the loan. Else if he wishes the gratuitous use of that thing in addition to repayment, it is the same as if he took money for lending, and that is usury; unless perhaps it were such a thing as friends are wont to lend to one another gratis, as in the case of the loan of a book.

Reply Obj. 7. If a man wish to sell his goods at a higher price than that which is just, so that he may wait for the buyer to pay, it is manifestly a case of usury: because this waiting for the payment of the price has the character of a loan, so that whatever he demands beyond the just price in consideration of this delay, is like a price for a loan, which pertains to usury. In like manner if a buyer wishes to buy goods at a lower price than what is just, for the reason that he pays for the goods before they can be delivered, it is a sin of usury; because again this anticipated payment of money has the character of a loan, the price of which is the rebate on the just price of the goods sold. On the other hand if a man wishes to allow a rebate on the just price in order that he may have his money sooner, he is not guilty of the sin of usury.

THIRD ARTICLE.

Whether a man is bound to restore whatever profits he has made out of money gotten by usury?

We proceed thus to the Third Article:—

Objection 1. It would seem that a man is bound to restore whatever profits he has made out of money gotten by usury. For the Apostle says (Rom. xi. 16): *If the root be holy, so are the branches.* Therefore likewise if the root be rotten so are the branches. But the root was infected with usury. Therefore whatever profit is made therefrom is infected with usury. Therefore he is bound to restore it.

Obj. 2. Further, It is laid down (Extra, *De Usuris,* in the Decretal: *Cum tu sicut asseris*): *Property accruing from usury must be sold, and the price repaid to the persons from whom the usury was extorted.* Therefore, likewise, whatever else is acquired from usurious money must be restored.

Obj. 3. Further, That which a man buys with the proceeds of usury is due to him by reason of the money he paid for it. Therefore he has no more right to the thing purchased than to the money he paid. But he was bound to restore the money gained through usury. Therefore he is also bound to restore what he acquired with it.

On the contrary, A man may lawfully hold what he has lawfully acquired. Now that which is acquired by the proceeds of usury is sometimes lawfully acquired. Therefore it may be lawfully retained.

I answer that, As stated above (Article 1), there are certain things whose use is their consumption, and which do not admit of usufruct, according to law (*ibid., ad* 3). Wherefore if such-like things be extorted by means of usury, for instance money, wheat, wine and so forth, the lender is not bound to restore more than he received (since what is acquired by such things is the fruit not of the thing but of human indus-

try), unless indeed the other party by losing some of his own goods be injured through the lender retaining them: for then he is bound to make good the loss.

On the other hand there are certain things whose use is not their consumption: such things admit of usufruct, for instance house or land property and so forth. Wherefore if a man has by usury extorted from another his house or land, he is bound to restore not only the house or land but also the fruits accruing to him therefrom, since they are the fruits of things owned by another man and consequently are due to him.

Reply Obj. 1. The root has not only the character of matter, as money made by usury has; but has also somewhat the character of an active cause, in so far as it administers nourishment. Hence the comparison fails.

Reply Obj. 2. Further, Property acquired from usury does not belong to the person who paid usury, but to the person who bought it. Yet he that paid usury has a certain claim on that property just as he has on the other goods of the usurer. Hence it is not prescribed that such property should be assigned to the persons who paid usury, since the property is perhaps worth more than what they paid in usury, but it is commanded that the property be sold, and the price be restored, of course according to the amount taken in usury.

Reply Obj. 3. The proceeds of money taken in usury are due to the person who acquired them not by reason of the usurious money as instrumental cause, but on account of his own industry as principal cause. Wherefore he has more right to the goods acquired with usurious money than to the usurious money itself.

FOURTH ARTICLE.

Whether it is lawful to borrow money under a condition of usury?

We proceed thus to the Fourth Article:—

Objection 1. It would seem that it is not lawful to borrow money under a condition of usury. For the Apostle says (Rom. i. 32) that they *are worthy of death . . . not only they that do these sins, but they also that consent to them that do them.* Now he that borrows money under a condition of usury consents in the sin of the usurer, and gives him an occasion of sin. Therefore he sins also.

Obj. 2. Further, For no temporal advantage ought one to give another an occasion of committing a sin: for this pertains to active scandal, which is always sinful, as stated above (Question 43, Article 2). Now he that seeks to borrow from a usurer gives him an occasion of sin. Therefore he is not to be excused on account of any temporal advantage.

Obj. 3. Further, It seems no less necessary sometimes to deposit one's money with a usurer than to borrow from him. Now it seems altogether unlawful to deposit one's money with a usurer, even as it would be unlawful to deposit one's sword with a madman, a maiden with a libertine, or food with a glutton. Neither therefore is it lawful to borrow from a usurer.

On the contrary, He that suffers injury does not sin, according to the Philosopher (*Ethic.* v. II), wherefore justice is not a mean between two vices, as stated in the same book (ch. 5). Now a usurer sins by doing an injury to the person who borrows from him under a condition of usury. Therefore he that accepts a loan under a condition of usury does not sin.

I answer that, It is by no means lawful to induce a man to sin, yet it is lawful to make use of another's sin for a good end, since even God uses all sin for some good, since He draws some good from every evil as stated in the *Enchiridion* (xi.). Hence when Publicola asked whether it were lawful to make use of an oath taken by a man swearing by false gods (which is a manifest sin, for he gives Divine honour to them) Augustine (*Ep.* xlvii.) answered that he who uses, not for a bad but for a good purpose, the oath of a man that swears by false gods, is a party, not to his sin of swearing by demons, but to his good compact whereby he kept his word. If however he were to induce him to swear by false gods, he would sin.

Accordingly we must also answer to the question in point that it is by no means lawful to induce a man to lend under a condition of usury: yet it is lawful to borrow for usury from a man who is ready to do so and is a usurer by profession; provided the borrower have a good end in view, such as the relief of his own or another's need. Thus too it is lawful for a man who has fallen among thieves to point out his property to them (which they sin in taking) in order to save his life, after the example of the ten men who said to Ismahel (Jerem. xli. 8): *Kill us not: for we have stores in the field.*

Reply Obj. 1. He who borrows for usury does not consent to the usurer's sin but makes use of it. Nor is it the usurer's acceptance of usury that pleases him, but his lending, which is good.

Reply Obj. 2. He who borrows for usury gives the usurer an occasion, not for taking usury, but for lending; it is the usurer who finds an occasion of sin in the malice of his heart. Hence there is passive scandal on his part, while there is no active scandal on the part of the person who seeks to borrow. Nor is this passive scandal a reason why the other person should desist from borrowing if he is in need, since this passive scandal arises not from weakness or ignorance but from malice.

Reply Obj. 3. If one were to entrust one's money to a usurer lacking other means of practising usury; or with the intention of making a greater profit from his money by reason of the usury, one would be giving a sinner matter for sin, so that one would be a participator in his guilt. If, on the other hand, the usurer to whom one entrusts one's money has other means of practising usury, there is no sin in entrusting it to him that it may be in safer keeping, since this is to use a sinner for a good purpose. ♦

QUESTIONS

1. Under what circumstances, if any, does Aquinas think it is acceptable to receive or pay interest on borrowed money?

2. Can gifts or other benefits substitute for money paid as interest when interest itself is not legitimate?

3. What important earlier works does Aquinas draw upon in developing and justifying his views?

FROM *THE WORKS OF BENJAMIN FRANKLIN*

Benjamin Franklin (1706–1790)

XXI

Necessary hints to those that would be rich

The use of money is all the advantage there is in having money.

For six pounds a year you may have the use of one hundred pounds, provided you are a man of known prudence and honesty.

He that spends a groat a day idly spends idly above six pounds a year, which is the price for the use of one hundred pounds.

He that wastes idly a groat's worth of his time per day, one day with another, wastes the privilege of using one hundred pounds each day.

He that idly loses five shillings' worth of time loses five shillings, and might as prudently throw five shillings into the sea.

He that loses five shillings, not only loses that sum, but all the advantage that might be made by turning it in dealing, which, by the time that a young man becomes old, will amount to a considerable sum of money.

Again, he that sells upon credit asks a price for what he sells equivalent to the principal and interest of his money for the time he is to be kept out of it; therefore he that buys upon credit pays interest for what he buys, and he that pays ready money might let that money out to use; so that he that possesses any thing he has bought, pays interest for the use of it.

Yet, in buying goods, it is best to pay ready money, because he that sells upon credit expects to lose five per cent by bad debts; therefore he charges, on all he sells upon credit, an advance that shall make up that deficiency.

Those who pay for what they buy upon credit pay their share of this advance.

He that pays ready money escapes, or may escape, that charge.

A penny saved is two pence clear,
A pin a day's a groat a year.

XXII

The way to wealth

As clearly shown in the preface of an old Almanac entitled "Poor Richard Improved" [1]

Courteous Reader:

I have heard that nothing gives an author so great pleasure as to find his works respectfully quoted by others. Judge, then, how much I must have been gratified by an incident I am going to relate to you. I stopped my horse lately where a great number of people were collected at an auction of merchants' goods. The hour of the sale not being come, they were conversing on the badness of the times; and one of the company called to a plain, clean, old man, with white locks: "Pray, Father Abraham, what think you of the times? Will not these heavy taxes quite ruin the country? How shall we ever be able to pay them? What would you advise us to do?" Father Abraham stood up and replied: "If you would have my advice, I will give it you in short; for *A word to the wise is enough,* as Poor Richard says." They joined in desiring him to speak his mind, and gathering round him he proceeded as follows:

"Friends," said he, "the taxes are indeed very heavy, and if those laid on by the government were the only ones we had to pay, we might more easily discharge them, but we have many others and much more grievous to some of us. We are taxed twice as much by our idleness, three times as much by our pride, and four times as much by our folly, and from these taxes the commissioners cannot ease or deliver us by allowing an abatement. However, let us hearken to good advice and something may be done for us; *God helps them that help themselves,* as Poor Richard says.

"I. It would be thought a hard government that should tax its people one-tenth part of their time, to be employed in its service, but idleness taxes many of us much more; sloth by bringing on diseases, absolutely shortens life. *Sloth, like rust, consumes faster than labor wears, while the used key is always bright,* as Poor Richard says. *But dost thou love life, then do not squander time, for that is the stuff life is made of,* as Poor Richard says. How much more than is necessary do we spend in sleep, forgetting that *The sleeping fox catches no poultry,* and that *There will be sleeping enough in the grave,* as Poor Richard says.

10 "*If time be of all things the most precious, wasting time must be,* as Poor Richard says, *the greatest prodigality,* since, as he elsewhere tells us, *Lost time is never found again, and what we call time enough always proves little enough.* Let us then up and be doing, and doing to the purpose; so by diligence shall we do more with less perplexity. *Sloth makes all things difficult, but industry all things easy;* and *He that riseth late must trot all day, and shall scarce overtake his business at night;* while *Laziness travels so slowly that* 20 *Poverty soon overtakes him. Drive thy business, let not that drive thee;* and *Early to bed and early to rise, makes a man healthy, wealthy, and wise,* as Poor Richard says.

"So what signifies wishing and hoping for better times? We may make these times better if we bestir ourselves. *Industry need not wish, and he that lives upon hopes will die fasting. There are no gains without pains; then help, hands, for I have no lands;* or if I have they are smartly taxed. 30 *He that hath a trade hath an estate, and he that hath a calling hath an office of profit and honor,* as Poor Richard says; but then the trade must be worked at and the calling followed, or neither the estate nor the office will enable us to pay our taxes. If we are industrious we shall never starve, for *At the working man's house hunger looks in but dares not enter.* Nor will the bailiff nor the constable enter, for *Industry pays debts, while despair increaseth them.* What though you 40 have found no treasure, nor has any rich relation left you a legacy, *Diligence is the mother of good luck, and God gives all things to industry. Then plough deep while sluggards sleep, and you shall have corn to sell and to keep.* Work while it is called to-day, for you know not how much you may be hindered to-morrow. *One to-day is worth two to-morrows,* as Poor Richard says; and further, *Never leave that till to-morrow which you can do to-day.* If you were a servant would not you 50 be ashamed that a good master should catch

you idle? Are you then your own master? Be ashamed to catch yourself idle when there is so much to be done for yourself, your family, your country, and your king. Handle your tools without mittens; remember that *The cat in gloves catches no mice,* as Poor Richard says. It is true there is much to be done, and perhaps you are weak-handed, but stick to it steadily and you will see great effects; for *Constant dropping wears away stones;* and *By diligence and patience* 60 *the mouse ate in two the cable;* and *Little strokes fell great oaks.*

"Methinks I hear some of you say, 'Must a man afford himself no leisure?' I will tell thee, my friend, what Poor Richard says: *Employ thy time well, if thou meanest to gain leisure; and, since thou art not sure of a minute, throw not away an hour.* Leisure is time for doing something useful; this leisure the diligent man will obtain, but the lazy man never; for *A life of leisure and a* 70 *life of laziness are two things. Many, without labor, would live by their wits only, but they break for want of stock;* whereas industry gives comfort and plenty and respect. *Fly pleasures, and they will follow you. The diligent spinner has a large shift; and now I have a sheep and a cow, everybody bids me good morrow.*"

"II. But with our industry we must likewise be steady, settled, and careful, and oversee our own affairs with our own eyes, and not trust 80 too much to others; for, as Poor Richard says:

> I never saw an oft -removed tree,
> Nor yet an oft-removed family,
> That throve so well as those that settled be.

And again, *Three removes as are bad as a fire;* and again, *Keep thy shop, and thy shop will keep thee;* and again: *If you would have your business done, go; if not, send.* And again:

> *He that by the plough would thrive,*
> *Himself must either hold or drive.*   90

And again, *The eye of a master will do more work than both his hands;* and again, *Want of care does us more damage than want of knowledge;* and again, *Not to oversee workmen is to leave them your purse open.* Trusting too much to others' care is the ruin of many; for, *In the affairs of this world men are saved, not by faith, but by the want of it;* but a man's own care is profitable; for, *If you would have a faithful servant, and one that you like, serve yourself. A little neglect may breed great mischief; for want of a nail the shoe was lost; for want of a shoe the horse was lost; and for want of a horse the rider was lost, being overtaken and slain by the enemy; all for want of a little care about a horse-shoe nail.*

"III. So much for industry, my friends, and attention to one's own business; but to these we must add frugality, if we would make our industry more certainly successful. A man may, if he knows not how to save as he gets, keep his nose all his life to the grindstone and die not worth a groat at last. *A fat kitchen makes a lean will;* and

> *Many estates are spent in the getting,*
> *Since women for tea forsook spinning and*
> *knitting,*
> *And men for punch forsook hewing and splitting.*

If you would be wealthy, think of saving as well as of getting. The Indies have not made Spain rich, because her outgoes are greater than her incomes.

"Away then with your expensive follies, and you will not then have so much cause to complain of hard times, heavy taxes, and chargeable families; for

> *Women and wine, game and deceit,*
> *Make the wealth small and the want great.*

And further, *What maintains one vice would bring up two children.* You may think, perhaps, that a little tea, or a little punch now and then, diet a little more costly, clothes a little finer, and a little entertainment now and then, can be no great matter; but remember, *Many a little makes a mickle.* Beware of little expenses: *A small leak will sink a great ship,* as Poor Richard says; and again, *Who dainties love, shall beggars prove;* and moreover, *Fools make feasts, and wise men eat them.*

"Here you are all got together at this sale of fineries and knick-knacks. You call them *goods;* but if you do not take care they will prove *evils* to some of you. You expect they will be sold cheap, and perhaps they may for less than they cost; but if you have no occasion for them they must be dear to you. Remember what Poor Richard says: *Buy what thou hast no need of, and ere long thou shalt sell thy necessaries.* And again, *At a great pennyworth pause a while.* He means, that perhaps the cheapness is apparent only, and not real; or the bargain, by straitening thee

in thy business, may do thee more harm than good. For in another place he says, *Many have been ruined by buying good pennyworths.* Again, *It is foolish to lay out money in a purchase of repentance;* and yet this folly is practised every day at auctions for want of minding the Almanac. Many a one, for the sake of finery on the back, have gone with a hungry belly and half-starved their families. *Silks and satins, scarlet and velvets, put out the kitchen fire,* as Poor Richard says.

"These are not the necessaries of life; they can scarcely be called the conveniences; and yet, only because they look pretty, how many want to have them! By these and other extravagances the genteel are reduced to poverty and forced to borrow of those whom they formerly despised, but who, through industry and frugality, have maintained their standing; in which case it appears plainly that *A ploughman on his legs is higher than a gentleman on his knees,* as Poor Richard says. Perhaps they have had a small estate left them, which they knew not the getting of: they think, *It is day, and will never be night;* that a little to be spent out of so much is not worth minding; but *Always taking out of the meal-tub, and never putting in, soon comes to the bottom,* as Poor Richard says; and then, *When the well is dry, they know the worth of water.* But this they might have known before, if they had taken his advice. *If you would know the value of money, go and try to borrow some; for he that goes a borrowing goes a sorrowing,* as Poor Richard says; and indeed so does he that lends to such people, when he goes to get it again. Poor Dick further advises and says,

> *Fond pride of dress is sure a very curse;*
> *Ere fancy you consult, consult your purse.*

And again, *Pride is as loud a beggar as Want, and a great deal more saucy.* When you have bought one fine thing you must buy ten more, that your appearance may be all of a piece; but Poor Dick says, *It is easier to suppress the first desire than to satisfy all that follow it.* And it is as truly folly for the poor to ape the rich, as for the frog to swell in order to equal the ox.

> *Vessels large may venture more,*
> *But little boats should keep near shore.*

It is, however, a folly soon punished; for, as Poor Richard says, *Pride that dines on vanity sups on contempt. Pride breakfasted with Plenty, dined with Poverty, and supped with Infamy.* And after all, of what use is this pride of appearance, for which so much is risked, so much is suffered? It cannot promote health, nor ease pain; it makes no increase of merit in the person; it creates envy; it hastens misfortune.

"But what madness must it be to *run in debt* for these superfluities! We are offered by the terms of this sale six months' credit; and that, perhaps, has induced some of us to attend it, because we cannot spare the ready money, and hope now to be fine without it. But ah! think what you do when you run in debt; you give to another power over your liberty. If you cannot pay at the time, you will be ashamed to see your creditor; you will be in fear when you speak to him; you will make poor, pitiful, sneaking excuses, and by degrees come to lose your veracity, and sink into base, downright lying; for, *The second vice is lying, the first is running in debt*, as Poor Richard says; and again, to the same purpose, *Lying rides upon Debt's back*; whereas a free-born Englishman ought not to be ashamed nor afraid to see or speak to any man living. But poverty often deprives a man of all spirit and virtue. *It is hard for an empty bag to stand upright.*

"What would you think of that prince or of that government who should issue an edict forbidding you to dress like a gentleman or gentlewoman, on pain of imprisonment or servitude? Would you not say that you were free, have a right to dress as you please, and that such an edict would be a breach of your privileges, and such a government tyrannical? And yet you are about to put yourself under such tyranny when you run in debt for such dress! Your creditor has authority, at his pleasure, to deprive you of your liberty by confining you in gaol till you shall be able to pay him. When you have got your bargain you may perhaps think little of payment, but, as Poor Richard says, *Creditors have better memories than debtors; creditors are a superstitious sect, great observers of set days and times.* The day comes round before you are aware, and the demand is made before you are prepared to satisfy it; or, if you bear your debt in mind, the term, which at first seemed so long, will, as it lessens, appear extremely short.

Time will seem to have added wings to his heels as well as his shoulders. *Those have a short Lent who owe money to be paid at Easter.* At present, perhaps, you may think yourselves in thriving circumstances, and that you can bear a little extravagance without injury, but—

> *For age and want save while you may;*
> *No morning sun lasts a whole day.*

Gain may be temporary and uncertain, but ever, while you live, expense is constant and certain; and *It is easier to build two chimneys than to keep one in fuel*, as Poor Richard says; so, *Rather go to bed supperless than rise in debt.*

> *Get what you can, and what you get hold;*
> *'Tis the stone that will turn all your lead into gold.*

And, when you have got the Philosopher's stone, sure you will no longer complain of bad times or the difficulty of paying taxes.

"IV. This doctrine, my friends, is reason and wisdom; but, after all, do not depend too much upon your own industry and frugality and prudence, though excellent things, for they may all be blasted, without the blessing of Heaven; and therefore ask that blessing humbly, and be not uncharitable to those that at present seem to want it, but comfort and help them. Remember Job suffered and was afterwards prosperous.

"And now, to conclude, *Experience keeps a dear school, but fools will learn in no other*, as Poor Richard says, and scarce in that, for it is true *We may give advice, but we cannot give conduct.* However, remember this, *They that will not be counselled cannot be helped*; and further, that *If you will not hear Reason, she will surely rap your knuckles*, as Poor Richard says."

Thus the old gentleman ended his harangue. The people heard it and approved the doctrine, and immediately practised the contrary, just as if it had been a common sermon; for the auction opened, and they began to buy extravagantly. I found the good man had thoroughly studied my Almanacs, and digested all I had dropped on these topics during the course of twenty-five years. The frequent mention he made of me must have tired any one else, but my vanity was wonderfully delighted with it, though I was conscious that not a tenth part of the wisdom was my own which he ascribed to me, but rather the gleanings that I had made of the sense of all ages and nations. However, I resolved to be the better for the echo of it, and though I had at first determined to buy stuff for a new coat, I went away resolved to wear my old one a little longer. Reader, if thou wilt do the same thy profit will be as great as mine. I am, as ever, thine to serve thee,

Richard Saunders.

ENDNOTE

1. In December of the year 1732 Franklin commenced the publication of what he styled *Poor Richard's Almanac,* price 5 pence. It attained an astonishing popularity at once. Three editions were sold within the month of its appearance. The average sale for twenty-five years was ten thousand a year. He was sometimes obliged to put it to press in October to get a supply of copies to the remote colonies by the beginning of the year. It has been translated into nearly if not quite every written language, and several different translations of it have been made into the French and German. It contains some of the best fun as well as the wisest counsel that ever emanated from his pen. ♦

QUESTIONS

1. At what rate of interest does Franklin say a person of good credit can borrow funds?

2. How much should a lender expect to lose in bad debts?

3. What are Franklin's ways to wealth?

4. For what purpose is it a good idea to borrow?

Of Riches and Of Usury from *The Essays*

Francis Bacon (1561–1626)

XXXIV.
Of Riches

I cannot call riches better than the baggage of virtue; the Roman word is better, *impedimenta*. For as the baggage is to an army, so is riches to virtue. It cannot be spared, nor left behind, but it hindreth the march; yea, and the care of it sometimes loseth or disturbeth the victory. Of great riches there is no real use, except it be in the distribution; the rest is but conceit. So saith Solomon: "Where much is, there are many to consume it, and what hath the owner but the sight of it with his eyes?" The personal fruition in any man cannot reach to feel great riches. There is a custody of them, or a power of dole and donative of them, or a fame of them, but no solid use to the owner. Do you not see what feigned prices are set upon little stones and rarities? and what works of ostensation are undertaken because there might seem to be some use of great riches? But then, you will say, they may be of use to buy men out of dangers or troubles. As Solomon saith, "Riches are as a strong hold in the imagination of the rich man." But this is excellently expressed, that it is in imagination, and not always in fact; for certainly great riches have sold more men than they have bought out. Seek not proud riches, but such as thou mayest get justly, use soberly, distribute cheerfully, and leave contentedly; yet have no abstract nor friarly contempt of them, but distinguish, as Cicero saith well of Rabirius Posthumus: *In studio rei amplificandoe, apparebat, non avaritice proedam, sed instrumentum bonitati quoeri.* Hearken, also, to Solomon, and beware of hasty gathering of riches: *Qui festinat ad divitias, non erit insons.* The poets feign that when Plutus (which is riches) is sent from Jupiter, he limps and goes slowly; but when he is sent from Pluto, he runs and is swift of foot. Meaning, that riches gotten by good means and just labor pace slow ly; but when they come by the death of others (as by the course of inheritance, testaments, and the like) they come tumbling upon a man. But it might be applied likewise to Pluto, taking him for the devil; for when riches come from the devil (as by fraud, and oppression, and unjust means) they come upon speed. The ways to enrich are many, and most of them foul. Parsimony is one of the best, and yet is not innocent, for it withholdeth men from works of liberality and charity. The improvement of the ground is the most natural obtaining of riches, for it is our great mother's blessing, the earth's; but it is slow. And yet, where men of great wealth do stoop to husbandry, it multiplieth riches exceedingly. I knew a nobleman in England that had the greatest audits of any man in my time—a great grazier, a great sheep-master, a great timber-man, a great collier, a great corn-master, a great lead-man, and so of iron, and a number of the like points of husbandry, so as the earth seemed a sea to him in respect of the perpetual importation. It was truly observed by one, "that himself came very hardly to a little riches, and very easily to great riches;" for when a man's stock is come to that, that he can expect the prime of markets, and overcome those bargains which for their greatness are few men's money, and be partner in the industries of younger men, he cannot but increase mainly. The gains of ordinary trades and vocations are honest, and furthered by two things: chiefly, by diligence; and by a good name for good and fair dealing. But the gains of bargains are of a more doubtful nature; when men shall wait upon others' necessity, broke by servants and instruments to draw them on, put off others cunningly that would be better chapmen, and the like practices, which are crafty and naught. As for the chopping of bargains, when a man buys, not to hold but to sell over again, that commonly grindeth double, both upon the seller and upon the buyer. Sharings do greatly enrich, if the hands be well chosen that are trusted. Usury is the certainest means of gain, though one of the worst, as that whereby a man doth eat his bread, *In sudore vultus alieni,* and besides doth plough upon Sundays. But yet, certain though it be, it hath flaws; for that the scriveners and brokers do value unsound men to serve their own turn. The fortune in being the first in an invention, or in a privilege, does cause sometimes a wonderful overgrowth in riches; as it was with the first sugar-man in the Canaries. Therefore, if a man can play the true logician, to have as well judgment as invention, he may do great matters, especially if the times be fit. He that resteth upon gains certain shall hardly grow to great riches; and he that puts all upon adventures, doth oftentimes break and come to poverty. It is good, therefore, to guard adventures with certainties that may uphold losses. Monopolies, and coemption of wares for resale where they are not restrained, are great means to enrich, especially if the party have intelligence what things are like to come into request, and so store himself beforehand. Riches gotten by service, though it be of the best, rise; yet when they are gotten by flattery, feeding humors, and other servile conditions, they may be placed amongst the worst. As for fishing for testaments and exec-utorships (as Tacitus saith of Seneca, *Testamenta et orbos, tangnam indagine capi*), it is yet worse; by how much men submit themselves to meaner persons than in service. Believe not much them that seem to despise riches; for they despise them that despair of them, and none worse when they come to them. Be not penny-wise; riches have wings, and some-times they fly away of themselves; sometimes they must be set flying to bring in more. Men leave their riches either to their kindred or to the public; and moderate portions prosper best in both. A great state left to an heir is as a lure to all the birds of prey round about to seize on him, if he be not the better estab-lished in years and judgment. Likewise, glo-rious gifts and foundations are like sacrifices without salt, and but the painted sepulchres of alms, which soon will putrefy and corrupt inwardly. Therefore, measure not thine advancements by quantity, but frame them by measure; and defer not charities till death; for certainly, if a man weigh it rightly, he that doth so is rather liberal of another man's than of his own. . . .

XLI.
Of Usury

Many have made witty invectives against usury. They say that it is pity the devil should have God's part, which is the tithe. That the usurer is the greatest Sabbath-breaker, because his plough goeth every Sunday. That the usu-rer is the drone that Virgil speaketh of—

Ignavum fucos à praesepibus arcent.

That the usurer breaketh the first law that was made for mankind after the Fall, which was, *In sudore vultûs tui comedes panem tuum; not In sudore vultûs alieni.* That usurers should have orange-tawny bonnets, because they do Judaise. That it is against nature for money to beget money, and the like. I say this only, that usury is a *concessum propter duritiem cordis,* for since there must be borrowing and lend-ing, and men are so hard of heart as they will not lend freely, usury must be permitted. Some others have made suspicious and cun-ning propositions of banks, discovery of men's estates, and other inventions; but few have spoken of usury usefully. It is good to set before us the incommodities and com-modities of usury, that the good may be either weighed out or culled out; and warily to pro-vide that while we make forth to that which is better, we meet not with that which is worse.

The discommodities of usury are: first, that it makes fewer merchants—for were it not for this lazy trade of usury, money would not lie still, but would, in great part, be employed upon merchandizing, which is the *vena porta* of wealth in a state. The second, that it makes poor merchants; for as a farmer cannot husband his ground so well if he sit at a great rent, so the merchant cannot drive his trade so well if he sit at great usury. The third is incident to the other two; and that is, the decay of customs of king or states, which ebb or flow with merchandizing. The fourth, that it bringeth the treasure of a realm or state into a few hands; for the usurer being at certainties, and others at uncertainties at the end of the game, most of the money will be in the box, and ever a state flourisheth when wealth is more equally spread. The fifth, that it beats down the price of land; for the employment of money is chiefly either merchandizing or purchasing, and usury way-lays both. The sixth, that it doth dull and damp all industries, improvements, and new inventions, wherein money would be stirring if it were not for this slug. The last, that it is the canker and ruin of many men's estates, which in process of time breeds a public poverty.

On the other side, the commodities of usury are: first, that howsoever usury in some respect hindereth merchandizing, yet in some other it advanceth it; for it is certain that the greatest part of trade is driven by young merchants upon borrowing at interest; so as if the usurer either call in or keep back his money, there will ensue presently a great stand of trade. The second is, that were it not for this easy borrowing upon interest, men's necessities would draw upon them a most sudden undoing, in that they would be forced to sell their means (be it land or goods) far under foot; and so, whereas usury doth but gnaw upon them, bad markets would swallow them quite up. As for mortgaging, or pawning, it will little mend the matter, for either men will not take pawns without use, or if they do, they will look precisely for the forfeiture. I remember a cruel moneyed man in the country that would say, "The devil take this usury; it keeps us from forfeitures of mortgages and bonds." The third and last is, that it is a vanity to conceive that there would be ordinary borrowing without profit; and it is impossible to conceive the number of inconveniences that will ensue if borrowing be cramped. Therefore, to speak of the abolishing of usury is idle. All States have ever had it, in one kind of rate or other; so as that opinion must be sent to Utopia.

To speak now of the reformation and reglement of usury—how the discommodities of it may be best avoided, and the commodities

retained. It appears, by the balance of commodities and discommodities of usury, two things are to be reconciled. The one, that the tooth of usury be grinded, that it bite not too much; the other, that there be left open a means to invite moneyed men to lend to the merchants for the continuing and quickening of trade. This cannot be done except you introduce two several sorts of usury, a less and a greater. For if you reduce usury to one low rate, it will ease the common borrower, but the merchant will be to seek for money; and it is to be noted that the trade of merchandize, being the most lucrative, may bear usury at a good rate; other contracts not so.

To serve both intentions the way would be briefly thus: that there be two rates of usury, the one free, and general for all; the other, under license only, to certain persons, and in certain places of merchandizing. First, therefore, let usury, in general, be reduced to five in the hundred; and let that rate be proclaimed to be free and current; and let the State shut itself out, to take any penalty for the same. This will preserve borrowing from any general stop or dryness. This will ease infinite borrowers in the country. This will, in good part, raise the price of land, because land purchased at sixteen years' purchase will yield six in the hundred, and somewhat more, whereas this rate of interest yields but five. This by like reason will encourage and edge industrious and profitable improvements; because many will rather venture in that kind than take five in the hundred, especially having been used to greater profit. Secondly, let there be certain persons licensed to lend to known merchants upon usury at a higher rate; and let it be with the cautious following: let the rate be, even with the merchant himself, somewhat more easy than that he used formerly to pay; for, by that means, all borrowers shall have some ease, by this reformation, be he merchant, or whosoever. Let it be no bank or common stock, but every man be master of his own money: not that I altogether mislike banks, but they will hardly be brooked, in regard of certain suspicions. Let the State be answered, some small matter, for the license, and the rest left to the lender; for if the abatement be but small, it will no whit discourage the lender. For he, for example, that took before ten or nine in the hundred will sooner descend to eight in the hundred than give over his trade of usury, and go from certain gains to gains of hazard. Let these licensed lenders be in numbers indefinite, but restrained to certain principal cities and towns of merchandizing; for then they will be hardly able to color other men's moneys in the country: so as the license of nine will not suck away the current rate of five; for no man will lend his moneys far off, nor put them into unknown hands.

If it be objected that this doth, in a sort, authorize usury, which before was in some places but permissive, the answer is, that it is better to mitigate usury by declaration than to suffer it to rage by connivance. ◆

QUESTIONS

1. According to Bacon, do riches tend to facilitate or to hinder virtue?

2. What are the ways to become wealthy, according to Bacon?

3. Which of these ways is the least admirable? Explain.

4. What are the seven ways in which lending money at interest hurts a society?

5. What are the three ways in which lending at interest is useful for a society?

6. What rate of interest does Bacon recommend as reasonable?

OF PROFITS
FROM *THE PRINCIPLE OF POLITICAL ECONOMY*

John Stuart Mill (1806–1873)

§1. . . . [We] proceed to the share of the capitalist; the profits of capital or stock; the gains of the person who advances the expenses of production—who, from funds in his possession, pays the wages of the labourers, or supports them during the work; who supplies the requisite buildings, materials, and tools or machinery; and to whom, by the usual terms of the contract, the produce belongs, to be disposed of at his pleasure. After indemnifying him for his outlay, there commonly remains a surplus, which is his profit; the net income from his capital: the amount which he can afford to spend in necessaries or pleasures, or from which by further saving he can add to his wealth.

As the wages of the labourer are the remuneration of labour, so the profits of the capitalist are properly, according to Mr. Senior's well-chosen expression, the remuneration of abstinence. They are what he gains by forbearing to consume his capital for his own uses, and allowing it to be consumed by productive labourers for their uses. For this forbearance he requires a recompense. Very often in personal enjoyment he would be a gainer by squandering his capital, the capital amounting to more than the sum of the profits which it will yield during the years he can expect to live. But while he retains it undiminished, he has always the power of consuming it if he wishes or needs; he can bestow it upon others at his death; and in the meantime he derives from it an income, which he can without impoverishment apply to the satisfaction of his own wants or inclinations.

Of the gains, however, which the possession of a capital enables a person to make, a part only is properly an equivalent for the use of the capital itself; namely, as much as a solvent person would be willing to pay for the loan of it. This, which as everybody knows is called interest, is all that a person is enabled to get by merely abstaining from the immediate consumption of his capital, and allowing it to be used for productive purposes by others. The remuneration which is obtained in any country for mere abstinence, is measured by the current rate of interest on the best security: such security as precludes any appreciable chance of losing the principal. What a person expects to gain, who superintends the employment of his own capital, is always more, and generally much more, than this. The rate of profit greatly exceeds the rate of interest. The surplus is partly compensation for risk. By lending his capital, on unexceptionable security, he runs little or no risk. But if he embarks in business on his own account, he always exposes his capital to some, and in many cases to very great, danger of partial or total loss. For this danger he must be compensated, otherwise he will not incur it. He must likewise be remunerated for the devotion of his time and labour. The control of the operations of industry usually belongs to the person who supplies the whole or the greatest part of the funds by which they are carried on, and who, according to the ordinary arrangement, is either alone interested, or is the person most interested (at least directly), in the result. To exercise this control with efficiency, if the concern is large and complicated, requires great assiduity, and often, no ordinary skill. This assiduity and skill must be remunerated.

The gross profits from capital, the gains returned to those who supply the funds for production, must suffice for these three purposes. They must afford a sufficient equivalent for abstinence, indemnity for risk, and remuneration for the labour and skill required for superintendence. These different compensations may be either paid to the same, or to different persons. The capital, or some part of it, may be borrowed: may belong to some one who does not undertake the risks or the trouble of business. In that case, the lender or owner is the person who practises the abstinence; and is remunerated for it by the interest paid to him, while the difference between the interest and the gross profits remunerates the exertions and risks of the undertaker. Sometimes, again, the capital, or a part of it, is supplied by what is called a sleeping partner; who shares the risks of the employment, but not the trouble, and who, in consideration of those risks, receives not a mere interest, but a stipulated share of the gross profits. Sometimes the capital is supplied and the risk incurred by one person, and the business carried on exclusively in his name, while the trouble of management is made over to another, who is engaged for that purpose at a fixed salary. Management, however, by hired servants, who have no interest in the result but that of preserving their salaries, is proverbially inefficient, unless they act under the inspecting eye, if not the controlling hand, of the person chiefly interested: and prudence almost always recommends giving to a manager not thus controlled a remuneration partly dependent on the profits; which virtually reduces the case to that of a sleeping partner. Or finally, the same person may own the capital, and conduct the business; adding, if he will and can, to the management of his own capital, that of as much more as the owners may be willing to trust him with. But under any or all of these arrangements, the same three things require their remuneration, and must obtain it from the gross profit: abstinence, risk, exertion. And the three parts into which profit may be considered as resolving itself, may be described respectively as interest, insurance, and wages of superintendence.

§2. The lowest rate of profit which can permanently exist, is that which is barely adequate, at the given place and time, to afford an equivalent for the abstinence, risk, and exertion implied in the employment of capital. From the gross profit has first to be deducted as much as will form a fund sufficient on the average to cover all losses incident to the employment. Next, it must afford such an equivalent to the owner of the capital for forbearing to consume it, as is then and there a sufficient motive to him to persist in his abstinence. How much will be required to form this equivalent depends on the comparative value placed, in the given society, upon the present and the future: (in the words formerly used) on the strength of the effective desire of accumulation. Further, after covering all losses, and remunerating the owner for forbearing to consume, there must be something left to recompense the labour and skill of the person who devotes his time to the business. This recompense too must be sufficient to enable at least the owners of the larger capitals to receive for their trouble, or to pay to some manager for his, what to them or him will be a sufficient inducement for undergoing it. If the surplus is no more than this, none but large masses of capital will be employed productively; and if it did not even amount to this, capital would be withdrawn from production, and unproductively consumed, until, by an indirect consequence of its diminished amount, to be explained hereafter, the rate of profit was raised.

Such, then, is the minimum of profits: but that minimum is exceedingly variable, and at some times and places extremely low; on account of the great variableness of two out of its three elements. That the rate of necessary remuneration for abstinence, or in other words the effective desire of accumulation, differs widely in different states of society and civilization, has been seen in a former chapter. There is a still wider difference in the element which consists in compensation for risk. I am not now speaking of the differences in point of risk between different employments of capital in the same society, but of the very different degrees of security of property in different states of society. Where, as in many of the governments of Asia, property is in perpetual danger of spoliation from a tyrannical government, or from its rapacious and ill-controlled officers; where to possess or to be suspected of possessing wealth, is to be a mark not only for plunder, but perhaps for personal ill-treatment to extort the disclosure and surrender of hidden valuables; or where, as in the European Middle Ages, the weakness of the government, even when not itself inclined to oppress, leaves its subjects exposed without protection or redress to active spoliation, or audacious withholding of just rights, by any powerful individual; the rate of profit which persons of average dispositions will require, to make them forego the immediate enjoyment of what they happen to possess, for the purpose of exposing it and themselves to these perils, must be something very considerable. And these contingencies affect those who live on the mere interest of their capital, in common with those who personally engage in production. In a generally secure state of society, the risks which may be attendant on the nature of particular employments seldom fall on the person who lends his capital, if he lends on good security; but in a state of society like that of many parts of Asia, no security (except perhaps the actual pledge of gold or jewels) is good; and the mere possession of a hoard, when known or suspected, exposes it and the possessor to risks, for which scarcely any profit he could expect to obtain would be an equivalent; so that there would be still less accumulation than there is, if a state of insecurity did not also multiply the occasions on which the possession of a treasure may be the means of saving life or averting serious calamities. Those who lend under these wretched governments, do it at the utmost peril of never being paid. In most of the native states of India, the lowest terms on which any one will lend money, even to the government, are such, that if the interest is paid only for a few years, and the principal not at all, the lender is tolerably well indemnified. If the accumulation of principal and compound interest is ultimately compromised at a few shillings in the pound, he has generally made an advantageous bargain.

§3. The remuneration of capital in different employments, much more than the remuneration of labour, varies according to the circumstances which render one employment more attractive, or more repulsive, than another. The profits, for example, of retail trade, in proportion to the capital employed, exceed those of wholesale dealers or manufacturers, for this reason among others, that there is less consideration attached to the employment. The greatest, however, of these differences, is that caused by difference of risk. The profits of a gunpowder manufacturer must be considerably greater than the average, to make up for the peculiar risks to which he and his property are constantly exposed. When, however, as in the case of marine adventure, the peculiar risks are capable of being, and commonly are, commuted for a fixed payment, the premium of insurance takes its regular place among the charges of production, and the compensation which the owner of the ship or cargo receives for that payment, does not appear in the estimate of his profits, but is included in the replacement of his capital.

The portion, too, of the gross profit, which forms the remuneration for the labour and skill of the dealer or producer, is very different in different employments. This is the explanation always given of the extraordinary rate of apothecaries' profit; the greatest part, as Adam Smith observes, being frequently no more than the reasonable wages of professional attendance; for which, until a late alteration of the law, the apothecary could not demand any remuneration, except in the prices of his drugs. Some occupations require a considerable amount of scientific or technical education, and can [1848] only be carried on by persons who combine with that education a considerable capital. Such is the business of an engineer, both in the original sense of the term, a machine-maker, and in its popular or derivative sense, an undertaker of public works. These are always the most profitable employments. There are cases, again, in which a considerable amount of labour and skill is required to conduct a business necessarily of limited extent. In such cases, a higher than common rate of profit is necessary to yield only the common rate of remuneration. "In a small seaport town," says Adam Smith, "a little grocer will make forty or fifty per cent upon a stock of a single hundred pounds, while a considerable wholesale merchant in the same place will scarce make eight or ten per cent upon a stock of ten thousand. The trade of the grocer may be necessary for the convenience of the inhabitants, and the narrowness of the market may not admit the employment of a larger capital in the business. The man, however, must not only live by his trade, but live by it suitably to the qualifications which it requires. Besides possessing a little capital, he must be able to read, write, and account and must be a tolerable judge, too, of perhaps fifty or sixty different sorts of goods, their prices, qualities, and the markets where they are to be had cheapest. Thirty or forty pounds a year cannot be considered as too great a recompense for the labour of a person so accomplished. Deduct this from the seemingly great profits of his capital, and little more will remain, perhaps, than the ordinary profits of stock. The greater part of the apparent profit is, in this case, too, real wages."

All the natural monopolies (meaning thereby those which are created by circumstances, and not by law) which produce or aggravate the disparities in the remuneration of different kinds of labour, operate similarly between different employments of capital. If a business can only be advantageously carried on by a large capital, this in most countries limits so narrowly the class of persons who can enter into the employment, that they are enabled to keep their rate of profit above the general level. A trade may also, from the nature of the case, be confined to so few hands, that profits may admit of being kept up by a combination among the dealers. It is well known that even among so numerous a body as the London booksellers, this sort of combination long continued to exist. I have already mentioned the case of the gas and water companies.

§4. After due allowance is made for these various causes of inequality, namely, differences in the risk or agreeableness of different employments, and natural or artificial monopolies; the rate of profit on capital in all employments tends to an equality. Such is the proposition usually laid down by political economists, and under proper explanations it is true.

That portion of profit which is properly interest, and which forms the remuneration for abstinence, is strictly the same, at the same time and place, whatever be the employment. The rate of interest, on equally good security, does not vary according to the destination of the principal, though it does vary from time to time very much according to the circumstances of the market. There is no employment in which, in the present state of industry, competition is so active and incessant as in the lending and borrowing of money. All persons in business are occasionally, and most of them constantly, borrowers: while all persons not in business, who possess monied property, are lenders. Between these two great bodies there is a numerous, keen, and intelligent class of middlemen, composed of bankers, stockbrokers, discount brokers, and others, alive to the slightest breath of probable gain. The smallest circumstance, or the most transient impression on the public mind, which tends to an increase or diminution of the demand for loans either at the time or prospectively, operates immediately on the rate of interest: and circumstances in the general state of trade, really tending to cause this difference of demand, are continually occurring, sometimes to such an extent, that the rate of interest on the best mercantile bills has been known to vary in little more than a year (even without the occurrence of the great derangement called a commercial crisis) from four, or less, to eight or nine per cent. But, at the same time and place, the rate of interest is the same, to all who can give equally good security. The market rate of interest is at all times a known and definite thing.

It is far otherwise with gross profit; which, though (as will presently be seen) it does not vary much from employment to employment, varies very greatly from individual to individual, and can scarcely be in any two cases the same. It depends on the knowledge, talents, economy, and energy of the capitalist himself, or of the agents whom he employs; on the accidents of personal connexion; and even on chance. Hardly any two dealers in the same trade, even if their commodities are equally good and equally cheap, carry on their business at the same expense, or turn over their capital in the same time. That equal capitals give equal profits, as a general maxim of trade, would be as false as that equal age or size gives equal bodily strength, or that equal reading or experience gives equal knowledge. The effect depends as much upon twenty other things, as upon the single cause specified.

But though profits thus vary, the parity, on the whole, of different modes of employing capital (in the absence of any natural or artificial monopoly) is, in a certain and a very important sense, maintained. On an average (whatever may be the occasional fluctuations) the various employments of capital are on such a footing as to hold out, not equal profits, but equal expectations of profit, to persons of average abilities and advantages. By equal, I mean after making compensation for any inferiority in the agreeableness or safety of an employment. If the case were not so; if there were, evidently, and to common experience, more favourable chances of pecuniary success in one business than in others, more persons would engage their capital in the business, or would bring up their sons to it; which in fact always happens when a business, like that of an engineer at present [1848], or like any newly established and prosperous manufacture, is seen to be a growing and thriving one. If, on the contrary, a business is not considered thriving; if the chances of profit in it are thought to be inferior to those in other employments; capital gradually leaves it, or at least new capital is not attracted to it; and by this change in the distribution of capital between the less profitable and the more profitable employments, a sort of balance is restored. The expectations of profit, therefore, in different employments, cannot long continue very different: they tend to a common average, though they are generally oscillating from one side to the other side of the medium.

This equalizing process, commonly described as the transfer of capital from one employment to another, is not necessarily the onerous, slow, and almost impracticable operation which it is very often represented to be. In the first place, it does not always imply the actual removal of capital already embarked in an employment. In a rapidly progressive state of capital, the adjustment often takes place by means of the new accumulations of each year, which direct themselves in preference towards the more thriving trades. Even when a real transfer of capital is necessary, it is by no means implied that any of those who are engaged in the unprofitable employment relinquish business and break up their establishments. The numerous and multifarious channels of credit, through which, in commercial nations, unemployed capital diffuses itself over the field of employment, flowing over in greater abundance to the lower levels, are the means by which the equalization is accomplished. The process consists in a limitation by one class of dealers or producers, and an extension by the other, of that portion of their business which is carried on with borrowed capital. There is scarcely any dealer or producer on a considerable scale, who confines his business to what can be carried on by his own funds. When trade is good, he not only uses to the utmost his own capital, but employs, in addition, much of the credit which that capital obtains for him. When, either from over-supply or from some slackening in the demand for his commodity, he finds that it sells more slowly or obtains a lower price, he contracts his operations, and does not apply to bankers or other money dealers for a renewal of their advances to the same extent as before. A business which is increasing holds out, on the contrary, a prospect of profitable employment for a larger amount of this floating capital than previously, and those engaged in it become applicants to the money dealers for larger advances, which, from their improving circumstances, they have no difficulty in obtaining. A different distribution of floating capital between two employments has as much effect in restoring their profits to an equilibrium, as if the owners of an equal amount of capital were to abandon the one trade and carry their capital into the other. This easy, and as it were spontaneous, method of accommodating production to demand, is quite sufficient to correct any inequalities arising from the fluctuations of trade, or other causes of ordinary occurrence. In the case of an altogether declining trade, in which it is necessary that the production should be, not occasionally varied, but greatly and permanently diminished, or perhaps stopped altogether, the process of extricating the capital is, no doubt, tardy and difficult, and almost always attended with considerable loss; much of the capital fixed in machinery, buildings, permanent works, being either not applicable to any other purpose, or only applicable after expensive alterations; and time being seldom given for effecting the change in the mode in which it would be effected with least loss, namely, by not replacing the fixed capital as it wears out. There is besides, in totally changing the destination of a capital, so great a sacrifice of established connexion, and of acquired skill and experience, that people are always very slow in resolving upon it, and hardly ever do so until long after a change of fortune has become hopeless. These, however, are distinctly exceptional cases, and even in these the equalization is at last effected. It may also happen that the return to equilibrium is considerably protracted, when, before one inequality has been corrected, another cause of inequality arises; which is said to have been continually the case, during a long series of years, with the production of cotton in the Southern States of North America; the commodity having been upheld at what was virtually a monopoly price, because the increase of demand, from successive improvements in the manufacture, went on with a rapidity so much beyond expectation that for many years the supply never completely overtook it. But it is not often that a succession of disturbing causes, all acting in the same direction, are known to follow one another with hardly any interval. Where there is no monopoly, the profits of a trade are likely to range sometimes above and sometimes below the general level, but tending always to return to it; like the oscillations of the pendulum.

In general, then, although profits are very different to different individuals, and to the same individual in different years, there cannot be much diversity at the same time and place in the average profits of different employments, (other than the standing differences necessary to compensate for difference of attractiveness), except for short periods, or when some great permanent revulsion has overtaken a particular trade. If any popular impression exists that some trades are more profitable than others, independently of monopoly, or of such rare accidents as have been noticed in regard to the cotton trade, the impression is in all probability fallacious, since if it were shared by those who have greatest means of knowledge and motives to accurate examination, there would take place such an influx of capital as would soon lower the profits to the common level. It is true that, to persons with the same amount of original means, there is more chance of making a large fortune in some employments than in others. But it would be found that in those same employments, bankruptcies also are more frequent, and that the chance of greater success is balanced by a greater probability of complete failure. Very often it is more than balanced: for, as was remarked in

another case, the chance of great prizes operates with a greater degree of strength than arithmetic will warrant, in attracting competitors; and I doubt not that the average gains, in a trade in which large fortunes may be made, are lower than in those in which gains are slow, though comparatively sure, and in which nothing is to be ultimately hoped for beyond a competency. The timber trade of Canada is [1848] one example of an employment of capital partaking so much of the nature of a lottery, as to make it an accredited opinion that, taking the adventurer in the aggregate, there is more money lost by the trade than gained by it; in other words, that the average rate of profit is less than nothing. In such points as this, much depends on the characters of nations, according as they partake more or less of the adventurous, or, as it is called when the intention is to blame it, the gambling spirit. This spirit is much stronger in the United States than in Great Britain; and in Great Britain than in any country of the Continent. In some Continental countries the tendency is so much the reverse, that safe and quiet employments probably yield a less average profit to the capital engaged in them, than those which offer greater gains at the price of greater hazards.

It must not however be forgotten, that even in the countries of most active competition, custom also has a considerable share in determining the profits of trade. There is sometimes an idea afloat as to what the profit of an employment should be, which though not adhered to by all the dealers, nor perhaps rigidly by any, still exercises a certain influence over their operations. There has been in England a kind of notion, how widely prevailing I know not, that fifty per cent is a proper and suitable rate of profit in retail transactions: understand, not fifty per cent on the whole capital, but an advance of fifty per cent on the wholesale prices; from which have to be defrayed bad debts, shop rent, the pay of clerks, shopmen, and agents of all descriptions, in short all the expenses of the retail business. If this custom were universal, and strictly adhered to, competition indeed would still operate, but the consumer would not derive any benefit from it, at least as to price; the way in which it would diminish the advantages of those engaged in the retail trade, would be by a greater subdivision of the business. In some parts of the Continent the standard is as high as a hundred per cent. The increase of competition however, in England at least, is rapidly tending to break down customs of this description. In the majority of trades (at least in the great emporia of trade), there are now numerous dealers whose motto is, "small gains and frequent"—a great business at low prices, rather than high prices and few transactions; and by turning over their capital more rapidly, and adding to it by borrowed capital when needed, the dealers often obtain individually higher profits; though they necessarily lower the profits of those among their competitors who do not adopt the same principle. Nevertheless, competition . . . has, as yet, but a limited dominion over retail prices; and consequently the share of the whole produce of land and labour which is absorbed in the remuneration of mere distributors, continues exorbitant; and there is no function in the economy of society which supports a number of persons so disproportioned to the amount of work to be performed.

§5. The preceding remarks have, I hope, sufficiently elucidated what is meant by the common phrase, "the ordinary rate of profit;" and the sense in which, and the limitations under which, this ordinary rate has a real existence. It now remains to consider what causes determine its amount.

To popular apprehension it seems as if the profits of business depended upon prices. A producer or dealer seems to obtain his profits by selling his commodity for more than it cost him. Profit altogether, people are apt to think, is a consequence of purchase and sale. It is only (they suppose) because there are purchasers for a commodity, that the producer of it is able to make any profit. Demand—customers—a market for the commodity, are the cause of the gains of capitalists. It is by the sale of their goods, that they replace their capital, and add to its amount.

This, however, is looking only at the outside surface of the economical machinery of society. In no case, we find, is the mere money which passes from one person to another, the fundamental matter in any economical phenomenon. If we look more narrowly into the operations of the producer, we shall perceive that the money he obtains for his commodity is not the cause of his having a profit, but only the mode in which his profit is paid to him.

The cause of profit is, that labour produces more than is required for its support. The reason why agricultural capital yields a profit, is because human beings can grow more food than is necessary to feed them while it is being grown, including the time occupied in constructing the tools, and making all other needful preparations: from which it is a consequence, that if a capitalist undertakes to feed the labourers on condition of receiving the produce, he has some of it remaining for himself after replacing his advances. To vary the form of the theorem: the reason why capital yields a profit, is because food, clothing, materials, and tools, last longer than the time which was required to produce them; so that if a capitalist supplies a party of labourers with these things, on condition of receiving all they produce, they will, in addition to reproducing their own necessaries and instruments, have a portion of their time remaining to work for the capitalist. We thus see that profit arises, not from the incident of exchange, but from the productive power of labour; and the general profit of the country is always what the productive power of labour makes it whether any exchange takes place or not. If there were no division of employments, there would be no buying or selling, but there would still be profit. If the labourers of the country collectively produce twenty per cent more than their wages, profits will be twenty per cent, whatever prices may or may not be. The accidents of price may for a time make one set of producers get more than the twenty per cent, and another less, the one commodity being rated above its natural value in relation to other commodities, and the other below, until prices have again adjusted themselves; but there will always be just twenty per cent divided among them all.

I proceed, in expansion of the considerations thus briefly indicated, to exhibit more minutely the mode in which the rate of profit is determined.

§6. I assume, throughout, the state of things, which, where the labourers and capitalists are separate classes, prevails, with few exceptions, universally; namely, that the capitalist advances the whole expenses, including the entire remuneration of the labourer. That he should do so, is not a matter of inherent necessity; the labourer might wait until the production is complete, for all that part of his wages which exceeds mere necessaries; and even for the whole, if he has funds in hand, sufficient for his temporary support. But in the latter case, the labourer is to that extent really a capitalist, investing capital in the concern, by supplying a portion of the funds necessary for carrying it on; and even in the former case he may be looked upon in the same light, since, contributing his labour at less than the market price, he may be regarded as lending the difference to his employer, and receiving it back with interest (on whatever principle computed) from the proceeds of the enterprise.

The capitalist, then, may be assumed to make all the advances, and receive all the produce. His profit consists of the excess of the produce above the advances; his *rate* of profit is the ratio which that excess bears to the amount advanced. But what do the advances consist of?

It is, for the present, necessary to suppose, that the capitalist does not pay any rent; has not to purchase the use of any appropriated natural agent. This indeed is scarcely ever the exact truth. The agricultural capitalist, except when he is the owner of the soil he cultivates, always, or almost always, pays rent: and even in manufactures, (not to mention ground-rent), the materials of the manufacture have generally paid rent, in some stage of their production. The nature of rent, however, we have not yet taken into consideration; and it will hereafter appear, that no practical error, on the question we are now examining, is produced by disregarding it.

If, then, leaving rent out of the question, we inquire in what it is that the advances of the capitalist, for purposes of production, consist, we shall find that they consist of wages of labour.

A large portion of the expenditure of every capitalist consists in the direct payment of wages. What does not consist of this, is composed of materials and implements, including buildings. But materials and implements are produced by labour; and as our supposed capitalist is not meant to represent a single employment, but to be a type of the productive industry of the whole country, we may suppose that he makes his own tools, and raises his own materials. He does this by means of previous advances, which, again, consist wholly of wages. If we suppose him to buy the materials and tools instead of producing them, the case is not altered: he then repays to a previous producer the wages which that previous producer has paid. It is true, he repays it to him with a profit; and if he had produced the things himself, he himself must have had that profit, on this part of his outlay, as well as on every other part. The fact, however, remains, that in the whole process of production, beginning with the materials and tools, and ending with the finished product, all the advances have consisted of nothing but wages; except that certain of the capitalists concerned have, for the sake of general convenience, had their share of profit paid to them before the operation was completed. Whatever, of the ultimate product, is not profit, is repayment of wages.

§7. It thus appears that the two elements on which, and which alone, the gains of the capitalists depend, are, first, the magnitude of the produce, in other words, the productive power of labour; and secondly, the proportion of that produce obtained by the labourers themselves; the ratio which the remuneration of the labourers bears to the amount they produce. These two things form the data for determining the gross amount divided as profit among all the capitalists of the country; but the *rate* of profit, the percentage on the capital, depends only on the second of the two elements, the labourer's proportional share, and not on the amount to be shared. If the produce of labour were doubled, and the labourers obtained the same proportional share as before, that is, if their remuneration was also doubled, the capitalists, it is true, would gain twice as much; but as they would also have had to advance twice as much, the rate of their profit would be only the same as before.

We thus arrive at the conclusion of Ricardo and others, that the rate of profits depends on wages: rising as wages fall, and falling as wages rise. In adopting, however, this doctrine, I must insist upon making a most necessary alteration in its wording. Instead of saying that profits depend on wages, let us say (what Ricardo really meant) that they depend on the *cost of labour*.

Wages, and the cost of labour, what labour brings in to the labourer, and what it costs to the capitalist; are ideas quite distinct, and which it is of the utmost importance to keep so. For this purpose it is essential not to designate them, as is almost always done, by the same name. Wages, in public discussions, both oral and printed, being looked upon from the point of view of the payers, much oftener than from that of the receivers, nothing is more common than to say that wages are high or low, meaning only that the cost of labour is high or low. The reverse of this would be oftener the truth: the cost of labour is frequently at its highest where wages are lowest. This may arise from two causes. In the first place, the labour, though cheap, may be inefficient. In no European country are wages so low as they are (or at least were) in Ireland: the remuneration of an agricultural labourer in the west of Ireland not being more than half the wages of even the lowest-paid Englishman, the Dorsetshire labourer. But if, from inferior skill and industry, two days' labour of an Irishman accomplished no more work than an English labourer performed in one, the Irishman's labour cost as much as the Englishman's, though it brought in so much less to himself. The capitalist's profit is determined by the former of these two things, not by the latter. That a difference to this extent really existed in the efficiency of the labour, is proved not only by abundant testimony, but by the fact, that notwithstanding the lowness of wages, profits of capital are not understood to have been higher in Ireland than in England.

The other cause which renders wages, and the cost of labour, no real criteria of one another, is the varying costliness of the articles which the labourer consumes. If these are cheap, wages, in the sense which is of importance to the labourer, may be high, and yet the cost of labour may be low; if dear, the labourer may be wretchedly off, though his labour may cost much to the capitalist. This last is the condition of a country over-peopled in relation to its land; in which, food being dear, the poorness of the labourer's real reward does not prevent labour from costing much to the purchaser, and low wages and low profits coexist. The opposite case is exemplified in the United States of America. The labourer there enjoys a greater abundance of comforts than in any other country of the world, except some of the newest colonies; but owing to the cheap price at which these comforts can be obtained (combined with the great efficiency of the labour), the cost of labour to the capitalist is at least not higher, nor the rate of profit lower, than in Europe.

The cost of labour, then, is, in the language of mathematics, a function of three variables: the efficiency of labour; the wages of labour (meaning thereby the real reward of the labourer); and the greater or less cost at which the articles composing that real reward can be produced or procured. It is plain that the cost of labour to the capitalist must be influenced by each of these three circumstances, and by no others. These, therefore, are also the circumstances which determine the rate of profit; and it cannot be in any way affected except through one or other of them. If labour generally became more efficient, without being more highly rewarded; if, without its becoming less efficient, its remuneration fell, no increase taking place in the cost of the articles composing that remuneration; or if those articles became less costly, without the labourer's obtaining more of them; in any one of these three cases, profits would rise. If, on the contrary, labour became less efficient (as it might do from diminished bodily vigour in the people, destruction of fixed capital, or deteriorated education); or if the labourer obtained a higher remuneration, without any increased cheapness in the things composing it; or if, without his obtaining more, that which he did obtain became more costly; profits, in all these cases, would suffer a diminution. And there is no other combination of circumstances, in which the general rate of profit of a country, in all employments indifferently, can either fall or rise.

The evidence of these propositions can only be stated generally, though, it is hoped, conclusively, in this stage of our subject. It will come out in greater fullness and force when, having taken into consideration the theory of Value and Price, we shall be enabled to exhibit the law of profits in the concrete—in the complex entanglement of circumstances in which it actually works.... ◆

QUESTIONS

1. According to Mill, what are the three components of profits?

2. How can these three components be apportioned to different people?

3. What are the three components to the cost of labor?

4. Why does Mill think that there is a natural or necessary minimum to the rate of profits? Why does this minimum vary from time to time and place to place?

5. What assumptions lie behind Mill's claim that the expectations of profit from various alternative ventures are generally equal?

6. What does Mill mean when he uses the word *equilibrium*?

7. Why might reaching equilibrium sometimes be a rather slow process?

Selection from: *The Business Guide*

J. L. Nichols (1851-1895) self-published Naperville, Ill 1893

Jay Gould.

How Money Grows at Interest

If one dollar be invested and the interest added to the principal annually, at the rates named, we shall have the following result as the accumulation of one hundred years.

One dollar, 100 years at 1 per cent	....	$ 2¾
One dollar, 100 years at 2 per cent	....	7¼
One dollar, 100 years at 3 per cent	....	19¼
One dollar, 100 years at 4 per cent	....	50½
One dollar, 100 years at 5 per cent	....	181½
One dollar, 100 years at 6 per cent	....	340
One dollar, 100 years at 7 per cent	....	868
One dollar, 100 years at 8 per cent	....	2,203
One dollar, 100 years at 9 per cent	....	5,513
One dollar, 100 years at 10 per cent	....	13,809
One dollar, 100 years at 15 percent	....	1,174,405
One dollar, 100 years at 18 per cent	....	15,145,000
One dollar, 100 years at 24 percent	....	2,551,799,404

SELECTION FROM: *THE BUSINESS GUIDE*

J. L. Nichols (1851–1895) self-published Naperville, Ill 1893

THE CREDIT SYSTEM

The Credit System—Its Advantages and Disadvantages.

1. There are many good reasons why people should pay cash for everything purchased. Hopeful people will always buy more freely if they can get it on credit, and are never anxious about pay day to come around.

2. Remember that those who sell on credit *must charge from ten to fifteen percent more for goods* in order to cover the interest and risks. It has been found that from seven to ten per cent of trusted out accounts become worthless.

3. It is always uncertain which of the trusted persons will fail to pay his account, and consequently all persons buying on credit have to share the extra prices, in order to meet the losses which all business men sustain that do a credit business.

4. Remember, the man who can pay cash for goods, or whatever purchase he may make, *can always secure a better bargain than the man who buys on credit.* It therefore will be a great saving if everyone could manage, by rigid economy if necessary, to pay cash for everything they buy. It would pay a high rate of interest on everything purchased.

5. Persons who buy real estate, or merchants who buy large quantities of goods, may often find it necessary to buy on credit. Many of our wealthiest farmers and business men made their money largely in having the benefit of credit, but, at the same time, if cash could be paid for everything purchased, whether real estate or other articles, it would be a great saving to the purchaser.

6. *Keep your word as good as a bank and you will always have credit when you desire it, and friends when you need them.*

SELECTION FROM: *THE BUSINESS GUIDE*

J. L. Nichols (1851–1895) self-published Naperville, Ill 1893

HOW TO DO BUSINESS WITH A BANK

1. National Banks are required by the United States to deposit interest-bearing bonds with the Treasurer at Washington in proportion to the capital stock paid in.

2. Banks of "circulation and deposit" have the use under certain restrictions of capital paid in by the stockholders, the money belonging to the depositors and the notes of their own circulation.

3. Make your deposits in the bank as early in the day as possible, and never without your bank-book.

4. Always use the deposit tickets furnished by the bank. When checks are deposited, the banks require them to be indorsed, whether drawn to his order or not.

5. Keep your check-book under lock and key.

6. Draw as few checks as possible; when several bills are to be paid, draw the money in one check.

7. Do not allow your bank-book to run too long without balancing. Compare it with the account of the bank.

8. In filling up checks, do not leave space in which the amount may be raised.

9. Write your signature with the usual freedom, and never vary the style of it.

10. Every check is paid by the bank at its own risk. If forged the bank must lose the amount.

11. If a raised check is paid by the bank, it can only charge the depositor the amount for which he drew.

12. Always keep the stub of your check book, and in issuing a check always fill the stub out first.

THE TULIPOMANIA
FROM EXTRAORDINARY POPULAR DELUSIONS AND THE MADNESS OF CROWDS

Charles Mackay (1814–1889)

QUIS FUROR, Ô CIVES!—LUCAN.

The tulip—so named, it is said, from a Turkish word, signifying a turban—was introduced into western Europe about the middle of the sixteenth century. Conrad Gesner, who claims the merit of having brought it into repute,—little dreaming of the commotion it was shortly afterwards to make in the world,—says that he first saw it in the year 1559, in a garden at Augsburg, belonging to the learned Counsellor Herwart, a man very famous in his day for his collection of rare exotics. The bulbs were sent to this gentleman by a friend at Constantinople, where the flower had long been a favourite. In the course of ten or eleven years after this period, tulips were much sought after by the wealthy, especially in Holland and Germany. Rich people at Amsterdam sent for the bulbs direct to Constantinople, and paid the most extravagant prices for them. The first roots planted in England were brought from Vienna in 1600. Until the year 1634 the tulip annually increased in reputation, until it was deemed a proof of bad taste in any man of fortune to be without a collection of them. Many learned men, including Pompeius de Angelis, and the celebrated Lipsius of Leyden, the author of the treatise "De Constantia," were passionately fond of tulips. The rage for possessing them soon caught the middle classes of society, and merchants and shopkeepers, even of moderate means, began to vie with each other in the rarity of these flowers and the preposterous prices they paid for them. A trader at Harlaem was known to pay one-half of his fortune for a single root, not with the design of selling it again at a profit, but to keep in his own conservatory for the admiration of his acquaintance.

One would suppose that there must have been some great virtue in this flower to have made it so valuable in the eyes of so prudent a people as the Dutch; but it has neither the beauty nor the perfume of the rose—hardly the beauty of the "sweet, sweet-pea:" neither is it as enduring as either. Cowley, it is true, is loud in its praise. He says—

> The tulip next appeared, all over gay,
> But wanton, full of pride, and full of play;
> The world can't show a dye but here has place;
> Nay, by new mixtures, she can change her face;
> Purple and gold are both beneath her care,
> The richest needlework she loves to wear;
> Her only study is to please the eye,
> And to outshine the rest in finery.

This, though not very poetical, is the description of a poet. Beckmann, in his *History of Inventions*, paints it with more fidelity, and in prose more pleasing than Cowley's poetry. He says, "There are few plants which acquire, through accident, weakness, or disease, so many variegations as the tulip. When uncultivated, and in its natural state, it is almost of one colour, has large leaves, and an extraordinarily long stem. When it has been weakened by cultivation, it becomes more agreeable in the eyes of the florist. The petals are then paler, smaller, and more diversified in hue; and the leaves acquire a softer green colour. Thus this masterpiece of culture, the more beautiful it turns, grows so much the weaker, so that, with the greatest skill and most careful attention, it can scarcely be transplanted, or even kept alive."

Many persons grow insensibly attached to that which gives them a great deal of trouble, as a mother often loves her sick and ever-ailing child better than her more healthy offspring. Upon the same principle we must account for the unmerited encomia lavished upon these fragile blossoms. In 1634, the rage among the Dutch to possess them was so great that the ordinary industry of the country was neglected, and the population, even to its lowest dregs, embarked in the tulip trade. As the mania increased, prices augmented, until, in the year 1635, many persons were known to invest a fortune of 100,000 florins in the purchase of forty roots. It then became necessary to sell them by their weight in *perits,* a small weight less than a grain. A tulip of the species called *Admiral Liefken,* weighing 400 *perits,* was worth 4400 florins; an *Admiral Van der Eyck,* weighing 446 *perits,* was worth 1260 florins; a *Childer* of 106 *perits* was worth 1615 florins; a *Viceroy* of 400 *perits,* 3000 florins; and, most precious of all, a *Semper Augustus,* weighing 200 *perits,* was thought to be very cheap at 5500 florins. The latter was much sought after, and even an inferior bulb might command a price of 2000 florins. It is related that, at one time, early in 1636, there were only two roots of this description to be had in all Holland, and those not of the best. One was in the possession of a dealer in Amsterdam, and the other in Harlaem. So anxious were the speculators to obtain them, that one person offered the fee-simple of twelve acres of building-ground for the Harlaem tulip. That of Am-sterdam was bought for 4600 florins, a new carriage, two grey horses, and a complete set of harness. Munting, an industrious author of that day, who wrote a folio volume of one thousand pages upon the tulipomania, has preserved the following list of the various articles, and their value, which were delivered for one single root of the rare species called the *Viceroy:*

		Florins
Two lasts of wheat	....	448
Four lasts of rye	....	558
Four fat oxen	....	480
Eight fat swine	....	240
Twelve fat sheep	....	120
Two Hogsheads of wine	....	70
Four tuns of beer	....	32
Two tuns of butter	....	192
One thousand lbs. of cheese	....	120
A complete bed	....	00
A suit of clothes	....	80
A silver drinking-cup	....	60
		2500

People who had been absent from Holland, and whose chance it was to return when this folly was at its maximum, were sometimes led into awkward dilemmas by their ignorance. There is an amusing instance of the kind related in Blainville's *Travels.* A wealthy merchant, who prided himself not a little on his rare tulips, received upon one occasion a very valuable consignment of merchandise from the Levant. Intelligence of its arrival was brought him by a sailor, who presented himself for that purpose at the counting-house, among bales of goods of every description. The merchant, to reward him for his news munificently made him a present of a fine red herring for his breakfast. The sailor had, it appears, a great partiality for onions, and seeing a bulb very like an onion lying upon the counter of this liberal trader, and thinking it, no doubt, very much out of its place among silks and velvets, he slyly seized an opportunity and slipped it into his pocket, as a relish for his herring. He got clear off with his prize, and proceeded to the quay to eat his breakfast. Hardly was his back turned when the merchant missed his valuable *Semper Augustus,* worth three thousand florins, or about 280*l* sterling. The whole establishment was instantly in an uproar; search was everywhere made for the precious root, but it was not to be found. Great was the merchant's distress of mind. The search was renewed, but again without success. At last some one thought of the sailor.

The unhappy merchant sprang into the street at the bare suggestion. His alarmed household followed him. The sailor, simple soul! had not thought of concealment. He was found quietly sitting on a coil of ropes, masticating the last morsel of his *"onion."* Little did he dream that he had been eating a breakfast whose cost might have regaled a whole ship's crew for a twelvemonth; or, as the plundered merchant himself expressed it, "might have sumptuously feasted the Prince of Orange and the whole court of the Stadtholder." Anthony caused pearls to be dissolved in wine to drink the health of Cleopatra; Sir Richard Whittington was as foolishly magnificent in an entertainment to King Henry V; and Sir Thomas Gresham drank a diamond dissolved in wine to the health of Queen Elizabeth, when she opened the Royal Exchange; but the breakfast of this roguish Dutchman was as splendid as either. He had an advantage, too, over his wasteful predecessors: *their* gems did not improve the taste or the wholesomeness of *their* wine, while *his* tulip was quite delicious with his red herring. The most unfortunate part of the business for him was, that he remained in prison for some months on a charge of felony preferred against him by the merchant.

Another story is told of an English traveller, which is scarcely less ludicrous. This gentleman, an amateur botanist, happened to see a tulip-root lying in the conservatory of a wealthy Dutchman. Being ignorant of its quality, he took out his penknife, and peeled off its coats, with the view of making experiments upon it. When it was by this means reduced to half its size, he cut it into two equal sections, making all the time many learned remarks on the singular appearances of the unknown bulb. Suddenly the owner pounced upon him, and, with fury in his eyes, asked him if he knew what he had been doing? "Peeling a most extraordinary onion," replied the philosopher. *"Hundert tausend duyvel!"* said the Dutchman; "it's an *Admiral Van der Eyck."* "Thank you," replied the traveller, taking out his note-book to make a memorandum of the same; "are these admirals common in your country?" "Death and the Devil!" said the Dutchman, seizing the astonished man of science by the collar; "come before the syndic, and you shall see." In spite of his remonstrances, the traveller was led through the streets followed by a mob of persons. When brought into the presence of the magistrate, he learned, to his consternation, that the root upon which he had been experimentalising was worth four thousand florins; and, notwithstanding all he could urge in extenuation, he was lodged in prison until he found securities for the payment of this sum.

The demand for tulips of a rare species increased so much in the year 1636, that regular marts for their sale were established on the Stock Exchange of Amsterdam, in Rotterdam, Harlaem, Leyden, Alkmar, Hoorn, and other towns. Symptoms of gambling now became, for the first time, apparent. The stock-jobbers, ever on the alert for a new speculation, dealt largely in tulips, making use of all the means they so well knew how to employ to cause fluctuations in prices. At first, as in all these gambling mania, confidence was at its height, and every body gained. The tulip-jobbers speculated in the rise and fall of the tulip stocks, and made large profits by buying when prices fell, and selling out when they rose. Many individuals grew suddenly rich. A golden bait hung temptingly out before the people, and one after the other, they rushed to the tulip-marts, like flies around a honey-pot. Every one imagined that the passion for tulips would last for ever, and that the wealthy from every part of the world would send to Holland, and pay whatever prices were asked for them. The riches of Europe would be concentrated on the shores of the Zuyder Zee, and poverty banished from the favoured clime of Holland. Nobles, citizens, farmers, mechanics, seamen, footmen, maid-servants, even chimney-sweeps and old clotheswomen, dabbled in tulips. People of all grades converted their property into cash, and invested it in flowers. Houses and lands were offered for sale at ruinously low prices, or assigned in payment of bargains made at the tulip-mart. Foreigners became smitten with the same frenzy, and money poured into Holland from all directions. The prices of the necessaries of life rose again by degrees: houses and lands, horses and carriages, and luxuries of every sort, rose in value with them, and for some months Holland seemed the very antechamber of Plutus. The operations of the trade became so extensive and so intricate, that it was found necessary to draw up a code of laws for the guidance of the dealers. Notaries and clerks were also appointed, who devoted themselves exclusively to the interests of the trade. The designation of public notary was hardly known in some towns, that of tulip-notary usurping its place. In the smaller towns, where there was no exchange, the principal tavern was usually selected as the "show-place," where high and low traded in tulips, and confirmed their bargains over sumptuous entertainments. These dinners were sometimes attended by two or three hundred persons, and large vases of tulips, in full bloom, were placed at regular intervals upon the tables and sideboards for their gratification during the repast.

At last, however, the more prudent began to see that this folly could not last for ever. Rich people no longer bought the flowers to keep them in their gardens, but to sell them again at cent percent profit. It was seen that somebody must lose fearfully in the end. As this conviction spread, prices fell, and never rose again. Confidence was destroyed, and a universal panic seized upon the dealers. *A* had agreed to purchase ten *Semper Augustines* from *B,* at four thousand florins each, at six weeks after the signing of the contract. *B* was ready with the flowers at the appointed time; but the price had fallen to three or four hundred florins, and *A* refused either to pay the difference or receive the tulips. Defaulters were announced day after day in all the towns of Holland. Hundreds who, a few months previously, had begun to doubt that there was such a thing as poverty in the land suddenly found themselves the possessors of a few bulbs, which nobody would buy, even though they offered them at one quarter of the sums they had paid for them. The cry of distress resounded every where, and each man accused his neighbour. The few who had contrived to enrich themselves hid their wealth from the knowledge of their fellow-citizens, and invested it in the English or other funds. Many who, for a brief season, had emerged from the humbler walks of life, were cast back into their original obscurity. Substantial merchants were reduced almost to beggary, and many a representative of a noble line saw the fortunes of his house ruined beyond redemption.

When the first alarm subsided, the tulip-holders in the several towns held public meetings to devise what measures were best to be taken to restore public credit. It was generally agreed that deputies should be sent from all parts to Amsterdam, to consult with the government upon some remedy for the evil. The government at first refused to interfere, but advised the tulip-holders to agree to some plan among themselves. Several meetings were held for this purpose; but no measure could be devised likely to give satisfaction to the deluded people, or repair even a slight portion

of the mischief that had been done. The language of complaint and reproach was in every body's mouth, and all the meetings were of the most stormy character. At last, however, after much bickering and ill-will, it was agreed at Amsterdam, by the assembled deputies, that all contracts made in the height of the mania, or prior to the month of November, 1636, should be declared null and void, and that, in those made after that date, purchasers should be freed from their engagements, on paying ten per cent to the vendor. This decision gave no satisfaction. The vendors who had their tulips on hand were, of course, discontented, and those who had pledged themselves to purchase, thought themselves hardly treated. Tulips which had, at one time, been worth six thousand florins, were now to be procured for five hundred; so that the composition of ten per cent was one hundred florins more than the actual value. Actions for breach of contract were threatened in all the courts of the country, but the latter refused to take cognizance of gambling transactions.

The matter was finally referred to the Provincial Council at the Hague, and it was confidently expected that the wisdom of this body would invent some measure by which credit should be restored. Expectation was on the stretch for its decision, but it never came. The members continued to deliberate week after week, and at last, after thinking about it for three months, declared that they could offer no final decision until they had more information. They advised, however, that, in the meantime, every vendor should, in the presence of witnesses, offer the tulips *in natura* to the purchaser for the sums agreed upon. If the latter refused to take them, they might be put up for sale by public auction, and the original contractor held responsible for the difference between the actual and the stipulated price. This was exactly the plan recommended by the deputies, and which was already shown to be of no avail. There was no court in Holland which would enforce payment. The question was raised in Amsterdam, but the judges unanimously refused to interfere, on the ground that debts contracted in gambling were no debts in law.

Thus the matter rested. To find a remedy was beyond the power of the government. Those who were unlucky enough to have had stores of tulips on hand at the time of the sudden reaction were left to bear their ruin as philosophically as they could; those who had made profits were allowed to keep them; but the commerce of the country suffered a severe shock, from which it was many years ere it recovered.

The example of the Dutch was imitated to some extent in England. In the year 1636 tulips were publicly sold in the Exchange of London, and the jobbers exerted themselves to the utmost to raise them to the fictitious value they had acquired in Amsterdam. In Paris also the jobbers strove to create a tulipomania. In both cities they only partially succeeded. However, the force of example brought the flowers into great favour, and amongst a certain class of people tulips have ever since been prized more highly than any other flowers of the field. The Dutch are still notorious for their partiality to them, and continue to pay higher prices for them than any other people. As the rich Englishman boasts of his fine race-horses or his old pictures, so does the wealthy Dutchman vaunt him of his tulips.

In England, in our day, strange as it may appear, a tulip will produce more money than an oak. If one could be found, rara in terris, and black as the black swan of Juvenal, its price would equal that of a dozen acres of standing corn. In Scotland, towards the close of the seventeenth century, the highest price for tulips, according to the authority of a writer in the supplement to the third edition of the Encyclopedia Britannica, was ten guineas. Their value appears to have diminished from that time till the year 1769, when the two most valuable species in England were the Don Quevedo and the Valentinier, the former of which was worth two guineas and the latter two guineas and a half. These prices appear to have been the minimum. In the year 1800, a common price was fifteen guineas for a single bulb. In 1835, a bulb of the species called the Miss Fanny Kemble was sold by public auction in London for seventy-five pounds. Still more remarkable was the price of a tulip in the possession of a gardener in the King's Road, Chelsea—in his catalogues it was labelled at two hundred guineas. ♦

QUESTIONS

1. What led to the increase in the prices of Dutch tulips in the seventeenth century?

2. Who shared the enthusiasm for tulips within Dutch society?

3. What led to the eventual decline in prices?

4. Were the government's responses effective in dealing with this decline in the prices of tulips?

5. Who, if anyone, kept the money from the sale of tulips at high prices?

Confusión de Confusiones

Joseph De La Vega (1650–1692)

It is especially worth noting that there are two classes of gamblers in these joints, so opposite to one another that they represent antipodes in their decisions and, I imagine, also in their fortunes. The first is that of the bulls or *liefhebberen* (which means "lovers" in Flemish),[1] and are those who always begin their business buying, because as lovers of the Nation, the State, and the Company, they continuously desire stocks to rise; they expect that with good news the market will suddenly climb, and prices will quickly increase. The second faction is that of the bears or *contraminores* (called this way owing to the fact that the Indies are considered a mine and they act as if yearning to exhaust this mine), and are those who always begin their business selling, some of them surpassing Timon of Athens, who loved Alcibiades solely to share his mission, namely, to be the executioner of his native land. It is necessary to flee them like the plague and not imitate them ever if not for exceptional occasions like, for example, when grabbing a *Bichile* (which is the Dutch word meaning butterfly for children). This expression is used to designate an opportunity for quick benefit, an opportunity that will flit around if not caught in flight, and will escape if not exploited.

Bulls are like the giraffe that is scared by nothing or like the magician of the Elector of Cologne, who in his mirror makes ladies appear much more beautiful than they really are. They love it all, praise it all, exaggerate it all. And as Bias fooled the ambassador of Alyattes in the siege of Priene by showing him mountains of sand covered in wheat to make him believe that a city in which abundance flourished could not be surrendered because of hunger, bulls make people believe that their artifices are riches and that crops grow in tombs. When attacked by serpents, they, like the Indians, consider them an exquisite and tasty delicacy. . . A fire does not impress them nor does a debacle disturb them.

Bears, to the contrary, are completely dominated by fear, inquietude, and nervousness. Rabbits turn into elephants, tavern fights into rebellions, and shadows appear to them as signs of chaos. But if in Africa there are ewes that serve as donkeys and rams that serve as horses, what is miraculous about the probability of every dwarf transforming into a giant in the eyes of bears?

Endnote

1. Translator's note: the actual Flemish word for lovers is *liefhebbers*.

QUESTIONS

1. According to De La Vega, who are the bulls and who are the bears in a market?

2. What emotions are expressed by the bulls?

3. What emotions are expressed by the bears?

4. Are either bulls or bears realistic in their assessments of market opportunities and risks?

FROM *THE GENERAL THEORY OF EMPLOYMENT, INTEREST, AND MONEY*

John Maynard Keynes (1883–1946)

In practice we have tacitly agreed, as a rule, to fall back on what is, in truth, a *convention*. The essence of this convention—though it does not, of course, work out quite so simply—lies in assuming that the existing state of affairs will continue indefinitely, except in so far as we have specific reasons to expect a change. This does not mean that we really believe that the existing state of affairs will continue indefinitely. We know from extensive experience that this is most unlikely. The actual results of an investment over a long term of years very seldom agree with the initial expectation. Nor can we rationalise our behaviour by arguing that to a man in a state of ignorance errors in either direction are equally probable, so that there remains a mean actuarial expectation based on equi-probabilities. For it can easily be shown that the assumption of arithmetically equal probabilities based on a state of ignorance leads to absurdities. We are assuming, in effect, that the existing market valuation, however arrived at, is uniquely *correct* in relation to our existing knowledge of the facts which will influence the yield of the investment, and that it will only change in proportion to changes in this knowledge; though, philosophically speaking, it cannot be uniquely correct, since our existing knowledge does not provide a sufficient basis for a calculated mathematical expectation. In point of fact, all sorts of considerations enter into the market valuation which are in no way relevant to the prospective yield.

Nevertheless the above conventional method of calculation will be compatible with a considerable measure of continuity and stability in our affairs, *so long as we can rely on the maintenance of the convention.*

For if there exist organised investment markets and if we can rely on the maintenance of the convention, an investor can legitimately encourage himself with the idea that the only risk he runs is that of a genuine change in the news *over the near future*, as to the likelihood of which he can attempt to form his own judgment, and which is unlikely to be very large. For, assuming that the convention holds good, it is only these changes which can affect the value of his investment, and he need not lose his sleep merely because he has not any notion what his investment will be worth ten years hence. Thus investment becomes reasonably "safe" for the individual investor over short periods, and hence over a succession of short periods however many, if he can fairly rely on there being no breakdown in the convention and on his therefore having an opportunity to revise his judgment and change his investment, before there has been time for much to happen. Investments which are "fixed" for the community are thus made "liquid" for the individual.

QUESTIONS

1. How does Keynes suggest that the convention of thinking that the current value of an investment is correct is related to the expectation of relatively slow change in the value of that investment?

2. Why does relatively slow change depend, in turn, on the maintenance of that convention?

3. What sorts of considerations might Keynes think enter into market prices that are not relevant to the financial return of an investment?

Selection from: *The Business Guide*

J. L. Nichols (1851–1895) self-published Naperville, Ill 1893

New York Stock Exchange

Boards of Trade and Stock Exchanges.

Boards of Trade and Stock Exchanges were originally organized to facilitate trade in the various commercial interests of the country; but unfortunately instead of blessing and benefiting mankind they have become gigantic engines of robbery and oppression. Members are elected by ballot and the admission fees vary in different organizations from nothing to $3,000.00.

Dealing in Futures.

This is simply a "high-toned" form of gambling, or in other words a system of "marked guessing" in which the best guesser wins. The game, like all other popular gambling games, is exceedingly simple. You simply bet on the market if it goes up or down, you win or lose just as you have staked your money.

Margins.

Margins are sums of money put up as a forfeit to secure the winner. When the margin is exhausted so that further loss is not guaranteed, it is the custom to close the trade and the winner "rakes in the pot" using the gambler's way of putting it.

Option Trading.

"Seller's option" gives the person selling the privilege of making delivery at any time before the expiration of the contract by giving one day's notice. "Buyer's option" gives the purchaser a claim for delivery at any time before the maturity of the contract.

Corners.

Thousands of bushels of grains are bought and sold for every bushel brought into the elevators. Chicago Board of Trade sells every day as much wheat as the State of Illinois harvests in a year. It can then be easily seen how "commerce" can be forced. In a Board of Trade each buyer buys upon the supposition that each seller is selling what he has not got, and the buyer is buying what he does not want. Now it is easy for a set of men with an unlimited amount of money to combine and "corner" any article in the market. It simply consists of buying more than can be delivered, and then making the sellers deliver or forfeit their margins. A "bull" is one who operates to raise the market—so called from the nature of the bull to toss with his horn. A "bear" is one who tries to lower the market, so called from the nature of the bear to tear down with his claws. A "lame-duck" is a member unable to fulfill his contracts, and is therefore expelled.

Bucket Shops.

These are Boards of Trade and Stock Exchanges for the boys and poor clerks, generally kept by a broken down broker who lost all his self-respect with his fortune. Here the poorest can try his luck in betting upon the markets. These shops are not reliable; they doctor the markets with false figures and deceive and take in whoever falls into their power. They are demoralizing gambling dens and in no way can they be safe.

VII

MANAGEMENT

INTRODUCTION: THE ART OF GETTING THINGS DONE THROUGH PEOPLE

The moment humanity made the discovery that hunting in packs produced a higher animal kill rate and a lower hunter mortality rate than hunting alone, it must have become apparent that some form of effective management for pack hunting was necessary. Concerns about sufficient and motivated labor power, and reliable and adequate armaments, both requirements for the predictability of successful hunting expeditions, must have imposed themselves on the uncultivated minds of those hard and limited hunters who naturally took the lead in making the kills. We can only imagine some of the organizational difficulties faced by these "alpha" leaders:

1. There are ten of us in this hunting pack. Can we find and kill enough today so that all our families will have enough to last through the week? We need a *sales forecast*.

2. Do we have enough of the right kinds of stones and branches for weapon production? We need a *raw material inventory*.

3. Do our weapons appear adequate to the task of making the kills? We need a check on the *condition of equipment*.

4. Yesterday, half of our hunting pack "slept in" so that they were of no use to us. Should we seek temporary help today? We need an *analysis of labor power*.

5. On our last hunt, Zorg, one of our hunters, threw his weapon at the animal and missed. Unfortunately, the weapon hit our brother-in-law, Gog, and killed him. Even worse, the animal took advantage of Zorg's surprise and ate him. Should we train our hunters? We need some kind of *training* and *quality control*.

Studying the problems experienced by the hunting pack is part of the process of understanding the tasks of management. But this is just the beginning. Clarifying, structuring, and satisfying the organizational needs requisite to the success of the pack, or any group, are some of the tasks inherent in the study of management. Those who understand this most fully, while building and effectuating "employee-friendly" and "market-oriented" management systems, position their organizations for success.

Because *any* group can profit from the execution of management principles, it stands to reason that sound management—let's call it managing for efficiency and effectiveness—can also produce disastrous results. On the political stage, for instance, managerial skillfulness has sometimes accounted for the rapid diffusion of radical and fanatical ideologies and the active construction, and even restoration, of sick societies. Just as often, however, the successful practice of political management has produced good doctrine and healthy environments. It is no different in the world of business. Well-managed companies have sometimes engaged in the production and sales of services and products that have led to unhealthy attitudes and narcotic-like dependencies. Still, we do not have to engage in much of a search to find organizations whose managers, through skill and dedication, have provided thoughtfully and meaningfully for all of us.

Abraham Lincoln displays such thoughtfulness in his "Letter to Horace Greeley." He leaves no room for doubt about his management philosophy; he says that the only manifest that matters is to save the country. Some might call that a mission statement. For Lincoln, it is managerial purpose or strategy. The tactics are far less important than the strategy—though the tactics matter as well. He tells us that tactically, he would prefer to deal a death blow to slavery. Still, the managerial strategy is to save the country, regardless of the slavery decision.

We often associate the name of Niccolo Machiavelli with power—and not the nice kind. *The Prince*, an opus that Machiavelli composed primarily to regain good relations with the very powerful Medici family, causes many modern readers to wince. This is not surprising because we find that he advocates a pragmatic managerial style that includes everything from cunning and guile to deception and scapegoating. It is possible that our discomfort with his advice is disingenuous. Machiavelli thinks princes—no, all of us—are insincere, faithless, and radically self-interested utility-maximizers. Thus, our distemper for unvirtuous, power strategies may be a veil that conceals our own tendency and talent for just those kinds of strategies!

Machiavelli suggests, therefore, that a leader should stress appearance over reality. A manager's purpose and mission will frequently be undermined by others. It is wise, he says, to appear to think and act one way—regardless of actual design—and to maintain this disguise in order to protect oneself from the fraudulence and faithlessness of others. It is really about getting the job done. This is not so different from what Lincoln tells Horace Greely. The manager must get the job done, and whatever works turns out to be what is best. This is something like early twentieth-century American pragmatism, where whatever works might be thought of as "the truth." However, truth is not the issue here. Efficient and effective action is what matters.

Plato, in our return to *The Republic*, offers a dialogue on the nature of managerial power or, to be more precise, who it is that finally leads and why. This short but fascinating conversation introduces a thought about leadership that transcends remuneration, social status, and control. The leader, we learn, leads by virtue of fear! This fear, it turns out, is that someone worse than oneself might lead instead. We ponder this and, with a bit of help from Socrates (as interpreted by Plato), come to understand that leadership, when it works best, works because it is designed to serve the constituency more than the leader, the employee more than the employer. Were we to be the constituency, would we want leadership that seeks to serve itself over its constituents? The fear that this could happen should be what drives excellent managerial leadership. This might sound ironic; then again, the notion of "Socratic irony" was well understood by Plato, Socrates' most famous student.

We know enough about Confucius to know that we don't know enough about him. Still, in *The Analects*, his students have collected some of the best Confucian ideas passed along over time. It doesn't take much to sense the moral tilt of the man. What we in the West think of as the golden rule almost always finds a place in these analects. Books XII and XX help us to know at least this: these additions to the Confucian lexicon are easily modernized as managerial principles. Even when they don't rise to the level of putative statements on the subject of management, they continue to stand as good advice for leaders—or anyone else who looks forward to a leadership position.

Everything about leadership can be summed up as good conduct—inside and outside the organization. But good conduct is not an act or a design just to get a result. It comes from wanting what is good—really wanting it—for oneself and for others. A leader who governs from these good desires cannot help but create good designs, and this is what gets good results. Good desires begin with love—not some sappy, soporific version of the stuff but the real thing. Good rulers love humanity. But they know humans, too. So love combined with knowledge becomes a powerful catalyst for leadership. Some might call this the psychology of leadership. Fine. Call it that. But if it is gestural only, it will not, in Confucian terms, create the well-managed organization (Machiavelli would, almost certainly, disagree). This is not to suggest that rules don't matter, but rules are insufficient to the drama of managing great organizations.

The foundations of management are, in great part, built on the dual concepts of efficient organizational structure and effective employee motivation. Andrew Carnegie, whose stewardship of the early steel industry and his Horatio Alger–like success made him one of the richest men in the United States, is always aware of the part that money plays in the balancing of these concepts. If the firm is not responsive to the need for fair compensation as a critical motivator, then no organizational structure is going to remain intact when labor strikes or walks off the job. Carnegie's investigation of "the labor question" produces a balanced document that affirms the dignity of labor and the purposes of capital, or management. This relationship between labor and capital must, according to Carnegie, evolve for the sake of the community. He recognizes that good management should produce an environment where strikes and boycotts would be unimaginable. The time, 1889, is not yet ripe, he says, for profit sharing, which would be the ideal solution. In the absence of such an ideal, there must be arbitration. Carnegie sketches a plan—including the acceptance of trade unions and a sliding scale of compensation—for peaceful relations between labor and capital that serves, even today, as a foundation for conduct and cooperation.

George Lorimer presents, in his *Letters from a Self-Made Merchant to His Son*, the letters of John Graham to his son, who is just "getting his feet wet" in the business world. Graham speaks from the perspective of advanced age and experience; he understands the "dual concepts" and what it takes to build a prosperous company in the late nineteenth century.

Graham's letter of September 1, 189_, quickly gets to the heart of how a firm's organizational hierarchy is determined. He is particularly complete and masterful in his methodical listing of the best practices for hiring and motivating employees. A natural storyteller, Graham prompts us, through his tale of Lem, to remember that management is something of an art and that managers must possess or develop the artist's introspective nature before assuming authority positions.

When relations between labor and capital are poor, people suffer. They suffer as managers and laborers, as producers and consumers—they suffer as people. The causes of poor relations may be traced to larger causes, as Carnegie explains, or smaller, more personal causes, as Graham details. Regardless of cause, there are more losers than winners when management fails.

R. H. Tawney asks us to consider these failures and to remember that social good comes from effective management and honorable purpose. He calls for a reassessment of the values of labor, incentives, rewards, and all other inducements to work productively. He entreats us to review the uses of tyranny and fear as general workplace motivators. Tawney believes that acquisitive societies, where people are primarily motivated by the desire for pecuniary gain, are not reflective enough about these things. Inducement, or motivation, matters, he says, and motivation is not always about money. The research, he tells us, is incomplete on the matter, and he offers us several ideas that might be effective employee motivators.

The laborers who work in the early twentieth-century English coal mines—colliers—are victims of the kind of management that both Carnegie and Tawney abhor. Such management is structured to get maximum work out of laborers at the lowest cost, while denying them even the meanest supports that might make their jobs less dangerous and more tolerable. This is management operating on the assumption that labor has little or no choice in the matter. It is unsympathetic to the pains it inflicts. D. H. Lawrence, an English writer known for his exploration of cultural manners and interior motivations, is aware of the devastation that such labor–capital discord can bring to the lives of powerless people.

D. H. Lawrence introduces us to Sir Clifford, an archetypal aristocrat of a manager whose views on the proper principles of management might horrify contemporary readers. Today, we think of these views as representative—in the extreme—of a certain managerial style. Yet, for Lawrence (and for Tawney, too), Sir Clifford's harsh *capitalist* values must be measured against Lady Chatterly's warm *Fabian/socialist* values. It is important that we do not fall into the trap of viewing Sir Clifford as an anachronistic symbol who is, thankfully, out of place in the modern world. Sir Clifford's workplace tyranny still has its proponents.

Tyranny is sometimes directly related to elements of unintended sociopolitical exploitation in the workplace. Frederick Taylor's vocabulary of managerial productivity experimentation is often thought of as a herald of the new managerial age, but some think of it as just another variety of tyranny—engineered to decrease manufacturing costs and to increase return on assets and unit profitability while straitjacketing workers to strict production behaviorisms. This kind of tyranny can produce an unhealthy inverse relationship— where worker productivity increases as worker satisfaction decreases.

The term *organization man* is less an everyday business expression now as it was when it was first introduced to the American business lexicon in 1956 by William H. Whyte, author of *The Organization Man* (not represented in this book). Whyte is an observer of the corporate culture of the 1950s, when American industrial imperialism was enthroned and rarely challenged in any global sense. He uses personification to describe the corporate managerial "body" of the period, seemingly fit and sitting there like an organizational Gargantua waiting for a physical examination.

As first understood, the meaning of *organization man* depends on one's mind-set about the requirements of business. Whyte describes him as a clearly conforming, quietly ambitious character—the type demanded by any large, bureaucratic organization. Like others affected by "organizationitis," he is viewed as diagnos-able but not especially treatable. To some, organizationitis is seen as a peculiarly American business disease; to others, it is an extraordinary American business cure.

At present, in this age of languishing loyalty to the corporation and lack of faith in the concept of upward mobility through the ranks of the corporate hierarchy, the organization man is perceived increasingly as a vanishing type—another reminder of an unenlightened era. We are passing from the age of the "old organizationalists" to the "new individualists."

Theories of management have been articulated and published in profusion since the publication of William Whyte's *Organization Man*. Many of these notions have been undernourished by indifference, some have been sacrificed to passionately argued criticism, and still others have been lost because management theory and practice change often. Even those that have found a more lasting place in the lexicon of management theories are not protected from revision or reconstruction. Yet the X and Y Theories of Douglas McGregor (whose *The Human Side of Enterprise* is a reading selection) sit on the alter like holy icons— untouchable and unalterable. This is true, in part, because McGregor's theories are built on historical fact and precedent. Nobody can argue away the supportive points for Theories X and Y because both theories have the historical record on their side. Theory Y is an evolutionary adaptation of Theory X. So they both sink or swim together, and in this case, they both swim. Here are some facts that give them buoyancy:

The nineteenth century was a time of capital hoarding and exploitation of labor, so the twentieth century was a time of budding cooperation between capital and labor and a period of good corporate citizenship. Theory X is an outgrowth of nineteenth-century ignorance, which disregarded the benefits of education and the potentialities of productive power inherent in a motivated labor force. Theory Y is the adaptive replacement for Theory X (an evolutionary improvement) and it recognizes the opportunities inherent in higher education, which, in itself, clues management into the benefits of directing the behavior of labor so that it favors organizational goals while providing limited autonomy—all for the purpose of improving productivity and building a cooperative *esprit de corps* (Tawney refers to this concept, too).

Some might argue this interpretation, but most do not. As McGregor says, the difference between Theory X and Theory Y "is the difference between treating people as children and treating them as adults." Maturation is typically a by-product of time, so the adaptation process in McGregor's theories is really just a factor of time and growth. The analogies should be obvious. The only real discussion here is the one that serves to predict the next transformational stage.

Chester Barnard is remembered for his magnum opus *The Functions of the Executive*. Though it is a product of the 1930s depression era, it treats the subject of the organization as if it were an eternal verity, defined by efficiency—which for Barnard means various types of cooperation. Efficiency and cooperation are the ingredients for success—that is the answer for the ages. And both are derived from moral codes of conduct. While McGregor might differentiate management as infantile or mature, Barnard differentiates by moral standards. We might infer from this that the best managers *and* the best employees can be found because of their moral natures. Their cooperation is ensured by their mutual responsibility and commitment to morality and by the codes that canonize it. How could an organization fail to succeed when its foundations are moral? More important, if its foundations are moral, it is because we are made of "the right stuff." ◆

Letter to Horace Greeley

Abraham Lincoln (1809–1865)

Executive Mansion,
Washington, August 22, 1862.

Hon. Horace Greeley:

Dear Sir.

I have just read yours of the 19th. addressed to myself through the New-York Tribune. If there be in it any statements, or assumptions of fact, which I may know to be erroneous, I do not, now and here, controvert them. If there be in it any inferences which I may believe to be falsely drawn, I do not now and here, argue against them. If there be perceptable [sic] in it an impatient and dictatorial tone, I waive it in deference to an old friend, whose heart I have always supposed to be right.

As to the policy I "seem to be pursuing" as you say, I have not meant to leave any one in doubt.

I would save the Union. I would save it the shortest way under the Constitution. The sooner the national authority can be restored; the nearer the Union will be "the Union as it was." If there be those who would not save the Union, unless they could at the same time *save* slavery, I do not agree with them. If there be those who would not save the Union unless they could at the same time *destroy* slavery, I do not agree with them. My paramount object in this struggle *is* to save the Union, and is *not* either to save or to destroy slavery. If I could save the Union without freeing *any* slave I would do it, and if I could save it by freeing *all* the slaves I would do it; and if I could save it by freeing some and leaving others alone I would also do that. What I do about slavery, and the colored race, I do because I believe it helps to save the Union; and what I forbear, I forbear because I do *not* believe it would help to save the Union. I shall do *less* whenever I shall believe what I am doing hurts the cause, and I shall do *more* whenever I shall believe doing more will help the cause. I shall try to correct errors when shown to be errors; and I shall adopt new views so fast as they shall appear to be true views.

I have here stated my purpose according to my view of *official* duty; and I intend no modification of my oft-expressed *personal* wish that all men everywhere could be free.

Yours,
A. Lincoln.

QUESTIONS

1. What does Lincoln identify as his duty as president?

2. What does he say his personal wishes are?

3. How does he balance his duty and his personal desires?

4. Why does he distinguish between his official duty and his personal wishes?

FROM *THE PRINCE*

Niccolo Machiavelli (1469–1527)

CONCERNING THE WAY IN WHICH PRINCES SHOULD KEEP FAITH

Every one admits how praiseworthy it is in a prince to keep faith, and to live with integrity and not with craft. Nevertheless our experience has been that those princes who have done great things have held good faith of little account, and have known how to circumvent the intellect of men by craft, and in the end have overcome those who have relied on their word. You must know there are two ways of contesting, the one by the law, the other by force; the first method is proper to men, the second to beasts; but because the first is frequently not sufficient, it is necessary to have recourse to the second. Therefore it is necessary for a prince to understand how to avail himself of the beast and the man. This has been figuratively taught to princes by ancient writers, who describe how Achilles and many other princes of old were given to the Centaur Chiron to nurse, who brought them up in his discipline; which means solely that, as they had for a teacher one who was half beast and half man, so it is necessary for a prince to know how to make use of both natures, and that one without the other is not durable. A prince, therefore, being compelled knowingly to adopt the beast, ought to choose the fox and the lion; because the lion cannot defend himself against snares and the fox cannot defend himself against wolves. Therefore, it is necessary to be a fox to discover the snares and a lion to terrify the wolves. Those who rely simply on the lion do not understand what they are about. Therefore a wise lord cannot, nor ought he to, keep faith when such observance may be turned against him, and when the reasons that caused him to pledge it exist no longer. If men were entirely good this precept would not hold, but because they are bad, and will not keep faith with you, you too are not bound to observe it with them. Nor will there ever be wanting to a prince legitimate reasons to excuse this nonobservance. Of this endless modern examples could be given, showing how many treaties and engagements have been made void and of no effect through the faithlessness of princes; and he who has known best how to employ the fox has succeeded best.

But it is necessary to know well how to disguise this characteristic, and to be a great pretender and dissembler; and men are so simple, and so subject to present necessities, that he who seeks to deceive will always find someone who will allow himself to be deceived. One recent example I cannot pass over in silence. Alexander VI did nothing else but deceive men, nor ever thought of doing otherwise, and he always found victims; for there never was a man who had greater power in asserting, or who with greater oaths would affirm a thing, yet would observe it less; nevertheless his deceits always succeeded according to his wishes, because he well understood this side of mankind.

Therefore it is unnecessary for a prince to have all the good qualities I have enumerated, but it is very necessary to appear to have them. And I shall dare to say this also, that to have them and always to observe them is injurious, and that to appear to have them is useful; to appear merciful, faithful, humane, religious, upright, and to be so, but with a mind so framed that should you require not to be so, you may be able and know how to change to the opposite.

And you have to understand this, that a prince, especially a new one, cannot observe all those things for which men are esteemed, being often forced, in order to maintain the state, to act contrary to fidelity, friendship, humanity, and religion. Therefore it is necessary for him to have a mind ready to turn itself accordingly as the winds and variations of fortune force it, yet, as I have said above, not to diverge from the good if he can avoid doing so, but, if compelled, then to know how to set about it.

For this reason a prince ought to take care that he never lets anything slip from his lips that is not replete with the above-named five qualities, that he may appear to him who sees and hears him altogether merciful, faithful, humane, upright, and religious. There is noth-
10 ing more necessary to appear to have than this last quality, inasmuch as men judge generally more by the eye than by the hand, because it belongs to everybody to see you, to few to come in touch with you. Every one sees what you appear to be, few really know what you are, and those few dare not oppose themselves to the opinion of the many, who have the majesty of the state to defend them; and in the actions of all men, and especially of princes, which it is not prudent to challenge, one judges 30
by the result.

For that reason, let a prince have the credit of conquering and holding his state, the means will always be considered honest, and he will be praised by everybody; because the vulgar are always taken by what a thing seems to be and by what comes of it; and in the world there are only the vulgar, for the few find a place there only when the many have no ground to rest on. 40

One prince of the present time, whom it is not well to name, never preaches anything else but peace and good faith, and to both he is most hostile, and either, if he had kept it, would have deprived him of reputation and kingdom many a time. ♦

QUESTIONS

1. Why does Machiavelli think it is not necessary that one always keeps one's word?

2. Why does Machiavelli think that it is useful not to have good qualities but rather just to appear to have them?

3. What animals does Machiavelli suggest that those in power need to emulate? Why?

From The Republic

Plato (428–349 BC)

Ruling as an Art

Surely the sole concern of the shepherd's art is to do the best for the charges put under its care; its own best interest is sufficiently provided for, so long as it does not fall short of all that shepherding should imply. On that principle it followed, I thought, that any kind of authority, in the state or in private life, must, in its character of authority, consider solely what is best for those under its care. Now what is your opin-
10 ion? Do you think that the men who govern states—I mean rulers in the strict sense—have no reluctance to hold office?

I don't think so, he replied; I know it.

Well, but haven't you noticed, Thrasymachus, that in other positions of authority no one is willing to act unless he is paid wages, which he demands on the assumption that all the benefit of his action will go to his charges? Tell me: Don't we always distinguish one form
20 of skill from another by its power to effect some particular result? Do say what you really think, so that we may get on.

Yes, that is the distinction.

And also each brings us some benefit that is peculiar to it: medicine gives health, for example; the art of navigation, safety at sea; and so on.

Yes.

And wage-earning brings us wages; that is
30 its distinctive product. Now, speaking with that precision which you proposed, you would not say that the art of navigation is the same as the art of medicine, merely on the ground that a ship's captain regained his health on a voyage, because the sea air was good for him. No more would you identify the practice of medicine with wage-earning because a man may keep his health while earning wages, or a physician attending a case may receive a fee.
40 No.

And, since we agreed that the benefit obtained by each form of skill is peculiar to it, any common benefit enjoyed alike by all these practitioners must come from some further practice common to them all?

It would seem so.

Yes, we must say that if they all earn wages, they get that benefit in so far as they are engaged in wage-earning as well as in practis-
50 ing their several arts.

He agreed reluctantly.

This benefit, then—the receipt of wages—does not come to a man from his special art. If we are to speak strictly, the physician, as such, produces health; the builder, a house; and then each, in his further capacity of wage-earner, gets his pay. Thus every art has its own function and benefits its proper subject. But suppose the practitioner is not paid; does he then
60 get any benefit from his art?

Clearly not.

And is he doing no good to anyone either, when he works for nothing?

No, I suppose he does some good.

Well then, Thrasymachus, it is now clear that no form of skill or authority provides for its own benefit. As we were saying some time ago, it always studies and prescribes what is good for its subject—the interest of the weaker party, not of the stronger. And that, my friend,
70 is why I said that no one is willing to be in a position of authority and undertake to set straight other men's troubles, without demanding to be paid; because, if he is to do his work well, he will never, in his capacity of ruler, do, or command others to do, what is best for himself, but only what is best for the subject. For that reason, if he is to consent, he must have his recompense, in the shape of money or honour, or of punishment in case of refusal.
80 What do you mean, Socrates? asked Glaucon. I recognize two of your three kinds of reward; but I don't understand what you mean by speaking of punishment as a recompense.

Then you don't understand the recompense required by the best type of men, or their motive for accepting authority when they do consent. You surely know that a passion for honours or for money is rightly regarded as something to be ashamed of.

Yes, I do.

For that reason, I said, good men are unwilling to rule, either for money's sake or for honour. They have no wish to be called mercenary for demanding to be paid, or thieves for making a secret profit out of their office; nor yet will honours tempt them, for they are not ambitious. So they must be forced to consent under threat of penalty; that may be why a readiness to accept power under no such constraint is thought discreditable. And the heaviest penalty for declining to rule is to be ruled by someone inferior to yourself. That is the fear, I believe, that makes decent people accept power; and when they do so, they face the prospect of authority with no idea that they are coming into the enjoyment of a comfortable berth; it is forced upon them because they can find no one better than themselves, or even as good, to be entrusted with power. If there could ever be a society of perfect men, there might well be as much competition to evade office as there now is to gain it; and it would then be clearly seen that the genuine ruler's nature is to seek only the advantage of the subject, with the consequence that any man of understanding would sooner have another to do the best for him than be at the pains to do the best for that other himself. On this point, then, I entirely disagree with Thrasymachus' doctrine that right means what is to the interest of the stronger. ♦

Questions

1. What does Socrates argue is the true concern of those who are in a position of authority?

2. What does Socrates mean when he distinguishes between the benefit that comes of any occupation versus the money that is made through that occupation?

3. What does the fact that good comes of a product or service, even if it is not paid for, signify for Plato?

4. How does Socrates explain the willingness of good people to accept a position of leadership?

FROM *THE ANALECTS*

K'ung Fu-tzu also known as *Confucius (551–479 BC)*

BOOK XII

1. Yen Yuan asked about perfect virtue. The Master said, To subdue one's self and return to propriety, is perfect virtue. If a man can for one day subdue himself and return to propriety, all under heaven will ascribe perfect virtue to him. Is the practice of perfect virtue from a man himself, or it is from others?

Yen Yuan said, "I beg to ask the steps of that process." The Master replied, "Look not at what is contrary to propriety; listen not to what is contrary to propriety; speak not what is contrary to propriety; make no movement which is contrary to propriety." Yen Yuan then said, "Though I am deficient in intelligence and vigour, I will make it my business to practice this lesson."

2. Chung-kung asked about perfect virtue. The Master said, "It is, when you go abroad, to behave to every one as if you were receiving a great guest; to employ the people as if you were assisting at a great sacrifice; not to do to others as you would not wish done to yourself; to have no murmuring against you in the country, and none in the family." Chung-kung said, "Though I am deficient in intelligence and vigour, I will make it my business to practice this lesson."

* * *

7. Tsze-kung asked about government. The Master said, "The requisites of government are that there be sufficiency of food, sufficiency of military equipment, and the confidence of the people in their ruler."

Tsze-kung said, "If it cannot be helped, and one of these must be dispensed with, which of the three should be foregone first?" "The military equipment," said the Master.

Tsze-kung again asked, "If it cannot be helped, and one of the remaining two must be dispensed with, which of them should be foregone?" The Master answered, "Part with the food. From of old, death has been the lot of all men; but if the people have no faith in their rulers, there is no standing for the State."

8. Chi Tsze-chang said, "In a superior man it is only the substantial qualities which are wanted; why should we seek for ornamental accomplishments?"

Tsze-kung said, "Alas! Your words, sir, show you to be a superior man, but for horses cannot overtake the tongue.

"Ornament is as substance; substance is as ornament. The hide of a tiger or leopard stripped of its hair, is like the hide of a dog or goat stripped of its hair."

* * *

14. Tsze-chang asked about government. The Master said, "The art of governing is to keep its affairs before the mind without weariness, and to practice them with undeviating consistency."

15. The Master said, "By extensively studying all learning, and keeping himself under the restraint of the rules of propriety, one may thus likewise not err from what is right."

16. The Master said, "The superior man seeks to perfect the admirable qualities of men, and does not seek to perfect their bad qualities. The mean man does the opposite of this."

17. Chi K'ang asked Confucius about government. Confucius replied, "To govern means to rectify. If you lead on the people with correctness, who will dare not to be correct?"

18. Chi K'ang, distressed about the number of thieves in the State, inquired of Confucius how to do away with them. Confucius said, "If you, sir, were not covetous, although you should reward them to do it, they would not steal."

19. Chi K'ang asked Confucius about government saying, "What do you say to killing the unprincipled for the good of the principled?" Confucius replied, "Sir, in carrying on your government, why should you use

killing at all? Let your evinced desires be for what is good, and the people will be good. The relation between superiors and inferiors, is like that between the wind and the grass. The grass must bend, when the wind blows across it."

20. Tsze-chang asked, "What must the officer be, who may be said to be distinguished?"

The Master said, "What is it you call being distinguished?"

Tsze-chang replied, "It is to be heard of through the State, to be heard of throughout his clan."

The Master said, "That is notoriety, not distinction.

"Now the man of distinction is solid and straightforward, and loves righteousness. He examines people's words, and looks at their countenances. He is anxious to humble himself to others. Such a man will be distinguished in the country; he will be distinguished in his clan.

"As to the man of notoriety, he assumes the appearance of virtue, but his actions are opposed to it, and he rests in this character without any doubts about himself. Such a man will be heard of in the country; he will be heard of in the clan."

* * *

BOOK XV

17. The Master said, "The superior man in everything considers righteousness to be essential. He performs it according to the rules of propriety. He brings it forth in humility. He completes it with sincerity. This is indeed a superior man."

18. The Master said, "The superior man is distressed by his want of ability. He is not distressed by men's not knowing him."

19. The Master said, "The superior man dislikes the thought of his name not being mentioned after his death."

20. The Master said, "What the superior man seeks, is in himself. What the mean man seeks, is in others."

21. The Master said, "The superior man is dignified, but does not wrangle. He is sociable, but not a partisan."

22. The Master said, "The superior man does not promote a man simply on account of his words, nor does he put aside good words because of the man."

23. Tsze-kung asked, saying, "Is there one word which may serve as a rule of practice for all one's life?" The Master said, "Is not RECIPROCITY such a word? What you do not want done to yourself, do not do to others."

24. The Master said, "In my dealings with men, whose evil do I blame, whose goodness do I praise, beyond what is proper? If I do sometimes exceed in praise, there must be ground for it in my examination of the individual." . . .

* * *

BOOK XX

1. Yao said, "Oh! You, Shun, the Heaven-determined order of succession now rests in your person. Sincerely hold fast the due Mean. If there shall be distress and want within the four seas, the Heavenly revenue will come to a perpetual end."

Shun also used the same language in giving charge to Yu.

T'ang said, "I, the child Li, presume to use a dark-coloured victim, and presume to announce to Thee, O most great and sovereign God, that the sinner I dare not pardon, and thy ministers, O God, I do not keep in obscurity. The examination of them is by they mind, O God. If, in my person, I commit offences, they are not to be attributed to you, the people of the myriad regions. If you in the myriad regions commit offences, these offences must rest on my person."

Chau conferred great gifts, and the good were enriched.

"Although he has his near relatives, they are not equal to my virtuous men. The people are throwing blame upon me, the One man."

He carefully attended to the weights and measures, examined the body of the laws, restored the discarded officers, and the good government of the kingdom took its course.

He revived States that had been extinguished, restored families whose line of succession had been broken, and called to office those who had retired into obscurity, so that throughout the kingdom the hearts of the people turned towards him.

What he attached chief importance to, were the food of the people, the duties of mourning, and sacrifices.

By his generosity, he won all. By his sincerity, he made the people repose trust in him. By his earnest activity, his achievements were great. By his justice, all were delighted.

2. Tsze-chang asked Confucius, saying, "In what way should a person in authority act in order that he may conduct government properly?" The Master replied, "Let him honour the five excellent, and banish away the four bad, things; then may he conduct government properly." Tsze-chang said, "What are meant by the five excellent things?" The Master said, "When the person in authority is beneficent without great expenditure; when he lays tasks on the people without their repining; when he pursues what he desires without being covetous; when he maintains a dignified ease without being proud; when he is majestic without being fierce."

Tsze-chang said, "What is meant by being beneficent without great expenditure?" The Master replied, "When the person in authority makes more beneficial to people the things from which they naturally derive benefit; is not this being beneficent without great expenditure? When he chooses the labours which are proper, and makes them labour on them, who will repine? When his desires are set on benevolent government, and he secures it, who will accuse him of covetousness? Whether he has to do with many people or few, or with things great or small, he does not dare to indicate any disrespect; is not this to maintain a dignified ease without any pride? He adjusts his clothes and cap, and throws a dignity into his looks, so that, thus dignified, he is looked at with awe; is not this to be majestic without being fierce?"

Tsze-chang then asked, "What are meant by the four bad things?" The Master said, "To put the people to death without having instructed them; this is called cruelty. To require from them, suddenly, the full tale of work, without having given them warning; this is called oppression. To issue orders as if without urgency, at first, and, when the time comes, to insist on them with severity; this is called injury. And, generally, in the giving pay or rewards to men, to do it in a stingy way; this is called the part of a mere official."

3. The Master said, "Without recognizing the ordinances of Heaven, it is impossible to be a superior man.

"Without an acquaintance with the rules of Propriety, it is impossible for the character to be established.

"Without knowing the force of words, it is impossible to know men." ◆

QUESTIONS

1. According to Confucius, food, weapons, and trusted leadership have what order of priority in a society?

2. Why does Confucius suggest what we call the golden rule as a principle of good management?

3. According to Confucius, does culture or inborn qualities make the person?

4. What leads to being influential?

5. According to Confucius, what are the five lovely things and the four ugly things?

AN EMPLOYER'S VIEW OF THE LABOR QUESTION FROM *THE GOSPEL OF WEALTH*

Andrew Carnegie (1835–1919)

The struggle in which labor has been engaged during the past three hundred years, first against authority and then against capital, has been a triumphal march. Victory after victory has been achieved. Even so late as in Shakespeare's time, remains of villeinage or serfdom still existed in England. Before that, not only the labor but the person of the laborer belonged to the chief. The workers were either slaves or serfs; men and women were sold with the estate upon which they worked, and became the property of the new lord, just as did the timber which grew on the land. In those days we hear nothing of strikes or of trade-unions, or differences of opinion between employer and employed. The fact is, labor then had no right which the chief, or employer, was bound to respect. Even as late as the beginning of this century, the position of the laborer in some departments was such as can scarcely be credited. What do our laboring friends think of this, that down to 1779 the miners of Britain were in a state of serfdom. They "were compelled by law to remain in the pits as long as the owner chose to keep them at work there, and were actually sold as part of the capitol invested in the works. If they accepted an engagement elsewhere, their master could always have them fetched back and flogged as thieves for having attempted to rob him of their labor. This law was modified in 1779, but was not repealed till after the acts passed in 1797 and 1799" (*The Trades-Unions of England*, p. 119). This was only ninety-seven years ago. Men are still living who were living then. Again, in France, as late as 1806, every workman had to procure a license; and in Russia, down to our own days, agricultural laborers were sold with the soil they tilled.

Consider the change, nay, the revolution! Now the poorest laborer in America and England, or indeed, throughout the civilized world, who can handle a pick or a shovel, stands upon equal terms with the purchaser of his labor. He sells or withholds it as may seem best to him. He negotiates, and thus rises to the dignity of an independent contractor. When he has performed the work he bargained to do, he owes his employer nothing, and is under no obligation to him. Not only has the laborer conquered his political and personal freedom: he has achieved industrial freedom as well, as far as the law can give it, and he now fronts his master, proclaiming himself his equal under the law.

But, notwithstanding this complete revolution, it is evident that the permanent relations to each other of labor and capital have not yet evolved. The present adjustment does not work without friction, and changes must be made before we can have industrial peace. To-day we find collisions between these forces, capital and labor, when there should be combination. The mill hands of an industrial village in France have just risen against their employers, attacked the manager's home and killed him. The streets of another French village are barricaded against the expected forces of order. The ship-builders of Sunderland, in England, are at the verge of starvation, owing to a quarrel with their employers; and Leicester has just been the scene of industrial riots. In our country, labor disputes and strikes were never so numerous as now. East and West, North and South, everywhere, there is unrest, showing that an equilibrium has not yet been reached between employers and employed.

A strike or lockout is, in itself, a ridiculous affair. Whether a failure or a success, it gives no direct proof of its justice or injustice. In this it resembles war between two nations. It is simply a question of strength and endurance between the contestants. The gage of battle, or the duel, is not more senseless, as a means of establishing what is just and fair, than an industrial strike or lockout. It would be folly to conclude that we have reached any permanent adjustment between capital and labor until strikes and lockouts are as much things of the past as the gage of battle or the duel have become in the most advanced communities.

Taking for granted, then, some further modifications must be made between capital and labor, I propose to consider the various plans that have been suggested by which labor can advance another stage in its development in relation to capital. And, as a preliminary, let it be noted that it is only labor and capital in their greatest masses which it is necessary to consider. It is only in large establishments that the industrial unrest of which I have spoken ominously manifests itself. The farmer who hires a man to assist him, or the gentleman who engages a groom or butler, is not affected by strikes. The innumerable cases in which a few men only are directly concerned, which comprise in the aggregate the most of labor, present upon the whole a tolerably satisfactory condition of affairs. This clears the ground of much, and leaves us to deal with the immense mining and manufacturing concerns of recent growth, in which capital and labor often array themselves in alarming antagonism.

Among expedients suggested for their better reconciliation, the first place must be assigned to the idea of coöperation, or the plan by which the workers are to become part owners in enterprises, and share their fortunes. There is no doubt that if this could be effected it would have the same beneficial effect upon the workman which the ownership of land has upon the man who hitherto tilled the land for another. The sense of ownership would make of him more of a man as regards himself, and hence more of a citizen as regards the commonwealth. But we are here met by a difficulty which I confess I have not yet been able to overcome, and which renders me less sanguine than I should like to

be in regard to coöperation. The difficulty is this, and it seems to me inherent in all gigantic manufacturing, mining, and commercial operations. Two men or two combinations of men will erect blast-furnaces, iron-mills, cotton-mills, or piano manufactories adjoining each other, or engage in shipping or commercial business. They will start with equal capital and credit; and to those only superficially acquainted with the personnel of these concerns, success will seem as likely to attend the one as the other. Nevertheless, one will fail after dragging along a lifeless existence, and pass into the hands of its creditors; while the neighboring mill or business will make a fortune for its owners. Now, the successful manufacturer, dividing every month or every year a proportion of his profits among his workmen, either as a bonus or as dividends upon shares owned by them, will not only have a happy and contented body of operatives, but he will inevitably attract from his rival the very best workmen in every department. His rival, having no profits to divide among his workmen, and paying them only a small assured minimum to enable them to live, finds himself despoiled of foremen and of workmen necessary to carry on his business successfully. His workmen are discontented and, in their own opinion, defrauded of the proper fruits of their skill, through incapacity or inattention of their employers. Thus, unequal business capacity in the management produces unequal results.

It will be precisely the same if one of these manufactories belongs to the workmen themselves; but in this case, in the present stage of development of the workmen, the chances of failure will be enormously increased. It is, indeed, greatly to be doubted whether any body of working-men in the world could to-day organize and successfully carry on a mining or manufacturing or commercial business in competition with concerns owned by men trained to affairs. If any such coöperative organization succeeds, it may be taken for granted that it is principally owing to the exceptional business ability of one of the managers, and only in very small degree to the efforts of the mass of workmen-owners. This business ability is excessively rare, as is proved by the incredibly large proportion of those who enter upon the stormy sea of business only to fail. I should say that twenty coöperative concerns would fail to every one that would succeed. There are, of course, a few successful establishments, notably two in France and one in England, which are organized upon the coöperative plan, in which the workmen participate in the profits. But these were all created by the present owners, who now generously share the profits with their workmen, and are making the success of their manufactories upon the coöperative plan the proud work of their lives. What these concerns will become when the genius for affairs is no longer with them to guide, is a matter of grave doubt and, to me, of foreboding. I can, of course, picture in my mind a state of civilization in which the most talented business men shall find their most cherished work in carrying on immense concerns, not primarily for their own personal aggrandizement, but for the good of the masses of workers engaged therein, and their families; but this is only a foreshadowing of a dim and distant future. When a class of such men has evolved, the problem of capital and labor will be permanently solved to the entire satisfaction of both. But as this manifestly belongs to a future generation, I cannot consider coöperation or common ownership, as the next immediate step in advance which it is possible for labor to make in its upward path.

The next suggestion is that peaceful settlement of differences should be reached through arbitration. Here we are upon firmer ground. I would lay it down as a maxim that there is no excuse for a strike or lockout until arbitration of differences has been offered by one party and refused by the other. No doubt serious trouble attends even arbitration at present, from the difficulty of procuring suitable men to judge intelligently between the disputants. There is a natural disinclination among business men to expose their businesses to men in whom they have not their entire confidence. We lack, so far, in America a retired class of men of affairs. Our vile practice is to keep accumulating more dollars until we die. If it were the custom here, as it is in England, for men to withdraw from active business after acquiring a fortune, this class would furnish the proper arbitrators. On the other hand, the ex-presidents of trade-unions, such as Mr. Jarrett or Mr. Wihle, after they have retired from active control, would commend themselves to the manufacturers and to the men as possessed of the necessary technical knowledge, and educated to a point where commercial reasons would not be without their proper weight upon them. I consider that of all the agencies immediately available to prevent wasteful and embittering contests between capital and labor, arbitration is the most powerful and most beneficial.

The influence of trades-unions upon the relations between employer and employed has been much discussed. Some establishments in America have refused to recognize the right of men to form themselves into these unions, although I am not aware that any concern in England would dare to take this position. This policy, however, may be regarded as only a temporary phase of the situation. The right of the working-men to combine and to form trades-unions is no less sacred then the right of the manufacturer to enter into associations and conferences with his fellows, and it must sooner or later be conceded. Indeed, it gives one but a poor opinion of the American workman if he permits himself to be deprived of a right which his fellow in England long since conquered for himself. My experience has been that trades-unions, upon the whole, are beneficial both to labor and to capital. They certainly educate the working-men, and give them a truer conception of the relations of capital and labor than they could otherwise form. The ablest and best workmen eventually come to the front in these organizations; and it may be laid down as a rule that the more intelligent the workman the fewer the contests with employers. It is not the intelligent workman, who knows that labor without his brother capital is helpless, but the blatant ignorant man, who regards capital as the natural enemy of labor, who does so much to embitter the relations between employer and employed; and the power of this ignorant demagogue arises chiefly from the lack of proper organization among the men through which their real voice can be expressed. This voice will always be found in favor of the judicious and intelligent representative. Of course, as men become intelligent more deference must be paid to them personally and to their rights, and even to their opinions and prejudices; and, upon the whole, a greater share of profits must be paid in the day of prosperity to the intelligent than to the ignorant workman. He cannot be imposed upon so readily. On the other hand, he will be found much readier to accept reduced compensation when business is depressed; and it is better in the long run for capital to be served by the highest intelligence, and to be made aware of the fact that it is dealing with men who know what is due to them, both as to treatment and compensation.

One great source of trouble between employers and employed arises from the fact that the immense establishments of to-day, in which alone we find serious conflicts between capital and labor, are not managed by their owners, but by salaried officers, who cannot possibly have any permanent interest in the welfare of the working-men. These officials are chiefly anxious to present a satisfactory balance-sheet at the end of the year, that their hundreds of shareholders may receive the usual dividends, and that they may therefore be secure in their positions, and be allowed to manage business without unpleasant interference either by directors or by shareholders. It is notable that bitter strikes seldom occur in small establishments where the owner comes into direct contact with his men, and knows their qualities, their struggles, and their aspirations. It is the chairman, situated hundreds of miles away from his men, who only pays a flying visit to the works and perhaps finds time to walk through the mill or mine once or twice a year, that is chiefly responsible for the disputes which break out at intervals. I have noticed that the manager who confers oftenest with a committee of his leading men has the least trouble with his workmen. Although it may be impracticable for the presidents of these large corporations to know the working-men personally, the manager at the mills, having a committee of his best men to present their suggestions and wishes from time to time, can do much to maintain and strengthen amicable relations, if not interfered with from headquarters. I, therefore, recognize in trades-unions, or, better still, in organizations of the men of each establishment, who select representatives to speak for them, a means, not of further embittering the relations between employer and employed, but of improving them.

It is astonishing how small a sacrifice upon the part of the employer will sometimes greatly benefit the men. I remember that at one of our meetings with a committee, it was incidentally remarked by one speaker that the necessity for obtaining credit at the stores in the neighborhood was a grave tax upon the men. An ordinary workman, he said, could not afford to maintain himself and family for a month, and as he only received his pay monthly, he was compelled to obtain credit and to pay exorbitantly for everything, whereas, if he had the cash, he could buy at twenty-five per cent less. "Well," I said, "why cannot we overcome that by paying them every two weeks?" The reply was: "We did not like to ask it, because we have always understood that it would cause too much trouble; but if you do that it will be worth an advance of five per cent in our wages." We have paid semi-monthly since. Another speaker happened to say that although they were in the midst of coal, the price charged for small lots delivered at their houses was a certain sum per bushel. The price named was double what our best coal was costing us. How easy for us to deliver to our men such coal as they required, and charge them cost! This was done without a cent's loss to us, but worth much gain to the men. Several other points similar to these have arisen by which their labors might be lightened or products increased, and others suggesting changes in machinery or facilities which, but for the conferences referred to, would have been unthought of by the employer and probably never asked for by the men. For these and other reasons I attribute the greatest importance to an organization of the men, through whose duly elected representatives the managers may be kept informed from time to time of their grievances and suggestions. No matter how able the manager, the clever workman can often show him how beneficial changes can be made in the special branch in which that workman labors. Unless the relations between manager and workmen are not only amicable but friendly, the owners miss much; nor is any man a first-class manager who has not the confidence and respect, and even the admiration, of his workmen. No man is a true gentleman who does not inspire the affection and devotion of his servants. The danger is that such committees may ask conferences too often; three or four meetings per year should be regarded as sufficient.

I come now to the greatest cause of the friction which prevails between capital and labor in the largest establishments, the real essence of the trouble, and the remedy I have to propose.

The trouble is that the men are not paid at any time the compensation proper to that time. All large concerns necessarily keep filled with orders, say for six months in advance, and these orders are taken, of course, at prices prevailing when they are booked. This year's operations furnish perhaps the best illustration of the difficulty. Steel rails at the end of last year for delivery this year were $29 per ton at the works. Of course the mills entered the orders freely at this price, and kept entering them until the demand growing unexpectedly great carried prices up to $35 per ton. Now, the various mills in America are compelled for the next six months or more to run upon orders which do not average $31 per ton at the seaboard and Pittsburg, and pay $34 at Chicago. Transportation, ironstone, and prices of all kinds have advanced upon them in the meantime, and they must therefore run the bulk of the year upon very small margins of profit. But the men, noticing in the papers the "great boom in steel rails," very naturally demand their share of the advance, and, under existing faulty arrangements between capital and labor, they have secured it. The employers, therefore, have grudgingly given what they know under proper arrangements they should not have been required to give, and there has been friction, and still is dissatisfaction upon the part of the employers. Reverse this picture. The steel-rail market falls again. The mills have six months' work at prices above the prevailing market, and can afford to pay men higher wages than the existing state of the market would apparently justify. But having just been amerced in extra payments for labor which they should not have paid, they naturally attempt to reduce wages as the market price of rails goes down, and there arises discontent among the men, and we have a repetition of the negotiations and strikes which have characterized the beginning of this year. In other words, when the employer is going down the employee insists on going up, and vice versa. What we must seek is a plan by which the men will receive higher wages when their employers are receiving higher prices for their product, and hence are making large profits; and, *per contra*, when the employers are receiving low prices for product, and therefore small if any profits, the men will receive low wages. If this plan can be found, employers and employed will be "in the same boat," rejoicing together in their prosperity, and calling into play their fortitude together in adversity. There will be no room for quarrels, and instead of a feeling of antagonism there will be a feeling of partnership between employers and employed.

There is a simple means of producing this result, and to its general introduction both employers and employed should steadily bend their energies. Wages should be based upon a sliding scale, in proportion to the net prices received for product month by month. And I here gladly pay Mr. Potter, president of the North Chicago Rolling Mill Company, the great compliment to say that he has already taken a step in this direction, for to-day he is working his principle mill upon this plan. The result is that he has had no stoppage whatever this year, nor any dissatisfaction. All has gone smoothly along, and this in itself is worth at least as much to the manufacturer and to the men as the differences in wages one way or another which can arise from the new system.

The celebrated Crescent Steel Works of Pittsburg, manufacturers of the highest grades of tool steel, pay their skilled workmen by a sliding scale, based upon prices received for product—an important factor in the eminent success of that firm. The scale adopted by the iron manufacturers and workmen is only an approach to the true sliding scale; nevertheless, it is a decided gain both to capital and labor, as it is adopted from year to year, and hence eliminates strikes on account of wages during the year, and limits these interruptions from that cause to the yearly negotiation as to the justice or injustice of the scale. As this scale, however, is not based upon the prices actually received for the product, but upon the published lists of prices, which should be received in theory, there is not complete mutuality between the parties. In depressed times, such as the iron industry has been passing through in recent years, enormous concessions upon the published card prices have been necessary to effect sales, and in these the workmen have not shared with their employers. If, however, there was added to the scale, even in its present form, a stipulation that all causes of difference which could not be postponed till the end of the year, and then consid-

ered with the scale, should be referred to arbitration and that, in case of failure of the owners and workmen to agree at the yearly conference, arbitration should also be resorted to, strikes and lockouts would be entirely eliminated from the iron business; and if the award of the arbitrators took effect from the date of reference the works could run without a day's interruption.

Dismissing, therefore, for the present all consideration of coöperation as not being within measurable distance, I believe that the next steps in the advance toward permanent, peaceful relations between capital and labor are:

First. That compensation be paid the men based upon a sliding scale in proportion to the prices received for product.

Second. A proper organization of the men of every works be made, by which the natural leaders, the best men, will eventually come to the front and confer freely with the employers.

Third. Peaceful arbitration to be in all cases resorted to for the settlement of differences which the owners and the mill committee cannot themselves adjust in friendly conference.

Fourth. No interruption ever to occur to the operations of the establishment, since the decision of the arbitrators shall be made to take effect from the date of reference.

If these measures were adopted by an establishment, several important advantages would be gained:

First. The employer and employed would simultaneously share their prosperity or adversity with each other. The scale once settled, the feeling of antagonism would be gone, and a feeling of mutuality would ensue. Capital and labor would be shoulder to shoulder, supporting each other.

Second. There could be neither strike nor lockout, since both parties had agreed to abide by a forthcoming decision of disputed points. Knowing that in the last resort strangers were called in to decide what should be a family affair, the cases would, indeed be few which could not be amicably adjusted by the original parties without calling in others to judge between them.

Whatever the future may have in store for labor, the evolutionist, who sees nothing but certain and steady progress for the race, will never attempt to set bounds to its triumphs, even to its final form of complete and universal industrial coöperation, which I hope is some day to be reached. But I am persuaded that the next step forward is to be in the direction I have ventured to point out; and as one who is now most anxious to contribute his part toward helping forward the day of amicable relations between the two forces of capital and labor, which are not enemies, but are really auxiliaries who stand or fall together, I ask at the hands of both capital and labor a careful consideration of these views. ♦

QUESTIONS

1. What does Carnegie mean by "the labor question"?

2. According to Carnegie, against whom has labor struggled?

3. Did Carnegie have a solution to the problem of incompetent management negatively affecting even the best workers?

4. What six ways did Carnegie suggest for reconciling the interests of labor and those of companies' owners?

FROM *LETTERS FROM A SELF-MADE MERCHANT TO HIS SON*

George Lorimer (1867–1937)

LETTER XV

Chicago September 1, 189—

Dear Pierrepont: I judge from yours of the twenty-ninth that you must have the black bass in those parts pretty well terrorized. I never could quite figure it out, but there seems to be something about a fish that makes even a cold-water deacon see double. I reckon it must be that while Eve was learning the first principles of dressmaking from the snake, Adam was off bass fishing and keeping his end up by learning how to lie.

Don't overstock yourself with those four-pound fish yarns, though, because the boys have been bringing them back from their vacations till we've got enough to last us for a year of Fridays. And if you're sending them to keep in practice, you might as well quit, because we've decided to take you off the road when you come back, and make you assistant manager of the lard department. The salary will be fifty dollars a week, and the duties of the position to do your work so well that the manager can't run the department without you, and that you can run the department without the manager.

To do this you will have to know lard; to know yourself; and to know those under you. To some fellows lard is just hog fat, and not always that, if they would rather make a dollar to-day than five to-morrow. But it was a good deal more to Jack Summers, who held your new job until we had to promote him to canned goods.

Jack knew lard from the hog to the frying pan; was up on lard in history and religion; originated what he called the "Ham and theory," proving that Moses' injunction against pork must have been dissolved by the Circuit Court, because Noah included a couple of shoats in his cargo, and called one of his sons Ham, out of gratitude, probably, after tasting a slice broiled for the first time; argued that all the great nations lived on fried food, and that America was the greatest of them all, owing to the energy-producing qualities of pie, liberally shortened with lard.

It almost broke Jack's heart when we decided to manufacture our new cottonseed oil product, Seedoiline. But on reflection he saw that it just gave him an extra hold on the heathen that he couldn't convert to lard, and he started right out for the Hebrew and vegetarian vote. Jack had enthusiasm, and enthusiasm is the best shortening for any job; it makes heavy work light.

A good many young fellows envy their boss because they think he makes the rules and can do as he pleases. As a matter of fact, he's the only man in the shop who can't. He's like the fellow on the tight-rope—there's plenty of scenery under him and lots of room around him, but he's got to keep his feet on the wire all the time and travel straight ahead.

A clerk has just one boss to answer to—the manager. But the manager has just as many bosses as he has clerks under him. He can make rules, but he's the only man who can't afford to break them now and then. A fellow is a boss simply because he's a better man than those under him, and there's a heap of responsibility in being better than the next fellow.

No man can ask more than he gives. A fellow who can't take orders can't give them. If his rules are too hard for him to mind, you can bet they are too hard for the clerks who don't get half so much for minding them as he does. There's no alarm clock for the sleepy man like an early rising manager; and there's nothing breeds work in an office like a busy boss.

Of course, setting a good example is just a small part of a manager's duties. It's not enough to settle yourself firm on the box seat—you must have every man under you hitched up right and well in hand. You can't work individuals by general rules. Every man is a special case and needs a special pill.

When you fix up a snug little nest for a Plymouth Rock hen and encourage her with a nice porcelain egg, it doesn't always follow that she has reached the fricassee age because she doesn't lay right off. Sometimes she will respond to a little red pepper in her food.

I don't mean by this that you ever want to drive your men, because the lash always leaves its worst soreness under the skin. A hundred men will forgive a blow in the face where one will a blow to his self-esteem. Tell a man the truth about himself and shame the devil if you want to, but you won't shame the man you're trying to reach, because he won't believe you. But if you can start him on the road that will lead him to the truth he's mighty apt to try to reform himself before any one else finds him out.

Consider carefully before you say a hard word to a man, but never let a chance to say a good one go by. Praise judiciously bestowed is money invested.

Never learn anything about your men except from themselves. A good manager needs no detectives, and the fellow who can't read human nature can't manage it. The phonograph records of a fellow's character are lined in his face, and a man's days tell the secrets of his nights.

Be slow to hire and quick to fire. The time to discover incompatibility of temper and curl-papers is before the marriage ceremony. But when you find that you've hired the wrong man, you can't get rid of him too quick. Pay him an extra month, but don't let him stay another day. A discharged clerk in the office is like a splinter in the thumb—a centre of soreness. There are no exceptions to this rule, because there are no exceptions to human nature.

Never threaten, because a threat is a promise to pay that it isn't always convenient to meet, but if you don't make it good it hurts your credit. Save a threat till you're ready to act, and then you won't need it. In all your dealings, remember that to-day is your opportunity; to-morrow some other fellow's.

Keep close to your men. When a fellow's sitting on top of a mountain he's in a mighty dignified and exalted position, but if he's gazing at the clouds, he's missing a heap of interesting and important doings down in the valley. Never lose your dignity, of course, but tie it up in all the red tape you can find around the office, and tuck it away in the safe. It's easy for a boss to awe his clerks, but a man who is feared to his face is hated behind his back. A competent boss can move among his men without having to draw an imaginary line between them, because they will see the real one if it exists.

Besides keeping in touch with your office men, you want to feel your salesmen all the time. Send each of them a letter every day so that they won't forget that we are making goods for which we need orders; and insist on their sending you a line every day, whether they have anything to say or not. When a fellow has to write in six times a week to the house, he uses up his explanations mighty fast, and he's pretty apt to hustle for business to make his seventh letter interesting.

Right here I want to repeat that in keeping track of others and their faults it's very, very important that you shouldn't lose sight of your own. Authority swells up some fellows so that they can't see their corns; but a wise man tries to cure his own while remembering not to tread on his neighbors'.

In this connection, the story of Lemuel Hostitter, who kept the corner grocery in my old town, naturally comes to mind. Lem was probably the meanest white man in the State of Missouri, and it wasn't any walk-over to hold the belt in those days. Most grocers were satisfied to adulterate their coffee with ground peas, but Lem was so blamed mean that he adulterated the peas first. Bought skin-bruised hams and claimed that the bruise was his private and particular brand, stamped in the skin, showing that they were a fancy article, packed expressly for his fancy family trade. Ran a soda-water fountain in the front of his store with home-made syrups that ate the lining out of the children's stomachs, and a blind tiger in the back room with moonshine whiskey that pickled their daddies' insides. Take it by and large, Lem's character smelled about as various as his store, and that wasn't perfumed with lily-of-the-valley, you bet.

One time and another most men dropped into Lem's store of an evening, because there wasn't any other place to go and swap lies about the crops and any of the neighbors who didn't happen to be there. As Lem was always around, in the end he was the only man in town whose meanness hadn't been talked over in that grocery. Naturally, he began to think that he was the only decent white man in the county. Got to shaking his head and reckoning that the town was plum rotten. Said that such goings on would make a pessimist of a goat. Wanted to know if public opinion couldn't be aroused so that decency would have a show in the village.

Most men get information when they ask for it, and in the end Lem fetched public opinion all right. One night the local chapter of the W. C. T. U. [Woman's Christian Temperance Union] borrowed all the loose hatchets in town and made a good, clean, workmanlike job of the back part of his store, though his whiskey was so mean that even the ground couldn't soak it up. The noise brought out the men, and they sort of caught the spirit of the happy occasion. When they were through, Lem's stock and fixtures looked mighty sick, and they had Lem on a rail headed for the county line.

I don't know when I've seen a more surprised man than Lem. He couldn't cuss even. But as he never came back, to ask for any explanation, I reckon he figured it out that they wanted to get rid of him because he was too good for the town.

I simply mention Lem in passing as an example of the fact that when you're through sizing up the other fellow, it's a good thing to step back from yourself and see how you look. Then add fifty per cent to your estimate of your neighbor for virtues that you can't see, and deduct fifty per cent, from yourself for faults that you've missed in your inventory, and you'll have a pretty accurate result.

Your affectionate father,
John Graham. ◆

QUESTIONS

1. What three things are essential to know if you want to be a good manager?

2. Who has the harder job, the manager or the subordinate?

3. What are workers especially sensitive to?

4. What things must a good manager do to be successful?

SELECTION FROM: *THE BUSINESS GUIDE*

J. L. Nichols (1851–1895) self-published Naperville, Ill 1893

BUSINESS ENERGY

"Blest work, if ever thou wert a curse of God, what must His blessings be!"—J. B. Selkirk

"Our greatest glory is not in never falling: but in rising every time we fall."—Confucius

We love our upright, energetic business men. Pull them this way and then that way and the other they only bend but never break. Trip them down and in a trice they are on their feet. Bury them in the mud, and in an hour they will be out and bright. They are not ever yawning away existence, or walking about the world as if they had come into it with only half their soul; you can not keep them down; you can not destroy them. But for these the world would soon degenerate. They are the salt of the earth. Who but they start any noble project? They build our cities and rear our manufactories. They whiten the ocean with their sails, and blacken the heavens with the smoke of their steam-vessels and furnace-fires. They draw treasures from the mines. They plow the earth. Blessings on them.

THE CONDITION OF EFFICIENCY
FROM *THE ACQUISITIVE SOCIETY*

R. H. Tawney (1880–1962)

Thus it is not only for the sake of the producers, on whom the old industrial order weighed most heavily, that a new industrial order is needed. It is needed for the sake of the consumers, because the ability on which the old industrial order prided itself most and which is flaunted most as an argument against change, the ability to serve them effectively, is itself visibly breaking down. It is breaking down at what was always its most vulnerable point, the control of the human beings whom, with characteristic indifference to all but their economic significance, it distilled for its own purposes into an abstraction called "Labor." The first symptom of its collapse is what the first symptom of economic collapses has usually been in the past—the failure of customary stimuli to evoke their customary response in human effort.

Till that failure is recognized and industry reorganized so that new stimuli may have free play, the collapse will not correct itself, but, doubtless with spasmodic revivals and flickerings of energy, will continue and accelerate. The cause of it is simple. It is that those whose business it is to direct economic activity are increasingly incapable of directing the men upon whom economic activity depends. The fault is not that of individuals, but of a system, of Industrialism itself. During the greater part of the nineteenth century industry was driven by two forces, hunger and fear, and the employer commanded them both. He could grant or withhold employment as he pleased. If men revolted against his terms he could dismiss them, and if they were dismissed what confronted them was starvation or the workhouse. Authority was centralized; its instruments were passive; the one thing which they dreaded was unemployment. And since they could neither prevent its occurrence nor do more than a little to mitigate its horrors when it occurred, they submitted to a discipline which they could not resist, and industry pursued its course through their passive acquiescence in a power which could crush them individually if they attempted to oppose it.

That system might be lauded as efficient or denounced as inhuman. But, at least, as its admirers were never tired of pointing out, it worked. And, like the Prussian State, which alike in its virtues and deficiencies it not a little resembled, as long as it worked it survived denunciations of its methods, as a strong man will throw off a disease. But today it is ceasing to have even the qualities of its defects. It is ceasing to be efficient. It no longer secures the ever-increasing output of wealth which it offered in its golden prime, and which enabled it to silence criticism by an imposing spectacle of material success. Though it still works, it works unevenly, amid constant friction and jolts and stoppages, without the confidence of the public and without full confidence even in itself, a tyrant who must intrigue and cajole where formerly he commanded, a gaoler who, if not yet deprived of whip, dare only administer moderate chastisement, and who, though he still protests that he alone can keep the treadmill moving and get the corn ground, is compelled to surrender so much of his authority as to make it questionable whether he is worth his keep. For the instruments through which Capitalism exercised discipline are one by one being taken from it. It cannot pay what wages it likes or work what hours it likes. In well-organized industries the power of arbitrary dismissal, the very center of its authority, is being shaken, because men will no longer tolerate a system which makes their livelihood dependent on the caprices of an individual. In all industries alike the time is not far distant when the dread of starvation can no longer be used to cow dissatisfied workers into submission, because the public will no longer allow involuntary unemployment to result in starvation.

And if Capitalism is losing its control of men's bodies, still more has it lost its command of their minds. The product of a civilization which regarded "the poor" as instruments, at worst of the luxuries, at best of the virtues, of the rich, its psychological foundation fifty years ago was an ignorance in the mass of mankind which led them to reverence as wisdom the very follies of their masters, and an almost animal incapacity for responsibility. Education and experience have destroyed the passivity which was the condition of the perpetuation of industrial government in the hands of an oligarchy of private capitalists. The workman of today has as little belief in the intellectual superiority of many of those who direct industry as he has in the morality of the system. It appears to him to be not only oppressive, but wasteful, unintelligent and inefficient. In the light of his own experience in the factory and the mine, he regards the claim of the capitalist to be the self-appointed guardian of public interests as a piece of sanctimonious hypocrisy. For he sees every day that efficiency is sacrificed to shortsighted financial interests; and while as a man he is outraged by the inhumanity of the industrial order, as a professional who knows the difference between good work and bad he has a growing contempt at once for its misplaced parsimony and its misplaced extravagance, for the whole apparatus of adulteration, advertisement and quackery which seems inseparable from the pursuit of profit as the main standard of industrial success.

So Capitalism no longer secures strenuous work by fear, for it is ceasing to be formidable. And it cannot secure it by respect, for it has ceased to be respected. And the very victories by which it seeks to reassert its waning prestige are more disastrous than defeats. Employers may congratulate themselves that they have maintained intact their right to freedom of management, or opposed successfully a demand for public ownership, or broken a movement for higher wages and shorter hours. But what is success in a trade dispute or in a political struggle is often a defeat in the workshop: the workmen may have lost, but it does not follow that their employers, still less that the public, which is principally composed of workmen, have won. For the object of industry is to produce goods, and to produce them at the lowest cost in human effort. But there is no alchemy which will secure efficient production from the resentment or distrust of men who feel contempt for the order under which they work. It is a commonplace that credit is the foundation of industry. But credit is a matter of psychology, and the workman has his psychology as well as the capitalist. If confidence is necessary to the investment of capital, confidence is not less necessary to the effective performance of labor by men whose sole livelihood depends upon it. If they are not yet strong enough to impose their will, they are strong enough to resist when their masters would impose theirs. They may work rather than strike. But they will work to escape dismissal, not for the greater glory of a system in which they do not believe; and, if they are dismissed, those who take their place will do the same.

That this is one cause of a low output has been stated both by employers and workers in the building industry, and by the representatives of the miners before the Coal Commission. It was reiterated with impressive emphasis by Mr. Justice Sankey. Nor is it seriously contested by employers themselves. What else, indeed, do their repeated denunciations of "restriction of output" mean except that they have failed to organize industry so as to secure the efficient service which it is their special function to provide? Nor is it appropriate to the situation to indulge in full-blooded denunciations of the "selfishness" of the working classes. "To draw an indictment against a whole nation" is a procedure which is as impossible in industry as it is in politics. Institutions must be adapted to human nature, not human nature to institutions. If the effect of the industrial system is such that a large and increasing number of ordinary men and women find that it offers them no adequate motive for economic effort, it is mere pedantry to denounce men and women instead of amending the system.

Thus the time has come when absolutism in industry may still win its battles, but loses the campaign, and loses it on the very ground of economic efficiency which was of its own selection. In the period of transition, while economic activity is distracted by the struggle between those who have the name and habit of power, but no longer the full reality of it, and those who are daily winning more of the reality of power but are not yet its recognized repositories, it is the consumer who suffers. He has neither the service of docile obedience, nor the service of intelligent co-operation. For slavery will work—as long as the slaves will let it; and freedom will work when men have learned to be free; but what will not work is a combination of the two. So the public goes short of coal not only because of the technical deficiencies of the system under which it is raised and distributed, but because the system itself has lost its driving force—because the coal owners can no longer persuade the miners into producing more dividends for them and more royalties for the owners of minerals, while the public cannot appeal to them to put their whole power into serving itself, because it has chosen that they should be the servants, not of itself, but of shareholders.

And, this dilemma is not, as some suppose, temporary, the aftermath of war, or peculiar to the coal industry, as though the miners alone were the children of sin which in the last few months they have been described to be. It is permanent; it has spread far; and, as sleeping spirits are stirred into life by education and one industry after another develops a strong corporate consciousness, it will spread further. Nor will it be resolved by lamentations or menaces or denunciations of leaders whose only significance is that they say openly what plain men feel privately. For the matter at bottom is one of psychology. What has happened is that the motives on which the industrial system relied for several generations to secure efficiency, secure it no longer. And it is as impossible to restore them, to revive by mere exhortation the complex of hopes and fears and ignorance and patient credulity and passive acquiescence, which together made men, fifty years ago, plastic instruments in the hands of industrialism, as to restore innocence to any others of those who have eaten of the tree of knowledge.

The ideal of some intelligent and respectable business men, the restoration of the golden sixties, when workmen were docile and confiding, and trade unions were still half illegal, and foreign competition meant English competition in foreign countries, and prices were rising a little and not rising too much, is the one Utopia which can never be realized. The King may walk naked as long as his courtiers protest that he is clad; but when a child or a fool has broken the spell a tailor is more important than all their admiration. If the public, which suffers from the slackening of economic activity, desires to end its malaise, it will not laud as admirable and all-sufficient the operation of motives which are plainly ceasing to move. It will seek to liberate new motives and to enlist them in its service. It will endeavor to find an alternative to incentives which were always degrading, to those who used them as much as to those upon whom they were used, and which now are adequate incentives no longer. And the alternative to the discipline which Capitalism exercised through its instruments of unemployment and starvation is the self-discipline of responsibility and professional pride.

So the demand which aims at stronger organization, fuller responsibility, larger powers for the sake of the producer as a condition of economic liberty, the demand for freedom, is not antithetic to the demand for more effective work and increased output which is being made in the interests of the consumer. It is complementary to it, as the insistence by a body of professional men, whether doctors or university teachers, on the maintenance of their professional independence and dignity against attempts to cheapen the service is not hostile to an efficient service, but, in the long run, a condition of it. The course of wisdom for the consumer would be to hasten, so far as he can, the transition. For, as at present conducted, industry is working against the grain. It is compassing sea and land in its efforts to overcome, by ingenious financial and technical expedients, obstacles which should never have existed. It is trying to produce its results by conquering professional feeling instead of using it. It is carrying not only its inevitable economic burdens, but an ever increasing load of ill will and skepticism. It has in fact "shot the bird which caused the wind to blow" and goes about its business with the corpse round its neck. Compared with that psychological incubus, the technical deficiencies of industry, serious though they often are, are a bagatelle, and the business men who preach the gospel of production without offering any plan for dealing with what is now the central fact in the economic situation, resemble a Christian apologist who should avoid disturbing the equanimity of his audience by carefully omitting all reference either to the fall of man or the scheme of salvation. If it is desired to increase the output of wealth, it is not a paradox, but the statement of an elementary economic truism to say that active and constructive cooperation on the part of the rank and file of workers would do more to contribute to that result than the discovery of a new coal-field or a generation of scientific invention.

The first condition of enlisting on the side of constructive work the professional feeling which is now apathetic, or even hostile to it, is to secure that when it is given its results accrue to the public, not to the owner of property in capital, in land, or in other resources. For this reason the attenuation of the rights at present involved in the private ownership of industrial capital, or their complete abolition, is not the demand of ideologues, but an indispensable element in a policy of economic efficiency, since it is the condition of the most effective functioning of the human beings upon whom, though, like other truisms, it is often forgotten, economic efficiency ultimately depends. But it is only one element. Co-operation may range from mere acquiescence to a vigilant and zealous initiative. The criterion of an effective system of administration is that it should succeed in enlisting in the conduct of industry the latent forces of professional pride to which the present industrial order makes little appeal, and which, indeed, Capitalism, in its war upon trade union organization, endeavored for many years to stamp out altogether.

Nor does the efficacy of such an appeal repose upon the assumption of that "change in human nature," which is the triumphant *reducio ad absurdum* advanced by those who are least satisfied with the working of human nature as it is. What it does involve is that certain elementary facts should be taken into account, instead of, as at present, being ignored. That all work is distasteful and that "every man desires to secure the largest income with the least effort" may be as axiomatic as it is assumed to be. But in practice it makes all the difference to the attitude of the individual whether the collective sentiment of the group to which he belongs is on the side of effort or against it, and what standard of effort it sets. That, as employers complain, the public opinion of considerable groups of workers is against an intensification of effort as long as part of its result is increased dividends for shareholders, is no doubt, as far as mere efficiency is concerned, the gravest indictment of the existing industrial order. But, even when public ownership has taken the place of private capitalism, its ability to command effective service will depend ultimately upon its success in securing not merely that professional feeling is no longer an opposing force, but that it is actively enlisted upon the side of maintaining the highest possible standard of efficiency which can reasonably be demanded.

To put the matter concretely, while the existing ownership of mines is a positive inducement to inefficient work, public ownership administered by a bureaucracy, if it would remove the technical deficiencies emphasized by Sir Richard Redmayne as inseparable from the separate administration of 3,000 pits by 1,500 different companies, would be only too likely to miss a capital advantage which a different type of administration would secure. It would lose both the assistance to be derived from the technical knowledge of practical men who know by daily experience the points at which the details of administration can be improved, and the stimulus to efficiency springing from the corporate pride of a profession which is responsible for maintaining and improving the character of its service. Professional spirit is a force like gravitation, which in itself is neither good nor bad, but which the engineer uses, when he can, to do his work for him. If it is foolish to idealize it, it is equally short-sighted to neglect it. In what are described *par excellence* as "the services" it has always been recognized that *esprit de corps* is the foundation of efficiency, and all means, some wise and some mischievous, are used to encourage it: in practice, indeed, the power upon which the country relied as its main safeguard in an emergency was the professional zeal of the navy and nothing else. Nor is that spirit peculiar to the professions which are concerned with war. It is a matter of common training, common responsibilities, and common dangers. In all cases where difficult and disagreeable work is to be done, the force which elicits it is normally not merely money, but the public opinion and tradition of the little society in which the individual moves, and in the esteem of which he finds that which men value in success.

To ignore that most powerful of stimuli as it is ignored today, and then to lament that the efforts which it produces are not forthcoming, is the climax of perversity. To aim at eliminating from industry the growth and action of corporate feeling, for fear lest an organized body of producers should exploit the public, is a plausible policy. But it is short-sighted. It is "to pour away the baby with the bath," and to lower the quality of the service in an attempt to safeguard it. A wise system of administration would recognize that professional solidarity can do much of its work for it more effectively than it can do it itself, because the spirit of his profession is part of the individual and not a force outside him, and would make it its object to enlist that temper in the public service. It is only by that policy, indeed, that the elaboration of cumbrous regulations to prevent men doing what they should not, with the incidental result of sometimes preventing them from doing what they should—it is only by that policy that what is mechanical and obstructive in bureaucracy can be averted. For industry cannot run without laws. It must either control itself by professional standards, or it must be controlled by officials who are not of the craft and who,

however zealous and well-meaning, can hardly have the feel of it in their fingers. Public control and criticism are indispensable. But they should not be too detailed, or they defeat themselves. It would be better that, once fair standards have been established, the professional organization should check offenses against prices and quality than that it should be necessary for the State to do so. The alternative to minute external supervision is supervision from within by men who become imbued with the public obligations of their trade in the very process of learning it. It is, in short, professional in industry.

For this reason collectivism by itself is too simple a solution. Its failure is likely to be that of other rationalist systems.

> "Dann hat er die Teile in seiner Hand,
> Fehlt leider! nur das geistige Band."
> [Then he has the parts in his hand,
> Lacks, unfortunately, only the spiritual
> bond.]

If industrial reorganization is to be a living reality, and not merely a plan upon paper, its aim must be to secure not only that industry is carried on for the service of the public, but that it shall be carried on with the active co-operation of the organizations of producers. But co-operation involves responsibility, and responsibility involves power. It is idle to expect that men will give their best to any system which they do not trust, or that they will trust any system in the control of which they do not share. Their ability to carry professional obligations depends upon the power which they possess to remove the obstacles which prevent those obligations from being discharged, and upon their willingness, when they possess the power, to use it.

Two causes appear to have hampered the committees which were established in connection with coal mines during the war to increase the output of coal. One was the reluctance of some of them to discharge the invidious task of imposing penalties for absenteeism on their fellow-workmen. The other was the exclusion of faults of management from the control of many committees. In some cases all went well till they demanded that, if the miners were penalized for absenteeism which was due to them, the management should be penalized similarly when men who desired to work were sent home because, as a result of defective organization, there was no work for them to do. Their demand was resisted as "interference with the management," and the attempt to enforce regularity of attendance broke down. Nor, to take another example from the same industry, is it to be expected that the weight of the miners' organization will be thrown on to the side of greater production, if it has no power to insist on the removal of the defects of equipment and organization, the shortage of trams, rails, tubs and timber, the "creaming" of the pits by the working of easily got coal to their future detriment, their wasteful layout caused by the vagaries of separate ownership, by which at present the output is reduced.

The public cannot have it both ways. If it allows workmen to be treated as "hands" it cannot claim the service of their wills and their brains. If it desires them to show the zeal of skilled professionals, it must secure that they have sufficient power to allow of their discharging professional responsibilities. In order that workmen may abolish any restrictions on output which may be imposed by them, they must be able to insist on the abolition of the restrictions, more mischievous because more effective, which, as the Committee on Trusts has recently told us, are imposed by organizations of employers. In order that the miners' leaders, instead of merely bargaining as to wages, hours and working conditions, may be able to appeal to their members to increase the supply of coal, they must be in a position to secure the removal of the causes of low output which are due to the deficiencies of the management, and which are today a far more serious obstacle than any reluctance on the part of the miner. If the workmen in the building trade are to take combined action to accelerate production, they must as a body be consulted as to the purpose to which their energy is to be applied, and must not be expected to build fashionable houses, when what are required are six-roomed cottages to house families which are at present living with three persons to a room.

It is deplorable, indeed, that any human beings should consent to degrade themselves by producing the articles which a considerable number of workmen turn out today, boots which are partly brown paper, and furniture which is not fit to use. The revenge of outraged humanity is certain, though it is not always obvious; and the penalty paid by the consumer for tolerating an organization of industry which, in the name of efficiency, destroyed the responsibility of the workman, is that the service with which he is provided is not even efficient. He has always paid it, though he has not seen it, in quality. Today he is beginning to realize that he is likely to pay it in quantity as well. If the public is to get efficient service, it can get it only from human beings, with the initiative and caprices of human beings. It will get it, in short, in so far as it treats industry as a responsible profession.

The collective responsibility of the workers for the maintenance of the standards of their profession is, then, the alternative to the discipline which Capitalism exercised in the past, and which is now breaking down. It involves a fundamental change in the position both of employers and of trade unions. As long as the direction of industry is in the hands of property-owners or their agents, who are concerned to extract from it the maximum profit for themselves, a trade union is necessarily a defensive organization. Absorbed, on the one hand, in the struggle to resist the downward thrust of Capitalism upon the workers' standard of life, and denounced, on the other, if it presumes, to "interfere with management," even when management is most obviously inefficient, it is an opposition which never becomes a government and which has neither the will nor the power to assume responsibility for the quality of the service offered to the consumer. If the abolition of functionless property transferred the control of production to bodies representing those who perform constructive work and those who consume the goods produced, the relation of the worker to the public would no longer be indirect but immediate, and associations which are now purely defensive would be in a position not merely to criticize and oppose but to advise, to initiate and to enforce upon their own members the obligations of the craft.

It is obvious that in such circumstances the service offered the consumer, however carefully safeguarded by his representation on the authorities controlling each industry, would depend primarily upon the success of professional organizations in finding a substitute for the discipline exercised today by the agents of property-owners. It would be necessary for them to maintain by their own action the zeal, efficiency and professional pride which, when the barbarous weapons of the nineteenth century have been discarded, would be the only guarantee of a high level of production. Nor, once this new function has been made possible for professional organizations, is there any extravagance in expecting them to perform it with reasonable competence. How far economic motives are balked today and could be strengthened by a different type of industrial organization, to what extent, and under what conditions, it is possible to enlist in the services of industry motives which are not purely economic, can be ascertained only after a study of the psychology of work which has not yet been made. Such a study, to be of value, must start by abandoning the conventional assumptions, popularized by economic textbooks and accepted as self-evident by practical men, that the motives to effort are simple and constant in character, like the pressure of steam in a boiler, that they are identical throughout all ranges of economic activity, from the stock exchange to the shunting of wagons or laying of bricks, and that they can be elicited and strengthened only by directly economic incentives. In so far as motives in industry have been considered hitherto, it has usually been done by writers who, like most exponents of scientific management, have started by assuming that the categories of business psychology could be offered with equal success to all classes of workers and to all types of productive work. Those categories appear to be derived from a simplified analysis of the mental processes of the company promoter, financier or investor, and their validity as an interpretation of the motives and habits which determine the attitude to his work of the bricklayer, the miner, the dock laborer or the engineer, is precisely the point in question.

Clearly there are certain types of industry to which they are only partially relevant. It can hardly be assumed, for example, that the degree of skill and energy brought to his work by a surgeon, a scientific investigator, a teacher, a medical officer of health, an Indian civil servant and a peasant proprietor are capable of being expressed precisely and to the same degree in terms of the economic advantage which those different occupations offer. Obviously those who pursue them are influenced to some considerable, though uncertain, extent by economic incentives. Obviously, again, the precise character of each process or step in the exercise of their respective avocations, the performance of an operation, the carrying out of a piece of investigation, the selection of a particular type of educational method, the preparation of a report, the decision of a case or the care of live stock, is not immediately dependent upon an exact calculation of pecuniary gain or loss. What appears to be the case is that in certain walks of life, while the occupation is chosen after a consideration of its economic advantages, and while economic reasons exact the minimum degree of activity needed to avert dismissal from it or "failure," the actual level of energy or proficiency displayed depend largely upon conditions of a different order. Among them are the character of the training received before and after entering the occupation, the customary standard of effort demanded by the public opinion of one's fellows, the desire for the esteem of the small circle in which the individual moves and to be recognized as having "made good" and not to have "failed," interest in one's work, ranging from devotion to a determination to "do justice" to it, the pride of the craftsman, the "tradition of the service."

It would be foolish to suggest that any considerable body of men are uninfluenced by economic considerations. But to represent them as amenable to such incentives only is to give a quite unreal and bookish picture of the actual conditions under which the work of the world is carried on. How large a part such considerations play varies from one occupation to another, according to the character of the work which it does and the manner in which it is organized. In what is called *par excellence* industry, calculations of pecuniary gain and loss are more powerful than in most of the so-called professions, though even in industry they are more constantly present to the minds of the business men who "direct" it, than to those of the managers and technicians, most of whom are paid fixed salaries, or to the rank and file of wage-workers. In the professions of teaching and medicine, in many branches of the public service, the necessary qualities are secured, without the intervention of the capitalist employer, partly by pecuniary incentives, partly by training and education, partly by the acceptance on the part of those entering them of the traditional obligations of their profession as part of the normal framework of their working lives. But this difference is not constant and unalterable. It springs from the manner in which different types of occupation are organized, on the training which they offer, and the morale which they cultivate among their members. The psychology of a vocation can in fact be changed; new motives can be elicited, provided steps are taken to allow them free expression. It is as feasible to turn building into an organized profession, with a relatively high code of public honor, as it was to do the same for medicine or teaching.

The truth is that we ought radically to revise the presuppositions as to human motives on which current presentations of economic theory are ordinarily founded and in terms of which the discussion of economic question is usually carried on. The assumption that the stimulus of imminent personal want is either the only spur, or a sufficient spur, to productive effort is a relic of a crude psychology which has little warrant either in past history or in present experience. It derives what plausibility it possesses from a confusion between work in the sense of the lowest *quantum* of activity needed to escape actual starvation, and the work which is given, irrespective of the fact that elementary wants may already have been satisfied, through the natural disposition of ordinary men to maintain, and of extraordinary men to improve upon, the level of exertion accepted as reasonable by the public opinion of the group of which they are members. It is the old difference, forgotten by society as often as it is learned, between the labor of the free man and that of the slave. Economic fear may secure the minimum effort needed to escape economic penalties. What, however, has made progress possible in the past, and what, it may be suggested, matters to the world today, is not the bare minimum which is required to avoid actual want, but the capacity of men to bring to bear upon their tasks a degree of energy, which, while it can be stimulated by economic incentives, yields results far in excess of any which are necessary merely to avoid the extremes of hunger or destitution.

That capacity is a matter of training, tradition and habit, at least as much as of pecuniary stimulus, and the ability of a professional association representing the public opinion of a group of workers to raise it is, therefore, considerable. Once industry has been liberated from its subservience to the interests of the functionless property-owner, it is in this sphere that trade unions may be expected increasingly to find their function. Its importance both for the general interests of the community and for the special interests of particular groups of workers can hardly be exaggerated. Technical knowledge and managerial skill are likely to be available as readily for a committee appointed by the workers in an industry as for a committee appointed, as now, by the shareholders. But it is more and more evident today that the crux of the economic situation is not the technical deficiencies of industrial organization, but the growing inability of those who direct industry to command the active good will of the personnel. Their co-operation is promised by the conversion of industry into a profession serving the public, and promised, as far as can be judged, by that alone.

Nor is the assumption of the new and often disagreeable obligations of internal discipline and public responsibility one which trade unionism can afford, once the change is accomplished, to shirk, however alien they may be to its present traditions. For ultimately, if by slow degrees, power follows the ability to wield it; authority goes with function. The workers cannot have it both ways. They must choose whether to assume the responsibility for industrial discipline and become free, or to repudiate it and continue to be serfs. If, organized as professional bodies, they can provide a more effective service than that which is now, with increasing difficulty, extorted by the agents of capital, they will have made good their hold upon the future. If they cannot, they will remain among the less calculable instruments of production which many of them are today. The instinct of mankind warns it against accepting at their face value spiritual demands which cannot justify themselves by practical achievements. And the road along which the organized workers, like any other class, must climb to power, starts from the provision of a more effective economic service than their masters, as their grip upon industry becomes increasingly vacillating and uncertain, are able to supply. ♦

QUESTIONS

1. According to Tawney, what motivated workers in the nineteenth century?

2. Why does Tawney think that those forces lost their power to motivate?

3. What possible alternatives might motivate workers to contribute enthusiastically to the industrial process?

4. What makes that the workers' enthusiastic contribution unlikely?

5. What does Tawney suggest for enlisting the cooperation of labor more fully?

FROM *LADY CHATTERLEY'S LOVER*

D. H. Lawrence (1885–1930)

On Sunday Clifford wanted to go into the wood. It was a lovely morning, the pear blossom and plum had suddenly appeared in the world, in a wonder of white here and there.

It was cruel for Clifford, while the world bloomed, to have to be helped from chair to bath-chair. But he had forgotten, and even seemed to have a certain conceit of himself in his lameness. Connie still suffered, having to lift his inert legs into place. Mrs. Bolton did it now, or Field.

She waited for him at the top of the drive, at the edge of the screen of beeches. His chair came puffing along with a sort of valetudinarian slow importance. As he joined his wife he said:

"Sir Clifford on his foaming steed!"

"Snorting, at least!" she laughed.

He stopped and looked round at the facade of the long, low old brown house.

"Wragby doesn't wink an eyelid!" he said. "But then why should it! I ride upon the achievements of the mind of man, and that beats a horse."

"I suppose it does. And the souls in Plato riding up to heaven in a two-horse chariot would go in a Ford car now," she said.

"Or a Rolls-Royce: Plato was an aristocrat!"

"Quite! No more black horse to thrash and maltreat. Plato never thought we'd go one better than his black steed and his white steed, and have no steeds at all, only an engine!"

"Only an engine and gas!" said Clifford.

"I hope I can have some repairs done to the old place next year. I think I shall have about a thousand to spare for that: but work costs so much!" he added.

"Oh, good!" said Connie. "If only there aren't more strikes!"

"What would be the use of their striking again! Merely ruin the industry, what's left of it: and surely the owls are beginning to see it!"

"Perhaps they don't mind ruining the industry," said Connie.

"Ah, don't talk like a woman! The industry fills their bellies, even if it can't keep their pockets quite so flush," he said, using turns of speech that oddly had a twang of Mrs. Bolton.

"But didn't you say the other day that you were a conservative-anarchist," she asked innocently.

"And did you understand what I meant?" he retorted. "All I meant is, people can be what they like and feel what they like and do what they like, strictly privately, so long as they keep the *form* of life intact, and the apparatus."

Connie walked on in silence a few paces. Then she said, obstinately:

"It sounds like saying an egg may go as addled as it likes, so long as it keeps its shell on whole. But addled eggs do break of themselves."

"I don't think people are eggs," he said. "Not even angels' eggs, my dear little evangelist."

He was in rather high feather this bright morning. The larks were trilling away over the park, the distant pit in the hollow was fuming silent steam. It was almost like old days, before the war. Connie didn't really want to argue. But then she did not really want to go to the wood with Clifford either. So she walked beside his chair in a certain obstinacy of spirit.

"No," he said. "There will be no more strikes, if the thing is properly managed."

"Why not?"

"Because strikes will be made as good as impossible."

"But will the men let you?" she asked.

"We shan't ask them. We shall do it while they aren't looking: for their own good, to save the industry."

"For your own good too," she said.

"Naturally! For the good of everybody. But for their good even more than mine. I can live without the pits. They can't. They'll starve if there are no pits. I've got other provision."

They looked up the shallow valley at the mine, and beyond it, at the black-lidded houses of Tevershall crawling like some serpent up the hill. From the old brown church the bells were ringing: Sunday, Sunday, Sunday!

"But will the men let you dictate terms?" she said.

"My dear, they will have to: if one does it gently."

"But mightn't there be a mutual understanding?"

"Absolutely: when they realize that the industry comes before the individual."

"But must you own the industry?" she said.

"I don't. But to the extent I do own it, yes, most decidedly. The ownership of property has now become a religious question: as it has been since Jesus and St. Francis. The point is not: take all thou hast and give to the poor, but use all thou hast to encourage the industry to give work to the poor. It's the only way to feed all the mouths and clothe all the bodies. Giving away all we have to the poor spells starvation for the poor just as much as for us. And universal starvation is no high aim. Even general poverty is no lovely thing. Poverty is ugly."

"But the disparity?"

"That is fate. Why is the star Jupiter bigger than the star Neptune? You can't start altering the makeup of things!"

"But when this envy and jealousy and discontent has once started," she began.

"Do your best to stop it. Somebody's *got* to be boss of the show."

"But who is boss of the show?" she asked.

"The men who own and run the industries." There was a long silence.

"It seems to me they're a bad boss," she said.

"Then you suggest what they should do."

"They don't take their boss-ship seriously enough," she said.

"They take it far more seriously than you take your ladyship," he said.

"That's thrust upon me. I don't really want it," she blurted out. He stopped the chair and looked at her.

"Who's shirking their responsibility now!" he said. "Who is trying to get away now from the responsibility of their own boss-ship, as you call it?"

"But I don't want any boss-ship," she protested.

"Ah! But that is funk. You've got it: fated to it. And you should live up to it. Who has given the colliers all they have that's worth having: all their political liberty, and their education, such as it is, their sanitation, their health conditions, their books, their music, everything. Who has given it them? Have colliers given it to colliers? No! All the Wragbys and Shipleys in England have given their part, and must go on giving. There's your responsibility."

Connie listened, and flushed very red.

"I'd like to give something," she said. "But I'm not allowed. Everything is to be sold and paid for now; and all the things you mention now, Wragby and Shipley *sells* them to people, at a good profit. Everything is sold. You don't give one heartbeat of real sympathy. And besides, who has taken away from the people their natural life and manhood, and given them this industrial horror? Who has done that?"

"And what must I do?" he asked, green. "Ask them to come and pillage me?"

"Why is Tevershall so ugly, so hideous? Why are their lives so hopeless?"

"They built their own Tevershall, that's part of their display of freedom. They built themselves their pretty Tevershall, and they live their own pretty lives. I can't live their lives for them. Every beetle must live its own life."

"But you make them work for you. They live the life of your coal mine."

"Not at all. Every beetle finds its own food. Not one man is forced to work for me."

"Their lives are industrialised and hopeless, and so are ours," she cried.

"I don't think they are. That's just a romantic figure of speech, a relic of the swooning and die-away romanticism. You don't look at all a hopeless figure standing there, Connie my dear."

Which was true. For her dark blue eyes were flashing, her colour was hot in her cheeks, she looked full of a rebellious passion far from the dejection of hopelessness. She noticed, in the tussocky places of the grass, cottony young cowslips standing up still bleared in their down. And she wondered with rage, why it was she felt Clifford was so *wrong*, yet she couldn't say it to him, she could not say exactly *where* he was wrong.

"No wonder the men hate you," she said.

"They don't!" he replied. "And don't fall into errors: in your sense of the word, they are *not* men. They are animals you don't understand, and never could. Don't thrust your illusions on other people. The masses were always the same, and will always be the same. Nero's slaves were extremely little different from our collier or the Ford motorcar workmen. I mean Nero's mine slaves and his field slaves. It is the masses: they are the unchangeable. An individual may emerge from the masses. But the emergence doesn't alter the mass. The masses are unalterable. It is one of the most momentous facts of social science. *Panem et circenses!* Only today education is one of the bad substitutes for a circus. What is wrong today, is that we've made a profound hash of the circuses part of the programme, and poisoned our masses with a little education."

When Clifford became really roused in his feelings about the common people, Connie was frightened. There was something devastatingly true in what he said. But it was a truth that killed.

Seeing her pale and silent, Clifford started the chair again, and no more was said till he halted again at the wood gate, which she opened.

"And what we need to take up now," he said, "is whips, not swords. The masses have been ruled since time began, and till time ends, ruled they will have to be. It is sheer hypocrisy and farce to say they can rule themselves."

"But can you rule them?" she asked.

"I? Oh yes! Neither my mind nor my will is crippled, and I don't rule with my legs. I can do my share of ruling: absolutely, my share; and give me a son, and he will be able to rule his portion after me."

"But he wouldn't be your own son, of your own ruling class; or perhaps not," she stammered.

"I don't care who his father may be, so long as he is a healthy man not below normal intelligence. Give me the child of any healthy, normally intelligent man, and I will make a perfectly competent Chatterley of him. It is not who begets us, that matters, but where fate places us. Place any child among the ruling classes, and he will grow up, to his own extent, a ruler. Put kings' and dukes' children among the masses, and they'll be little plebeians, mass products. It is the overwhelming pressure of environment."

"Then the common people aren't a race, and the aristocrats aren't blood," she said.

"No, my child! All that is romantic illusion. Aristocracy is a function, a part of fate. And the masses are a functioning of another part of fate. The individual hardly matters. It is a question of which function you are brought up to and adapted to. It is not the individuals that make an aristocracy: it is the functioning of the aristocratic whole. And it is the functioning of the whole mass that makes the common man what he is."

"Then there is no common humanity between us all!"

"Just as you like. We all need to fill our bellies. But when it comes to expressive or executive functioning, I believe there is a gulf and an absolute one, between the ruling and the serving classes. The two functions are opposed. And the function determines the individual."

Connie looked at him with dazed eyes.

"Won't you come on?" she said.

And he started his chair. He had said his say. Now he lapsed into his peculiar and rather vacant apathy, that Connie found so trying. In the wood, anyhow, she was determined not to argue. ♦

QUESTIONS

1. According to Lord Chatterley, does culture or inborn qualities make the person?

2. What metaphors does Chatterley use in describing workers?

2. For whose sake do managers do their work and owners invest?

THE HUMAN SIDE OF ENTERPRISE

Douglas M. McGregor (1906–1964)

3

THEORY X: THE TRADITIONAL VIEW OF DIRECTION AND CONTROL

Behind every managerial decision or action are assumptions about human nature and human behavior. A few of these are remarkably pervasive. They are implicit in most of the literature of organization and in much current managerial policy and practice:

1. *The average human being has an inherent dislike of work and will avoid it if he can.*

This assumption has deep roots. The punishment of Adam and Eve for eating the fruit of the Tree of Knowledge was to be banished from Eden into a world where they had to work for a living. The stress that management places on productivity, on the concept of "a fair day's work," on the evils of featherbedding and restriction of output, on rewards for performance—while it has a logic in terms of the objectives of enterprise—reflects an underlying belief that management must counteract an inherent human tendency to avoid work. The evidence for the correctness of this assumption would seem to most managers to be incontrovertible.

2. *Because of this human characteristic of dislike of work, most people must be coerced, controlled, directed, threatened with punishment to get them to put forth adequate effort toward the achievement of organizational objectives.*

The dislike of work is so strong that even the promise of rewards is not generally enough to overcome it. People will accept the rewards and demand continually higher ones, but these alone will not produce the necessary effort. Only the threat of punishment will do the trick.

The current wave of criticism of "human relations," the derogatory comments about "permissiveness" and "democracy" in industry, the trends in some companies toward recentralization after the postwar wave of decentraliza-tion—all these are assertions of the underlying assumption that people will only work under external coercion and control. The recession of 1957–1958 ended a decade of experimentation with the "soft" managerial approach, and this assumption (which never really was abandoned) is being openly espoused once more.

3. *The average human being prefers to be directed, wishes to avoid responsibility, has relatively little ambition, wants security above all.*

This assumption of the "mediocrity of the masses" is rarely expressed so bluntly. In fact, a good deal of lip service is given to the ideal of the worth of the average human being. Our political and social values demand such public expressions. Nevertheless, a great many managers will give private support to this assumption, and it is easy to see it reflected in policy and practice. Paternalism has become a nasty word, but it is by no means a defunct managerial philosophy.

I have suggested elsewhere the name Theory X for this set of assumptions. … Theory X is not a straw man for purposes of demolition, but is in fact a theory which materially influences managerial strategy in a wide sector of American industry today. Moreover, the principles of organization which comprise the bulk of the literature of management *could only have been derived from assumptions such as those of Theory X.* Other beliefs about human nature would have led inevitably to quite different organizational principles.

Theory X provides an explanation of some human behavior in industry. These assumptions would not have persisted if there were not a considerable body of evidence to support them. Nevertheless, there are many readily observable phenomena in industry and elsewhere which are not consistent with this view of human nature.

Such a state of affairs is not uncommon. The history of science provides many examples of theoretical explanations which persist over long periods despite the fact that they are only partially adequate. Newton's laws of motion are a case in point. It was not until the development of the theory of relativity during the present century that important inconsistencies and inadequacies in Newtonian theory could be understood and corrected.

The growth of knowledge in the social sciences during the past quarter century has made it possible to reformulate some assumptions about human nature and human behavior in the organizational setting which resolve certain of the inconsistencies inherent in Theory X. While this reformulation is, of course, tentative, it provides an improved basis for prediction and control of human behavior in industry.

Some Assumptions about Motivation

At the core of any theory of the management of human resources are assumptions about human motivation. This has been a confusing subject because there have been so many conflicting points of view even among social scientists. In recent years, however, there has been a convergence of research findings and a growing acceptance of a few rather basic ideas about motivation. These ideas appear to have considerable power. They help to explain the inadequacies of Theory X as well as the limited sense in which it is correct. In addition, they provide the basis for an entirely different theory of management.

The following generalizations about motivation are somewhat oversimplified. If all of the qualifications which would be required by a truly adequate treatment were introduced, the gross essentials which are particularly significant for management would be obscured. These generalizations do not misrepresent the facts, but they do ignore some complexities of human behavior which are relatively unimportant for our purposes.

Man is a wanting animal—as soon as one of his needs is satisfied, another appears in its place. This process is unending. It continues from birth to death. Man continuously puts forth effort—works, if you please—to satisfy his needs.

Human needs are organized in a series of levels—a hierarchy of importance. At the lowest level, but preeminent in importance when they are thwarted, are the physiological needs. Man lives by bread alone, when there is no bread. Unless the circumstances are unusual, his needs for love, for status, for recognition are inoperative when his stomach has been empty for a while. But when he eats regularly and adequately, hunger ceases to be an important need. The sated man has hunger only in the sense that a full bottle has emptiness. The same is true of the other physiological needs of man—for rest, exercise, shelter, protection from the elements.

A satisfied need is not a motivator of behavior! This is a fact of profound significance. It is a fact which is unrecognized in Theory X and is, therefore, ignored in the conventional approach to the management of people. I shall return to it later. For the moment, an example will make the point. Consider your own need for air. Except as you are deprived of it, it has no appreciable motivating effect upon your behavior.

When the physiological needs are reasonably satisfied, needs at the next higher level begin to dominate man's behavior—to motivate him. These are the safety needs, for protection against danger, threat, deprivation. Some people mistakenly refer to these as needs for security. However, unless man is in a dependent relationship where he fears arbitrary deprivation, he does not demand security. The need is for the "fairest possible break." When he is confident of this, he is more than willing to take risks. But when he feels threatened or dependent, his greatest need is for protection, for security.

The fact needs little emphasis that since every industrial employee is in at least a partially dependent relationship, safety needs may assume considerable importance. Arbitrary management actions, behavior which arouses uncertainty with respect to continued employment or which reflects favoritism or discrimination, unpredictable administration of policy—these can be powerful motivators of the safety needs in the employment relationship at every level from worker to vice president. In addition, the safety needs of managers are often aroused by their dependence downward or laterally. This is a major reason for emphasis on management prerogatives and clear assignments of authority.

When man's physiological needs are satisfied and he is no longer fearful about his physical welfare, his social needs become important motivators of his behavior. These are such needs as those for belonging, for association, for acceptance by one's fellows, for giving and receiving friendship and love.

Management knows today of the existence of these needs, but it is often assumed quite wrongly that they represent a threat to the organization. Many studies have demonstrated that the tightly knit, cohesive work group may, under proper conditions, be far more effective than an equal number of separate individuals in achieving organizational goals. Yet management, fearing group hostility to its own objectives, often goes to considerable lengths to control and direct human efforts in ways that are inimical to the natural "groupiness" of human beings. When man's social needs—and perhaps his safety needs, too—are thus thwarted, he behaves in ways which tend to defeat organizational objectives. He becomes resistant, antagonistic, uncooperative. But this behavior is a consequence, not a cause.

Above the social needs—in the sense that they do not usually become motivators until lower needs are reasonably satisfied—are the needs of greatest significance to management and to man himself. They are the egoistic needs, and they are of two kinds:

1. Those that relate to one's self-esteem: needs for self-respect and self-confidence, for autonomy, for achievement, for competence, for knowledge
2. Those that relate to one's reputation: needs for status, for recognition, for appreciation, for the deserved respect of one's fellows

Unlike the lower needs, these are rarely satisfied; man seeks indefinitely for more satisfaction of these needs once they have become important to him. However, they do not usually appear in any significant way until physiological, safety, and social needs are reasonably

satisfied. Exceptions to this generalization are to be observed, particularly under circumstances where, in addition to severe deprivation of physiological needs, human dignity is trampled upon. Political revolutions often grow out of thwarted social and ego, as well as physiological, needs.

The typical industrial organization offers only limited opportunities for the satisfaction of egoistic needs to people at lower levels in the hierarchy. The conventional methods of organizing work, particularly in mass production industries, give little heed to these aspects of human motivation. If the practices of "scientific management" were deliberately calculated to thwart these needs—which, of course, they are not—they could hardly accomplish this purpose better than they do.

Finally—a capstone, as it were, on the hierarchy—there are the needs for self-fulfillment. These are the needs for realizing one's own potentialities, for continued self-development, for being creative in the broadest sense of that term.

The conditions of modern industrial life give only limited opportunity for these relatively dormant human needs to find expression. The deprivation most people experience with respect to other lower-level needs diverts their energies into the struggle to satisfy *those* needs, and the needs for self-fulfillment remain below the level of consciousness.

4

THEORY Y: THE INTEGRATION OF INDIVIDUAL AND ORGANIZATIONAL GOALS

To some, the preceding analysis will appear unduly harsh. Have we not made major modifications in the management of the human resources of industry during the past quarter century? Have we not recognized the importance of people and made vitally significant changes in managerial strategy as a consequence? Do the developments since the twenties in personnel administration and labor relations add up to nothing?

There is no question that important progress has been made in the past two or three decades. During this period the human side of enterprise has become a major preoccupation of management. A tremendous number of policies, programs, and practices which were virtually unknown thirty years ago have become commonplace. The lot of the industrial employee—be he worker, professional, or executive—has improved to a degree which could hardly have been imagined by his counterpart of the nineteen twenties. Management has adopted generally a far more humanitarian set of values; it has successfully striven to give more equitable and more generous treatment to its employees. It has significantly reduced economic hardships, eliminated the more extreme forms of industrial warfare, provided a generally safe and pleasant working environment, *but it has done all these things without changing its fundamental theory of management.* There are exceptions here and there, and they are important; nevertheless, the assumptions of Theory X remain predominant throughout our economy.

Management was subjected to severe pressures during the Great Depression of the thirties. The wave of public antagonism, the open warfare accompanying the unionization of the mass production industries, the general reaction against authoritarianism, the legislation of the New Deal produced a wide "pendulum swing." However, the changes in policy and practice which took place during that and the next decade were primarily adjustments to the increased power of organized labor and to the pressures of public opinion.

Some of the movement was away from "hard" and toward "soft" management, but it was short-lived, and for good reasons. It has become clear that many of the initial strategic interpretations accompanying the "human relations approach" were as naïve as those which characterized the early stages of progressive education. We have now discovered that there is no answer in the simple removal of control—that abdication is not a workable alternative to authoritarianism. We have learned that there is no direct correlation between employee satisfaction and productivity. We recognize today that "industrial democracy" cannot consist in permitting everyone to decide everything, that industrial health does not flow automatically from the elimination of dissatisfaction, disagreement, or even open conflict. Peace is not synonymous with organizational health; socially responsible management is not coextensive with permissive management.

Now that management has regained its earlier prestige and power, it has become obvious that the trend toward "soft" management was a temporary and relatively superficial reaction rather than a general modification of fundamental assumptions or basic strategy. Moreover, while the progress we have made in the past quarter century is substantial, it has reached the point of diminishing returns. The tactical possibilities within conventional managerial strategies have been pretty completely exploited, and significant new developments will be unlikely without major modifications in theory.

The Assumptions of Theory Y

There have been few dramatic break-throughs in social science theory like those which have occurred in the physical sciences during the past half century. Nevertheless, the accumulation of knowledge about human behavior in many specialized fields has made possible the formulation of a number of generalizations which provide a modest beginning for new theory with respect to the management of human resources. Some of these assumptions were outlined in the discussion of motivation in Chapter 3. Some others, which will hereafter be referred to as Theory Y, are as follows:

1. *The expenditure of physical and mental effort in work is as natural as play or rest.* The average human being does not inherently dislike work. Depending upon controllable conditions, work may be a source of satisfaction (and will be voluntarily performed) or a source of punishment (and will be avoided if possible).

2. *External control and the threat of punishment are not the only means for bringing about effort toward organizational objectives. Man will exercise self-direction and self-control in the service of objectives to which he is committed.*

3. *Commitment to objectives is a function of the rewards associated with their achievement.* The most significant of such rewards, e.g., the satisfaction of ego and self-actualization needs, can be direct products of effort directed toward organizational objectives.

4. *The average human being learns, under proper conditions, not only to accept but to seek responsibility.* Avoidance of responsibility, lack of ambition, and emphasis on security are generally consequences of experience, not inherent human characteristics.

5. *The capacity to exercise a relatively high degree of imagination, ingenuity, and creativity in the solution of organizational problems is widely, not narrowly, distributed in the population.*

6. *Under the conditions of modern industrial life, the intellectual potentialities of the average human being are only partially utilized.*

These assumptions involve sharply different implications for managerial strategy than do those of Theory X. They are dynamic rather than static: They indicate the possibility of human growth and development; they stress the necessity for selective adaptation rather than for a single absolute form of control. They are not framed in terms of the least common denominator of the factory hand, but in terms of a resource which has substantial potentialities.

Above all, the assumptions of Theory Y point up the fact that the limits on human collaboration in the organizational setting are not limits of human nature but of management's ingenuity in discovering how to realize the potential represented by its human resources. Theory X offers management an easy rationalization for ineffective organizational performance: It is due to the nature of the human resources with which we must work. Theory Y, on the other hand, places the problems squarely in the lap of management. If employees are lazy, indifferent, unwilling to take responsibility, intransigent, uncreative, uncooperative, Theory Y implies that the causes lie in management's methods of organization and control.

The assumptions of Theory Y are not finally validated. Nevertheless, they are far more consistent with existing knowledge in the social sciences than are the assumptions of Theory X. They will undoubtedly be refined, elaborated, modified as further research accumulates, but they are unlikely to be completely contradicted.

On the surface, these assumptions may not seem particularly difficult to accept. Carrying their implications into practice, however, is not easy. They challenge a number of deeply ingrained managerial habits of thought and action.

***

Acceptance of Theory Y does not imply abdication, or "soft" management, or "permissiveness." As was indicated above, such notions stem from the acceptance of authority as the *single* means of managerial control, and from attempts to minimize its negative consequences. Theory Y assumes that people will exercise self-direction and self-control in the achievement of organizational objectives *to the degree that they are committed to those objectives.* If that commitment is small, only a slight degree of self-direction and self-control will be likely, and a substantial amount of external influence will be necessary. If it is large, many conventional external controls will be relatively superfluous, and to some extent self-defeating. Managerial policies and practices materially affect this degree of commitment

Authority is an inappropriate means for obtaining commitment to objectives. Other forms of influence—help in achieving integration, for example—are required for this purpose. Theory Y points to the possibility of lessening the emphasis on external forms of control to the degree that commitment to organizational objectives can be achieved. Its underlying assumptions emphasize the capacity of human beings for self-control, and the consequent possibility of greater managerial reliance on other means of influence. Nevertheless, it is clear that authority *is* an appropriate means for control under certain circumstances—particularly where genuine commitment to objectives cannot be achieved. The assumptions of Theory Y do not deny the appropriateness of authority, but they do deny that it is appropriate for all purposes and under all circumstances.

Many statements have been made to the effect that we have acquired today the know-how to cope with virtually any technological problems which may arise, and that the major industrial advances of the next half century will occur on the human side of enterprise. Such advances, however, are improbable so long as management continues to organize and direct and control its human resources on the basis of assumptions—tacit or explicit—like those of Theory X. Genuine innovation, in contrast to a refurbishing and patching of present managerial strategies, requires first the acceptance of less limiting assumptions about the nature of the human resources we seek to control, and second the readiness to adapt selectively to the implications contained in those new assumptions. Theory Y is an invitation to innovation. ◆

QUESTIONS

1. What are the components of Theory X and Theory Y?

2. What is the hierarchy of human needs presented by McGregor?

SELECTION FROM: *THE BUSINESS GUIDE*

J. L. Nichols (1851–1895) self-published Naperville, Ill 1893

HOW TO DO BUSINESS

One cannot do successfully what he does not perfectly understand. He may have competent employees or trusted attorneys to do his business, but they may do his work imperfectly, or seek their own ease or profit at his expense, and he not being able to detect their malpractices must suffer the loss, or perhaps fail. Or he may attempt to manage everything himself, commit fatal errors, as he will be almost sure to do and thereby sustain a still greater loss. "First understand every detail of your business, and then go ahead."

A wealthy farmer said, when asked how he made his money, "Sir, *I understand my business* and attend to it." In that reply is the sum and substance of all true success.

THE NATURE OF EXECUTIVE RESPONSIBILITY
FROM *THE FUNCTIONS OF THE EXECUTIVE*

Chester I. Barnard (1886–1961)

Let us apply these definitions and observations in an illustration that may be recognized as typical of common experience. Mr. A, a citizen of Massachusetts, a member of the Baptist Church, having a father and mother living, and a wife and two children, is an expert machinist employed at a pump station of an important water system. For simplicity's sake, we omit further description. We impute to him several moral codes: Christian ethics, the patriotic code of the citizen, a code of family obligations, a code as an expert machinist, a code derived from the organization engaged in the operation of the water system. He is not aware of these codes. These intellectual abstractions are a part of his "system," ingrained in him by causes, forces, experiences, which he has either forgotten or on the whole never recognized. Just what they are, in fact, can at best only be approximately inferred by his actions, preferably under stress. He has no idea as to the order of importance of these codes, although, if pressed, what he might say probably would indicate that his religious code is first in importance, either because he has some intellectual comprehension of it, or because it is socially dominant. I shall hazard the guess, however, that their order of importance is as follows: his code as to the support and protection of his own children, his code of obligations to the water system, his code as a skilled artisan, his code with reference to his parents, his religious code, and his code as a citizen. For his children he will kill, steal, cheat the government, rob the church, leave the water plant at a critical time, botch a job by hurrying. If his children are not directly at stake, he will sacrifice money, health, time, comfort, convenience, jury duty, church obligations, in order to keep the water plant running; except for his children and the water plant, he cannot be induced to do a botch mechanical job— wouldn't know how; to take care of his parents, he will lie, steal, or do anything else contrary to

his code as a citizen or his religious code; if his government legally orders him to violate his religious code, he will go to jail first. He is, however, a very responsible man. It not only takes extraordinary pressure to make him violate any of his codes, but when faced with such pressure he makes great effort to find some solution that is compatible with all of them; and because he makes that effort and is capable he has in the past succeeded. Since he is a very responsible man, knowing his codes you can be fairly sure of what he will do under a rather wide range of conditions.

Now if we introduce a single disturbing factor, the use of alcoholic beverages, we have a considerable change. Our "case" becomes rather irresponsible. The use of alcohol does not violate any of his codes. Because of it, however, he neglects the children, he botches his work, he has been discharged from the water system as undependable, his parents are on public support, he steals for liquor, etc., etc. He is irresponsible; but for the present his codes remain still the same. He will even fight about them if challenged, though intoxicated. He is as moral now as before. He sincerely believes all his conduct has become reprehensible and is sick with genuine remorse when sober; but he is irresponsible, nevertheless.

It may seem to some reader an exaggeration to call devotion to a water system a moral code. Many persons appear unaware of the force of such codes derived from organization associations. But organizations depend greatly upon such moral codes. I recall a telephone operator on duty at a lonely place from which she could see in the distance the house in which her mother lay bedridden. Her life was spent in taking care of her mother and in maintaining that home for her. To do so, she chose employment in that particular position, against other inclinations. Yet she stayed at her switchboard while she watched the house burn down.[1] No code, public or organizational, that has any general validity under such circumstances governed her conduct, and she certainly violated some such codes, as well as some of her own. Nevertheless, she showed extraordinary "moral courage," we would say, in conforming to a code of her organization—the *moral* necessity of uninterrupted service. This was high responsibility as respects that code.

These illustrations suggest the usefulness of considering the relation of sanctions to codes and to responsibility. Some codes, being the accumulated effect of custom, general opinion, and similar "states of mind" of society, and of *informal* organizations of large and small size, have usually no specific sanctions associated with them which support their moral power. Other codes arise from experience and contact with *formal* organizations. These often have specific sanctions related to some details of conduct pertinent to them. For example, the code of citizenship is somewhat reinforced by penalties for violations or failure to conform. The codes related to industrial organizations are partly reinforced by possibilities of discharge, etc. It may be said that these sanctions help to establish codes, but not responsibility. Thus where conformance is secured by fear of penalties, what is operating is not the moral factor in the sense of the term as used here, but merely negative inducements or incentives. In practice, it is often, perhaps usually, impossible to distinguish the reasons for compliance; but it is quite well understood that good citizenship, for example, is not obtainable by such specific inducements. Only the deep convictions that operate regardless of either specific penalties or specific rewards are the stuff of high responsibility.

The private code of morals which derives from a definite formal organization is one aspect of what we have previously referred to as the "organization personality." It is also an aspect of the "zone of indifference." Those who have a strong attachment to an organization, however it comes about, are likely to have a code or codes derived from it if their connection has existed long; but whether they appear responsible with respect to such codes depends upon the general capacity for responsibility and upon their place in the spectrum of personal codes.

Hence, the assent of an individual to an order or requirement of an organization, that is, the question of whether he will grant authority to it, is very complex. It depends upon the effect of the order or requirement as a positive or negative incentive, modified by the sanctions, if any, involved in denying authority to it; upon whether or not the individual has a code of morals derived from the organization; upon whether there is conflict of his codes in respect to the specific requirements; upon how important the organization code is as compared with others; upon his sense of responsibility; and so on. If the sense of responsibility is generally weak, conflict of codes is not important but specific incentives and sanctions are. If the sense of responsibility is strong, conflict of codes will result in denial of authority if the organization code is the less important, and specific incentives in that event will usually be unimportant influences. ◆

ENDNOTE

1. The mother was rescued.

QUESTIONS

1. What are the four guiding codes that Barnard imputes to his example worker?

2. In what way is each code "moral"?

3. Why might Barnard think that you can predict a person's behavior if you know her or his moral codes?

4. In what way did the telephone operator described by Barnard exhibit moral courage?

Selection from: *The Business Guide*

J. L. Nichols (1851–1895) self-published Naperville, Ill 1893

How to Apply for a Situation

1. Fit yourself by securing a fair knowledge of Arithmetic, Geography, Grammar, United States History, Bookkeeping, and master Penmanship sufficiently so as to write neatly and rapidly. Obtain a good commercial education in some reliable institution if you possibly can.

2. Secure a few letters of recommendation from your friends and prominent business men if possible.

3. Make up your mind what business you desire to follow and get a list of the best houses in this line, and then make preparation to apply.

4. Then put on your best clothes, see that they are neatly brushed, that your linen is faultless, your boots blacked, your hands and face clean, and your finger-nails properly trimmed.

5. Go to the best houses first. Walk directly to the office and ask for the proprietor. If he is not in or is busy and cannot see you, say that you may call again and politely leave. Make a note of your call and then go to the next place on your list.

VIII

PRODUCTION

INTRODUCTION: TAKE THIS JOB AND LOVE IT

Ralph Borsodi, a mid-twentieth-century supporter of plain living and high thinking, defines the modern industrial production system as a group of manufacturing methods of which the most obvious are: "(a) systematic production; (b) standardization to insure uniformity; (c) division of labor." Though Borsodi goes on to decry the horrors that mass production creates, such as neurotic dependencies engendered by mass distribution of products and services, and the subversion of popular taste dedicated to mass consumption, he does acknowledge that, without a production orientation, most of the luxuries and some of the necessities of modern civilization would be in short supply.

Since the introduction of manufacturing systemization in the United States during the late eighteenth century and early nineteenth century, there have been many outspoken critics of production: from the older anti-establishment writing of Henry David Thoreau, countercultural communes like Brook Farm and Fruitlands in the 1840s, the newer anti-establishment writing of Paul Goodman, and the reestablishment of a form of neo-Jeffersonian agrarianism practiced in the country living of Scott and Helen Nearing. And one thing has been clear: There are intelligent arguments against the production model.

However, there are equally intelligent arguments in favor of production. Who would deny that modern forms of manufacturing have eliminated much of the misery of labor? Who would refuse to acknowledge the advances made by the marriage of technology to factory production and the concomitant contribution to health, wealth, and even the pursuit of happiness? And is there anyone who would argue that mechanized manufacturing has not freed us to pursue more conscious, thoughtful, and meaningful leisure activities?

The Travels of Marco Polo is an astonishing first-person account of the first meeting between East and West, represented by the 1275 journey of Marco Polo from Italy to China to observe the "other world" of Kublai Khan. *The Travels* is a hybrid adventure yarn and a critical summary of observations and experiences. Marco Polo chronicles, for example, the many modes of manufacturing throughout a fairly large territorial swath of China and finds an "extensive manufacture of silks" with an advanced distribution system of the output for a people who "subsist entirely by trade." He explains how they collect the raw supplies, like coal and wood, and how these supplies are routed and distributed for both production and leisure purposes. Polo is at his best when he details a "production process" such as the collection and manufacture of salt. It is all surprisingly modern.

Marco Polo is quick to recognize that, in China, one finds a society with advanced notions of production for both needs and wants. Providing goods for utility and profit, he discovers, is an important unifying principle for Kublai Khan and his people. And it pleases Polo to note a commonality between China and the early trade capitals of Europe: The profits from the production and exchange of goods bring happiness and contentment.

The marketplace of China is every bit as advanced and interesting as anything Marco Polo might find in Europe. In his account of "the abundant quantity of game of all kinds," he is describing well-managed inventories. In his description of the extraordinary variety of goods to be found in the marketplace, he is revealing the antecedents of retailing strategy. In his assertion that the "inhabitants of the city are idolators" who are "always clothed in silk," Polo is studying consumer motivation and reminding modern readers that a commercial society, with its emphasis on production, distribution, and the marketing of fetishistic, status goods, is not the invention of materialistic twenty-first-century advertisers.

David Hume's eighteenth-century empiricism plays well to a modern audience which has lost its taste for rationalism of the Cartesian kind that asks us only to think something, even the existence of an ineffable god, for it to be so. Hume, like many others of his eighteenth-century Augustan age, is not prepared to accept sensation as knowledge—particularly given the multiplicity of sensations in the world. We cannot, Hume argues, draw any final conclusions from what we think, or what we reason to be so. At best, we can, for the sake of convenience and what appears to work empirically, draw conclusions based upon probabilities. The teacher and philosopher, Henry Thomas has given concise expression to Hume's brand of skepticism which, he says: ". . . ends with the idea that we cannot rely upon any of our ideas. There is no fundamental difference, he [Hume] suggests, between sanity and insanity. The martyr who tries to save humanity and the madman who tries to destroy it are, according to Hume, equally unable to prove their point. Let no one therefore assume that he alone has discovered the truth. Modesty is the beginning of wisdom. The philosopher should accept probabilities, and refrain from assuming certainties."

Although the writing of David Hume is not represented in this book, his thoughts on the subject of production are important to your understanding of the subject because they reflect the same hue as his philosophical speculations on the relationship of reality and probability. There are manufacturing and commercial principles, he tells us, that, "if just and sound, must always prevail in the general course of things, though they may fail in particular cases . . . ." And these principles must be tolerated without prejudice because "the greatness of a state, and the happiness of its subjects, how independent so ever they may be supposed in some respects, are commonly allowed to be inseparable with regard to commerce. . . ."

Manufacturing is an empiric requirement in a just society, according to Hume, because without it, people are reduced to an indolent and unmotivated condition in which they are not inspired to improve "their skill and industry." Such a state of affairs is a prescription for political powerlessness and personal unhappiness. Manufacturing increases labor and output and the "more labour [sic], therefore, is employed beyond mere necessaries, the more powerful is any state." While such thinking is antithetical to classical notions of the primacy of need-satisfaction over want-creation, it is important to remember that Hume does not grant Plato and Aristotle any special dispensation: He is not prepared to agree with either of them that states should be limited to manufacturing only those things that are necessary to the household.

It is probable, Hume thinks, that manufacturing and its inevitable counterpart, foreign trade, serve to distribute wealth more evenly, mitigating the burden of taxes. Beyond this most practical issue, the production of goods neutralizes, at least in part, the potential for riches to concentrate in the hands of only a few. Hume's own experience suggests that: ". . . where the riches are in few hands, these must enjoy all the power, and will readily conspire to lay the whole burthen [sic] on the poor, and oppress them still farther, to the discouragement of industry."

For Hume, therefore, manufacturing is a requisite of health and happiness for the majority.

We can hear Hume in Alexander Hamilton's *Report on Manufacturism*, a well-reasoned 1790 argument in favor of augmenting America's early agrarian economy with the creation of a manufacturing base. Alexander is not interested in moving away from agriculture as an economic preoccupation; he just wants to supplement it with another mode of labor that, if applied appropriately, would yield substantial benefits to all Americans.

It may seem odd that Hamilton is compelled, in this matter, to write an official letter to the House of Representatives and, in doing so, make a special appeal to Thomas Jefferson. But you must consider the circumstances. Prior to the Revolutionary War, the English had prohibited the American colonists from manufacturing most industrial goods. The English wanted the colonies to serve as a market for English-manufactured goods, not as a lower-cost producer of identical or superior home-produced products. It stands to reason that such a prohibition would naturally direct most Americans toward agrarian lives. Thomas Jefferson believes, however, in the agrarian life. He knows firsthand how a simple life of the soil can promote proper republican virtues (do not confuse this use of the word *republican* with any notions about the modern twenty-first-century Republican)—that plain living will, indeed, produce high thinking. Jefferson is deeply suspicious of the English manufacturing model and its modern techniques for the creation and dissemination of products. Such mass production naturally requires mass consumption and, he thinks inevitably promotes thoughtless acquisitiveness and avarice—vices he does not want to see become commonplace in the nascent American democracy.

The French historian, politician, and ethnographer Alexis de Tocqueville is still considered one of the most shrewd observers of the American scene. His magnum opus on the subject of American social mores and political values, *Democracy in America*, was published more than 170 years ago (in two parts, in 1835 and 1840, respectively), so his stature is no mean phenomenon. His observations include insights into the American moral and intellectual disposition. It is clear that he admires deeply the "habits of the heart" he finds among common men and women, although he expresses some concern that individualism and self-reliance might, while working for the economic benefit of the nation, have the effect of isolating men and women within the confines of their own families and friends. Such insulation might disintegrate communities and lead to the fall of civic responsibility. He is equally concerned that, where manufacturing and production are taking hold in the new age of industrialization, the capitalist owners of factories and shops are developing into a de facto aristocracy. The production paradigm, he observes, tends to diminish the fundamental abilities for workers. Such an arrangement in a democratic country, so suffused with the ideology of equality, seems uncharacteristic and even dangerous to Tocqueville. It might surprise some to know that Adam Smith expresses a similar concern in his *Wealth of Nations*.

As we read Tocqueville, we ask ourselves if division of labor, which he cites as a particularly culpable production concept, is as mentally debilitating as suggested. Judging from the dual premises of Karl Marx's *Alienated Labor* —that factory workers live miserable lives as commodities and that factory owners who profit from worker misery are members of the elect, propertied class—you might infer that by the mid-nineteenth century, manufacturing had proven to be more a disease than a cure. Marx argues against a production system that alienates, agitates, and automates human labor and in the process, transforms people from subjects to objects. He does not deny that technological production has made some positive advances, but he demands an examination of the relationship between modern manufacturing and the laborers it alienates. As always, Marx is on the side of the men and women who actually make the products.

While it is easy for the contemporary mind to summarily, if erroneously, dismiss Marx as the father of a political/economic system that failed, his intelligent sociological investigation into the world of modern production should *not* be ignored. He is one of the first writers to think deeply about how factory automation sets the stage for impersonal, estranged relations between people. Marx is concerned about more than the archetypal class struggle—he opens an early discussion on the subject of meaning in the modern world.

Recognizing that unproductive manufacturing plant conditions and their impact on human thought and energy reduce worker productivity, Taylor introduces scientific management, which employs devices such as time and motion studies to ascertain optimum plant/labor and management/labor conditions to produce surplus profits for all stakeholders. Taylor's so-called new-style management is presented as yet another means of creating generally more equitable and amicable relations between the business parties—especially between labor and management. However, some would say that Taylor has further entrenched the idea of people as "human capital."

The four principles Taylor introduces are revolutionary and evolutionary in the world of management. They turn the manufacturing plant polity on its head and clear a path for the head to lead the rest of the body—bringing sense and sensibility to a still undeveloped and unevolved state of managerial affairs. If this is so, then how might such progressive notions lead to a possible continuation of nineteenth-century practices of "labor as exploitation." Is this interpretation of affairs mistaken? How can a scientific system that produces more equitable workplace relations be perceived by some as just another tyranny designed for the twentieth-century mind?

Henry Ford is often thought of as the first man to put mass production into practice on a global scale. If this were all he had done, certainly, it would be enough. But he was more than a mechanic with vision. Ford believed that the populist dream of creating decent, simple lives for people—lives given to useful work, abetted by a good wage and plenty of leisure time for interesting personal pursuits and the promotion of Jeffersonian virtue—was not a dream at all. He believed it could become reality for the masses if his production system could become the model for all industrial manufacturing. He wanted to be more than the most efficient producer of automobiles; he wanted to solve the populist problem that had nagged at production for many years.

The reading from Henry Ford's autobiography, *My Life and Work,* outlines in easy detail how unskilled labor can be applied to one of the most important production objectives: increasing productivity. The careful attention to principles of assembly and the declaration of developments that followed from their application must have seemed like a miracle to manufacturers looking for a way to maintain profits in competitive markets. Still, it must have seemed a divine inspiration to others who simply wondered what would become of the many unskilled laborers who might be left behind by an increasingly technical civilization.

We might credit Henry Ford with solving the populist problem—creating jobs for otherwise useless people (made useless now from everything from technology to outsourcing). But the human use of human beings does not look at all appealing when we examine the downward spiral of Lily Bart, a central character Edith Wharton's 1905 novel *The House of Mirth.* Even if we did not know that her life was in a tailspin from both ill-considered and virtuous decisions, we, as moderns, would not be tempted to view her arduous and, sometimes, humiliating labors as enviable. The work she does is referred to as "mean work"— especially "for anybody with a headache." But alienating labor, particularly as we now understand it, would generate a headache for anybody whose purpose in life is not singularly to work and thus generate an income. The act of production does not automatically mean an improvement in the life of the worker-producer, although it may mean some kind of economic advancement. And the remuneration may not provide an opportunity for later improvement. It may be that some kinds of production alter the meanings of our lives in sad and, sometimes, desperate ways.

The lives of working women in early, industrializing countries of the twentieth and twenty-first centuries is not always a healthy affair (this is not true for women alone). It cannot escape anyone's notice that the opening of the workplace to women has often meant a lower cost of production in the workplace and horrid conditions for women (and other) employees. As a foundation, however, it has also made women essential to the world of commerce. In some places, it has meant that the world of executive leadership is now open to women.

Elizabeth Butler is notable as a member of the first-wave feminists of early twentieth-century America. Her book *Women and the Trades* provides an assessment of women in the workplace. It is a pioneering effort on behalf of American egalitarianism and early production research. Butler introduces the idea that women have become a necessary and valuable foundation of the industrial life of the United States. Such a place clarifies the productive capacity of women and offers, as proof, another supportive fact applicable to their natural political empowerment.

Beyond the social implications of Butler's unemotional and unbiased writing, there is the quality of her observations within a manufacturing setting. She details production processes that reflect increasing productivity while warning that productive technologies tend to erode employment opportunities for both women and men. Finally, she offers a cogent argument for workplace training as an antidote to low wages and diminishing worker satisfaction.

The reading entitled "Man and Machine" by Mohandas Gandhi is a lucid expression of the fear experienced by those who see base materialism as the most persistent outgrowth of factory systems and mass production. Although Gandhi, whose history bespeaks a passionate commitment to passive resistance and simple virtues, writes from personal experience, you should keep in mind that he attempts to represent the views of a huge, early twentieth-century contingent of Indians and that a Gandhian pronouncement could, in its time, marshal powerful human resistance. Thus, when he equates industrialization with exploitation, he is suggesting potential resistance, if not inciting it.

Yet Gandhi is of two minds. Like Jefferson, he fears that mass production promotes "mammon worship" and the dispossession of high thinking. Like Hamilton, however, he sees that machinery could be put to labor-saving and productive uses. Though Gandhi does not settle the conflict between production and values, he does offer some hope that everything can come out right in the end. ◆

From *The Travels of Marco Polo*

Marco Polo (1254–1324)

CHAPTER 59

OF THE CITIES OF CHINTIGUI SIDIN-FU-GIN-GUI AND PAZAN-FU

You travel for twelve days by a river, on each side of which lie many towns and castles, and at length you reach the large and handsome city of Chintigui. The inhabitants are traders and artisans. They make cloth of the bark of certain trees, which looks well, and is the ordinary summer clothing of both sexes. The men are brave warriors. They have no other kind of money than the stamped paper of the Great Khan.

In this province the tigers are so numerous, that the inhabitants, from apprehension of their ravages, cannot venture to sleep at night out of their towns; and those who navigate the river dare not go to rest with their boats moored near the banks. These animals have been known to plunge into the water., swim to the vessel, and drag the men out.

In this country are likewise found the largest and fiercest dogs that can be met with. So courageous and powerful are they, that a man, with a couple of them, may be an over-match for a tiger. Armed with a bow and arrows, and thus attended, should he meet a tiger, he sets on his bold dogs, who instantly advance to the attack. The animal instinctively seeks a tree, against which to place himself, in order that the dogs may not be able to get behind him, and that he may have his enemies in front. With this intent, as soon as he perceives the dogs, he makes towards the tree, but with a slow pace, and by no means running, that he may not show any signs of fear, which his pride would not allow. During this deliberate movement, the dogs fasten upon him, and the man shoots him with his arrows. He, in his turn, endeavours to seize the dogs, but they are too nimble for him, and draw back. By this time he has been wounded by so many arrows, and so often bitten by the dogs, that he falls through weakness and from loss of blood. By these means it is that he is captured.

There is here an extensive manufacture of silks, which are exported in large quantities to other parts by the navigation of the river, which flows through towns and castles. The people subsist entirely by trade. At the end of twelve days, you arrive at the city of Sidin-fu, of which an account has been already given. From thence, in twenty days, you reach Gin-gui, in which we were, and in four days more the city of Pazan-fu, which belongs to Cathay, and lies towards the south, in returning by the other side of the province. The inhabitants worship idols, and burn the bodies of their dead. They are subjects of the Great Khan, and his paper money is current among them. They gain their living by trade and manufacture, having silk in abundance, of which they weave tissues mixed with gold, and also very fine scarfs. This city has many towns and castles under its jurisdiction: a great river flows beside it, by means of which large quantities of merchandise are conveyed to the city of Kanbalu [Peking]; for by the digging of many canals it is made to communicate with the capital. But we shall take our leave of this, and, proceeding three days' journey, speak of another city named Chan-glu.

CHAPTER 60

OF THE CITY OF CHAN-GLU

Chan-glu is a large city situated towards the south, and is in the province of Cathay. It is under the dominion of the Great Khan. The inhabitants worship idols, and burn the bodies of their dead. The stamped paper of the Emperor is current amongst them.

In this city and the district surrounding it they make great quantities of salt, by the following process: in the country is found a salty earth; upon this, when laid in large heaps, they pour water, which in its passage through the mass imbibes the particles of salt, and is then collected in channels and is conveyed to very wide pans, not more than four inches in depth. In these it is well boiled, and then left to crystallize. The salt thus made is white and good, and is exported to various parts. Great profits are made by those who manufacture it, and the Great Khan derives from it a considerable revenue.

This district produces abundance of well-flavoured peaches, of such a size that one of them will weigh two pounds troy-weight. . . .

CHAPTER 76

OF THE NOBLE AND MAGNIFICENT CITY OF KIN-SAI

Upon leaving Va-giu you pass, in the course of three days' journey, many towns, castles, and villages, all of them well inhabited and opulent. The people have abundance of provisions. At the end of three days you reach the noble and magnificent city of Kin-sai [capital; Hang-chaul,] a name that signifies "The Celestial City," and which it merits from its pre-eminence to all others in the world, in point of grandeur and beauty, as well as from its abundant delights, which might lead an inhabitant to imagine himself in paradise.

This city was frequently visited by Marco Polo, who carefully and diligently observed and inquired into every circumstance respecting it, all of which he recorded in his notes, from whence the following particulars are briefly stated. According to common estimation, this city is an hundred miles in circuit. Its streets and canals are extensive, and there are squares, or market-places, which being necessarily proportioned in size to the prodigious concourse of people by whom they are frequented, are exceedingly spacious. It is situated between a lake of fresh and very dear water on the one side, and a river of great magnitude on the other, the waters of which, by a number of canals, large and small, are made to run through every quarter of the city, carrying with them all the filth into the lake, and ultimately to the sea. This furnishes a communication by water, in addition to that by land, to all parts of the town. The canals and the streets being of sufficient width to allow of boats on the one, and carriages in the other, to pass easily with articles necessary for the inhabitants.

It is commonly said that the number of bridges, of all sizes, amounts to twelve thousand. Those which are thrown over the principal canals and are connected with the main streets, have arches so high, and built with so much skill, that vessels with their masts can pass under them. At the same time, carts and horses can pass over, so well is the slope from the street graded to the height of the arch. If they were not so numerous, there would be no way of crossing from one place to another.

Beyond the city, and enclosing it on that side, there is a ditch about forty miles in length, very wide, and full of water that comes from the river before mentioned. This was excavated by the ancient kings of the province, in order that when the river should overflow its banks, the superfluous water might be diverted into this channel. This serves at the same time as a measure of defence. The earth dug out from thence was thrown to the inner side, and has the appearance of many hillocks, surrounding the place.

There are within the city ten principal squares or market-places, besides innumerable shops along the streets. Each side of these squares is half a mile in length, and in front of them is the main street, forty paces in width, and running in a direct line from one extremity of the city to the other. It is crossed by many low and convenient bridges. These market-squares are at the distance of four miles from each other. In a direction parallel to that of the main street, but on the opposite side of the squares, runs a very large canal, on the nearer bank of which capacious warehouses are built of stone, for the accommodation of the merchants who arrive from India and other parts with their goods and effects. They are thus conveniently situated with respect to the market-places. In each of these, upon three days in every week, there is an assemblage of from forty to fifty thousand persons, who attend the markets and supply them with every article of provision that can be desired.

There is an abundant quantity of game of all kinds, such as roebucks, stags, fallow deer, hares, and rabbits, together with partridges, pheasants, francolins, quails, common fowls, capons, and such numbers of ducks and geese as can scarcely be expressed; for so easily are they bred and reared on the lake, that, for the value of a Venetian silver groat, you may purchase a couple of geese and two couple of ducks.

There, also, are the shambles, where they slaughter cattle for food, such as oxen, calves, kids, and lambs, to furnish the tables of rich persons and of the great magistrates. As to the people of the lower classes, they eat every kind of meat, without any discrimination.

At all seasons there is in the markets a great variety of herbs and fruits, and especially pears of an extraordinary size, weighing ten pounds each, that are white in the inside, like paste, and have a very fragrant smell. There are peaches also, in their season, both of the yellow and white kind, and of a delicious flavour. Grapes are not produced there, but are brought in a dried state, and very good, from other parts. This applies also to wine, which the natives do not hold in estimation, being accustomed to their own liquor prepared from rice and spices. From the sea, which is fifteen miles distant, there is daily brought up the river, to the city, a vast quantity of fish; and in the lake also there is abundance, which gives employment at all times to persons whose sole occupation it is to catch them. The sorts are various according to the season of the year. At the sight of such an importation of fish, you would think it impossible that it could be sold ; and yet, in the course of a few hours, it is all taken off, so great is the number of inhabitants, even of those classes which can afford to indulge in such luxuries, for fish and flesh are eaten at the same meal.

Each of the ten market-squares is surrounded with high dwelling-houses, in the lower part of which are shops, where every kind of manufacture is carried on, and every article of trade is sold; such, amongst others, as spices, drugs, trinkets, and pearls. In certain shops nothing is vended but the wine of the country, which they are continually brewing, and serve out fresh to their customers at a moderate price. The streets connected with the market-squares are numerous, and in some of them are many cold baths, attended by servants of both sexes. The men and women who frequent them, have from their childhood been accustomed at all times to wash in cold water, which they reckon highly conducive to health. At

these bathing places, however, they have apartments provided with warm water, for the use of strangers, who cannot bear the shock of the cold. All are in the daily practice of washing their persons, and especially before their meals.

In other streets are the quarters of the courtesans who are here in such numbers as I dare not venture to report. Not only near the squares, which is the situation usually appropriated for their residence, but in every part of the city they are to be found, adorned with much finery, highly perfumed, occupying well-furnished houses, and attended by many female domestics. These women are accomplished, and are perfect in the arts of caressing and fondling which they accompany with expressions adapted to every description of person. Strangers who have once tasted of their charms, remain in a state of fascination, and become so enchanted by their wanton arts, that they can never forget the impression. Thus intoxicated with sensual pleasures, when they return to their homes they report that they have been in Kin-sai, or The Celestial City, and look forward to the time when they may be enabled to revisit this paradise.

In other streets are the dwellings of the physicians and the astrologers, who also give instructions in reading and writing, as well as in many other arts. They have apartments also amongst those which surround the market-squares. On opposite sides of each of these squares there are two large edifices, where officers appointed by the Great Khan are stationed, to take immediate notice of any differences that may happen to arise between the foreign merchants, or amongst the inhabitants of the place. It is their duty likewise to see that the guards upon the several bridges in their respective vicinities are duly placed, and in cases of neglect, to punish the offenders at their discretion.

On each side of the principal street, already mentioned as extending from one end of the city to the other, there are houses and mansions of great size, with their gardens, and near to these, the dwellings of the artisans, who work in shops, at their several trades; and at all hours you see such multitudes of people passing and repassing, on their various avocations, that the providing food in sufficiency for their maintenance might be deemed an impossibility. It is observed, however, that on every market-day, the squares are crowded with tradespeople, who cover the whole space with the articles brought by carts and boats, for all of which they find sale. From, the single article of pepper, some notion may be formed of the whole quantity of provisions, meat, wine, groceries, and the like, required for the consumption of the inhabitants of Kin-sai. Marco Polo learned from an officer employed in the Great Khan's customs, the daily amount of pepper bought was forty-three loads, each load being two hundred and forty-three pounds.

The inhabitants of the city are idolaters, and they use paper money as currency. The men as well as the women have fair complexions, and are handsome. The greater part of them are always clothed in silk, in consequence of the vast quantity of that material produced in the territory of Kin-sai, exclusively of what the merchants import from other provinces.

Amongst the handicraft trades exercised in the place, there are twelve considered to be superior to the rest, as being more generally useful. There are a thousand workshops for each craft, and each shop furnishes employment for ten, fifteen, or twenty workmen, and in a few instances as many as forty, under their respective masters. The opulent masters in these shops do not labour with their own hand but, on the contrary, assume airs of gentility and affect parade. Their wives equally abstain from work.

They have much beauty, as has been remarked, and are brought up with delicate and languid habits. The costliness of their dresses, in silks and jewelry, can scarcely be imagined. Although the laws of their ancient kings ordained that each citizen should exercise the profession of his father, yet they were allowed, when they acquired wealth, to avoid manual labour, provided they kept up the establishment, and employ persons to work at their paternal trades.

Their houses are well built and richly adorned with carved work. So much do they delight in ornaments of this kind, in paintings, and fancy buildings, that the sums they lavish on such objects are enormous.

The natural disposition of the native inhabitants of Kin-sai is peaceful, and by the example of their former kings, who were themselves unwarlike, they have been accustomed to habits of tranquility. The management of arms is unknown to them, nor do they keep any in their houses. They conduct their mercantile and manufacturing concerns with perfect candour and honesty. They are friendly towards each other, and persons who inhabit the same street, both men and women, from the mere circumstance of neighbourhood, appear like one family.

In their domestic manners they are free from jealousy or suspicion of their wives, to whom great respect is shown, and any man would be accounted infamous who should presume to use indecent expressions to a married woman. To strangers also, who visit their city in the way of commerce, they give proofs of cordiality, inviting them freely to their houses, showing them friendly attention, and furnishing them with the best advice and assistance in their mercantile transactions. On the other hand, they dislike the sight of soldiery, not excepting the guards of the Great Khan, for they remind them that they were deprived of the government of their native kings and rulers.

On the borders of the lake are many handsome and spacious edifices belonging to men of rank and great magistrates. There are likewise many idol temples, with their monasteries, occupied by a number of monks, who perform the service of the idols. Near the central part are two islands, upon each of which stands a superb building, with an incredible number of apartments and separate pavilions. When the inhabitants of the city have occasion to celebrate a wedding, or to give a sumptuous entertainment, they resort to one of these islands, where they find ready for their purpose every article that can be required, such as vessels, napkins, table linen, and the like, which are provided and kept there at the common expense of the citizens, by whom also the buildings were erected. It may happen that at one time there are a hundred parties assembled there, at wedding or other feasts, all of whom, notwithstanding, are accommodated with separate rooms or pavilions, so judiciously arranged that they do not interfere with each other.

In addition to this, there are upon the lake a great number of pleasure vessels or barges, calculated for holding ten, fifteen, to twenty persons, being from fifteen to twenty paces in length, with a wide and flat flooring, and not liable to heel to either side in passing through the water. Such persons as take delight in the amusement, and mean to enjoy it, either in the company of their women or that of their male companions, engage one of these barges, which are always kept in the nicest order, with proper seats and tables, together with every other kind of furniture necessary for giving an entertainment. The cabins have a flat roof or upper deck, where the boatmen take their place, and by means of long poles, which they thrust to the bottom of the lake, which is not more than one or two fathoms in depth, they shove the barges along, until they reach the desired spot. These cabins are painted inside with various colours and with a variety of figures; all parts of the vessel are likewise adorned with painting. There are windows on each side, which may either be kept shut, or opened, to give an opportunity to the company, as they sit at table, of looking out in every direction and feasting their eyes on the variety and beauty of the scenes as they pass them. And truly the gratification afforded in this manner, upon the water, exceeds any that can be derived from the amusements on the land; for as the lake extends the whole length of the city, on one side, you have a view, as you stand in the boat, at a certain distance from the shore, of all its grandeur and beauty, its palaces, temples, convents, and gardens, with trees of the largest size growing down to the water's edge, whilst at the same time you enjoy the sight of other boats of the same description, continually passing you, filled in like manner with parties in pursuit of amusement. In fact, the inhabitants of this place, as soon as the labours of the day have ceased, or their mercantile transactions are closed, think of nothing else than of passing the remaining hours in parties of pleasure, with their wives or their mistresses, either in these barges, or about the city in carriages . . . .

CHAPTER 78

OF THE REVENUES OF THE GREAT KHAN

We shall now speak of the revenue which the Great Khan draws from the city of Kin-sai and the places within its jurisdiction, constituting the ninth division or kingdom of Manji. In the first place, upon salt, the most productive article, he levies a yearly duty of eighty tomans of gold, each toman being eighty thousand saggi, and each saggio fully equal to a gold florin, and consequently amounting to six million four hundred thousand ducats. This vast produce is occasioned by the distance of the province to the sea, and the number of salt lakes or marshes, in which, during the heat of summer, the water becomes crystallized, and from whence a quantity of salt is taken, sufficient for the supply of five of the other divisions of the province.

There is here cultivated and manufactured a large quantity of sugar, which pays, as do all other groceries, three and one-third percent. The same is also levied upon the wine, or fermented liquor, made of rice. The twelve classes of artisans, of whom we have already spoken, as having each a thousand shops, and also the merchants, as well those who import the goods into the city, in the first instance, as those who carry them from thence to the interior, or who export them by sea, pay, in like manner, a duty of three and one-third per cent. But goods coming by sea from distant countries and regions, such as from India, pay ten per cent. So likewise all native articles of the country, as cattle, the vegetable produce of the soil, and silk, pay a tax to the king.

The account being made up in the presence of Marco Polo, he had an opportunity of seeing that the revenue of his Majesty, exclusively of that arising from salt, already stated, amounted in the year to the sum of two hundred and ten tomans, or sixteen million eight hundred thousand ducats. . . .

CHAPTER 80

OF THE KINGDOM OF KON-CHA AND ITS CAPITAL CITY NAMED FU-GIU

Upon leaving the last city of the kingdom of Kin-sai, named Gie-za, you enter that of Kon-cha, the principal city of which is named

Fu-giu. In the course of six days' journey through this country, in a south-east direction, over hills and along valleys, you continually pass towns and villages, where the necessaries of life are in abundance, and there is much field sport, particularly of birds. The people are subjects of the Great Khan, and are engaged in commerce and manufactures.

In these parts there are tigers of great size and strength. Ginger and also galangal are produced in large quantities, as well as other drugs. For money equal in value to a Venetian silver groat you may have eighty pounds weight of fresh ginger, so common is its growth. There is also a vegetable which has all the properties of the true saffron, as well the smell as the colour, and yet it is not really saffron. It is held in great estimation, and being an ingredient in all their dishes, it bears, on that account, a high price.

The people in this part of the country are addicted to eating human flesh, esteeming it more delicate than any other, provided the death of the person has not been occasioned by disease. When they advance to combat they throw loose their hair about their ears, and they paint their faces of a bright blue colour. They arm themselves with lances and swords, and all march on foot excepting their chief, who rides on horse-back. They are a most savage race of men, insomuch that when they slay their enemies in battle, they are anxious to drink their blood, and afterwards they devour their flesh. Leaving this subject, we shall now speak of the city of Kue-lin-fu.

The journey of six days being accomplished, you arrive at the city of Kue-lin-fu, which is of considerable size, and contains three very handsome bridges, upwards of a hundred paces in length, and eight paces in width. The women of the place are very handsome, and live in a state of luxurious ease. There is much raw silk produced here, and it is manufactured into silk pieces of various sorts. Cottons are also woven, of coloured threads, which are carried for sale to every part of the province of Manji. The people employ themselves extensively in commerce, and export quantities of ginger and galangal.

I have been told, but did not myself see the animal, that there are found at this place a species of domestic fowls which have no feathers; their skins clothed with black hair, resembling the fur of cats. Such a sight must be extraordinary.[1] They lay eggs like other fowls, and they are good to eat. The multitude of tigers renders travelling through the country dangerous, unless a number of persons go in company.

CHAPTER 81

OF THE CITY OF UN-GUEN

Upon leaving the city of Kue-lin-fu, and travelling three days, during which you are continually passing towns and castles, of which the inhabitants are idolaters, have silk in abundance, and export it in considerable quantities, you reach the city of Un-guen. This place is remarkable for a great manufacture of sugar, which is sent from thence to the city of Kanbalu for the supply of the court. Previously to its being brought under the dominion of the Great Khan, the natives were unacquainted with the art of manufacturing sugar of a fine quality, and boiled it in such an imperfect manner, that when left to cool it remained in the state of a dark-brown paste. But at the time this city became subject to his Majesty's government, there happened to be at the court some persons from Babylon who were skilled in the process, and who, being sent thither, instructed the inhabitants in the mode of refining the sugar by means of the ashes of certain woods.

Travelling fifteen miles further in the same direction, you come to the city of Kan-giu, which belongs to the kingdom or viceroyalty of Kon-cha, one of the nine divisions of Manji. In this place is stationed a large army for the protection of the country and to be always in readiness to act, in the event of rebellion.

Through the midst of it passes a river, a mile in breadth, upon the banks of which, on either side, are extensive and handsome buildings. In front of these, great numbers of ships are seen lying, having merchandise on board, and especially sugar, of which large quantities are manufactured here also. Many vessels arrive at this port from India, freighted by merchants who bring with them rich assortments of jewels and pearls, upon the sale of which they obtain a considerable profit. This river empties into the sea, at no great distance from the port named Zai-tun. The ships coming from India ascend the river as high up as the city, which abounds with every sort of provision, and has delightful gardens, producing exquisite fruits.

CHAPTER 82

OF THE CITY AND PORT OF ZIA-TUN AND THE CITY OF TIN-GUI

Upon leaving the city of Kan-giu and crossing the river to proceed in a south-easterly direction, you travel during five days through a well-inhabited country, passing towns, castles, and substantial dwellings, well supplied with all kinds of provisions. The road lies over hills, across plains, and through woods, in which are found many of those shrubs from whence the camphor is procured. The country abounds also with game. The inhabitants are subjects of the Great Khan, and within the jurisdiction of Kan-giu.

At the end of five days' journey, you arrive at the noble and handsome city of Zai-tun, which has a port on the seacoast celebrated for the resort of shipping, loaded with merchandise, that is afterwards distributed through every part of the province of Manji. The quantity of pepper imported there is so considerable, that what is carried to Alexandria, to supply the demand of the western parts of the world, is trifling in comparison, perhaps not more than the hundredth part. It is indeed impossible to convey an idea of the number of merchants and the accumulation of goods in this place, which is held to be one of the largest ports in the world. The Great Khan derives a vast revenue from this place, as every merchant is obliged to pay ten per cent. upon the amount of his investment. The ships are freighted by them at the rate of thirty per cent. for fine goods, forty-four for pepper, and for sandalwood, and other drugs, as well as articles of trade in general, forty per cent. It is computed by the merchants, that their charges, including customs and freight, amount to half the value of the cargo; and yet upon the half that remains to them their profit is so considerable, that they are always disposed to return to the same market with a further stock of merchandise.

The country is delightful. The people are idolaters, and have all the necessaries of life in plenty. Their disposition is peaceable, and they are fond of ease and indulgence. Many persons arrive in this city from the interior parts of India for the purpose of having their persons ornamented by puncturing with needles . . ., as it is celebrated for the number of its artists skilled in that practice.

The river that flows by the port of Zai-tun is large and rapid, and is a branch of that which passes the city of Kin-sai. At the place where it separates from the principal channel stands the city of Tin-gui. Of this place there is nothing further to be observed, than that cups or bowls and dishes of porcelainware are there manufactured. The process was explained to be as follows. They collect a certain kind of earth, as it were, from a mine, and laying it in a great heap, suffer it to be exposed to the wind, the rain, and the sun, for thirty or forty years, during which time it is never disturbed. By this it becomes refined and fit for being wrought into the vessels above mentioned. Such colours as may be thought proper are then laid on, and the ware is afterwards baked in ovens or furnaces. Those persons, therefore, who cause the earth to be dug, collect it for their children and grandchildren. Great quantities of the manufacture are sold in the city, and for a Venetian groat you may purchase eight porcelain cups.[2]

We have now described the viceroyalty of Kon-cha, one of the nine divisions of Manji, from whence the Great Khan draws as ample a revenue as even from that of Kin-sai. Of the others we shall not attempt to speak, because Marco Polo did not himself visit any of their cities, as he has done those of Kin-sai and Kon-cha. It should be observed that throughout the province of Manji one general language prevails, and one uniform manner of writing, yet in the different parts of the country there is a diversity of dialect, similar to what is found between the Genoese, the Milanese, the Florentine, and the dialects of other Italian states, whose inhabitants, although they have each their peculiar speech, can make themselves reciprocally understood.

Not having yet completed the subjects upon which Marco Polo purposed to write, he will now bring this Second Book to a close, and will commence another with a description of the countries and provinces of India, dividing it into the Greater, the Lesser, and the Middle India. These parts he visited whilst employed in the service of the Great Khan, who ordered him thither upon different occasions of business, and afterwards again when, accompanied by his father and uncle, on their returning journey escorting the queen destined for King Axgon.

He will have the opportunity of relating many extraordinary circumstances observed by himself personally in those countries, but at the same time will not omit to notice others of which he was informed by persons worthy of credit, or which were pointed out to him in the sea-chart of the coasts of India. ♦

ENDNOTES

1. These birds are known to poultry-fanciers as the *Fleecy Persian*. The Chinese call them velvet-hair fowls but only a white variety exists today.
2. Porcelain is mentioned in Chinese books of the Han dynasty (B.C. 206–A.D. 220), but it was about a hundred years after Marco Polo during the Ming dynasty that the great porcelain age of China flourished.

QUESTIONS

1. What were some of the main products that Marco Polo saw being produced and traded in China?

2. Tax on the production and sale of which product in particular brought much revenue to the Chinese emperor?

3. What countries does Polo mention as international trading partners of China?

4. What three attributes does Polo identify as indicators of the well-ordered nature of China's society?

Manufactures
from *The Works of Alexander Hamilton*

Alexander Hamilton (1757–1804)

The Secretary of the Treasury, in obedience to the order of the House of Representatives, of the 15th day of January, 1790, has applied his attention, at as early a period as his other duties would permit, to the subject of Manufactures, and particularly to the means of promoting such as will render the United States independent of foreign nations for military and other essential supplies; and he thereupon respectfully submits the following report:

The expediency of encouraging manufactures in the United States, which was not long since deemed very questionable, appears at this time to be pretty generally admitted. The embarrassments which have obstructed the progress of our external trade, have led to serious reflections on the necessity of enlarging the sphere of our domestic commerce. The restrictive regulations, which, in foreign markets, abridge the vent of the increasing surplus of our agricultural produce, serve to beget an earnest desire that a more extensive demand for that surplus may be created at home; and the complete success which has rewarded manufacturing enterprise in some valuable branches, conspiring with the promising symptoms which attend some less mature essays in others, justify a hope that the obstacles to the growth of this species of industry are less formidable than they were apprehended to be, and that it is not difficult to find, in its further extension, a full indemnification for any external disadvantages which are or may be experienced, as well as an accession of resources, favorable to national independence and safety.

There still are, nevertheless, respectable patrons of opinions unfriendly to the encouragement of manufactures. The following are, substantially, the arguments by which these opinions are defended:

"In every country (say those who entertain them) agriculture is the most beneficial and productive object of human industry. This position, generally, if not universally true, applies with peculiar emphasis to the United States, on account of their immense tracts of fertile territory, uninhabited and unimproved. Nothing can afford so advantageous an employment for capital and labor, as the conversion of this extensive wilderness into cultivated farms. Nothing, equally with this, can contribute to the population, strength, and real riches of the country.

"To endeavor, by the extraordinary patronage of government, to accelerate the growth of manufactures, is, in fact, to endeavor, by force and art, to transfer the natural current of industry from a more to a less beneficial channel. Whatever such a tendency, must necessarily be unwise; indeed, it can hardly ever be wise in government to attempt to give a direction to the industry of its citizens. This, under the quick-sighted guidance of private interest, will, if left to itself, infallibly find its own way to the most profitable employment; and it is by such employment, that the public prosperity will be most effectually promoted. To leave industry to itself, therefore, is, in almost every case, the soundest as well as the simplest policy. . . ."

***

It has been maintained that agriculture is not only the most productive, but the only productive, species of industry. The reality of this suggestion, in either respect, has, however, not been verified by any accurate detail of facts and calculations; and the general arguments which are adduced to prove it, are rather subtle and paradoxical, than solid or convincing.

Those who maintain its exclusive productiveness are to this effect:

Labor bestowed upon the cultivation of land produces enough not only to replace all the necessary expenses incurred in the business, and to maintain the persons who are employed in it, but to afford, together with the ordinary profit on the stock or capital of the farmer, a net surplus or rent for the landlord or proprietor of the soil. But the labor of artificers does nothing more than replace the stock which employs them (or which furnishes materials, tools, and wages), and yields the ordinary profit upon that stock. It yields nothing equivalent to the rent of the land; neither does it add any thing to the total value of the whole annual produce of the land and labor of the country. The additional value given to those other parts of the produce of land which are wrought into manufactures, is counterbalanced by the value of those other parts of that produce which are consumed by the manufacturers. It can, therefore, only be by saving or parsimony, not by the positive productiveness of their labor, that the classes of artificers can, in any degree, augment the revenue of the society.

To this it has been answered:

1. "That, inasmuch as it is acknowledged that manufacturing labor reproduces a value equal to that which is expended or consumed in carrying it on, and continues in existence the original stock or capital employed, it ought, on that account, alone, to escape being considered wholly unproductive. That, though it should be admitted, as alleged, that the consumption of the produce of the soil, by the classes of artificers or manufacturers, is exactly equal to the value added by their labor to the materials upon which it is exerted, yet it would not thence follow that it added nothing to the revenue of the society, or to the aggregate value of the annual produce of its land and labor. If the consumption, for any given period, amounted to a given sum, and the increased value of the produce manufactured, in the same period, to a like sum, the total amount of the consumption and production, during that period, would be equal to the two sums, and consequently double the value of the agricultural produce consumed; and though the increment of value produced by the classes of artificers should, at no time, exceed the value of produce of the land consumed by them, yet there would be, at every moment, in consequence of their labor, a greater value of goods in the market than would exist independent of it."

2. "That the position, that artificers can augment the revenue of a society only by parsimony, is true in no other sense than in one which is equally applicable to husbandmen or cultivators. It may be alike affirmed of all these classes, that the fund acquired by their labor, and destined for their support, is not, in an ordinary way, more than equal to it. And hence it will follow that augmentations of the wealth or capital of the community (except in the instances of some extraordinary dexterity or skill) can only proceed, with respect to any of them, from the savings of the more thrifty and parsimonious."

3. "That the annual produce of the land and labor of a country can only be increased in two ways—by some improvement in the productive powers of the useful labor which actually exists within it, or by some increase in the quantity of such labor. That, with regard to the first, the labor of artificers being capable of greater subdivision and simplicity of operation than that of cultivators, it is susceptible, in a proportionably greater degree, of improvement in its productive powers, whether to be derived from an accession of skill or from the application of ingenious machinery; in which particular, therefore, the labor employed in the culture of land can pretend to no advantage over that engaged in manufactures. That, with regard to an augmentation of the quantity of useful labor, this, excluding adventitious circumstances, must depend essentially upon an increase of capital, which again must depend upon the savings made out of the revenues of those who furnish or manage that which is at any time employed, whether in agriculture or in manufactures, or in any other way."

But while the exclusive productiveness of agricultural labor has been thus denied and refuted, the superiority of its productiveness has been conceded without hesitation. As this concession involves a point of considerable magnitude, in relation to maxims of public administration, the grounds on which it rests are worthy of a distinct and particular examination.

One of the arguments made use of in support of the idea may be pronounced both quaint and superficial. It amounts to this: That, in the productions of the soil, nature cooperates with man; and that the effect of their joint labor must be greater than that of the labor of man alone.

This, however, is far from being a necessary inference. It is very conceivable that the labor of man alone, laid out upon a work requiring great skill and art to bring it to perfection, may be more productive, in value, than the labor of nature and man combined, when directed towards more simple operations and objects; and when it is recollected to what an extent the agency of nature, in the application of the mechanical powers, is made auxiliary to the prosecution of manufactures, the suggestion which has been noticed loses even the appearance of plausibility.

It might also be observed, with a contrary view, that the labor employed in agriculture is, in a great measure, periodical and occasional, depending on seasons, and liable to various and long intermissions; while that occupied in many manufactures is constant and regular, extending through the year, embracing, in some instances, night as well as day. It is also probable that there are, among the cultivators of land, more examples of remissness than among artificers. The farmer, from the peculiar fertility of his land, or some other favorable circumstance, may frequently obtain a livelihood, even with a considerable degree of carelessness in the mode of cultivation; but the artisan can with difficulty effect the same object, without exerting himself pretty equally with all those who are engaged in the same pursuit. And if it may likewise be assumed as a fact, that manufactures open a wider field to exertions of ingenuity than agriculture, it would not be a strained conjecture, that the labor employed in the former, being at once more constant, more uniform, and more ingenious, than that which is employed in the latter, will be found, at the same time, more productive.

But it is not meant to lay stress on observations of this nature; they ought only to serve as a counterbalance to those of similar complex-ion. Circumstances so vague and general, as well as so abstract, can afford little instruction in a matter of this kind.

Another, and that which seems to be the principal argument offered for the superior productiveness of agricultural labor, turns upon the allegation, that labor employed on manufactures yields nothing equivalent to the rent of land, or to that net surplus, as it is called, which accrues to the proprietor of the soil.

But this distinction, important as it has been deemed, appears rather verbal than substantial.

It is easily discernible, that what, in the first instance, is divided into two parts, under the denominations of the ordinary profit of the stock of the farmer and rent to the landlord, is, in the second instance, united under general appellation of the ordinary profit on the stock of the undertaker; and that this formal or verbal distribution constitutes the whole difference in the two cases. It seems to have been overlooked, that the land is itself a stock or capital, advanced or lent by its owner to the occupier or tenant, and that the rent he receives is only the ordinary profit of a certain stock in land, not managed by the proprietor himself, but by another, to whom he lends or lets it, and who, on his part, advances a second capital, to stock and improve the land, upon which he also receives the usual profit. The rent of the landlord and the profit of the farmer are, therefore, nothing more than the ordinary profits of two capitals belonging to two different persons, and united in the cultivation of a farm; as, in the other case, the surplus which arises upon any manufactory, after replacing the expenses of carrying it on answers to the ordinary profits of one or more capitals engaged in the prosecution of such manufactory. It is said one or more capitals, because, in fact, the same thing which is contemplated in the case of the farm, sometimes happens in that of a manufactory. There is one who furnishes a part of the capital or lends a part of the money by which it is carried on, and another who carries it on with the addition of his own capital. Out of the surplus which remains after defraying expenses, an interest is paid to the money-lender, for the portion of the capital furnished by him, which exactly agrees with the rent paid t o the landlord; and the residue of that surplus constitutes the profit of the undertaker or manufacturer, and agrees with what is denominated the ordinary profits on the stock of the farmer. Both together make the ordinary profits of two capitals employed in a manufactory; as, in the other case, the rent of the landlord and the revenue of the farmer compose the ordinary profits of two capitals employed in the cultivation of a farm.

The rent, therefore, accruing to the proprietor of the land, far from being a criterion of exclusive productiveness, as has been argued, is no criterion even of superior productiveness. The question must still be, whether the surplus, after defraying expenses, of a given capital, employed in the purchase and improvement of a piece of land, is greater or less than that of a like capital, employed in the prosecution of a manufactory; or whether the whole value produced from a given capital and a given quantity of labor, employed in one way, be greater or less than the whole value produced from an equal capital and an equal quantity of labor, employed in the other way; or rather, perhaps, whether the business of agriculture, or that of manufactures, will yield the greater product, according to a compound ratio of the quantity of the capital and the quantity of labor which are employed in the one or in the other.

The solution of either of these questions is not easy; it involves numerous and complicated details, depending on an accurate knowledge of the objects to be compared. It is not known that the comparison has ever been made upon sufficient data, properly ascertained and analyzed. To be able to make it, on the present occasion, with satisfactory precision, would demand more previous inquiry and investigation than there has been hitherto either leisure or opportunity to accomplish.

Some essays, however, have been made towards acquiring the requisite information, which have rather served to throw doubt upon, than to confirm, the hypothesis under examination. But it ought to be acknowledged that they have been too little diversified, and are too imperfect to authorize a definitive conclusion either way; leading rather to probable conjecture than to certain deduction. They render it probable that there are various branches of manufactures, in which a given capital will yield a greater total product, and a considerably greater net product, than an equal capital invested in the purchase and improvement of lands; and that there are also some branches, in which both the gross and the net produce will exceed that of agricultural industry, according to a compound ratio of capital and labor. But it is on this last point that there appears to be the greatest room for doubt. It is far less difficult to infer generally, that the net produce of capital engaged in manufacturing enterprises is greater than that of capital engaged in agriculture.

The foregoing suggestions are not designed to inculcate an opinion that manufacturing industry is more productive than that of agriculture. They are intended rather to show that the reverse of this proposition is not ascertained; that the general arguments which are brought to establish it are not satisfactory; and, consequently, that a supposition of the superior productiveness of tillage ought to be no obstacle to listening to any substantial inducements to the encouragement of manufactures, which may be otherwise perceived to exist, through an apprehension that they may have a tendency to divert labor from a more to a less profitable employment.

It is extremely probable that, on a full and accurate development of the matter, on the ground of fact and calculation, it would be discovered that there is no material difference between the aggregate productiveness of the one and of the other kind of industry; and that the propriety of the encouragements which may, in any case, be proposed to be given to either, ought to be determined upon considerations irrelative to any comparison of that nature.

. . . But, without contending for the superior productiveness of manufacturing industry, it may conduce to a better judgment of the policy which ought to be pursued respecting its encouragement, to contemplate the subject under some additional aspects, tending not only to confirm the idea that this kind of industry has been improperly represented as unproductive in itself but to evince, in addition, that the establishment and diffusion of manufactures have the effect of rendering the total mass of useful and productive labor, in a community, greater than it would otherwise be. In prosecuting this discussion, it may be necessary briefly to resume and review some of the topics which have been already touched.

To affirm that the labor of the manufacturer is unproductive, because he consumes as much of the produce of lands as he adds value to the raw material which he manufactures, is not better founded than it would be to affirm that the labor of the farmer, which furnishes materials to the manufacturer, is unproductive, because he consumes an equal value of manufactured articles. Each furnishes a certain portion of the produce of his labor to the other, and each destroys a corresponding portion of the produce of the labor of the other. In the meantime, the maintenance of two citizens, instead of one, is going on; the State has two members instead of one; and they, together consume twice the value of what is produced from the land.

If, instead of farmer and artificer, there were a farmer only, he would be under the necessity of devoting a part of his labor to the fabrication of clothing and other articles, which he could procure of the artificer, in the case of there being such a person; and of course he would be able to devote less labor to the cultivation of his farm, and would draw from it a proportionately less product. The whole quantity of production, in this state of things, in provisions, raw materials, and manufactures, would certainly not exceed in value the amount of what would be produced in provisions and raw materials only, if there were an artificer as well as a farmer.

Again, if there were both an artificer and a farmer, the latter would be left at liberty to pursue exclusively the cultivation of his farm. A greater quantity of provisions and raw materials would, of course, be produced, equal, at least, as has been already observed, to the whole amount of the provisions, raw materials, and manufactures, which would exist on a contrary supposition. The artificer, at the same time, would be going on in the production of manufactured commodities, for the provisions and materials which were procured from him, but to furnish the artificer himself with a supply of similar commodities for his own use. Thus, then, there would be two quantities or

values in existence, instead of one; and the revenue and consumption would be double, in one case, what it would be in the other.

If, in place of both of these suppositions, there were supposed to be two farmers and no artificer, each of whom applied a part of his labor to the culture of land and another part to the fabrication of manufactures; in this case, the portion of the labor of both, bestowed upon land, would produce the same quantity of provisions and raw materials only, as would be produced by the entire sum of the labor of one, applied in the same manner; and the portion of the labor of both, bestowed upon manufactures, would produce the same quantity of manufactures only, as would be produced by the entire sum of the labor of one, applied in the same manner. Hence, the produce of the labor of the two farmers would not be greater than the produce of the farmer and artificer; and hence it results that the labor of the farmer, and as positively productive as that of the farmer, and as positively augments the revenue of the society.

The labor of the artificer replaces to the farmer that portion of his labor with which he provides the materials of exchange with the artificer, and which he would otherwise have been compelled to apply to manufactures; and while the artificer thus enables the farmer to enlarge his stock of agricultural industry, a portion of which he purchases for his own use, he also supplies himself with the manufactured articles of which he stands in need. He does still more. Besides this equivalent, which he gives for the portion of agricultural labor consumed by him, and this supply of manufactured commodities for his own consumption, he furnishes still a surplus, which compensates for the use of the capital advanced, either by himself or some other person, for carrying on the business. This is the ordinary profit of the stock employed in the manufactory, and is, in every sense, as effective an addition to the income of the society as the rent of land.

The produce of the labor of the artificer, consequently, may be regarded as composed of three parts: one, by which the provisions for his subsistence and the materials for his work are purchased of the farmer; one, by which he supplies himself with manufactured necessaries;

and a third, which constitutes the profit of the stock employed. The two last portions seem to have been overlooked in the system which represents manufacturing industry as barren and unproductive.

In the course of the preceding illustrations, the products of equal quantities of the labor of the farmer and artificer have been treated as if equal to each other. But this is not to be understood as intending to assert any such precise equality. It is merely a manner of expression, adopted for the sake of simplicity and perspicuity. Whether the value of the produce of the labor of the farmer be somewhat more or less than that of the artificer, is not material to the main scope of the argument, which, hitherto, has only aimed at showing that the one, as well as the other, occasions a positive augmentation of the total produce and revenue of the society.

It is now proper to proceed a step further, and to enumerate the principal circumstances from which it may be inferred that manufacturing establishments not only occasion a positive augmentation of the produce and revenue of the society, but that they contribute essentially to rendering them greater than they could possibly be without such establishments. These circumstances are:

1. The division of labor.
2. An extension of the use of machinery.
3. Additional employment to classes of the community not ordinarily engaged in the business.
4. The promoting of emigration from foreign countries.
5. The furnishing greater scope for the diversity of talents and dispositions, which discriminate men from each other.
6. The affording a more ample and various field for enterprise.
7. The creating, in some instances, a new, and securing, in all, a more certain and steady demand for the surplus produce of the soil.

Each of these circumstances has a considerable influence upon the total mass of industrious effort in a community; together, they add to it a degree of energy and effect which is not easily conceived. . . . ◆

QUESTIONS

1. With what main question was Hamilton concerned?

2. Did Hamilton think that we could rely on Adam Smith's concept of the invisible hand to order the economy?

3. What advantages did Hamilton identify for agriculture and manufacturing, respectively?

"Manufactures"
The present state of
manufactures, commerce,
interior and exterior trade?

Thomas Jefferson (1743–1826)

We never had an interior trade of any importance. Our exterior commerce has suffered very much from the beginning of the present contest. During this time we have manufactured within our families the most necessary articles of clothing. Those of cotton will bear some comparison with the same kinds of manufacture in Europe; but those of wool, flax and hemp are very coarse, unsightly, and unpleasant: and such is our attachment to agriculture, and such our preference for foreign manufactures, that be it wise or unwise, our people will certainly return as soon as they can, to the raising of raw materials, and exchanging them for finer manufactures than they are able to execute themselves.

The political economists of Europe have established it as a principle that every state should endeavour to manufacture for itself: and this principle, like many others, we transfer to America, without calculating the difference of circumstance which should often produce a difference of result. In Europe the lands are either cultivated, or locked up against the cultivator. Manufacture must therefore be resorted to of necessity not of choice, to support the surplus of their people. But we have an immensity of land courting the industry of the husbandman. Is it best then that all our citizens should be employed in its improvement, or that one half should be called off from that to exercise manufactures and handicraft arts for the other? Those who labour in the earth are the chosen people of God, if ever he had a chosen people, whose breasts he has made his peculiar deposit for substantial and genuine virtue. It is the focus in which he keeps alive that sacred fire, which otherwise might escape from the face of the earth. Corruption of morals in the mass of cultivators is a phaenomenon of which no age nor nation has furnished an example. It is the mark set on those, who not looking up to heaven, to their own soil and industry, as does the husbandman, for their subsistence, depend for it on the casualties and caprice of customers. Dependence begets subservience and venality, suffocates the germ of virtue, and prepares fit tools for the designs of ambition. This, the natural progress and consequence of the arts, has sometimes perhaps been retarded by accidental circumstances: but, generally speaking, the proportion which the aggregate of the other classes of citizens bears in any state to that of its husbandmen, is the proportion of its unsound to its healthy parts, and is a good-enough barometer whereby to measure its degree of corruption. While we have land to labour then, let us never wish to see our citizens occupied at a work-bench, or twirling a distaff. Carpenters, masons, smiths, are wanting in husbandry: but, for the general operations of manufacture, let our work-shops remain in Europe. It is better to carry provisions and materials to workmen there, than bring them to the provisions and materials, and with them their manners and principles. The loss by the transportation of commodities across the Atlantic will be made up in happiness and permanence of government. The mobs of great cities add just so much to the support of pure government, as sores do to the strength of the human body. It is the manners and spirit of a people which preserve a republic in vigour. A degeneracy in these is a canker which soon eats to the heart of its laws and constitution. ◆

QUESTIONS

1. Does Jefferson think that the United States should encourage manufacturing or agriculture?

2. What relevant difference is there between the European and the American contexts that leads Jefferson to his recommendation?

3. What virtues does Jefferson think that agriculture helps develop in a people?

THAT ARISTOCRACY MAY BE ENGENDERED BY MANUFACTURES FROM *DEMOCRACY IN AMERICA*

Alexis de Tocqueville (1805–1859)

I have shown that democracy is favourable to the growth of manufactures, and that it increases without limit the numbers of the manufacturing classes: we shall now see by what sideroad manufacturers may possibly in their turn bring men back to aristocracy. It is acknowledged that when a workman is engaged every day upon the same detail, the whole commodity is produced with greater ease, promptitude, and economy. It is likewise acknowledged that the cost of the production of manufactured goods is diminished by the extent of the establishment in which they are made, and by the amount of capital employed or of credit. These truths had long been imperfectly discerned, but in our time they have been demonstrated. They have been already applied to many very important kinds of manufactures, and the humblest will gradually be governed by them. I know of nothing in politics which deserves to fix the attention of the legislator more closely than these two new axioms of the science of manufactures.

When a workman is unceasingly and exclusively engaged in the fabrication of one thing, he ultimately does his work with singular dexterity; but at the same time he loses the general faculty of applying his mind to the direction of the work. He every day becomes more adroit and less industrious; so that it may be said of him, that in proportion as the workman improves the man is degraded. What can be expected of a man who has spent twenty years of his life in making heads for pins? and to what can that mighty human intelligence, which has so often stirred the world, be applied to him, except it be to investigate the best method of making pins' heads? When a workman has spent a considerable portion of his existence in this manner, his thoughts are for ever set upon the object of his daily toil; his body has contracted certain fixed habits, which it can never shake off: in a word, he no longer belongs to himself, but the calling which he has chosen. It is in vain that laws and manners have been at the pains to level all barriers round such a man, and to open to him on every side a thousand different paths to fortune; a theory of manufactures more powerful than manners and laws binds him to a craft, and frequently to a spot, which he cannot leave: it assigns to him a certain place in society, beyond which he cannot go: in the midst of universal movement it has rendered him stationary.

In proportion as the principle of the division of labour is more extensively applied, the workman becomes more weak, more narrow-minded, and more dependent. The art advances, the artisan recedes. On the other hand, in proportion as it becomes more manifest that the productions of manufactures are by so much the cheaper and better as the manufacture is larger and the amount of capital employed more considerable, wealthy and educated men come forward to embark in manufactures which were heretofore abandoned to poor or ignored handicraftsmen. The magnitude of the efforts required, and the importance of the results to be obtained, attract them. Thus at the very time at which the science of manufactures lowers the class of workmen, it raises the class of masters.

Whereas the workman concentrates his faculties more and more upon the study of a single detail, the master surveys a more extensive whole, and the mind of the latter is enlarged in proportion as that of the former is narrowed. In a short time the one will require nothing but physical strength without intelligence; the other stands in need of science, and almost of genius, to ensure success. This man resembles more and more the administrator of a vast empire—that man, a brute. The master and the workman have then here no similarity, and their differences increase every day. They are only connected as the two rings at the extremities of a long chain. Each of them fills the station which is made for him, and out of which he does not get: the one is continually, closely, and necessarily dependent upon the other, and seems as much born to obey as that other is to command. What is this but aristocracy?

As the conditions of men constituting the nation become more and more equal, the demand for manufactured commodities becomes more general and more extensive; and the cheapness which places these objects within the reach of slender fortunes becomes a great element of success. Hence there are every day more men of great opulence and education who devote their wealth and knowledge to manufactures; and who seek, by opening large establishments, and by a strict division of labour, to meet the fresh demands which are made on all sides. Thus, in proportion as the mass of the nation turns to democracy, that particular class which is engaged in manufactures becomes more aristocratic. Men grow more alike in the one—more different in the other; and inequality increases in the less numerous class in the same ratio in which it decreases in the community. Hence it would appear, on searching to the bottom, that aristocracy should naturally spring out of the bosom of democracy.

But this kind of aristocracy by no means resembles those kinds which preceded it. It will be observed at once, that as it applies exclusively to manufactures and to some manufacturing callings, it is a monstrous exception in the general aspect of society. The small aristocratic societies which are formed by some manufacturers in the midst of the immense democracy of our age, contain, like the great aristocratic societies of former ages, some men who are very opulent, and a multitude who are wretchedly poor. The poor have few means of escaping from their condition and becoming rich; but the rich are constantly becoming poor, or they give up business when they have realised a fortune. Thus the elements of which the class of the poor is composed are fixed; but the elements of which the class of the rich is composed are not so. To say the truth, though there are rich men, the class of rich men does not exist; for these rich individuals have no feelings or purposes in common, no mutual traditions or mutual hopes; they are therefore members, but no body.

Not only are the rich not compactly united amongst themselves, but there is no real bond between them and the poor. Their relative position is not a permanent one; they are constantly drawn together or separated by their interests. The workman is generally dependent on the master, but not on any particular master; these two men meet in the factory, but know not each other elsewhere; and whilst they come into contact on one point, they stand very wide apart on all others. The manufacturer asks nothing of the workman but his labour; the workman expects nothing from him but his wages. The one contracts no obligation to protect, nor the other to defend; and they are not Permanently connected either by habit or by duty. The aristocracy created by business rarely settles in the midst of the manufacturing population which it directs: the object is not to govern that population, but to use it. An aristocracy thus constituted can have no great hold upon these whom it employs; and even if it succeed in retaining them at one moment, they escape the next: it knows not how to will, and it cannot act. The territorial aristocracy of former ages was either bound by law, or thought itself bound by usage, to come to the relief of its serving-men, and to succor their distresses. But the manufacturing aristocracy of our age first impoverishes and debases the men who serve it, and then abandons them to be supported by the charity of the public.

This is a natural consequence of what has been said before. Between the workman and the master there are frequent relations, but no real partnership.

I am of opinion, upon the whole, that the manufacturing aristocracy which is growing up under our eyes, is one of the harshest which ever existed in the world; but at the same time it is one of the most confined and least dangerous. Nevertheless the friends of democracy should keep their eyes anxiously fixed in this direction; for if ever a permanent inequality of conditions and aristocracy again penetrate into the world, it may be predicted that this is the channel by which they will enter. ♦

QUESTIONS

1. According to de Tocqueville, what effects on workers does the division of labor have when coupled with industrialization?

2. What does de Tocquevile mean by a manufacturing, rather than a territorial, aristocracy?

3. Why might a manufacturing aristocracy prove to be the harsher of the two?

ALIENATED LABOR

Karl Marx (1818–1883)

We began with the premises of political economy. Accepting its terminology and its laws, we presupposed private property, the separation of labor, capital, and land; and of wages, profit and rent; the division of labor, competition, the concept of exchange-value: From political economy itself and in its own terms, we showed how the worker sinks to the level of a commodity, and indeed the most wretched of all commodities, since the harder he labors and the more he produces, the more miserable he becomes. We saw also that competition inevitably results in the accumulation of capital in a few hands, and hence the restoration of monopoly in a more terrible form; and finally, that the distinction between capitalist and landlord—like the difference between farm laborer and factory worker—melts away; and the whole of society divides basically into two classes: property owners and propertyless workers.

Political economy begins with the fact of private property without in any way accounting for that fact. Instead, it takes the material processes of private property as they actually occur, presents these processes in general, abstract formulas, and then offers these formulas as laws. It does not comprehend these laws, that is, it fails to show how they arise out of the nature of private property. Political economy tells us nothing about the source of the distinction of labor from capital, or of capital from land. When, for example, economists define the relationship of wages to profit, they take the interests of capitalists as the basis; in other words, they take for granted what they should explain. Similarly, competition is accounted for by external circumstances. Political economy never tells us whether these external and seemingly accidental circumstances are perhaps a necessary development. To economists, exchange itself seems an accidental fact. The only moving forces that political economy recognizes are human greed and the war among the greedy—competition.

Precisely because political economy fails to grasp the interconnections within the system, it was possible to counterpose the doctrine of competition to the doctrine of monopoly, the doctrine of freedom of crafts to that of the guilds, the doctrine of the division of landed property to that of the great estates; because competition, freedom of crafts and the division of landed property were seen merely as chance developments brought about by contrivance and force, rather than as the necessary, inevitable and natural consequences of monopoly, the guild system, and feudal property.

Thus we now have to understand the essential connection between private property, greed, the separation of labor, capital and land, exchange and competition, value and the devaluation of men, monopoly and competition—between this whole system of alienation and the money system.

Let us begin our explanation not as the economist does, with some legendary primordial situation, which clarifies nothing, but merely removes the question to a gray and nebulous distance. The economist takes for granted what remains to be demonstrated, namely, the necessary relationship between two things—between, for example, division of labor and exchange. In the same way theology explains the origin of evil by the fall of man, that is, it takes as a premise what it should explain.

We shall begin with a contemporary economic fact. The worker becomes all the poorer the more wealth he produces, the more his production increases in power and volume. The worker becomes an ever cheaper commodity the more commodities he creates. As the world of things increases in value, the human world becomes devalued. For labor not only produces commodities; it makes a commodity of the work process itself, as well as of the worker—and indeed at the same rate as it produces goods.

This means simply that the object produced by man's labor—its product—now confronts him in the shape of an alien thing, a power independent of the producer. The product of labor is labor given embodiment in a material form; this product is the objectification of labor. The performance of work is thus at the same time its objectification. In the sphere of political economy, the performance of work appears as a material loss, a departure from reality for the worker; objectification appears both as deprivation of the object and enslavement to it; and appropriation of the product by others as alienation.

The reduction of labor to a mere commodity—in short, the dehumanization of work— goes so far that the worker is reduced to the point of starving to death. So remote from life has work become that the worker is robbed of the real things essential not only for his existence but for his work. Indeed, work itself becomes something which he can obtain only with the greatest difficulty and at intervals. And so much does appropriation of his product by others appear as alienation that the more things the worker produces, the fewer can he possess and the more he falls under the domination of the wealth he produces but cannot enjoy—capital.

All these consequences flow from the fact that the worker is related to the product of his labor as to an alien thing. From this premise it is clear that the more the worker exerts himself, the more powerful becomes the world of things which he creates and which confront him as alien objects; hence the poorer he becomes in his inner life, and the less belongs to him as his own. It is the same with religion. The more man puts into God, the less he retains in himself. The worker puts his life into the things he makes; and his life then belongs to him no more, but to the product of his labor. The greater the worker's activity, therefore, the more pointless his life becomes. Whatever the product of his labor, it is no longer his own. Therefore, the greater this product, the more he is diminished. The alienation of the worker from his product means not only that this labor becomes an impersonal object and takes on its own existence, but that it exists outside himself, independently, and alien to him, and that it opposes itself to him as an autonomous power. The life which he has conferred on the object confronts him in the end as a hostile and alien force.

Let us now look more closely at the phenomenon of objectification and its result for the worker: alienation and, in effect, divorce from the product of his labor. To understand this, we must realize that the worker can create nothing without nature, without the sensuous, external world which provides the raw material for his labor. But just as nature provides labor with means of existence in the sense of furnishing raw material which labor processes, so also does it provide means for the worker's physical subsistence. Thus the more the worker by his labor appropriates the external, sensuous world of nature, the more he deprives himself of the means of life in two respects: first, that the sensuous external world becomes progressively detached from him as the medium necessary to his labor; and secondly, that nature becomes increasingly remote from him as the medium through which he gains his physical subsistence.

In both respects, therefore, the worker becomes a slave of things; first, in that labor itself is something he obtains—that is, he gets work; and secondly, in that he obtains thereby the physical means of subsistence. Thus, things enable him to exist, first as a worker, and secondly, as one in bondage to physical objects. The culmination of this process of enslavement is that only as a worker can he maintain himself in his bondage and only as a bondsman to things can he find work.

In the laws of political economy, the alienation of the worker from his product is expressed as follows: the more the worker produces, the less he has to consume; the more value he creates, the more valueless, the more unworthy he becomes; the better formed is his product, the more deformed becomes the worker; the more civilized his product, the more brutalized becomes the worker; the mightier the work, the more powerless the worker; the more ingenious the work, the duller becomes the worker and the more he becomes nature's bondsman.

Political economy conceals the alienation in labor by avoiding any mention of the evil effects of work, on those who work. Thus, whereas labor produces miracles for the rich, for the worker it produces destitution. Labor produces palaces, but for the worker, hovels. It produces beauty, but it cripples the worker. It replaces labor by machines, but how does it treat the worker? By throwing some workers back into a barbarous kind of work, and by turning the rest into machines. It produces intelligence, but for the worker, stupidity and cretinism.

Fundamentally, the relationship of labor to the product of labor is the relationship of the worker to the object of his production. The relationship of property owners to the objects of production and to production itself is only a consequence of this primary relationship, and simply confirms it. We shall consider this other aspect later. When we ask, then, what is the essential relationship of labor, we are concerned with the relationship of the worker to production.

Thus far we have considered only one aspect of the alienation of the worker, namely, his relationship to the product of his labor. But his estrangement is manifest not only in the result, but throughout the work process—within the productive activity itself. How could the worker stand in an alien relationship to the product of his activity if he were not alienated in the very act of production? The product after all is but the résumé of his activity, of production. Hence if the product of labor is alienation, production itself must be active alienation—the alienation of activity, the activity of alienation. The alienation of the product of labor merely sums up the alienation in the work process itself.

What then do we mean by the alienation of labor? First, that the work he performs is extraneous to the worker, that is, it is not personal to him, is not part of his nature; therefore he does not fulfill himself in work, but actually denies himself; feels miserable rather than content, cannot freely develop his physical and mental powers, but instead becomes physically exhausted and mentally debased. Only while not working can the worker be himself; for while at work he experiences himself as a stranger. Therefore only during leisure hours does he feel at home, while at work he feels homeless. His labor is not voluntary, but coerced, forced labor. It satisfies no spontaneous creative urge, but is only a means for the satisfaction of wants which have nothing to do with work. Its alien character therefore is revealed by the fact that when no physical or other compulsion exists, work is avoided like the plague. Extraneous labor, labor in which man alienates himself, is a labor of self-sacrifice, of mortification. Finally, the alienated character of work for the worker is shown by the fact that the work he does is not his own but another's, and that at work he belongs not to himself, but to another. Just as in religion the spontaneous activity of human imagination, of the human brain and heart, is seen as a force from outside the individual reacting upon him as the alien activity of gods or devils, so the worker's labor is no more his own spontaneous activity; but is something impersonal, inhuman and belonging to another. Through his work the laborer loses his identity.

As a result, man—the worker—feels freely active only in his animal functions—eating, drinking, procreating, or at most in his dwelling and personal adornment—while in his human and social functions he is reduced to an animal. The animal becomes human, and the human becomes animal. Certainly eating, drinking and procreating are also genuinely human functions; but abstractly considered, apart from all other human activities and regarded as ultimate ends in themselves, they are merely animal functions.

We have considered the alienation of practical human activity or labor from two aspects. First, the relationship of the worker to the product of labor as an alien object which dominates him. This relationship implies at the same time a relationship to the sensuous external world of nature as an alien and hostile world. Second, the relationship of labor to the act of production within the work process. This is the relationship of the worker to his own activity as something alien, and not belonging to him, it is activity as misery, strength as weakness, creation as emasculation; it is the worker's own physical and mental energy, his personal life (for what is life but activity?) as an activity which is turned against himself, which neither depends on nor belongs to him. Here we have self-alienation as opposed to alienation from things.

And now we see that yet a third aspect of alienated labor can be deduced from the two already considered. For man is a creature of his species [*Gattungswesen*] not only because in practice and in theory he adopts mankind as the object of his creation—indeed his field is the whole of nature—but also because within himself he, one man, represents the whole of mankind and therefore he is a universal and a free being.

The life of the species, for man as for animals, has its physical basis in the fact that man, like the animals, lives on nature; and since man is more universal than animals, so too the realm of nature on which he lives is more universal. Just as plants, animals, stones, the air, light, etc. theoretically form a part of human consciousness, as subjects for natural science and art, providing man with intellectual and spiritual nourishment from the nonhuman world—nourishment which he must first prepare and transform before he can enjoy and absorb it—so too this non-human world is a practical part of human life and activity, since man also subsists physically on nature's products in the form of food, heat, clothing, shelter, etc. The universality of man in practice is seen in the universality which makes the whole of nature conceivable as man's inorganic body, since

nature is first, his direct means of existence, and second, the raw material, the field, the instrument of his vital activity. Nature is man's inorganic body, that is, nature apart from the human body itself. To say that man lives on nature means that nature is his body with which he must remain in constant and vital contact in order not to die. And to say that man's physical and spiritual life is linked to nature is simply an expression of the interdependence of all natural forces, for man himself is part of nature.

Just as alienated labor separates man from nature and from himself—his own active functions and life activity—so too it alienates him from the species, from other men. It degrades all the life of the species and makes some cold and abstract notion of individual life and toil into the goal of the entire species, whose common life also then becomes abstract and alienated.

What happens in the end is that man regards his labor—his life-activity, his productive life—merely as a means of satisfying his drive for physical existence. Yet productive life is the real life of the species. We live in order to create more living things. The whole character of a species is evident in its particular type of life-activity; and free, conscious activity is the generic character of human beings. But alienated labor reduces this area of productive life to a mere means of existence.

Among animals there is no question of regarding one part of life as cut off from the rest; the animal is one with its life-activity. Man, on the other hand, makes his life-activity the object of his conscious will; and this is what distinguishes him from animals. It is because of this free, conscious activity that he is a creature of his species. Or perhaps it is because he is a creature of his species that he is a conscious being, that he is able to direct his life-activity and that he treats his own life as subject matter and as an object of his own determination. Alienated labor reverses this relationship: man, the self-conscious being, turns his chief activity—labor, which should express his profound essence—into a mere means of physical existence.

In manipulating inorganic nature and creating an objective world by his practical activity, man confirms himself as a conscious creature of his species, that is, as a member of his whole species, a being who regards the whole of mankind as involved in himself, and himself as part of mankind. Admittedly animals also produce, building, as do bees, ants or beavers, their nests or dens. But animals produce only for their own immediate needs or for those of their young. Animal production is limited, while man's production is universal. The animal produces only under compulsion of direct physical need, while man produces even when free from physical need, and only truly produces or creates when truly free from such need. Animals produce or reproduce only themselves, while man reproduces the whole of nature. Whatever animals produce—nests or food—is only for their own bodies; but man's creations supply the needs of many species. And whereas animals construct only in accordance with the standards and needs of their kind, man designs and produces in accordance with the standards of all known species and can apply the standards appropriate to the subject. Man therefore designs in accordance with the laws of beauty.

Thus it is precisely in shaping the objective world that man really proves himself as a creature of his species; for in this handiwork resides his active species-life. By means of man's productivity, nature appears to him as his work and his reality. The true object of man's labor therefore is the objectification of man's species-life—his profound essence; for in his labor man duplicates himself not merely intellectually, in consciousness, but also actively, in reality; and in the world that he has made man contemplates his own image. When, therefore, alienated labor tears away from man the object of his production, it snatches from him his species—life—the essence of his being—and transforms his advantage over animals into a disadvantage, insofar as his inorganic body, nature, is withdrawn from him.

Hence, in degrading labor—which should be man's free, spontaneous activity—to a mere means of physical subsistence, alienated labor degrades man's essential life to a mere means to an end. The awareness which man should have of his relationship to the rest of mankind is reduced to a state of detachment in which he and his fellows become simply unfeeling objects. Thus alienated labor turns man's essential humanity into a nonhuman property. It estranges man from his own human body, and estranges him from nature and from his own spiritual essence—his human being.

An immediate consequence of man's estrangement from the product of his labor is man's estrangement from man. When man confronts himself, he confronts other men. What characterizes his relationship to his work, to the product of his labor, and to himself also characterizes his relationship to other men, their work, and the products of their labor.

In general, the statement that man is alienated from the larger life of his species means that men are alienated from each other and from human nature. Man's self-estrangement—and indeed all his attitudes to himself—first finds expression in his relationship to other men. Thus in the relationship of alienated labor each man's view of his fellows is determined by the narrow standards and activities of the work place.

We started with an economic fact, the separation of the worker from the means of production. From this fact flows our concept of alienated or estranged labor; and in analyzing this concept, we merely analyzed a fact of political economy.

Let us now see how alienated labor appears in real life. If the product of my labor is alien to me, if it confronts me as an alien power, to whom then does it belong? If my own activity belongs not to me, but is an alien, forced activity, to whom does it then belong? It must belong to a being other than me. Who then is this being?

Is it the gods? In ancient times the major productive effort was evidently in the service of the gods—for example, temple building in Egypt, India, Mexico; and the product of that effort belonged to the gods. But the gods were never the lords of labor. Neither was nature ever man's task-master. What a contradiction it would be if man—as he more and more subjugated nature by this labor, rendering divine miracles superfluous by the wonders of industry—if man were then to renounce his pleasure in producing and his enjoyment of the product merely in order to continue serving the gods.

Hence, the alien being to whom labor and the product of labor belong, in whose service labor is performed and for whose enjoyment the product of labor serves—this being can only be man himself. So, if the product of labor does not belong to the worker, if it confronts him as an alien power, this must mean that it belongs to a man other than the worker. If the worker's activity is a torment to him, it must be a source of enjoyment and pleasure to another man. Neither the gods nor nature but only man himself can be this alien power over men.

Let us consider our earlier statement that man's relation to himself first becomes objectified, embodied and real through his relation to other men. Therefore, if he is related to the product of his objectified labor as to an alien, hostile, powerful and independent object, then he is related in such a way that someone else is master of this object—someone who is alien, hostile, powerful and independent of him. If his own activity is not free, then he is related to it as an activity in the service, and under the domination, coercion and yoke, of another man.

The alienation of man from himself and from nature appears in his relationship with other men. Thus religious self-alienation necessarily appears in the relationship between laymen and priest—or—since we are here dealing with the spiritual world—between laymen and intercessor. In the everyday, practical world, however, self-alienation manifests itself only through real, practical relationships between men. The medium through which alienation occurs is itself a practical one. As alienated laborer, man not only establishes a certain relationship to the object and process of production as to alien and hostile powers; he also fixes the relationship of other men to his production and to his product; and the relationship between himself and other men. Just as he turns his own production into a real loss, a punishment, and his own product into something not belonging to him; so he brings about the domination of the non-producer over production and its product. In becoming alienated from his own activity, he surrenders power over the activity to a stranger.

So far we have considered this alienated relationship only from the worker's standpoint. Later we shall also consider it from the standpoint of the non-worker, since through the process of alienating his labor the worker brings forth another man who stands outside the work process. The relationship of the worker to work also determines the relationship of the capitalist—or whatever one chooses to call the master of labor—to work. Private property thus is essentially the result, the necessary consequences of alienated labor and of the extraneous relationship of the worker to nature and to himself. Hence private property results from the phenomenon of alienated labor—that is, alienated labor, alienated life and alienated man.

We took the concept of alienated labor and alienated life from political economy and from an analysis of the movement of private property. But analysis of this movement shows that although private property appears to be the source and cause of labor's alienation, it is really the consequence—just as the gods are originally not the cause but the effect of man's intellectual confusion. Later on, however, this relationship becomes reciprocal.

Only at the final stage of the development of private property is its secret revealed, namely, that on the one hand it is the product of alienated labor, and on the other hand it is the means by which labor becomes estranged, and by which the estrangement is perpetuated.

This development illuminates several unresolved conflicts. Political economy starts with labor as the real soul of production, yet attributes nothing to labor and everything to private property. Faced with this contradiction, Proudhon decided in favor of labor and against private property. We suggest, however, that this apparent contradiction is really a contradiction within alienated labor itself, and that political economy has merely formulated the laws of alienated labor.

We also suggest that wages and private property are identical: when the product or object of labor pays for labor itself, wages are only a necessary consequence of labor's alienation. In the wage system labor does not appear as an end in itself but as the servant of wages. We shall develop this point later on. Meanwhile, what are the consequences?

An enforced rise in wages—disregarding all other difficulties, especially the fact that such an anomaly could only be maintained by force—would therefore be nothing but a better payment of slaves and would not restore, either for the worker or for work, human significance and dignity. Indeed, even the equality of wages demanded by Proudhon would only transform the relationship of the present-day worker to his labor into the relationship of all men to labor. Society then would be conceived as an abstract capitalist. Wages are an immediate consequence of the alienation of labor, and alienated labor is the immediate cause of private property. The downfall of one means the downfall of the other.

From the relationship of alienated labor to private property it also follows that the emancipation of society from private property and hence from servitude takes the political form of the emancipation of the workers. This is not because the emancipation of workers alone is at stake, but because their liberation means the emancipation of all humanity. All human servitude is involved in the relationship of the worker to production, and all forms of servitude are only modifications and consequences of this relationship.

Just as we have derived the concept of private property from our analysis of alienated labor, so every category of political economy can be developed with the help of these two factors; and in each of these categories—trade, competition, capital, money—we find only a particular expression of these basic factors.

Before considering this framework, however, let us try to solve two problems. First, we wish to ascertain the general nature of private property as it has resulted from alienated labor and as it relates to truly human, social property. Second, we have taken as a fact and analyzed the alienation of labor. We now ask, how does man come to alienate his labor? How is this estrangement rooted in the nature of human development? We moved toward solving this problem when we transformed our question about the origin of private property into a question about the relation of alienated labor to the course of human development. For in speaking of private property one may think he is dealing with something external to man. But in speaking of labor, one is directly concerned with man himself. This new formulation of the question contains its own solution.

As to the first problem—the general nature of private property and its relation to truly human property—we have divided estranged labor into two elements which condition each other, or rather constitute different expressions of the same relationship. Appropriation appears as alienation, or as estrangement; and estrangement appears to be appropriation, the adoption of one's product by someone else for his own use exclusively.

We have considered one aspect—alienated labor in relation to the worker himself, that is, estranged labor as it affects the working man. And we found that the necessary consequence of this relation was the property relation of the non-worker to the worker and to work. Private property as the concrete, condensed expression of estranged labor includes both relations—the relationship of the worker to work, to his product, and to the non-worker; and the relationship of the non-worker to the worker and to the worker's product.

We saw that to the worker who appropriates nature by his labor, this appropriation appears as alienation, his own spontaneous activity belongs to another man, vitality becomes a sacrifice of life, and production of the object becomes loss of the object to an alien power or person. Let us now consider the relation of this alien man to the worker, to labor, and to the object of labor.

First, it must be noted that everything which for the worker becomes an alienated activity, for the non-worker becomes an alienated state of mind. Second, what for the worker is a highly practical attitude toward production and the product of labor becomes for the non-worker a mere theoretical attitude. Third, the non-worker does everything against the worker which the latter does against himself, but the non-worker does not do against himself what he does against the worker. . . . ◆

QUESTIONS

1. According to Marx, what is the difference between how people live outside their roles as workers versus in their roles as workers?

2. What is the difference between personal property and private property? What is different about the motivation to produce each?

3. According to Marx, what is the sole motivation recognized by economics?

4. What are objectification and alienation of labor?

5. Who alienates labor?

6. What happens to the worker as production increases?

From *The Principles of Scientific Management*

Frederick Taylor (1856–1915)

By far the most important fact which faces the industries of our country, the industries, in fact of the civilized world, is that not only the average worker, but nineteen out of twenty workmen throughout the civilized world firmly believe that it is for their best interests to go slow instead of to go fast. They firmly believe that it is for their interest to give as little work in return for the money that they get as is prac-
10 tical. The reasons for this belief are two-fold, and I do not believe that the workingmen are to blame for holding these fallacious views.

If you will take any set of workmen in your own town and suggest to those men that it would be a good thing for them in their trade if they were to double their output in the coming year, each man turn out twice as much work and become twice as efficient, they would say, "I do not know anything about other people's
20 trades; what you are saying about increasing efficiency being a good thing may be good for other trades, but I know that the only result if you come to our trade would be that half of us would be out of a job before the year was out." That to the average workman is an axiom, it is not a matter subject to debate at all. And even among the average business men of this country that opinion is almost universal. They firmly believe that that would be the result of a
30 great increase in efficiency, and yet directly the opposite is true.

The Effect of Labor Saving Devices

Whenever any labor-saving device of any kind has been introduced into any trade—go back into the history of any trade and see it—even though that labor-saving device may turn out ten, twenty, thirty times that output that was originally turned out by men in that trade, the
40 result has universally been to make work for more men in that trade, not work for less men.

Let me give you one illustration. Let us take one of the staple businesses, the cotton industry. About 1840 the power loom succeeded the old hand loom in the cotton industry. It was invented many years before, somewhere about 1780 or 1790, but it came in very slowly. About 1840 the weavers of Manchester, England, saw that the power loom was coming, and in 1860
50 they knew it would turn out three times the yardage of cloth in a day that the hand loom turned out. And what did they do, these five thousand weavers of Manchester. England, who saw starvation staring them in the face? They broke into the establishments into which those machines were being introduced, they smashed them, they did everything possible to stop the introduction of the power loom. And the same result followed that follows every attempt to interfere with the introduction of
60 any labor-saving device, if it is really a labor-saving device. Instead of stopping the introduction of the power loom, their opposition apparently accelerated it, just as opposition to scientific management all over the country, bitter labor opposition to-day, is accelerating the introduction of it instead of retarding it. History repeats itself in that respect. The power loom came right straight along.

And let us see the result in Manchester.
70 Just what follows in every industry when any labor-saving device is introduced. Less than a century has gone by since 1840. The population of England in that time has now more than doubled. Each man in the cotton industry in Manchester, England, now turns out at a restricted estimate ten yards of cloth for every yard of cloth that was turned out in 1840. In 1840 there were 5,000 weavers in Manchester. Now there are 265,000. Has that
80 thrown men out of work? Has the introduction of labor-saving machinery, which has multiplied the output per man by ten-fold, thrown men out of work?

What is the real meaning of this? All that you have to do is to bring wealth into this world and the world uses it. That is the real meaning. The meaning is that where in 1840 cotton goods were a luxury to be worn only by rich people when they were hardly ever seen on the street, now every man, woman and child all over the world wears cotton goods as a daily necessity.

Nineteen-twentieths of the real wealth of this world is used by the poor people, and not the rich, so that the workingman who sets out as a steady principle to restrict output is merely robbing his own kind. That group of manufacturers which adopts as a permanent principle restriction of output, in order to hold up prices, is robbing the world. The one great thing that marks the improvement of this world is measured by the enormous increase in output of the individuals in this world. There is fully twenty times the output per man now that there was three hundred years ago. That marks the increase in the real wealth of the world; that marks the increase of the happiness of the world, that gives us the opportunity for shorter hours, for better education, for amusement, for art, for music, for everything that is worthwhile in the world—goes right straight back to this increase in the output of the individual. The workingmen of today live better than the king did three hundred years ago. From what does the progress the world has made come? Simply from the increase in the output of the individual all over the world.

THE DEVELOPMENT OF SOLDIERING

The second reason why the workmen of this country and of Europe deliberately restrict output is a very simple one. They, for this reason, are even less to blame than they are for the other. If, for example, you are manufacturing a pen, let us assume for simplicity that a pen can be made by a single man. Let us say that the workman is turning out ten pens per day, and that he is receiving $2.50 a day for his wages. He has a progressive foreman who is up to date, and that foreman goes to the workman and suggests, "Here, John, you are getting $2.50 a day, and you are turning out ten pens. I would suggest that I pay you 25 cents for making that pen." The man takes the job, and through the help of his foreman, through his own ingenuity, through the help of his friends, at the end of the year he finds himself turning out twenty pens instead of ten. He is happy, he is making $5.00, instead of $2.50 a day. His foreman is happy because, with the same room, with the same men he had before, he has doubled the output of his department, and the manufacturer himself is sometimes happy, but not often. Then someone on the board of directors asks to see the payroll, and he finds that we are paying $5.00 a day where other similar mechanics are only getting $2.50, and in no uncertain terms he announces that we must stop ruining the labor market. We cannot pay $5.00 a day when the standard rate of wages is $2.50; how can we hope to compete with surrounding towns? What is the result? Mr. Foreman is sent for, and he is told that he has got to stop ruining the labor market of Cleveland. And the foreman goes back to his workman in sadness, in depression, and tells his workman, "I am sorry, John, but I have got to cut the price down for that pen; I cannot let you earn $5.00 a day; the board of directors has got on to it, and it is ruining the labor market; you ought to be willing to have the price reduced. You cannot earn more than $3.00 or $2.75 a day, and I will cut your wages so that you will only get $3.00 a day." John, of necessity accepts the cut, but he sees to it that he never makes enough pens to get another cut.

CHARACTERISTICS OF THE UNION WORKMAN

There seem to be two divergent opinions about the workmen of this country. One is that a lot of the trade unions' workmen, particularly in this country, have become brutal, have become dominating, careless of any interests but their own, and are a pretty poor lot. And the other opinion which those same trade unionists hold of themselves is that they are pretty close to little gods. Whichever view you may hold of the workingmen of this country, and my personal view of them is that they are a pretty fine lot of fellows; they are just about the same as you and I. But whether you hold the bad opinion or the good opinion, it makes no difference. Whatever the workingmen of this country are or whatever they are not, they are not fools. And all that is necessary is for a workingman to have but one object lesson, like that I have told you, and he soldiers for the rest of his life.

There are a few exceptional employers who treat their workmen differently, but I am talking about the rule of the country. Soldiering is the absolute rule with all workmen who know their business. I am not saying it is for their interest to soldier. You cannot blame them for it. You cannot expect them to be large enough minded men to look at the proper view of the matter. Nor is the man who cuts the wages necessarily to blame. It is simply a misfortune in industry.

THE DEVELOPMENT OF SCIENTIFIC MANAGEMENT

There has been, until comparatively recently, no scheme promulgated by which the evils of rate cutting could be properly avoided, so soldiering has been the rule.

Now the first step that was taken toward the development of those methods of those principles, which rightly or wrongly have come to be known under the name of scientific management, the first step that was taken was taken in an earnest endeavor to remedy the evils of soldiering; an earnest endeavor to make it unnecessary for workmen to be hypocritical in this way to deceive themselves, to deceive their employers, to live day in and day out a life of deceit forced upon them by conditions—the very first step that was taken toward the development was to overcome that evil. I want to emphasize that, because I wish to emphasize the one great fact relating to scientific management, the greatest factor, namely, that scientific management is not a new set of theories that has been tried on by any one at every step. Scientific management at every step has been an evolution, not a theory. In all cases the practice has preceded the theory, not succeeded it. In every case one measure after another has been tried out, until the proper

remedy has been found. That series of proper eliminations, that evolution, is what is called scientific management. Every element of it has had to fight its way against the element that preceded it, and prove itself better or it would not be there tomorrow.

All the men that I know of who are in any way connected with scientific management are ready to abandon any scheme, any theory in favor of anything else that could be found that is better. There is nothing in scientific management that is fixed. There is no one man, or group of men, who has invented scientific management.

What I want to emphasize is that all of the elements of scientific management are an evolution, not an invention. Scientific management is in use in an immense range and variety of industries. Almost every type of industry in this country has scientific management working successfully. I think I can safely say that on the average in those establishments in which scientific management has been introduced, the average workman is turning out double the output he was before. I think that is a conservative statement.

THE WORKMEN: THE CHIEF BENEFICIARIES

Three or four years ago I could have said there were about fifty thousand men working under scientific management, but now I know there are many more. Company after company is coming under it, many of which I know nothing about. Almost universally they are working successfully. This increasing of the output per individual in the trade results, of course, in cheapening the product; it results, therefore, in larger profit usually to the owners of the business; it results also, in many cases, in a lowering of the selling price, although that has not come to the extent it will later. In the end the public gets the good. Without any question, the large good which so far has come from scientific management has come to the worker. To workmen has come, practically right off as soon as scientific management is introduced, an increase in wages amounting from 33 to 100 per cent, and yet that is not the greatest good that comes to the workmen from scientific management. The great good comes from the fact that, under scientific management they look upon their employers as the best friends they have in the world; the suspicious watchfulness which characterizes the old type of management, the semiantagonism, or the complete antagonism between workmen and employers is entirely superseded, and in its place comes genuine friendship between both sides. That is the greatest good that has come under scientific management. As a proof of this in the many businesses in which scientific management has been introduced, I know of not one single strike of workmen working under it after it had been introduced, and only two or three while it was in process of introduction. In this connection I must speak of the fakers, those who have said they can introduce scientific management into a business in six months or a year. That is pure nonsense. There have been many strikes stirred up by that type of man. Not one strike has ever come, and I do not believe ever will come, under scientific management.

WHAT SCIENTIFIC MANAGEMENT IS

What is scientific management? It is no efficiency device, nor is it any group or collection of efficiency devices. Scientific management is no new scheme for paying men, it is no bonus system, no piece-work system, no premium system of payment; it is no new method of figuring costs. It is no one of the various elements by which it is commonly known, by which people refer to it. It is not time study nor man study. It is not the printing of a ton or two of blanks and unloading them on a company and saying, "There is your system, go ahead and use it." Scientific management does not exist and cannot exist until there has been a complete mental revolution on the part of the workmen working under it, as to their duties toward themselves and toward their employers, and a complete mental revolution in the outlook of the employers toward their duties, toward themselves, and toward their workmen. And until

this great mental change takes place, scientific management does not exist. Do you think you can make a great mental revolution in a large group of workmen in a year, or do you think you can make it in a large group of foremen and superintendents in a year? If you do, you are very much mistaken. All of us hold mighty close to our ideas and principles in life and we change very slowly toward the new, and very properly too.

Let me give you an idea of what I mean by this change in mental outlook. If you are manufacturing a hammer or a mallet, into the cost of that mallet goes a certain amount of raw materials, a certain amount of wood and metal. If you will take the cost of the raw materials and then add to it that cost which is frequently called by various names—overhead expense, general expense, indirect expense: that is, the proper share of taxes, insurance, light, heat, salaries of officers and advertising—and you have a sum of money. Subtract that sum from the selling price, and what is left over is called the surplus. It is over this surplus that all of the labor disputes in the past have occurred. The workman naturally wants all he can get. His wages come out of that surplus. The manufacturer wants all he can get in the shape of profits and it is from the division of this surplus that all the labor disputes have come in the past— the equitable division.

The new outlook that comes under scientific management is this: The workmen, after many object lessons, come to see, and the management comes to see that this surplus can be made so great, providing both sides will stop their pulling apart, will stop their fighting and will push as hard as they can to get as cheap an output as possible, that there is no occasion to quarrel. Each side can get more than ever before. The acknowledgment of this fact represents a complete mental revolution.

INTELLIGENT OLD-STYLE MANAGEMENT

There is one more illustration of the new and great change which comes under scientific management. I can make it clearer, perhaps, by contrasting it with what I look upon as the best of the older types of management. If you have a company employing five hundred or a thousand men, you will have in that company perhaps fifteen different trades. The workmen in those trades have learned absolutely all that they know, not from books, not by being taught, but they have learned it traditionally. It has been handed down to them, not even by word of mouth in many cases, but by seeing what other men do. One man stands alongside of another man and imitates him. That is the way the trades are handed down, and my impression is that trades are now picked just as they were in the Middle Ages.

The manufacturer, the manager or the foreman who knows his business realizes that his chief function as a manager—I am talking now of the old-fashioned manager—ought to be to get the true initiative of his workman. He wants the initiative of the workman, their hard work, their good will, their ingenuity, their determination to do all they can for the benefit of his firm. If he knows anything about human nature, if he has thought over the problems, he must realize that in order to get the initiative of his workman, in order to modify their soldiering, he must do something more for his men than other employers are doing for their men under similar circumstances. The wise manager, under the old type of management, deliberately sets out to do something better for his workmen than his competitors are doing, better than he himself has ever done before. It takes a good while for the workmen to stop (being suspicious) . . . but if the manager keeps at them for a sufficiently long time he will get the confidence of the men, and when he does workmen of all kinds will respond by giving a great increase in output. When he sets out to do better for his men than other people do for theirs, the workmen respond liberally when that time comes. I refer to this case as being the highest type of management, the case in which the managers deliberately set out to do something better for their workmen than other people are doing, and to give them a special incentive of some kind, to which the workmen respond by giving a share at least of their initiative.

What Scientific Management Will Do

I am going to prove to you that even that type of management has not a ghost of a chance in competition with the principles of scientific management. Why? In the first place under scientific management, the initiative of the workmen, their hard work, their good will, their best endeavors are obtained with absolute regularity. There are cases all the time where men will soldier, but they become the exception, as a rule, and they give their true initiative under scientific management. That is the least of the two sources of gain. The greatest source of gain under scientific management comes from the new and almost unheard-of duties and burdens which are voluntarily assumed, not by the workmen, but by the men on the management side. These are the things which make scientific management a success. These new duties, these new burdens, undertaken by the management have rightly or wrongly been divided into four groups, and have been called the principles of scientific management.

The first of the great principles of scientific management, the first of the new burdens which are voluntarily undertaken by those on the management side, is the deliberate gathering together of the great mass of traditional knowledge which, in the past has been in the heads of the workmen, recording it, tabulating it, reducing it in most cases to rules, laws, and in many cases to mathematical formulae, which, with these new laws, are applied to the cooperation of the management to the work of the workmen. This results in an immense increase in the output, we may say, of the two. The gathering in of this great mass of traditional knowledge, which is done by the means of motion study, time study, can be truly called the science.

Let me make a prediction. I have before me the first book, so far as I know, that has been published on motion study and on time study. That is, the motion study and time study of the cement and concrete trades. It contains everything relating to concrete work. It is of about seven hundred pages, and embodies the motions of men, the time and the best way of doing that sort of work. It is the first case in which a trade has been reduced to the same condition that engineering data of all kinds have been reduced, and it is this sort of data that is bound to sweep the world.

I have before me something which has been gathering for about fourteen years, the time or motion study of the machine shop. It will take probably four or five years more before the first book will be ready to publish on that subject. There is a collection of sixty or seventy thousand elements affecting machine shop work. After a few years, say three, four or five years more, some one will be ready to publish the first book giving the laws of the movements of men in the machine shop—all the laws, not only a few of them. Let me predict, just as sure as the sun shines, that is going to come in every trade. Why? Because it pays, for no other reason. That results in doubling the output in any shop. Any device which results in an increased output is bound to come in spite of all opposition, whether we want it or not. It comes automatically.

THE SELECTION OF THE WORKMAN

The next of four principles of scientific management is the scientific selection of the workman, and then his progressive development. It becomes the duty under scientific management, of not one, but of a group of men on the management side, to deliberately study the workmen who are under them; study them in the most careful, thorough and painstaking way, and not just leave it to the poor overworked foreman to go out and say, "Come on, what do you want? If you are cheap enough I will give you a trial."

That is the old way. The new way is to take a great deal of trouble in selecting the workmen. The selection proceeds year after year. And it becomes the duty of those engaged in scientific management to know something about the workmen under them. It becomes their duty to set out deliberately to train the workmen in their employ to be able to do a better and still better class of work than ever before, and to then pay them higher wages than ever before. This deliberate selection of the workmen is the second of the great duties that devolve on the management under scientific management.

BRINGING TOGETHER THE SCIENCE AND THE MAN

The third principle is the bringing together of this science of which I have spoken and the trained workmen. I say bringing because they don't come together unless some one brings them. Select and train your workmen all you may, but unless there is some one who will make the men and the science come together, they will stay apart. The "make" involves a great many elements. They are not all disagreeable elements. The most important and largest way of "making" is to do something nice for the man whom you wish to make come together with the science. Offer him a plum, something that is worth while. There are many plums offered to those who come under scientific management—better treatment, more kindly treatment, more consideration for their wishes, and an opportunity for them to express their wants freely. That is one side of the "make." An equally important side is, whenever a man will not do what he ought, to either make him do it or stop it. If he will not do it let him get out. I am not talking of any mollycoddle. Let me disabuse your minds of any opinion that scientific management is a mollycoddle scheme.

I have a great many union friends. I find they look with especial bitterness on this word "make." They have been used to doing the "making" in the past. That is the attitude of the trade unions, and it softens matters greatly when you can tell them the facts, namely, that in our making the science and the men come together, nine-tenths of our trouble comes with the men on the management side in making them do their new duties. I am speaking of those who have been trying to change from the old system to the new. Nine-tenths of our troubles come in trying to make the men on the management side do what they ought to do, to make them do the new duties, and take on these new burdens, and give up their old duties. That softens this word "make."

THE PRINCIPLE OF THE DIVISION OF WORK

The fourth principle is the plainest of all. It involves a complete redivision of the work of the establishment. Under the old scheme of management, almost all of the work was done by the workmen. Under the new, the work of the establishment is divided into two large parts. All of that work which formerly was done by the workmen alone is divided into two large sections, and one of those sections is handed over to the management. They do a whole division of the work formerly done by the workmen. It is this real cooperation, this genuine division of the work between the two sides, more than any other element which accounts for the fact that there never will be strikes under scientific management. When the workman realizes that there is hardly a thing he does, that does not have to be preceded by some act of preparation on the part of the management, and when that workman realizes when the management falls down and does not do its part, that he is not only entitled to a kick, but that he can register that kick in the most forcible possible way, he cannot quarrel with the men over him. It is team work. There are more complaints made every day on the part of the workmen that the men on the management side fail to do their duties, than are made by the management that the men fail. Every one of the complaints of the men have to be heeded, just as much as the complaints from the management that the workmen do not do their share. That is characteristic of scientific management. It represents a democracy, cooperation, a genuine division of work which never existed before in this world. ♦

QUESTIONS

1. What are the principles of scientific management?

2. Does Taylor think workers are correct to fear increased productivity?

3. How do workers resist efforts to increase productivity?

From *My Life and Work*

Henry Ford (1863–1947)

If a device would save in time just 10 per cent. or increase results 10 per cent., then its absence is always a 10 percent. tax. If the time of a person is worth fifty cents an hour, a 10 per cent. saving is worth five cents an hour. If the owner of a skyscraper could increase his income 10 per cent., he would willingly pay half the increase just to know how. The reason why he owns a skyscraper is that science has proved that certain materials, used in a given way, can save space and increase rental incomes. A building thirty stories high needs no more ground space than one five stories high. Getting along with the old-style architecture costs the five-story man the income of twenty-five floors. Save ten steps a day for each of twelve thousand employees and you will have saved fifty miles of wasted motion and misspent energy.

Those are the principles on which the production of my plant was built up. They all come practically as of course. In the beginning we tried to get machinists. As the necessity for production increased it became apparent not only that enough machinists were not to be had, but also that skilled men were not necessary in production, and out of this grew a principle that I later want to present in full.

It is self-evident that a majority of the people in the world are not mentally—even if they are physically—capable of making a good living. That is, they are not capable of furnishing with their own hands a sufficient quantity of the goods which this world needs to be able to exchange their unaided product for the goods which they need. I have heard it said, in fact I believe it is quite a current thought, that we have taken skill out of work. We have not. We have put in skill. We have put a higher skill into planning, management, and tool building, and the results of that skill are enjoyed by the man who is not skilled. This I shall later enlarge on.

We have to recognize the unevenness in human mental equipments. If every job in our place required skill the place would never have existed. Sufficiently skilled men to the number needed could not have been trained in a hundred years. A million men working by hand could not even approximate our present daily output. No one could manage a million men. But more important than that, the product of the unaided hands of those million men could not be sold at the price in consonance with buying power. And even if it were possible to imagine such an aggregation and imagine its management and correlation, just think of the area that it would have to occupy! How many of the men would be engaged, not in producing, but in merely carrying from place to place what the other men had produced? I cannot see how under such conditions the men could possibly be paid more than ten or twenty cents a day—for of course it is not the employer who pays wages. He only handles the money. It is the product that pays the wages and it is the management that arranges the production so that the product may pay the wages.

The more economical methods of production did not begin all at once. They began gradually—just as we began gradually to make our own parts. "Model T" was the first motor that we made ourselves. The great economies began in assembling and then extended to other sections so that, while today we have skilled mechanics in plenty, they do not produce automobiles—they make it easy for others to produce them. Our skilled men are the tool makers, the experimental workmen, the machinists, and the pattern makers. They are as good as any men in the world—so good, indeed, that they should not be wasted in doing that which the machines they contrive can do better. The rank and file of men come to us unskilled; they learn their jobs within a few hours or a few days. If they do not learn within that time they will never be of any use to us. These men are, many of them, foreigners, and all that is required before they are taken on is that they should be potentially able to do enough work to pay the overhead charges on the floor space they occupy. They do not have to be able-bodied men. We have jobs that require great physical strength—although they are rapidly lessening; we have other jobs that require no strength whatsoever—jobs which, as far as strength is concerned, might be attended to by a child of three.

It is not possible, without going deeply into technical processes, to present the whole development of manufacturing, step by step, in the order in which each thing came about. I do not know that this could be done, because something has been happening nearly every day and nobody can keep track. Take at random a number of the changes. From them it is possible not only to gain some idea of what will happen when this world is put on a production basis but also to see how much more we pay for things than we ought to, and how much lower wages are than they ought to be, and what a vast field remains to be explored. The Ford Company is only a little way along on the journey.

A Ford car contains about five thousand parts—that is counting screws, nuts, and all. Some of the parts are fairly bulky and others are almost the size of watch parts. In our first assembling we simply started to put a car together at a spot on the floor and workmen brought to it the parts as they were needed in exactly the same way that one builds a house. When we started to make parts it was natural to create a single department of the factory to make that part, but usually one workman performed all of the operations necessary on a small part. The rapid press of production made it necessary to devise plans of production that would avoid having the workers falling over one another. The undirected worker spends more of his time walking about for materials and tools than he does in working; he gets small pay because pedestrianism is not a highly paid line.

The first step forward in assembly came when we began taking the work to the men instead of the men to the work. We now have two general principles in all operations—that a man shall never have to take more than one step, if possibly it can be avoided, and that no man need ever stoop over.

The principles of assembly are these:

1. Place the tools and the men in the sequence of the operation so that each component part shall travel the least possible distance while in the process of finishing.

2. Use work slides or some other form of carrier so that when a workman completes his operation, he drops the part always in the same place—which place must always be the most convenient place to his hand—and if possible have gravity carry the part to the next workman for his operation.

3. Use sliding assembling lines by which the parts to be assembled are delivered at convenient distances.

The net result of the application of these principles is the reduction of the necessity for thought on the part of the worker and the reduction of his movements to a minimum. He does as nearly as possible only one thing with only one movement.

Along about April 1, 1913, we first tried the experiment of an assembly line. We tried it on assembling the fly-wheel magneto. We try everything in a little way first—we will rip out anything once we discover a better way, but we have to know absolutely that the new way is going to be better than the old before we do anything drastic.

I believe that this was the first moving line ever installed. The idea came in a general way from the overhead trolley that the Chicago packers use in dressing beef. We had previously assembled the fly-wheel magneto in the usual method. With one workman doing a complete job he could turn out from thirty-five to forty pieces in a nine-hour day, or about twenty minutes to an assembly. What he did alone was then spread into twenty-nine operations; that cut down the assembly time to thirteen minutes, ten seconds. Then we raised the height of the line eight inches—this was in 1914—and cut the time to seven minutes. Further experimenting with the speed that the work should move at cut the time down to five minutes. In short, the result is this: by the aid of scientific study one man is now able to do somewhat more than four did only a comparatively few years ago. That line established the efficiency of the method and we now use it everywhere. The assembling of the motor, formerly done by one man, is now divided into eighty-four operations—those men do the work that three times their number formerly did. In a short time we tried out the plan on the chassis.

About the best we had done in stationary chassis assembling was an average of twelve hours and twenty-eight minutes per chassis. We tried the experiment of drawing the chassis with a rope and windlass down a line two hundred fifty feet long. Six assemblers travelled with the chassis and picked up the parts from piles placed along the line. This rough experiment reduced the time to five hours fifty minutes per chassis. In the early part of 1914 we elevated the assembly line. We had adopted the policy on "man-high" work; we had one line twenty-six and three quarter inches and another twenty-four and one half inches from the floor—to suit squads of different heights. The waist-high arrangement and a further subdivision of work so that each man had fewer movements cut down the labour time per chassis to one hour thirty-three minutes. Only the chassis was then assembled in the line. The body was placed on in "John R. Street"—the famous street that runs through our Highland Park factories. Now the line assembles the whole car.

It must not be imagined, however, that all this worked out as quickly as it sounds. The speed of the moving work had to be carefully tried out; in the fly-wheel magneto we first had a speed of sixty inches per minute. That was too fast. Then we tried eighteen inches per minute. That was too slow. Finally we settled on forty-four inches per minute. The idea is that a man must not be hurried in his work—he must have every second necessary but not a single unnecessary second. We have worked out speeds for each assembly, for the success of the chassis assembly caused us gradually to overhaul our entire method of manufacturing and to put all assembling in mechanically driven lines. The chassis assembling line, for instance, goes at a pace of six feet per minute; the front axle assembly line goes at one hundred eighty-nine inches per minute. In the chassis assembling are forty-five separate operations or stations. The first men fasten four mud-guard brackets to the chassis frame; the motor arrives on the tenth operation and so on in detail. Some men do only one or two small operations, others do more. The man who places a part does not fasten it—the part may not be fully in place until after several operations later. The man who puts in a bolt does not put on the nut; the man who puts on the nut does not tighten it. On operation number thirty-four the budding motor gets its gasoline; it has previously received lubrication; on operation number forty-four the radiator is filled with water, and on operation number forty-five the car drives out onto John R. Street.

Essentially the same ideas have been applied to the assembling of the motor. In October, 1913, it required nine hours and fifty-four minutes of labour time to assemble one motor; six months later, by the moving assembly method, this time had been reduced to five hours and fifty-six minutes. Every piece of work in the shops moves; it may move on hooks on overhead chains going to assembly in the exact order in which the parts are required; it may travel on a moving platform, or it may go by gravity, but the point is that there is no lifting or trucking of anything other than materials. Materials are brought in on small trucks or trailers operated by cut-down Ford chassis, which are sufficiently mobile and quick to get in and out of any aisle where they may be required to go. No workman has anything to do with moving or lifting anything. That is all in a separate department—the department of transportation.

We started assembling a motor car in a single factory. Then as we began to make parts, we began to departmentalize so that each department would do only one thing. As the factory is now organized each department makes only a single part or assembles a part. A department is a little factory in itself. The part comes into it as raw material or as a casting, goes through the sequence of machines and heat treatments, or whatever may be required, and leaves that department finished. It was only because of transport ease that the departments were grouped together when we started to manufacture. I did not know that such minute divisions would be possible; but as our production grew and departments multiplied, we actually changed from making automobiles to making parts. Then we found that we had made another new discovery, which was that by no means all of the parts had to be made in one factory. It was not really a discovery—it was something in the nature of going around in a circle to my first manufacturing when I bought the motors and probably ninety per cent. of the parts. When we began to make our own parts we practically took for granted that they all had to be made in the one factory—that there was some special virtue in having a single roof over the manufacture of the entire car. We have now developed away from this. If we build any more large factories, it will be only because the making of a single part must be in such tremendous volume as to require a large unit. I hope that in the course of time the big Highland Park plant will be doing only one or two things. The casting has already been taken away from it and has gone to the River Rouge plant. So now we are on our way back to where we started from—excepting that, instead of buying our parts on the outside, we are beginning to make them in our own factories on the outside.

This is a development which holds exceptional consequences, for it means . . . that highly standardized, highly subdivided industry need no longer become concentrated in large plants with all the inconveniences of transportation and housing that hamper large plants. A thousand or five hundred men ought to be enough in a single factory; then there would be no problem of transporting them to work or away from work and there would be no slums or any of the other unnatural ways of living incident to the overcrowding that must take place if the workmen are to live within reasonable distances of a very large plant.

Highland Park now has five hundred departments. Down at our Piquette plant we had only eighteen departments, and formerly at Highland Park we had only one hundred and fifty departments. This illustrates how far we are going in the manufacture of parts.

Hardly a week passes without some improvement being made somewhere in machine or process, and sometimes this is made in defiance of what is called "the best shop practice." I recall that a machine manufacturer was once called into conference on the building of a special machine. The specifications called for an output of two hundred per hour.

"This is a mistake," said the manufacturer, "you mean two hundred a day—no machine can be forced to two hundred an hour."

The company officer sent for the man who had designed the machine and they called his attention to the specification. He said,

"Yes, what about it?"

"It can't be done." said the manufacturer positively, "no machine built will do that—it is out of the question."

"Out of the question!" exclaimed the engineer, "if you will come down to the main floor you will see one doing it; we built one to see if it could be done and now we want more like it."

The factory keeps no record of experiments. The foreman and superintendents remember what has been done. If a certain method has formerly been tried and failed, somebody will remember it—but I am not particularly anxious for the men to remember what someone else has tried to do in the past, for then we might quickly accumulate far too many things that could not be done. That is one of the troubles with extensive records. If you keep on recording all of your failures you will shortly have a list showing that there is nothing left for you to try—whereas it by no means follows because one man has failed in a certain method that another man will not succeed.

They told us we could not cast gray iron by our endless chain method and I believe there is a record of failures. But we are doing it. The man who carried through our work either did not know or paid no attention to the previous figures. Likewise we were told that it was out of the question to pour the hot iron directly from the blast furnace into mould. The usual method is to run the iron into pigs, let them season for a time, and then remelt them for casting. But at the River Rouge plant we are casting directly from cupolas that are filled from the blast furnaces. Then, too, a record of failures—particularly if it is a dignified and well-authenticated record—deters a young man from trying. We get some of our best results from letting fools rush in where angels fear to tread.

None of our men are "experts." We have most unfortunately found it necessary to get rid of a man as soon as he thinks himself an expert—because no one ever considers himself an expert if he really knows his job. A man who knows a job sees so much more to be done than he has done, that he is always pressing forward and never gives up an instant of thought to how good and how efficient he is. Thinking always ahead, thinking always of trying to do more, brings a state of mind in which nothing is impossible. The moment one gets into the "expert" state of mind a great number of things become impossible.

I refuse to recognize that there are impossibilities. I cannot discover that any one knows enough about anything on this earth definitely to say what is and what is not possible. The right kind of experience, the right kind of technical training, ought to enlarge the mind and reduce the number of impossibilities. It unfortunately does nothing of the kind. Most technical training and the average of that which we call experience, provide a record of previous failures and, instead of these failures being taken for what they are worth, they are taken as absolute bars to progress. If some man, calling himself an authority, says that this or that cannot be done, then a horde of unthinking followers start the chorus: "It can't be done."

Take castings. Casting has always been a wasteful process and is so old that it has accumulated many traditions which make improvements extraordinarily difficult to bring about. I believe one authority on moulding declared—before we started our experiments—that any man who said he could reduce costs within half a year wrote himself down as a fraud.

Our foundry used to be much like other foundries. When we cast the first "Model T" cylinders in 1910, everything in the place was done by hand; shovels and wheelbarrows abounded. The work was then either skilled or unskilled; we had moulders and we had labourers. Now we have about five per cent. of thoroughly skilled moulders and core setters, but the remaining 95 per cent. are unskilled, or to put it more accurately, must be skilled in exactly one operation which the most stupid man can learn within two days. The moulding is all done by machinery. Each part which we have to cast has a unit or units of its own—according to the number required in the plan of production. The machinery of the unit is adapted to the single casting; thus the men in the unit each perform a single operation that is always the same. A unit consists of an overhead railway to which at intervals are hung little platforms for the moulds. Without going into technical details, let me say the making of the moulds and the cores, and the packing of the cores, are done with the work in motion on the platforms. The metal is poured at another point as the work moves, and by the time the mould in which the metal has been poured reaches the terminal, it is cool enough to start on its automatic way to cleaning, machining, and assembling. And the platform is moving around for a new load.

Take the development of the piston-rod assembly. Even under the old plan, this operation took only three minutes and did not seem to be one to bother about. There were two benches and twenty-eight men in all; they assembled one hundred seventy-five pistons and rods in a nine-hour day—which means just five seconds over three minutes each. There was no inspection, and many of the piston and rod assemblies came back from the motor assembling line as defective. It is a very simple operation. The workman pushed the pin out of the piston, oiled the pin, slipped the rod in place, put the pin through the rod and piston, tightened one screw, and opened another screw. That was the whole operation. The foreman, examining the operation, could not discover why it should take as much as three minutes. He analyzed the motions with a stop-watch. He found that four hours out of a nine-hour day were spent in walking. The assembler did not go off anywhere, but he had to shift his feet to gather in his materials and to push away his finished piece. In the whole task, each man performed six operations. The foreman devised a new plan; he split the operation into three divisions, put a slide on the bench and three men on each side of it, and an inspector at the end. Instead of one man performing the whole operation, one man then performed only one third of the operation— he performed only as much as he could do without shifting his feet. They cut down the squad from twenty-eight to fourteen men. The former record for twenty-eight men was one hundred seventy-five assemblies a day. Now seven men turn out twenty-six hundred assemblies in eight hours. It is not necessary to calculate the savings there!

Painting the rear axle assembly once gave some trouble. It used to be dipped by hand into a tank of enamel. This required several handlings and the services of two men. Now one man takes care of it all on a special machine, designed and built in the factory. The man now merely hangs the assembly on a moving chain which carries it up over the enamel tank, two levers then thrust thimbles over the ends of the ladle shaft, the paint tank rises six feet, immerses the axle, returns to position, and the axle goes on to the drying oven. The whole cycle of operations now takes just thirteen seconds.

The radiator is a complex affair and soldering it used to be a matter of skill. There are ninety-five tubes in a radiator. Fitting and soldering these tubes in place is by hand a long operation, requiring both skill and patience. Now it is all done by a machine which will make twelve hundred radiator cores in eight hours; they are soldered in place by being carried through a furnace by a conveyor. No tinsmith work and so no skill [is] required.

We used to rivet the crank-case arms to the crank-case, using pneumatic hammers which were supposed to be the latest development. It took six men to hold the hammers and six men to hold the casings, and the din was terrific. Now an automatic press operated by one man, who does nothing else, gets through five times as much work in a day as those twelve men did.

In the Piquette plant the cylinder casting travelled four thousand feet in the course of finishing; now it travels only slightly over three hundred feet.

There is no manual handling of material. There is not a single hand operation. If a machine can be made automatic, it is made automatic. Not a single operation is ever considered as being done in the best or cheapest way. At that, only about ten per cent. of our tools are special; the others are regular machines adjusted to the particular job. And they are placed almost side by side. We put more machinery per square foot of floor space than any other factory in the world—every foot of space not used carries an overhead expense. We want none of that waste. Yet there is all the room needed—no man has too much room and no man has too little room.

Dividing and subdividing operations, keeping the work in motion—those are the keynotes of production. But also it is to be remembered that all the parts are designed so that they can be most easily made. And the saving? Although the comparison is not quite fair, it is startling. If at our present rate of production we employed the same number of men per car that we did when we began in 1903—and those men were only for assembly—we should to-day require a force of more than two hundred thousand. We have less than fifty thousand men on automobile production at our highest point of around four thousand cars a day! ♦

10

QUESTIONS

1. What were Ford's claims about opportunity costs, the application of scientific management principles, and recordkeeping?

2. What did Ford think of the division of labor?

3. What assertion did Ford make about work that "the most stupid man can learn within two days"?

4. Why was the assembly line so important for Ford?

SELECTION FROM: *THE BUSINESS GUIDE*

J. L. Nichols (1851–1895) self-published Naperville, Ill 1893

HOW TO ESTIMATE THE CONTENTS OF A PILE OF GRAIN, POTATOES, HAY OR WOOD

Rule—Put the commodity in the form of a heap. Then multiply the diameter in feet by itself, and then again by height in feet, and divide the result by 4, and you have the approximate contents in bushels.

Example:—How many bushels in a heap of grain 6 feet in diameter and 3 feet high?

Solution: $6 \times 6 \times 3 \div 4 = 27$ bushels. Ans.

From *The House of Mirth*

Edith Wharton (1862–1937)

Look at those spangles, Miss Bart—every one of 'em sewed on crooked."

The tall forewoman, a pinched perpendicular figure, dropped the condemned structure of wire and net on the table at Lily's side, and passed on to the next figure in the line.

There were twenty of them in the workroom, their fagged profiles, under exaggerated hair, bowed in the harsh north light above the utensils of their art; for it was something more than an industry, surely, this creation of ever-varied settings for the face of fortunate womanhood. Their own faces were sallow with the unwholesomeness of hot air and sedentary toil, rather than with any actual signs of want: they were employed in a fashionable millinery establishment, and were fairly well clothed and well paid; but the youngest among them was as dull and colourless as the middle-aged. In the whole work-room there was only one skin beneath which the blood still visibly played; and that now burned with vexation as Miss Bart, under the lash of the forewoman's comment, began to strip the hat-frame of its over-lapping spangles.

To Gerty Farish's hopeful spirit a solution appeared to have been reached when she remembered how beautifully Lily could trim hats. Instances of young lady-milliners establishing themselves under fashionable patronage, and imparting to their "creations" that indefinable touch which the professional hand can never give, had flattered Gerty's visions of the future, and convinced even Lily that her separation from Mrs. Norma Hatch need not reduce her to dependence on her friends.

The parting had occurred a few weeks after Selden's visit, and would have taken place sooner had it not been for the resistance set up in Lily by his ill-starred offer of advice. The sense of being involved in a transaction she would not have cared to examine too closely had soon afterward defined itself in the light of a hint from Mr. Stancy that, if she "saw them through," she would have no reason to be sorry. The implication that such loyalty would meet with a direct reward had hastened her flight, and flung her back, ashamed and penitent, on the broad bosom of Gerty's sympathy. She did not, however, propose to lie there prone, and Gerty's inspiration about the hats at once revived her hopes of profitable activity. Here was, after all, something that her charming listless hands could really do; she had no doubt of their capacity for knotting a ribbon or placing a flower to advantage. And of course only these finishing touches would be expected of her: subordinate fingers, blunt, grey, needle-pricked fingers, would prepare the shapes and stitch the linings, while she presided over the charming little front shop—a shop all white panels, mirrors, and moss-green hangings—where her finished creations, hats, wreaths, aigrettes and the rest, perched on their stands like birds just poising for flight.

But at the very outset of Gerty's campaign this vision of the green-and-white shop had been dispelled. Other young ladies of fashion had been thus "set-up," selling their hats by the mere attraction of a name and the reputed knack of tying a bow; but these privileged beings could command a faith in their powers materially expressed by the readiness to pay their shop-rent and advance a handsome sum for current expenses. Where was Lily to find such support? And even could it have been found, how were the ladies on whose approval she depended to be induced to give her their patronage? Gerty learned that whatever sympathy her friend's case might have excited a few months since had been imperilled, if not lost, by her association with Mrs. Hatch. Once again, Lily had withdrawn from an ambiguous situation in time to save her self-respect, but too late for public vindication. Freddy Van Osburgh was not to marry Mrs. Hatch; he had been rescued at the eleventh hour—some said by the efforts of Gus Trenor and Rosedale—and despatched to Europe with old Ned Van Alstyne; but the risk he had run would always be ascribed to Miss Bart's connivance, and would somehow serve as a summing-up and corroboration of the vague general distrust of her. It was a relief to those who had hung back from her to find themselves thus justified, and they were inclined to insist a little on her connection with the Hatch case in order to show that they had been right.

Gerty's quest, at any rate, brought up against a solid wall of resistance; and even when Carry Fisher, momentarily penitent for her share in the Hatch affair, joined her efforts to Miss Farish's, they met with no better success. Gerty had tried to veil her failure in tender ambiguities; but Carry, always the soul of candour, put the case squarely to her friend.

"I went straight to Judy Trenor; she has fewer prejudices than the others, and besides she's always hated Bertha Dorset. But what *have* you done to her, Lily? At the very first word about giving you a start she flamed out about some money you'd got from Gus; I never knew her so hot before. You know she'll let him do anything but spend money on his friends: the only reason she's decent to me now is that she knows I'm not hard up.—He speculated for you, you say? Well, what's the harm? He had no business to lose. He *didn't* lose? Then what on earth—but I never *could* understand you, Lily!"

The end of it was that, after anxious enquiry and much deliberation, Mrs. Fisher and Gerty, for once oddly united in their effort to help their friend, decided on placing her in the work-room of Mme. Regina's renowned millinery establishment. Even this arrangement was not effected without considerable negotiation, for Mme. Regina had a strong prejudice against untrained assistance, and was induced to yield only by the fact that she owed the patronage of Mrs. Bry and Mrs. Gormer to Carry Fisher's influence. She had been willing from the first to employ Lily in the show-room: as a displayer of hats, a fashionable beauty might be a valuable asset. But to this suggestion Miss Bart opposed a negative which Gerty emphatically supported, while Mrs. Fisher, inwardly unconvinced, but resigned to this latest proof of Lily's unreason, agreed that perhaps in the end it would be more useful that she should learn the trade. To Regina's work-

room Lily was therefore committed by her friends, and there Mrs. Fisher left her with a sigh of relief, while Gerty's watchfulness continued to hover over her at a distance.

Lily had taken up her work early in January: it was now two months later, and she was still being rebuked for her inability to sew spangles on a hat-frame. As she returned to her work she heard a titter pass down the tables. She knew she was an object of criticism and amusement to the other work-women. They were, of course, aware of her history—the exact situation of every girl in the room was known and freely discussed by all the others—but the knowledge did not produce in them any awkward sense of class distinction: it merely explained why her untutored fingers were still blundering over the rudiments of the trade. Lily had no desire that they should recognize any social difference in her; but she had hoped to be received as their equal, and perhaps before long to show herself their superior by a special deftness of touch, and it was humiliating to find that, after two months of drudgery, she still betrayed her lack of early training. Remote was the day when she might aspire to exercise the talents she felt confident of possessing; only experienced workers were entrusted with the delicate art of shaping and trimming the hat, and the forewoman still held her inexorably to the routine of preparatory work.

She began to rip the spangles from the frame, listening absently to the buzz of talk which rose and fell with the coming and going of Miss Haines's active figure. The air was closer than usual, because Miss Haines, who had a cold, had not allowed a window to be opened even during the noon recess; and Lily's head was so heavy with the weight of a sleepless night that the chatter of her companions had the incoherence of a dream.

"I *told* her he'd never look at her again; and he didn't. I wouldn't have, either—I think she acted real mean to him. He took her to the Arion Ball, and had a hack for her both ways. . . . She's taken ten bottles, and her headaches don't seem no better—but she's written a testimonial to say the first bottle cured her, and she got five dollars and her picture in the paper. . . . Mrs. Trenor's hat? The one with the green Paradise?

Here, Miss Haines—it'll be ready right off . . . . That was one of the Trenor girls here yesterday with Mrs. George Dorset. How'd I know? Why, Madam sent for me to alter the flower in that Virot hat—the blue tulle: she's tall and slight, with her hair fuzzed out—a good deal like Mamie Leach, only thinner. . . . "

On and on it flowed, a current of meaningless sound, on which, startlingly enough, a familiar name now and then floated to the surface. It was the strangest part of Lily's strange experience, the hearing of these names, the seeing the fragmentary and distorted image of the world she had lived in reflected in the mirror of the working-girls' minds. She had never before suspected the mixture of insatiable curiosity and contemptuous freedom with which she and her kind were discussed in this underworld of toilers who lived on their vanity and self-indulgence. Every girl in Mme. Regina's workroom knew to whom the headgear in her hands was destined, and had her opinion of its future wearer, and definite knowledge of the latter's place in the social system. That Lily was a star fallen from that sky did not, after the first stir of curiosity had subsided, materially add to their interest in her. She had fallen, she had "gone under" and true to the ideal of their race, they were awed only by success—by the gross tangible image of material achievement. The consciousness of her different point of view merely kept them at a little distance from her, as though she were a foreigner with whom it was an effort to talk.

"Miss Bart, if you can't sew those spangles on more regular I guess you'd better give the hat to Miss Kilroy."

Lily looked down ruefully at her handiwork. The forewoman was right: the sewing on of the spangles was inexcusably bad. What made her so much more clumsy than usual? Was it a growing distaste for her task, or actual physical disability? She felt tired and confused: it was an effort to put her thoughts together. She rose and handed the hat to Miss Kilroy, who took it with a suppressed smile.

"I'm sorry; I'm afraid I am not well," she said to the forewoman.

Miss Haines offered no comment. From the first she had augured ill of Mme. Regina's consenting to include a fashionable apprentice among her workers. In that temple of art no raw beginners were wanted, and Miss Haines would have been more than human had she not taken a certain pleasure in seeing her forebodings confirmed.

"You'd better go back to binding edges," she said drily.

Lily slipped out last among the band of liberated workwomen. She did not care to be mingled in their noisy dispersal: once in the street, she always felt an irresistible return to her old standpoint, an instinctive shrinking from all that was unpolished and promiscuous. In the days—how distant they now seemed!—when she had visited the Girls' Club with Gerty Farish, she had felt an enlightened interest in the working-classes; but that was because she looked down on them from above, from the happy altitude of her grace and her beneficence. Now that she was on a level with them, the point of view was less interesting.

She felt a touch on her arm, and met the penitent eye of Miss Kilroy.

"Miss Bart. I guess you can sew those spangles on as well as I can when you're feeling right. Miss Haines didn't act fair to you."

Lily's colour rose at the unexpected advance: it was a long time since real kindness had looked at her from any eyes but Gerty's.

"Oh, thank you: I'm not particularly well, but Miss Haines was right. I *am* clumsy."

"Well, it's mean work for anybody with a headache." Miss Kilroy paused irresolutely. "You ought to go right home and lay down. Ever try orangeine?"

"Thank you." Lily held out her hand. "It's very kind of you—I mean to go home."

She looked gratefully at Miss Kilroy, but neither knew what more to say. Lily was aware that the other was on the point of offering to go home with her, but she wanted to be alone and silent—even kindness, the sort of kindness that Miss Kilroy could give, would have jarred on her just then.

"Thank you," she repeated as she turned away.

She struck westward through the dreary March twilight, toward the street where her boarding-house stood. She had resolutely refused Gerty's offer of hospitality. Something of her mother's fierce shrinking from observation and sympathy was beginning to develop in her, and the promiscuity of small quarters and close intimacy seemed, on the whole, less endurable than the solitude of a hall bedroom in a house where she could come and go unremarked among other workers. For a while she had been sustained by this desire for privacy and independence; but now, perhaps from increasing physical weariness, the lassitude brought about by hours of unwonted confinement, she was beginning to feel acutely the ugliness and discomfort of her surroundings. The day's task done, she dreaded to return to her narrow room, with its blotched wall-paper and shabby paint; and she hated every step of the walk thither, through the degradation of a New York street in the last stages of decline from fashion to commerce. ◆

QUESTIONS

1. Where did Lily Bart come from and where is she headed?

2. What does Wharton mean by "the degradation of a New York street in the last stages of decline from fashion to commerce"?

3. How does Lily's situation compare to Wharton's image of New York?

ECONOMIC FOOTHOLD
FROM *WOMEN AND THE TRADES*

Elizabeth Beardsley Butler (1854–1932)

Wages, hours, and factory conditions which affect health concern the public well-being too closely to be utterly neglected by a community whose women go out at labor. This much our survey of employments in Pittsburgh makes clear. Bound up in these considerations is the question of workmanship—the processes assigned to women, their skill, and the economic foothold which they have gained.

In interpreting these employments, I have discussed them as parts of the different industries. Yet while I have called them for convenience by the name of their products, as candy making and lamp making, these are not really the women's occupations. A closer analysis shows that very nearly identical processes run through many of these employments. Women are pasting labels not only in canneries, but in paper box, cigar and paint factories. They are tending machines no less in cracker making and cork cutting than in the metal works. Here we have a basis for recapitulating our employments in a way that will afford a fairer index of how far women have actually come into the industrial life of the district as factors in production. They may be grouped according to the nature of their occupations as skilled workers, workers at a handicraft, hand workers at a process which requires speed or dexterity, machine operators, machine tenders, wrappers and labelers, and hand workers at a process which requires no intelligence.

The following table gives the number of workers in each of these groups:[1]

NUMBER OF WOMEN WORKERS IN VARIOUS OCCUPATIONS		
GROUPS		
Kind of Work	*No. of Women*	*Percentage*
Skilled work	139	.8
Handicraft	305	1.9
Hand work requiring dexterity	3641	23.2
Machine operating	4885	31.1
Machine tending	2188	13.9
Wrapping and labeling	2118	13.3
Hand work requiring no dexterity	2475	15.8
	15,651	100.0

The only women in the trades considered who can be called skilled in any true sense are the millinery trimmers and telegraph operators. Both these must serve an apprenticeship until they have learned the routine work of their occupation; and having learned the work they must serve a still longer time to gain mastery of its details. They must have intelligence and an aptitude for what they do; beyond that they must have training.

The group of women who possess a handicraft is also conspicuously small. Makers of hand stogies, expert makers in millinery houses, and fine ironers in laundries, have occupations for which they must spend time in training. They do the whole of the thing. Although speed in execution counts in these occupations as in all others, quality of product is emphasized. The workers must think of the workmanship first, and of the quantity second.

Added together, however, the women of these two groups make less than 3 percent of the 22,185 under consideration in Pittsburgh; and from their work we can scarcely judge of the nature of women's work as a whole. That work is, as a rule, of a nature to require neither strength, endurance, intelligence nor training.

As we take up hand work which in contrast requires speed or dexterity and only that, we find that the percentage of women has jumped to nearly one-fourth of the total. The women in this group are bottling pickles, dipping chocolates, icing cakes, rolling stogies, making bandeaux for hats, shaping sand cores, winding wire, pasting paper boxes, sorting corks. They learn what they have to do sometimes in a week, sometimes in two or three months. In six months they work rapidly; in a year they have often reached their maximum output. They work by hand, it is true, but at the kind of hand work in which they repeat continuously a simple, undiversified motion.

The machine operators are the largest group of all. Many of them run sewing machines by power; they press the treadle and hold the cloth in place. Others cut tin, or bunch stogies, or run ironing machinery or wind coils. As more and more machines have been equipped with power, thus making muscular strength unnecessary, the increasing employment of women has become possible. Even when an additional man is employed to keep the machines in repair, the total outlay for wages and power is less than the total outlay for the wages of hand workers and the material which they use.

To increase the automatic efficiency of the machine so that not an operator but merely a machine tender is necessary, is the next step. Labor cost to the manufacturer is saved not only by the employment of fewer people, but by the payment of lower wages to those who remain. One Pittsburgh paper box factory has reduced its force one-half by the introduction of new covering machines, and by the introduction of still other machines it might reduce its force a third more; yet the output of the factory has steadily increased. The marking machine has dispensed with from one-half to three-fourths of the checkers in four laundries. In the cork factory, new tapering machines are being put in. For each of the old machines, one operator was necessary, but four of the new machines can be tended by one girl. Instances without number from Pittsburgh's industrial experience could be cited affirming how machinery is labor-saving both of human strength and of the numbers of employes. By thus cheapening the cost of the product, it stimulates demand and ultimately results in an actual increase both of machines and employes. But it should also be borne in mind that machinery is wage-saving. Not only fewer people relative to output are employed, but those few are paid the wages, not of skilled, but of unskilled labor.

One woman puts fifty hinges a minute through a machine. Each second a hinge is lifted out and slipped into place, the hand drawn back as the machine moves, another hinge lifted and slipped into place—this for ten hours each working day. Other women spread out a tobacco leaf on the suction plate, put the half made bunch in the leaf, press the treadle and push the rolled stogy aside; spread out another leaf, cut, put the bunch in place, press the treadle and push aside. Still others steady tile paper in a box-covering machine, guide it according to the gauge, replace it when the strip runs out, guide it according to the gauge, and so on. Such work not only requires no thought; it is stupefying. The operative who has become in truth an adjunct of the machine, works with a machine-like precision, and with machine-like absence of thought. Work which demands nothing of the intelligence, costs the intelligence more than work which demands too much.

There are 2000 machine tenders in Pittsburgh. Closely akin to them, and of equal numbers, are the women who wrap and label. They pack crackers, candy, glass, lamps, with quick, machine-taught, unvarying motions, lifting, wrapping, putting in place, for ten hours a day.

Lowest of all, perhaps, in grade of intelligence are the hand workers of whom neither training nor dexterity is required. They are the preparation hands in canneries, the strippers in stogy factories, the hand-washers and starchers in laundries, the miscellaneous hands in printing establishments, and the women day laborers in the metal works. These women can be set at their jobs without preliminary explanation and can do these jobs adequately, for the occupations are of a sort, whether slicing pickles, stemming tobacco, or screwing nuts on bolts, at which they soon gain their maximum speed.

With the development of machinery, then, which has disintegrated many of the skilled men's trades, and along with that subdivision of labor which, in districts like this about Pittsburgh, has put ten immigrants at the machines for every all-around mechanic set to work, women are called into factories in large numbers, but they are called to simple, unskilled, and unstimulating labor. In discussing wages paid in the Pittsburgh district it was clear that women had displaced men altogether in many of these occupations; that they had been hired because they would work for less; that they could work for less when their living expenses were met by family or by outsiders; and that they were often forced to work for less, because, through lack of strength or training, they were limited in their chance for work to a small group of industries, and to certain restricted levels in most of those industries, where the labor market has naturally become glutted.

It remains to discuss here more in detail the reasons which have kept women in this limited range of occupations. Some of these occupations require greater dexterity than others, and some emphasize speed, but the overwhelmingly large proportion require in their women employes neither training, nor stability, nor intelligence.

Skill, judgment, the way of a machine, and the relation of one machine to another cannot be learned in three to six months. The understanding of these things belongs to men who have years of working time before them. But to a woman who hopes to be out and away from her employment in factory or shop before the end of six or eight years, knowledge of several different processes in the same shop and training in the organization of a department, have no apparent utility.

Women are a shifting body of workers, first, because they give up their industrial work at marriage, and second, because of their consequent lack of ambition. Together these facts produce among them an unprofessional attitude, a conscious instability. For these reasons, women are undesirable apprentices, and since it does not pay to take them for the greater part of a year step by step through the intricacies of a trade, they can be employed profitably only at such occupations as are quickly learned.

They may be allowed from three to six months in which to gain the requisite speed, but in most cases the actual operation is learned in a few weeks.

Their opportunities for employment are still further circumscribed by the opposition of men's unions.[2] Telegraph operators and press feeders admit women on the same terms as men, but neither union has succeeded in enforcing the closed shop, or in gaining a large following among Pittsburgh women workers. The National Stogy Makers have barred women from their union. The broom makers do not include in their union the subsidiary employment at which women are engaged. The core makers have not only kept women out of their union, but are attempting to close all shops against them. The bookbinders' union admits only men. All these are unions of skilled workmen. Either they include only such parts of the trade as are really skilled (as among the bookbinders who admit finishers, forwarders and rulers), or they include all the workmen at a single process (as among stogy makers and core makers), but specifically prohibit the admission of women to their union.

Three conditions then—the more obvious lack of physical strength which interferes to some extent with a woman's operation of heavy machinery, opposition from men's unions, and, most important of all, industrial instability—have combined to leave to women the subsidiary processes, and the mechanical operations which demand little of the intelligence.

Cause and effect in their case work in a circle. Expectation of marriage, as a customary means of support, stunts professional ambition among women. This lack of ambition can have no other effect than to limit efficiency, and restricts them to subsidiary, uninteresting, and monotonous occupations. The very character of their work in turn lessens their interest in it. Without interest, they least of all feel themselves integral parts of the industry and in consequence assume no responsibility, affect no loyalty. They do not care to learn; opportunity to learn is not given them; both are causes and both are effects. Women see only a fight for place, and very uncertain advantage if they gain it; wages are low, again both cause and effect of their dependence in part on others for their support. They shift about on lower levels of industry from packing room to metal work, from metal work to laundry work; a very few through unwonted good fortune, unwonted determination, break through the circle and rise.

The physical effect of long hours under high speed pressure is comparable to the mental effect of continuous unstimulating work. We cannot afford that the work which women do should leave them with a deficit in health; nor can we afford that it should leave them with a deficit in mental alertness. Suggestions have been made for possible checks and safeguards against trade dangers in order to standardize the health of the workers. To standardize intelligence is a far more subtle problem, but one which there is reason to hope will be met in part by the newer educational ideals.

The experiments which have been made in trade training, for women as well as for men, suggest one fairly defined way of advance and improvement. By trade training is not meant the sort of training often most in demand, class work in amateur cooking, dressmaking, and millinery. The training meant is class work comparable to that of trade-trained men, which reacts to the benefit both of industry and of customer, by improving the quality of the product. This should develop in women industrial intelligence by teaching them the practice and the significance of allied industrial processes. To be concrete: Pittsburgh women are largely employed in printing and bookbinding establishments, but as feeders, not as rulers. Why not teach them to mix inks, to fill pens, to manage the ruling machines, as well as to slip into place one piece of ledger paper after another in rhythmic succession? Women are employed for sorting and sizing in broom factories. Why should they not be taught to dye and wash and stack the corn, so that they could rise, if they had opportunity, to positions of responsibility in the sorting department? Women are employed in machine shops and foundries. Why are they not taught the principles on which sand cores are made, the combinations of sand, the kinds of sand for different sorts of work, the necessary allowance for shrinkage, and the combinations of simple into

complex cores? Women are employed in garment factories. Why should they not be taught to cut out garments as well as to run the machines; to plan and direct as well as to execute? Women are employed to sell goods. Why should they not be taught the plan of store organization, differences in fabric, the psychology of meeting a customer's needs? Such an educational program implies building on the present occupations of women to increase the efficiency of women at present employed. It would not mean merely manual training; nor would it mean a feminizing of trade courses. It would mean cooperation between trade schools and manufacturers, which should result, through the success of a few women, in wider opportunity for the many.

Were such trade training general, the depressive mental effect of much factory work might in part be overcome. The worker would understand the relation of her occupation to others and the relation of her industry to others; she would cease to be an altogether unintelligent cog in the wheel. An occupation that calls for a little knowledge as well as for dexterity becomes immediately a stimulus to the intelligence.

It is not my purpose to suggest that all women would profit by trade training. Many, no doubt, under any circumstances, would tend to move from unskilled work to unskilled work, and out to uncared-for homes. Nor would I, in looking for economic as well as psychological effects, claim that were all workers trained in their trades, wages would magically rise. The wages of trained workers are relatively high today because the trained are few; were they many, their payment might be on a different basis. My belief is simply that, were trade training general, one reason for the present low wages of working women would be removed. The advocates of equal pay for equal work would have more instances of equal work to show, and could with justice demand for skilled workers what for unskilled workers they cannot. These skilled workers would be equipped to demand with justice more for themselves, and with larger show of success.

A girl's well grounded self-reliance, even in a semi-skilled trade, such as garment making, is enough to extend her six possible working years to ten, and to lead her ambition far. The tendency toward lengthening the term of woman's working life seems likely to be strengthened among trained and skilful workers. The resulting conflict between trade opportunities and domestic responsibilities must be met by further adjustment. Yet pending such adjustment, we shall do well to remember that inferior and monotonous work processes are no preparation for intelligent home making. Higher earnings and increased industrial efficiency go far toward developing in working women a sense of responsibility, personal and social, toward whichever group they choose to become a part. ♦

ENDNOTES

1. The 6534 saleswomen in mercantile houses are not included in this enumeration.

2. An exception to this is the United Garment Workers of America, which has many women members, and in Pittsburgh has been notably successful.

QUESTIONS

1. What did Butler notice about the work that women did in early twentieth-century Pittsburgh?

2. What are the reasons that managers did not want to invest in training women?

3. What are the reasons why women could only work in relatively poor jobs compared to men?

Man and Machine
from *All Men Are Brothers*

Mohandas Gandhi (1869–1948)

I must confess that I do not draw a sharp line or any distinction between economics and ethics. Economics that hurt the moral well-being of an individual or a nation are immoral and, therefore, sinful. Thus, the economics that permit one country to prey upon another are immoral.

The end to be sought is human happiness combined with full mental and moral growth. I use the adjective moral as synonymous with spiritual. This end can be achieved under decentralization. Centralization as a system is inconsistent with a non-violent structure of society.

I would categorically state my conviction that the mania for mass production is responsible for the world crisis. Granting for the moment that the machinery may supply all the needs of humanity, still, it would concentrate production in particular areas, so that you would have to go about in a roundabout way to regulate distribution, whereas, if there is production and distribution both in the respective areas where things are required, it is automatically regulated, and there is less chance for fraud, none for speculation.

Mass production takes no note of the real requirement of the consumer. If mass production were in itself a virtue, it should be capable of indefinite multiplication. But it can be definitely shown that mass production carries within it its own limitations. If all countries adopted the system of mass production there would not be a big enough market for their products. Mass production must then come to a stop.

I don't believe that industrialization is necessary in any case for any country. It is much less so for India. Indeed I believe that independent India can only discharge her duty towards a groaning world by adopting a simple but ennobled life by developing her thousands of cottages and living at peace with the world. High thinking is inconsistent with a complicated material life, based on high speed imposed on us by Mammon worship. All the graces of life are possible, only when we learn the art of living nobly.

There may be sensation in living dangerously. We must draw the distinction between living in the face of danger and living dangerously. A man who dares to live alone in a forest infested by wild beasts and wilder men without a gun and with God as his only help, lives in the face of danger. A man who lives perpetually in mid-air and dives to the earth below to the admiration of a gaping world lives dangerously. One is a purposeful, the other a purposeless life.

What is the cause of the present chaos? It is exploitation, I will not say of the weaker nations by the stronger, but of sister nations by sister nations. And my fundamental objection to machinery rests on the fact that it is machinery that has enabled these nations to exploit others.

I would destroy that system today, if I had the power. I would use the most deadly weapons, if I believed that they would destroy it. I refrain only because the use of such weapons would only perpetuate the system, though it may destroy its present administrators. Those who seek to destroy men rather than manners, adopt the latter and become worse than those whom they destroy under the mistaken belief that the manners will die with the men. They do not know the root of the evil.

Machinery has its place; it has come to stay. But it must not be allowed to displace necessary human labour: An improved plough is a good thing. But if by some chance one man could plough up, by some mechanical invention of his, the whole of the land of India and control all the agricultural produce and if the millions had no other occupation, they would starve and being idle, they would become dunces, as many have already become. There is hourly danger of many more being reduced to that unenviable state.

I would welcome every improvement in the cottage machine, but I know that it is criminal to displace hand-labour by the introduction of power-driven spindles unless one is at the same time ready to give millions of farmers some other occupation in their homes.

What I object to, is the 'craze' for machinery, not machinery as such. The craze is for what they call labour-saving machinery. Men go on 'saving labour' till thousands are without work and thrown on the open streets to die of starvation. I want to save time and labour, not for a fraction of mankind, but for all; I want the concentration of wealth, not in the hands of a few, but in the hands of all. Today machinery merely helps a few to ride on the back of millions. The impetus behind it all is not the philanthropy to save labour, but greed. It is against this constitution of things that I am fighting with all my might.

The supreme consideration is man. The machine should not tend to make atrophied the limbs of man. For instance, I would make intelligent exceptions. Take the case of the Singer Sewing Machine. It is one of the few useful things ever invented, and there is a romance about the device itself. Singer saw his wife labouring over the tedious process of sewing and seaming with her own hands, and simply out of his love for her he devised the sewing machine in order to save her from unnecessary labour. He, however, saved not only her labour but also the labour of everyone who could purchase a sewing machine.

It is an alteration in the condition of labour that I want. This mad rush for wealth must cease, and the labourer must be assured, not only of a living wage, but a daily task that is not a mere drudgery. The machine will, under these conditions, be as much a help to the man working it as to the State, or the man who owns it. The present mad rush will cease, and the labourer will work (as I have said) under attractive and ideal conditions. This is but one of the exceptions I have in mind. The sewing machine had love at its back. The individual is the one supreme consideration. The saving of labour of the individual should be the object, and the honest humanitarian consideration, and not greed, the motive. Replace greed by love and everything will come right.

Hand-spinning does not, it is not intended that it should, compete with, in order to displace, any existing type of industry; it does not aim at withdrawing a single able-bodied person, who can otherwise find a remunerative occupation from his work. The sole claim advanced on its behalf is that it alone offers an immediate, practicable, and permanent solution of that problem of problems that confronts India, viz., the enforced idleness for nearly six months in the year of an overwhelming majority of India's population, owing to lack of a suitable supplementary occupation to agriculture and the chronic starvation of the masses that results therefrom.

I have not contemplated, much less advised, the abandonment of a single healthy, life-giving industrial activity for the sake of hand-spinning. The entire foundation of the spinning wheel rests on the fact that there are scores of semi-employed people in India. And I should admit that if there were none such, there would be no room for the spinning wheel.

A starving man thinks first of satisfying his hunger before anything else. He will sell his liberty and all for the sake of getting a morsel of food. Such is the position of millions of the people of India. For them, liberty, God and all such words are merely letters put together without the slightest meaning. They jar upon them. If we want to give these people a sense of freedom we shall have to provide them with work which they can easily do in their desolate home and which would give them at least the barest living. This can only be done by the spinning wheel. And when they have become self-reliant and are able to support themselves, we are in a position to talk to them about freedom, about Congress, etc. Those, therefore, who bring them work and means of getting a crust of bread will be their deliverers and will be also the people who will make them hunger for liberty.

Little do town-dwellers know how the semi-starved masses of India are slowly sinking to lifelessness. Little do they know that their miserable comfort represents the brokerage they get for the work they do for the foreign exploiter, that the profits and the brokerage are sucked from the masses. Little do they realize that the government established by law in British India is carried on for this exploitation of the masses. No sophistry, no jugglery in figures can explain away the evidence that the skeletons in many villages present to the naked eye. I have no doubt whatsoever that both England and the town-dwellers of India will have to answer, if there is a God above, for this crime against humanity which is perhaps unequaled in history.

I would favour the use of the most elaborate machinery if thereby India's pauperism and resulting idleness be avoided. I have suggested hand-spinning as the only ready means of driving away penury and making famine of work and wealth impossible. The spinning wheel itself is a piece of valuable machinery, and in my own humble way I have tried to secure improvements in it in keeping with the special conditions of India.

I would say that if the village perishes, India will perish too. India will be no more India. Her own mission in the world will get lost. The revival of the village is possible only when it is no more exploited. Industrialization on a mass scale will necessarily lead to passive or active exploitation of the villagers as the problems of competition and marketing come in. Therefore we have to concentrate on the village being self-contained, manufacturing mainly for use. Provided this character of the village industry is maintained, there would be no objection to villagers using even the modern machines and tools that they can make and can afford to use. Only they should not be used as a means of exploitation of others. ◆

Questions

1. What did Gandhi think was the goal of economics?

2. What did Gandhi think of industrial production as a means to achieve that goal?

3. Why is hand-spinning important for Gandhi?

Selection from: *The Business Guide*

J. L. Nichols (1851–1895) self-published Naperville, Ill 1893

Business Maxims

1. Your first ambition should be the acquisition of knowledge, pertaining to your business.
2. Above all things acquire a good, correct epistolary style, for you are judged by the business world according to the character, expression, and style of your letters.
3. During business hours attend to nothing but business, but be prompt in responding to all communications, and never suffer a letter to remain without an answer.
4. Never fail to meet a business engagement, however irksome it may be at the moment.
5. Undertake no business without mature reflection, and confine your capital closely to the business you have established.
6. Lead a regular life, avoid display, and choose your associates discreetly, and prefer the society of men of your own type.
7. Avoid litigation as much as possible, study for yourself the theory of commercial law, and be your own lawyer.
8. Never run down a neighbor's property or goods and praise up your own. It is a mark of low breeding, and will gain you nothing.
9. Never misrepresent, falsify, or deceive; have one rule of moral life, never swerve from it, whatever may be the acts or opinions of other men.
10. Watch the course of politics in national affairs, read the papers, but decline acceptance of political positions if you desire to succeed in a certain line of business. Never be an office-seeker.
11. Be affable, polite and obliging to everybody. Avoid discussions, anger, and pettishness. Interfere with no disputes the creation of others.

12. Never form the habit of talking about your neighbors, or repeating things that you hear others say. You will avoid much unpleasantness, and sometimes serious difficulties.

13. Endeavor to be perfect in the calling in which you are engaged.

14. Make no investments without a full acquaintance with their nature and condition; and select such investments as have intrinsic value.

15. Never sign a paper for a stranger. Think nothing insignificant which has a bearing upon your success.

16. There is more in the use of advantages, than in the measure of them.

17. Of two investments, choose that which will best promote your regular business.

18. Never refuse a choice when you can get it.

19. Goods well bought are half-sold.

20. Goods in store are better than bad debts.

21. By prosecuting a useful business energetically, humanity is benefited.

22. Keep accurate accounts, and know the exact conditions of your affairs.

23. Be economical: a gain usually requires expense; what is saved is clear.

24. Reality makes no allowance for wishes or bad plans.

25. Write a good, plain, legible hand.

26. Never gamble or take chances on the Board of Trade.

27. Never take any chances on another man's game.

28. Never sign a paper without first reading it carefully.

29. Keep your word as good as a bank.

30. Remember that an honest man is the noblest work of God.

INDEX